MEETING OF GENERALS

MEETING OF GENERALS

Tony Foster

Ⅲ METHUEN
Toronto New York London Sydney Auckland

Canadian Cataloguing in Publication Data

Foster, Tony, 1932–
    Meeting of generals

Bibliography: p.
Includes index.
ISBN 0-458-80520-3

1. Foster, Harry Wickwire. 2. Meyer, Kurt, 1919–1961.
3. Generals—Canada—Biography. 4. Canada.
Canadian Army—Biography. 5. Generals—Germany—
Biography. 6. War crime trials—Germany—Aurich.
7. Caen, Battle of, 1944. I. Title.

D804.G43M49 1986   940.5405   C86-094171-X

Design and maps: Robin Brass
Printed and bound in Canada
1 2 3 4   86   90 89 88 87

For the grandchildren—who never knew them.

CONTENTS

MAPS

ACKNOWLEDGMENTS

Baker, Rev. Lorne, Captain, Chaplain (ret.). Dorchester, N.B., Canada

Bell-Irving, Hon. H.P., Brigadier, Lieutenant-Governor of British Columbia (ret.). Vancouver, B.C., Canada

Bundesarchiv, Koblenz. West Germany.

Cambridge Military Library, RA Park, Halifax, N.S., Canada

Campbell, Clarence S., Lieutenant-Colonel (deceased)

Dietz, Robert, Wehrmacht Sergeant (ret.). Halifax, N.S., Canada

Douglas, Dr. W.A.B. Ottawa, Ont., Canada

Dudka, Stanley, Sergeant (ret.). Lawrencetown, N.S., Canada

Eberbach, Heinrich, General of Panzer Troops (ret.). Notzingen, West Germany

Eberbach, Ursula, née Meyer. Notzingen, West Germany

Foster, Harry W., Major-General (deceased)

Fromm, Dr. Günter, Waffen-ss Sergeant (ret.). Ratingen, West Germany

Fulton, Hon. E. Davie. Vancouver, B.C., Canada

Glenbow Museum, Calgary, Alta., Canada

Golding, Jack (deceased).

Halifax Citadel Army Museum, Halifax, N.S., Canada

Huntley, Brown (deceased)

Johnston, Ian S., Brigadier (deceased)

Kitching, George, Major-General (ret.). Victoria, B.C., Canada

Lehmann, Wadi, Captain (ret.). Surrey, B.C., Canada

Lord Strathcona Horse (Royal Canadian) Archives, Canadian Forces Base, Calgary, Alta., Canada

Macdonald, Bruce J.S., Lieutenant-Colonel and County Court Judge (deceased)

Mansell, Dennis, Sergeant (ret.). North Vancouver, B.C., Canada

Melski, Anthony. Porter's Lake, N.S., Canada

Meyer, Hubert, Waffen-ss Colonel (ret.). Leverkusen, West Germany

Meyer, Kate. Hagen, West Germany

Meyer, Kurt Jr. Rotenburg/Fulda, West Germany

Moncel, Robert, Lieutenant-General (ret.). Murder Point, N.S., Canada

MUNIN-Verlag, Osnabrück, West Germany

Murdock, Scott, Brigadier (ret.). London, Ont., Canada

Pollock, Caitlin. Halifax, N.S., Canada

Pollock, Dr. Gordon, Spy (ret.). Halifax, N.S., Canada

Proctor, John W., Brigadier (ret.). Calgary, Alta., Canada
Public Archives of Canada, Ottawa, Ont., Canada
Richter, Friedrich, Waffen-SS Major (ret.). Uetze, West Germany
Roberts, J.A., Brigadier (ret.). Château d'Oex, Switzerland
Robinson, MacKenzie, Brigadier (ret.). Hamilton, Ont., Canada
Russell, Arthur, Major (ret.). Langley, B.C., Canada
Silverstein, Dr. Harvey. Halifax, N.S., Canada
Sparling, Allan H., Major-General (ret.). Oakville, Ont., Canada
Vokes, Christopher, Major-General (deceased)
Voss, Waffen-SS Major. Hagen, West Germany
Westropp, L. Charles A., Captain. Halifax, N.S., Canada
Wickwire, Alice (deceased)
Wickwire, James L. (ret.). Halifax, N.S., Canada
Wilson, Barbara. Public Archives of Canada, Ottawa, Ont., Canada
Wilson, Jack, Lieutenant-Colonel (ret.). Halifax, N.S., Canada
Winters, Walter N., Lieutenant, Commander RCN (ret.). Southampton, Ont.,
    Canada
Woita, Melanie, née Meyer. Grossmoor, West Germany

Special thanks are due to Ben Greenhous, Götz Eberbach and Greg Cable,
whose generous advice and assistance turned a disjointed 1,200-page manuscript into—one hopes—a smooth error-free book.

My thanks also to Joseph Reddy and Hubert Maier, two astonishingly
persistent researchers, without whose efforts this story could never have been
assembled.

Finally, I am deeply indebted to Ludwig Kosche for his invaluable advice,
voluntary research, correcting my errors, and chiding me for some of my
more flamboyant prose. During four years his vast knowledge of Canadian
and German military history kept me on track, and his patience and meticulous
correcting of the final manuscript and galleys provided me with a first-class
product.

Academic critics may complain about my lack of footnotes throughout the text. I make no apology for their omission. Most leisure readers find copious footnotes distracting to a story narrative. I have tried to present what I feel is a sensible balance between what needed to be given as a source reference and what was obvious. The bulk of the story concerns Generals Meyer and Foster. Since everything said, written or attributed to them comes from family conversations, letters, diaries, tapes or personal recollections by those who knew or served with them, a succession of "Ibid." footnotes seems a bit silly when the source of such material is self-evident.

On the other hand, the historical background references I have included and listed in the bibliography were used only to set the stage on which the two men acted out their parts and I make no claim to the accuracy of that material. As to whether the various unit War Diaries, trial transcripts, personal memoirs, published histories—with copious footnotes—and documents I used in setting that stage are without flaw, I leave for the reader to decide.

PREFACE

FIRST DAWNINGS of physical awareness. That moment when the human consciousness begins to record the memory of people and events.

I walk a dusty road on a summer day toward a white clapboard church. Nanny holds my hand. Her name is Kathy and she towers above me. It is early summer. The day is hot and buzzing with insects. A prairie sun scorches the roadway. I can feel its heat through the soles of my new red shoes. Single-strap, one-button jobs that squeak as I cross the polished hardwood floor to the front pews. Everyone stares. I can't stop the squeaks. I try walking flat-footed. Squeak, squeak, squeak, squeak. It is my brother's christening ceremony. I am two and a half years old.

My mother holds a squalling bundle of white lace and satin. Beside her my father sits straight and tall. He is dressed in uniform. All men dress in uniform. It isn't until I reach five that I realize there is another world where men wear other types of clothing. Civilians.

The church is very quiet. My father hasn't seen my new shoes. I hold up a foot so he'll be sure to notice. He doesn't.

"Look at my new shoes!"

Slowly he turns his head and stares at me. A finger touches his lips. "Shhhhh!" And then he winks. Under the trim moustache his lips tighten into a smile. Content, I lean back against the seat and admire my gorgeous red shoes.

I see him astride his horse at the front of a long column of mounted soldiers. The 11th of November 1936. Clop-clop-clippity-clop. Sunlight glints across the white plumed helmets and metal work. The air is cool. Every horse is breathing smoke like a dragon. Clop-clop-clippity-clop. Spurs jingle, harnesses jangle, saddles creak. The column swings into line abreast and stops in front of a cold stone monument. A single bugle plays a brief lament. Then there is silence, except for the horses who snort and toss their heads impatiently. I see grown men in khaki uniforms kneeling on the pavement. Their heads are bowed. They look like they have no legs. Some are weeping. Not loudly like children. Just tears streaming down their faces from their memories and the autumn cold. Everyone sings in sorrow: "Oh God, our help in ages past. . . ." And I am crying too because even a four-year-old can sense when something terrible has happened.

Throughout the war I went to boarding schools. One was Vernon Prep School in British Columbia's Okanagan Valley. Eighty-five boys with their

xiii

fathers overseas. Field Marshal Montgomery's nephew was there, a sixth-former with facial characteristics similar to the hero of El Alamein. Each day at noon the radio was turned on over lunch. Whenever the Field Marshal's name was mentioned, as invariably it was, all the boys clapped and our "Monty" modestly lowered his head. Then, on 6 June 1944 my father's name was announced as the brigadier leading the troops of the 7th Infantry Brigade ashore on the Normandy beaches. The boys applauded my brother and me. I knew exactly how poor "Monty" had felt. Somehow it seemed improper for a son to be accepting accolades earned by a father. I was terribly embarrassed, although secretly terribly proud.

Then the war ended. A number of fathers didn't return. Their sons carried dog-eared photographs of graveyards and tidy white crosses with their fathers' names in bold black lettering. At bedtime before lights out the photographs would be studied thoughtfully then carefully put away. Later some of the boys wept. Racking sobs that wrenched the soul.

My father didn't come home until 1946. He had been ordered to act as president of a courtmartial assembled to hear evidence against ss Brigade-führer und Generalmajor der Waffen-ss Kurt Meyer. There appeared to be little doubt as to Meyer's guilt. During the trial the noonday radio referred to him as a fanatical Nazi, a ruthless ss general who killed for the sheer joy of killing, a member of the same group that ran the concentration camps and burned the Jews in ovens. When he was convicted and sentenced to death, everybody I knew felt that justice had been served. The uproar that followed the commutation of his sentence to a life behind bars in New Brunswick's Dorchester Penitentiary seemed like a reproach to my father's military integrity. Although only 13 at the time, I considered myself an authority on the war and military justice.

Time passed. Meyer was forgotten. I grew into manhood. The war years dimmed for those who had not been directly involved. Articles on Meyer appeared in the newspapers from time to time: his release from Dorchester to finish his sentence in Germany, his parole from prison, his job as a salesman for a brewery, then, in 1961, his death.

I was visiting my father over the Christmas holidays when word of Meyer's passing arrived. The radio and newspaper reporters who phoned the house were given a brusque "No comment!" Later that evening I asked him to tell me of his Normandy battles against Meyer's 12th ss Division, the courtmartial, the death sentence. I asked if there had ever been any doubt in his mind of Meyer's guilt.

"Not the slightest," he replied. "He was just as guilty of murder as I was at the time . . . or any other senior officer in the field during a battle. The difference between us was that I was on the winning side. That makes a big difference."

Had the courtmartial been a sham then? Vindictiveness by the victor over the vanquished?

My father sighed and sipped his port reflectively. "I don't believe Meyer pulled the trigger on his captives or gave orders to execute any of them. But I'm sure he knew what happened. ss discipline was such that he couldn't help but know. But does that make him guilty of murder any more than I'm guilty for knowing about the German prisoners my troops killed?"

"Then why did you convict him?"

"Because I had no choice according to those rules of warfare dreamt up by a bunch of bloody barrackroom lawyers who never heard a shot fired in anger. In wartime a commanding officer is responsible for the actions of his men."

"But that's absurd!"

"It's also military justice."

"Then where is the truth?"

"Ah!" He nodded as if the question had troubled him too. "I suppose in the final analysis it lies in the conscience of the victor."

Twenty years after that conversation I wrote a letter to Frau Käthe (Kate) Meyer in Hagen, West Germany. I told her I was seeking the truth. From Frau Meyer, her daughters, her son Kurt who visited me in Halifax, and from scores of officers and men of the Waffen-ss and the Canadian army, I learned that there are two sides to every story. I leave the matter of truth to the conscience of the reader.

PRELUDE

AURICH, GERMANY: The Canadian military courtmartial of Kurt Meyer began at exactly 10:30 on a grey overcast morning, 10 December 1945. It had been designed by a nation weary of war as a showcase for fair play and justice toward a defeated enemy. Although no one spoke about it, there was little doubt in anybody's mind what verdict ultimately would be handed down or what the sentence would be.

To a world still blinking in disbelief at the misery and slaughter of millions of innocents by German political and military forces, anyone who held a command position became a suspect. Meyer was an ideal candidate. So far as public opinion was concerned and those newspapers that claimed to reflect it, he personified the evil that had brought Germany to defeat and disgrace. Troops of the 12th ss Panzer Division (Hitlerjugend)* under his command had murdered at least 41 Canadian soldiers the previous year during the first days after the Allied landings in Normandy. Witnesses came forward to testify to these facts, and bodies had been exhumed from shallow graves. In view of the carefully documented evidence, a trial seemed irrelevant, but it was important that the facts be aired publicly so that justice could be seen to be done.

At ten o'clock the doors opened to allow German civilians entry ahead of everyone else. Their presence, the authorities felt, provided a sense of democratic legitimacy to the proceedings. Twenty seats in one row had been reserved for them exclusively. All had been designated "non-Nazi" by the Allied occupation forces. "Tame" Germans they were called. In 1945 there were no "good" Germans.

A pair of enormous guards in gleaming boots let the rest of the spectators in at 10:15. The German civilians fell silent as the surrounding seats were taken by uniformed officers and enlisted men of the Canadian and Allied armed forces. Some were there as official observers for their governments, others out of curiosity. The rest came because they had nothing better to do and this was the only worthwhile show in town. Senior officers conversed among themselves in guarded tones while junior officers listened respectfully.

A special press box had been provided for reporters. Most of the major Canadian and British dailies were represented, faces and names familiar to the millions of readers who had followed the unfolding tragedy of war through

---

*Hitler Youth

their words over the past six years. The newsmen talked above the general conversational murmur with that easy self-assurance of professional spectators.

The younger ones scribbled background notes on their impressions of the surroundings to provide "flavour" for their reports " . . . walls—beautiful dark oak panelling—large oil paintings in heavy gilt frames—matching draperies—chandeliers overhead—modern indirect lighting—raised dais for judge's bench—large Canadian flag on wall behind." One idealistic reporter wrote that "the overall effect was of a solemn sobriety comparable to any County Court in Canada."

To overcome language barriers and speed the judicial process, simultaneous translation services were provided in German, French and English. The new system had been developed for use during the trials in the Bavarian city of Nuremberg where, since 20 November, the British, Americans and Russians had been playing out their final scenes of World War II by dispensing justice to the principal players of the Third Reich* charged with war crimes against humanity.

Possessed with only one bona fide *war criminal*, Canada's judicial and publicity requirements were modest. Compared with Nuremberg's medieval magnificence, the town of Aurich paled into insignificance. The North Sea lay less than 20 miles away. Bitterly cold winter winds swept down across the agricultural flatlands surrounding the town. Nearby, the Ems-Jade Canal linked the seaports of Wilhelmshaven on the east with Emden on the west. Aurich owed its recent economic livelihood to the Kriegsmarine.† But as the German navy's fortunes fell, so did the town's. By the time Grand Admiral Doenitz, as head of state, had authorized the final surrender document, most of the district's naval establishments had been abandoned for lack of personnel—the personnel having left for lack of ships. From the small-town Canadian viewpoint, Aurich was an ideal place for a war crimes trial.

Hastily, an ornate conference room in one of the deserted naval barracks was converted into a court of law, witnesses were assembled, the accused was flown back from custody in England, members of the court were appointed, and members of the press notified. Finally, Canada was ready to give Kurt Meyer justice.

At precisely 10:30, five generals and a lieutenant-colonel entered the courtroom through a side door and took their places on the raised dais. Each of the generals had been decorated and held senior combat commands at a brigade or divisional‡ level. Each had served his country honourably and

---

*Reich—meaning empire. The first, the Holy Roman Empire, came to an end in 1806; the second, Bismarck's Hohenzollern Empire lasted, from 1871 to 1918; the third, proclaimed by the Nazis, lasted from 1933 to 1945.
†The German navy.
‡See Appendix A for description of army organizational structuring.

well, but none could claim to be a judge, although two were trained lawyers. The scholarly Lieut.-Col. W.B. Bredin of Victoria had been appointed by the legal branch of the Canadian army to act as judge advocate, advising the court on matters of procedure and law, while Brigadier-General Ian Johnston, temporarily commanding the 5th Armoured Division, had had a civil law practice in Toronto before the war. Officers appointed for the defence and prosecution were also qualified attorneys.

The members acknowledged salutes from officers at the defence and prosecution tables below the dais, then took their seats. The president, Major-General Harry Foster, commander of the 4th Armoured Division, sat at the centre of the long table with Lieut.-Col. Bredin on his immediate right. The four brigadier-generals were arrayed on either side: H.S. Sparling,* commander Royal Artillery 3rd Infantry Division; H.P. Bell-Irving,† commander 10th Infantry Brigade; J.A. Roberts, commander 8th Infantry Brigade; and I.S. Johnston, already mentioned. Never before in Canada's military history had such a group of senior officers sat in judgment of a former adversary of comparable rank.

There was a pause. A few coughs from the spectators. A hush of expectancy. Foster nodded to the prosecutor, Lieut.-Col. Bruce Macdonald, then to Lieut.-Col. Maurice Andrew of the defence. Both signified they were ready to proceed.

"Bring in the prisoner!"

Flanked by two escort officers from the Royal Winnipeg Rifles, Kurt Meyer marched into the room and halted before the bench. He stood bareheaded, as dictated by military convention for accused soldiers. He wore a plain field-grey German army uniform without rank badges or military decorations.

For a moment Meyer's gaze fixed directly on Foster. Their troops had met in battle. They knew each other by name, reputation and tactical ability in the field, but this was the first time they had met face to face. Two pairs of grey-blue eyes studied each other dispassionately. Then Meyer lowered his head in a short formal bow and took his seat in the prisoner's box.

Interpreters and court reporters were sworn by Bredin. A medical certificate was produced showing Meyer fit to stand trial. The convening orders and certificate of the Judge Advocate-General of the Canadian army were read, and members of the court answered to their names in turn. Bredin was sworn by Foster to secrecy on the votes and opinions of the court members, after which Bredin swore each member to try the case truly and fairly and maintain the same secrecy as he had sworn to uphold himself. Meyer was then brought to his feet and formally arraigned.

The accused, Brigadeführer [Major-General] Kurt Meyer, an officer in the former Waffen-ss, then part of the Armed Forces of the German Reich, now

---

*Later major-general and vice-chief of the General Staff
†Later lieutenant-governor of the Province of British Columbia.

in the charge of 4 Battalion, Royal Winnipeg Rifles, Canadian Army Occupation Force, Canadian Army Overseas, is charged with:

FIRST CHARGE: COMMITTING A WAR CRIME, in that he in the Kingdom of Belgium and Republic of France during the year 1943 and prior to the 7th day of June 1944, when Commander of 25 SS Panzer Grenadier Regiment, in violation of the laws and usages of war, incited and counselled troops under his command to deny quarter to Allied troops.

Meyer's features remained impassive as the first charge was translated. The gentlemen of the press nodded among themselves. They had all been briefed on the articles of the Hague and Geneva Conventions to which Germany had been a signatory. Hague Rule 23 (c) stated: "It is forbidden to kill or wound an enemy, who having laid down his arms, or having no longer means of defence has surrendered at discretion." Rule 23 (d) was even more specific: "It is forbidden to declare that no quarter will be given." The British and Canadian *Manual of Military Law* left no doubt of the intention of these two rules: "This prohibition is clear and distinct; there is no question of the moment up to which acts of violence may be contained without disentitling the enemy to be ultimately admitted to the benefit of quarter. War is for the purpose of overcoming resistance, and no vengeance can be taken because an individual has done his duty to the last but escaped injury."

Bredin read out the next charge:

SECOND CHARGE: COMMITTING A WAR CRIME, in that he in the Province of Normandy and the Republic of France on or about the 7th day of June, 1944 . . . was responsible for the killing of prisoners of war, in violation of the laws and usages of war, when troops under his command killed twenty-three Canadian prisoners of war at or near the villages of Buron and Authie.

Rules for the conduct of war had been observed by the major European powers since the Napoleonic Wars. A military force had the right to try, in the field, members of its own forces for breaches of military discipline as well as any members of its enemy's military forces who might become prisoners. In World War I both Germany and the Allied nations had recognized and exercised this right.

The law, by international understanding, permitted uniformed combatants who carried arms for either side to kill each other, but if captured, each side was entitled to the protected status of prisoners of war. Civilians, however, were accorded no such consideration. Those that took up arms against their country's foes in civilian dress did so at the risk of summary trial and execution by their opponents if they were caught. So too did an enemy who denied his uniformed opponents the protected status of prisoners of war.

In a world now teetering on the brink of nuclear annihilation, such legal ritualism appears preposterous; yet in 1945 observance of the international code of military wartime ethics was uppermost in everyone's mind.

THIRD CHARGE: COMMITTING A WAR CRIME in that he at his Headquarters at l'Ancienne Abbaye Ardenne in the Province of Normandy and Republic of France on or about the 8th day of June, 1944 . . . gave orders to troops under his command to kill seven prisoners of war, and as a result of such orders the said prisoners of war were thereupon shot and killed.

Section 441 in the *Manual of Military Law* states in ambiguous fashion that "the term 'war crime' is the technical expression for such an act of enemy soldiers and enemy civilians as may be visited by punishment on capture of the offenders. It is usual to employ this term, but it must be emphasized that it is used in the technical military and legal sense only, and not in the moral sense. For although some of these acts, such as abuse of privileges of the Red Cross badge, or the murder of prisoners, may be disgraceful, yet others, such as conveying information about the enemy, may be highly patriotic and praiseworthy. The enemy, however, is in any case entitled to punish these acts as war crimes."

The crowded spectator gallery had fallen silent. Even the occasional coughing stopped. An army news photographer with a Graflex camera tried to attract Foster's attention for permission to record the scene. But General Foster was staring at General Meyer. The photographer decided to take his picture anyway. Everyone on the bench gave an involuntary blink.

FOURTH CHARGE: (Alternative to Third Charge) COMMITTING A WAR CRIME, in that he in the Province of Normandy and Republic of France on or about the 8th day of June, 1944 . . . was responsible for the killing of prisoners of war . . . when troops under his command shot and killed seven Canadian prisoners of war at his Headquarters at l'Ancienne Abbaye Ardenne.

The *Manual of Military Law* divides war crimes into different classes under section 443: "killing of the wounded; refusal of quarter; maltreatment of dead bodies on the battlefield; ill treatment of prisoners of war. . . . It is important to note, however, that members of the armed forces who commit such violations of the recognized rules of warfare as are ordered by their Government, or by their commander, are not war criminals and cannot be punished by the enemy. He may punish the officials or commanders responsible for such orders if they fall into his hands, but otherwise he may only resort to the other means of obtaining redress." The defence of "superior orders" was not allowed at any Allied war crimes trial, however. In Canada's case, a regulation provided that superior orders should "not constitute an absolute defence or in mitigation of punishment if the military court . . . determines that justice so requires."

Section 449 of the manual insisted that "in every case, however, there must be a trial before the punishment and the utmost care must be taken to confine the punishment to the actual offender." Finally, under section 450: "All War Crimes are liable to be punished by death, but a more lenient penalty may be pronounced."

> FIFTH CHARGE: COMMITTING A WAR CRIME, in that he in the Province of Normandy and Republic of France on or about the 7th day of June 1944 . . . was responsible for the killing of prisoners of war . . . when troops under his command killed eleven Canadian prisoners of war (other than those referred to in the Third and Fourth Charges) at his Headquarters at l'Ancienne Abbaye Ardenne.

A second charge sheet accused Meyer of responsibility for the execution of seven more Canadian prisoners near the village of Mouen on 17 June 1944, after he had taken over as divisional commander of the 12th ss.

In a clear incisive voice, Meyer replied "*Nein!*" to all charges. Foster nodded that the accused could be seated. For an instant Meyer's gaze shifted as he examined the rows of spectators in the packed courtroom. Not a flicker of emotion crossed his face when he sat down. He had not the slightest doubt of his innocence nor the least doubt that he would be convicted. Such were the fortunes of the vanquished.

At the prosecutor's table, Lieut.-Col. Bruce Macdonald* came to his feet and began outlining his case. Macdonald, a native of Nova Scotia, had practised law in Windsor, Ontario, and had volunteered for active service with the Essex Scottish, his local county regiment, in 1939. He rose quickly in the ranks, and by 1944, during the early battles in Normandy, he had become the regiment's commanding officer. His appointment as chief prosecutor of war criminals for the Canadian forces came early in 1945 when, together with Lieut.-Col. Clarence Campbell† and Lieut.-Col. Dalton Dean, he assembled the case against Meyer. He knew Meyer was guilty. It was merely the degree of guilt that needed to be established.

> I reminded the Court of the importance of the case. It was the first of its kind to be tried by a Canadian Military Court. It would also be the first occasion in the prosecution of war criminals in Europe where an effort would be made to establish the immediate responsibility of a high ranking officer for crimes committed on his order, and also his vicarious responsibility for the commission of such crimes by troops under his command but where he had given no direct order for so doing . . . secondly, from his failure to exercise that measure of disciplinary control over his officers and men which is the duty of a commanding officer to exercise.[1]

Most of the murdered soldiers were members of the Regina and Royal Winnipeg Rifles Regiments captured during that first frantic 72 hours after the Normandy landings on D-Day. As part of the 7th Canadian Infantry

---

*Later crown attorney for Windsor and county court judge of Essex County.
†Later president of the National Hockey League.

Brigade, both units had been in the first wave of troops that came ashore at dawn on 6 June 1944. Harry Foster, then a brigadier, had been the brigade's commander. Some of the dead had been his soldiers.

"There was an irony to this whole distasteful affair," he said later. "Not because of what had happened to my men—that was inexcusable. But then war itself is inexcusable. What struck me as I sat in my comfortable chair looking down at this hardnosed Nazi was that not one of us sitting on the bench, with the exception of Bredin, could claim clean hands in the matter of war crimes or atrocities or whatever you want to call them. It hadn't all been one-sided. Our troops did some pretty dreadful things to the Germans. Didn't that make all of us who were commanding officers just as guilty as Meyer? I remember thinking at the time: you poor arrogant bastard. Except for an accident of birth and background our positions might have been reversed. In which case I would now be standing before you asking for justice at this meeting of generals."[2]

PART 1

IN THE SHADOW OF WAR

You smug-faced crowd with kindling eye
Who cheer when soldier lads march by
Sneak home and pray you'll never know
The hell where youth and laughter go.
                    SIEGFRIED SASSOON

JANIE! Control yourself. I'll not have our firstborn arrive on April Fools!"

And so Harry Wickwire Foster was born shortly after midnight, 2 April 1902, in the city of Halifax, Nova Scotia. His father, Gilbert Lafayette Foster—"Laffy" to his friends and family—had married Janie Wickwire the previous June at her family's home in Canning, a prosperous tree-shaded town in Nova Scotia's picturesque Annapolis Valley.

The Fosters and Wickwires traced their roots in a direct line through eight generations back to New London, Connecticut, a not uncommon genealogical feat for most Annapolis Valley families today. In 1755 the "Connecticut Planters" were offered free lands seized from the French in Nova Scotia during the Acadia Expulsion. After a brief visit of inspection in 1761, the Fosters and Wickwires along with several hundred other families migrated to Nova Scotia.

Yet despite this common heritage, local gossip insisted that "poor Janie had married quite beneath her." Her father, John Leander Wickwire, had been a member of Canada's young Parliament in 1872, a prominent merchant and shipbuilder with a Midas touch. Sleek square-rigged clippers built on the Bay of Fundy shore and manned by men of the Sheffield-Wickwire Company had sailed the oceans of the world and made the family rich. J.L.'s palatial home sat at the right end of town, and if he wasn't quite a millionaire, he was certainly "well fixed in his situation," as an obituary related upon his death in the spring of 1891.

Janie was 14 when her father died of a heart attack. A dark-haired girl with soft brown eyes and a pretty, intelligent face, she was perhaps a little too intelligent for her own good. Her quick wit and tongue seemed to scare every eligible bachelor away. Nonetheless, she remained an attractive catch for anyone with the courage and passion to pursue her. She had, together with her mother, elder sister and two brothers, inherited a sizeable sum in money and property.

Laffy, on the other hand, had little to offer in the way of financial security or material accomplishment. His father, George Foster, had died when Laffy was five, leaving the home farm at North Kingston village to his wife, Almira, and Edgar, the eldest of his 11 children. Of the nine boys and two girls, Laffy stood at the end of the inheritance line with his sisters.

Even though his mother raised them all very sternly as "solemn straight-backed Methodists fearing God and the Devil in equal dollops," he had had a happy childhood on the farm, later attending lessons, using chalk and slate, at the one-room village school. He discovered that he had an aptitude for learning, natural curiosity, and that he enjoyed reading immensely.

Only three of the children managed to make it through to higher education in Halifax: William, who eventually became the auditor for the City of Halifax; Mary Ann, who'd "been bitten by the Bible" and became a missionary; and Laffy, who entered medical school at Dalhousie University in the fall of 1892 because "it seemed the sensible thing to do at the time."

Halifax was then a small city of soot-encrusted clapboard houses and a few stone residential and public buildings. Ocean liners and cargo vessels—steam and sail—crowded the harbour and wharfs. Scheduled weekly sailings went to Boston, New York, the West Indies and England. The Royal Navy maintained a coaling station for its warships that restlessly prowled the Empire's sea lanes. Queen Victoria's reign had entered its 55th year, with Britain at the zenith of its power and glory and global influence. Four years earlier, Wilhelm II, Queen Victoria's grandson, had succeeded his father as king of Prussia and German emperor. The Second German Reich, created by Bismarck, had existed for exactly 21 years.

The Dominion of Canada was only four years older. A gigantic country, more than twice the size of all Europe and divided by a host of regional differences, its population was still reaching for the 5-million mark. Across the border the American population was approaching 70 million, but for the first time in years, Canadians no longer feared American adventurism turning in their direction for conquest. A third of the U.S. populace were

European born and hadn't the slightest interest in pursuing old colonial grievances. America's congressional hawks found that an invasion of Canada had lost its voter appeal.

Laffy graduated from Dalhousie with average grades in 1894. "But having M.D.C.M. after my name provided no guarantee for a prospective patient's survival. The more I learned the less I realized I knew." After a summer holiday back at the family farm, he took the steamer from Halifax to New York and for the next two years studied surgery at New York University. He graduated in 1896 and, following a year's internship at New York City Hospital, came home to set up practice, heavily in debt to his mother and brother Edgar for their years of financial support.

Standing a gangly six feet two inches tall, with soft brown hair, pink complexion and baby-blue eyes, he looked much too young to be taken seriously as a family GP and even less as a competent surgeon. He selected Canning to begin his practice. He rented rooms and crossed his fingers. "But as the year wore on, it became clear that the local citizens enjoyed remarkably good health. The old ones died quickly when their time came, and without complaint. The new arrivals were all handled by a physician 20 years my senior. I was left with the cuts, scrapes and broken limbs."

Life expectancy at the time was 47.3 years. Laffy had reached the halfway point and seemed to be getting nowhere. A new Liberal government under Wilfrid Laurier had swept into power in Ottawa the year before, and Dr. Frederick Borden, a native of Canning and the locally elected member, had been appointed minister of militia and defence by the new prime minister. During the parliamentary summer recess of 1897, Laffy met Dr. Borden. The old politician with the muttonchop whiskers took a liking to the impoverished young doctor.

Borden held the post of honorary lieutenant and surgeon-major in the 68th Kings County Battalion of Infantry of the Active Militia,* a position he'd been awarded at the start of his political career. In late July the 68th's assistant surgeon requested transfer to an exciting new cavalry regiment, and Borden suggested Laffy for the vacancy. The regiment's commanding officer (CO) could hardly refuse a request from the local member and cabinet minister. Laffy's formal acceptance was confirmed on 9 August 1897 by the Adjutant-General in Ottawa.

"The pay was meagre, the uniform rather splendid and the benefits enormous. Being a militia officer provided a solid introduction to every social function and level of local influence throughout the district." He met Harry Hamm Wickwire, the county's provincial government member and Janie's older brother, who took an instant liking to him. The gregarious and amusing

---

*Membership permitted regular civilian occupation unless the member was called to active service in times of national crisis.

Harry introduced Laffy to Janie. He fell in love. "But in my present circumstances there isn't a hell of a lot I can do about the situation," he wrote ruefully.

Still, being in the militia was a start. An act issued by the first government Assembly in Halifax had authorized the creation of a militia in 1758. The act required "all male persons, planters, and inhabitants, and their servants, between the ages of sixteen and sixty" to bear arms and attend all musters and military exercises. Combined with British regulars, the militia was used to oppose local Indians, the French and finally the threat of American invasion after the Thirteen Colonies' revolt in 1775. Officers received their commissions from the government in Halifax, and these were based as much on the social standing as on the tactical abilities of the recipients. After the Napoleonic Wars the militia's annual musters developed into little more than elaborate social gatherings for officers and their wives and jovial drinking parties for other ranks.

With the passage of the Militia Act in 1855, conscription was abolished in favour of volunteer regiments. After Confederation in 1867, when the four provinces united as the Dominion of Canada, administration of the militia was turned over to the central government in Ottawa. In 1871 the last British garrison regiments withdrew to England and the new Militia Act authorized a Canadian volunteer Permanent Force and militia for "defence of the Dominion." Thus, a large citizen army of amateurs evolved that could be called to arms in times of crisis and trained for battle by a small cadre of professional soldiers from the Permanent Force.

Laffy's militia membership was about to change his "present circumstances" for the better, providing him with the means and encouragement to ask the beautiful, dark-haired Janie to marry him.

2

In the summer of 1897 two ships arrived in Seattle and San Francisco carrying a number of ecstatic new millionaires lugging more gold than they could comfortably carry. Word of their riches fanned out across the continent like a prairie brush fire. The great Klondike Gold Rush was under way.

By early winter the population of Dawson in the Yukon Territory had swelled from under 200 to 20,000. Shortages of food, shelter and basic amenities for the thousands of gold-hungry adventurers pouring over the White and Chilcoot passes from Alaska created a potential for the breakdown of law and order.

The 600-mile border dividing Alaska and the Canadian Yukon had been policed by 20 members of the North-West Mounted Police since 1894. Reinforcements were needed desperately. More Mounties were sent north, but by the spring of 1898 their manpower resources had been stretched to the breaking point.

The situation was complicated by a dispute between Canada and the United States over ownership of the White and Chilcoot passes. As Yukon Commissioner Maj. J.M. Walsh observed: "The population here being chiefly American, many of them are not disposed to view with favour any restrictions placed upon them by the ordinary law of the country and some of them have been heard to say that it was high time the Union Jack was pulled down and the Stars and Stripes hoisted in its place."[1] Both California and Oregon had entered the American union by similar methods.

Virtually everybody in the area carried a weapon of some sort. One spark of antagonism, real or imagined, could touch off an explosion that might overwhelm Canadian authority. The nearest troops were units of the U.S. 14th Infantry Regiment at Dyea, Alaska. It would take only a formal request by U.S. citizens who feared for their safety to bring the American army over the mountains to the aid of a "provisional government." The Yukon could be lost. An armed and visible Canadian military presence was needed to enforce Canada's rights.

The country's regular army in 1898 consisted of 850 men of all ranks. None of its three Permanent Force regiments—the Royal Canadian Dragoons (RCD), the Royal Canadian Artillery and the Royal Regiment of Canadian Infantry—was in a position to meet the manpower requirements for a "Yukon Field Force." It was decided that detachments should be drawn from all three. Command went to Maj. T.B. Evans of the Royal Canadian Dragoons, who was promoted to lieutenant-colonel for the occasion. In addition to various civil servants, surveyors and private contractors, also included were four ladies from the Victorian Order of Nurses to provide medical services in the Yukon and Miss Faith Fenton of the *Toronto Globe* to record the events for her paper's readers.

Borden wrote Laffy and asked if he'd be interested in joining the expedition as surgeon-major. It meant a three-year posting, with the title of surgeon-major implying the position of senior medical officer rather than a promotion in rank. Still, only eight months in the militia and already he was being given a chance to prove himself. After waiting for the formality of the 68th's commanding officer's polite request to join the force, he sent off a telegram of acceptance.

The whole idea of a military intervention in the Yukon caught the nation's enthusiasm. Newspapers loved the story. It had romance, the mystery of vast and distant regions only vaguely known by the population, the glory of gold and perhaps even a military confrontation with the Americans at the end of the journey. There was no shortage of volunteers.

Laffy bid Janie a circumspect adieu, promised to write, then boarded a train to Ottawa, where members of the new force were assembling. He found

Borden in his office on Parliament Hill. The Minister of Militia and Defence was "quite taken aback by my enthusiasm and promptitude since the normal course of events would have been to wait until the appointment had been confirmed before showing up for work." Borden arranged lodgings for Laffy, and on 21 March his surgeon-major's status was confirmed. He was two months short of his 27th birthday.

At once Laffy threw himself into the task of organizing medical and supply requirements for the force's proposed complement of 200 men, supporting civil servants, and usual camp followers. Everyone in the unit received a thorough medical examination, and those who failed to meet the standards were quickly replaced. But his biggest headache turned out to be persuading the troopers to stay away from the ladies of Ottawa, who were "giving a few of our men a good deal more than the regular doses of love and understanding."

Finally, they were ready. After "a colourful parade and inspection by the Prime Minister" and another parade the following day for the Governor-General, they marched off to the Canadian Pacific Railway (CPR) station to board their train for the West.

"Arrived in Winnipeg Sunday AM after two days and nights of boredom. Men are beginning to settle down. We marched off to the RCD barracks through cheering crowds where a citizens welcoming committee had laid on a wagon load of beer for the troops. Lots of speeches and silliness. At last, filled with beer and good wishes everybody staggered back to the train accompanied by the band of the 90th Regiment playing 'The Maple Leaf Forever.' Shortly before 6:00 PM we swayed off across the prairies heading for Vancouver."

On the West Coast, officers were provided with first-class accommodations in one of the local hotels, while other ranks billeted at a shut-down vaudeville theatre. Several days were spent packing and labelling 60 tons of supplies, including two Maxim guns, that were to be loaded aboard the ss *Islander*. They sailed on 14 May and two days later hove to in Alaskan coastal waters while U.S. customs officers boarded the ship.

It was a matter of some political embarrassment that the force's access route to the Yukon lay through American lands and waters. However, since all arms and equipment on board were "in bond," the customs inspection became little more than a brief formality and they were allowed to proceed to Fort Wrangel, a coastal port on the Alaskan Panhandle.

"Troops from the local U.S. Army detachment—mostly coloureds—gave us a friendly welcome. Hard to believe these are members of the same enemy forces plotting to take over the Yukon. I wonder if it isn't all just a case of somebody in Ottawa crying 'Wolf! Wolf!' These fellows couldn't be nicer. But oh my, what a dreary dreadful place this is."

Lieutenant-Colonel Evans put his men to work transferring all cargo to a pair of shallow draft riverboats chartered to carry the force and its supplies up the Stikine River back into Canadian territory.

Two days thrashing upstream in the wood-burning sternwheelers brought them to Glendora, British Columbia, where the soldiers trained in marching with heavy backpacks single file over narrow broken trails while sustaining themselves on a diet of bully-beef and hardtack biscuits. In midday temperatures that reached 90 degrees Fahrenheit the troops marched and bitched and sweated.

At the beginning of June an advance guard of 50 was sent ahead to build a log barracks at Fort Selkirk, an old Hudson's Bay Company trading post at the junction of the Pelly and Yukon rivers that lay along the river route between Dawson and Whitehorse and the Alaskan port of Skagway 250 miles to the south. The main force followed during mid-June, with enough supplies to last them until winter. In the weeks that followed, they crossed mountains, swamps, rivers and lakes through blistering sun, torrential downpours, and clouds of famished mosquitoes. They built roads, bridges and boats, and hacked out mountain trails. Throughout it all, they were drilled on a regular basis "so that no one is permitted to forget that he is first and last a soldier of the Queen." Finally, on 11 September, as twilight crept across the mountains and autumn's first chill settled on the land, they reached their destination.

A quarter of the force, along with one of the Maxim guns, were sent downriver to Dawson to reinforce the Mounties. Laffy remained at Fort Selkirk where the winds howled and the thermometer sank like a stone. For weeks it hovered at 40 below zero. The men had little to do beyond housekeeping chores and keeping themselves fed, warm and amused. Laffy held regular sick parades every morning, but "unfortunately there is no known remedy for chronic boredom," he wrote Janie.

Then slowly the days began to lengthen. Temperatures and spirits rose, but plans were already afoot to have the force withdrawn. Dawson's gold rush had ended almost as quickly as it had begun. The Mounties had never really lost their iron grip on the local situation, nor had the Americans shown any inclination to invade or engineer a slick administrative takeover. The militia's commanding officer in Ottawa wanted the men back with their units. Holding a quarter of the country's Permanent Force in the Yukon had badly depleted the southern garrisons of manpower. Half the force was sent home in September and during October the headquarters was moved up to Dawson, leaving only a ten-man detachment at Fort Selkirk. Evans was ordered out by dogsled the following month.

"The boom town of Dawson has gone bust. A pest hole," Laffy complained. There were still plenty of prospectors working throughout the region but the *rush* was over. Another winter passed in the bitterly cold and seemingly endless nights. He wanted to quit the place. More exciting events were happening elsewhere in the world. "Damn!" he wrote. "If only I could have predicted the future."

Prime Minister Laurier had offered the British government a token force of 1,000 infantry plus two battalions of mounted riflemen to assist in quelling the Boer uprisings in South Africa. A first contingent had sailed from Quebec City at the end of October 1899. A second group of 600 men and horses left from Halifax in late February, with Dr. Borden's only son, "Handsome Harold," a lieutenant in the Dragoons, among them. Two surgeon-majors were included with the group. If Laffy hadn't been cooling his heels in the Yukon, he could have claimed one of the appointments.

At last, early in May, orders arrived in Dawson for the troops to turn over their weapons and supplies to the Mounties and report back to their regimental stations. The hundred remaining members boarded a riverboat for the trip out to Whitehorse and Skagway and arrived in Vancouver on 5 July. The great Yukon adventure had ended.

3

When Laffy reached home near the end of the month, he found the town of Canning in mourning. "Handsome Harold" had been killed leading a charge near Witpoort Ridge in the Transvaal. Laffy had enjoyed the dashing younger Borden's style, especially his reputation with the local young ladies. "Poor Doctor Borden. What a waste! This is the reality of war."

He spent a week or two visiting his mother and brothers in Kingston and reassuring himself that his feelings for Janie hadn't changed. Then he asked her to marry him. He'd managed to save nearly a thousand dollars from his pay, a considerable sum for the times.* Social convention required that he make a formal request for Janie's hand from her eldest brother, Harry Hamm Wickwire, H.H. as he was known by the electorate he represented in Kings County. "With money in my pocket and all of my debts paid to mother and Ed I felt much less of a pauper than when last I had spoken of the matter to H.H. and Mrs. Wickwire. Both seemed agreeable, if not wildly enthusiastic about the prospects of having me as an in-law."

H.H. used his political influence with the president of the Dominion Atlantic Railway to hire his prospective brother-in-law as the company's Halifax doctor overseeing its work camps. The job paid an annual retainer sufficient to support a decent city house and would allow him enough free time to develop a private practice. A wedding date was set for 13 June the following year to coincide with Janie's 26th birthday. Laffy rented an old house in Halifax close to the park, with stabling in the rear for his horse, sleigh and buggy.

Once Laffy had established himself, H.H. put him up for membership

---

*Roughly $50,000 purchasing power in 1986.

in the prestigious Halifax Club, a watering hole with fireplaces and leather chairs for members of the city's business and professional community. It was a place for a person to be seen, introduced and become known to the captains of industry, politics and finance. But in spite of his enthusiasm and introductions, the private practice he hoped for failed to materialize. He was too young, too new an arrival on the staid conservative scene. His only stories were about the Yukon "cold and gold while everybody else wanted to talk about the latest news from South Africa." By the following June his savings were gone and he was living solely on his retainer from the railway. The day before the wedding he reflected ruefully: "I am in nearly the same dreadful financial position as when we met. Also am starting to lose hair quite badly. Perhaps alopecia is desirable in a physician for building patient trust. I've tried just about everything else."

The wedding in Canning "went through without a hitch on an absolutely perfect day filled with sunshine, smiles and dozens of aunts, uncles, cousins and newly minted in-laws." They took the train to Halifax to spend two nights at the Queen's Hotel, then went aboard a steamer to Boston. From Boston they rode on to New York, staying for two weeks with one of Laffy's college pals who had set himself up in an enormously successful Manhattan practice. He needed a partner. Fifty-fifty on everything. Would Laffy be interested? No more financial worries. It was tempting, but Janie put her foot down. She hadn't married him to live in New York, but he was free to make up his own mind. Laffy gave in. Sailing home in late July, she told him that she was pregnant, adding as an afterthought, "You didn't really want our firstborn to be an American, did you?"

"Of course not!" he replied stoutly.

They settled comfortably into the routine of married life. In his diary entry for 13 January 1904, he wrote: "Gave little Harry his bath. He is such a joy to us." But his practice was not going well. A few days later, he wrote: "Clear and fine but cold. Harry is playing with his kitten and is happy as he can be, tho' I am uncertain about where to go or what to do. I do not feel depressed. I must do something else to bring in more money. Patients never pay." It was his pride more than their finances that was suffering. Janie's income from her father's estate guaranteed they'd always have a roof over their heads and food on the table, but he was supposed to be the breadwinner. He realized he had little aptitude for business and absolutely no stomach for making patients pay their bills. It was an age when gentlemen, especially doctors, didn't press for money from their debtors. His spirits rose a little, but he still didn't know "what we are to do."

On 16 February 1905 their second son was born. Janie decided to name him after Laffy, but for simplicity's sake she shortened the more formal Gilbert Lafayette to "Gil." "Not as robust a lad as little Harry and rather a quiet baby."

That fall an opening occurred in the Army Medical Corps of the Permanent Force. Laffy was asked by Borden—now Sir Frederick Borden, K.C.M.G. — if he'd be interested. Since his return from the Yukon, he'd been promoted to surgeon-captain in the 68th King's Infantry Militia, faithfully attended the summer manoeuvres each year at Camp Aldershot outside Kentville, and remained on call to active duty in case of a national emergency. But being a member of the Permanent Force would give him a career.

Borden had managed to get the Pensions Act passed in 1901, giving members of the armed forces a basic security that until then had been lacking. Since Canada's spectacular contribution during the Boer War and the impressive decorations earned by men of the tiny force—several Victoria Crosses (vcs) among them—soldiering for all ranks had become a respectable profession for the first time. By offering security and a decent living wage, the Permanent Force could pick and choose its recruits. Its 2,500 members were the best to be had from a population now close to 6 million.

Borden's offer would give Laffy the rank of major, a batman,* government transportation and stabling, plus an adequate income. Instead of dealing with nonpaying patients and his weekly assortment of railway workers' injuries, he'd be dealing with professional soldiers who "would at the very least report on sick parade bathed and cleaned." After talking it over with Janie, he accepted. His appointment was confirmed on 1 October 1905. No longer did he consider himself a failure. He knew he'd never get rich but neither would he have to grovel for money.

Pride and self-esteem recovered, he set about reorganizing the Halifax garrison's medical services into the army's finest. His tactful ability to bring others around to his way of thinking, together with natural organizational skills, caught the attention of the Director General of Medical Services during one of his regular inspection tours. As a result, in 1907 he was promoted to lieutenant-colonel and later made assistant medical officer of the 6th Divisional Area (the Province of Nova Scotia). "Which means I now get to do all the work and the Colonel collects all the credit."

He and his family moved into a spacious three-storey home directly across the road from the Halifax Ladies College. Little Harry had reached school age, and as the college accepted boys up to the age of ten, he was enrolled. Brother Gil followed as soon as he was old enough. Harry remained in the college for five years, graduating in 1912 and placing fourth in a class comprised of himself and 11 girls. He received a diploma suitably tied with pink ribbon. In later years, proud of his attendance, he would turn up in his dress uniform at annual alumni meetings and introduce himself as "an old girl."

The boys developed very different personalities. Gil, the "quiet baby" as

---

*Valet, servant—usually a private in rank.

described by his father, turned into a bright ball of enthusiasm filled with energy and curiosity about the world around him. By comparison Harry appeared dull, far more taciturn and phlegmatic in his approach to life. While Harry did well in school, Gil excelled, always remaining far out in front of his older brother in brains, ability and personality.

They spent their summers visiting Annapolis Valley relations, first Grandmother Almira Foster at the farm in North Kingston, then the Wickwires at Kentville. Janie's two brothers, H.H. (after whom young Harry had been named) and Fred, owned large comfortable homes across the road from each other on the main highway into Kentville. Both played at being farmers and operated sizeable acreages of apple orchards and valuable dikelands for pasturing their livestock. The Foster boys had seven cousins, four girls and three boys, between the two Wickwire families, all roughly the same ages as themselves. To confuse matters, H.H. had named his eldest son Harry too. He had been born almost exactly one year after Harry Foster.

With a fine sense of the dramatic, H.H. took the Foster boys around the country to introduce them to their family roots. A visit to the local graveyards where their ancestors were buried. Views from the wharfs at Canning, Kingsport and Scott Bay where the great clipper ships of Sheffield-Wickwire had berthed and loaded their cargoes of apples and lumber for England and the world. Every old retired sea captain and mate had a story to tell of high adventure, thundering seas and roaring winds, sparkling islands dotting a rimless blue Pacific.

"Uncle Harry's stories were as good as anything we heard from the sailors," Harry remembered. "His stories were outrageous. To hear him talk, he'd been to sea on every ship that Grandfather Wickwire ever owned; pilot, captain, mate and bosn'—he'd done it all. I don't remember whether or not I believed what he told us then but I do know Uncle Harry's tall tales decided me on going to sea as soon as I was old enough to leave home. Joining the army was the furthest thing from my mind."

4

The third of August 1914 was Monday Bank Holiday in England, another hot summer day. Race drivers roared their cars around the track at Brooklands. Young men in straw boaters punted along the Thames while their girls, in summer dresses, lazed beneath parasols. The Brighton beaches were packed with swimmers and bathing-machine houses. King George V was in the fourth year of his reign, and cigarettes cost five and a half pennies a pack.

Britain had reached the zenith of its global power, a power greater than the world had ever known. More magnificent than either Greece or Rome, more powerful than the Mongol hordes and the armies of Islam combined, the British Empire covered a quarter of the earth's land surface and controlled virtually all its oceans and seas. British influence extended everywhere. No nation made a unilateral decision on anything without due consideration of Britain's reaction. It was all about to change forever.

The House of Commons was in special session. At 5:03 p.m. a one-word telegram arrived at British military field headquarters in Aldershot: "Mobilize." Word went out to every unit in the country and to every member of Britain's enormous empire.

The next afternoon at 2:00 p.m., Lieut. Georges Picard of the Belgian army stared through his field glasses from his observation post on the German-Belgian frontier. Long columns of grey-uniformed German cavalry were streaming across the undefended border. It was the start of a great encircling movement planned by the German High Command to bypass the French army in the east and attack France from the north through Belgium. But Belgian neutrality had been guaranteed by the great European powers in a treaty of 1831, and as a signatory Britain now demanded that the Germans get out of Belgium before midnight or face war. The cabinet gathered at 10 Downing Street to await Germany's reply. Finally, at 15 minutes past midnight Berlin time, Britain's declaration of war was handed to the German ambassador in London.

The British Empire had always been somewhat of a mystery to most Europeans, an impression shared across the Atlantic by the Americans. How strong were the loyalties between the mother country and her self-governing offspring, people wondered? The declaration of war by Britain legally bound its colonies and dominions to battle, but there was no logical reason why Australia, Canada, New Zealand or South Africa should get involved in a conflict on the European mainland. German High Command counted on such a reaction. They were disappointed. With a speed and fervour that astonished the world, members of the Empire rallied to the clarion call.

Australia's defence minister said that "Australia wants the rest of the Empire to know that . . . all she possesses, to the last ear of corn and drop of blood, is freely offered to maintain the glory and greatness of the Empire, and to battle the righteous cause wherein she is engaged." Louis Botha, South Africa's prime minister, who only 15 years before had been battling British troops during the Boer War, promised to take on the German colonies of East and Southwest Africa. And ten days after the outbreak of hostilities, Prime Minister Richard Sedon had the first contingent of nearly 8,000 New Zealand troops on its way to England with a promise of more to follow in the months ahead.

Sir Robert Borden, Canada's prime minister,* wired London three days

---

*A cousin of Sir Frederick Borden from Grand Pré, Nova Scotia; Borden's Conservative government succeeded Sir Wilfrid Laurier's Liberals in 1911.

before the war began to promise his country's support and ask for suggestions on how he could help the cause. One division of 22,000 troops was offered and accepted. Borden promised to raise a half-million men by 1916.

Harry and Gil were on their summer holidays from school in Toronto. The previous year Laffy had been appointed assistant director of medical services of the 2nd Divisional Area (Central Ontario). He had moved the family to Toronto and placed the boys in a local school. Their "funny" East Coast accents resulted in seemingly endless fist fights "from which we acquitted ourselves with honour," Harry recounted. "Fortunately no one ever learned that our previous education came from a Ladies College or we'd have been doomed to an entire year of black eyes and bloody noses."

Toronto had grown to 400,000 people. An industrious but dreadfully parochial conservative city, it burgeoned with new industry, buildings, talent and a mass of hard-working European immigrants. After Halifax with its steep hills, bustling waterfront and ocean smells, Toronto seemed awfully dull. However, the mobilization orders that went out to all Canadian units on 1 August 1914 brought Toronto and the rest of the country to a level of excitement unknown since the glorious days of the Boer War.

An assembly area for the overseas expeditionary force that was to be sent to England was selected at Valcartier, a sandy plain 16 miles northwest of Quebec City. After the local farmers had been evacuated, construction began on 8 August, and a month later 33,000 men assembled from militia units across the nation. Laffy was appointed officer in charge of training medical personnel.

The boys and their mother went home to Nova Scotia by train. Uncle Fred offered them an old house next door to his own place for the duration, which everyone felt wouldn't be much beyond Christmas. Cousins Jim and Harry introduced them to other boys going to Kentville's elementary school, "where we were regarded with about the same degree of suspicion we'd endured back in Toronto because of our newly acquired flat Ontario accents." It was a no-win situation, but this time the brothers had cousins to back them up. The boys settled quickly into the familiar surroundings while their father went off to war.

At Valcartier all was chaos. Without enough tents or greatcoats to keep out the autumn frosts and rains, the keen but green militiamen soon came down with colds and fever. The Jacques Cartier River, which provided the camp's water, became polluted from latrine runoff. The army doctors had their hands full keeping the men fit and healthy at the makeshift camp. Forty medical officers were employed examining, vaccinating and inoculating the recruits.

Most of the time at Valcartier was spent in issuing clothing and equipment, in medical parades and in organizing or reorganizing the force for its voyage overseas. Scores of civilian contractors descended on Quebec, bringing in ton after ton of supplies that bore little relation to the army's needs. Every town and city across Canada wanted its share of the public purse. No system of quality control, long-range planning, or supervision had been arranged. The results were boots that after 12 parades turned into a mass of sodden pulp at the heels, where paper had been used instead of leather, and hundreds of new wagons for the baggage train, each with a turning radius wider than any road in Europe. Speed in getting the troops to England became the only principle of mobilization.

The troops started embarking from Quebec City in late September. Eleven days were needed to get the 30,621 members of the force on board the various ships. As each vessel was loaded, it moved down the St. Lawrence River to Gaspé Bay to anchor at the convoy assembly area. Finally, on 3 October, 32 ships, including Royal Navy cruiser escorts, sailed for Plymouth. Throughout the 11-day voyage the ocean remained ominously calm, but the trip passed without incident beyond the normal rumours of mines, submarines and German warships.

Once in England another 11 days were needed to unload the division and its strange equipment. Salisbury Plain had been designated for the Canadian campsite. Laffy, who'd faced the worst that Canada could offer in weather, was appalled. He wrote Janie and the boys: "This is a terribly desolate area. About 15 by 25 miles with not a fence, house, animal or person to be seen. All it seems to do is rain—rain—rain."

Although ideal for summer manoeuvres and heavy artillery practice, as winter quarters for an army under canvas tents Salisbury Plain was a disaster. A thin clay soil covered an underlying base of chalk limestone that prevented any rain runoff. Consequently, whenever and wherever the men marched, the ground became an oozing quagmire. In a 75-day period, only five were without rain. It turned out to be the wettest fall and winter in 60 years.

Laffy observed in a Christmas letter home: "Although our men are now crowded into makeshift wood frame and canvas covered huts which are better than living in the mud under tents everybody is still damp, bored and homesick. Influenza, subacute enteritis and meningitis have broken out. . . . For the first time I understand how England built her empire. It was done by men desperate to escape the English climate at any price."

The British War Office had been led to believe that the Canadians were fully equipped, trained and ready for action. One inspection on the Salisbury Plain quickly changed any thoughts of sending them off to France by December, which had been the original plan. Close to $5 million worth of supplies and materials purchased in Canada for the division—an enormous sum at the time—had to be abandoned and everything replaced with standard British army issue, from boots, blankets and clothing to vehicles, wagons and horse harnesses. Valcartier had been a mistake; Salisbury Plain was the consequence. It was an embarrassing beginning to Canada's participation in the Great War.

Meanwhile, problems were developing at home between Janie and the boys. Although doing her best, she was not a disciplinarian. A stern male presence was needed when the children stepped out of line, and neither of Janie's brothers could help. Fred had gone off to war and H.H. had to remain in Halifax during fall and winter sittings in the House of Assembly.

That spring Harry turned 13, a dangerous age for any boy, when the first rebellious stirrings against conventional authority begin. He started cutting classes and talked his cousin Jim into joining him. "We didn't do much," Jim admitted, "just fooled around until it was time to go home." But before it got out of hand, the mothers decided to take action. Harry, Gil and Jim were enrolled as boarders at King's College School in Windsor, 25 miles from Kentville. The mothers were advised by the Headmaster, "Any funny business from the lads and they'll feel the sting of six of the best across their backsides."

With a sense of foreboding, the boys prepared themselves for the worst when their summer holidays ended. Harry remembered 1915 as the last days of his boyhood, the sudden transition from child to youth. "We spent that summer roaming the county on our bikes, picking strawberries, then raspberries when they came in season. We went swimming at Kingsport Beach or Starr's Point. Sundays were for visiting grownups around a large dinner table and listening to their stories. On rainy days we played darts in the loft of Uncle Harry's barn."

5

By 17 November, while the Canadian 1st Division sat soaked and waiting on Salisbury Plain, the battle in Europe had changed from a fluid movement of men, guns and horses to a series of trenches, barbed wire and shell holes stretching from the coast of Belgium to the Swiss frontier, a distance of over 300 miles. During the next four years, changes along the front lines would be measured in yards as the vast opposing armies settled in to wear each other down. The front might bend and bulge a little from time to time as either side probed for weakness in its enemy's defences, but every small advantage was always short-lived. The battered defenders would rouse themselves through some supreme effort and counterattack to regain the lost ground.

In February 1915 the British War Office decided finally that its Canadian troops were trained and equipped sufficiently to be sent to France. The division sailed from Avonmouth and arrived in the port of St. Nazaire. It reached the front line on 3 March, where a few days later men of the Princess

Patricia's Canadian Light Infantry (composed largely of ex-British regulars who had been in France the previous two months serving with the British 29th Division) stopped a fierce counterattack at St. Floi, near the town of Ypres. The British generals conducting the campaign appeared satisfied with this performance. One of them wrote his corps commander: "Our Canadian troops have been blooded nicely and their line has held."

If any lingering doubt remained about the Canadians, it was dispelled a week after the 1st Division took over a sector of the front line in the northern face of the Ypres salient on 17 April. Laffy, who had been promoted to temporary colonel the week before, was still suffering from the aftereffects of having his tonsils removed in mid-March. Offered a 30-day recuperative leave in England, he had turned it down in favour of remaining with the action. Quickly, he positioned his casualty clearing stations and field ambulance services at various points 1,000 yards behind the trenches.

The Allied spring offensive had petered out the month before. The British offensive began at the village of Neuve Chapelle on 10 March, but a week later, when the dust settled, all that had been gained was a small village and strip of land three miles wide and a mile deep. The French offensive, farther east in the Woevre and Alsace regions, was of no greater value to the general campaign. To add to Allied woes, a Russian offensive in the east had failed miserably. Suddenly, it became essential that something be done quickly to prevent the Germans sending more troops from the Western Front to deal the Russian army its death blow. With Russia out of the war, the Germans would have sizeable reinforcements to pour into their trenches in the west. After hurried discussions among the Allied Army Commands in early April, Lille was selected as the point for renewed Allied activity. The Germans, however, anticipated the move and at once began preparations for a massive counterattack in the Ypres sector.

For the first two days after the Canadians arrived in the line, both armies exchanged desultory fire across no-man's-land, testing each other's defences. "Men died and men were wounded," Laffy wrote, "but no more than had been dying and wounded since the last big thrust took us nowhere. Sometimes I have my doubts that the men leading our armies know what they are about. Nevertheless, we must depend on our British generals to come up with the right answers or we are all lost."

The German bombardment opened along the front at dawn on 22 April 1915 as prelude to their counterattack. The troops hunkered down and waited. Hour after hour for the next three days and nights the shells screamed down, churning the soft ground and trenches into a horror of cratered cesspools filled with black-water mud and splattered bodies. "The human destruction and suffering is beyond description. Wagon loads of amputated limbs and mutilated bodies covered with tarps leave the Clearing Stations twice each day. Some take a direct hit on their way back to the burial disposal area.

When this happens the orderlies load what's left into other wagons and push the dead horses into the first available shell hole of which there is never any shortage. The dead, dying and wounded continue on to the sector Field Hospital. It is heartbreaking work for all of us trying to patch up bodies before life drains away."

Near twilight on 22 April the shelling ceased suddenly. An eerie quiet descended over the front. Down the line in either direction the muffled crump of heavy guns continued, their sound deadened by distance. But on the Ypres sector even the rifle fire had stopped. Cautiously, the men peered through periscopes from their dugouts. Overhead skies were grey with a light breeze blowing from the east. A strange dirty yellow fog appeared in front of the German lines. It thickened and drifted slowly toward the Canadian trenches. Fascinated, the soldiers watched the dark mass as it slid through the barbed wire, crossed the sandbagged trenches, then settled down upon them. Within seconds they were scrambling to escape the deadly, choking chlorine gas.

All along the front, British, French and Canadians came running from their trenches in a wild panic of confusion and terror. Troops manning the second line of trenches watched in bewilderment. Their comrades staggered in over the parapets and collapsed, gasping for breath as they died in the agonies of suffocation. Some urinated in their socks or undershirts and wrapped them around their faces to keep out the fumes. Others tried holding their breath until the main cloud had passed and found that what gas was left behind in the trenches remained at waist level until it dissipated. Behind the cloud of creeping gas and wearing new protective masks came the German infantry.

Some of the fiercest fighting of the war took place in the days that followed. By next afternoon the Germans had pushed back the French and British to a point where the Canadians were forced to fight on three fronts between St. Julien and Grafenstafel. On 24 April they delivered another gas attack and St. Julien had to be abandoned. Then the wind changed and the prevailing westerlies prevented further gas attacks. The Canadians held their positions until relieved by British troops on 29 April.

Canadian casualties killed, wounded and missing were 3,000 men. Laffy was mentioned in dispatches and awarded a CB (Companion of the Bath) in recognition of his direction of the Allied medical services that had saved so many lives during the horrors on the Ypres sector that spring.

Back in Canada, school started the first week of September. Harry, Gil and cousin Jim arrived by train at Windsor to begin their first term as King's boarders. To their sons' embarrassment, both mothers had decided to come along and supervise an orderly transfer of authority. The fact that Prime Minister Borden himself was a King's old boy cut no ice with the cousins. Just because his parents wanted to be rid of Sir Robert a half century earlier didn't make things any easier for new boys in 1915.

During the first week they were forced through a series of disgusting initiation ceremonies given to all new boys but managed to retain both their sense of humour and perspective. Harry and cousin Jim were put in grade 8; Gil, two grades behind them. By Christmas Gil had advanced to grade 7. Harry always found his young brother's ability to excel almost effortlessly at everything he attempted oddly amusing. "Instead of being jealous of the little bugger I had to admire him. Only in athletics was I better."

Most of the boys had fathers and uncles serving overseas, and an underlying anxiety was always present whenever the daily papers arrived. Every few weeks a boy would be called out of class by the Head and led away to his study. After a comforting arm had been laid around the young lad's shoulder, the Head, as gently as possible, would tell him quietly that his father had been killed in France. With red-rimmed eyes the poor boy had to pack his belongings under the sympathetic stares of his dormitory mates, then catch the first train home. For a few days a pall of sorrow descended over the school until the natural resilience of youth regained the upper hand. The threat of losing a father on the battlefield remained constantly in every boy's mind.

For the June 1916 graduation day, Harry stood second in a class of 16 and received a prize for English and history. Cousin Jim came third, also collecting awards. Gil breezed to the top of his class and picked up first prize for overall proficiency. He was so far ahead of everyone else in his group that the Head made a recommendation he skip a grade and start his next school year in the same class as his brother and cousin. But by the time September 1916 arrived the Foster boys were in England.

The war had dragged on for two years, and there was nothing to indicate that it wouldn't go on for another two in exactly the same way. Laffy had been appointed deputy director of medical services during the fall of 1915 with a posting to Canadian Army Headquarters in France. His new job placed him far back from the front lines and involved monthly trips to England for various staff meetings. He decided to arrange passage for Janie and the boys. At least in England he would be able to see them every month during his brief leaves. He was sure now that "barring some peculiar accident that could happen to anyone anywhere I shall survive this business and live to a respectable age with you at my side, dear Janie." Except for the U-boat dangers in crossing the Atlantic, which he considered a minimal but calculated risk, there was really nothing to keep the family apart any longer.

The boys arrived with their mother at Liverpool in a convoy of 24 ships from Halifax on 27 July 1916. Laffy met them dockside and took them to London where he had rented a furnished flat in Hampstead Garden. After they were settled comfortably, he returned to France. It wasn't much of a reunion but it was better than nothing.

6

What remained of the summer was spent by the boys and their mother seeing the sights in and around London, a practice they continued every holiday during their three-year stay. The sidewalks were jammed with uniformed men from across the Empire—young, sad-eyed soldiers on leave from the front; walking wounded; older officers sporting campaign ribbons from the Boer War. Ladies' skirts were worn above the ankles and parasols and wide-brimmed hats were still in fashion. The streets rumbled with smoking buses, trucks, taxis, motorbikes and noisy private cars, while carriages and sleekly curried horses clopped around St. James and Hyde Park. Everyone appeared to have a fatalistic disregard about the future. Men and women laughed and shopkeepers went on with business as usual. The only visible signs of war were the gun emplacements scattered in city parks as protection against air attacks by German Zeppelins. And at night there was a blackout.

Mindful of what the Headmaster at King's had said about putting her sons in the same grade, Janie wisely decided to enter them in different schools. She realized that Harry accepted Gil's academic brilliance as a matter of course and had learned to live with it, but there was no reason to rub his nose in it. To compete and lose against a brother three years his junior would make him look ridiculous. Consequently, in September, while Gil stayed home to attend Orme Square School in West Kensington as a day boy, Harry went off as a boarder to Berkhamsted.

Berkhamsted grammar school, on the outskirts of London, dated from the reign of Henry VIII and reeked with those traditional values that had made England great. Nearly 400 years of British history had passed through its classrooms in the admirals, doctors, explorers, scientists, generals and statesmen who had formed the cornerstones of the Empire. As a visiting "colonial" Harry felt himself to be small-fry indeed. For a second time he endured the initiation punishment handed out to new boys. Berkhamsted's turned out to be far more brutal than King's. "But then they've had two hundred years longer to perfect it," he observed in a letter to his mother. In their first year, new boys were expected to act as lackeys for the sixth-formers.

"We were on call at any hour of the day or night to shine their shoes, make beds, press clothes and run errands. Tardiness or disobedience resulted in a painful caning by one of the seniors. Sixth-formers ran the school after classroom hours and so long as the brutality stopped short of permanent physical damage or death our seniors were allowed to do what they wanted with the new boys. . . . I became a particularly enticing target because of my colonial accent and the fact I was a good deal older than most of the other new boys."

But he soon got the hang of it and adapted to his new surroundings. Discipline, team spirit, fair play, gentlemanly conduct and hard work were instilled in the Berkhamsted boys. The effect on Harry was profound. In later years he regarded his time at the school as the turning point of his life.

Every weekday morning before classes the entire school assembled in the chapel for prayers and to hear any announcements from the Headmaster.

"At least once each week the Head read out the name of an old boy who had died in France, most of them not much older than me. At first they were just names and faces that boys who remembered them would point out in one of the school photos. But by the end of the war many of the dead and wounded were sixth-formers whom I had known and cheered on the football field; even one who'd caned me for failing to polish the brasswork on his cadet uniform. It seemed to me then that the finest thing a man could do with his life was join the army and serve his King."

In Canada Harry had thrilled to the stories and heroic adventures in G.A. Henty and *Boys Own Annual*, memorized the poems of Robert W. Service and Rudyard Kipling, and dreamed of sailing in a tall ship like those his grandfather had built. At Berkhamsted his interests switched to military history and the biographies of great generals. And although only managing to come first in his class standings one term during 1917, he kept himself in the top third throughout his Berkhamsted years.

Schoolwork never came easy to him and to achieve even the margin of success he enjoyed required much greater effort than he saw being put into it by most of the other boys. "How I envy them!" he wrote his father. "I feel very thick in the head." But any shortcomings he felt in his academic abilities were more than offset by his athletic accomplishments. He had developed into a slim-waisted, long-legged teenager with prodigious strength in the arms and shoulders and an astonishing capacity for absorbing punishment on the football field. In his first year his enthusiasm resulted in a broken nose. Halfway through the next season he managed to fracture a shoulder. Even so, he became a superb gymnast and distance runner and a valuable member of the school's cricket, swimming and football teams.

In November 1918, following a match against a military training unit stationed near the town, he was awarded the coveted School 1st XV Colours along with fellow classmate George Mills.* An assessment of their competitive abilities appeared in the school yearbook.

H.W. Foster ('18) A hard-working forward of the light type, who shoved hard, and was particularly good in the loose. Often came to the help of the outsides with his tackling.

---

*Later Sir George H. Mills, Air Chief Marshal of the RAF, and upon his retirement, Gentleman of the Black Rod in the House of Commons.

G.H. Mills ('18) A sturdy but slow forward, who was never very conspicuous, but could be relied upon to do his share. Useful with his feet.

Fifty-five years later the team captain still remembered Harry as "well mannered . . . self-sufficient and somewhat reserved apart from his enthusiasm for sport . . . an admirable member of the team, keen and cooperative. He played with dash and skill and was always a stayer."

Laffy had been posted back to Canadian Headquarters at Shorncliffe in England as director-general of medical services and temporary surgeon-general. The post warranted promotion to major-general. He took over his new posting from the outgoing director, Maj.-Gen. G.C. Jones, on 11 February 1917. Nearly 20 years had passed since Sir Frederick Borden had persuaded him to join the local county militia as surgeon-lieutenant. He had reached the top of his profession. In the Canadian Army Medical Corps major-general was as high as anyone could go.

Across the Channel the war swayed on. Great and bloody battles had been fought. Unknown towns, rivers and places had suddenly become focal points in the massive, pointless slaughter as the best and bravest of a generation perished. Gallipoli, in the Turkish Dardanelles, became the Ypres for Australian, British and New Zealand troops; after seven months of tactical insanity and over 100,000 casualties, the forces were withdrawn. At the battles of Verdun, nearly 700,000 French and German soldiers were lost in an unbelievable orgy of death and destruction. Seven entire villages disappeared from the face of the earth. On the Somme, an experiment in British and French cooperative incompetence along a 25-mile battlefront cost the British army 500,000 casualties in five months. There seemed to be no end to the slaughter. At Lys, Passchendaele, one place after another, generals gambled away their armies in disastrous, ill-conceived, poorly executed attacks or counterattacks that produced little more for either side than longer lists of casualties. No wonder the French army mutinied after the disastrous Nivelles offensive in April 1917.

The wounded, maimed and dying poured back across the Channel to military hospitals throughout Britain. In the tens of thousands they came, blinded, shell-shocked, gassed, burned and tortured beyond belief or human endurance. And for the first time since the Napoleonic Wars each nation's army found itself starved for reserves to replace the appalling losses at the front.

France and Germany had traditionally relied on conscripts to fill the army's ranks, but Britain had introduced a Military Service Bill in 1916 only when voluntary recruiting methods proved inadequate. Canada remained steadfast in its concept of a volunteer citizen army. But by the summer of 1917 the shortage of replacements was causing ominous political rumblings at home.

The problem lay with the French Canadians of Quebec. Of the 300,000

Canadian soldiers serving overseas in 1917 less than 15,000 were French Canadian, although French Canadians comprised a full 20 percent of the nation's population. "The French aren't pulling their weight!" trumpeted the English-speaking *Montreal Gazette*. It was an issue that threatened to tear the country's shaky confederation apart.

Yet the fault lay not so much with French Canada's distaste for a European war as with the bigotry of English Canada's defence establishment, who flatly refused to allow the Quebecois to serve together in their own regimental and battalion groups. The initial patriotic enthusiasm of French Canadian volunteers prepared to fight the "Prussians of Europe" had given way to deep suspicions of the "Prussians of Ontario." Politicians and churchmen who had encouraged Quebec's overseas volunteers during 1914 now fought like tigers to prevent the Conscription Bill from passing. In the end, the bill passed, but by then the young French lads at whom it was directed had vanished deep into the Quebec forests like their *coureurs de bois* ancestors, prepared to wait out the war. As it turned out, it was the Germans themselves who indirectly managed to solve the critical shortage of reserves for the Allied armies by bringing the United States into the war.

In May 1915 the Cunard liner *Lusitania*, equipped as an auxiliary warship, mounting guns and carrying a cargo of ammunition in her hold, was torpedoed off the Head of Kinsale by a German submarine. She sank in 45 minutes with a loss of 1,198 lives, including 124 Americans. Germany's ambiguously worded apology and reminder that the arming of merchant ships would be treated as a hostile act was unacceptable to President Woodrow Wilson. Three months later another U-boat, without warning, sank the White Star liner *Arabic* off Cape Clear. Among the passengers who lost their lives were 26 Americans. On 4 September another liner, the *Hesperian*, was torpedoed. Two American citizens were among her crew. The politically popular stance of U.S. neutrality began to change. In financial circles a concern developed that in the event of a German victory, England and France would be unable to honour their war debts to the U.S.

Finally, the German blunder of the Zimmermann Telegram dangling chunks of American territory before Mexico, combined with the declaration of unrestricted submarine warfare, brought the United States into the war on 6 April 1917. Within five months 1.5 million men were in training camps across the country. The first contingent landed in France during late June. Although it took the better part of a year for the full force of American mobilization to be felt in Europe, by the summer of 1918, 300,000 troops a month were crossing the Atlantic. Germany was finished.

The Honour Roll at Berkhamsted in July 1918 stated proudly that 1,145 old boys were serving with the country's armed forces; 184 had been killed in

action, 177 wounded. Gallantry awards included 84 MCs, 18 DSOs,* and one
VC. The VC winner was of particular interest to Harry, since its recipient,
Capt. George R. Pearkes,† although born in England, had emigrated to Canada
in 1906. A great fuss was made over Harry by some of the school's masters
when word was received in January that old boy Pearkes had won the Empire's
highest award for bravery. "As though being a general's son and fellow
Canadian produced some magic that placed me automatically in the same
league as George Pearkes. . . . All of it very embarrassing and a bit silly."

7

Janie, meanwhile, had started fretting over her sons' lack of appreciation
for the finer things in life. A French tutoress was engaged for the two summer
months in the hope of providing the boys with an eclectic "cultural wash."
Gil was enthusiastic, Harry vaguely suspicious. The young lady, Mademoiselle
Vernier, came from a good family, highly recommended by the wife of the
French ambassador. *La pauvre* Annette—as she was introduced—had been
visiting England with her parents in 1914 when the Germans marched into
France, occupying their town. They decided to remain in England until the
war ended and by early 1917 were out of funds and forced to find employment.

Annette was 19, three years older than Harry but light years ahead of
him in maturity. Tall for a French woman, she had shining, shoulder-length
black hair, ivory skin, a voluptuous figure and enormous brown eyes that
danced with suppressed mischief. Her heavily accented English oozed with
carnal promise. Both brothers fell instantly in love.

A series of afternoon and evening cultural sorties were arranged with
Annette and—worse luck—their mother. They visited museums, art galleries
and sculpture exhibitions, attended concerts at the Royal Albert Hall, and
were introduced to the spectacle of opera at Covent Garden. "Our abilities
in converstional French increased by leaps and bounds."

In late August a message arrived from Shorncliffe that Laffy had fallen
ill with an attack of influenza. Janie took the first train down to Kent, leaving
Annette in charge at the Kensington flat. Since Harry was away at school
most of the year, the boys shared a room with twin beds. But on the first
night Annette insisted they sleep separately and ordered Gil off grumbling
to the small guest room. Near midnight she tiptoed in to see Harry.

"I was petrified. She peeled off her clothes. Peeled off the bed covers and

*Military Cross and Distinguished Service Order.
†Later major-general during World War II, Canadian defence minister in 1957 and lieutenant-
governor of British Columbia in 1960.

tore the buttons off my pajama top trying to undress me." The last thing he remembered before being engulfed by lust was how mad his mother would be when she discovered the missing buttons. Brother Gil found them in bed together in the morning. A Bible was produced and Gil compelled to swear eternal silence. His admiration for Harry soared.

"What was it like?" Gil demanded later.

"Oh, it was all right, I suppose," Harry told him modestly.

"Jesus!" Gil rolled his eyes with envy. "I wish to God I was 16."

Two weeks later they were back in school. Two months later the war was over.

By the spring of 1919 only the last vestiges of the mighty Allied forces remained in England. Sprawling camps and manning depots lay silent, littered with refuse abandoned by the departing armies. All that remained were headquarters and hospital staff along with the last of the bedridden battle casualties too sick to move.

Laffy stayed on at Shorncliffe, organizing the final disbandment of Canadian hospitals throughout England and assembling all Canadian personnel working in British hospitals for transfer home. "Like the 'ten little indians' the trick was to clear us all out of England without disruption or danger to the stretcher cases until only one person was left. Me."

His command position as director-general of medical services meant a posting to Ottawa when he got home. It wasn't something he anticipated enjoying. Military politics and backstabbing in Ottawa during the war had been bad enough. "The thought of sitting in the middle of it all during peacetime is enough to dampen anyone's enthusiasm for the job." He decided the boys should return with their mother when the school term ended. He would follow later.

He considered himself lucky to have survived the war with nothing more than a shrapnel cut across the bridge of his nose—a memento from a visit to the front in 1916. In recognition of his services to France he was awarded the Legion of Honour and Croix de Guerre. Britain added the Order of St. John of Jerusalem, awarded for services in the cause of humanity throughout the Commonwealth.

Despite the cessation of hostilities in Europe, the world remained in turmoil. Canadian troops were in Siberia fighting against the Bolsheviks. An influenza epidemic raged across the globe, killing more people in four months than had been lost during the entire war by all the nations involved. On 21 June the German fleet was scuttled by its officers and men at Scapa Flow in a final gesture of defiance. In Paris the Allies fretted impatiently for the Germans to sign a final peace treaty. Things were not going well.

Across the Atlantic the Riot Act was read in the city of Winnipeg, placing it under martial law, when a bitter strike ended with a police charge that left one man dead and two others badly hurt. In Toronto a tram-car strike had paralyzed the city. Even Halifax had its share of problems: a general vaccination had been ordered to combat an outbreak of smallpox.

Janie and the boys sailed for home in July to spend what remained of the summer with their family in the Annapolis Valley. "It was like coming home to heaven," Harry remembered. "Everything seemed to be moving at an unhurried orderly pace. In England I had the feeling of being merely one individual within a group. But arriving back in Canada I felt for the first time that I belonged. Until then 'King and Country' had been just words. Now I knew exactly what they meant."

It was strawberry-picking time. Roadside banks lay covered with wild flowers. The afternoons were hot and breathless. Fat robins gorged themselves and sang.

The boys were paraded around the district to visit relations like prodigal sons. Both had developed pronounced English accents, which drew amused smiles from aunts and uncles and imitative teasing from all the cousins, who insisted that they were trying to act "stuck up."

When September came, the boys were sent off to separate schools. Janie reasoned that since Ottawa would be the family's residence until Laffy finished his service career, their schooling should be in the same general area. She sent Harry as a boarder to Bishop's College School in Lennoxville, Quebec, east of Montreal, while Gil entered high school in Ottawa. Both were still in the same grade.

Harry's strength and size placed him on the Bishop's football team a week after his arrival. The first season he did well; as the school magazine reported: "[It was] his first year at the Canadian game but he picked it up very quickly and developed into one of the best linesmen we had. He is a rangy player."

In early October Laffy fell ill with the strain of influenza sweeping the world. For several weeks he hovered near death. Janie made arrangements to sail on the next available ship, but before she could embark, a telegram arrived from Shorncliffe: "Patient has survived. Sailing for home November 19 with Xmas presents for all."

He was still very weak. The illness had affected his heart in some odd way, so that it was skipping one beat in every four. "An uncomfortable sensation," he complained. Instead of visiting London one last time to say goodbye to his friends and associates, he went directly to Southampton and boarded his ship.

His friend, Sir William Osler, the great Canadian diagnostician, wrote to him from London two days before he sailed: "I am desolate not to see you and say 'Good-bye' in person. Hearty thanks for all the good work you have done. You took over a tough job and have pulled it through."

When Sir Andrew MacPhail wrote *The Medical Services (The Official History of the Canadian Forces in the Great War, 1914–19)*, he concluded his volume with the words "The Service had been created in time of peace by Bergin, Neilson, Fiset and Jones; in time of war by Jones and Foster."

"Imagine that!" Laffy wrote, obviously pleased. "A farm boy from North Kingston helping to create the Army's Medical Services—and a Major General to boot!"

8

Harry and Gil had made up their minds to join the army and chose to enter Royal Military College (RMC) in Kingston as the starting point of their careers. The college had been turning out Canadian officers and gentlemen since 1876. Standards were high, discipline severe, and the camaraderie among cadets invaluable for those intending to make the army their profession.

If their father had reached the top, neither boy saw any reason why he couldn't do the same. Laffy was enormously proud of their decision. Yet the old problem of Gil's brilliance overshadowing Harry remained to be solved. If they graduated from their respective high schools in the same year, they would enter RMC together. The solution was provided by Gen. Sir Arthur Currie, the new principal of McGill University in Montreal. Currie had ended the war as Canadian Army Corps commander and knew Laffy well.

In 1920 the Board of Governors of McGill—after some prompting from Sir William Osler—invited Laffy to receive an Honorary Doctor of Laws degree in recognition of his service to the nation. He accepted. The award held a peculiar irony for him. Back in 1892 when he had entered Dalhousie University as a medical student, he had claimed he had received his mandatory two years premedical university training at McGill. He had never been near the place and had arrived in Halifax straight off the farm, believing all he needed to qualify for medical school was his high school graduation certificate and tuition money. No one had told him about the prerequisite of two years training in arts and science. He couldn't ask his family for more money, nor could he afford to waste an extra two years reaching his goal. He crossed his fingers and decided to bluff it, hoping the Dalhousie Registrar would be too busy to check with McGill. The bluff worked.

"Think what might have happened if you had told the truth!" Currie exclaimed.

"I know very well what would have happened, General. I'd have become a farmer working for my brother Ed."

He explained his concern over Harry's RMC entry to Currie. The old corps commander thought a moment and smiled. "Laffy, you're trying to circumvent the system again, aren't you?"

Laffy agreed that he was.

"Then why not send him to McGill first and RMC later, instead of the other way around?"

The military college's four-year scholastic course did not provide graduates with degrees in a variety of subjects. A further year of study was needed at a recognized civilian university. Theoretically, if Harry took his extra year at McGill first, he could be credited with two years at RMC, placing him a class ahead of Gil. It would be twisting the procedures but it was worth a shot.

But RMC's commandant, Lieut.-Gen. A.C. Macdonell, was aghast when Laffy proposed this educational "fiddle" on behalf of his eldest son. "It's not playing the game!" Macdonell complained when Laffy visited him in Kingston.

"It's for the lad's own good," Laffy countered.

They reached a compromise. If Harry could pass his first year applied science course at McGill with an 80 percent average and find himself a militia unit willing to grant him an appointment as lieutenant, then Macdonell would see to it that RMC accepted him as a third-year student entrant. Pleased with himself, Laffy returned to Ottawa.

Eight months of Ottawa was all he could stomach. Beyond the usual political intrigues raging on all sides, there didn't seem to be much for him to do that really mattered. Gradually, he found himself giving way to cynicism about the importance politicians now placed on the armed forces. The Allied treaty signed at Versailles effectively bankrupted the German people into total submission. Simultaneously, the League of Nations had been founded with the objective of "providing a lasting peace between all peoples of the earth." Other than quelling the odd riot, a country's armed forces appeared superfluous in these new enlightened times, according to the politicians.

The truth was that after the pressures and excitement of war Laffy had become bored with peace. The thought of spending the rest of his active career in Ottawa pushing paper and intriguing with bureaucrats appalled him. He was only 49 and still in reasonably good health. There were bound to be other things he could do. He decided the time had come to leave the army.

On the last day of May 1921 the government made his departure official. His $3,638.54 per annum pension was generous* and, when added to Janie's income, provided enough for them to live comfortably. They packed their things and returned to the old house in Kentville.

Harry graduated from Bishop's in June, winning the Lieutenant-Governor's Medal for French. He attributed this single academic success to the basic grounding received in the language from *la pauvre* Annette back in England.

---

*Skilled tradesmen earned $2,500 per annum in 1921.

The rest of his marks were in the low 60s. Gil, on the other hand, collected every available prize from his school as well as a 96 percent average. The brothers headed back to Kentville for their holidays.

Arranging for Harry to enter McGill posed no problem. But a bona fide commission in a militia regiment was considerably more difficult. Fortunately, a horse called Ginger solved the matter for him. Ginger and Starbuck were a pair of magnificent chargers Laffy had received as a parting gift from the British Army Medical Corps in 1919. They came with him on the ship to Halifax and were sent to Fred Wickwire for stabling until Laffy could make up his mind what to do with them. Much later he learned that the animals had been superbly trained at the Royal Equestrian College in Weedon and were in fact worth a considerable sum.

Harry discovered their jumping, hunting and showmanship abilities quite by accident the year after they moved back to Kentville. He pronounced Ginger the best of the pair, certainly better trained than any other horse in Nova Scotia. Laffy respected his judgment. Harry had been riding since the age of seven and at age nine had fearlessly handled an enormous black stallion.

Word of Ginger's abilities spread around the county. That summer Laffy had a visit from the colonel of the local militia based at Camp Aldershot nearby. The King's (Nova Scotia) Mounted Rifles were starting their summer training exercises and needed horses to train recruits. Each year the army rented whatever horses were required from the surrounding district. Naturally, owners brought in their worst old plugs and pastured drays for military use.

"Can't say as I blame them, General," the Colonel conceded. "Only a damn fool would turn over a good horse for some ploughboy to practise his cavalry charges. But just for once I'd like to have a decent mount for the summer."

Laffy smelled the possibility of a horse trade. "Tell you what, Colonel. You can have both horses for the summer camp provided you take my son Harry with Ginger and give him a commission. No charge for the horses."

"Done, by God!" the Colonel exclaimed and rode out on Starbuck.

By summer's end Provisional Lieut. Harry Foster had proved to be a competent cavalryman. "I can match anyone in the unit when it comes to horsemanship," he bragged, and the boast included brother Gil, who was petrified of the animals.

Gil went away to RMC in August. The following month Harry left for McGill. Laffy drove Harry to the station to catch the train for Halifax and Montreal, impressing upon him the importance of doing well at school, but saying nothing about his agreement with Lieutenant-General Macdonell or about his having to make an 80 percent average. "If he'd told me that, I might have thrown in the sponge then and there. I had never made an 80 percent average in my life."

Harry took a room on Sherbrooke Street within walking distance of the university. He had a letter for General Currie from his father, with instructions to deliver it in person. Sir Arthur received him graciously, scanned the contents, then delivered a stinging 15-minute lecture on the importance of celibacy throughout his year of studies and on the evils of Montreal's night life . . . which were considerable.

The Principal needn't have worried. Harry had already decided to prove his stunted academic abilities were correctable. By the Christmas holidays he had managed an 82 percent average, and for his final exams, an astonishing 91 percent. Elated, he returned home to discover just how much had been riding on the outcome of his year at McGill.

True to his word, Macdonell enrolled him as a "gentleman cadet" at RMC one class ahead of his brother. His formal army career began on 4 September 1922 when he arrived at Kingston on the train with Gil and checked into the college as a third-year student. He was under no illusions about the manner in which he had managed to enter and knew that the staff and other cadets of his class would be gauging his performance carefully. Sons of senior army officers—brats as they were called—were expected to excel. Failure would be unthinkable, the disgrace unbearable.

On his second day Harry paraded before Macdonell. To his men in France Macdonell had been known as "Batty Mac" because of a variety of eccentricities. To those who irritated him, he'd bark out: "You're fired!" and then apologize later. The cadets adored him. He had graduated from RMC back in 1886, standing fourth in his class and winning an honours diploma. For 20 years he had served with the Royal North-West Mounted Police (RNWMP) before taking over command of the 1st Division in France to become one of Canada's greatest fighting soldiers. Whenever he spoke of the Mounties, the 1st Division or his monarch, he clicked his heels like a Prussian martinet and came solemnly to attention.

"You intend to make the army your career, Foster?"

"Yes, sir!"

"Admirable ambition. And how far do you intend to venture in the service, may I ask?"

"I intend to become a general, sir."

At this brash impertinence a smile ghosted Macdonell's features. For a moment the thin lips beneath the heavy white moustache pursed thoughtfully.

"In that case, young man, make very sure that you become a good one! Don't become an idler. We have quite enough idlers and rascals in the service already. Bear that in mind."

Harry promised that he would.

PART 2
BATTLE'S WAKE

Man in portions can foresee,
His own funereal destiny.

BYRON

KURT ADOLF WILHELM MEYER was born on 23 December 1910 in the village of Jerxheim, 30 kilometres southeast of Braunschweig* as the crow flies. His father, Otto, was a happy-go-lucky man with a wide smile, grey eyes and unusual musical talents. Without any professional training he managed to teach himself to play a variety of instruments and to play them well. Every wedding, village dance or holiday gathering used Otto's one-man band as the main attraction. The pay was poor but he always had a good time.

Otto had little formal education. His five brothers and two sisters had acquired a respectable status in the community through hard work, but Otto preferred living from day to day, letting the future take care of itself. He wasn't lazy. He just never got around to getting properly organized to follow a career.

Jerxheim lay surrounded by huge fields of corn, potatoes and cabbages. Flat farmland stretched from one horizon to the other, its monotony broken by a few lonesome trees and low buildings. A coalminers' settlement bordered

---

*The city of Brunswick in Brunswick State, of which Jerxheim was a part.

the village. The coal was of a low-grade quality and burned too quickly, giving off clouds of sulphurous black smoke that ruined the lines of fresh washing on laundry days. The only other local industries were a sugar beet processing plant and coal briquet factory nearby at Offleben.

Otto's father, a mild-mannered farmer, encouraged his son to seek the security of a job with a future. Something stable and permanent. The sugar beet factory looked like his best bet. It was a sensible suggestion, provided a position could be found that required no unusual ability or profound dedication. Otto made a cautious inquiry and was hired immediately as an unskilled labourer. It suited his teenage temperament exactly.

He had been on the job four years when one of the local farm girls caught his eye. Alma Weihe was 18 years old and the exact opposite to Otto, which was probably why they found each other so appealing. Where Otto was careless, Alma was careful. While he ignored the future, she planned for it. A woman of quick perception and great determination, she set her sights on the musically romantic Otto. Alma had three brothers and a sister. Her mother worked on one of the local farms, but her father, a mason by profession, had been killed in an accident while employed as a lumberman one winter.

Alma believed Otto could do much better for himself and her by giving up his job in the sugar beet factory and joining the Kaiser's expanding army. At least in the army Otto would have a chance of advancement and a decent wage. Without wealth and family connections, he could never aspire to the officers' corps, but a senior noncommissioned rank was certainly within reach of his abilities. Anything would be better than working as a labourer. Besides, Otto could garner a degree of respect in the community by wearing the Emperor's uniform.

Otto had other ideas. Despite his desire to please Alma, he put his foot down when it came to enlisting. A life of 24-hour duty under strict Prussian military discipline held scant interest for the easygoing Meyer, in spite of the attraction of a uniform. The matter resolved itself quickly when Alma discovered herself with child. How could Otto, in all decency, leave for military service at such a time? Enlistment plans were suspended until after the baby arrived.

In Germany in 1910, the death rate for children up to the age of seven was the highest in Europe. But Alma's firstborn was blessed with a sturdy constitution and a healthy pair of lungs. She stayed home nursing the baby until he could digest solid food, then went to work at the sugar beet factory with Otto. During his mother's daily absences young Kurt was left to the care of his paternal grandmother. Germany provided compulsory old age pensions after 1889, but most working-class families had one or more elderly members living under the same roof.

Although Otto was prepared to accept responsibility for fathering young Kurt, he had not the least intention of marrying Alma—at least for the moment. He considered marriage a state a man did not venture into lightly. He needed time to think about it. (It was not until the outbreak of war in 1914 that he finally made up his mind and proposed. They had a "war wedding" at Goslar.)

Things were not easy for Alma, being the mother of an illegitimate child in a small conservative village. There was gossip. Her mother defended her. Local wagging tongues suggested that she should turn the baby over to an institution for proper care, for how else could the child survive? But Alma refused. Fortunately, she had always been a good worker, so the manager of the sugar beet plant gave her permission to keep the baby with her in the workers' quarters provided by the company.

Once again Alma began pressuring her Otto to join the army. Only this time she was careful not to become pregnant before a decision had been made. Gradually, she wore away at his defences. Her arguments were hard to challenge. After all, what future did either of them have in their present jobs? Did he want them to spend the rest of their lives amid the sweet rotting pungency of sugar beets? The army had to be better. Once in its uniform, he'd become a respected member of the community. Steady wages. Security. Even early promotion was possible when his superiors discovered his musical talents. Didn't every soldier love to sing?

At last Otto gave in. He packed his instruments away and took a train to Magdeburg where he enlisted in the infantry for the minimum service term of 12 years. Anything to keep Alma happy.

2

As Alma had anticipated, Otto Meyer's presence in the Kaiser's army had caught the eye of his superior officer. Everyone liked Otto. Fellow soldiers came to him with their problems, looked to him for advice, and admired his musical accomplishments and relaxed approach to life. Yet when there was a job to be done, he went at it quickly and efficiently. He rose quickly through the ranks of noncommissioned officers, which in the closely structured and socially conscious German army was no mean accomplishment.

His son adored him. Not quite four, Kurt already imagined himself a soldier. Otto made him a wooden sword with a real metal guard cut from a tin can. Brandishing the weapon, Kurt strutted around the house issuing orders to imaginary legions and the family dog.

During late July 1914 Otto's regiment received orders to move out and occupy positions along the French border. He kissed Kurt, Alma and his new baby girl, Melanie, goodbye and went off to war. After he had gone, Alma wept.

"Why are you crying, Mama?" Kurt asked. He saw nothing strange in his father's departure to fight the French. That was what soldiers were supposed to do, wasn't it? "Don't worry, Mama. If my daddy gets wounded or killed, then I'll shoot all Frenchmen. I'll teach them, if they dare touch my daddy!"

After nearly half a century of peaceful and prosperous development without serious interruption, the German Empire found itself at war with half the world. Spontaneously, 67 million Germans rose as one in a wave of enthusiasm that swept aside every difference of class, age, religion and political belief. It was without parallel in German history.

There was no hatred or hostility. As a nation the German people were neither politically minded nor politically trained. Decisions on foreign policy were matters best left to the Kaiser's diplomatic experts, so far as his subjects were concerned. Whatever the problem, the people had no doubt about the essential righteousness of the German cause—whatever it was. In spite of the Kaiser's military flamboyance, they believed that at the bottom of his Teutonic heart he was a man of peace. Any decision to take up arms must have been forced upon him. Without this unshakeable conviction the German people could never have found the strength to hold on for so long against the overwhelming coalition of forces arrayed against them.

Yet, however politically unprepared Germany may have been to fight a war, its General Staff operated with clockwork precision. For five days and nights the officer in charge of mobilization plans remained at his post in the Ministry of War, ready to answer any questions that might arise during the massive troop movements. But so smoothly did the military machine function that not a single inquiry was received.

German success depended upon a swift encircling movement based on the famous Schlieffen Plan.[1] But von Moltke, chief of the General Staff, was no Schlieffen and his watered-down version of Schlieffen's tactically brilliant idea resulted in the German retreat from the Marne six weeks later. The mobile form of warfare, which for a hundred years had been the special preserve of the Prusso-German army, was replaced by a stationary trench warfare once the original plan had miscarried.

If Gen. Erich von Falkenhayn, the Prussian minister of war who took over from the broken von Moltke, had followed his first instincts and resumed the offensive, in all probability he could have brought the war to a successful conclusion on the Western Front during the autumn of 1914; but because he went on the defensive, the immediate advantage in training and leadership held by a superb German army over the first weeks of the war was lost. The tactic gave the Allies time to bring up their overwhelming reserves of men and resources until at last, through sheer numbers and abundance of material, Germany would be forced to capitulate. Falkenhayn's decision taken on the morning of 15 September 1914 sealed the German defeat four years later.

On the Eastern Front, however, the dashing Eighth Army under Gen. Paul von Hindenburg managed to maintain its mobility against Russia. In the battle of Tannenberg at the end of August, General Samsonov's Second Russian Army was surrounded and nearly destroyed. The Germans captured 92,000 prisoners. Yet by the time Russia's army collapsed in 1917 it was too late to provide any material advantage to the German army on the Western Front.

Nevertheless, the horror of the trenches, the battles of Ypres, Verdun, the Somme and the Argonne ultimately drained the nation's reserves of men and material. The dream of a new and better Germany so strong among the volunteers who had flocked to the Kaiser's banners died on pockmarked battlefields in Poland and Flanders. Of all the losses that befell Germany, the greatest was the loss of the idealistic and brave young men who should have been its future leaders.

The last gasp of the German army came on 15 July 1918 when both prongs of an attack at Rheims collapsed with severe losses. Acceptance of defeat might have saved something from the chaos that eventually followed Gen. Erich von Ludendorff's last gamble. But Hindenburg's operational commander was a stubborn man. Like Napolean at Waterloo, when all reasonable chance of avoiding defeat had vanished, he refused to admit that he was beaten. For three months he wavered between bursts of acute depression and blind optimism.

Inside the country social order began to break down. Mobs of disillusioned and hungry people roamed the streets inside the major cities of the north, shouting revolutionary slogans and setting fires. U.S. President Wilson demanded that a democratic government be established to arrange a peace in accordance with his 14-point program. Faced with the inevitable, Kaiser Wilhelm agreed. As the *Götterdämmerung* approached, the Kaiser appointed Prince Max of Baden to the chancellorship of the nation's first democratic government with orders to negotiate for a cessation of hostilities. But he had waited too long. When Wilson demanded Wilhelm's abdication, revolution broke out and spread like wildfire across the country. On 4 November the fleet mutinied at Kiel. Finally, on 9 November, the last vestiges of government were overthrown in Berlin, and from the balcony of the Imperial Castle Germany was declared a republic. Prince Max announced the Kaiser's abdication and departure with his family into exile. The Hohenzollern dynasty was finished.

3

Otto survived the war, an astonishing accomplishment for an Oberfeldwebel* who had crossed into Belgium with the main force of infantry on 4 August 1914. He received four wounds, one during each year of service at the front lines. The last, a bullet through his right lung taken during the final days of fighting nearly finished him. The medics put an army greatcoat over him and sent him away. He arrived home bloodsoaked and weary.

The Meyers moved from Jerxheim to the larger town of Schöningen, where Otto recuperated at home. Too ill to work and with no military pension to sustain his family, he turned to Alma for suggestions on how they were to survive. With single-minded determination, she enrolled in an 18-month course at the Brunswick School of Midwifery. While she was away, her mother and young Kurt looked after Otto and Melanie. Midwifery students were not supposed to be married, and visiting males were forbidden on the premises. The nurses made an exception in Alma's case. When Otto turned up for a visit, they helped smuggle him into her room and provided a little extra food. She passed her final exams with good marks and returned home.

In the bureaucratic upheaval that followed the revolutionary movement, anyone with the least talent could profess expertise in any occupation and bluff it out, although actually finding work within a chosen profession was quite another matter. Undaunted, Alma persuaded the authorities of her competence and became the family's principal breadwinner. It meant leaving the house at odd hours and placing her ten-year-old son in charge of things while Otto was sick.

Proudly, Kurt rose to the situation: "Mummy, you go to work, I'll look after Melanie and Papa. Everything will be all right." And so it was except for periodic moments when the boy within him gained the upper hand and he gave his sister his schoolbag and disappeared off into the woods to play. These lapses seldom lasted more than two or three days before the school principal would drop by the house inquiring after Kurt's health. Kurt accepted the punishment that followed without complaint.

"Did it hurt?" Melanie inquired after one thrashing.

"Yes. But not enough to make me cry!"

By spring Otto's health had improved to a point where he could sit in a chair by the window and watch the bleak winter's accumulation of coal dust being washed away by the April rains. Kurt enjoyed marching into the room and performing the sword drills his father had taught him while on leave during the war.

"Go on with you!" Otto laughed. "You're not a soldier or an officer yet."

---

*Sergeant-major.

"But I will be one day. You'll see!"

Revolution in 1918 ended all thought of further resistance by the army but failed to bring about its dissolution. The OHL* remained intact and at its post and directed the march back from the Rhine in perfect order within the short time allowed to it by the Allies' armistice terms.

However, the course of revolution was far from smooth. Moderates and radicals throughout the country struggled desperately to assert their dominance, the former trying to re-establish law and order, the latter attempting to extend the revolutionary movement. A "Council of People's Delegates" had replaced the Imperial government in Berlin, but its more moderate members found it impossible to work with radicals backed by armed revolutionary guards and street mobs. In desperation, Ebert, head of the moderates, turned to the army for help.

The problem lay in locating officers with forces that could be relied upon to remain loyal at a time when a general demoralization had infected the service. Units that had marched back into Germany as disciplined formations had dissolved to rabble and disappeared once they had reached their home garrisons and been exposed to the ravings of the civilian population. On Christmas Eve, 1918, the first attempt to clear the Imperial Palace of revolutionary guards turned into a rout. The army could no longer be relied upon. A new method of restoring law and order had to be devised. And quickly.

It came through creation of the *Freikorps*,† groups of voluntary forces serving alongside remnants of the old army. Their leaders were mainly junior officers and NCOs (noncommissioned officers) demobilized only a month or two earlier from various branches of the military service. Although their training, strength and discipline varied widely, all were committed to defending Germany's eastern frontiers from Polish incursions and to breaking the revolutionary terror at home. They shared a fanatical hatred for the Republic and its lifeless provisional government which didn't trust them.

Paradoxically, a new republic rose out of these counterrevolutionary *Freikorps*, which provided the embattled Ebert government with time to arrange a constitutional assembly in the Thuringian town of Weimar.

During February 1919 *Freikorps* units made their first appearance in Bremen, smashing revolutionary forces that had occupied the old Hanseatic town. Westphalia and Halle were the next to fall. By March, after a week of bloody street fighting that left 1,200 dead, Berlin had been cleared. The cities of Magdeburg and Brunswick, both centres of extreme radicalism, were targeted in April, and by the end of the month 30,000 Prussians, Bavarians

---

*German Army High Command.
†Free Corps.

and South Germans were concentrated against Munich. The 60,000 Soviet Red Guards assembled at Dachau were overthrown on 7 April and the *Freikorps* swept on to conquer Saxony in May. By summer their numbers had risen to 400,000 men. Order was restored, the revolutionary guards disarmed, and conservative elements in each locale persuaded to assist local authorities in maintaining law and order.

In Weimar, meanwhile, the Constitutional Assembly enacted a law covering a "provisional Reichswehr" (German army), which confirmed the legitimacy of the *Freikorps*. It provided for a voluntary enlistment of six or nine years, promotion of privates and NCOs to commissioned rank, and the creation of special military schools with an emphasis on sport instead of army drills. Given the legal authority to act, work began at once on the military foundations of the resurrected German army.

On 7 May 1919 at the Versailles treaty conference the Allied powers handed the German delegation a thunderbolt. In the draft of the peace treaty, German military forces were to be limited to 100,000 long-term volunteers, including 4,000 officers. Permissible armaments were listed down to the last detail: no tanks, aircraft or heavy artillery. Only a minimum of light weapons and cavalry units would be allowed. The General Staff was to be dissolved and all military schools throughout the nation were to be closed with four exceptions. All preparations for mobilization were to be strictly forbidden. Finally, Germany was to admit responsibility for causing the war and surrender its wartime leaders for trial before an Allied tribunal.

These last two "honour clauses" infuriated the Reichswehr. They announced their readiness to sacrifice themselves in a hopeless struggle rather than stand by and see the country dishonour itself by signing such an outrageous document. Most of the generals spoke of open revolt. Plans were even discussed for setting up an independent state in East Prussia and trying to hold out in a last battle to the death against Allied and Polish forces. Hindenburg collapsed in paroxysms of indecision. Only Army Chief of Staff General Groener kept his head, realizing that any plan born of desperation could result in the total dismemberment of Germany. Despite abuse from every quarter, Groener had the courage to do what under existing circumstances was unavoidable. He capitulated to the Allied treaty demands and set about doing his best to fulfil their conditions.

The uneasy alliance between the Weimar Republic and the army had received a heavy blow. At every rank, soldiers felt they had been betrayed by the very government they had put in power. Even the national colours were changed to republican black, red and gold. Then, on 6 March 1920, under the conditions of the peace treaty, the government ordered the first reduction of the Reichswehr to 200,000 men. Once again the spark of revolution was ignited.

Conspirators, led by General von Lüttwitz, head of the Berlin Command,

and Dr. Kapp of the East Prussian administration, decided to overthrow the government and set up a national dictatorship. Warnings of the coup gave the government time to dismiss von Lüttwitz and Commander Ehrhardt, leader of the naval brigade stationed on the outskirts of Berlin, but before the orders could take effect the naval brigade marched on the city. Gen. Hans von Seeckt* saved the situation by asking Noske, the war minister, at the 11th hour: "There can surely be no idea of letting Reichswehr fight against Reichswehr. Do you, Minister . . . intend to let troops meet each other in battle . . . men who a year and a half ago were fighting shoulder to shoulder against the enemy?"

Noske cancelled his combat orders and left for Dresden at 4:30 a.m. to wait out events. Von Seeckt went on leave. A general strike was organized throughout Germany, and Kapp, Lüttwitz and Ehrhardt took over the seat of government in Berlin. They lasted three days. Only a small part of the Reichswehr followed Lüttwitz. Army commanders in the south and west of the country remained loyal to the legitimate government of Weimar. Even Lüttwitz's son-in-law refused to obey his orders. On the third day the "*Kapp-Putsch*" was over. Kapp fled to Sweden and von Seeckt came back from leave to arrange the orderly withdrawal of Ehrhardt's naval brigade to its quarters, where he had it disarmed and later disbanded. An unsettled peace returned.

Although Schöningen lay less than 40 kilometres from both Magdeburg and Brunswick, it was far enough off the main roads to miss most of the revolutionary unrest that continued to plague the major population centres. Both Otto and Alma were anti-Soviet and far from naive politically. In spite of the colossal failures of the monarchist government that had destroyed Germany in war and the weak ineffectual leadership of its Weimar replacement in peace, the Meyers were, like most small-town people, suspicious of the panaceas being offered by revolutionaries from either left or right. In Alma's opinion, honest hard work was the best solution to the nation's ills.

"No one gets something for nothing," she told Kurt. "In the end someone always has to pay a price."

The village of Offleben had no doctor, and modern medicines were nonexistent. Those who fell ill either got better or died. But once a year the government medical officer turned up to vaccinate the latest crop of babies. As local midwife, Alma became the officer's official contact in the community.

Word came by post that the medical officer would arrive at 10:00 a.m. the next day with his entourage of doctors and nurses to set up at the local school. Alma set Kurt off on his bicycle to alert the new mothers. Along

---

*President of the Preparatory Commission for the Peace Army and of the Truppenamt, which replaced the former General Staff.

the way he was stopped by a few of his pals who were going to a pond near the coal factory to catch tadpoles. They needed help. Someone to climb down the three-metre hole on the end of a rope and scoop the water. So far they had no volunteers. Would Kurt be interested?

"Let's go!" he told them. His reputation soared among his peers. Everyone shared the tadpoles.

When the medical officer arrived next morning none of the mothers appeared. A runner was dispatched to the Meyer household.

"Kurt!" Otto roared.

His ten-year-old son backed away. "I forgot, Papa. Wait a minute before you beat me."

He rushed outside, jumped on his bicycle, raced through the village to alert the missing mothers about the medical officer's arrival, then rode home to collect his thrashing.

Although he demonstrated an unusual degree of recklessness for a young lad, he did have one weakness: fear of the dark. Shortages after the war of just about everything produced armies of professional thieves. Anything that wasn't set in concrete was considered fair game for removal and resale.

One night Kurt awoke with a start. There were noises on the roof above the bedroom he shared with his sister. Men's voices. Thieves were taking down the lightning rod. Quickly he nipped out of bed and shook Melanie.

"They're here to murder us," he announced hoarsely. "Go get Grandma!"

The old lady was a year shy of her 70th birthday, but his youthful logic told him that a scream or two from her would be far more effective than anything a terrified soprano-voiced boy of 11 could produce. His sister padded off to wake their grandmother. Kurt waited, shivering in bed. By the time the old lady sorted herself out, the thieves were gone, along with the lightning rod.

"Why on earth didn't you shout, Kurt?"

"Because, Grandma, I was frightened. Supposing they decided to kill me? I had no gun."

"Supposing they decided to kill me?"

"No one would kill you. You're an old lady. That would not be correct."

It never occurred to him to wake his father or mother. Otto needed his rest and Alma might have insisted that her son lead the attack. In daylight he wouldn't have hesitated, but in the dark he was afraid.

He had a fascination for weapons, although his first encounter with live ammunition nearly turned into a disaster. During the third year of the war, Otto had returned from the front for a brief leave. Members of the armed forces were permitted to wear their weapons at all times, and Otto carried a pistol in a shiny leather holster. Kurt badgered him endlessly for permission to fire it. "When you're older and can shoot straight enough to kill Frenchmen then we can discuss it," his father said.

There wasn't a Frenchman within kilometres of the place. But there were plenty of dogs running wild. Ideal targets for pistol practice. And there was Fritz, the family's pet. Poor old Fritz had long passed the canine equivalent of three score and ten years. Sick, blind and arthritic, he dragged himself around the house in constant pain. Alma asked that the poor thing be put out of its misery, but Otto procrastinated.

"Papa, the dog has to be shot," Kurt reminded him one afternoon toward the end of his leave.

Otto sighed. "Very well. I'll take care of it after my nap."

Kurt waited until he was asleep, then crept into the bedroom and removed the pistol from its holster. Old Fritz was led out to the back garden and tied to a fence post. Releasing the safety catch the way his father had showed him, Kurt raised the weapon, steadying it with both hands. He closed his eyes and squeezed the trigger. Fritz howled. The bullet went wild. He fired again. His second shot hit the fence post. On the third try the dog dropped with a bullet through his brain.

Otto came running from the house with Kurt's grandmother, yanked the gun out of the boy's hands and began beating him with a stick. Kurt stood his ground. When it ended, he nodded.

"You are right to beat me, Papa. But it is not for taking your pistol, is it?"

"Isn't it?" Otto demanded. "What exactly do you think it's for?"

"Because I missed the first two shots. For that I am sorry. But you see I need more practice."

Slowly, his father pocketed the pistol. "Get a shovel and bury the dog, son." He went back to the house shaking his head.

4

The Treaty of Versailles stands as a classic example of how the destruction of a nation can be accomplished. Besides the limitations imposed on Germany as a military power, the treaty provided reprisals of unprecedented severity. The vast coalfields of the Saar Basin were to be handed over to France for 15 years, after which its inhabitants would decide their political future by referendum. Germany was stripped of all its colonial possessions, plus a broad slice of territory separating East Prussia from the rest of the country, which became a Polish province. More than a million Germans were expelled from this "Polish Corridor." The Baltic port of Danzig was detached from Germany and established as a demilitarized "Free City" under the League of Nations' protection. Although most of the city's 400,000 citizens were German, the treaty gave Poland joint control of Danzig harbour and over the foreign relations of its civic government. Finally, and most devastating of all, Germany was required to pay the Allies reparations for the war, amounting to 132 billion gold marks.

Allied propaganda at war's end had insisted that the fight had been with the Kaiser and German militarism, not with the German people. The war had been to save the world for the democratic ideal, and once the nation became a constitutional democracy, the German people were assured Allied friendship. On 4 July 1918, U.S. President Wilson had stated that no territorial changes would take place without the consent of the populations living within those territories. German soldiers returning from the battlefields of Europe were welcomed home by the slogan "God's blessing, you brave fighters. God and Wilson will help us now."

But it was not to be. The Allies decided that the German people had to be punished. Plebiscites were held in the dismembered territories of Schleswig, Eupen, Malmédy and in large portions of East Prussia, which resulted in resounding German victories. But the newly founded Austrian Republic, the Sudeten and South Tyrol Germans, who had voted by over 90 percent for German union, were forbidden to proceed. Austria was forced to change its name from Deutschösterreich to Österreich—Austria as distinct from German-Austria.

By late summer of 1919 the basic ingredients for another war were firmly in place. It required only a leader to appear who would promise to expunge what was perceived by its citizens as Germany's disgrace and national dishonour at the hands of its enemies and the whole ghastly business would once more be set in motion.

The government of the Weimar Republic lurched from calamity to calamity. In violation of the plebiscite decision given in 1921, Poland refused to return Upper Silesia to Germany. First Danzig, then Upper Silesia. How the Germans hated the Poles!

In January 1923 French and Belgian troops occupied the industrialized Ruhr Valley in retaliation for Germany's default on its war debt. Now the Germans hated the French and Belgians too.

To make matters worse, the country had entered a period of hyperinflation, the prelude to complete economic collapse. In 1914 the German mark, French and Swiss franc, Italian lira and English shilling were all about equal in value, with an exchange rate of four or five to the U.S. dollar. Nine years later when Germany's inflation had peaked, the exchange rate had reached one trillion marks to the dollar! Walter Levy, a German-born New York oil consultant, remembered: "My father was a lawyer and had taken out an insurance policy in 1903. . . . Every month he made the payments faithfully. It was a 20-year policy and when it came due he cashed it and bought a single loaf of bread."

"You'd better order two schnapps, friend, if you want to save money," a barman told a Canadian traveller to Frankfurt in 1923, "because by the time you're ready for your second drink the price will have climbed again."

Industrial workers were paid daily at noon from the back of trucks. A company accountant and his clerks climbed over the tailgates and threw out bundles of freshly printed notes to the men, who then raced to the nearest shop to buy something—anything—of value.

School teachers, paid during the morning recess each school day, arranged to have their relatives meet them at the playground to collect their bundles of currency and hurry off to buy the day's food. Lawyers, doctors and dentists began charging for their services in produce: chicken, eggs, butter—whatever was of real value.

Normally law-abiding citizens throughout the countryside turned to petty larceny. Gasoline was siphoned from cars and trucks. Copper pipes, electronic cables, steel rails and manhole covers disappeared. Nothing was sacred. Not even the lightning rod on the Meyers' roof.

Publisher Leopold Illstein wrote:

> People just didn't understand what was happening. All the economic theory that had been taught didn't provide for the phenomenon. There was a feeling of utter dependence on anonymous powers—almost as a primitive people believed in magic—that somebody must be in the know, and that this small group of "somebodies" must be a conspiracy.[2]

Into this bewildering state of affairs and uncertainty during November 1923 stepped Adolf Hitler.

Born in Braunau-am-Inn, Austria, near the German border, Hitler was the son of a minor Austrian customs official who, until mid-life, went by the name of Schicklgruber. Adolf was the product of his third marriage. His father died when the boy was 14, leaving a little money. Hitler received his basic education in Linz. After his mother died, he received a small orphan's pension and moved to Vienna, hoping to become an architect. He ended up working as a freelance artist, selling his sketches through an acquaintance, Reinhold Hanisch, for a pittance.

In May 1913, when he was 24, he abandoned Vienna for Munich. His years of Viennese penury and artistic failure, together with the violent anti-Semitism so prevalent in the city at the time,[3] produced in him a warped philosophy toward life. He considered his lack of recognition in Austria to be the fault of others rather than his own glaring artistic mediocrity. Since most of the talented artists and musicians in Vienna were Jewish, as were many of the city's successful businessmen, he considered the Jews responsible for frustrating his ambitions.

At the outbreak of World War I, he joined a Bavarian reserve regiment and saw action at the front lines. He fought in the trenches, acted as a dispatch runner and reached the rank of Gefreiter (lance-corporal). He was wounded in the Battle of Somme in 1916 and gassed during the last months of the war.

After the armistice he convinced himself that the German defeat had been due to Jewish and Marxist socialists betraying the nation at home while the soldiers were giving their lives. Returning to Bavaria, he attended and later conducted courses designed to keep ex-servicemen from joining the Bolshevik movement. He came under the influence of Gottfried Feder, intellectual father of the Nazi movement, and joined a tiny political group in Munich calling itself the German Workers Party. Although the new party had few definite ideas, it did have a clear insight into the value of media and public manipulation. Hitler quickly distinguished himself within the group as a spellbinding orator. His accent was lower-class Bohemian, but his message was hypnotic for the hundreds of ex-soldiers who came to hear him speak at various Munich beer halls.

Through officers such as Capt. Ernst Röhm and Col. Franz von Epp, he maintained close contacts with the Reichswehr that were to stand him in good stead later. In 1921 he ousted the party's founding leader and took over himself, changing its name to the National Socialist German Workers' Party (NSDAP). Its platform became Hitler's anti-Marxist and anti-Semitic creed, liberally mixed with a dose of bombastic nationalism.

Thinking that the Weimar Republic was on the verge of collapse in November 1923, Hitler made his first attempt to seize power in an alliance with Röhm, General Ludendorff and Hermann Göring, a much-respected and decorated air ace and the last commander of the Richthofen Flying Circus squadron. The intention was to make Ludendorff the German dictator. This Munich beer hall *Putsch*—as it came to be known—was easily quelled by the local authorities. Göring was wounded and fled into Swedish exile. Hitler, Ludendorff and other instigators were arrested two days later and tried for treason. Hitler received a five-year "fortress"* term and was packed off to Landsberg Fortress.

The postwar depression years bypassed most of Germany's rural towns and villages. Money had never been plentiful among country folk in the best of times, and now that money was virtually worthless, people relied on their ingenuity and the soil to see them through the hard times.

Alma moved the family to the village of Offleben, five kilometres northeast of Schöningen. Otto was still too weak to hold a steady job, but the district provided a wider scope of opportunity for Alma's professional services. They moved into a modest rented house near the town centre and enrolled the children in the local school.

Luxury foods were scarce and very expensive, fresh meat practically nonexistent. But there was no shortage of staples such as milk, butter, cheese,

---

*A fortress term instead of prison meant that the judge acknowledged the deed was done out of honourable motives.

flour, cabbages and potatoes from local farmers. As village midwife, Alma's credit was good with every shopkeeper. She made her daily rounds by bicycle, a relic from the war. It had a rusty crossbar and a worn, brown leather saddle. One Sunday after church Kurt offered to clean it.

"When I finish, Mama, it will be like new!" Alma seemed doubtful but reluctantly gave him permission to go ahead.

On the front steps under a warm morning sun he set up his workshop and proceeded to take the bicycle to pieces. Every part was sanded, scrubbed, polished, then oiled. By midafternoon he had finished and reassembled the machine. Proudly, he called his mother to inspect the results.

"Like new, isn't it?"

She agreed. An assortment of cotter pins, screws and nuts lay on the bottom step. "Where did those come from?"

Kurt shrugged. "From the bicycle. They don't seem to fit anywhere now. I'll save them for spare parts. You never know when we might need them."

To replace old Fritz, a new dog was purchased from a butcher in Magdeburg—a ferocious Doberman who snapped at anyone who came within biting distance of the end of his chain. It was hoped that in time the animal would settle into his new surroundings. His food dish was pushed to within gobbling range by a steel rod impervious to canine incisors. For Kurt, the challenge of taming the beast became overpowering. He spent hours—out of snapping range—talking softly to the brute, gradually calming, soothing, until at last he could place his hands on the dog's bristled fur and rub his ears lightly. Slowly the mutt responded.

Whooping with pride he called his father out to the garden shed where the animal was chained.

"I've tamed him, Papa. Watch this!"

Boldly he walked over to the dog, but the unusual sight of two people inside his shed brought him instantly to his feet with a growl. Once Kurt came within range, the dog leaped, fangs bared, and tore a strip of flesh from his throat. If Otto hadn't stepped in with the steel rod, the dog would have killed his son. Two weeks later, with Kurt's neck still swathed in bandages, the dog struck again, sinking his fangs into Kurt's foot. The resulting injury caused problems for the rest of his life, for without special orthopedic shoes he was never able to walk any distance. The dog was taken back to the butcher.

Christmas morning, 1923. While Alma prepared the dinner, a runner arrived for help with an early delivery by a woman not due until the New Year. Alma washed her hands and left Kurt in charge of the kitchen with instructions to finish peeling the apples for her pie. When she had gone, Kurt turned to Melanie.

"Froschle, you're supposed to help me."

"I am not. Mama put you in charge."

"So I'm ordering you to help."

"I won't. It's your job."

Impasse.

Was he prepared to allow his young sister to gain the upper hand? In the laneway outside the kitchen window sat a large dish-shaped tub brimming with cement grouting being used by the neighbour to repair a crumbling wall. It beckoned him invitingly.

"If you don't help, I'll put you into that cement!"

"Hah! You wouldn't dare."

Challenged, he had no alternative but to proceed. Melanie was hauled kicking and clawing outdoors where he swung her into the middle of the grey, slimy muck. She screamed as her skin burned and the cement hardened. Neighbours came running. Otto appeared grim-faced.

"What the devil do you think you're up to? Get her out of that tub at once!"

Kurt obeyed; pants rolled up, he scrubbed her with cold water under his father's supervision while the neighbours clucked in disapproval. Finally, when Melanie had been rubbed red and clean and had stopped crying, Otto escorted both children into the house, Melanie to change her clothes, Kurt for a good hiding. Later, after dinner, when the stings of cement and punishment had subsided and they were alone, Kurt asked, "It wasn't that bad, was it, Froschle?"

"It hurt."

"But I didn't mean to hurt you. I just wanted you to help."

"I know. Next time ask. Don't order. You're not in the army yet."

"One day I will be, Froschle. You'll see."

5

An amnesty in the late summer of 1924 reduced Hitler's five-year sentence to eight months and freedom. He had passed the time in comfortable quarters working with his friend Rudolf Hess on the final draft of *Mein Kampf* (*My Struggle*), destined to become the bible of the Nazi movement. But beyond the walls of Landsberg Fortress, his party had disintegrated. He set to work at once rebuilding it. For a time Strasser, creator of the northern wing of the Nazi party, held more influence in party ranks than Hitler. But gradually, through the rest of 1924 and 1925, Hitler managed to recover the ground he had lost during his imprisonment. Although the Nazis held only 12 seats in the Reichstag, a few wealthy industrialists were already beginning to take an interest in Hitler's career.

In March 1925 Kurt received his confirmation into the Protestant church. He was 14 years old, with a thick muscular body already grown to its full adult height of five feet nine inches. For the first time he began asserting his independence. The confirmation ceremony required candidates to dress formally in a dark suit and hat for the procession through the village to the church. One look at himself in the mirror was enough. Already taller than his schoolmates, the addition of a high hat made him look absurd.

"Impossible! I'm not wearing this hat!"

His parents pleaded. Over and above his intransigence and the cost of the hat, there was the matter of their neighbours to consider. All the other boys would respect conformity and be wearing formal hats. Why not their son?

"Because I refuse to make a spectacle of myself. A laughingstock in the village."

"But you are leading the procession into church!"

"And so I will. But not in this hat, Mama."

"But you must wear a hat. It is expected," Alma insisted.

"Then I shall wear my school hat."

"A red hat?" Even Otto was shocked at such sacrilege.

"If it's good enough to wear to school, Papa, it's good enough to wear to church. I'm sure God won't mind."

His school days ended that summer. His marks weren't high enough for a scholarship to continue grade school. Not that he failed. Far from it. He excelled in history and got on well with his teacher, but in 1924 state academic scholarships were limited to those at the very top of the class. Average students were expected to select a suitable trade and enter into an apprenticeship program. Missing out on a scholarship turned out to be the best thing that could have happened for his military career, although at the time entering an apprenticeship program seemed the least likely method of achieving his ambitions.

For an assertive personality brimming with self-confidence and having no patience for stupidity, entry into an apprenticeship program could be disastrous. Contract terms between employer and apprentice lasted from three to four years, depending on the trade, after which the apprentice could become a journeyman, then a master. It could be a long, frustrating road. During his time with the employer and while still under legal age, the apprentice was compelled by law to obey orders without question and work long and irregular hours for a pittance while absorbing the fundamentals of his trade. The relationship was little better than bondage. Not all employers were tyrants, but those who were made life unbearable for their apprentices.

Kurt's first career choice remained the army, but that required influence and money, and the Meyers had neither. With the new German army limited to 100,000, only the very brilliant or privileged could expect admission into the officers' training school, and Kurt did not have the required secondary school certificate.

His mother knew how bitterly disappointed he felt. Since he had been old enough to walk, the army had been his all-consuming passion. Yet she also knew that her husband would never recover from his war wound. Otto was slowly dying. The sooner her children were apprenticed into useful trades and able to support themselves the better.

Melanie had inherited her father's musical talent and had developed a beautiful, sensitive voice. Alma decided that her daughter should study to become a concert singer, a highly respected profession with good pay and one where her physical handicap would be less of a problem than in other traditional female careers. (She wore a steel brace on her left leg and walked with great difficulty.) Alma doubted that Melanie would ever find herself a husband unless she could claim something unique to compensate her physical imperfection. It was a cruel thought.

Kurt, she decided, would apprentice as a shopkeeper's assistant and join the white-collar work force to become a respectable merchant like his Uncle Willi, Otto's older brother, who operated a shop in the village of Oehnhausen. He agreed to take Kurt in as his apprentice but later withdrew the offer, fearing he would not be able to train his nephew with sufficient discipline and severity for him to learn anything. But, like his brother, Willi was a mild-mannered and sincere man who took his family responsibilities seriously, so he made arrangements with a business acquaintance in the town of Minden, west of Hannover, to accept Kurt's apprenticeship contract.

"You're lucky to have such a position," Alma told Kurt when the news arrived by post that he could leave immediately for Minden.

"I'd still prefer the army."

"You're too young. Wait until you're older. When your apprenticeship with Herr Hagler is finished and if you still feel the same, we'll see what can be done."

It was a slim enough hope to sustain him for the four years of servitude that faced him. He didn't argue or question his mother's arrangements. She helped him pack, squeezed him into his confirmation suit and took him in to receive his father's blessing.

The Allied bullet in Otto's lung allowed him to do light work on a temporary basis. Since 1919, he had worked off and on as a railway officer. Although the pay was poor, the job was not physically taxing and provided him with a degree of financial security and a sense of worth. From 1920 to 1924 he had served in a part-time capacity as a parish worker in Offleben. Because his TB was not considered to have resulted from his war wound, his request for a disability pension had been refused. During the previous winter his physical condition had suddenly begun to deteriorate and he took to his bed. The doctors could find nothing wrong and simply prescribed rest. Without X-rays there was no way to see the spiky tubercular viruses eating away at his lungs.

"You will not dishonour the Meyer name," Otto told him.

"No, Vati."*

"You will do what you're told cheerfully and willingly."

"Yes, Vati."

"And you will write home regularly."

"Every week," Kurt promised.

Satisfied, Otto nodded. "Good luck then."

Kurt hugged him tightly for a moment, then left the room quickly before the tears blinded his eyes.

"Your father is dying," Alma told him at the train station.

"I know, Mama."

"He has a year—maybe two—left."

The train puffed past them, swirling the platform in steam. They shook hands formally. It was considered undignified to exhibit emotion publicly—and this applied even to 14-year-olds leaving home for the first time. Kurt saved his tears until the train was moving and he could hide himself in the washroom and suppress the sounds of his sorrow by several lengthy flushings.

His employer in Minden turned out to be a brute whose own three sons had already deserted him because of his ruthless nature and sour disposition. Hagler made arrangement for Kurt's room and board with Frau Hirtz, a widow who ran a Spartan establishment catering to apprentices on the outskirts of town. What miserable sums of money Kurt managed to extract from Hagler were turned over to Frau Hirtz for "extras" at mealtime. His working day at Hagler's shop started at 7:00 a.m. and ended at 7:00 p.m., with 20 minutes off for lunch. Sundays were free. However, both Herr Hagler and Frau Hirtz expected him to attend church with the other boys. "Which is it to be, Meyer? God fearing or God damned?" Hagler thundered at the end of his first week. It wasn't much of a choice. His employer presented an infinitely more persuasive argument for attending church than the Almighty could ever hope to achieve.

Six months passed before Hagler allowed him a weekend home in Offleben. The visit created great excitement for the family. A mass murderer named Hamann was reported in the newspapers to be operating in the Hannover area. Realizing Kurt would have to pass through that city on his way home, changing trains late at night on what was certain to be a deserted platform, Alma was beside herself with worry until Kurt appeared safe and sound. At once her concern shifted to his return trip. Exasperated by his mother's constant carping about the dangers he faced, Kurt snapped, "If you don't shut up about this Hamann, Mum, I'll go find him and ask him to make me into frankfurters and send you some!"

He had been with Hagler two years, stoically enduring the man's abuse

---

*Daddy.

and constant criticism, when he found cause to rebel. It was a matter of principle. One summer morning while he was decorating the shop window, another boy appeared out on the sidewalk. After watching Kurt for several minutes, the boy began making faces and shouting insults. Kurt ignored him and continued working. Frustrated, the boy hurled a cobblestone through the window, showering Kurt with broken glass, then took to his heels, disappearing down the street.

"You fool!" Hagler howled. "Look what you've done!"

"I didn't do it, Herr Hagler."

"Don't lie to me. Of course you did it!" He refused to hear Kurt's side of the story. But even more humiliating was the letter Hagler posted to the Meyers demanding payment in full for the cost of replacing the store's front window broken by their son!

Kurt had had enough. Next morning, instead of going to work, he walked through Minden and headed southeast toward the Czechoslovakian border. Four days and nights he walked, hitching rides on trains or with local farmers and lorry drivers, moving through strange countryside, begging for food. By the fifth day he could hardly move. His shoes were worn out and he was desperately hungry. Shortly after sunrise he stopped in a village to gaze at the front window of a shoemaker's shop. There were sturdy boots, thick-soled shoes and patent leather pumps on display. A pair of tall elegant boots caught his eye. He looked up and down the street. No one was about. "Should I steal them?" he wondered. So easy to do. Everyone in the village asleep. Momentary sound of breaking glass, then a quick grab for the boots and he'd be off and running like the wind. But he couldn't bring himself to do it, and with a sigh he limped on out of the village. The sun rose, warming his shoulders. He lay down in the new grass bordering the road and fell asleep.

That same morning in Offleben Melanie tried to cheer her father out of one of his bouts of depression. "You look so sad, Papa. Let's play and sing 'Der Mai ist gekommen'" ("May Has Come"). While Otto accompanied her on his cello, she played and sang. They had only just started when there was a knock at the door. A grim-faced local constable stepped into the house and announced that Kurt had been reported missing. Alma immediately assumed he'd been murdered and burst into tears.

Next day Alma and Otto took the train to Minden to be on hand when their son's body was discovered. Local police had begun a complete search, even to dragging the Weser River that divided the town in case the young apprentice had committed suicide, not an unusual event among depressed teenagers living away from home and contracted into a lonely servitude. But dragging the river produced nothing except an assortment of garbage and a few abandoned bicycles. Several more days passed with no sign of the missing apprentice. Kurt, meanwhile, had holed up at the railway station in the border city of Hof. Near midnight he fell asleep at a table in the station's restaurant. The proprietor called the police, and in due course an officious Bavarian constable arrested him as a vagrant and carted him off to jail.

The jail, a dank, stinking pesthole, had been built during medieval times and offered nothing in the way of basic amenities. No sooner had the jailer locked him into one of the narrow cells than Kurt vomited from the smell of the place. Fortunately, a police inspector turned up later in the morning, berated the jailer for treating the boy as a criminal and took him to his own home for a decent meal. When Kurt had eaten and washed, the inspector suggested he tell him what had happened.

"I've done nothing wrong!" Kurt insisted and then proceeded to tell him the story of Herr Hagler and the shop window.

A policeman accompanied Kurt on the train from Hof to Minden and delivered him back into Herr Hagler's clutches. Hagler's first impulse was to administer a severe beating for all the trouble his apprentice had caused, to say nothing of the enormous expenses incurred by the Meyers in travelling costs and the futile search for their son.

"Okay, beat me if you want, Herr Hagler. I deserve it for all the trouble I caused. I'm very sorry. But I did not break your window."

Looking at Otto Meyer, so obviously marked for death, Hagler too felt sorry. Kurt went back to work without his beating and the Meyers returned to Offleben.

Kurt promised to remain with Hagler until his apprenticeship ended. "But not a day longer!" he warned his mother. "I'd rather starve than work as a shop-assistant."

The purgatory ended in April 1928. He passed his exams as a shopkeeper's assistant. On his last day Hagler frostily wished him good luck and even shook his hand. Kurt was free. He caught the first train out of Minden for home.

PART 3

THE MAKING OF A WARRIOR: I

*Education: the receiving capacity
becomes the amount received and the
receiver's desire determines his capacity.*
A. MACLAREN, D.D.

THE FIRST THING Harry Foster discovered at the Royal Military College was that the time allotted during any one week was never enough to complete the activities laid down in the curriculum. A conflict of philosophies developed between Macdonell, as commandant, and Ivor Martin, the director of studies. Martin felt the emphasis of the four-year program should be directed toward academic excellence, with the military aspect given a secondary and much lower priority. Macdonell believed exactly the opposite. He saw no reason why the college couldn't produce both. As commandant, Macdonell had final authority over Martin's plans to expand the academic curriculum but was reluctant to embarrass Martin in public. In the end, the cadets suffered from overloaded work schedules.

A second matter concerned "hazing" and the privilege given to the graduating class of administering discipline and punishment. For Harry, who had experienced the worst types of hazing from Canadian and British private schools, RMC's historic rituals seemed little more than petty annoyances. However, most cadets entering RMC had never seen a boarding school. The indignities of hazing and corporal punishment given by young men not much older than themselves came as a nasty shock. Lectures on the necessity of instilling instant obedience to orders from a senior officer—the very foundation of the military command system—gradually swayed the reluctant cadets to the army's way of thinking. But not always.

Harry realized that "one either played the game their way, accepting all the rubbish that went along with it or got out. No officer is qualified to give orders until he has learned to take orders."

The orderly, fast-paced life suited him to a T. Although weak in most of his academic subjects, he made up for it in the military training program, which in his opinion was by far the most important. "Captain Bray of the Royal Horse Artillery was our riding instructor. He spent most sessions swearing at either the Gentlemen Cadets or their mounts. To an inexperienced horseman his 'riding free' exercise was torture. Riding without stirrups, arms crossed and reins dropped, a rider was expected to direct his mount by thigh pressure alone. Without training and well-conditioned thigh muscles the cadet fell off his horse within minutes. I was one of the few who never did."

Although the era of horseman and lance had ended during the war, its principles were still taught at RMC. The lances were eight-foot bamboo poles tipped with triangular grooved steel blades. A steel butt fitted into a lance bucket fastened to the right stirrup. At full gallop, with the lance held snugly against the body, a wrist strap securing it to the killing arm (always the right), the lancer was expected to drive the tip into his mounted or dismounted adversary. "After impaling his target, the rider, still at full gallop, swung lance and body right to disengage, leaving the corpse behind him. If he forgot to swing, the force of contact knocked him off the horse. A useful drill for teaching someone Newton's Laws of Motion where they applied to riding a polo pony but for military purposes it was a waste of time."

In the college's athletic program he delivered the same intense effort that he had at boarding school, giving a good account of himself during the traditional visit and sports competition held between RMC and West Point cadets.

He was not especially popular, although his ability to recite scores of lengthy verses from Kipling, Bliss Carman and Robert Service gave him a feature spot in any social gathering. At one time he had over 150 poems and verses in his repertoire. Competitive memory work had been one of the forms of mental exercise used on the boys of Berkhamsted, and Harry had a knack for remembering rhyming couplets. Unfortunately, this *idiot savant* ability didn't extend into his regular academic studies.

Most of the nearly 300 cadets sported moustaches—at least those who had enough hair to grow something presentable. Harry had always felt his upper lip too wide for his face and decided a slim, tidy military moustache would solve the problem. So pleased was he with the results that he wore it for the rest of his life.

He had developed a dry, puckish sense of humour more British than Canadian, masking it behind a somewhat solemn exterior. His voice was deep, his speech pattern clipped into short sentences with a trace of an English accent. He had an unnerving habit of coming directly to the point in any conversation. Diplomacy would never be one of his strong points. Yet for all his obvious physical strength and directness, he remained basically shy, hiding whatever inadequacies of personality he believed he had behind a brusque imperturbable exterior. It was all an act developed over the years to compete with Gil.

"Harry was always a dour sonofabitch," Chris Vokes, a classmate of Gil's remembered. "He was a distant second in everything to his younger brother." Vokes thought Gil the most brilliant man he had ever met. Sixty-five years later his opinion hadn't changed.

But Gil, in the class behind Harry, had finally met his match in Guy Granville Simonds, an intense humourless young Englishman with a passion for detail bordering on mania. Simonds's father, a lieutenant-colonel in the Royal Artillery, had brought the family to Canada in 1912. The young Simonds went to Ottawa's exclusive—and very expensive—Ashbury College for his basic education and graduated with honours.

To Harry, "Guy had that type of abrasive personality that refuses to suffer the company of fools at any time. But you had to admire his single-mindedness and dedication at whatever he attempted. No one liked him particularly, but everyone respected him. There was not the least doubt that he, like Gil, would reach senior command eventually. But while Guy always managed to place himself at the top of his class by sheer determination, Gil's close second by comparison appeared almost effortless. He had a much broader general knowledge than Guy, and of course a far more sociable personality."

Oddly, Simonds seemed to prefer Harry's company to Gil's, possibly because he realized Harry admired him and posed no real competitive threat.

Back in Kentville, Laffy found something to keep himself busy. He became an apple broker. He started by helping Janie's brother, Fred Wickwire, who owned considerable orchard acreage on the outskirts of town. Fred had never been much for the tedious minutiae of business and was happy to have Laffy shoulder the responsibility for him. After careful assessment of his performance other growers came forward at the end of the first year. There was a certain novelty to having a full-blown general acting as an apple agent.

Laffy was delighted. It suited his need to be working at organizational details. There was the added bonus of a handsome income and the legitimate excuse to travel about the district's dusty roads in his Model T, socializing. By 1923 business had increased to such a profitable extent he decided to move back to Halifax and closer to the shipping action. He felt an urgency to be active. Tragically, H.H. had died of a heart attack in 1922 at the age of 54 and two of Laffy's brothers had succumbed to early old age. "My contemporaries are dropping like flies around me," he wrote. His theory for longevity was to keep active with "regular purges and good food."

When the boys came home from RMC for their summer leave, discussions ensued as to what regiments they intended joining after their graduation. It was an important decision. Whatever regiment a young officer selected became *his* regiment for the rest of his army career. The regiment served as master, mistress, lover, family and his all-consuming passion. Its pride and traditions, its battles won and lost, its heroes and its cowards, all were a part of each regiment's character. To gain membership into such an exclusive little gathering of men became a matter of careful thought and consideration by both parties to the association. In the most exclusive British army cavalry and guards regiments, the list of applicants was always ten times as long as the vacancies. A regiment wanted young officers who "fitted" into its social and military style of activities and upheld its carefully nurtured traditions, no matter how absurd or bizarre they might appear to those on the outside.

Officers, on the other hand, wanted the prestige of being associated with a "good" regiment, preferably one with its senior officers nearing retirement age. This way they stood a better chance at early promotion. "Good" meant dashing dress uniforms, decent postings to comfortable peacetime quarters, amiable companionship, acceptance into the highest levels of society, plus a variety of interesting soldiering activities throughout the year to prevent boredom. During wartime men might serve their King and Country, but they died for their regiments.

Harry had decided already on the Royal Canadian Dragoons, one of the Permanent Force's two splendid cavalry regiments. The Dragoons were based at Stanley Barracks in Toronto and at St. Jean, Quebec. During the summers of '22 and '23 the regiment had been ordered up to Cape Breton Island to prevent outbreaks of lawlessness by striking miners of the British Empire Steel and Coal Company. Backing the local police turned out to be a thankless task. From a moral perspective, the miners were right in the stand they had taken against the company's venality and shoddy management practices. They were overworked, underpaid and unmercifully victimized by a greedy consortium of absentee owners. Unfortunately, the law was on the side of the company. Yet in spite of being labelled "black-legs" and "scabs," the Dragoons acquitted themselves in gentlemanly fashion. To Harry, reading about it in the newspapers, it sounded exciting work. He was neither for nor against the miners.

The Royal Canadian Regiment (RCR), an infantry unit, became Gil's final choice. The RCR had its four companies distributed between Halifax, Montreal, Toronto and London, Ontario. He was persuaded by his mother as much as anything else. As the youngest, Gil had always been her favourite. Since the RCRs kept a permanent establishment in Halifax, Gil's membership in the regiment offered a good chance of a posting close to home.

At once Laffy saw that their choices presented an awkward problem. Canada was a vast country, but its Permanent Force army was very small—3,611 men and 756 horses. The horses didn't know each other but most of the men did. And therein lay the problem. If both sons served with regiments located in the eastern half of the country, it would not be long before senior officers would be comparing Harry unfavourably with his brother. His career could be stunted before it started.

Harry spent the last weeks of summer at Camp Aldershot with the Mounted Rifles militia. When he finished training, he was granted a temporary commission as second lieutenant. It wasn't much but at least it represented a start up the ladder. A day or two before he and Gil were to return to RMC, Laffy suggested gently that he should consider an alternative to the Dragoons.

"I was not so blind that I didn't understand his reasons. The whole business with Gil was beginning to exasperate me. I wanted to shout: 'Why can't you let me compete with him, dammit! He may be smarter but that doesn't make him better!' But I simply could not speak like that to Dad. So when he trotted out his idea of my joining the Lord Strathconas instead of the Dragoons I agreed and returned to RMC feeling like a horse's ass for having given in so easily."

Only after he had been back at the college several weeks did he learn that the officer who had led the Strathconas overseas in 1914 had been Macdonell. Shortly before the Christmas break the old general stopped him in the corridor on his way to a lecture about troop hygiene.

"Understand you're being accepted by the Straths, Foster."

It was news to Harry. "I hope so, sir."

"I recommended you. So you can count on it."

"Thank you, sir."

"It's a good regiment. Do it proud."

2

In 1900 Lord Strathcona offered to pay the complete cost of raising, equipping and sending a mounted unit from Western Canada to the Boer War. This public-spirited gesture was accepted by the government, and Major Sam Steele* of the Royal North-West Mounted Police was appointed to command. Recruits were drawn from local cowboys, ranchers, officers and men of the RNWMP. Strictly speaking, the Strathcona unit was not Canadian at all but

---

*Later Maj.-Gen. Sir Sam Steele.

rather a British army regiment recruited in Canada and paid for by an overly generous Canadian citizen.

Although the regiment was officially disbanded in Halifax after its return from the South African War, the war had made mounted rifle regiments popular. The Canadian Mounted Rifles was added to the Permanent Force in 1901 and based in Winnipeg. In 1909 it was re-badged Strathcona's Horse (Royal Canadians), and two years later it added the prefix "Lord" to its designation. Macdonell, then a major, took over command the following year from the colourful Sam Steele.

During the Great War members of the regiment covered themselves with glory, earning two VCs, 15 DSOs, 21 MCs and scores of other decorations for gallantry. The regiment's actions as part of the Canadian Cavalry Brigade at Moreuil Wood in France in 1918 had been especially brilliant. General Ludendorff, the German High Command strategist, wrote in his memoirs that having been prevented by this action from capturing Amiens, the great spring offensive "was brought to a standstill."

Harry's official posting as lieutenant to the Straths came on 2 July 1924 when he graduated from RMC. His new regiment had two cavalry squadrons: A Squadron based in Winnipeg at Fort Osborne Barracks; and B Squadron at the regiment's headquarters based on the Sarcee Plain just outside Calgary. His orders were to join B Squadron. He said goodbye to Gil, who was heading home to Halifax, and promised to write all the news when he reached the West.

Canada's population passed the 9-million mark in 1924. The flyleaf of every English school reader in the country contained the motto "One Flag, One King, One Country." King George V was in the 14th year of his reign, still occupied with his two favourite pastimes: shooting grouse and stamp collecting. His son David, Prince of Wales, had become the world's most eligible bachelor. With 107 nations, commonwealths, protectorates, colonies, and island administrations in all, the British Empire's population amounted to a half-billion people, roughly one-quarter of the earth's population. Global maps were predominantly British Empire red. To English-speaking Canadians, the French were still Frogs; to French Canadians, the English remained *les maudits anglais*.

Cal Coolidge had become the 30th president of the United States a year earlier. The tight-lipped Republican insisted on a stringent economy until the national debt had been reduced, and he maintained an austere indifference to proposed social and government reforms; yet his frugal policies brought a gradual return to prosperity.

Canada had a Liberal government in Ottawa headed by Mackenzie King, grandson of William Lyon Mackenzie, the great rebel and reformer in the days before Confederation. King bore no resemblance to his illustrious grandparent. A short, uninspiring little man with a high-pitched voice and weasel-worded policies, he was nonetheless a master politician who understood that the key to remaining in power depended on ruling by consensus. He had spent the war years safely ensconced in the United States with a comfortable job working for the Rockefeller Foundation.

Some of Coolidge's tightfistedness must have rubbed off on King because in 1924 his government decided that not even the army should be exempt from budget cuts. A 50-cent per day reduction was ordered for men in the ranks. This new rate gave recruits $1.20 per day, while soldiers with six years service collected $1.50 plus uniforms, room and board. In some units 90 percent of the men below the rank of corporal resigned after being given the option of returning to civilian life or remaining in the service at the new rates.

Young officers were not much better off. The army was certainly no place for men seeking a comfortable, well-paid job. Formal mess dinners attended in evening clothes, debutante balls attended in full-dress uniform and the camaraderie of fun and games during various interunit sporting events were only a small part of a subaltern's life. They were the things that made it all worthwhile. Then there was the other part, where he spent the bulk of his time training himself, his troops and—if he was cavalry—his horse.

Training himself meant constant studying, attending every conceivable type of course—from weaponry and tactical field exercises, using live ammunition, to organizing food and transport for men and horses on a three-week bivouac. Throughout it all, his every move, action and interaction was monitored and graded by his commanding officer. Each promotion came only after long hours of study, exams and patience.

Training his troops meant training not only men of his regiment but also those of the various militia units scattered throughout the region for which his regiment was responsible. He could never allow himself to forget that the sole purpose of his existence—of his regiment's existence—was to provide that necessary nucleus of experts capable of mobilizing the militia units rapidly into a fighting wartime army. But in 1924 war seemed a long, long way off. Some politicians doubted there would ever be another.

Training his horse meant hours of curry comb and brushing, saddle soap and harness oil for the leather fastenings and saddle, and teaching his horse to obey the slightest nudge of knee, rein or spur in all kinds of weather and under simulated battle conditions. He had a groom and batman to assist him, but the bulk of the work he had to do himself. He was the one who had to ride the animal.

He was underpaid, constantly in debt to his tailor, his mess, his brother officers and his family. Military Headquarters in Ottawa made things very clear in one of its discouraging directives: "It is preferable that subalterns have some form of private means upon which to draw as supplement to their army pay." Most did.

If a young officer had no such supplement and his family was unable or unwilling to provide that little extra needed to sustain him, then the only respectable alternative to resigning from the service was to "marry money."

"This required a very rapid courtship before the novelty of a uniform, gleaming boots and silver spurs paled and the unfortunate girl discovered what sort of lifestyle she'd be inflicting on her family and herself by marrying the poor sod," Harry reflected. "Every young impecunious officer worth his salt kept a weather eye peeled for money-marrying opportunities . . . myself included."

By contemporary standards such outright opportunism appears chauvinistic. Yet the system seemed to work. Initial mutual attractions developed quickly into love, respect and understanding that usually lasted a lifetime.

Calgary's population in 1924 was already 10,000 more than that of Halifax. In 30 years it had grown from a few ramshackle houses and tents alongside the CPR (Canadian Pacific Railway) tracks to a metropolis of 66,000 people. Yet, for all its growth it still remained a clapboard prairie town of Potëmkin storefronts and Chinese laundries. A ceaseless wind came down from the Rocky Mountains, blowing hot or cold year-round. In July it blew hot and dry, carrying a fine grainy dust that sifted into every facial crease and household cranny. The city's streets, except for the downtown shopping district, were powdered and unpaved. When it rained, the powder turned to thick yellow gumbo that stuck like glue to feet, wheels and horses' hoofs.

This was Harry's first trip to the prairies. From his uncomfortable wicker seat on the train he had watched with fascination as its vast emptiness unfolded. "Hour after hour of flat pancake yellow land with afternoon temperatures close to a hundred under a blazing sun." The train reached Calgary midmorning of the third day. He phoned the regimental orderly office to inquire about transport. The Adjutant came on the line.

"Ah, yes. Foster. You're the RMC chappie, aren't you. Well we don't provide transport. If both your legs are functioning I suggest you try using them."

He had brought a large kitbag and tin trunk and had no intention of lugging them across town on his shoulders. He decided on the luxury of a taxi. Headquarters and troop billeting were set up in the local armouries. No funds had been allocated from Ottawa for building a proper barracks. Horse barns and the regiment's parade square were a mile away from the armouries and next to the city's garbage dump. The CPR tracks ran alongside.

"My heart sank at the sight of the stabling. Instead of proper barns I found a row of tumbledown sheds roofed with rusty tin. Dirt, dust and bits of paper blew about the pebbled parade square like something out of a nightmare. I felt like weeping after coming so far and expecting so much only to find that I had been cheated."

His commanding officer, known as "Hooch" MacDonald, had won two DSOs and an MC in France, ending the war as lieutenant-colonel.

"You're our first RMC laddie since the war. Glad to have you along," he greeted Harry. "Did they teach you how to ride?"

"Yes, sir."

"Ummm. We'll see about that."

He was sent off to meet the officer commanding B Squadron, Lionel Page. A brevet* lieutenant-colonel, Page had won three DSOs in France and had a habit of smacking his thick riding breeches with his swagger stick when emphasizing a point. Harry found him in the drill hall conducting a lecture. At midday the coolest place in Calgary was inside the armoury drill hall. When the lecture ended, the Adjutant introduced Harry.

"We're going to have to teach you to ride all over again (*smack*), Foster. Those RMC instructors from the Horse Artillery turn out riders that look like clothespegs instead of cavalrymen (*smack*). Can't have that (*smack*). 'Cock Roberts' will straighten you out. Got yourself a mount? No? Well, never mind, you can go looking tomorrow."

Mystified, Harry was shown to his quarters. Next day he found himself listed in orders as a cavalry recruit assigned to basic training under "Cock Roberts." Sergeant-Major Roberts, MC, turned out to be a short, bandy-legged man with a barrel chest and a voice like a trumpet. In France he had served as a regimental captain in the front lines but dropped back to company sergeant-major after the war in order to remain in the service. Being outranked by an RMC graduate lieutenant must have been a bitter experience for the worldly-wise Cock Roberts.

"As far as I'm concerned," he informed Harry, "you're just another dumb farm recruit who'll ride his horse like a jackass until he's properly trained by me, sir!" NCO instructors were permitted to say whatever they wanted to officer recruits as long as their diatribes were suffixed with the word "sir." That made it acceptable, according to the *King's Regulations Manual*.

Harry picked his horse from a compound of wild mustangs brought in off the range periodically by local cowboys coming into town for a piss-up. The army paid for saddle, harness and stabling only. Officers were expected to pay for their own mounts. Target, an enormous black stallion with fire in his eyes, cost him $50—nearly a month's pay. After almost killing himself breaking and gelding the animal, he had to learn to ride him the "Lord Strathcona way."

But he never seemed to be able to satisfy the Sergeant-Major. Over the next weeks Roberts harassed him unmercifully. "Bend that back. Not that

---

*A promotion granted as an honour without increase of pay.

way! You look like a bullfrog trying to hump a bass drum, sir!" The Sergeant-Major tried everything he could to make him lose his temper in front of the other recruits. Wisely, Harry held his tongue.

Finally, one day in September after a particularly hard two hours of riding exercises during which Roberts had been roaring at him practically nonstop, the Sergeant-Major strutted over to him at the stables. For several minutes he stood watching Harry rub down Target. The air stank of sweating animals and men. Enormous green bottle flies feasted noisily on the fresh horse droppings.

"I stiffened. Waiting for his next outburst. Instead, he walked over and saluted, then smiled. I returned it, somewhat dumbfounded. 'You'll do, Lieutenant,' he said. 'Glad to have you with our regiment.' It was the first time he'd called me lieutenant instead of sir. I realized then that I'd made it."

Calgary's citizens considered the army a collection of social parasites. Soldiers—particularly cavalry soldiers—were too indolent or too stupid for useful employment in the "real" world. At every opportunity the men were ridiculed for their blind acceptance of the absurd military discipline that emasculated "real" men. Their childish toy-soldier uniforms, their unproductive playing at foolish war games, all of it was anathema to local citizenry. The cavalry's stylized horsemanship appeared sissified to the district's cowboys. While cavalry gentlemen put in a relaxing three hours playing soldier, cowboys spent up to 12 hours a day in the saddle working for a living.

Even the CPR engineers managed to get into the act. Each felt honour bound to blow his train whistle or release clouds of steam as he rolled past the Strathconas' parade ground. As the terrified horses plunged and reared, throwing riders and troop formations into chaos, the trainmen hooted their derision.

There could also be a serious side to this sort of razzing. One autumn afternoon Sgt. "Bogie" Allen was giving Harry and the new recruits a demonstration in the art of "tent-pegging." The object of this exercise was to teach sword point accuracy to mounted cavalrymen in dispatching ground troops during a charge. A row of wooden tent pegs was hammered lightly into the ground to represent enemy soldiers. Then, at full gallop, each cavalryman was expected to lean from his saddle and in quick succession flick out the tent pegs using his sword tip. It needed a good eye, steady hand and superb horsemanship.

A basic precaution for this exercise was the removal of the leather sword straps from each man's wrist so that in the event of a tumble his sword would be thrown clear. Unfortunately Bogie forgot to clear the leather from his own wrist. He had flicked the sixth peg at a full gallop when a passing CPR trainman caught sight of the action and pulled his whistle long and hard. The horse bolted for the six-foot perimeter fence and tried to jump it. It somersaulted into the wire, throwing Bogie to the ground. As he landed, the attached sword whizzed across his face severing the end of his nose.

"Bogie was out like a light. Quick as a wink, Charlie Brown, our instructing officer, galloped over and dismounted. He found the piece of nose lying on the gravel, picked it up, wiped it off on the seat of his riding britches and slapped it back on Bogie's face. Two men were detailed to cart Bogie off to the medical officer for stitches. Of course, his nose was never quite the same, but at least he had a nose. A formal complaint was laid against the CPR. But nothing ever came of it, although after that the engineers did stop blowing their steam and whistles. God! How we hated Calgary and the CPR."

3

Gil graduated from RMC the following year, together with Chris Vokes and Simonds. As expected, Guy collected the Sword of Honour and Governor-General's Silver Medal. Gil was just behind him in grades. "No one gets a prize for coming second," he wrote Harry. "I made up for it by getting drunk."

To please his father, Simonds chose a posting to B Battery of the Royal Canadian Horse Artillery Regiment based in Kingston, less than a mile from the college. Vokes took his posting with the Royal Canadian Engineers, but instead of joining the regiment he decided to finish his education at McGill for a Bachelor of Science degree.

Gil had already made arrangements to join the Royal Canadian Regiment. Although its regimental headquarters and one company were based at London, Ontario, it had three other companies in Montreal, Toronto and Halifax. Gil's posting was to A Company in Halifax. For his parents, it turned out to be a happy choice. Laffy and Janie had rented a handsome home directly across the road from Dalhousie University. The shipping and brokerage business had flourished, so that for the first time since their marriage they were in a position to buy a house of their own. Gil was billeted at the officers' quarters in Royal Artillery Park and came for lunch or dinner nearly every day.

He was young, handsome and filled with fun. Girls came flocking. There were dances at least twice a week at one of the hotels or golf clubs, and always a party going on somewhere each evening. He made it a point to try and attend everything. And wherever he went, he drank. His father chided him gently, pointing to H.H.'s early demise due in part to a fondness for "the creature," and to Gil's cousin Harry who had already drunk his way out of Dalhousie in disgrace. "I'm afraid it's the curse of the Wickwires," Laffy said, preferring to blame Janie's side of the family. "Be careful or it will destroy you!"

His mother said nothing. To her he could do no wrong. Besides, she reasoned logically, he was only 22. Wasn't it natural for a young man to sow a few wild oats before finding himself a nice girl and settling down?

Harry returned home on leave in the spring of 1926 to find his brother well on the way to becoming an alcoholic. "Gil could put away a quart of whisky without any apparent effect. His eyes got a bit brighter, his face a bit redder, but that was all." Everyone drank in the service. An officer was expected to drink. To be able to drink more than anyone else in the officers' mess and remain upright was regarded as an admirable accomplishment and worthy of respect. "The key to drinking was knowing when to stop before you fell over and made a fool of yourself. Or were sick. Then admiration turned to scorn and it took some considerable time before an offender could hold his head up in the mess again."

The officers' mess. Everything revolved around the mess. Mess dinners. Mess social events. Mess bar. It was every regiment's central gathering place for exchanging ideas, jokes, scandals and complaints. There were happy messes, sad messes, stuffy messes and casual messes. But there were no nonalcoholic messes in the Canadian or British armies.

So far the drinking hadn't hurt Gil's career. He had enough sense to keep himself sober during working hours or when he needed to study for the courses he was taking. He had already written and passed his exams for captain, although it would be another three years before the promotion would come through. Harry hadn't even begun studying for his captaincy. "It was a bit difficult for me to discuss Gil's drinking with him when he'd already accomplished more in his career drunk than I had sober."

At the end of his leave, Harry stopped off in Ottawa to visit his cousin Alice Wickwire, H.H.'s elder daughter, who worked as private secretary to the Minister of National Defence. Looking very natty in his uniform, he took a cab to Defence Headquarters. The building was divided into two sections—civilian employees at one end, military personnel at the other. He entered through the military section. As he walked the hallways, icy stares from senior army officers followed his passage. He found Alice typing at her desk just outside the Minister's private office. For a half hour they chatted about his new posting to A Squadron in Winnipeg and how happy he would be to get out of Calgary. He had heard the social life in Winnipeg was much better. Alice wished him luck. He returned past the icy stares and caught a cab back to the railway station.

Three days later, after the regular mounted morning parade at Fort Osborne Barracks in Winnipeg, he was ordered to report to his commanding officer. "Look here, young fellow, I don't know what the hell you've been doing while you were down east. But by God, the District Officer Commanding wants to see you." It sounded serious. At 1130 hours he and the CO were paraded before Arthur Henry Bell, the GOC (general officer commanding). Angrily,

Bell came straight to the point. "You have been reported to the Chief of Staff as having gone directly over the heads of your superiors—including the Adjutant-General—to see the Minister of National Defence in Ottawa. Now just what in hell is all this about? Eh?"

Harry's knees felt weak. He wanted to laugh at the absurdity of it all. Carefully he explained the reason for his visit to Defence Headquarters. Bell blinked uncertainly.

"That's all?"

"That's all, sir."

"Hummmph!" An embarrassed pause. "Well then, no harm done. Hummmph! Carry on!"

The episode taught him a valuable lesson: "If you want to stay clear of trouble, stay out of Ottawa. I resolved there and then that never under any circumstances would I ever serve in Ottawa. The place reeked of hypocrisy, corruption and intrigue."

Winnipeg indeed turned out to be a vast improvement over Calgary. In 1926 it was still the third-largest city in the nation with a population close to 200,000. Besides being the West's largest industrial, agricultural and railway centre, it had an enormous cultural and social awareness, no doubt attributable to the sense of isolation its citizens felt from the rest of the country. There were highly professional ballet and opera companies, a talented theatre group, two vaudeville music halls and a number of movie theatres. Debutantes "came out" each season at Government House, and the St. Charles Golf and Country Club sponsored regular dances for the young *in* crowd. Winnipeg's social calendar was considered the best west of Toronto. Some said Winnipeg's was better.

Winnipeg had the widest main street in Canada, the country's windiest corner at Portage and Main, and also a rabbit warren of a permanent army barracks at Fort Osborne. Amazingly, the populace treated troops with civility and even pride during their occasional public appearances for Remembrance Day, musical rides at summer fairs or polo matches against American army teams that visited the city.

Harry became a member of the army's polo team. Though economy measures forced team members to use their cavalry mounts instead of properly trained polo ponies, they managed to give a good account of themselves whenever they met the Americans. "The poor Yankees never had a chance against us at any time. Prohibition had done them in."

Since 1919 America had been dry, at least theoretically. Orange, grapefruit, tomato or pineapple juice was served at officers' messes throughout the United States, so young officers never learned how to drink "properly." The Canadian army polo team showed them how. Before each home game, members of both teams were toasted ceremoniously in the Strathconas' mess. "After several stiff drinks, which courtesy compelled the Americans to accept, we all trooped out to the polo field. Normally, we'd have the game won by the end of the first chukker."*

Each summer the Strathconas' eligible officers were invited to the Winnipeg Debutantes' Ball, one of the season's most prestigious events. Everyone who was anyone turned up. Toronto's monthly *haut prétentieux* magazine, *Mayfair*, always provided an in-depth account with photographs and cloying captions. Winnipeg's two newspapers sent their reporters and photographers decked out in tie and tails. And why not when the most beautiful, most desirable and wealthiest girls in the city would be there? The organizers provided the best orchestra, the best canapes and the best champagne, with dancing well past midnight. It couldn't help but turn the head and heart of every impoverished young subaltern. Harry was no exception.

He had been away on a training exercise the previous year and missed the event. He had no intention of missing it a second time. Since the war, a number of Strathcona officers had found wives through attending the Debutantes' Ball. To a young woman embarking on life, could anything appear more handsome and attractive than a young cavalry officer in dress uniform and gleaming buttons? That summer of 1927 Harry was ripe for plucking.

On the evening of the ball he presented his embossed invitation at the door of the St. Charles Country Club and joined the crush of guests waiting for the debs to appear as their names were called. In the reception hall at the bottom of the wide staircase photographers stood poised. At each name, perfumed and sweating bodies pressed forward—proud parents, doting uncles, lusty young men.

"The whole business struck me as a bit of a horse auction. I could just imagine how the poor girls felt coming down the stairs in their long dresses, trying not to trip over themselves. My God, but they were beautiful!"

Margaret Ruth Muir—"Margo" for short—was three months shy of her 18th birthday. She had just graduated from the Bishop Strachan School for young ladies in Toronto. She planned now to go on to law at the University of Manitoba in the fall. She was very bright, very beautiful and very rich. Her grandfather had been one of the founding members of the Winnipeg Grain Exchange and died a millionaire, leaving the estate to his sons. The youngest, Arthur, had died of wounds in France. Robert—Margo's father—became sole heir. He had none of his father's business acumen nor flair for the financial advantage and was regarded more of a charming playboy than a serious businessman. He and his wife, Jean, had two children: Margo, their firstborn, and Bill, three years younger. Margo, called "Duchess" by her father because of her dark-eyed arrogance and imperious gypsy-like beauty,

---

*A polo game is divided into six seven-and-a-half minute periods or "chukkers."

was very tall—over five feet ten inches in her stocking feet—with naturally wavy black hair and a long, oval face. From the moment he clapped eyes on her, Harry was smitten.

"Since her name began with M, she was well back in the pack. The others were all beautiful. But she was much more than that. Standing at the top of the staircase waiting for her name to be called, she looked like a princess out of some fairy tale. I decided it was not a moment to stand on ceremony. As she reached the bottom step and paused for a moment holding her bouquet while the flashbulbs popped, I came forward and took her by the hand. Suddenly, my mind went blank. I couldn't think of a thing to say."

Instead of trying, he took the dance program dangling from her wrist on a silver string and, beginning with the second dance, wrote his name on every other line. Some of the debs standing nearby giggled. He ignored them and kept writing. When he finished, she glanced briefly at the name, then without a word went off to rejoin her parents.

"I was crushed. I trailed her around the room like a moonstruck calf trying for some sign of recognition or acceptance. She ignored me. Local lads in evening dress flocked around laughing and looking back at me. I felt like running them through with my sabre. Then the orchestra started."

Margo swept onto the floor with her father. They were a beautifully matched couple. Harry watched enviously until the waltz ended and her father delivered her back to the crowd of admirers. Frustrated, he wandered away to the bar and ordered himself a double rye and water. She wasn't in his league, he decided regretfully. Much too high class. Probably a snob. The music started again. But he refused to turn around and face the competition from the smart young men. Then someone tapped his arm. He turned. It was Margo. She wore a smile as wide and bright as a prairie sky.

"I think this is our dance, Lieutenant."

4

It proved to be a lengthy courtship. Her father had far more ambitious plans for his "Duchess" than marriage to some destitute cavalry officer from Nova Scotia. What were his social connections, his income, his family background? Being a general's son just wasn't good enough, particularly a retired medical general who was now no more than a common tradesman!

"Apples, you say?"

"Yes, sir," Harry replied.

"But why would he want to sell apples if he was a surgeon and a general?"

"I suppose because people want to buy apples, Mr. Muir."

Robert, who had never done a day's work in his life outside of cashing dividend checks from the family's business interests, viewed Harry's offhand acceptance of Laffy's strange behaviour with deep suspicion. If a Muir had to change her name through marriage, then at least it should be for a name as proud and worthy as Muir, Robert believed. There were few Muirs in Winnipeg or anywhere else for that matter. But every voters' list in the country had a couple of dozen Fosters on it. Common.

Whenever Harry came to call for Margo, he would be forced to sit and listen to another litany on the Muir lineage from her father. "I couldn't decide whether he was trying to bore me into staying away from the house or encouraging me to trot out my own ancestors and compete." In the end he decided to remain silent.

Despite pretentions of still being an important part of the city's economic and social vitality, the Muir family with Robert at its helm had already entered a final eclipse. Still, Robert considered himself a practical man. He visualized Margo as a practising lawyer with one of the city's better legal firms after she had graduated from university. Later, he intended—surreptitiously—to arrange a marriage for her into one of Winnipeg's socially acceptable and monied families. For her to end up an army wife with a husband who after retirement had no prospects beyond his military pension except as an apple salesman or the like, just wasn't in the cards.

As always, he discussed his concerns with Maj. Murray Ross. Ross was an enigma. A spare, saturnine man who insisted always on being addressed by his former military rank, Ross had arrived on the Muirs' doorstep in the early winter of 1920, claiming to have been Arthur Muir's closest friend at the front line in France during the war and to have been with him at the time he was mortally wounded. Just before slipping into final unconsciousness, Arthur, so Ross maintained, had made him promise to visit Robert and Jean in Winnipeg. His two-year delay in arriving had been due to the recovery time necessary for his own war wounds. Quite naturally, Robert invited him in.

Over the following weeks the Major told the Muirs a series of compelling war stories about his pal Arthur. Robert couldn't hear enough of Ross's tales. After a few months, when it became obvious their houseguest had no intention of leaving and the Major kept remembering new "Arthur stories," Jean became sceptical about the man's authenticity. But Robert wouldn't hear of it and insisted that Ross be treated henceforth as a family member.

Thus, the ubiquitous Major Ross became a permanent household fixture with his own private room and maid service. Worse, he became Robert's confidant and financial and business advisor as well. He had no apparent business credentials and no source of income. When Jean questioned him about the military pension to which he was entitled because of his wounds, Ross turned evasive. In the end, Robert offered to help, and the Major's entire existence came to depend upon Robert's generosity and openheartedness. With the passing of years the children learned to accept this bizarre relationship between Ross and their father. Not surprisingly, their mother never could.

Ross's advice on the dangerous infatuation between Margo and Harry was for Robert to say and do nothing. He felt certain that once Margo got to university and realized that there were a lot more fish in the sea, her passion would cool and she would come to her senses. As always, Robert agreed.

On 21 May 1927 Laffy recorded in his diary: "Captain Lindbergh passed over Halifax on his way to Paris . . . only 25 years old!!! The same age as Harry."

His 56th birthday came and went and for the first time he started feeling the effects of his own mortality. After much searching, he finally found a retirement home for Janie and himself in the pleasant little town of Wolfville, less than a 15-minute drive from Kentville. The house was huge and, for a couple approaching their 60s, wildly impractical, particularly since they intended to spend their winters at the house they had rented in Halifax. Yet for the first time in his life Laffy had money to spend frivolously. It was important for his self-esteem to be able to give Janie a home at least as grand as the one she and her brothers had grown up in back at Canning. He settled into the life of a country squire with unabashed pleasure.

Gil organized a motor trip for them all the way to Kingston so that he could attend the RMC June ball. Laffy and Janie were enthusiastic. They travelled on gravel roads through New Brunswick and Quebec into Ontario. Gil was offered an instructor's job at the college—which was quite an honour for one so young. The ball turned out to be a roaring success. Chris Vokes graduated from McGill and came down from Montreal for the party. Guy Simonds was still at his posting with B Battery and just as serious-minded as ever. Gil laughed a lot and drank a lot but managed the return trip to Halifax without incident. He could still control his liquor.

In November Harry finally wrote home with the first news of Margo Muir and his intention of asking her to marry him. Janie was delighted—more so when she learned that the girl's family had money. If only Gil could find the same sort of girl in Halifax. But Gil was away in Ottawa taking a course at the Small Arms School. Janie offered Harry her grandmother's engagement ring with a caveat that if Margo decided later not to go through with the wedding the ring would be returned. If Harry didn't use the ring, maybe Gil would. Janie had other rings to offer the boys, but the one from her grandmother was her favourite.

On Christmas Eve at the mess dance Harry proposed to Margo. His primary assault successful, he wired home: "Margo accepted. Tackling Mr. Muir today over dinner. Merry Xmas to all. Love. Harry."

A pall of silence fell across the Muirs' Christmas dinner table when Margo waved her ringed finger in front of the family. Brother Bill offered enthusiastic congratulations. Her mother expressed a polite interest. Major Ross and

Robert continued eating. Harry felt like a leper.

After several weeks of acrimonious family debates chaired by Major Ross, Harry was informed that if Margo still felt the same about him in two years, her father would give them permission to marry. Would he accept these terms? Harry had little choice. "On my pay I couldn't afford the price of an elopement ladder much less the cost of a honeymoon to some secluded hideaway far from Major Ross and the Muirs."

The Major remained convinced Margo would come to her senses or that Harry would be transferred back to the Strathconas' B Squadron at Calgary and the entire matter would die a natural death. But Margo was made of sterner stuff, and Harry remained in Winnipeg as the steadfast suitor. At last, in the spring of 1929, after Margo finished her second year of university and announced she had no intention of becoming a lawyer, her father threw in the towel. A wedding date was set for 7 September—six days short of her 20th birthday.

The "nuptials," as the newspapers insisted on calling the wedding, turned out to be one of Winnipeg's most spectacular social events that year. Harry, who had been promoted brevet captain in May, was given a full military wedding by the regiment. All military personnel wore dress uniforms.[1] The effect was dazzling.

Margo's ivory satin wedding dress had a 15-foot train. Inside the church she was accompanied by a matron of honour and five bridesmaids. Enormous floral bouquets spilled across the altar front of St. George's Anglican Church, filled to overflowing with uniforms, clanking swords and squeaking leather, social lions, tattle-tale reporters, the invited and uninvited. Even the street outside was packed with spectators.

Chris Vokes acted as best man. Guy Simonds, who had been transferred the year before to the Royal Canadian Artillery's C Battery in Winnipeg, acted as one of the ushers. Both men would marry local girls during their tours of duty in the city.

An imposing coach drawn by six mounted chargers waited outside until the church doors were flung open and Mendelssohn's wedding march burst out across Crestwood Avenue. Hand in hand the newlyweds paused for a moment on the church steps while an honour guard of Strathconas formed an archway of crossed swords out to the sidewalk and carriage. Afternoon sunshine glinted from the polished helmets and sabres. People clapped and cheered as the couple boarded their coach in a shower of rice and good wishes.

At the reception, speeches and congratulatory telegrams mingled with the champagne and liquor. Jean Muir wept nonstop. Major Ross managed one or two frosty smiles and a handshake for Harry. Robert kept shaking his head like a swimmer trying to dislodge a water block from one ear.

A Nova Scotian honeymoon had been agreed upon, and they caught the six o'clock eastbound express with less than a minute to spare. Major Ross felt Niagara Falls more suitable, but one of Harry's brother officers had offered them the use of a secluded cabin directly across from Halifax on the Northwest Arm. No charge. Major Ross caved in.

At two o'clock next morning as the train thundered through the night and they lay spent in each other's arms, there came a sudden knock at the door of their drawingroom compartment. An urgent telegram, the conductor shouted.

"Slide it under the door!" Harry told him.

It was from Gil in England. He had gone overseas on a two-year exchange posting with the RCR's affiliate British regiment, the Gloucestershires. Somehow he had managed to arrange a precise delivery time: "WOOF WOOF. ETC. GIL." With a smile Harry went back to bed.

Fifty-four days later the New York stock market crashed and Robert Muir lost most of his family's fortune.

5

Mackenzie King's Liberal government went down to defeat in 1930. The Conservatives, headed by R.B. Bennett, took over the country on behalf of a thoroughly frightened electorate. Yet the canny King turned out to be the real winner. The switch to the Conservatives had had little to do with policy solutions to the disastrous economic times facing the country. There were no jobs and no prospect of jobs. An entire generation grew up in frustration, powerless to change their circumstances and angry at those in charge who had allowed it all to happen.

But the army, like the civil service it represented, remained well insulated from the country's economic plight. If the worst should happen—violent social unrest, a breakdown of law and order, a descent into mob rule—then a well-disciplined army would be required by the government to bring order out of chaos. It was a bond, unwritten and unspoken, but clearly understood by both parties. "We in government will insulate and protect you from the harsh economic realities of the real world. But in turn you must protect us whenever we call upon you to serve our needs." It provided a powerful moral incentive for cooperation.

While individual members of the armed forces might disagree with their government's policy or with orders from their superior officers or feel a reluctance to take part in volatile social situations they might be thrust into, they felt honour bound to obey. Moralists could argue that every man or woman must bear final responsibility for his or her actions. Soldiers knew better. When the army was called out in successive years to Cape Breton Island to prevent civil strife and protect property owned by local mining interests, whom exactly did it represent? The starving strikers in virtual serfdom to the companies? The provincial and municipal governments wanting to maintain the status quo? The federal government? The greedy and selfish mine owners? It was not a matter to concern the army.

Soldiers were given their orders and were expected to obey them regardless of any legal or moral interpretation. Disobedience in peacetime meant courtmartial, imprisonment and dishonourable discharge; during wartime it could mean a firing squad. Armies functioned through a chain of command based on strict discipline and obedience. This was what separated an army from a rabble. In exchange for the protection and security of serving, a soldier gave up his right to freedom of expression and choice.

If Harry had any moral misgivings, he kept them to himself. He had joined the army because he loved the life, the companionship, the enjoyment of working with others who thought and felt as he did about the regimented society they had chosen. It was almost a make-believe world, a world of pretense and pretension, learning how to train others to fight a war that no one really believed would occur.

After they returned to Winnipeg in October, the Muirs gave them a new two-bedroom white stucco house and the latest two-passenger Ford with a rumbleseat. The $400 from the Fosters in Wolfville went on household furnishings and two yappy Scottish terrier puppies. They settled comfortably into married life, unaffected by the misery or social upheaval that surrounded them. Although Harry's pay was never quite enough to live on, any shortfall could still be made up by the Muirs or, in a pinch, the Fosters. Neither Margo nor Harry had any hesitation about asking for money from either set of parents when it was needed.

For a time Margo considered returning to university and finishing her degree but gave up the idea as impractical. A B.A., she decided, would lead nowhere and accomplish nothing aside from making her father happy and providing her with the modest satisfaction of proving she could do it. Her marriage was satisfaction enough. Her father's earlier academic interests for her had been replaced by the prospect of grandchildren. Besides, wives— especially army wives—were expected to stay home, cook, look after the house, act as hostesses to their husband's friends, and raise children. She had been taught to be conventional and accepted her condition. Nor was there anything unconventional in Harry's thinking to encourage her to do otherwise.

Two years slipped by. Laffy and Janie gave up the Halifax house and settled permanently in Wolfville. Gil came home from England to be confirmed as captain and adjutant of the RCRs in Halifax. Gil's drinking was now a worry to both his parents. There wasn't a single respectable girl in Halifax who would have anything to do with him after eight o'clock in the evening when he was usually too drunk to stand. Only his daytime brilliance saved him from disaster.

Chris Vokes had been posted to the Halifax garrison. "If I had a best friend in Halifax it was Gil. And the old general and his wife treated me like their own son. But oh, how Gil broke their hearts! He just couldn't stay away from the booze. After a few months of watching him drown in alcohol, I suddenly found myself sliding down the same precipice to disaster. It sneaks up on you, y'know."

One day in the Royal Artillery Park officers' mess, Gil's commanding officer took Chris to one side. "Look here, Vokes, you know Foster better than anyone. He's a drunk. I'm going to have to cashier him. Could you break it to him first. I don't want a scene."

"Don't do it, sir!" Vokes pleaded.

"Why not? We've already got enough drunks in the Permanent Force."

"Because he's too young and too good to throw into the trash heap."

"Hmmm. Think you can straighten him out?"

"I can try."

Frightened by the threat of a dishonourable discharge, Gil stayed relatively sober over the next few months. At least while he was with Chris.

Over the Muirs' Sunday dinner table Major Ross grew steadily more somber, predicting an imminent worldwide economic collapse. Harry, whose knowledge and understanding of international finance were marginal at best, always tried steering these discussions to military matters, about which Ross also considered himself an expert.

Margo's father, on the other hand, found military discussions boring. He wanted to know when Harry intended "putting Duchess in pod" as he indelicately termed it. The same inane question came up every weekend until Harry began finding excuses to avoid the Sunday dinner ritual. Margo sided with Harry. For a year family relations remained strained. Finally, in late January 1932, the situation resolved itself when Margo announced she was expecting a baby. Even Major Ross's stonefaced countenance came alive at the news.

A broken shoulder blade from a fall during a match against the U.S army team finished Harry's polo career, but he still travelled to the U.S. on regular exchange visits with U.S. cavalry units, participating on the jumping teams, precision displays of horsemanship and musical rides. The annual public events were popular on both sides of the border, and whenever it could be arranged, Margo and the other wives went along on these tours like "well-bred camp followers."

Yet the important work for Permanent Force officers remained the training of the nation's militia units for that distant war no one believed would come. It was a vague generality upon which to base a career. It required a special temperament to withstand the never-ending public ridicule of professional "soldier boys." The men learned to accept it, although it stung their pride.

There were courses to attend. Updates on new weapons and their uses. Lectures on tactics by experts visiting from England and the United States. Hundreds of new facts and figures to be learned and remembered and passed on to the militia's "Sunday Soldiers." Despite outward appearances, very little had changed in military thinking since 1918. The summer weeks before every harvest were spent out in the field training the prairie militia units. District Headquarters issued the movement orders: "Captain H.W. Foster, L.S.N. (RC), will proceed to Maple Creek, Saskatchewan."

At 2:30 a.m. the train stopped for ten minutes to take on water. In the coach-class section a conductor awakened Harry from a fitful sleep. He yawned and climbed down onto a wood platform in the middle of nowhere. The night sky stretched high and cloudless from rim to rim with not a tree in sight. And the creek had been dry since June. He collected his saddle and kitbag from the baggage car. The locomotive sighed and wheezed in repose. A string-bean-pole man with enormous jug ears appeared from under the yellow station lights.

"Howdo! You that cavalry instructor they sent us from Winnipeg?" The man's ears braced the rim of his battered stetson.

"I am."

"Well, ah'm Owry Cansgood, Cap'n. Pleasetameetcha!"

He had splayed front teeth and hard callused hands. Everything was closed at this time of night, he explained. "But I been detailed to look after you. So guess we best get along to Mrs. Smith's afore we decide what to do next. You thirsty?"

Harry allowed that he was. He threw his gear in back of the buckboard and climbed up beside Owry.

America's prohibition fanaticism had spilled across the border, turning Saskatchewan dry as a prairie drought. Mrs. Smith and her daughter ran the local knocking shop on the edge of town. Everyone in Maple Creek patronized Mrs. Smith, including the local Royal Canadian Mounted Police (RCMP) constabulary. Owry introduced Harry and ordered a bottle of rotgut whisky. Near dawn they ordered a second bottle. Cansgood was anything but the hayseed he appeared. As an infantryman in France he had won the Military Cross for valour. But like the rest of his militia group, he had always wanted to be a cavalryman. Harry sympathized. By 6:00 a.m. they had emptied the second bottle. Owry announced it was time they reported to the Colonel. Mrs. Smith fixed some breakfast and arranged for her daughter to drive them out to where the militiamen had pitched their tents in the Cypress Hills, 25 miles south of town. A rooster tail of yellow dust chased the Model A as it bumped along the dry empty road to the campsite.

Instead of a proper cavalry layout with tents set in rows so that troops could muster to their horses on the double, Harry found them pitched in an infantry hollow-square formation. Not good. Weren't these supposed to be cavalry trainees? A small brackish creek ambled past the edge of the campground. It provided drinking water at one end and disposal for liquid waste on the downstream side. Didn't the commanding officer understand the basics of troop hygiene in the field? Where did the horses drink?

They found Colonel Greenway on a knoll seated on the skin of his favourite horse, which had been draped over a hay bale. The Colonel sucked on a straw. He came to his feet when Harry reported. He had a large angular face and stood nearly six and a half feet tall. Owry introduced them.

"Isn't this a cavalry camp, Colonel?" Harry inquired.

"That's right, buster."

"Then why is it laid out in a hollow square, sir?"

"Tell you what, buster. When you've turned these boys of mine into cavalrymen, then I'll change the camp design. That suit you?"

Harry agreed.

From under the horsehide Greenway produced a bottle of yellow liquid. He offered Harry a swig. It tasted like nothing he'd experienced.

"Slew water from that creek mixed with Eno's Fruit Salts to give it a little sparkle. Couldn't drink it otherwise," Greenway explained. "Gives everybody the shits but what the hell, it's better than nothing."

"Where are the horses?" Harry asked.

"Oh, they'll be along later. You go find yourself a cot in the officers' tent and get yourself settled, then we'll talk."

Daytime temperatures in the teepee-type Bell tents reached 120 degrees Fahrenheit at midday. It was cooler outside under the blazing sun. Near seven o'clock that evening the horses appeared, a stampede of 300 wild mustangs flushed over the preceding days from their grazing places among the Cypress Hills. The energetic cowboys selected the meanest stallion from the herd and delivered him to Harry.

"Gentlest creature of the lot, Cap'n. My word on it!"

After Harry subdued his animal in a spectacular 20-minute contest of wills to the cheers of the militiamen, the Colonel strode over as he dismounted and thumped him on the back approvingly.

"That was one hell of a performance, buster. Now all you've got to do is get the right man mounted on the right horse and you're in business. I expect to see everyone mounted and on parade tomorrow morning at 0800 hours. If you need me, I'll be in my tent."

Two weeks later the military district's general officer commanding arrived to inspect the new South Saskatchewan Light Horse. Men and horses performed superbly—squadron drill at the gallop, cavalry charges, virtually flawless horsemanship.

"Damn good show, Greenway!"

"Thank you, sir," the Colonel replied, modestly accepting the praise on behalf of his men.

While Colonel Greenway took the accolades, Owry Cansgood took Harry back to Maple Creek to catch the train for Winnipeg.

A half a world away in Silesia, Lieut.-Col. Heinz Guderian* was busy experimenting in armoured tactics, using trucks covered with wood and canvas to represent tanks and anti-tank guns. The concept of mechanized armour used in tactical formations during wartime was a revolutionary idea. Guderian knew the day of cavalry had passed. Mobility was the key to success in any future conflict. Self-propelled guns, tanks and armoured vehicles would change forever the face of war. "We had at first to rely on exercises carried out with dummies: originally these had been canvas dummies pushed about by men on foot, but now at least they were motorized dummies of sheet metal."[2]

The real tanks would come later.

6

They named their first child Anthony after Anthony Farrier, Harry's closest friend. Margo would have preferred an acceptable family name from either the Muir or Foster antecedents, but Harry insisted.

His confirmation from brevet captain to captain came in July 1934. It gave him a bit more pay but not much else. "Five ruddy years to move up one rung on the ladder! I'll be an old man before I get anywhere," he complained. One evening he sat down with Margo and worked out exactly how long it might take him to become colonel of the regiment. Allowing for his seniority and normal retirement attrition, 1963 seemed to be the earliest. All very depressing.

During the Turner Valley oil boom of 1929 a few of his pals had left the regiment to make their fortunes in the Alberta oil fields. He had been asked to join but had hesitated too long. Several became millionaires and went on to make other fortunes in real estate and industry, apparently able to thrive in a depressed economy. Throughout his life, Harry remained mystified by the ability of successful businessmen to create orderly profit out of economic chaos. His brain simply didn't work along such lines. Yet he respected and admired those abilities in others, even to the point of being a bit envious of their talents. In the end, he made up his mind that "come hell or high water I'll stick at being a professional soldier."

But if he intended reaching senior command, he would have to get himself into one of the Imperial Staff Colleges. Nobody went anywhere in the Empire's armies until he had graduated from a Staff College. There were two: one in Camberley, England, on the busy London-to-Portsmouth highway; the other in Quetta, India, near the Afghanistan border in the northwest.

---

*Creator of Hitler's panzer divisions and *Blitzkrieg* concept.

Acceptance criteria for Canadian army applicants were based on competitive examinations for officers between the ages of 25 and 33 who had attained their captaincy. Canada was permitted to fill no more than three vacancies a year, and final selection went to the three officers with the highest exam marks.

RMC provided preparatory courses at Kingston for prospective applicants. Harry had attended the 1929 summer session soon after his promotion to brevet captain. It all seemed perfectly straightforward: he would pass in the top three and be off to England in December. But when the final exam results were posted, to his embarrassment he saw his name at the bottom. Getting good marks wasn't good enough. He had to be among the best.

Three years passed. He studied every free minute, memorizing whole paragraphs from *King's Regulations* and the *Manual of Military Justice*. In 1932 he tried again, this time managing to place himself halfway up the grading list. Better, but not nearly good enough. Chris Vokes wrote and passed in 1933. Infuriating. Vokes now became senior to Harry on the appointments list. Another try in 1934 had the same results. Because of the age limitation, time was running out. He had only one more chance.

The Strathconas transferred him back to Calgary. Hardship country. Margo was expecting another child in May. They moved into comfortable married quarters in the city's expanding suburbs. Throughout March and April he sat up nights with cold wet towels around his head to keep himself awake and studied. God how he studied! He had decided to leave the army if he failed again.

The day arrived. He sat down at a trestle table in one of the classrooms at the Calgary Armouries with five other nervous officers. He opened his exam packet and began to write. At the other end of the country, Gil was writing his first attempt. Guy Simonds was sitting, too. Tough competition. If he could just come in third. Five hours later he handed in his papers and went off to Kelowna, British Columbia, for a tactical exercise.

He left Margo to hold on until his return. She couldn't wait. The baby arrived on 18 May two weeks early and nine days before Harry was due back. For months they had argued over names. Harry had decided on Gilbert Lafayette to please his father if it was a boy, Janie if it turned out to be a girl. Margo wanted some acknowledgment of her family's contribution.

By the time Harry returned, David Muir Foster's birth had been officially recorded with the Alberta government. It was too late to change anything.

"But why David?"

"Because David slew Goliath," she told him mischievously. After thinking about that for a moment, he decided to drop the subject.

Gil was in Ottawa on a course at the Small Arms School when the exam results were announced. His heart sank. Quickly he dashed off a letter to Laffy.

My Dear Dad: Harry and I both passed but here is the catch. 1st Simonds—
2nd Gerrard—3rd self—4th Harry. The Director of Training said I would go
to Quetta. I said I'd waive my place in favour of Harry because it was his last
chance. He said my proposal couldn't be considered but that he would make
a strong recommendation that Harry be permitted to write again next year.
Rotten isn't it? I don't want to go to India and if I hadn't written the exams
Harry could have gone. I should feel very pleased at being successful my first
time. But I don't. Wish things could have turned out differently. I'm writing
Harry. Say nothing about my feelings. All goes well and I'm not celebrating.
Lots of love to you and mother. Gilbert.

It meant that Vokes, Simonds and Gil were all senior to Harry now. A
great gloom descended over the Calgary household. He felt certain his career
was finished. At best he might make major by his retirement age. Resignation
from the army was his only honourable course of action. But what was he
qualified to do besides ride a horse well and shout troop commands? He
was 33 years old and knew nothing but the army.

However, before he managed to put his resignation into writing and submit
it to his commanding officer, word arrived from the Director of Training
at Ottawa confirming the promise made to Gil. Not only would he be given
another chance for Staff College, but he was to be appointed as GSO3* at
London, Ontario, to learn the basics of being a competent staff officer. There
still appeared to be a chance—a slim chance in his own mind—he might
be able to make something of himself after all.

The new posting became effective in late October. He timed his annual
leave to coincide with the transfer, giving the family three weeks together
in Wolfville. Gil arranged to take his leave from the RCRs at the same time.
"Never was I so glad to see the last of a place as Calgary."

Fall is the most beautiful time of the year in Nova Scotia. On clear, crisp
nights, "frost bugs" are about to nip the leaves near dawn with splashes
of gold and pink and saffron. The apple-harvest days are cool and mellow,
and the air holds a chill of quiet breathlessness. It is the hunting season
for moose, deer and duck. Off Shelburne the big Atlantic tuna swirl after
bait. And in hundreds of peaceful lakes and rivers the trout and salmon are
awake and feeding after their summer somnolence.

The big house in Wolfville filled with life and the sounds of laughter.
Laffy smiled contentedly. It was for just such a purpose he had bought the
place. Janie arranged family weekends so that all the Valley relatives could
bring each other up to date on their happenings and introduce their new
offspring. It felt good to belong. Even the petty jealousies and tart remarks
made between bloodlines were incapable of inflicting more than fleeting
injury.

---

*General Staff officer, grade 3.

The worst of the Depression was past, so the older men told one another wisely. The credit belonged to Germany. Its new chancellor, Adolf Hitler, seemed to have things moving again. Local sawmills had received sizeable orders for mine pit props from several German buyers. Money, although far from plentiful, was available for investment. A collective sigh of optimism could be heard across the country.

Cousin Alice still worked in Ottawa with her cabinet minister. Cousin Harry had turned into a bothersome drunk and family mooch only barely tolerated. Cousin Jim had become a civil engineer with the highways department and was busy designing the new paved roads promised to the electorate by the Liberal government. He and his wife had a baby girl.

Between Laffy's fishing and hunting expeditions with Harry and Gil and Janie's weekend buffets on the broad front lawn, their holidays slipped by quickly. It was to be the last time they would meet together as a family.

On a fishing trip near the end of their leave Gil confided to Harry that he had never wanted to join the army.

"I'm bored to death with it. Did you know that?"

Harry admitted that he didn't. Then why had he joined?

"For the same reason you did. It was expected. Dad wants us both to be generals. Carry on the tradition. That sort of nonsense. So I obliged."

"You can always resign."

Gil shook his head. "Too late, big brother. Too late. I chose the wrong career. The army's all I know. I'm too old now for anything new. Just one of life's little tragedies."

Harry thought he was joking. He wasn't. Gil's face pleaded for understanding. He didn't want to go to India. He sensed disaster. In Quetta, cut off from the family support, there would be nowhere for him to run, no idolizing mother and father willing to overlook his transgressions, no reason to stay sober. Two years in India. A long ocean voyage out and back through the Suez.

He drank far too much, not just in the afternoons and evenings, but all day every day. Never so much that he staggered or slurred his words in front of company, but enough to put away a 40-ounce bottle of whisky during his waking hours.

"India will finish me," he muttered.

"Then for God's sake don't go!"

They were seated on the riverbank, tossing their lines into the drifting current. Fish were jumping but not biting. Beyond the river's edge the rich brown Valley land lay resting after fall plowing. Gil reached into the wicker picnic basket Janie had packed that morning and removed the ubiquitous bottle. He took a long swallow. His eyes brightened. He offered his brother a drink. Harry took a judicious nip and passed it back.

Gil sighed. "I envy you, big brother. Do you know that? For you it's all black and white. No shades of grey. You may never reach the top but mark my words you'll be among the chosen few."

"So will you if you'd put your mind to it," Harry countered.

Gil gave a sad smile. "Don't be an ass."

The family settled into married quarters at Wolseley Barracks in London, Ontario, an imposing three-storey granite structure that served as the RCRs headquarters. Broad lawns sloped away to the edge of the CPR tracks. Giant elms provided nesting for a million starlings. The officers shot them for sport on Sunday afternoons. The wives, wearing tweed skirts and heavy cablestitch pullovers against the autumn chill, clustered on the grass, discussing husbands, careers, offspring and social calendars.

Each woman observed a pecking order according to her husband's rank. The army classified them as *dependants*, and certainly they were that. They developed the odd habit of referring to one another formally as "Mrs. Major Carolina-Jones" or "Mrs. Captain Margo-Foster" during introductions. All deferred to the Colonel's robust, red-faced dependant, who held strong opinions on just about anything and aired them loudly with all the authority of a regimental sergeant-major.

As the newest recruit, Margo remained cautiously on the sidelines, refusing to be drawn into any argument where she might disgrace Harry inadvertently by using her intellect. Army wives were not supposed to be intellectual, only logical. After the years of easy informality among prairie society she found the social pretensions of these easterners ludicrous. But she played the game.

They made a strange pair. Margo was full of energy, conversation and curiosity. When she wasn't knitting, reading, dressmaking, running the household, or disciplining the children, she was busy organizing social events and committees for a dozen different activities. By comparison Harry seemed dull. He had learned to control his youthful enthusiasms because he considered them to be "unmilitary." With time and practice he had managed to mask every emotion he considered a sign of weakness behind a wall of taciturn imperturbability. To those who didn't know him well, he seemed aloof and coldly distant. It was a hell of an act and served him well throughout his career.

GSO3 meant paperwork. Harry hated paperwork. Any time spent sitting behind a desk he considered wasted unless there was something to learn. However, he was astute enough to manufacture a little enthusiasm for the new job and make the best of it, while at the same time retaining his sense of perspective. The deception worked. Although he detested the job, his CO's year-end performance report made the effort worthwhile: "Although this officer has only been in the District for appx. 2 mos. he has shown considerable aptitude for the work. He is keen and interested and a very good instructor. He is, in my opinion, above average."

So far he'd made all the right moves.

7

In January 1936 King George V died at his Sandringham country estate in Norfolk. David, the popular Prince of Wales, succeeded him to become Edward VIII of England and the Dominions, Emperor of India and Defender of the Faith.

Two months later Jean Muir died in Winnipeg. Margo took the train west to attend the funeral. If she felt any deep loss over her mother's passing, she kept it to herself. Her mother had suffered so much for so long that the release of death seemed more an occasion for relief than sorrow. But in the week that followed, her father sank into a deep depression and refused to be consoled. She was reluctant to leave him in such a state. Major Ross suggested a distraction. A hobby. Something to take his mind off his loss. An aviary.

"Birds?"

"Why not?" the Major demanded. "People breed dogs and cats. Why not birds?"

While Ross designed steel-mesh cages and supervised the workmen down in the basement, Margo scoured the pet shops for exotic birds. As the tempo of activity surged around him, Robert Muir's interest in the strange project stirred. Within days he had taken charge of the operation and was telephoning commercial aviaries all over the continent for mating pairs. By the time Margo caught the train back to London, the house had a collection of caged songbirds to rival any zoo in the country.

She arrived at Wolseley Barracks to the howls of her four-year-old son, Tony, sick in bed with a raging earache and soaring temperature. Even Harry looked worried. The base medical officer had tried aspirin and hot compresses without success. The boy had been crying steadily for three days and nights. She took him straight to hospital.

By the time a civilian specialist was called in, the infection had spread into the mastoid bone. Without an immediate operation, they were told, their son would die. In the days before antibiotics, survival rates for mastoid operations were two out of five. There was no alternative. It took an hour of cutting, sawing and scraping, but the boy survived with only a modest scar as a reminder.

No sooner had their son arrived home than Laffy phoned from Wolfville to say that Janie had fallen seriously ill. He didn't sound optimistic. Could Harry take emergency leave and come at once? His mother was asking for him. Alarmed, Harry dashed off a wire to Gil in Quetta and left immediately by car for the East Coast.

Two days and a night of practically nonstop driving brought him to his mother's bedside. She looked terribly frail with the pasty yellow complexion and black-ringed eyes of someone suffering acute jaundice. In dreadful pain and unable to keep anything in her stomach, Janie didn't recognize her eldest son.

"Gilbert?" she whispered. Always the favourite.

"It's Harry," Laffy corrected. "Gilbert's in India. Remember?"

"Massage my feet, Gilbert, will you please? No one massages my feet the way you do it, dear."

Harry obliged until she fell into a troubled morphine-induced sleep, all the while muttering endearments to his younger brother. Not once had she spoken his name. It hurt him deeply. He glanced over at his father. The old general appeared oblivious to her omission. Later, sometime before dawn, he awoke with a start, hearing his mother's cries of pain. Another morphine injection and she was quiet. Father and son retired to the library to talk until breakfast time.

The political situation in Europe had turned grave. Adolf Hitler had denounced the armament clauses of the Treaty of Versailles the year before and re-established compulsory military service. In a lunatic policy of appeasement the British government was allowing Germany to build a new navy up to 35 percent of Britain's naval strength. Less than two months earlier Hitler had repudiated the Locarno Pact.[3] German troops had reoccupied the demilitarized Rhineland Zone.

"There will be another war, Harry. Mark you! And it will be a long and bloody one unless England wakes up before it's too late."

Then they spoke of Gil and how much pleasure his letters from India brought his mother. Laffy handed Harry a few to read. His brother wrote amusingly and well, poking fun at the various Indian and British army institutions and pretensions. He had a keen eye for detail and an appreciation for the absurd. The GSO1 at Staff College he described as "a pompous needle-nosed martinet with a piercing voice and abhorrence of meat and alcohol—particularly alcohol, which of course does little for his popularity. But he certainly knows his stuff. His name is Montgomery." Gil's descriptions of India were pure Kipling.

"Your brother should have become a writer," Laffy observed regretfully.

"You mean instead of a drunk?" They were the only vicious words Harry had ever uttered about his brother.

During his emergency leave, he divided the time between his mother, while she was awake and lucid, and his father, when his mother slept. Uncles, aunts and cousins glided in and out of the house, their faces long with concern, their voices hushed in sympathy. At week's end, reluctantly, he headed back to Ontario, promising to phone each day for progress reports.

Laffy kept hoping for the best, yet his physician's common sense told him that his wife was dying and there was nothing he could do about it except keep her free from pain and provide whatever comfort he could when she was awake. Day by day she wasted away. Finally, he decided on the last resort. Exploratory surgery was set for 10 June.

When it was over he wrote painfully in his diary: "8:00 AM. Visited Janie who was quite free from pain and glad the operation was to be early. 8:30. Said goodbye to the dearest girl on earth. Dr. W. & Dr. S. operated and found conditions so grave decided to establish a drainage shunt. Sudden heart failure. She passed away on the operating table. Sent wires to Harry and Gilbert and relations."

Harry drove Margo and Tony back for the funeral. Gil had wired that he was prepared to chuck Staff College, resign his commission and return home immediately to help out. Laffy sent off a swift refusal, ordering him to stay put and finish his course. He should have accepted. It might have saved Gil from disaster.

During July and August militia camps across the nation opened for business. Men of all ages and professions arrived for two-week refresher courses and training in the arts of war. With Germany rearming, a tingle of anticipation stirred the men in every unit. The diehards were certain war was coming, the novices weren't so sure. Both agreed the European situation appeared volatile.

The RCRs' camp lay in flat open fields on the east side of Wolseley Barracks. Tents were pitched in orderly rows, field kitchens set up, medical inspection undertaken for every new arrival. Horses were procured for cavalry training. But the new emphasis was on mechanization. The Department of National Defence had reorganized the country's field formations to meet contemporary doctrine and expectations. Four cavalry regiments were converted to armoured car units, and six infantry regiments were designated as tank battalions. The units would not be receiving any equipment, but they could begin to regard themselves as mechanized. In the case of armoured car regiments, training was accomplished by using private civilian vehicles and pretending. There were, of course, no tanks.

However, 12 British-built Carden-Lloyd "tankettes" had been turned over to the RCRs for use as support vechicles with the idea of improving the regiment's mobility with machine guns. The tiny two-man machines tore around the fields raising considerable dust and enthusiasm but nothing in the way of tactical innovation. Tactical mobility was still regarded by senior officers as a function of cavalry.

But there were heretics to this philosophy. Capt. E.L.M. Burns* of the Royal Canadian Engineers had written an article back in 1924 on "The Mechanization of Cavalry." He had announced boldly that "the inefficient and obsolete horse . . . is a weapon that has had its day." He proposed cavalry units be equipped with vehicles capable of carrying four or five men and

---

*Later lieutenant-general and commander of the Canadian I Corps in Italy, 1944.

a machine gun across country at 15 miles per hour, relying on speed rather than armour for protection. "A cavalry mounted on such machines . . . would be able to reconnoitre, pursue, escape easily in rearguard actions, cooperate with and protect the movement of tanks, and most important of all, attack unshaken infantry in lightly wired [barbed wire] positions with excellent chances of success."[4]

In 1936 Lieut.-Col. F.F. Worthington,* new commander of the Permanent Force's tank school at Wolseley Barracks, advocated converting the Permanent Force cavalry regiments to tanks. This was still regarded as heresy. Thus, when the commanding officers of the two cavalry units—Royal Canadian Dragoons and Lord Strathcona Horse—were consulted, both were violently opposed to the idea. They argued that the mobility and flexibility of horsemen could never be matched by tanks or armoured cars. Horse-drawn two-pounder anti-tank guns—so the theory went—gave cavalry the edge against any tank. They had apparently forgotten the tragic 90-minute lesson given at the Moreuil Wood in France where 300 troopers and 800 horses had gone down under German machine-gun fire. The day of the dashing horse soldier was over, but its thousand-year tradition died hard.

Meanwhile, the German army had authorized its first three panzer divisions to be equipped in part with Pzkw† IIs, mounting 20 mm cannon and 14 mm of armour plate. Prototypes of the Pzkw III with a larger 37 mm cannon were undergoing field trials in Silesia even while Harry galloped his trainees through complicated cavalry manoeuvres in Ontario's hot humid summer.

Every officers' mess has its self-appointed know-it-all, an insufferable condescending individual whom everyone dislikes but tolerates for the sake of mess harmony. At Wolseley Barracks' mess the know-it-all was Capt. Charles Foulkes. "His mouth was as mean and narrow as his hard-shelled Baptist mind. He had a sneering supercilious attitude toward anyone his own rank or below but grovelled to everybody over the rank of major," Harry recalled. "One of the few people in this life that I thoroughly disliked."

In the mess one afternoon they nearly came to blows. Although talking shop was considered bad form, at a table nearby Foulkes sat lecturing a trio of subalterns on his idea of cavalry tactics. "Not only didn't he know what he was talking about but the poor militia subalterns were taking it all in as the gospel." Harry made the mistake of waiting until Foulkes left to go to the bathroom and then leaned over to tell the junior officers not to put too much stock in what he had said but to read their cavalry orders. It was all laid out in proper form in the book. A discussion ensued. Foulkes returned and, after hearing a few moments of argument from his recent tactical converts, accused Harry of trying to undermine his position and authority.

---

*Later major-general and commander of the 4th Armoured division in England, 1942.
†Panzerkampfwagen—literally, "armour-plated battle carriage"—a tank.

Words were exchanged: laconic ones from Harry, outrage from Foulkes. A circle of amused officers gathered. Finally, the red-faced Foulkes challenged Harry to "settle matters in a gentlemanly fashion."

"You mean a duel?"

"I mean boxing gloves," Foulkes shouted.

Harry finished his drink and stood up. "I refuse. It would be an uneven match. You'd lose your teeth, and your mouth would be even smaller than it is already. Besides, I never fight with an inferior, especially a jackass." A round of applause followed him out the door. Foulkes left the mess in a cold fury.

"It was a silly damn thing to do," Harry admitted, "but how was I to know that the conniving sonofabitch would wind up one day as chairman of the Canadian Chiefs of Staff."*

On 10 December Edward VIII announced over the radio his abdication of the throne so that he might wed the twice-divorced American Wallis Simpson. His shy younger brother, the Duke of York, assumed the crown as George VI.

On the same day, Laffy arrived by train in London, Ontario, for a visit. He was lonely. The Wolfville house had been put up for sale, and he had taken up residence in Kentville at the Cornwallis Inn, a comfortable CPR hotel with broad, shaded wood verandahs and lush sloping lawns fronting the town's main street. He had given up his apple brokerage business, except for his own crop and brother-in-law Fred Wickwire's. He missed Janie. He missed Gil.

He had spent the summer driving about the province, visiting old army friends and seeing how the country had changed. He suffered from phlebitis in both legs, making long car trips painful. Not wanting to intrude on Harry and Margo, he took a room at the Hotel London, a half-hour walk from Wolseley Barracks. He stayed four months, visiting daily to play with his grandchildren or talk to Margo while Harry was away at work.

Harry took him on several week-long regular militia inspection tours, visiting small-town armouries around southwestern Ontario where indoor formations of weekend soldiers crashed to attention and performed nearly flawless drills followed by close-order marching around the concrete floors past the reviewing stands.

"Can they do anything else?" Laffy inquired after they had reviewed a dozen different units in a dozen different towns.

"Spout the King's Regulations and guard duty challenges. That's about all," Harry admitted. "Some can ride a horse."

"But if war comes, will they fight?"

---

*From 1951 to 1960 as a general.

Harry thought a moment. Then shook his head. "I don't know, Dad. If they don't, then everything I've been doing has been a waste of time."

8

By spring, 1937, the first phase of Hitler's war economy was completed. Using Keynesian deficit-spending policies to rebuild and rearm Germany, a point of virtual "full employment" had been reached. German industrialists such as Fritz Thyssen and Gustav Krupp reaped enormous rewards for supporting the Nazi regime. Over 100,000 employees at the Krupp works in Essen were producing armaments on a scale unsurpassed anywhere else in the world.

Emboldened by his previous unopposed successes, Hitler next embarked on a policy of piecemeal absorption of European territories. Strange tales were coming out of Germany. Refugees claiming to be escaping from Nazi persecution told of murder in the streets and exile to secret concentration camps. Few people believed them. The refugees were mostly Jews. No one paid much attention. Besides, the appeasement policies advocated by the Western nations in dealing with Germany tolerated no confrontation.

Confirmation of Harry's Staff College appointment arrived in early July. He wrote his father: "I can't believe it! After seven years of wishful thinking." He was 35 and already too old for serious consideration as anything more than a competent militia instructor, but the Director of Training in Ottawa had kept his word. However, there was a tuition fee of $1,500 payable in three equal installments upon arrival in England. Britain's encouragement of colonial staff officers at the college didn't extend to free enrollment. What to do?

With some misgivings, he composed a carefully worded letter home for help. He had never asked for such a sum before and hadn't the least idea how he could repay his father. He needn't have worried. Not only did Laffy agree to provide the funds but announced that he had decided to accompany them on the boat to England for a holiday.

His depression over Janie's death had passed. He'd run into an old childhood sweetheart from North Kingston, Agnes Stoop. She and Laffy had rekindled their youthful passions, although, as Laffy hastened to explain, "on a considerably higher emotional plane than we enjoyed 50 years ago."

The only event to mar Harry's last months at Wolseley Barracks came in late August when Tony burned down the horse barns while playing with matches. Capt. Rodney Keller,* his wife and young son—also named Tony and the same age as Harry's eldest—were visiting, and while the grownups

---

*Later major-general and D-Day commander of the 3rd Canadian Division.

talked, the boys were sent off to explore, the resident Tony acting as guide. After viewing the stabling barns, they climbed up to the hayloft to play. The fire was a beaut—fire engines, bells, terrified horses, water hoses, cursing men and livid parents. Fortunately, all the animals were taken out before the roof collapsed. The Tonys received "a pair of damn good hidings," Harry reported in a letter to Laffy.

Lieutenant-Colonel Worthington, who had been away in England on a course with the Royal Tank Corps, said later that "Tonys Foster and Keller had probably done more to advance the cause of armoured forces over cavalry at London, Ontario, than any other single event." The horse barns were never rebuilt and the following summer the Canadian Armoured Fighting Vehicle School was moved to Camp Borden, Ontario, with Worthington firmly in command.

Harry sailed for England on the ss *Ausonia* on 12 December 1937. Laffy, Harry and Margo were seated at the captain's table for the seven-day voyage. Near the end, as the ship approached the mouth of the Thames making for the Tilbury docks, Laffy admitted awkwardly his intention of marrying Agnes. If that would be all right? "I need someone to share my old age," he explained. Was he asking his son's permission to remarry?

He was.

Stiffly self-conscious, Harry gave him his formal blessing.

Five days later they were seated with the children around the dining room table in their new home at Camberley for Christmas. The roof leaked. The taps leaked. The floors creaked. There was no central heating. There were mice in the cellar and drafts around each door and window. Fortunately, the weather outside remained mild. They were happy.

Classes at Staff College began in the New Year.

While Harry and Margo had been packing their steamer trunks at Wolseley Barracks in November, Gil had been packing his bags in Quetta for the long voyage home from Bombay. Colonel Montgomery's assessment of Gil's Staff College performance said it all: "This officer is brilliant. But he drinks." He certainly did, literally falling off the boat when it docked in England in early January. His father was there to meet him.

Shocked at the emaciated drunken figure that stumbled down the gangway and toppled over at his feet, Laffy bundled him into a taxi and took him straight to a London clinic specializing in "drying out" alcoholics. It was wildly expensive and in Gil's case a complete waste of money. He had passed the point of no return. Two weeks in the clinic, two days without a drink, then a four-day bender followed by another week in the clinic. Gil's brain needed alcohol just to function.

In lucid moments he apologized, weeping for the disgrace he had brought down upon his father. India had destroyed him—the terrible boredom and isolation of a foreign land with little to do for diversion but sightsee and party. He had passed the course but lost his own private war.

On 18 February 1938 Laffy wrote in his diary: "Gilbert left on the 10:40 AM boat-train from Euston to sail C.P. from Liverpool tonight. Looks fit and strong. I feel his treatments have been of great help and trust he will do good work in Canada."

Pure self-deception.

Agnes joined Laffy in London for the rest of his visit—two 67-year-olds enjoying a holiday at the Crown Hill Hotel. The hotel, close to Kensington Gardens, held happy memories of his war years when he and Janie and the children had stayed there when they first arrived from Canada and the world had been much less complicated.

On 25 March Laffy and Agnes sailed for Canada. Margo and Harry came up to London the evening before with the children for a farewell dinner. The conversation—as always—centred around Gil. Laffy was optimistic. "You'll see. He'll straighten himself out once he gets back to the regiment and sees all his old friends." Neither Harry nor Margo commented, and the children were too young to understand.

Since his return from India and subsequent to sailing for Halifax, Gil had once again become his father's single consuming interest. Margo resented it. She had never shared the family's admiration for her brother-in-law. In her eyes Gil was "a drunken bum who squandered his talents because he lacked guts." Whenever his name came up in conversation, she would purse her lips disapprovingly and remain silent. Harry had long since grown used to the fact that in his father's eyes he'd never be more than a pinch-hitter for Gil, regardless of what he accomplished on his own.

The evening remained fixed in Harry's mind: Margo coldly silent, Agnes listening politely to Laffy's stories about Gilbert, and the children bored into restlessness and yawning over their cake and ice-cream. Then it was time to go. Almost as an afterthought in the midst of their goodbyes Laffy wished him luck on his staff course. Harry thanked him courteously. He promised to write. It was the last time father and son would meet.

On 31 October 1938 Gil was formally cashiered from the army. He celebrated the occasion by drinking himself senseless. Three days later he sobered up enough to catch the train to Wolfville. Laffy wrote in his diary: "Gilbert arrived from Halifax. His condition was such I called Dr. C. in Kentville and we took him to the hospital infirmary in Halifax and called Dr. W. to attend him. Condition grave. He is now turned out of the service which has been his ruin." Laffy felt crushed under a great and terrible sorrow, blaming himself for Gil's destruction.

Harry passed his first year at Staff College and took Margo to the French Riviera for a holiday to celebrate. The Staff College commandant's report on Harry's abilities, while not exactly laudatory, was encouraging. "Professional ability average, but he is slow in applying it. Has common-sense: mentally inclined to be slow. A good and willing worker. Very strong physically. Able to stand up to a lot of work. Should do well on active service." Harry vowed to himself to be a bit more dazzling during his second year.

That May, the King and Queen set off for North America on a seven-week tour arranged by a nervous British government. Its purpose was to reinforce England's ties with its closest dominion while at the same time provide Americans with their first glimpse of the fairy-tale magic of a reigning British monarch. If and when war came, his island kingdom would need all the help it could get in defending its shores.

The Royal couple sailed aboard the *Empress of Australia* on 6 May from Portsmouth. Harry drove Margo and the children down to the coast to see their departure. Tens of thousands of people lined the beaches of Gosport, Hayling and the Isle of Wight as capital ships from the Royal Navy accompanied the brightly painted Cunard liner out of Portsmouth Harbour. A formation of long-range, four-motored Sunderland flying boats flew overhead, dipping their wings on each pass over the fleet. The children waved and cheered, which was rather silly, as someone pointed out, for the vessels were at least a mile offshore, but the excitement was infectious. Everyone up and down the shore waved and cheered enthusiastically at the receding vessels.

The following month, while fishing at one of his favourite pools, Laffy suffered a sudden blood clot in his left leg. It took him hours to crawl out to the highway for help. After two days of unsuccessful surgical attempts to clear the clot, gangrene set in. His leg was amputated above the knee.

"The prognosis is not good," he wrote. "I fear my days are now numbered. Without constant exercise to maintain good blood circulation other clots will form." He had moved back to the big house in Wolfville with Agnes after their return from England. No one wanted to buy the place, it seemed. Too big and too expensive to maintain. Gil moved in with them, helping around the place when he was sober.

Agnes listened patiently to Laffy's litany of complaints, encouraging him to try his new crutches. But he was just too old to start hoisting his bulk about with his arms and shoulders, especially while he suffered painful attacks of bursitis. He spent his days sitting in the garden talking to Gil and Agnes or indoors reading when it rained. Friends and relations came to call, shook their heads and went away.

"They don't understand," he wrote Margo. "All the excitement is gone. I'm just a tired old man waiting for the end."

The peaceful English summer of 1939 was drawing to a close. Every free weekend Harry took Margo and the children off on some expedition the way his mother and father had done when he and Gil were lads. His boys were too young to appreciate most of what they saw, but Margo was game for everything. Whether boating on the River Streatley, swimming in the ocean at Hayling Island or visiting Stonehenge, the departure from Camberley was always arranged so that they would reach their destination in time for a noonday picnic. But the days of picnics and sightseeing were coming to a close.

PART 4

THE MAKING OF A WARRIOR: II

Youth is the season of credulity.
WILLIAM PITT (THE ELDER)

Aɴʏ ʜᴏᴘᴇs assistant shopkeeper Kurt Meyer had of joining the army in 1928 were dashed when he discovered there were thousands of young men across the country—most better qualified than he—waiting for vacancies in the 100,000-man force. The army could afford to pick and choose. He put in his application anyway, then went over to the National Socialist German Workers' Party offices in Schöningen and signed up with the Sturmabteilung (sᴀ).*

He had joined the ɴsᴅᴀᴘ as a Hitler Youth in 1925, shortly after his confirmation. He did so more as a protest than through any political convictions about the Nazi party. But all the same he found the idea of nazism, of a jackbooted and uniformed political party providing disciplined camaraderie for the working classes, appealing. Never mind that its leaders were for the most part social misfits or that its platform remained obscured behind a smoky gauze of nationalistic beer hall rhetoric. At the time Kurt joined the movement, it was the next best thing to being in the army.

The sᴀ had evolved as the party's shock troops. Dressed in distinctive

---

*Storm troopers.

brown uniforms, caps and jackboots, and often armed with truncheons, the SA provided protection or intimidation at party meetings, and head bashing during street marches if challenged by the Communists or Social Democrats. It was all grand fun so long as one remembered to keep one's head down during the street battles.

As an SA member Kurt was expected to buy his own uniform, attend local political rallies when his name appeared on the duty roster, and turn up for regular drills and weekend marches. Party members were supposed to find employment for themselves and pay their monthly dues, although in cases of extreme hardship this last requirement could be waived by the local secretary.

Kurt found himself a job as a construction worker building roads. The work paid well but was very hard, and by early summer he had spent enough time on the end of a shovel to realize there were easier ways of making a living. He applied for a job as a mailman and to his surprise was accepted. Poor pay but easy working hours. If he walked quickly, he could finish his deliveries by early afternoon and take the rest of the day off. He needed all the free time he could get to fulfil his obligations to the Nazi movement.

Otto didn't approve of his son's political activities. He considered Kurt too young to be out all night. Neither he nor Alma had any idea where he went every evening or what he was doing. Finally, a young woman next door to the Meyers told Alma not to be upset. "Your son knows my fiancé. They are with the Nazis. They have meetings and stuff like that. It's all quite harmless." Nevertheless, Otto and Alma worried. Their son was still only 17. "At least he isn't a Communist or one of those noisy Socialists," Alma observed. The Nazis were regarded as a group of rising militant nationalists. Few people were clear about their motives or aims, or how wide their support among the working classes.

From time to time Kurt appeared at the breakfast table with black eyes and assorted minor injuries from fighting with local competing political parties. "Terrible night again," he'd tell his parents enthusiastically over coffee. "But we gave them a good licking."

Otto's physical condition continued to deteriorate. Two years earlier Alma had become alarmed by his weight loss and breathing difficulties. She insisted on a proper diagnosis by government doctors, together with X-rays. When the results were known, Otto was sent immediately to Stege in the Harz Mountains for a rest cure at a hospital specializing in lung diseases. He left on a Tuesday. By Thursday afternoon he was home. "Are you tough enough to hear the truth, Herr Meyer?" the hospital's chief resident had inquired after viewing his X-rays. "You have a year, no more."

Two summers had passed since that diagnosis and still he held on to life.

One Sunday afternoon Melanie lay resting in a hammock on the front verandah. Kurt kept teasing her by turning the hammock and dumping her onto the floor. Fed up with her brother's antics, she went indoors to complain to Otto, who as usual was in bed. "Papa, Kurt keeps tipping me out of the hammock . . ." She never finished the sentence. Her father had turned a deathly grey. Quickly she ran and fetched her mother and Kurt. They gathered around the twin beds.

"Push the beds apart, then sit down and listen. I have something to say to you all," he whispered. For a moment he paused, catching his breath. "Melanie, you keep studying your music. Feel free to buy a new piano. Kurt, you must somehow go into the military and become a soldier. I want you to take care of the family. Mother, continue doing your job as a midwife. It is an honourable profession." His voice faded. A few minutes later he spoke his last words: "I want a military funeral with music. A salute with ten rifles at my graveside. And Kurt, if they don't fire in proper unison tell them how it's done. And Melanie, wear a red dress at my funeral. I can't bear the thought of you in black."

He died that afternoon. The air was hot and very humid, with a threat of thunderstorms from the west. Across the road through an open window a phonograph played Mozart.

They buried him in a corner of the Offleben cemetery and entered his name on the war memorial inside the church. An honour guard of six war veterans fired their volleys in perfect unison over his grave.

Alma and Melanie wore black.

The Munich *Putsch* (uprising) of 1923 had shown Hitler that his belief in the army's indifference to political rebellion against the Republic had been a serious miscalculation. Much as the Reichswehr disliked the Weimar government, it was prepared to shoot any person or group trying to overthrow it.

"When I resume active work," Hitler told a fellow prisoner in Landsberg Fortress, "it will be necessary to pursue a new policy. Instead of working to achieve power by armed coup, we shall have to hold our noses and enter the Reichstag against the Catholic and Marxist deputies. If outvoting them takes longer than outshooting them, at least the results will be guaranteed by their own constitution. Any lawful process is slow. . . . Sooner or later we will have a majority—and after that Germany."

His idea of following a legal road to power was not shared by the paramilitary groups within the Nazi movement. His friend and supporter, Ernst Röhm, leader of the SA, remained convinced that by maintaining the storm troops as a secret army the day would come when they could join the Reichswehr to overthrow the Weimar Republic and establish a dicta-torship. Röhm, an unpleasant, porcine-faced man, was one of the original members of the party. He had served during the war as an officer and exhibited an extraordinary organizational ability in putting together the paramilitary

Kampfbund* and SA groups out of members of the *Freikorps* and Nazi party. He was jailed for his part in the Munich *Putsch*. Upon release, his insistence that the SA as a military arm should have equal standing with the political wing of the Nazi movement led to Hitler's replacing him with a more complaisant commander. Röhm left in disgust for Bolivia to organize that country's military establishment along Germanic lines.

Unfortunately, his replacement, Captain Pfeffer, also an ex-wartime officer, proved no more flexible than Röhm in his view of the SA's role, and much less capable of keeping its brawling, beer-drinking membership under control.

Despite its reputation the SA was a result—not the author—of street-brawling politics. The street-fighting style was an invention of the left-wing parties, most of which were older than the Nazi party. Much of the middle and lower middle classes were sick of their violence. Nazi popularity soared when the SA was turned loose to counterattack its left-wing rivals. During 1926 a government ban on the movement was lifted with a resulting dramatic increase in membership. But there were grave risks, Hitler realized, in allowing the organization to become too strong too quickly.

Should the SA get out of hand, the government might decide to step in and suppress the entire Nazi movement. On the other hand, if membership swelled to such numbers that it matched the size of the Reichswehr, there was a good chance the generals would insist on its being disbanded. Finally, if Hitler leaned too heavily on his brownshirted SA legions, they might very well turn on him. It was a dilemma he could not resolve satisfactorily until he came to power. Meanwhile he needed his SA supporters. They provided constant visible evidence of his party's disciplined thrust toward political power. Yet he despaired at some of the SA's excesses. Brawls at their meetings and pitched street battles with their own ex-service leagues were a constant source of worry. At any moment the government in Berlin might decide they had had enough and bring in the army to demonstrate that they were still in control.

In Offleben Kurt became known as an ardent Nazi and SA brawler. One evening on his way home alone he was ambushed by six youthful Social Democrats armed with fence laths. He knew he didn't stand a chance and that in all probability they would kill him. Quickly he waded into battle, arms swinging. The first club hit his shoulder a glancing blow. Immediately, he dropped to the ground and played possum. In the darkness none of his attackers could see where the blows had landed but realized their victim lay motionless. They stopped swinging.

"My God, we've killed him!"

Hurling their weapons aside, they raced from the scene. When he was

---

*Small paramilitary fighting group.

certain they had gone, Kurt got to his feet and trotted home. Never again did he go out at night alone.

His political activities also cost him his job with the post office. The senior postmaster wanted no part of a brownshirted Nazi revolutionary in spite of Kurt's insistence that one day the National Socialists would be running the country.

"When that day happens, Herr Meyer, come and see me and I'll give you back your route."

For several weeks he searched the surrounding district for a white-collar job where his shopkeeping abilities could be put to use, but there was nothing available anywhere. In the end, he settled for a labourer's job in the local briquette factory—hard, dirty, dusty work bringing coarse coal from the nearby mines to the factory where it was processed into moulded briquettes and shipped off to regional wholesalers. His daily assignment consisted of heaving baskets of finished briquettes up from the moulding presses and placing them on a conveyor that transported them outdoors to be stacked for shipment. Strong as he was, it required all his stamina to last through the first week of ten-hour days until his mailman's muscles readjusted.

He pitied his older married co-workers with large families who were forced through circumstances to earn their living in such a fashion. He at least was single and had prospects for an easier life once the Reichswehr accepted his application for enlistment.

The longer he worked at the factory, the greater his sense of outrage at the owners' injustices against the workers. There were no safety regulations to protect the men and no first-aid equipment in case of accidents. Failure to appear on time for a shift resulted in dismissal. No excuses. There were lots of men waiting to fill the vacancies.

These were exactly the sort of inequities in the labour force that the Nazis intended changing when they came to power, Kurt explained to his fellow workers with all the idealism of a 17-year-old pumped full of political ideology. "Workers are human beings. Not animals. We have the right to be treated with respect. Without us the owners have nothing!"

"And without the owners we'd have no jobs!" came the shouted replies above the roar of machinery.

Most of the workers were older than Kurt, war veterans who were tired of fighting, disillusioned by government promises and political rhetoric. A teenage firebrand spouting clichés didn't interest them. Still, they admired his spirit.

Each Wednesday the Managing Director arrived from Magdeburg in his chauffeured Mercedes to inspect the factory's accounts. The factory's manager met the car and unctuously escorted the Director into the office. After an hour they emerged and the Director drove away.

"If you're so keen on change, Meyer, why don't you just nip over and tell

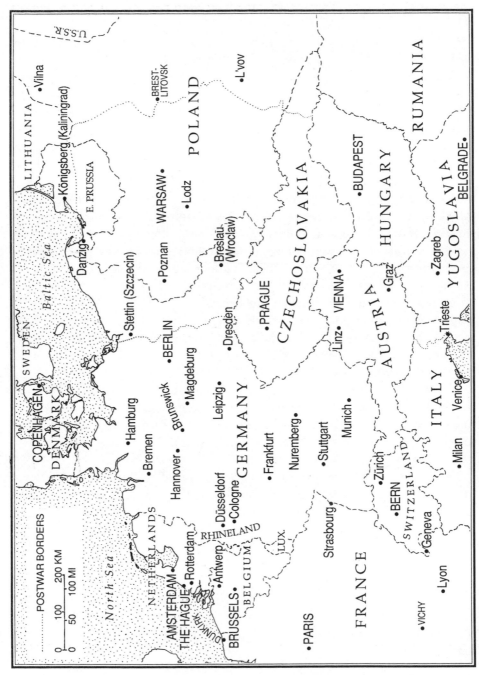

Germany and neighbouring countries in the prewar period.

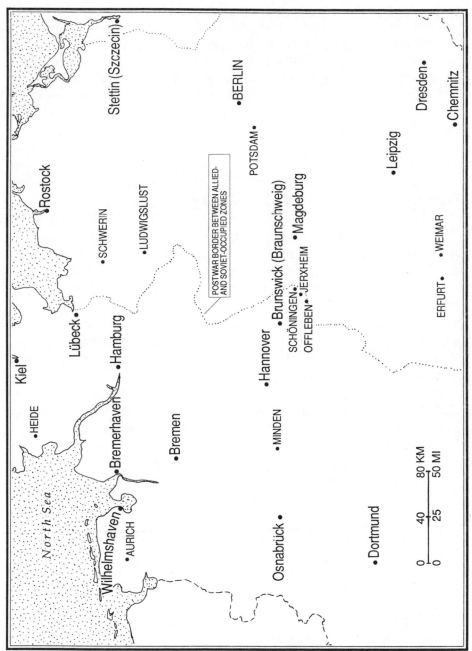

North-central Germany, where Kurt Meyer was raised.

the Manager what's wrong with this dump?" one of the older veterans suggested during a Wednesday's lunch break. At that moment there were about 30 filthy coal-faced workers in the yard. On impulse Kurt jumped up and loudly demanded their attention. Surprised, the men fell silent.

In a high-pitched voice he explained their options: "It is suggested that I tell Herr Hausser what needs to be done to improve working conditions. I will do this gladly but I need your support. All those against my speaking to Herr Hausser raise their hands!"

This psychological trick he had learned from the Nazis. Individuals in any group generally are incapable of action through fear of being singled out and ridiculed. Compliance for or against a proposal always had to be presented in such a way that lack of response signified acceptance.

No one raised his hand. He waited. Silence. "I accept your decision."

Squaring his shoulders, he marched across the yard and into the administration office. He decided to begin by asking for a single item: a fully equipped first-aid station. It was something that affected everyone yet pointed to no one individual as the complainant, other than himself. But that didn't count, as he explained firmly to the manager: "The men have elected me as their spokesman."

"I could dismiss you for insubordination, Herr Meyer."

"True. But then you would have to deal with someone else who might not be as nice as I am, Herr Hausser."

His training with the Nazis had taught him to hold his ground against superior forces. Bluffing makes believers. It was Hausser who cracked. He agreed to provide the necessary first-aid equipment and a washroom in the administration office.

"You're not a Communist, are you, Meyer?"

"Certainly not."

Hausser seemed relieved. "Good. I don't like Communists."

"Neither do I, Herr Hausser."

This single triumph brought him respect and recognition from the other workers as a young man who could get things done, the one to turn to for help. He had become the union leader of a group of workers who had no union. Meetings were arranged each weekend for discussions about other changes at the factory.

He found these gatherings exhilarating. He became their acknowledged leader, the one who made the final decisions. As a young lad playing soldier, defending a hill fort against other boys armed with wooden swords, he had always been the leader of his group. Everyone recognized he had that certain undefinable "something" that caused others to follow and obey. It puzzled him because he considered himself to be no better or worse than any other boy his own age. But at the Offleben briquette factory it dawned on him that he was a born leader. And the Nazi party had shown him how to use this power to his advantage. He was not an orator, his voice wasn't right. Nor would he ever make a good dramatic actor. Yet when he gave one of his impassioned speeches to the workers, his words came with such conviction and sincerity that his listeners agreed to whatever he proposed.

Within a few months the factory had become tightly unionized in everything but name, and Kurt its revered spokesman—a teenage demagogue. One by one Hausser agreed to the requests submitted from the men. However, being leader produced a lot of additional work and responsibility, but no extra wages for Kurt. He was also vulnerable. On several occasions Hausser had threatened to fire him and at the last minute cancelled the order. Kurt was sure that one day he would carry it through.

If only the Reichswehr would accept him—then he would be able to lead real soldiers. But he never heard from the army, and it seemed membership in the brawling brownshirts would lead him nowhere until the Nazis came to power. How long would that take? He felt trapped. A full year had passed since he had left Hagler, and nothing had been accomplished toward his goal. In April 1929 he decided to apply for the police force. It wasn't the army but it was better than the factory. With only eight years of formal schooling plus an apprenticeship, however, the highest rank he could attain would be sergeant; officers required a high school diploma.

Recruits were admitted to the Police School at Schwerin once a year in September after nationwide written and physical examinations. The entrance exams covered High German spelling, history, general knowledge and mathematics. They weren't difficult and he felt he'd done well. But a few days before the date set for his physical he started worrying about his foot. Would they detect his awkward gait?

"Nanni, watch me walk! Tell me if it looks normal to you. They mustn't know."

Melanie examined him with a critical eye as he strolled self-consciously back and forth across the room. He announced that he could feel a twinge when he turned on the ball of his foot, but she saw no visible impediment to his movement. For Melanie, crippled by polio, her brother's ailment was entirely in his mind.

By mid-August he received written notification that he had been accepted. His orders were to report to Schwerin on 1 September. He had beaten out all other local candidates in the exams. A train ticket and travelling expenses were attached. Elated, he took Melanie and Alma out to a restaurant for dinner. The following day he quit his job at the factory.

While 27-year-old Captain Harry Foster honeymooned in Nova Scotia, 18-year-old Police Cadet Kurt Meyer began his training at Schwerin, Mecklenburg, 30 kilometres from the Baltic Sea.

2

It was no honeymoon. *Polizeianwärter** were given a hard time. The curriculum covered everything from field-stripping weapons blindfolded to manning personnel carriers for riot control in narrow city streets. During basic training, cadets were kept so busy there wasn't time to think about politics, family or even romance. For each cadet who failed the course there were hundreds of applicants waiting to take his place.

Kurt teamed up with Fritz Richter—an attraction of opposites. Richter too was a member of the Nazi party and a storm trooper, but he lacked Kurt's flair for the grand gesture. Fritz admired and envied his new friend's impetuosity and enthusiasm for life, yet shrank from any thought of imitating his dash and style. On the other hand, Kurt enjoyed Richter's quiet humour and caustic pessimism. As their friendship developed, Fritz became a restraining influence on Kurt's periodic excesses that would in all probability have resulted in his being thrown out of the course.

Cadets were given a short holiday over Christmas. Kurt came home on the train dressed in his new uniform and anxious to impress his mother and sister. *Landespolizei*† members wore the dark green military uniform jackets of the Hunter's Guard from the time of Emperor Wilhelm. With accompanying blue breeches, braid, white gloves and sword, the effect was spectacular.

Bursting with pride, Kurt paused before alighting from his carriage at the Offleben station. Alma and Melanie stood waiting with beaming faces. Gravely he stepped onto the platform, tripped over his sword and fell flat on his face. Everyone within sight broke into laughter. Red-faced and covered with soot, he got to his feet, said "Shit!" and handed the impediments over to his mother to carry home for him.

"No longer a boy but still not quite a man," Alma observed.

"Nor a policeman," Kurt agreed.

The midpoint in the training came during March when half-term exams designed to weed out the deadwood were administered to everyone. Kurt breezed through. Richter failed by two miserable points, but his instructor took pity on him and let him stay if he promised to do well on his finals.

Their training ended in August. A formal graduation ceremony turned them into full-status civil servants and police officers with the rank of Unterwachtmeister.‡ The most promising from each class were kept at the school as instructors for the next year's recruit intake. Both Meyer and Richter were chosen. Their experience with SA, performing its drills and marches, had paid dividends. As new instructors they were appointed platoon leaders

---

*Police force cadets.   †Provincial police.
‡Lower sergeant—under-sergeant (corporal).

and placed on standby duty with the Police Training Squad to assist with crowd control when required.

Street fights between political factions were still commonplace. The Training Squad maintained itself at battalion strength, with its companies divided into *Korporalschaften* (platoons). If word came in that the *Reichsbanner** or SA was planning a march in a town or city, it was a safe bet that the Communists would be planning one from the opposite direction. When they collided, knifings and shootings resulted. A red alert would go out to the Training Squadron. All leaves cancelled. Combat dress and side arms. The nervous waited inside the barracks until called to action. With luck they could get away with setting up a few roadblocks and detour traffic to separate the marching factions. At worst they waded into the mob with truncheons swinging, trying to separate the warring opponents. It was dangerous work.

The *Rotfront* (Red Front) had the biggest and strongest men in their marches—quiet, grim-faced toughs who stepped out smartly with their arms locked, forming a solid phalanx of muscle and determination. At one march Meyer and Richter waited tensely as the *Rotfront* marchers approached. Tramp, tramp, tramp. The demonstrators rounded the corner marching in perfect step, arms linked, a few huge-bosomed women among them. The marchers wore shirts to show they weren't carrying concealed weapons. At the edge of the barriers they halted and allowed the police to search them. By police order, the women were exempt from physical contact. After the frisking, the police stood aside and the phalanx marched on. A block away they collided with the uniformed SA. Gunfire erupted. Bodies littered the street. The SA ran for their lives. Where had the weapons come from? As police raced to their personnel carriers and gave chase, Meyer collared one of the women while the men were being searched. Miraculously her bosom had changed in size and dimension.

"Madame, you appear to have shrunk."

As had the other women in the march. Each had been carrying a brace of pistols in her brassiere that they handed over to their men after the police search.

New police orders stated that henceforth females would be searched for weapons.

Meanwhile Hitler's star was on the ascent. While the world wallowed in economic chaos, the Nazis exploited the disillusioned masses and discontented middle class who saw their standard of living threatened by what they perceived as a weak and ineffectual government. Foreign loans that had

---

*Meaning "Empire's Flag," a left-wing group of mostly Social Democrats, composed of front-line soldiers from World War I.

restarted the country's economic recovery after the period of hyperinflation were now being withdrawn. Suddenly, a tide of unemployment threatened to overwhelm every resource that might be mobilized to relieve the situation.

In the Reichstag elections of September 1930, the Nazis won 107 seats. Hitler was now a power to be reckoned with. The fateful polarization of party politics had begun. Two extreme radical wings gained power at the expense of the moderate central parties. Formation of a majority government became impossible.

The chancellor, Heinrich Brüning, leader of the moderate Catholic Centre party and youngest chancellor ever to hold office, was not totally opposed to the Nazis. But his foreign policy plans prevented the inclusion of any Nazis in his cabinet. He was only able to command a Reichstag majority through an uneasy alliance with the Socialists.

With his new legitimacy confirmed by the electorate, Hitler found that the SA under Captain Pfeffer's direction was becoming an embarrassment. He sent word to Bolivia for Röhm to come home and take charge of matters again. Pfeffer stepped down and Röhm quickly brought things under control, dealing severely with anyone who stood in his way. Yet, as before, Röhm's ambition to share in political power worried Hitler. It also worried the Reichswehr's generals, who could see a day coming when SA membership would outnumber, and finally be in a position to outmanoeuvre, the country's legitimate armed forces.

It was difficult for Hitler to decide which was the lesser of the two evils: an incompetent Pfeffer·he could control but with an unruly SA he couldn't; or an ambitious Röhm he could never control but who would command a properly disciplined SA.

Frequently, police cadets were ordered to attend party rallies for both the left and right. Their job was to maintain law and order, since invariably the meetings would be broken up by political opponents. Before every rally they received the usual briefing by the police captain in charge. "If you are forced to draw your pistol, then for heaven's sake fire it! Don't fiddle around with it. Same goes for your club. If you draw it, use it. One blow alongside your fellow's hot head ought to cool him down."

Many of the platform speakers at these rallies were superb orators. Meyer and Richter were impressed by Fritz Montag, who owned a small shop in Dömitz but often came to Schwerin to speak. Still a young man, he had served in the front lines during the war and commanded great respect from all his listeners. Meyer and Richter visited him frequently at his home to discuss politics and listen to his storehouse of military experiences. His upright character and courteous consideration made a lasting impression on them both.

Kurt's first attendance at a party meeting as a civilian was on *Deutscher*

*Tag** at Gardebusch where the SA was holding a rally. Not wanting to look like civilians, he and Richter wore half their police uniforms topped by a civilian jacket. The boots and breeches allowed them to blend with the snappy, uniformed SA men while still officially dressed in mufti. The massed marching of the SA with its bands and banners was like nothing they had seen before. Company after company of men in crisply starched uniforms paraded under the swastika flags in precise unbroken lines, moving as a single irrepressible force. They found themselves caught up in a fever of nationalism by the sounds of marching bands, drum rolls and shouted orders. This was where Germany's destiny lay. The 30-man SA marches in Offleben and Burg (Richter's home town) paled by comparison.

Commands and troop drills were the same they used for training their police platoons, but the "brownshirts" were marching to a grander, more professional standard. Somehow they had to get involved, become part of its operational activities. They approached the local SA commander for permission to join the drills during their off-duty hours.

"You're both police officers?" He seemed sceptical. "Are you party members?"

They produced their cards and proof of SA membership. Kurt's NSDAP number had been issued back in 1925.† The Commander was impressed.

"Our weekends are generally free," Kurt explained.

"Excellent! We can always use a couple of good instructors. Report for duty next Saturday at 0800 hours."

To be drilling groups of a hundred or more tough SA men for five hours each weekend came as close to heaven as any 19-year-old Unterwachtmeister could imagine. More important, the experience they gained gave them that extra confidence needed to finish training their cadet platoons and obtain top marks along with the recognition of being fully qualified instructors.

During one of Kurt's weekends with the SA, a local senior party official asked him if he had heard the news. "Jupp Goebbels is going to be married here in Schwerin. Adolf Hitler is to be best man. What an honour for Mecklenburg!"

And what luck! Two of the top Nazi leaders and their entourage in the district. An opportunity to meet the men for whom he had been working for so long. He passed the news on to Richter and three other police officers who were also part-time SA members. All applied immediately for three days special leave.

Naturally, Hitler and Goebbels would have their own bodyguards, but Kurt and his friends knew all the local troublemakers and were sure their own presence as an added protection for the wedding party would be welcome.

---

*Literally, "German Day."

†In 1933 he was awarded the "Old Guard" badge with 1925 engraved on it in recognition of his political loyalty.

After discussing the matter among themselves, they decided the best approach would be to attend the Schwerin church as private citizens interested only in meeting their Führer and thereafter let things develop according to the reception they got.

Not only were they all welcomed at the wedding, but they were invited to attend the gala dinner reception that evening. There they were introduced as "officers" to the guests—Hitler, Goebbels, General von Epp, Ernst "Putzi" Hanfstaengl and Sepp Dietrich, the latter the commander of the Führer's bodyguard. After the dinner, in a flash of inspiration and with an eye to his own future, Corporal Meyer audaciously approached Corporal Hitler and asked if he would consider posing for a picture with his five loyal "officers" from Schwerin. The others held their breath. To everyone's astonishment Hitler agreed.

Kurt explained later to Richter: "One day he will lead Germany. I want to be certain that he remembers me."

3

Kurt became known as a ladies' man in Schwerin. The girls loved his flashing eyes, infectious laughter and enthusiasm for life. Richter disapproved. Liaisons with the opposite sex were supposed to be conducted along serious lines and not taken lightly. "You must give more importance to your love affairs."

"I'm trying, Fritz. Believe me, I'm trying. But there are so many to choose from it's hard to make up my mind."

Unlike the dour Richter, Kurt exuded an animal magnetism. He was the centre of attention. Among men this magnetism translated into a grudging acknowledgment that he was a leader; among women it translated into sex appeal. It was this that first attracted Kate Bohlmann.

The Bohlmanns of Schrampe were a family of some substance. They operated a large farm and village inn near the shores of beautiful Lake Arendt, halfway between Schwerin and Offleben. There were three children in the family: Fritz, the eldest, who managed the estate; Paul, who had entered the army in the fall of 1931 and was taking his basic Reichswehr training at Celle; and Kate, 19, tall, blond and gorgeous.

Kurt had been invited to visit his sister and her fiancé in nearby Arendsee over the Christmas holidays. He was glad to assume the duty of chaperone to keep local tongues from wagging. Richter, on his way home to Burg, came along to spend a few days and keep him company.

On their second day Kurt and Fritz went on a walking tour of the countryside, stopping in at the Bohlmanns' inn for lunch and a beer. Both were in uniform and looking very smart. It was an era when any uniform commanded respect. Paul Bohlmann, home on leave and also in uniform,

Janie and Harry Foster, 1902.

Alma and Kurt Meyer in Jerxheim, 1911.

Maj.-Gen. "Laffy" Foster, 1917. (Public Archives Canada/PA 7174)

Otto Meyer at the front in 1916.

Harry Foster at age 15 at Berkhamsted,
England.

Fifteen-year-old apprentice Kurt Meyer.

Royal Military College (RMC) student
Foster in 1923.

Police cadet Meyer in 1928.

RMC graduates of 1925: Gil Foster, Chris Vokes, Guy Simonds.

Harry Foster, Winnipeg, 1928.

Kurt on graduation from the ss Training
School in Berlin, 1935.

Margaret Muir, 1927.
The wedding coach-and-six awaits
Captain and Mrs. Harry Foster in
Winnipeg, 7 September 1929.

L.S.H "A Coy" Sarcee Camp Aug 1930
W.J. Ring Cirnut Photo "A Coy"

Harry Foster (mounted on the second horse, centre) with Lord Strathcona's Horse "A" Company. Sarcee Camp, Calgary, August 1930. (Lord Strathcona's Horse Regiment Archives)

Harry (third from left) and other members of the regiment's polo team, 1932. (Glenbow Archives/PA-2489-8)

Kurt Meyer, in black uniform at extreme right of the second column, takes part in the Ceremonial March of the SS and SA in Berlin, 1933.

Kurt (right) shortly after his appointment to Hitler's bodyguard in 1934. Leibstandarte Commander Sepp Dietrich is second from left.

Obersturmführer Meyer with two Leibstandarte sergeants in 1935.

In black ss uniform, Kurt (partially hidden) accompanies Hitler at a presentation in Nuremberg in 1934.

Hitler in his private railway car with members of the Leibstandarte behind.

Hitler, with Sepp Dietrich (left), inspects the Leibstandarte at the ss Lichterfelde Barracks in Berlin, December 1935. (Bundesarchiv/109-1-11)

Kurt, Ursula and Inge at the Leibstandarte's Berlin
housing estate, 1936.

(From left) Margo, Harry, David and Tony picnic on the
South Downs in the summer of 1939.

saw them enter and introduced himself. They promptly asked him to join them and for the rest of the afternoon traded stories about their careers and experiences.

Later, when his sister came on duty to help with the evening's customers, Paul told her about the two police officers from Schwerin. Kate was intrigued.

She saw Kurt the next afternoon sauntering along the road with her brother and Fritz Richter. The sword, white gloves and braidings on his green jacket made an instant hit with the impressionable girl. His open look, fascinating eyes and firm handshake fairly took her breath away.

For Kurt it was love at first sight, but an impossible match. He decided she was much too good for him. She had lived an orderly life, protected from the rough and tumble world in which he had grown up. Her childhood had been happy, without fear or want. She had acted in school plays, enjoyed dancing, cooking, needlework and helping with the family farm and inn. She was everything a man could possibly want in a wife.

He brought Melanie to meet her and asked, "Well, Nanni, what do you think?"

"I think she's wonderful. Just your type of woman. Marry her."

Easier said than done. He had nothing. No money and not much of a position. "Do you really think I should see her again?"

He began courting Kate seriously. It was an agonizingly slow courtship, destined to go on for three years. Finally, when Melanie married and was living in Arendsee, he had the perfect excuse to visit Kate instead of going to Offleben to see his mother. Alma understood.

Both Meyer and Richter were qualified Jujitsu fighters.* Their instructor at the Police School, Andreas Hecht, had been Germany's national champion in 1926, and Kurt fought in the middleweight class for the Police Force Championships during 1932. Competition was among police units from Rostock, Güstrow, Wismar and Schwerin. Kurt made it to the finals in his division. His opponent, a man named Spensson, was a superb athlete for whom Kurt was no match.

He decided to bluff his way through to a draw. The rules called for every stranglehold to be released after 20 seconds. Properly applied, a neck hold blocked blood to the brain, causing unconsciousness within seconds. At the start Kurt did well, managing to wriggle out from every dangerous situation. But in the last minute Spensson caught him in a fatal stranglehold. Kurt froze, swelling his neck muscles to keep the blood flowing into his brain. The 20 seconds passed. Spensson released him. Kurt staggered off to the dressing rooms undefeated. Spensson, the chagrined champion, was forced

---

*A form of unarmed combat developed by the Japanese that forces an opponent to use his weight against himself.

to share first prize with the mediocre but determined Meyer.

"You don't deserve this, Meyer," Spensson hissed when they came forward to collect their trophy. "I won!"

Kurt smiled. "Oh no you didn't. You lost. I won because you underestimated your opponent."

Spensson swore to get even. In the weeks that followed, he took every opportunity to humiliate and taunt Kurt in front of the other men. But Kurt was astute enough to realize that if he accepted the challenge for another bout, Spensson would in all probability try to kill him. How could he put him in his place without actually meeting him in unarmed combat?

An idea came to him. He would climb out onto the roof of the administration building and dump a pail of cold water on Spensson as he came up the walkway to class. The man would become a laughingstock. It was brilliant. If his antagonist lost his temper and started a fight, everyone would sympathize with Kurt and regard Spensson as a bad sport. On the other hand, if Spensson retaliated by dumping a bucket of water on him, they'd be even and that should end the man's bitterness.

That at least was his theory as he made his way across the roof of the three-storey building, lugging a pail of water. But the tiles were slippery. He lost his footing, dropped the pail and slithered down the roof and over the edge. At the last moment he made a grab for the eavestroughing. It held. The pail crashed onto the concrete below.

At ground level everyone stopped to stare in fascination at the swinging figure hanging precariously from the gutter. Each time he attempted to hoist his legs back onto the roof the eavestroughing pulled away from its anchor bolts. Finally, with a loud snap it broke. He made a complete somersault on his way down, landed on his feet, then fell forward unconscious.

Colonel Fuchs, the commandant, pushed his way through the throng of spectators to the crumpled figure lying on the cement. He felt Meyer's pulse. It was there but ever so faintly. Fuchs shook his head. "Take him away. There is nothing anyone can do now."

A stretcher party carried him to the military hospital where after one look at his injuries the doctor ordered him placed in an empty bathroom. "Let him die in peace."

Two hours later he regained consciousness and remembered what had happened. He felt no pain. He called for the doctors and demanded to know what they intended to do about his injuries. Still in severe shock but well aware of his condition and what would happen when the effects of shock wore off, he ordered the physicians to begin work on him immediately. "Because if you don't help me soon, I shall report you to the Nazis and send for Hildebrandt."

The doctors went to work at once. He had 22 fractures. When they had finished operating on his shattered bones, he was encased in plaster from his chest to his toes. And then the pain began. For a few days it was touch and go whether he would survive. Alma and Melanie were notified. Richter contacted Kate: "I write to you because Kurt had an accident. He fell off a roof and is in hospital. I'd like to surprise him with a visit from his Kate. Can you come?"

She arrived in Schwerin the next day. Alma and Melanie were already at his bedside. He didn't look at all well.

"Tell me truthfully, doctor. Is he going to die?" Alma asked.

"I doubt it, Frau Meyer. He's much too stubborn for that sort of nonsense."

Later, Josef Goebbels and *Gauleiter* Hildebrandt* visited him. After that he was treated like royalty by the hospital's staff. Spring turned to summer. The weeks slipped by. He read, he slept, he received visitors and fretted over his slow recovery. One day he had a visit from a beautiful countess he had met at one of the party's receptions. She had just heard about his accident and had come to see if there was anything he needed. She was a lovely creature, three years older than Kurt and attracted to him for reasons known only to herself. Wealthy, well educated and elegantly dressed, she moved in a rarefied social circle of friends and knew everyone of any consequence. Yet during her hospital visits she treated Kurt as her social equal. He announced to his mother that he had finally found the woman of his dreams.

Their affair was not illogical, he explained. Although he might be only a lowly police officer, he was also an old party member and highly regarded within its hierarchy as a young man to watch. He received invitations to every important meeting, reception, social event and public rally in the district. Once the Nazis achieved power, it was not inconceivable that he would be appointed to a position of considerable importance.

But Alma was outraged at the thought of her son involving himself with an older woman from the upper classes. It seemed a betrayal of her family's working-class background. "Are you out of your mind, you megalomaniac? What do you want with a countess? I absolutely forbid it!" Besides, she had already decided Kate to be the proper choice for her son.

Kurt said nothing.

On 23 August, Kate's birthday, he crawled painfully out of bed and telephoned his congratulations. She invited him to come to the farm when he was discharged and stay at Schrampe until he fully recovered. It seemed

---

*The Nazis divided Germany into 42 territorial units known as *Gaue*. In each, a *Gauleiter* (premier) was responsible for all political activities. Hildebrandt was one of the first freely elected district Nazi premiers and a friend of Meyer's from the early days of the party's activities.

the surest way of keeping him out of the countess's clutches. Chivalrously he accepted her offer.

Gradually the fractures healed, but there were problems with his left leg. It remained numb. Hours of ultraviolet heat treatments produced no improvement. His doctors considered amputation, fearing that gangrene would invade the lifeless limb.

"Listen, Fritz, if they decide to amputate, you must bring me a pistol," he told Richter during one visit. "I don't want to live with one leg." Richter refused.

A week before the doctors were to make their decision, Kurt pulled himself off the orthopedic bed and for several hours every night forced his leg to operate. By the time one of the nurses caught him at it, the leg had begun to respond. It was now slightly shorter than the other and he required a specially raised orthopedic shoe to compensate for the difference, but he could walk. That was the main thing. His left leg and hip were to trouble him to the end of his days.

"Well, little sister," he told Melanie ruefully after his release from hospital, "now I know what a hard time you have getting around."

With his return to active police duty now a foregone conclusion, the other officers nicknamed him "Panzermeyer"* in admiration of his incredible resilience. The name stuck. Even Spensson had been awed by his feat of survival.

He took recuperative leave with the Bohlmanns that fall. Short walks with a cane at first, then longer journeys around the shore of Lake Arendt. His strength returned. On his 22nd birthday he finally asked Kate to marry him.

The countess, never really a contender for his devotion, faded into little more than a pleasurable memory.

Chancellor Brüning meanwhile was being driven to rely more and more on forces outside the parliamentary system for the Republic's survival. These forces were the Reichswehr and the president, 84-year-old hero of Tannenberg Marshal Paul von Hindenburg.

Under section 48 of the Weimar Constitution, Hindenburg had authorization in cases of emergency to suspend constitutional guarantees temporarily. This right of legislation by presidential decree proved to be of immense political importance during the breakdown of normal government. Even the Weimar's die-hard supporters recognized the necessity for government stability. Over the months of political crisis the President's power was increased to a point where he had rights to appoint or dismiss a cabinet on his own authority, since that authority was recognized as being higher than any party's. As president he represented the nation as a whole, not

*Meaning tough-skinned—hard, shield.

simply its individual political interests. This aberrant constitutional provision carried in it the implicit right to dictatorial power for whoever decided to take advantage of the situation.

In executing these dictatorial powers Hindenburg was able to rely on Reichswehr support. The army was directly under his command and, like the President, claimed to represent the whole nation rather than a faction. Under Hindenburg's authority the Reichswehr had the power to intervene in the internal affairs of any district or region within the Republic. Almost imperceptibly, political power was transferred from a democratically elected parliamentary majority to a dictatorial form of government based on the benevolence of its aging president.

Despite the problems piling up against him, Brüning hoped to carry through his constitutional reforms and arrange to release the economic and military chains that still bound the nation under the Treaty of Versailles. Brüning might have succeeded had it not been for General von Schleicher and his underhanded intrigues. Schleicher, a brilliant staff officer and messmate of Hindenburg's son, rose to pre-eminence under Minister of War Groener.

Schleicher became disenchanted with Brüning after the Chancellor's refusal to include any representatives from the Nazi party in his cabinet. He believed the Reichswehr too weak to deal successfully with the combined forces of communism and national socialism and favoured cooperation with one against the other. In his opinion the only logical ally for the Reichswehr was the Nazis, whom the Ministry of War had always regarded as a kind of unruly group of comrades-in-arms.

Without informing the Chancellor, he began secret negotiations with Röhm to find some common ground for uniting the SA and Reichswehr for Germany's rearmament. Nazi representation in a new cabinet became a part of the discussions. In the summer of 1932 Schleicher naively believed that under a firm guiding hand the Nazis could provide a constructive influence in a democratic government. Groener, suffering from diabetes and forced to devote much of his time to the Ministry of Home Affairs, left the Ministry of War to Schleicher and his Machiavellian intrigues against the hard-pressed Chancellor. Patiently, Hitler waited for his moment.

Early in 1932 Brüning tried to have Marshal von Hindenburg's seven-year presidential term extended by a two-thirds majority of the Reichstag. Hitler was approached for his cooperation, which he gave, only to withdraw it a few days later. In the new electoral campaign that resulted, an angry polarization developed between the parties when Hitler became Hindenburg's chief rival for the presidency.

One day after the old marshal's re-election, Brüning moved to have the SA disbanded, following pressure from Groener and various ministers of Home Affairs throughout the German states. But the hapless Groener broke before the withering opposition mounted in the Reichstag by the Nazis. Coldly, he was informed by the Army Chief of Staff and the devious Schleicher that he could no longer count on the Reichswehr's confidence. Brüning and his government fell, done in by the Nazis, by Schleicher's intrigues and by the powerful Junkers landowners in the east whom Brüning had antagonized with plans for breaking up insolvent estates.

His departure came at the very moment limited German rearmament had been agreed upon in principle by the Allied powers. On the morning Brüning was to pay his last formal visit to Hindenburg and submit his resignation, word arrived from France—the last holdout to German rearmament—that the government had agreed to his proposals. A final chance for the legal re-establishment of the nation's military power vanished. Not that it would have made one tittle of difference as things worked out.

With Brüning gone, the Reichswehr proceeded with its rearmament in defiance of its Versailles treaty agreements. The stage was now set for the final scene of a Nazi political takeover. Hitler had only to make his move.

4

Before an account of the methods and series of events by which Hitler achieved power, it is worth examining the origins of the ss—*Schutzstaffel**—and its enigmatic commander, Heinrich Himmler, for Himmler was to be a major prop to Hitler's power.

During the early years Hitler had relied for personal protection on four or five professional thugs who took turns driving his car about the country when he attended political rallies. These toughs had recruited a group of similar muscular loyalists to assist in the Munich *Putsch* of 1923. Known as *Stosstruppe* Hitler,† their role had been to destroy the printing presses belonging to the city's Social Democrat newspaper. With Hitler's arrest and imprisonment they melted away.

After his release from jail Hitler reorganized the *Stosstruppe* and called it the *Schutzstaffel*. Compact branches of no more than 20 or 30 men were set up in various major cities for his use during speaking engagements. Their numbers were kept purposely small. By 1929 there were only 280 ss men in the party. In April of that same year Hitler appointed Himmler, still a minor party official, to command the group. Of all the monsters produced from Nazi party ranks Himmler stood without peer.

The sickly, myopic son of a Bavarian schoolmaster, Himmler had spent a short time as an officer cadet during the closing days of the war. After

---

*Protection Squads.
†Shock Troop Hitler.

demobilization he returned to school and by 1922 became a qualified farmer. Unable to find employment and without any special talent to compensate for his uninspiring physical appearance, he joined the politics of the right along with tens of thousands of similarly disillusioned young men of the time. He served in a Bavarian *Freikorps* during the revolutionary period and took part in the Munich *Putsch* as a member of the *Reichskriegsflagge** group.

Soon after Hitler's release from prison, Himmler joined the Nazi party and became secretary to the Strassers, Hitler's rivals for the party's leadership. Later, he worked as Goebbels's assistant in the propaganda service. He married a fellow vegetarian and set up a chicken farm, but both his farm and marriage failed miserably. He joined the SS in 1925 as number 168 and by 1929 had been promoted to second-in-command. When Heiden, one of Hitler's original bodyguards, was relieved of command, Himmler assumed the leadership.

Grateful to the point of servility for having been given the chance to prove his value, he was determined to make Hitler's SS a major force in the party's development. From the beginning, his strange fantasies and total acceptance of the crackpot racial theories advocated by Nazi philosophers Darré and Rosenberg[1] became the foundation of SS policy. While Hitler might not have been clear in his own mind exactly how the SS should develop and be used as an organ of the party, Himmler hadn't the slightest doubt. He wanted to create an elite group to compete with the SA.

He regarded his SS troops as Teutonic Knights, the vanguard of a new German Order. They were to be tall, blond, virile Nordics, sound of wind, limb, courage and loyalty. Although he insisted applicants be perfect physical specimens—even to a lack of fillings in their teeth—he never found enough young men to fulfil this fantasy.

He was particularly interested in attracting recruits from the aristocracy, advertising the SS as the social elite of the Nazi movement. Among his blue-blooded adherents, Himmler could count many a prince and lesser aristocrat. Later, at Wewelsburg Castle, he created an SS centre modelled after the Master's House of the Teutonic Knights, complete with a pagan order of chivalry for those members of higher rank. Ex-officers of the armed forces were also welcome.

One summer afternoon in 1931 a handsome young man arrived at Himmler's chicken farm to discuss career possibilities in the SS. The visitor, Reinhard Heydrich, was the personification of Himmler's Aryan fantasies. Captivated by Heydrich's cold-eyed personality, he offered him the job of setting up an inner-party intelligence service to be known as the *Sicherheitsdienst*, SD for short. The offer was made in the mistaken belief that Heydrich's previous post as a naval cypher officer was in some way involved

---

*Empire War Flag—a political Free Corps (*Freikorps*) of the right.

with counterespionage. The tight-lipped Heydrich agreed at once.

The majority of ss recruits accepted during the years prior to the Nazis' taking power seldom matched the physical standards imposed by ss regulations, which accounted for Kurt Meyer managing to join on 15 May 1931 as recruit number 17559. By January 1933 the ss had grown to over 50,000 members. At the time of his fall from the roof Kurt had been instructing both ss and sa recruits during his off-duty hours. The fact that he was five feet nine inches tall, had dark hair and wore an orthopedic shoe became irrelevant when compared to the need for qualified first-class drill instructors.

Hitler had little time for the philosophy of nazism or the racial mythology embraced by Himmler. Privately, he scorned such ravings. He lived for one thing only: power. With over 13 million voters behind him during the summer conflict of 1932, he was on the verge of achieving his political ambitions.

The new cabinet, after Brüning's fall, was completely authoritarian in composition, drawn mainly from the great industrialists and landowners. Franz von Papen became chancellor. Connected through marriage to one of the mighty industrial families of the Saar and a conservative monarchist to boot, he was much admired by Hindenburg. As an intriguer he was almost on a par with Schleicher, who now became minister of war.

Brüning's earlier ban on the sa was lifted to pacify the Nazis. However, seeing his plans for closer cooperation with the Nazis being thwarted, Schleicher met secretly with Hitler to work out an alternate arrangement. A subsequent meeting arranged between Hitler and Hindenburg misfired badly because of von Papen's counterintrigues. The Nazis went over to the official opposition, and the government was voted down at the opening of the newly elected Reichstag.

The next election produced an erosion of Nazi popular support for the first time, but no appreciable widening of the cabinet's parliamentary base. Von Papen proclaimed himself ready to carry on, placing his faith in Hindenburg's backing and the Reichswehr's bayonets. However, the army's leaders were opposed to supporting any cabinet against the clearly expressed will of the majority of the country's voters.

Hitler was then asked to become vice-chancellor. He failed to gain support. Finally, Schleicher took over the Chancellery with what was left of von Papen's cabinet. During the next two months he tried desperately to replace the parliamentary system with some other form of government that would guarantee a closer cooperation between the people and the Reichswehr— a coalition of trade unions, industrialists and the army.

This utopian concept collapsed in January 1933. Leipart, leader of the socialist trade unions, refused to endorse Schleicher's policies, and von Papen, still smarting from losing the chancellorship, met secretly with Hitler in Cologne where they made a pact to join forces against the Chancellor. In desperation Schleicher threatened to publish an investigative report about funds that had been given to the Junkers landholders during the time Schleicher had supported Brüning. These hereditary estate owners were the same group that had played a significant role in Brüning's downfall. Now they went after Schleicher.

Hindenburg finally had enough. On 28 January he dismissed Schleicher and two days later announced the new cabinet. Hitler became chancellor, von Papen his vice-chancellor. The days of the Third Reich had begun.

The Reichswehr had not been consulted on Hitler's appointment to the chancellorship, and last-minute attempts by General Hammerstein, head of Army Command, to influence the decision had been brushed aside by Hindenburg. What finally persuaded the army to give its approval to the new political master was the hope of his providing the military with the camouflage needed to mask German rearmament and the creation of a military dictatorship. Compared to the politically astute Nazi leadership, the Reichswehr's generals, like everyone else, were little better than babes in the wood for believing they would ever be in a position to use Hitler and the Nazi party to serve their own ends. Nor was the army the only group to suffer from the delusion of Nazi cooperation.

The Conservatives, the third group in the new government coalition with the army and Nazis, were composed of cynical political opportunists who believed that the time was at hand for the collapse of the Republic, along with the concept of representative government. With its demise and an alliance with the Nazis, they believed the threat of a revolution from the left would be eliminated while at the same time they would be provided with an unmolested opportunity to woo both the radical right and left over to the "National Conservative" cause.

The Nazis harboured no illusions about their ascribed role. A decade had been devoted to gaining sufficient government power through legal means in order to achieve their real revolutionary intentions. Nazi leaders stood head and shoulders above their political partners in organizational ingenuity and conspiratorial ability. Once admitted to a share of the supreme power, they intended to outfox and outmanoeuvre their secret enemies and political allies.

Within months the links binding the Nazis to the Nationalists and middle-of-the-road Conservatives were broken one by one, and with astonishing ease. A month after Hitler assumed the chancellorship, the Reichstag went up in flames. There was no proof that the Nazis did it, and a Communist culprit conveniently turned up to be accused of the crime. At the assembled cabinet meeting on 28 February, the morning after the fire, Hitler proposed "that a ruthless settlement with the KPD* was imperative. The psychologically

*The German Communist party.

correct moment for this settlement had come."

Hitler had his eye on the 5 March elections. A decree that banned the KPD ensured victory for the Nazis and their supporters on the right. Whether Hitler really believed in a Communist threat was irrelevant. His desire was to suppress Marxism, and the Reichstag fire provided the opportunity. The "Emergency Decree" and its exploitation by Goebbels brought a stampede of the frightened middle class into the Nazi camp. The decree effectively abolished fundamental rights to freedom and authorized the new government to take direct action against Communist organizations and other opponents. On the night/of 28 February Göring instructed his Berlin police to arrest all Communist deputies in the government and several thousand Communist officials.

On 23 March new emergency powers obtained by Hitler through false promises to the Catholic Centre party were given to the government for four years by the necessary two-thirds majority.[2] Supposedly directed against disgruntled elements of the Weimar Republic, they became the means by which all recognized political opposition to the Nazis was suppressed.

On 2 May the trade union buildings in Berlin were seized. The assets of the German Social Democratic party (SPD) were confiscated on 9 May. Later, on 22 June, it was banned. In the weeks that followed and into the autumn of 1933, Social Democrats, leaders of the Centre party, Royalists, Bavarian People's party, unpopular industrialists and government officials, wealthy middle-class and particularly Jewish lawyers, writers and academics were packed off to new concentration camps being set up around the country by the SA, SS and state police.

In Prussia alone during March and April over 25,000 people were taken into "protective custody." These did not include any of the summary and largely unreported arrests made by the SA and SS against their political foes in the larger cities. Their meeting places, homes and friends were already known, and the SA and SS lost no time in rounding them up, usually with violence and bloodshed.

Only the army still held the power to oust the Nazis. But the Reichswehr remained indifferent to this elimination of its civilian associates, still believing it had the power to step in at any time and stop the whole "experiment." The army stood contemptuous of the nation's willingness to tolerate the Nazis' reign of terror and maintained a haughty belief that nothing comparable to the Nazi excesses would ever be permitted within its own domain. Whenever a dispute arose with Hitler, it was necessary only to refer the matter to their joint superior, President von Hindenburg, and it would be decided in favour of the Reichswehr. Throughout the balance of the year an uneasy truce existed between Hitler and the generals.

Meanwhile, Himmler and his cold-eyed protégé, Heydrich, were organizing their own power base. Himmler's appointment to the Munich police presidency on 9 March and as Political Police commander for Bavaria three weeks later provided little scope for extending his power and influence. By comparison, Hitler's trusted friend and confidant, Hermann Göring, received the plum appointment of Prussian minister of the interior, and with it, command of the Berlin police. Göring had supplemented the city's constabulary with 10,000 of Himmler's SS men to ensure Nazi control of terror. An SS official, Daluege, had been given command of the group. Yet Daluege remained Göring's man.

Himmler and Heydrich decided to try for central power through the indirect approach. Their first step was to capture control of local political police authorities operating in the smaller states, such as the Schwerin-Mecklenburg force to which Kurt Meyer belonged. Their technique became one of intimidating city officials with a display of black-uniformed SS strength, designed to coerce an invitation to take over local police duties. The frightened burghers fell like nine pins.

Moving next to Berlin, Heydrich set up an SD office for his intelligence network right under Göring's nose on the pretext of having discovered an assassination plot against Göring that had been missed by his Berlin police. With this ploy Himmler then persuaded Hitler of the need to centralize control of all Political Police forces. Hitler agreed. Himmler was appointed head of the Berlin Secret Police. The power from this office, together with his expanding control over the smaller states and dossiers on every party member, friend and foe, would in time make him the second most powerful man in the Reich.

Next, Himmler organized a special body of jailers for the new concentration camp he had created in the stone huts on the grounds of an old gunpowder factory at Dachau, near Munich. Known as Totenkopf* guards, they were recruited from within the general SS body and commanded by Theodor Eicke. More concentration camps were being built at Oranienburg, Papenburg, Esterwegen, Kemma, Sachsenburg, Sonnenburg—all, he knew, would be needing SS guards.

Finally, he set up the first standing armed SS unit, known as the *Stabswache*.† Stationed originally in Munich, its 120 handpicked loyalists were brought to Berlin in March 1933 and comfortably billeted at the Alexander Barracks in Friedrichstrasse, a short distance from Hitler's official residence at the Reich Chancellery. Its commander, Joseph Dietrich—"Sepp" to his friends and comrades-in-arms—had been one of Hitler's rubber truncheon-equipped bodyguards from the party's head-bashing days. The SS *Stabswache*'s

---

*Meaning "Death's Head"—although used primarily for concentration camp duties, its members saw action in World War II as the Totenkopf Division led by Eicke.
†Staff Guard—later named SS Leibstandarte–Adolf Hitler.

duties were to guard Hitler and the Chancellery.

Sitting unobtrusively in his Berlin headquarters during the early summer of 1934, Himmler had managed in 16 months to create for himself an organization with its own prison system, an intelligence network spying over party, state and people, plus the nucleus of a private army in his Totenkopf and *ss Stabswache*.

Coincidentally, it had been assembled at the exact moment Hitler needed such an organization to neutralize Röhm and his SA.

5

Despite his ss and party activities Kurt's sole source of income remained his position as a civil service police officer.

Police School graduates were expected to sign a 25-year term of service contract. Although it meant financial security, it also meant bondage. Promotion dates could be anticipated, earnings could be determined to the pfennig for every year of service. It was a comfortable life, but boring. Everything became routine: instructing new cadets, red alerts at any time of the day or night, street patrols, clashes with demonstrators.

In the spring of 1933 he was promoted to police Wachtmeister—full sergeant. His injuries had healed and he was back playing sports and working full-duty shifts. Free time he divided between party interests and his beautiful Kate. He had managed to save enough to buy a secondhand motorcycle, a noisy machine with no muffler that could be heard for kilometres whenever he came visiting. The local farm lads were jealous. Kate belonged to them. She was much too lovely to be spirited away from under their noses by an outsider in police uniform.

"Yah! What's so great about your Kurt Meyer?" they teased. Kate smiled sweetly and said that she intended to marry him but still like them too. As a result, when Kurt arrived on his motorcycle, every rejected suitor within hearing distance descended on the inn to get even. They let the air out of his tires, teased the pair unmercifully when they were together, and generally made life unpleasant. So uncomfortable did this gauntlet become that he began shutting off the motor and pushing his bike for the last kilometre in and out of the village.

His silent arrivals and departures also helped prevent any confrontation with Kate's father. Fritz Bohlmann wasn't opposed to Kurt seeing his daughter, only suspicious of his motives. "One day he comes in a green uniform, the next day he arrives in a black one. He should make up his mind which one he prefers."

His friend from Dömitz, Fritz Montag, had been the one responsible for Kurt and the other three party loyalists at the Police School joining the expanding ss. Montag had allied himself with the Nazis and had been appointed local ss recruiting officer. To fill its ranks, he turned to the best men in the regional sa detachments and lured them into Himmler's new elite.

As Police School cadre and sa instructors, Kurt and his fellow officers were ideal candidates. Besides, Montag already knew them as friends and loyal supporters of the new German Order. They were flattered by his invitation to join the group. Their sa ties, although never severed, were altered to the point where most of their free time was spent drilling with the ss.

A staff car picked them up from barracks each evening and drove them to the drilling grounds where they put the ss recruits through their paces, after which they were chauffeured home. Montag encouraged Kurt and Richter to approach other friends and colleagues to join. Results of this sa poaching produced a very high calibre of recruits for the ss and a lot of animosity between the two organizations.

Not everyone who applied was accepted automatically. Nor did everyone who was accepted embrace Himmler's rabid racist philosophies. But as in any tightly structured organization, the piper called the tune and those who declined to dance to his melody were quickly asked to leave the party. The ss was no place for moralists.

Yet during one of Kurt's rare moments of introspection at Christmastime, 1933, he discovered to his surprise that in his four years at Schwerin with the police and the party the only exciting things that had happened were meeting Kate, falling off the roof and joining the ss. He had also received a seven-month duty suspension plus a fine for "conduct unbecoming a police officer" when he had been photographed in his green police uniform standing on the front steps of Schwerin Castle next to Adolf Hitler. Rather ruefully, he realized that his career was going nowhere. Even with the pay raise as Wachtmeister he didn't have enough to marry Kate. A full reassessment of his position and objectives was required. He discussed it with Richter.

"We're in a rut. Here we are, good party members, highly prized professional police instructors, and what have we got to show for it?"

Fritz scratched his head. "You want something more?"

"Don't you? Is a *Landespolizist* all you want to be for the rest of your life?"

Richter shrugged. Any change in the status quo made him uneasy. "Until I hear a better idea."

Kurt had one. They would apply to Sepp Dietrich in Berlin for permission to join the Leibstandarte. It was a bold move. The original *ss Stabswache* that Dietrich had brought to the city in March 1933 had evolved into a political elite that could be used for armed police and anti-terrorist work as well as for its normal duties at the Chancellery and protecting Hitler. On 2 September, at the "Congress of Victory" rally in Nuremberg, Hitler announced its new designation: the unit—now almost up to regimental strength—would be known as the SS Leibstandarte–Adolf Hitler. A few weeks later, in front of the Feldherrnhalle War Memorial where the Munich *Putsch* had ended exactly ten years before, the Leibstandarte took an oath of loyalty to Hitler unto death.

The problem with joining such a unit, as Richter saw it, was that as the arms-bearing branch of the SS, its members should have some sort of military background and training. Neither he nor Kurt qualified.

"We can pick it up as we go along," Kurt said airily. "Are you with me then? What have we got to lose?"

They made formal application to Dietrich.

Hitler described Dietrich as "a man unique, under whose swashbuckling appearance is a serious, conscientious, scrupulous character." Born in Upper Bavaria in 1892, the son of working-class parents, he received only the rudiments of an education before being apprenticed as a butcher. He hated the work and successively tried his hand as a farm labourer, waiter and handyman before joining the Imperial Army. He served with the 42nd Infantry Regiment as a foot soldier in 1914, later moved to one of the storm battalions where he fought with great distinction, and ended the war as Oberfeldwebel in the 13th Bavarian Tank Detachment with several decorations to his credit.

After discharge Dietrich found part-time work as a gas station attendant, a customs officer, and finally as foreman in a tobacco factory. But he missed the excitement of war, the close companionship of men in battle. He joined the *Freikorps* in 1919 and took part in the fighting against Polish annexationists in the Silesian dispute. Then in 1923 he participated in the Munich *Putsch* as an ardent nationalist, later joining the Nazi party.

Starting as one of Hitler's bodyguards in the SS, he rose quickly through its ranks until by 1930 he had become SS Oberführer* commanding all southern German SS units. The citizens of Lower Bavaria elected him to the Reichstag in September of that year. It was at this time that his close friendship with Hitler really began.

Promoted to SS Gruppenführer† in 1931, Dietrich was handed command of all northern SS groups together with the responsibility for Hitler's bodyguard. His leadership qualities and personal courage made a deep impression on the Führer, far more than any of the Reichswehr's monocled generals. As a former corporal, Hitler appreciated former sergeant-major Dietrich's coarse language, uproarious laughter and undeniable common touch with his subordinates: "He is one of my oldest companions in the struggle." When a decision had been made to organize an armed unit within the SS—

---

*Brigadier.
†Lieutenant-general—see Appendix B corresponding equivalents between Waffen-SS, U.S. and British ranks.

which was to become the Leibstandarte—it was only natural for Hitler to turn to Dietrich for its creation.

After reviewing the applications from Meyer and Richter, Dietrich set the necessary bureaucratic wheels in motion to arrange their transfer from the *Landespolizei*. Dietrich needed experienced instructors in Berlin just as badly as the SS unit did in Schwerin.

Kurt was promoted to Oberwachtmeister* in April 1934 and three weeks later was relieved of all duties in the police force pending his transfer to Berlin as SS Untersturmführer† in the Leibstandarte.

At Kurt's instigation, Dietrich accepted all four of the Police School's loyal party men. Ironically, their enthusiasm for joining produced serious consequences for them all in later years. As volunteers into what would be determined after World War II to have been a "criminal organization" they had inadvertently sacrificed their rights to full retirement pensions. Had they waited only six months, they could have "elected" transfer into the SS unit of their choice when the Schwerin-Mecklenburg *Landespolizei* became the first of many police groups to be disbanded and absorbed into other military organizations. Compulsory transfers were regarded as involuntary acts over which individuals had no control. Accordingly, transferees were entitled to full retirement benefits.

The Schwerin Police School quartet arrived in Berlin on 15 May 1934. After reporting into the Orderly Room, drawing down their bed linen and barrack assignments, they were taken by the duty officer to meet the CO.

"Your job is very simple," Dietrich explained. "It is to protect our Leader's life and guard the Chancellery against all enemies of the Reich."

Six weeks later they were to discover to their surprise that the Reich's enemies now included Ernst Röhm and the rest of the SA's leaders. But by then they were all at training camp in Jüterborg.

Röhm and his SA had become both an embarrassment and threat to Hitler— an embarrassment because of Röhm's high-profile homosexual activities, which, now that the Nazis were in power, gave the party an odious image with the population; and a threat because with a membership of over 3 million men the SA had become considerably more powerful than the Reichswehr. Even worse, now that Röhm felt confident of his position, he had been pushing for a merger of the SA, SS, army, navy and air force, with the SA as the senior Praetorian Guard and himself in command. The Reichswehr would be relegated to the role of a separate army filled with conscripts. Bluntly, the Reichswehr told Hitler to make up his mind as to which organization was going to be responsible for the nation's defence: the SA or the army.

---

*Senior police sergeant.
†Second lieutenant.

Playing cleverly on the army's fears, Hitler agreed to have Röhm's unification proposal withdrawn from cabinet (of which Röhm was a member) in exchange for the defence services agreeing to adopt his party's emblems of eagle and swastika for their uniforms and headwear. It was a triumph of political opportunism, and the army leadership failed to appreciate its implications. Such symbolic acceptance of Nazi leadership by the armed forces had a profound effect on the general population, many of whom regarded the untainted Reichswehr as the sole restraining influence on the Nazis. They now appeared to have joined forces.

Then, one more card played into Hitler's hand. Hindenburg's doctors advised that the old marshal's remaining time on earth could be measured in months. Without Hindenburg's presidential influence to hold Hitler in check, to whom could the Reichswehr turn as mediator? More importantly, who would replace Hindenburg as president?

After a number of discussions, deals and counterproposals the generals agreed to accept Hitler as Hindenburg's successor in exchange for Hitler's promise to "settle" the SA and left-wing of the Nazi party. Both were beginning to clamour loudly for a "second revolution." Even Röhm made no bones about his contempt for Hitler's dealings with the army. "Adolf is a *Schweinehund!*" he proclaimed loudly. "He'll give us all away. Old friends aren't good enough for him now. Chummy with the East Prussian generals. They've become his pals now."

Hitler felt distinctly uncomfortable with the barrage of criticism levelled at his leadership from within the party ranks. He ordered Göring and Himmler to make the necessary arrangements to eliminate everyone who they considered posed a threat to himself and the regime. In a cynical alliance of self-interest, Göring and Himmler took it upon themselves to include personal enemies, past enemies and possible future enemies in their hit lists. Where evidence of crimes appeared thin, Heydrich obligingly fabricated some. By mid-June, movements of their intended victims were carefully monitored, SS killer squads selected, and 30 June picked as the day of reckoning.

Dubbed the "Night of the Long Knives" by foreign correspondents, the purge began in the early hours before dawn. Heines, the SA leader of Silesia, was surprised naked in bed coupled to one of his handsome young SA men. Both were shot. Strasser, Hitler's old party rival, was murdered in his prison cell. Ex-chancellor General von Schleicher and his wife were caught in their Berlin villa and executed along with General von Bredow. All over Germany Hitler's enemies were rounded up. Röhm was sent to Stadelheim prison near Munich and given a pistol with a single bullet as he entered his cell. Fifteen minutes later, when two SS officers, Eicke and Lippert, saw that he had not elected to take his own life, they shot him.

In Berlin the Leibstandarte had been formed into commando groups to work with other SS units. Operating as mobile hit-and-run squads, they roared through the city's streets all morning, searching out their designated quarry. One team, headed by Kurt Gildisch, murdered a Transport Ministry director, who was president of the Catholic Action layman's organization. The man, Dr. Klausener, was caught in his office by SS Hauptsturmführer Gildisch and shot in the back when he turned around. The resourceful Gildisch then faked his suicide and strolled back to the street with his men to continue their search for the next victim.

Lichterfelde Barracks—the old officers' cadet school—became the interrogation centre for those arrested during the SS sweep, as well as a dumping ground for the bodies of those executed by Leibstandarte execution squads in the courtyard behind the main building. All members of the Leibstandarte participated in the action, with the exception of those on Chancellery duty. Dietrich made a personal decision not to use Meyer or Richter in the affair.

Dietrich's orders had been to take a detachment and pick up the senior SA leaders. But while the Leibstandarte was still on the road heading to the residences of those to be apprehended, Hitler decided to make the arrests himself. At 5:00 p.m. that afternoon he ordered Dietrich to collect an officer and six men with rifles for an execution squad and report to Stadelheim prison near Munich. Sepp arrived at the prison gates with his "six good shots to ensure nothing messy happened." There was a delay while the prison governor tried to interfere. Dietrich set him straight. Then, one by one, the SA leaders were led into the prison yard and stood against the wall. The courteous Leibstandarte officer read each his fate. "The Führer and Reich Chancellor has condemned you to death. The sentence will be carried out forthwith."

Dietrich found the entire business distasteful and later recounted: "Before it was Schneidhuber's turn I was off. I'd had enough."

By early morning on 2 July, the shootings had ended. Estimates of the dead ranged from 150 at Lichterfelde Barracks to 200 across the rest of the country. Hitler openly admitted in the Reichstag to 74 killed and three suicides. Recent research has uncovered the names of 85 people who were murdered as a result of Hitler's "list" that night.

Unwittingly, the army had purged itself of one threat only to subject itself to another. At best the SA had never been more than a heterogeneous unwieldy body rife with political frictions. The SS, on the other hand, although infinitely smaller, was a highly organized, well-disciplined and fanatical body made all the more dangerous by its relationships with the police and Gestapo.* With the SA gone, the SS was now free to grow.

The Reichswehr foolishly congratulated itself that the purges had been completed without involving any of its own men. Subsequent searches of

---

*Geheime Staatspolizei—Secret State Police; its chief was SS Obergruppenführer Heinrich Müller.

SA arms depositories uncovered over 177,000 rifles, almost twice as many as the Reichswehr stocked. The army had once more proved itself capable of wielding the ultimate power within the nation without interfering directly in its political affairs. Or so it still believed. General von Blomberg, minister of war and Hitler's personal handyman in the Reichswehr, expressed the army's thanks to Hitler in an order of the day on 1 July: "The Führer has personally attacked and wiped out the mutineers and traitors with soldierly decision and exemplary courage." The army, he reminded Hitler, remained the sole bearer of arms and intended to stay aloof from internal political conflict.

What remained of the SA membership soon shrank to little more than an association of old comrades to be trotted out for marches and to line parade routes on ceremonial occasions.

At the Jüterborg Training Depot Kurt was appointed a platoon leader in the 6th Training Company. Training never seemed to end. The formal drills and combat field exercises were not much different than those at Schwerin Police School. But specially appointed SS instructors provided the student officers with more exotic courses on secrecy, betrayal and counterintelligence. Heydrich's SD made certain nothing was missed in the art of deception. NCOs, on the other hand, were lectured on more mundane subjects: military conduct, handling of clothing and stores, health care, and prevention of venereal disease among troops.

The training camp dissolved in mid-October and all 12 companies transferred back to the Leibstandarte in Berlin. With an expanded force of nearly 2,500 men, the unit had become a full infantry regiment and the pride and showpiece of the Nazi party.

6

Whatever misgivings he may have had about the SA purges, Kurt kept them to himself. As one of the most junior of new junior officers in the Leibstandarte, and with his oath of obedience to Hitler still fresh in his mind, he was in no position to question orders. Besides, after years of longing for a military career, he had made it finally into Lichterfelde Barracks, not as an officer cadet with a high school graduation certificate (*Abitur*), but as a fully commissioned SS Untersturmführer. And with only a grade 8 education! What more did one need as proof of the opportunities provided to all through national socialism? The fact that few self-respecting Reichswehr officers, either retired or on active service, would have anything to do with "that uniformed party bunch of toy soldiers" appeared irrelevant.

Whether the army realized it or not, it was Hitler, not its generals, who commanded it. If the army had missed that point in July, it was made abundantly clear in August. Hindenburg died on 2 August 1934. Without consulting anyone in the Wehrmacht,* Hitler announced his merging of the offices of chancellor and president. On the same day he arranged to receive unconditional and personal oaths of allegiance from the heads of the armed forces, ensuring that the same oath would be administered to every soldier and sailor on active service. Like the SS, the nation's servicemen became vassals of Adolf Hitler.

In recognition of their meritorious service in squashing the SA, Hitler elevated the SS to the status "of an independent organization within the National Socialist German Workers' Party" in a decree of 20 July 1934. Himmler's craving for power and status had at last been fulfilled. He stood as leader of a recognized independent policing force, answerable only to Hitler. At once he set to work making plans for its expansion.

Throughout the summer Kurt drilled with the Leibstandarte. As a platoon leader he revelled in his new responsibilities. There were classroom lectures on tactics for assaulting and defending the Reich Chancellery, detailed weaponry courses, plus a host of rules and regulations to be learned covering everything from procedures during ceremonial drills to the correct way to make a bed and hang a uniform in the wardrobe.

Although political pedigrees and Aryan racial origins were firmly established before recruits were accepted, political propaganda still remained an integral part of the training curriculum. A procession of visiting senior party officials made certain that every man understood and appreciated Hitler's value to the nation. Himmler told them: "Your only purpose here is to ensure that our Führer lives to see the fulfilment of his dreams for the Third Reich. *Heil* Hitler!"

Provided with dramatic uniforms, good pay, comfortable quarters, first-class meals, pleasant companions and a secure future in a respected and powerful nation, what recruit in his right senses could argue against such maudlin political sentiment? All hail Hitler indeed.

Yet the main thrust of training was devoted to physical development. Mathematics, science, literature and philosophy were not considered subjects necessary for developing the attributes of leadership or healthy minds and bodies. "I don't expect you all to be athletes," Dietrich explained, "but I do expect you all to be athletic." Exercising began at first light—rain or shine. Everyone assembled on the parade square in their gym wear and after a half hour of vigorous calisthenics trotted off on an eight-kilometre run. A quick shower, a change into uniform, then breakfast in the vast 1,700-seat dining hall. Classroom lectures were scheduled during the mornings on

---

*The Reichswehr—literally, "Empire defence"—became known as the Wehrmacht, meaning "Defence power," i.e., the armed forces, including the navy and air force.

alternate working days. The rest of their time was spent playing sports, swimming in the splendid Lichterfelde pool or practising drills and marching.

The men marched in goose step for hours on end, up and down the long concrete road behind the church within the Lichterfelde grounds. Every boot had to be in line at a 90 degree angle from the ground on each step. "Not 84 or 87 degrees, you dimwits! I want 90. Nothing less or more. Let's try again, shall we?"

On they marched, dripping with perspiration from the afternoon sun but refusing any murmur of complaint lest it be considered a sign of weakness. At last, and just when every black-booted calf muscle began quivering in rebellious exhaustion, their company commander would call a halt for the day and march them back to the barracks. Week after week they marched and drilled until every company moved in perfect unison as one man.

To the military ss they were Hitler's pretty "Asphalt Soldiers," a derision tinged with envy. No regular army unit even came close to matching the disciplined precision of the black-uniformed phalanxes from Lichterfelde. Their knowledge of military tactics, battlefield organization and staff planning remained virtually nonexistent, but no one could deny the spectacular display of Germanic youth presented to the civilian population when they paraded through a city street. They were proud. They were tough. They were unique. And they knew it.

Richter, however, grew uneasy about his lack of basic knowledge and training. He persuaded himself that the day would come when experienced Wehrmacht officers would volunteer for the ss and novices such as he and Kurt would be left behind in the lower ranks until retirement. Realizing the limited knowledge of military affairs possessed by its officers, the ss prodded the Wehrmacht to offer—albeit reluctantly—a variety of officer training courses. Richter signed up for several in spite of Kurt's warnings.

"Mark my words. The army will do you in, Fritz. To them we're still just policemen. Do you think they'll welcome you as a comrade-in-arms when you arrive on course? Hah! It will never happen."

Kurt felt content to stay put, picking up what he lacked as he went along. Bound to be slower, but it was surer. The Leibstandarte would continue expanding and as long as he kept his nose clean and stayed out of trouble he could expand with it. He saw no urgency. He was still only 23.

But Richter remained unmoved. A short time later his transfer orders arrived from the Wehrmacht's training program. His arrival at the army depot as a black-uniformed junior ss officer was greeted with contemptuous amusement. Kurt's warnings had been right on the mark. But it was too late to change horses again. He had to stick it out. His career with the military went nowhere.

With his own future reasonably secure, Kurt now felt confident enough to go ahead with his plans to marry Kate. Alma was delighted that he had finally made up his mind. The Bohlmanns remained noncommittal. They admired Kurt's enthusiasm and obvious love for their daughter but were uneasy about the political side of his career and where it would ultimately lead. But since Kate was of age, Kurt's asking her parents permission was little more than a social courtesy.

Before setting the date, however, there were political procedures that had to be followed: an application to the RUSHA* branch of the SS to determine the bride's racial purity. Several weeks passed while Himmler's researchers delved into the Bohlmann family tree, searching for signs of Jewish or Slavic rot. Apparently there were none, or at least none that could be found by the SS. Permission was granted.

Their December wedding became the year's social event in Arendsee, with nearly 300 guests, including *Gauleiter* Hildebrandt and a group of Kurt's pals from the Leibstandarte who had driven down from Berlin. The Bohlmanns held the reception at their Schrampe inn. Alma and Melanie were on hand to weep and wish them happiness.

Kate took a potted flower growing in some of the moist dark soil from her family's garden on their honeymoon. "As insurance against homesickness," she explained.

Kurt remembered the same feeling the day he left Offleben to begin his apprenticeship. He smiled: "What you need is a baby. Otherwise I can see the day you'll leave me to run away back home."

The married quarters of the Leibstandarte became their new home; it was first-class accommodation by any standards: beautiful Victorian-style rooms with high ceilings, rich mahogany wood mouldings and doors, and a view of the traffic along the Finkensteiner Allee. Berlin was not new to Kate. She had spent a year at the "Bethesda" school as a teenager and later worked in a private house learning needlepoint. Nonetheless, during her first years of marriage the pangs of homesickness for the country were never far from the surface.

She tried making friends with the other wives but found that they had little in common. To make matters more difficult, Kurt seemed to spend more time with "his boys," as he called them, than he did with her. Either he was officer-of-the-guard over at the Chancellery or drilling for an approaching ceremonial parade. She passed the time exploring the city, endlessly cleaning the apartment and working at her sewing. She became bored.

With the approach of spring she discovered that she was going to have a baby. Suddenly, everything seemed worthwhile again. Inge, the first of their four daughters, arrived in October, six days after Kurt had been promoted

---

*See Appendix C, "Principal Organizations within the SS."

to SS Obersturmführer* and appointed as platoon leader of a motorcycle Tank-Hunter Company.

His promotional assessment report read in part:

Racial Appearance: Nordic.
Character: faultless, a quick-thinking stable and determined personality.
Commonsense: normal, good overall knowledge.
Perception: good.
National-socialist ideology: faultless.
Conduct in and out of Service: very good.
Athletics: very good.
Instructing Ability: very good.
Summation: suitable as Platoon Leader.

October 3, 1935.   signed: Dietrich.

In 1933, as a result of Himmler's announcement that the SS would guarantee "the security of Germany from the interior"—in other words, suppress any rebellious elements of the population swiftly and effectively—groups of "Political Action Squads" were formed in major centres throughout the country. Known as the SS Politische Bereitschaften, they were mobile units from 250 to 500 men trained in armed police duties. The Leibstandarte had been classified, trained and used in June and July 1934 as just such an armed political force. During December of that same year, after realizing the need for an overall command coordination, Himmler—with Hitler's approval—ordered his Action Squads formed into military-style battalions and integrated with the Leibstandarte. Hitler put a name to the group three months later: SS Verfügungstruppe,† SS-VT for short. To command the new body, he appointed Paul Hausser, one of the few high-ranking ex-army officers to join the SS.

The date, 16 March 1935, marked the transformation of the Nazi party's political police units into a military force under Hitler's exclusive control. Coincidentally, the date also marked the introduction of a general military conscription for Germany, in violation of the Versailles treaty.

Although neither Hitler nor Himmler voiced their reasons for creating a police force of three armed regiments at the moment the Wehrmacht had been ordered to expand its own ranks, the purpose was obvious. The general SS and SS-VT provided a counterbalance to any revolutionary ideas harboured in the minds of the army's senior officers. A military takeover of an unarmed civilian government was one thing. A successful coup against a disciplined political army was something else entirely.

To set the military minds at rest, Hitler reaffirmed that the Wehrmacht's role would remain "the security of Germany from its external enemies." As

*First lieutenant.
†Disposal Troops—Special Purpose Troops; no literal translation.

well, the army was given responsibility for the SS-VT military training, budgetary and equipment inspection rights, and promised that in the event of war all SS-VT units would be dispersed throughout the armed forces and placed under army command.

Indirectly the Wehrmacht also controlled the SS-VT's numerical growth through the manpower allocation rights that were vested with the Ministry of War. Over half of all recruits who qualified and asked to join the armed SS were refused and shunted into the army. Thus, with its autonomy from political interference still guaranteed by Hitler, the Wehrmacht offered no strenuous objections to the Führer's "private internal army."

The SS-VT formed into three regiments, each of three battalions— *Standarten** Germania stationed in Hamburg, Deutschland stationed at Munich, and the Leibstandarte still based in Berlin. Dietrich's long-standing relationship with Hitler gave the Leibstandarte a degree of autonomy not shared by the other two regiments, much to Himmler's annoyance. In addition, Dietrich outranked Hausser, his commanding officer, which complicated matters even more for the SS Reichsführer. During one heated discussion with Himmler over a Leibstandarte officer picked up by the Berlin police for being drunk and disorderly, Dietrich refused Himmler's insistence on disciplinary measures. His rationale: "My position as guard commander will no more allow your interference on security matters than it will upon the morality of my men. They are mine and we are his [Hitler's]. Now go back to your office and let us get on with the job."

Himmler later complained bitterly that the Leibstandarte was becoming "a complete law unto itself. It does and allows anything it likes without taking the slightest notice of orders from above."

But Hitler made it very clear where his sympathies lay when he wrote to Himmler: "Dietrich is master of his own house which, I would remind you, is also my house."

Even Hausser, the SS-VT's—and Leibstandarte's—nominal CO, found his way barred at the gates of Lichterfelde. Dietrich would tolerate no outside interference. So far as Dietrich was concerned, Hausser had his "authorization to attend Leibstandarte parades," nothing more.

Yet it was due to Hausser more than anyone that the country was able to produce a cadre of young colonels and generals whose tactical leadership abilities at the front were unmatched by even the Wehrmacht during the closing days of World War II.

Hausser had left the army in 1932 with the rank of lieutenant-general. He held specific views on the methods needed to instil soldierly virtues into SS-VT officer recruits. Curriculum at the SS Junkerschule† cadet training centres

*Regiment.

†Literally, School of Noblemen, another example of Himmler's flair for the dramatic.

became his responsibility. Himmler set up the first at Bad Tölz in Bavaria in April 1934 and a second at Brunswick, which Hausser directed the following November. He modelled them after English boarding schools, stressing the physical rather than academic accomplishments of trainees. The "sporting bond" that grew between officers and men of the ss did much to create a sense of brotherhood unlike anything provided in the Wehrmacht training programs. Cadets were brought out at 6:00 a.m. for an hour's physical training, followed by a Spartan breakfast of mineral water and porridge, both formulated especially for the ss. Weapons training, ideological schooling and sports activities took up the remainder of the day. Later in the course the men took part in field manoeuvres, using live ammunition, an innovation for the times. Hausser considered Himmler "a mighty queer bird with his feet firmly fixed six centimetres above the ground."

Because of Himmler's strict physical, racial and political requirements, finding acceptable candidates became a serious problem, and prior to 1938 nearly half of the cadets on the course had no more than a grade 8 education. For young men without social position, money or an *Abitur*,* the ss-vt offered the only opportunity to achieve senior officer rank, something they could never hope to attain in the Wehrmacht. Little wonder that most ss-vt officer graduates displayed a loyalty and devotion to the Nazi cause that at times bordered on fanaticism.

7

During his periodic leaves Kurt often left Kate in Berlin and drove down to Offleben to visit his mother and sister. Melanie's husband, Alfred Feindt, a civil engineer from Arendsee, held a responsible, well-paying position in the local coal mine. From the days when Kurt had carried Melanie as a little girl everywhere on his back because she couldn't walk, Kurt felt a responsibility for his sister. When Feindt had proposed, he had asked for his word of honour that he would never leave her; Alfred gave it. He should have extracted the same promise from his sister, who had inherited her father's easygoing nature.

On these visits home, Kurt usually turned up on his motorcycle with the detachable sidecar or in an automobile with two or three friends. Once he arrived in a tank, parking the monster on the street outside the house. Everyone in town came to gawk. Alma was enormously proud of him.

One visit he decided to show off. "Look, Nanni! Here's one of the things we do in the Leibstandarte with our motorbikes." Four men were selected from the crowd of onlookers. After hanging them from his shoulders, he

---

*High school diploma.

rode up a steep slope at the edge of town and back again. "Anyone else want to try?" Nobody did. Neither would any of the four ride his shoulders a second time. Bruno Grupenberg, a neighbour's son, was so impressed by the performance he decided to quit high school and join the Leibstandarte. Too shy to ask Kurt directly, he approached Melanie and asked her to intercede on his behalf.

"Are you sure you want to abandon your *Abitur*?" Kurt asked when he met the lad. Bruno stood six feet four inches tall and looked the ideal ss candidate. But with less than a year from earning his high school certificate, it seemed a pity to drop out now.

"Yes," Bruno replied adamantly.

"Right, then. Go home. Pack your stuff. I'm heading back to Berlin in the morning. You can ride with me."

Before taking him to the recruiting office, Kurt wanted to test the lad's courage with a jump from the ten-metre diving board at the Lichterfelde pool. It was one of the emotional tests he used on his own men. Leading his company up the diving tower ladder in full uniform—swimmers and nonswimmers alike—he marched them over the edge.

Bruno balked. "I can't jump from this height. I've never done it before. I just can't!"

Kurt patted his arm. "Listen, lad. I fell off a roof once. Three storeys. It was unintended. But I survived. I'll show you how it's done. Remember, it's only water."

After a moment of hesitation Bruno followed him down. Both climbed out, soaked but laughing, and went off to Kurt's apartment to change. "That wasn't so bad was it?"

Bruno agreed.

"In the Leibstandarte you'll discover that officers never ask their men to do anything they aren't prepared to do themselves. Do you still want to join?"

"Yes."

Grupenberg was accepted into the Leibstandarte.*

One evening, Kurt stumbled home and slumped into a chair. "It's all over, Mutti,"† he told Kate. "I'm being courtmartialed for fighting in the officers' mess. They'll probably boot me out of the service."

What started as a friendly discussion had developed into a loud drunken argument between himself and another junior officer. In exasperation, and before they came to blows, Kurt had poured a half-litre stein of beer over the man's head. Dietrich saw it happen and ordered him out of the mess, promising his arrest in the morning.

---

*And miraculously managed to survive World War II.
†Mummy.

Kate phoned the officers' mess and asked if Dietrich had left. While the mess orderly went to find him, she gathered her courage. When he answered the phone, her voice trembled but she came straight to the point: "Gruppenführer, please don't arrest my husband tomorrow."

"Why?"

"Because I'm pregnant again."

Sepp paused to digest this information. Kate held her breath. She heard a sigh in her ear.

"All right," he grunted. "I'll cancel the order."

"Thank you, Gruppenführer."

Their second daughter, Ursula, arrived on 12 December 1936.

By early 1935 tangible results of Hitler's economic miracle were visible across the nation. Germany had started rearming. Little enhances an economic miracle more than a nation preparing for war. It began surreptitiously at first, later more brazenly and without regard to the Versailles agreements.

By the thousands, then tens of thousands, people were going back to work. Factories that had been idle since 1918 opened their gates again. Automobiles, ships, trucks, engines, then tanks, guns and airplanes started rolling off the production lines. A network of four-lane superhighways (autobahn), revolutionary in design, was planned to link the country's major cities from east to west. Mines were reopened—with pit props ordered from Nova Scotia.

The 1935 plebiscite on the Saar had been the first step in reclaiming Germany's lost honour. Given to France for a 15-year exploitation period as compensation for the destruction of mines in northern France, the Saarland's inhabitants voted overwhelmingly to rejoin Germany. Hitler's political stock soared.

His next external venture was occupation of the demilitarized zone of Germany's Rhineland adjacent to the Saar. His generals hesitated at such an open breach of the Versailles treaty. A plebiscite was one thing, but how would the Allied powers react to a military occupation? Hitler had no doubts: "If the army is reluctant to lead the way, a suitable spearhead will be provided by the Leibstandarte."

Arrangements were made with Dietrich to move a company of men to the frontier. On 7 March 1936 the Leibstandarte raised the road barrier and crossed the Rhine to proceed unopposed into the city of Saarbrücken on the French border. They received an enthusiastic greeting. As Hitler expected, the Allies accepted the move with little more than a perfunctory complaint. The Leibstandarte returned home as heroes, while the Wehrmacht seethed at having handed over to Hitler's private army the opportunity to distinguish itself on a job exclusively within the Wehrmacht's mandate.

Not everyone shared in the economic boom. The Jewish population, its middle class in particular, was encouraged to emigrate through a combination of a subtle psychological threat of what the future might hold for them and a not so subtle public condemnation of their existence. According to the Nazis, Jewish greed and treachery had been one of the principal causes for losing the war. Their presence posed a threat of racial contamination to Aryan purity. Jews would no longer be welcome or tolerated in Germany. The message was received loud and clear and a mass exodus began by those who could afford the price of departure.

Himmler's seven concentration camps still housed less than 10,000 inmates,* mostly political opponents of the regime rounded up in 1933. Less than half were Jewish. In a nation of over 60 million (after the return of the Saar) the 10,000 behind barbed wire could be overlooked very easily.

The Berlin Summer Olympics of 1936 gave Hitler and the Nazi party a chance to demonstrate their new self-confidence to the world. The Leibstandarte opened the ceremonies as guard of honour. Visitors had seen nothing like them before—a juggernaut of goose-stepping soldiers wearing black boots, black uniforms tinged with gold and silver braidings, and red swastika armbands. Polished swords and ceremonial daggers flashed like a thousand sparklets in the sun. The masses in the grandstand roared their approval while the visitors clapped politely and felt strangely uneasy.

During his time as Obersturmführer, Kurt was often away from Berlin on Wehrmacht training courses designed to improve the military capabilities of SS-VT officers. Unlike the ones his friend Richter had elected to take, these were mandatory for all junior officers. Most lasted six weeks and gave the young Asphalt Soldiers their first real exposure to military professionalism in the Prussian tradition.

The Wehrmacht was more interested in developing potential SS-VT leaders with brains than muscles. Schoolboy games and athletics placed low on their training agenda. Courses covered basic staff planning, assessing military intelligence, and disposition of troops for attack or defence from the regimental down to the platoon level. In addition, there were programs designed for specific tactical requirements—training motorcycle riflemen to deploy during an attack, forward reconnaissance for hunting and destroying tanks, personnel training.

Each group of new SS arrivals was coolly received by the army instructors until individual officers had time to discover the calibre of the recruits. SS-VT men had to do much better on the course than their Wehrmacht counterparts in order to get the same grade. The army made no bones about their distaste for Himmler's black legions, but Kurt managed to make his mark. Maj.-Gen. Fritz Holzhauer remembered the young Meyer and in his retirement years wrote: "For the first few days the other participants were

---

*The mass extermination programs did not begin until after 1940.

reluctant to have anything to do with the young officer from the Leibstandarte Adolf Hitler. But he turned out to be a soldier at heart and in due
course a part of us. He was an excellent comrade. Moreover, his fellowship
with the Wehrmacht was maintained even after he'd been promoted several
ranks in the Waffen-SS over his army peers."

As the Leibstandarte expanded, a shortage of space developed at Lichterfelde.
Officers' married quarters were moved to a new housing development near
the Teltow Canal. Kate was delighted with their new home. No dust or dirt.
Everything was clean, compact and modern. Each house had two bedrooms,
separate dining room, large hallway, bright kitchen and private balcony that
led off the living room. No expense had been spared to ensure the family
comforts for Hitler's Praetorian Guard.

Kurt was promoted to Hauptsturmführer* of the 14th Kradschützen†
Company in December 1937, a few days short of his 27th birthday. The
intemperance of youth faded as he assumed more responsibilities at home
and in his career. There were still occasional outbursts of annoyance or
enthusiasm, but the emotional rollercoaster ride on which Kate had joined
him seemed to be slowing down. It made him a much more comfortable
person to have as a husband.

His daring with motorcycles resulted in his being appointed leader of a
stunt team the Leibstandarte provided for public performances in places such
as the huge Deutschlandhalle exhibition stadium and elsewhere across the
country on special occasions. To teach his men the different stunts in the
repertoire, Kurt demonstrated each himself so that they would know what
he asked was not impossible. "If an old man like me can do it, there's no
reason why you can't."

Every man collected his share of broken bones and bruises, but the gasps
of surprise and general applause they received at their exhibitions made up
for it. After the show he congratulated each of his men, then joined them
for a drink in the privates' canteen. Although he was their commanding
officer, they were all "his boys." He enjoyed sharing their successes and
comradeship.

This was not a pose conjured up for special occasions to get the best out
of the men. He had too much integrity for that sort of nonsense. A leader
can only command respect and obedience from a body of men if they believe
that their interests will always be his first consideration. Kurt not only
believed in such a doctrine, he practised it.

"Mutti," he told Kate on Christmas Eve, "before we start celebrating, I

---

*Captain (company commander).
†Literally, "Motorcycle Riflemen." A *Krad* was a motorcycle with sidecar capable of carrying
three fully equipped soldiers. It was the fastest mobile ground transport at the time for troop
movements.

have to visit my boys." Off he went with a big carton of gifts for those who had been stuck with guard duty over the holiday. Room by room he drifted through the barracks, pausing for a cigarette or a chat before returning home. Kate understood.

Her homesickness for Schrampe had passed. She was even beginning to enjoy the excitement of living in Berlin. Nearly every weekend in summer there seemed to be a parade somewhere in the city to commemorate something. Led by a band and a colour party bearing an array of magnificently tasselled flags came the marching men: SS-VT or the SA, Hitlerjugend or the Wehrmacht, with war veterans bringing up the rear. They all took their turn parading. The Nazis thrived on public spectacle.

Then there were special events like the Olympics when the city filled with visitors. At night the theatre marquees came alive. Sidewalks teemed with people looking for entertainment or simply gazing into shop windows at the evidence of prosperity's abundance.

In good weather Kate could arrange to leave the girls for an hour or two with a babysitter and meet Kurt at the Chancellery when he came off duty. They would go somewhere together, for a pastry or to see a movie. Guard duties had been altered to two-week cycles since the early days, and when Kurt's turn came up, he had to spend most of his time away from home checking on the men. Oddly, she never saw Hitler at the Chancellery, although Kurt met him frequently during his rounds when the Führer was in residence. He was on speaking terms with a number of the senior party officials who came and left at all hours of the day and night. Hitler, he discovered, rarely went to bed before 3:00 a.m. and seldom arose before midmorning.

The Goebbels family took a liking to Kurt and on several occasions invited him home for coffee and a chat. Their children each had a pet rabbit. For a time Kurt toyed with the idea of getting a pair for Inge and Ursula when they were old enough to look after them. But then the war intervened.

Kate could never accept her husband's enthusiasm for Hitler or believe his stories of the admiration he evoked from every woman he met. Her chance to see Hitler came when the Leibstandarte officers and their wives were ordered to attend a tear-jerking propaganda film produced by Goebbels's ministry. Titled *Hitlerjunge Quex,** it told the story of a boy who found comfort in the Hitler Youth movement after being rejected by everyone else, only to be murdered by his former Communist comrades. Not exactly first-class film fare. Nonetheless, it gave the ladies who had been invited a chance to wear their evening dresses and view the Nazi leaders seated in the theatre's upper gallery.

Ten minutes before showtime Hitler, accompanied by Goebbels and Göring with their wives, took his seat to thunderous applause. For the first time

---

Hitler Youth Quex.

Kate had an opportunity to study the country's vaunted leadership. To her eyes, Goebbels looked like an amiable ferret. Göring—overweight and wearing a garish uniform—appeared red-faced and jovial. Hitler sat without any expression, offering a few brief arm salutes to the cheering audience. Only then did she appreciate the magnitude of his personality. It was something she couldn't explain. A power that seemed to draw everyone near him into his orbit. Something about his eyes.

8

After the Rhineland occupation the German army had great difficulty preserving its High Command and General Staff from the embrace of the Nazis. The combined effects of the party encroachments and rearmament began taking their toll on the morality of the officers' corps. A dwindling minority of older senior officers remained confirmed monarchists with staunch conservative Christian ideals, but generals like Blomberg, the minister of war, Reichenau and others saw the party as a springboard for achieving their own ambitions. The masses of military personnel who stood between these viewpoints remained politically indifferent and were prepared to disregard the less appetizing aspects of the Nazi government.

A bigger problem existed among the younger officers who were now coming out of the war colleges by the thousands. Few came from social groups with traditions of leadership in public life. More often than not, they were lower middle class, the sons of farmers, tradespeople and labourers who in the past had been excluded from the officer ranks. They owed their career opportunities to Hitler's national socialism. Assimilating them socially and professionally into German military traditions proved a monumental task for the regimental commanders of the units to which they were assigned.

Every attempt by the army to maintain its traditional spirit produced the strongest opposition from the Nazis, even though fears of organized Wehrmacht opposition had faded; yet so long as it remained independent in its outlook and tradition, its potential as a rallying point for effective opposition posed a threat to Hitler. Despite his promises to honour its independence, he knew something had to be done to neutralize this potential for creating political problems. Ultimately, the ss provided the solution. In January 1938 the first opportunity to break the army's independence presented itself.

In the course of spying on everyone of any interest, Heydrich's SD security service had uncovered a juicy bit of scandal concerning the minister of war, Marshal von Blomberg. The Marshal's new bride had at one time been a prostitute. Blomberg was forced to resign. The natural choice for his successor was General Fritsch, the Commander-in-Chief of the Army. But Heydrich had a dossier on him as well. An SD informant was prepared to testify on the General's alleged homosexual practices. Hitler placed Fritsch on indefinite leave. Heydrich's informant admitted later that he had confused the General with a retired army captain, but before Fritsch could return to his post, Hitler abolished the War Ministry and incorporated its powers into a joint Defence Command over which he placed himself in control.

Gen. Walther von Brauchitsch became the new army commander, while senior officers of the other services retained their postings. As political and titular commander-in-chief of all armed forces, Hitler now had the legitimate right to replace one or all of them as he saw fit or to intervene directly in any service matter. He appointed the malleable Gen. Wilhelm Keitel as his chief of staff.

With the Wehrmacht satisfactorily neutralized and under his thumb he could now embark on the road to European conquest.

Austria became his first objective. Mobilization orders went out to Gen. Heinz Guderian's XVI Army Corps and the Leibstandarte. But the Austrian invasion was not entirely an unwelcome "act of aggression" within the strict meaning of the phrase.

The collapse of the Austro-Hungarian government in the closing months of 1918 had produced a flurry of political realignments within the carcass of the dying Empire. Austria was now one-eighth the size of the old Empire and centred in the city of Vienna. In the decade after the war the country had been locked in a chaotic struggle between factions dominated by the Social Democrats and Christian Socialists. The discord drove many moderate and patriotic Austrians into the extreme Pan-German camp, which believed the only path to economic stability lay in union with Germany.

The Austrian Parliament had unanimously voted for union with Germany in 1918, and the country's foremost political parties during the 1920s all supported German unification. In March 1931 plans for union with Germany were reintroduced together with a customs agreement, but after violent objections from France and Italy the project was shelved in September of the same year.

Engelbert Dollfus, leader of the Conservatives, became chancellor in 1932. A friend and admirer of Italian dictator Benito Mussolini, Dollfus adopted an independent stance vis-à-vis his own Conservative party and the Pan-Germans, who were by this time Nazi in character. When the Socialists made an unsuccessful attempt on his life in 1933 and launched an unsuccessful revolution the following year, he established a "corporate state"–style dictatorship satisfactory to no one. The Pan-German Nazis revolted, and Dollfus, who was being held hostage in the Vienna Chancellery, was murdered. With Dollfus's death the country's independence ceased. Political unrest continued and *Anschluss* (political union) had become a rallying cry for most of the population by 1937.

Confronted with Hitler's demand for Austrian annexation near the end of the year, the new chancellor, Kurt von Schuschnigg, resisted. Angrily, Hitler summoned him to Berchtesgaden on 12 February 1938, where after several hours of tantrums and threats by the German leader, Schuschnigg was compelled to sign an agreement clearing the way for nazism in Austria. On his return, he tried organizing a rather fraudulent national plebiscite against Hitler. The result, to the delight of the Pan-Germans, was movement orders for the forces mobilized and waiting under General Guderian and Gruppen-führer Dietrich.

Kurt received his orders on 9 March 1938. He would lead his 14th Kradschützen Company into Austria with one battalion of the Leibstandarte. Full battle order: weapons, ammunition, field supplies and vehicle support to carry the group for a seven-day period. It was to be regarded simply as another six-week field exercise for the troops. Austrian resistance could be considered minimal, according to intelligence reports. Then again one never knew.

The force assembled smoothly, and at dusk on 11 March, the battalion left Berlin for the Austrian border. At dawn next morning Guderian's columns crossed the border near Passau on the river Danube and headed for Vienna. The Leibstandarte provided rearguard coverage to the main column. At Linz they paused to act as honour guard for Hitler's arrival before proceeding on to Vienna.

The battalion covered 950 kilometres in 48 hours without incident and in full cooperation with the Wehrmacht. Even the grim-faced Guderian was impressed by the high calibre of organizational ability demonstrated by the Leibstandarte, the first instance of a senior army officer voicing approbation for the military qualities of Hitler's private army. Dietrich beamed with pleasure.

There were triumphal celebrations in the capital, and any glum faces among the citizenry were lost among the cheering crowds of well-wishers lining the parade routes. A majority of Austrians remained convinced that Germany's economic miracle under Hitler would now spill freely across their borders.

The battalion remained billeted in the Vienna area until well into April. Their task, as well as the army's, was to preserve law and order while the new Nazi administration organized its priorities for the country. These included dissolving the Austrian Diet (Parliament), incorporating the army with the Wehrmacht, substituting the reichsmark for the schilling, subordinating the nation to the Reich as the German province of Ostmark, and placing Chancellor Schuschnigg in prison.*

With a third bloodless conquest to Hitler's credit, even his worst critics

---

*Where he remained throughout the war. After 1945 he became professor of political science at St. Louis University in the U.S., and an American citizen in 1956.

were changing their opinions on his political acumen in foreign affairs.

Back in Berlin Kurt was given leave to recover from a sudden attack of appendicitis. Kate managed to get him into hospital before his appendix ruptured. The doctors operated on Wednesday afternoon. On Saturday morning he appeared at the doorstep. "Hello, Mutti. I'm back. Couldn't stand the place any longer, so I ran away."

A staff car with two drivers was arranged for them to go on tour. They drove to Offleben and spent a week with Alma and Melanie. His visits home had become local events. Alma's son was regarded as a colourful character, someone of whom the town could be proud. Three years earlier, after completing a pilot training course at his own expense designed to familiarize army officers with the advantages of aircraft for tactical support in a *Blitzkrieg*, he had appeared over Offleben in a light aircraft. After beating up the town at low level with some dramatic aerobatics, he picked a field on the outskirts and brought the machine in for a bumpy, gut-wrenching landing. The townspeople ran out to view the damage. There wasn't any. "Every landing you can walk away from is a success," he told them gravely, then went off to see his mother.

In Offleben his two drivers became bored. They were young teenagers who insisted that Melanie call them "drivers" and not "boys." Kurt and Kate were invited out for an evening with friends, and the boys were released to another evening of boredom. They had been hoping for permission to borrow the staff car and attend a dance at a town nearby, but neither had screwed up the courage to ask Kurt. Instead, they decided to try Melanie, inviting her to come along. It took only minutes to convince her and they were off.

Melanie assumed they would be out for a couple of hours and back before Kurt returned from his party. But the boys stayed until the last dance when the hall closed at three in the morning.

"Since when have you started giving orders to my men, Nanni?" Kurt demanded. The boys stood mute and trembling with fear and throbbing heads.

"I didn't think you'd mind."

"Well you were wrong. I do mind. Last night was the first and last time you do that. Understand?"

Melanie nodded. He smiled and told the boys to find some place to sit down before they fell down.

Berlin duty had its advantages. The Leibstandarte was hired to take part in the movie production *Der Alte Fritz* (*Frederick the Great*). It meant extra pay for every member of the regiment, little flirts with actresses and a chance to wear tailor-made historical uniforms. All great fun and such a success that the regiment was called in later for a return engagement in *Die Drei Musketiere* (*The Three Musketeers*).

Everyone who was anyone came to Berlin to pay homage to the German chancellor—kings, presidents, industrialists, movie stars, politicians, ambassadors. Few of them agreed with his policies, but none could deny his political and economic accomplishments for the Third Reich. While in Berlin and wherever they went with the Führer, the famous and not so famous were guarded by the Leibstandarte.

Hitler remained incessantly on the move, making speeches, attending rallies, confiding, honouring, scheming and always watching the bell-wether of opportunity. Wherever he travelled, a company of Leibstandarte went with him, whether by rail, by road or by air. On one six-week visit to Hitler's refuge at Obersalzberg in the Bavarian Alps, Dietrich sent Kurt with his entire 14th Company to provide guard duties during the Führer's stay.

There were no church services at Lichterfelde on Sundays. Himmler had decreed that national socialism and the church were incompatible. Good ss leaders were expected to choose between the party and their religion. Accordingly, Kurt and Kate abandoned the church. It was no great loss, as neither of them had spent much time in church since their marriage.

Instead of church on Sunday mornings Kurt took the girls for swimming lessons. They rode on his back like opossums while he breaststroked gently up and down the pool. When Inge cried, he chided her: "The only time you are permitted to cry is when you've lost your head. Have you lost your head?"

"No, Vati."

"Then stop crying."

9

The Jews were not a subject discussed by Kurt or Kate. They had little to do with Jews in any case, and those few they did know seemed nice enough. Yet "the evil of Judaism," as one of the basic planks in the party's platform and ss teachings, could not be ignored. Fortunately, the Meyer family was never placed in a position of having to take a public stand against the Jews either verbally or physically. Like the other Leibstandarte soldiers and their families insulated against the realities of "civvy street," they regarded the Jews as a political and ideological problem rather than a moral one.

Five years of carefully orchestrated Nazi indoctrination had convinced a majority of Germans that Jews actually were the source of most evils infecting the country, but always "with the exception of that nice Jewish family who lived next door and who had been ever so helpful and considerate until the Gestapo arrested them last night."

Hitler's first important speech way back on 13 August 1920 established his anti-Semitic policy firmly in the minds of his supporters:

We are convinced that scientific anti-Semitism, which recognizes clearly the frightful danger that that race represents to our people, can only be our guide. . . . Our task must be to arouse the mass instinct against the Jew, stir it up and keep it at the boil until it decides to support the movement.

The Jew became the object of the hate campaign that no totalitarian regime can ever do without. From 1933 on, Jews were gradually excluded from every facet of German life and encouraged to emigrate. By 1938 over 170,000 had left the country. Among those remaining, many could never bring themselves to believe that they could become outcasts in the land of their birth; many who were unable or unwilling to leave chose suicide. Posters everywhere fuelled the hate campaign. At the entrance to a Bavarian resort: FREE OF JEWISH TAINT. At public swimming pools: BATHING PROHIBITED TO DOGS AND JEWS. In restaurant windows: JEWS NOT WANTED HERE. Municipal authorities in a number of towns and cities ordered their employees to shun all social relations with Jews as a "moral and patriotic duty."

On 15 September 1935, at the Nazi party rally in Nuremberg, Hitler announced the Nuremberg Laws, the next step in his campaign to rid the country of its Jewish population. The Reich Citizenship Act stated: "No Jew can become a citizen of the Reich. The right to vote on political questions is not extended to him and he may not be appointed to any office of the State." Issued in tandem came the Act for Protection of German Blood and German Honour. It prohibited marriage and extramarital relations between German nationals and Jews, specifying further that no Jew was permitted to "employ a female national of German or allied blood under 45 years of age . . . within his household." Official justification for this piece of absurdity lay in protecting the "survival of the German race."

Throughout the rise of nazism, Hitler's position never altered. After one party rally and while the thunder of applause still rang in his ears, he confided to his circle of intimates: "Out with them from all the professions and into the ghetto with them. Fence them in somewhere where they can perish as they deserve while the German people look on, the way people stare at wild animals."[3]

The names of Jews who had given their lives in the war were not to be included in new war memorials, although an addendum to the original order stated that "out of a spirit of generosity Jewish names will not be removed from existing memorials." This merely provided overzealous officials with an excuse for erasing names to curry party favour.

A certain amount of backtracking ensued during the period immediately prior to and during the Olympic Games. The Games were vitally important to Hitler and the Nazis, and nothing was to be allowed to jeopardize Germany's image abroad. Heydrich's Gestapo ordered "hands off" the Jews "until after the conclusion of the Games."

After the Austrian *Anschluss*, proprietors of Jewish businesses were replaced across the country with incompetent party officials. Corruption became rife as Jews began selling their holdings to "Aryans" for nominal sums in order to continue operating. On 22 April 1938 an order was promulgated "For the Prevention of Camouflage Assistance to Jewish Undertakings," under which Germans who lent themselves to such corrupt practices were subject to fines and prison. A week later the "Order for Disclosure of Jewish Assets" provided for a deposit to be paid by Jewish asset holders to the government based on a percentage of holdings, supposedly as a surety bond. The plan, developed by Göring, complemented his earlier "Aryanization" of the economy to finance the nation's expanding war machine without raising general taxes.

Further decrees ordered special authorization for every sale or land lease, forestry concession, industrial operation, new factory or business enterprise being undertaken by a Jew. Jews were forbidden to lend money, deal in real estate, act as business managers, practise law, medicine or dentistry, or teach in schools or universities. In short, they became unemployed and unemployable. Göring put it succinctly at the Ministry of Aviation on 14 October when he demanded that the Jewish problem "be tackled energetically and forthwith. They must be driven out of the economy."

However, final exclusion of the Jews from German economic life could never be achieved while existing disbarment laws remained in effect. Some pretext was needed to finish off the Jews once and for all, and it came on 7 November when a 17-year-old Jew named Grünspan assassinated von Rath, secretary to the German legation in Paris. The *Völkischer Beobachter* newspaper wrote the same day: "Obviously the German people will be able to draw their own conclusions from this new outrage." A quick discussion among Hitler, Göring and Goebbels the next day resulted in the Reich Minister of Propaganda being selected as torchbearer to fan the flames of "spontaneous" anarchy.

In a passionate speech to the party faithful assembled at the Old Town Hall in Munich for their annual celebration of the 1923 *Putsch*, Goebbels launched the final destruction of the Jews' economic existence. Without actual orders being given by anyone, the *Reichskristallnacht** pogrom began. Later, an official report from the party High Court to Göring[4] made it clear everyone understood his role in the events that took place across the country on 9 and 10 November: "The words of the Reich Minister of Propaganda left no doubt to the party leaders that they were not to appear openly as the instigators of the demonstrations, although of course they were to organize them and see that they were carried through."

By 11 November when the dust finally settled and an assessment had been made of the havoc wreaked upon the Jews, the authorities determined that

---

*Crystal Night.

over 7,000 Jewish shops and businesses had been damaged, and synagogues in every Jewish district throughout Germany had been burned to the ground. Heydrich reported the death of 36 Jews, though this was later revised to 91.

Surprisingly, the ss had little to do with the actual operation of events. Its activities were confined to that of a back-up force where needed. The sa and the Nazi party were the prime instigators of the affair. In Berlin the Leibstandarte remained at Lichterfelde Barracks throughout the two-day period and took no part.

Privately, Himmler and Heydrich were appalled by the way the pogrom had been handled. They would have preferred to achieve the same results by means of innocuous bureaucratic terror. To prove their point, during the following weeks some 20,000 Jews—mainly wealthy middle class—were rounded up and placed in concentration camps. Most were quickly released after a payment to the ss and a promise of speedy emigration.

A week after Crystal Night the British chargé d'affaires in Berlin observed: "I have not yet met a single German from any walk of life who does not disapprove to some degree of what has occurred. But I fear that not even an unequivocal condemnation of professed National Socialists and senior officers in the armed forces will have any effect on the gang of madmen who are presently in control of Nazi Germany."[5]

Political union with Austria resulted in Czechoslovakia being uncomfortably surrounded by Germany on three sides. Hitler's next move was the absorption of Czechoslovakia's Sudetenland. Bohemia and Moravia, territories of what is today Czechoslovakia, had belonged to the First Empire since the Middle Ages, and German settlers had occupied the wild and virtually uninhabited mountain district in the west long before coming to Berlin. In 1918 they had formed independent provinces and asked to join Germany. A hurried occupation by Czech forces resulted, together with promises of local autonomy for the Sudeten-Germans from the government in Prague. The promises were never kept. Instead, the central government attempted to destroy the Germans economically. Pandit Nehru, visiting the Sudeten region in the early 1930s at the invitation of the German Social Democrats, wrote: "I have seen misery that reminds me of the worst scenes in India." Yet, even though by 1936 the Sudeten-Germans numbered slightly over 3 million—roughly one-fifth of the country's population—they controlled 40 percent of all national industries and, with some justification, were hostile to the Prague government. Henlein, the German-Sudeten leader, called on the Czech government to transfer the Sudeten region to the German Reich. His proposal was rejected, although Beneš, the Czech president, agreed that the Sudeten-Germans had some justification for complaining about the way they were being treated. Throughout the summer of 1938 the Sudeten-German Nazi party, supported vigorously by their kinsmen across the border, pressed for equal rights. In the end, their demands became so outrageous that Beneš flatly refused to discuss the matter further. Hitler threatened to occupy the country by force.

At this juncture British Prime Minister Neville Chamberlain flew to Berchtesgaden, Hitler's alpine retreat, to try reasoning with the German chancellor. Chamberlain and French Premier Edouard Daladier agreed to pressure the Czech government to surrender all districts in which more than 50 Germans resided. Hitler wanted more. Chamberlain flew to Germany a second time, meeting Hitler at Godesberg. Hitler's new demands were absurd. War with Germany loomed. France and Britain mobilized and recommended Czechoslovakia do the same.

Benito Mussolini stepped in as arbitrator and suggested another conference be held. Desperate to avoid war at any cost, Daladier and Chamberlain met with Hitler, Göring and Mussolini at Munich on 29 September. Hitler's new terms were only slightly modified, but they were accepted. Everyone signed. Chamberlain flew back to England with a worthless agreement in his pocket and the belief in his heart that he had brought back "peace in our time." The Czechs had been defeated without a shot being fired.

The Leibstandarte was ordered to participate in the occupation force that moved into the Sudetenland on 3 October. Kurt's company took the lead as they crossed the border to gain another bloodless victory for the Führer. Ecstatic Sudeten-Germans showered them with flowers, embraces and goodwill. At Carlsbad the Leibstandarte provided a guard of honour for Hitler's triumphal entry and speech. When the party ended, Kurt took his men back to Berlin. It was a proud moment to be a political soldier of the most powerful nation on earth.

The new border with Czechoslovakia as specified in the "Munich Pact" turned over the country's primary ring of fortress defences to Germany, the nation against which they had been designed. With their western defence in German hands the Czechs were vulnerable to invasion whenever Hitler decided the time was ripe. The 15th of March 1939 turned out to be that date. In total defiance of his Munich pledges, Hitler announced annexation of what remained of Czechoslovakia.

Wehrmacht forces rolled into the undefended country with such a display of military might that organized Czech resistance would have been impossible. Another bloodless conquest. Once more members of the Leibstandarte provided an honour guard for the Führer, this time in Prague, although judging by the cold reception given the Germans who rumbled into the city the guard was required more for Hitler's protection than to line the path of triumph.

The neighbouring territories of Bohemia and Moravia were declared protectorates of the Reich. Slovakia was permitted to retain its nominal independence and military force,[6] although as Hitler prepared for his invasion of Poland, Slovakian autonomy became a myth when German troops entered the country and declared martial law. Hitler had now become the most powerful dictator in Europe since Napoleon.

His next grab was the Lithuanian Baltic seaport of Klaipeda,* formerly owned by East Prussia but assigned to Lithuania under the Versailles treaty. "It belongs to Germany and I'll have it back," he said, and the Lithuanians bowed to the Nazi ultimatum and returned the area with its German-speaking majority to its original owner.

At home Hitler was now considered to be a political and military genius of the highest order. There seemed to be nothing he could not do once he set his mind to it. In spite of the ss terror, the concentration camps, the corrupt political practices, and the favouritism that flourished on all sides, most Germans were firmly behind their Führer. And why not? So far he had cost them nothing and given them everything. The country had gone back to work. People were prosperous. The future appeared golden. German honour had been finally restored, the country's lost territories recovered by the Third Reich.

The integrity of the new ss-vt had been seriously compromised by ss Brigadeführer Gottlob Berger, who had become head of ss recruiting in 1938. He was in fact founder of what was later to become the Waffen-ss, although ss generals in later years preferred to discount his contribution. Born in 1897, the son of a sawmill owner, Berger saw action in World War I as a lieutenant commanding a battle group and was severely wounded. A superb athlete and instructor, knowledgeable in military affairs, he had the typical Swabian tendency toward loquacity that tended to rub everybody the wrong way. Himmler was the exception. Berger shared Himmler's ambition of building the ss-vt into a full-scale army. The Wehrmacht was determined that such a threat to its prestige would never happen and did everything in its power to thwart Berger's expansion program, but "The Duke of Swabia"—as the ss called him—was a hard man to dissuade once he made up his mind. He knew exactly how to get around his Wehrmacht opposition.

Three categories of recruits were exempt from Wehrmacht service and responsible only to the Reichsführer-ss and Chief of the German Police: the concentration camp guards of the Totenkopfverbände, their reinforcements in times of war, and the *Ordnungspolizei*.† The Wehrmacht had no control over these organizations. Berger decided to use them as the basis upon which to build Himmler's private army. Two of Hitler's decrees provided the legitimacy for his action. The first, issued in August 1938, permitted that, in the event of war, units of the Totenkopfverbände would be used to reinforce the ss-vt. Then, in May 1939, Himmler was given additional authority to

---

*"Memel" in German.

†Literally, "Order Police"—regular uniformed police of the *Gendarmerie, Schutzpolizei,* Fire Police, and certain technical and auxiliary services.

call up 50,000 men of the Allgemeine-SS as Totenkopfverbände reinforcements.

By using the concentration camp guard units to reinforce the SS-VT, Berger managed to link the proudest SS unit with the most disreputable. This odious coupling was to have catastrophic results later for those who served willingly and unwillingly in what was to become the Waffen-SS. Many of the SS-VT commanders regarded the merger as an insult, but not one was brave enough to complain either to Berger or Himmler.

The Totenkopfverbände concentration camp guards were little better than thugs. Led by SS Gruppenführer Theodor Eicke, they had been created by him as the antithesis to militarism. Although both organizations developed from the party's original Action Squads—the *Politische Bereitschaften*—there was no similarity in their outlook. The SS-VT were trying valiantly to become a serious military organization, while Eicke's group assumed an anti-military stance.

Eicke, an irascible Alsatian with a coarse sarcastic tongue, had been a failure at everything he attempted, and he imbued his men with his life-long sense of deep resentment. In the Kaiser's army he served as a paymaster and developed a loathing for professional officers. The army had dismissed him. He failed as a policeman. The party considered him an argumentative troublemaker and had written him off. Only Himmler seemed to appreciate his value. Eicke viewed his collection of Totenkopf thugs as a counterbalance to the SS-VT. His men, for the most part, were uneducated country bumpkins, dull-witted aspiring policemen who had failed to make the grade, and the embittered unemployed. Whenever Eicke spouted tirades of hate against the Jews, Marxists or professional soldiers, they listened in respectful silence. They were brutal and they were vicious. And by decree they were now brothers-in-arms with the SS-VT.

10

Hitler turned covetously now to the east. The Free City of Danzig, a Baltic seaport situated on one arm of the Vistula River, had been incorporated into Prussia in 1793. With the exception of a seven-year period under Napoleon's rule, the city had been the capital of West Prussia and a part of Germany. But in 1919 the Treaty of Versailles awarded Danzig the status of "Free City" under a high commissioner appointed by the League of Nations. To give Poland a seaport the treaty allowed Polish jurisdiction of the area's railways and customs operations. In reality, this manoeuvre gave Danzig*

---

*Now known as Gdansk province, formed in 1945 out of Danzig and parts of Pomerania and the Polish province of Pomoroze.

to Poland together with a narrow strip of "no-man's-land" known as the "Polish Corridor" that separated the two countries. Hitler demanded road and railway access through the corridor to be followed by a plebiscite under international control.

Britain and France guaranteed Polish independence. The days of appeasement were over. Worse, England and France entered into negotiations with Russia to bolster their defence against the Reich.

Without some guarantee that Russia would not interfere with a German strike on Poland Hitler dared not invade. He had two choices: sign a nonaggression pact with Stalin in Moscow immediately, before the French and British concluded theirs, or abandon his claims to Danzig and the corridor and play a waiting game. He was too impatient to wait. Swallowing everything he had said previously about Russia's Bolshevist dictatorship, he ordered his foreign minister, Joachim von Ribbentrop, to fly to Moscow and cut a deal with Stalin.

Hitler's offer proved much more interesting than the moral grounds on which the French and British had approached the Russian dictator to sign their treaty. Poland would be divided more or less equally between Germany and Russia. Hitler would attack first in a lightning attack with 54 front-line divisions against Poland's 22 infantry divisions and seven cavalry brigades. When the bulk of Polish forces had been subdued in western Poland, the Red Army would invade from the east, stabbing in the back whatever Polish resistance remained.

It was exactly the type of double-dealing that Stalin appreciated. Germany took all the risks while Russia collected 50 percent of the winnings with minimum effort. While the French and British missions in Moscow were left cooling their heels, Germany and Russia signed a nonaggression pact on 23 August 1939. At last the way was cleared for Hitler to deliver Germany into war.

Like a giant curved scimitar of finely honed steel the German army lay bivouacked about the Polish frontiers in two huge army groups. Throughout the troubled month of August they waited for movement orders. The nights were warm and starlit, the days hot, dry and buzzing with insects and rumour.

The Leibstandarte had been assigned to Army Group South, under Gerd von Rundstedt. As a motorized regiment, it was placed under control of the 17th Infantry Division on the Eighth Army's right flank. In comparison to the mighty Wehrmacht masses, the Leibstandarte seemed very small potatoes indeed.

Late in August von Rundstedt, after inspecting his forward assault units, ordered extra reconnaissance forces to flesh out his Tenth Army's left wing, linking it closer to the Eighth Army. The Leibstandarte moved in to fill the frontal gap. Its assignment, in the event of hostilities—now a foregone conclusion—was to cross the Polish frontier near the Breslau area and capture all critical high ground behind the Prosna River.

The men passed their time playing games, checking and rechecking the motorbikes and writing letters home. "The tension is now electric," a soldier wrote. "When do we move? Will the Poles give in and surrender to the Führer's demands? A hundred questions. A hundred rumours each day and still no one knows anything. A sergeant from the unit next to us said he heard his major telling the company commander that September 1st is the big day. I'll be glad to move. The heat and flies from the horses tethered upwind from our camp will drive me mad if we don't get out of here soon."

The army waited. Finally, on 30 August, von Rundstedt received the coded words from German High Command setting D-day for 1 September at 0445 hours. Orders were passed down the army's chain of command to every unit: "Strike camp. Move out." By nightfall long columns of tanks, guns, trucks, horse-drawn supply wagons, motorcycles and marching men were heading toward Poland.

If the Colonel-General felt personal misgivings over his orders to invade, they were never recorded. Then 64, von Rundstedt had retired the previous summer after a career spanning 50 years of uninterrupted service to his country. During the first war he had held a variety of staff jobs and was regarded as steady, highly competent, but outspoken. When Hitler recalled him, stating, "I want only the best to command our new armies," von Rundstedt obediently reported for duty.

The Leibstandarte's new anti-tank company was awarded the spearhead position among the panzers for the attack, with Kurt Meyer riding at its point. He would be one of the first into Poland. An exciting thought, although he would have preferred the unit to be used exclusively in an armed forward reconnaissance role, operating more or less independently rather than being tied to the tanks.

"Does Poland have any tanks for us to destroy?" he asked Dietrich during the regiment's last briefing. Wouldn't his company be of more use in front of the army, seizing tactical opportunities as they presented themselves, rather than hanging back with the lumbering panzers? No luck. His request didn't even rate an indulgent explanation by Dietrich. The orders were final.

For two days and nights the men and machines moved up to the assembly areas located between five and eight kilometres from the frontier. Radio silence was strictly enforced. Goggled and steel-helmeted dispatch riders on noisy motorbikes hurtled up and down the dusty columns with last-minute orders for the battalion commanders. Everyone's spirits were high. More of a holiday atmosphere than that of an army marching to war.

One man wrote: "It feels more like another one of our usual exercises than a war. I suppose it will change but meantime I am enjoying every minute." Another enthusiastic letter home from an 18-year-old might have come from someone off on a camping expedition with the Hitlerjugend. "This is an exciting way to spend September. The weather is beautiful. No more 'spit and polish.' Even our NCOs are relaxed and enjoying themselves. Hope I brought enough film for my camera. There will be lots of interesting sights to photograph."

Shortly past midnight on 1 September, Kurt moved his company from the marshalling area and down the road to the border wire. They travelled without lights, slowly, each driver spacing himself from the blue exhaust flame of the vehicle in front. Engine noises staccatoed the night. Skies remained cloudless under a waning moon. They drew up a few hundred metres short of the customs barrier and parked well off the side of the road.

They waited. No smoking. Silence in the surrounding forests. Weapons were rechecked. Safety catches left on. One accidental shot and the enemy would be alerted. Already the Pole was the enemy. Friend or foe. For a soldier it was only a state of mind. An hour passed. Then two.

At 0430 hours they heard a faint rumble like the sound of a thunderstorm fretting just over the horizon. Tanks. Minutes passed. The rumbling grew. Two minutes to zero hour. The first tanks clanked past. Kurt raised his hand.

"*Achtung*! Panzers forward!" World War II was under way.

PART 5

THE WHIRLWIND

*In peace there's nothing so becomes a
  man
As modest stillness and humility:
But when the blast of war blows in our
  ears,
Then imitate the action of the tiger.*
WILLIAM SHAKESPEARE

BLITZKRIEG! Like a whirlwind they descended on Poland. Ninety minutes after crossing the border they were already six kilometres inland, the tanks beginning to fan out as they approached the first of the open flatlands. Impossible to defend but ideal for tanks. Where were the Polish tanks? Kurt raced ahead with his company searching for quarry.

He saw the first Polish dead lying in a ditch. Mangled bodies shredded by shellfire. Their khaki-green uniforms were soaked with blood. The Eagle of Poland badges on the dead men's field caps reflected the morning sunlight. His mind recorded their images more as a momentary curiosity than a horror. The motorcycles thundered past and were gone. In each village, chickens and farm animals scattered in terror. Where had the people gone? Were hidden faces peering from behind the closed windows? What had happened to the Polish tanks?

Once beyond the thin frontier defences, they collided with the first spirited resistance. Approaching the Prosna River, anti-tank guns of the Polish 10th Infantry Division opened up from fortified positions along the heights of the opposite shore. The morning mists drifting along both sides of the riverbank gave the Poles an advantage—their spotters were able to direct fire at specific targets, while the German tanks were forced to fire blind. Momentarily the advance slowed.

ss troops crossed the river and cleared the lower defences. Smoke mingled with the mist. There was a ten-minute wait while trucks brought in an assault battalion to scale the heights. When they were ready, the tanks ceased firing. The troops started up the slopes, each company covering the other as they leapfrogged forward. After a short bloody battle on the summit the Poles fled to regroup. The tanks moved forward. German dead were staked out for burial, the wounded carried carefully back down to the trucks.

The town of Boleslavecz was the next objective. It lay six kilometres to the northwest in an area defended by units of the 30th Infantry Division and 21st Infantry Regiment together with armoured cars of the Wolwyska Cavalry Brigade. They held the German advance to a crawl. ss companies that managed to smash through the Polish lines suddenly found themselves encircled and under fire. The Poles fought like demons in hand-to-hand combat, accepting terrible losses. One counterattack followed another.

They came toward the German lines nearly shoulder to shoulder, accepting the storm of bullets. Their men dropped like targets in a shooting gallery. As each fell, the gap left in the line was taken up by the men on either side. One of the German soldiers remembered: "They were brave. They came at us led by their officers and shouting their battle cry. Haaaaaah! It sounded like a long laugh. Over and over again they repeated it. When they came close enough we slaughtered them like sheep. Yes, they were very brave. But I think also very stupid." The outcome was never really in doubt. By ten that morning the Poles had given up. The Leibstandarte swept into town. Droves of prisoners were herded to the rear.

Their final objective for the day was Wieuroszov. It lay 11 kilometres farther north along the river. Leaving Boleslavecz, they split into three columns, the first advancing down a dusty dirt road that led to the town's eastern perimeter, a second swinging out past Opatov to make its way through the thick pine and birch forest and cut the road connection west of town. The main column proceeded down the riverbank in a direct route.

The terrain had changed from flat indefensible open countryside to a series of rolling hills and copses providing good defensive positions. Every bush and knoll was infested with small groups of determined Poles. Time after time the Leibstandarte's columns were forced to stop, dismount the men from the trucks, and attack the pockets of resistance. They were more of an annoyance than an impediment, although a number of casualties resulted. The delays kept them from reaching Wieuroszov until early evening. Picket patrols were established around the town's perimeter, and the men turned in for the night.

At the late-night briefing, Dietrich congratulated his company commanders.

The Polish campaign, showing the movements of Kurt Meyer's Leibstandarte.

Every objective had been taken and casualties kept to a minimum. Plans now called for the ss units to take up the flank guard position forward of the Wehrmacht's main force. Kurt had yet to fight an anti-tank battle. So far all he had run into were Polish cavalry units that acted as if they were still fighting the first war. They were no match for motorcycle riflemen and machine guns, even less so against tanks. Yet like packs of wolves circling a moving herd, they continued harassing the armoured columns even while realizing the hopelessness of their own position.

The western half of Poland formed a deep salient into German territory. Every Polish division committed to defending that salient was automatically outflanked by German armies to the north and south. Poland's High Command faced two choices: abandon the highly populated and industrialized western salient to make a stand farther inland or contest every foot of ground. They decided to make a fight of it. There wasn't a chance of winning anything beyond admiration for their courage.

On the ground they were outnumbered by more than 2 to 1 in men, over 4 to 1 in artillery and guns, and greater than 8 to 1 in armour. Their entire armoured forces consisted of two brigades of outdated eight-ton tanks and 29 companies of lightly armoured weapons carriers. Both sides employed horses for their supply wagons and guns. But where the Germans used as many trucks as animals, 90 percent of all wheeled transport in the Polish army remained horse-drawn.

Aerial reconnaissance of German ground movements by the Polish air force was nonexistent. Most of its planes had been bombed at their airfields by Luftwaffe Junkers 87 dive-bombers during the first hours of the German invasion. Warsaw sat undefended against Heinkel III bombers because all anti-aircraft guns had been moved out of the city to defend military positions. The country was unprepared for war. General mobilization had been ordered on 31 August. Only one-third of the country's 2 million first-line troops were in the field, the strategic passes over the Carpathia Mountains were unfortified, and, according to rumours, the country was full of German spies with underground radios. There were indeed German spies working inside Poland, but their numbers were highly exaggerated by the Germans themselves as a ploy for intimidation. Once the war started, the Poles used the rumours as an excuse for murdering thousands of Germans. These murders then became the pretext for the Germans murdering Polish civilians. Tit for tat.

During late August Polish generals had boasted to the nervous British Foreign Office that the German army was all bluff. They promised that if war came they would overwhelm them and march on to Berlin. Brave words. The Wehrmacht plan of attack had been organized in three stages. Step one encircled the Polish army in a double pincer movement east and west of Warsaw. Once the army had been contained, the next stage called for destroying its field forces in a confined area at a bend of the Vistula River. This was to be followed with destruction of fortresses around the Polish capital, concluding with the capture of Warsaw. OKH* estimated the entire operation should take no more than three weeks.

After a night spent beating off cavalry attacks around their perimeter defences, the Leibstandarte was on the road by 0600 hours, 2 September. Weeks of unseasonably hot dry weather had lowered rivers throughout the country. The Prosna, normally a natural barrier, proved no obstacle to the Eighth Army's main force when it forged across and headed to its next objective, a crossing of the Warta River.

"We fight from one shallow river to the next. Squadrons of their cavalry cover our flanks as we move. They are looking for openings. But horses are no match for tanks. Each time they come close our guns get their range. Down go their horses kicking and struggling. It's not a pretty sight. I feel sorry for the horses, not the Poles."

The Warta lay 32 kilometres farther east. Strongly fortified pillboxes and concrete gun emplacements lined its eastern bank. The river had been designated as the Polish army's primary defence line. By late afternoon, after two hours of bitter fighting, several holes were punched through the fortifications and the enemy began withdrawing.

Dietrich ordered the Leibstandarte ahead of the main column to fight its way through to the rail and road junction at Pabianice, a prosperous market town near the Ner River. Kurt roared off with his hunters. This was the sort of attack he enjoyed. Out in front of everybody. First man into the battlefield.

Six kilometres beyond the column they ran into a hailstorm of fire from the retreating enemy. Vehicles halted and men leapt out, scrambling for cover. The men took up position, using whatever they could find to keep clear of the zinging bullets. Kurt sent a dispatch rider back to advise the main force.

He lay in the grass beside his car, studying the rolling terrain with field glasses. The Rottenführer† beside him suddenly recoiled. "I've been hit, Haupsturmführer." Kurt pulled the man's bloodied hand away from his head. The bullet had grazed the temple just below the lip of his helmet. Kurt gave the wound an exploratory probe. It was nothing serious. Lots of blood but little damage. A medic was summoned forward to bandage the cut.

"A few more centimetres to the left and you'd be dead," the Rottenführer observed.

"Or a few more to the right and so would you."

---

*German Army High Command.
†Corporal.

North of Chestakova the Tenth Army began breaking through the Polish defences. On 3 September, lead elements from two panzer divisions crossed the Pilica River in a gap between the Polish armies of Lodz and Cracow. The panzers wheeled northeastward and headed for Warsaw. The German pincers were beginning to close on Poland's capital. Quickly, Polish High Command issued orders for their armies to fall back on a defence line running from Szczercov to Lenkava deep within Polish territory. The armies began withdrawing into a long, narrow and, although neither side realized it at the time, indefensible pocket allowing no escape.

Yet all was not clear sailing for the Wehrmacht. During D-day plus 4, von Rundstedt's intelligence reports showed seven Polish divisions in retreat before Army Group North between the Warta and Bzura rivers. Their presence posed an immediate threat to his flank. He ordered Army Group South to shift its front and meet the withdrawing Polish forces. Hastily, an assault on the city of Lodz was organized by the Eighth Army to hold the thrust against its northern flank while the centre and right wings were ordered to smash the enemy as they approached Lodz.

Pabianice, meanwhile, was proving a tough nut to crack for the Leibstandarte. Designated as part of the Pole's secondary defence ring outside Lodz, the town's garrison had recently been equipped with heavy anti-tank guns and bolstered by the 2nd Kaniov Rifle Regiment plus a number of units from those Polish divisions withdrawing before Army Group North. Their morale was high, and not without justification. For three days and nights they forced the Germans to contest every foot of ground at a bloody price.

Every SS battalion was placed in the line. For the first time the troops found they were fighting armed civilians as well as Polish riflemen. These civilians—mostly local farmers and woodsmen—knew every foot of the surrounding countryside and used it to good effect. Combining marksmen's skills with individual initiative, they concealed themselves in well-camouflaged positions and waited for the Germans to appear.

Their choice of tall, isolated treetops and open hillside dugouts was suicidal, but so intense was their hate for the invader that they gave their lives willingly. Their favourite targets were motorcycle dispatch riders, small five- to eight-man patrols travelling on foot or in staff cars driving the roads without escort. To combat the sharpshooters, effective countermeasures were swiftly developed. One of the Leibstandarte related: "They clung like body lice in the tops of tall trees. Every bush and wood became suspect. Two grenades or a few clips of ammunition was usually enough to settle our nerves. Either the Pole dropped out or enough foliage blew away that we could see the branches over which he was draped."

Large cultivated fields of corn and sunflowers surrounded the Pabianice district. Crops were desperately in need of rain. The tall, shimmering harvest now became a killing ground for Germans and Poles alike. Under hot cloudless skies and in uniforms stinking of sweat and fear, small groups stalked each other through the crackling plantings. Each waited patiently for the other to close within point-blank range. A sharp exchange of grenades and gunfire followed, accompanied by cries from the wounded. Then both sides regrouped in another section of another field where the same moves were repeated.

The SS began wearing their camouflage jackets and helmet covers. They were uncomfortably hot, but their colours blended beautifully with the green maize and sunflower stalks. One weary Unterscharführer* wrote: "Every field had nests of Poles. Some of their dugouts were connected by underground tunnels. No sooner had we blown up one with a grenade bundle than up they popped from another. Why a few dugouts even had crops growing on top of them and were impossible to see until you stepped on one! It took hours to clear the fields in our sector but it had to be done. We couldn't leave any of the enemy behind to stab us in the back."

On 7 September, Pabianice became Army Group South's main objective. The 23rd Panzer Regiment led the initial assault at midmorning. Polish fire was intense and well directed. The German tanks withdrew, leaving a number of blazing wrecks. New orders from Division instructed two Leibstandarte companies to pass through the tanks and take the Polish defences on foot. Under heavy artillery and mortar barrage the men moved forward in smooth tactical assault formations. They swept through the first line of defenders, flinging aside a hastily mounted counterattack as they reached the centre of town. Units on the flanks of the attack were unable to keep up with the main thrust, however, and the spearhead force had to leave small sections behind to shore up the walls of the salient that had been created. With the loss of these "drop offs" and steadily mounting casualties, the attack soon ran out of gas. The Poles charged in for a counterattack, using assorted infantry and cavalry units.

As one furious attack followed another, slowly the Leibstandarte was forced to give ground, backing down the same streets, past the same houses they had taken earlier. The Polish spearheads suffered terrible casualties. A final thrust at the edge of town brought them into the field where the Leibstandarte had set up its headquarters. Cooks, clerks and drivers, along with every available NCO and officer, were pressed into the battle.

Several times the Poles came within a whisker of overrunning the regimental command post and cutting off contact between HQ and the troops, but the Leibstandarte stood firm. Shortly past noon the attackers withdrew to regroup and replace the losses sustained by their assault companies. With relief the Germans did likewise.

Kurt had been in the thick of the fighting around regimental headquarters, pouring machine-gun fire into the relentlessly advancing Poles. "I jumped

*Sergeant.

up and shot into the advancing tanks. . . . To my right a Grenadier of 13th Company was shot through the neck while he fired. . . . Suddenly I was on the ground again with a slug in my left shoulder."

"You've been hit," a soldier told him as the Poles started to withdraw. Someone helped him to the dressing station. He had a grazing wound similar to the one his Rottenführer had collected two days before. Plenty of blood but not much damage.

Kate heard the news in Offleben. She had just given birth to Irmtraud, their third daughter, and was still confined to bed. Alma had been taking care of both Kate and the girls. Both women were enormously relieved.

At 1430 hours the Poles mounted a last desperate charge.

"They came at us through the smoke with heads held high like missionaries seeing a vision. They fell in hundreds until only a dozen or so were left. These too kept coming, looking neither left nor right. I hadn't the heart to kill the last of them. But then they were down and it was all over."

Pabianice garrison surrendered. Later that evening the SS entered the town. Everywhere the Poles were falling back. Tanks of the Tenth Army raced through a gap in the line at Petrov left by the retreating forces, capturing the country's best road leading to Warsaw. More motorized infantry were needed to support the tanks for the final assault, so the Leibstandarte was transferred to the Tenth Army's 4th Panzer Division. Forward elements reached the Warsaw suburb of Ochota at 1715 hours on 8 September.

2

The liner *Duchess of Athol* sailed from England for Canada on 8 September with Harry, Margo and the boys. Two days before, Harry had taken a morning train up to London with the rest of the Canadian officer contingent attending Staff College—Captains Sparling, Mann,* Lister and Snow—and reported in to Colonel Logie at Canada House on Trafalgar Square for instructions. Harry was handed steamship tickets and orders to report back to his regiment in Winnipeg.

Two days didn't give him much time to sell the car, terminate the house lease, pack the family's belongings and be ready to catch the boat-train for Liverpool. He took a noon train back to Camberley and, after getting Margo started on the packing, drove over to the Staff College. The commandant, Major-General Paget, brought the Canadians together for a brief address.

"We were told that we all would get our p.s.c. [passed Staff College certificate] and dagger. He bid us au revoir and said: 'This war will be won

---

*Later Brigadier-General Sparling, who sat with Harry on the Meyer courtmartial, and Major-General Mann, one of the principal planners of the Dieppe raid.

by morale. As staff officers you can contribute to high morale by personal liaison by insisting on a high standard of training; by facilitating honours and awards for the fighting troops.' It is quite obvious General Headquarters is at the College. Saw His Majesty, Lord Gort and Dill* in the hall. There are innumerable senior dugouts being assembled not to mention the steady arrival and departure of staff cars all driven by women of the Auxiliary Force."

Paget then handed each of the officers his final gradings and report to sign. Harry's stated in part: "A cheerful and popular officer with plenty of practical commonsense. Has a shrewd brain and a good working knowledge of his profession. Speaks well and with humour. A good team worker. Has definite powers of leadership. Is imperturbable and would stand up well to strain. Will make a good commander." He couldn't have asked for better if he'd written it himself.

They left the next day for London. "What a thrill to be leaving Camberley and its chiseling tradesmen. Got established in the Euston Hotel. A lousy joint. We're informed that sailing is postponed indefinitely. What to do? Go back to Camberley? No house. No car. Baggage all sitting dockside in Liverpool. Decided to stay put. The A.R.P. [air raid precaution] arrangements and dozens of barrage balloons drifting above the city look most reassuring."

The delay was due to the convoy assembling in the Mersey River estuary. A week dragged by under brilliant cloudless skies. Boredom and frustration set in. Finally, on 13 September—Margo's birthday—word arrived that the convoy was ready to sail. The boat-train departed Euston Station at 0730 hours the following morning. There were no arrangements for feeding passengers on the five-hour nonstop trip. The compartments were packed with anxious parents, fidgeting children and howling babies.

At Liverpool they queued for an hour and a half while officious bureaucrats checked everyone's ticket. Then they went aboard to find four bunks in a narrow second-class cabin with a single porthole. A teenage steward took charge of the boys. In late afternoon the ship cast off and dropped anchor opposite New Brighton at the mouth of the Mersey. The evening conversations among passengers centred around German submarines. Were there any about? Would they have the gall to torpedo another helpless passenger liner? (The *Athenia* had been torpedoed on 4 September.) The consensus was that they would. The Captain promised a departure for the following afternoon.

Next morning the *Duchess of York* passed upstream to pick up passengers. Like the *Athol* she too had been painted a solid grey and mounted one 4.7-inch gun forward and a four-barrel Bofors anti-aircraft gun aft. An hour later four minesweepers passed downstream on their way to sweep the convoy

---

*General Gort, vc, led the British Expeditionary Force to France in 1939; General Sir John Dill led i Corps of the BEF in France.

out to the Irish Sea. After lunch the ship weighed anchor and followed the procession of vessels heading for the submarine nets at the mouth of the Mersey. A navy sloop laden with depth charges slipped in behind the liner.

"Through glasses I can see large work parties on the northern shore filling sandbags along the beaches for use in Liverpool.... At about 1600 the *Duchess of York* overtakes us . . . out we go. The first Atlantic convoy of the war. The sea is calm. Visibility excellent—too damn excellent. Everyone excited. A very grim boat drill.... Life belts to be worn or carried at all times."

East of the Isle of Man they overtook the four minesweepers. Suddenly, against the bright light of the western sky one of their destroyer escorts hoisted a black flag and veered away at full speed. In seconds the convoy changed course 45 degrees and increased speed. The ship's guns were manned. Life jackets checked. The air was electric with suppressed excitement. A large mushroom of water erupted close astern of the destroyer, followed seconds later by a huge waterspout. Two depth charges. Two dull explosions on the flat oily sea.

"Some claim it shook the ship. I didn't notice it. The destroyer turns at full speed, racing back some hundreds of yards then turns again. Her black flag is lowered. She makes the signal 'oil.' The convoy resumes course. As darkness falls, the sea continues calm and visibility still too damn good. The ships, spaced at half mile intervals, are clearly visible although not a light can be seen."

Two days later a U-boat sank the British aircraft carrier *Courageous*. By then the convoy was well out in the Atlantic. The boat arrived at Quebec City on 22 September in bright sunshine and tied up next to the *Empress of Britain*. Every ship's whistle and siren in the harbour greeted the arrival. Most passengers remained on board until the ship docked next day in Montreal.

Harry deposited Margo and the children at the Windsor Hotel while he went over to Military District Headquarters to arrange for some expense money and train tickets to Winnipeg. HQ teemed with activity. Volunteers were enlisting by the thousands. "Frenchies too, believe it or not," a harried recruiting captain told him. "Problem is, we've got nothing to give anyone in the way of gear. Hell of a way to fight a war, isn't it?" Recruits were being told to go home and await further orders. The Liberal government of Mackenzie King had waited too long before "screwing up enough political courage to order what was needed to equip a proper military force."

Back at the hotel he phoned his father in Wolfville. Laffy sounded terribly down. The loss of his leg had made him morose and the crutches hurt his arms after a few brief steps. Margo got on the phone and did her best to cheer him up. It was no use. His circulatory problems were getting worse. He gave himself a year at the outside. And what of Gil, Harry inquired? "Your brother borrowed enough money for passage to England the day Hitler invaded Poland. He plans to join the Gloucestershires as a private—if they'll have him. I wished him luck."

So did Harry.

Margo's father and the ubiquitous Major Ross were at the station to meet them when they arrived in Winnipeg two days later. The day was overcast with a raw wind blowing out of the northwest, the first whisper of winter. Robert Muir and Ross insisted that they all move into the big house until Harry knew where he would be posted. A school for the boys was less than a five-minute walk.

The war news wasn't good. The Polish government had fled into Rumanian exile. The German army offered to evacuate all civilians in Warsaw, but the Poles refused. The city would not surrender. The Luftwaffe began bombing Warsaw, one sortie after another, ruthlessly and systematically obliterating huge residential sections of the city. Hitler had kept his word with Stalin. On 28 September the German-Soviet Boundary and Friendship Treaty divided Poland between them. France, Britain and their allies remained helpless.

Harry was ordered to prepare a lecture course on Staff College ideas for his regiment and organize an officers' training program at the University of Manitoba. From all parts of the province keen young men came flocking in to join their local militia units while the units worked frantically to organize themselves into active regiments. Chaos became epidemic. The few Permanent Force officers available rushed from one militia group to the next, trying to create some order out of the shambles.

By mid-October the weather turned very cold and still the shortages of clothing and equipment had not been resolved. Harry complained about "the disgraceful deficiencies . . . RCHA† and PPCLI‡ without caps. Cameron Highlanders drilling in civilian clothes for God's sake! And no issue boots. Two Bren guns in the entire district and we've been at war nearly two months. . . . Troops having to find their own billets all over Winnipeg." For a nation mobilizing to fight a war, the country was in a dismal state of preparedness.

What arms were available were nearly all of 1914–18 vintage. Mobile transport was virtually nonexistent. There were only 16 light tanks in the country. Yet on the day Hitler invaded Poland the Department of National Defence issued an order authorizing the creation of the "Canadian Active Service Force'" (CASF). It was to be composed of two divisions. Enlistment was voluntary, with most men entering directly from the Active Militia.

Late in September the Minister of National Defence announced that the 1st Division would be sent overseas while the 2nd Division was to be "kept under arms as a further measure of preparedness." A week later Maj.-Gen. A.G.L. McNaughton, former chief of the General Staff, was appointed as

---

†Royal Canadian Horse Artillery.
‡Princess Patricia's Canadian Light Infantry.

"Inspector General of the Units of the 1st Canadian Division." During the next two months McNaughton travelled from coast to coast, assessing the quality of training and unit organizations that were soon to be taken under his command.

On 20 October the War Office in London was advised that the 1st Division would be ready to sail early in December. A British suggestion that the troops be sent directly to southern France was vetoed by Ottawa. Canadian Army Command understood only too well the deficiencies of the men and equipment they intended shipping overseas. It was all beginning to resemble 1914 and the Salisbury Plain, with masses of poorly equipped and briefly trained Canadian soldiers looking to the British army for their salvation. Only this time the War Office allocated Camp Aldershot in Hampshire for the Canadian occupation.

Along with others of the Permanent Force who had been handed the task of assembling the new snowballing army, Harry worried. "I have fought the idea off but it grows persistently that the fine Empire spirit of Canada in this party is inspired by selfish motives. . . . Politicians make pretty speeches about the wonderful aid we are giving in resources but . . . all are being paid for by the British taxpayer. They are to make Canada the training centre for the Empire air forces. Secretly everyone rejoices because they see financial benefits. . . . Meanwhile thousands of splendid fellows drill furiously in poor clothing having given up good jobs to kill Germans. . . . It's going to be mighty interesting to see how it all works out. The men of the CASF are wonderful material. Wish I could say the same for our politicians."

3

For his wound and bravery under fire Kurt was awarded the Iron Cross Second Class. The German army had completed the most successful tactical military encirclement in history. At a bend on the Bzura River the armies of Poland had been annihilated. The last stage of the battle was the capture of Warsaw and surrounding fortresses. The Leibstandarte was shifted to the Modlin area to attack the fortress garrisons still insanely holding out.

Near Guzov, Hitler and Himmler visited the SS troops. They arrived in a convoy of Mercedes open touring cars with 20 bodyguards armed to the teeth who rode in front and back of the Führer's vehicle. The motorcycle company of the Leibstandarte was drawn up for inspection. Dietrich and Himmler made the rounds with Hitler, Dietrich introducing them to his officers, most of whom Hitler knew already. He gave the men a fiery pep talk before driving off to inspect another unit.

Dive-bombers from the Luftwaffe's 4th Air Fleet together with a massive artillery bombardment blasted the Poles inside the Modlin fortresses. Warsaw surrendered on 27 September, freeing the Germans to turn their full fury against the forts. Polish General Thomme surrendered two days later. All up and down the front the big guns fell silent. Soldiers on both sides sighed with relief. The campaign was over.

Then, strangely, after weeks of parched dry weather—"Hitler weather" the Poles had called it—it began to rain. A cool steady rain that cleansed the earth, redeemed the harvest and washed the bloated bodies of animals and men that had lain black and rotting under the sun.

Throughout the weeks in Poland Kurt had agitated for transfer to a more active role than hunting tanks. Several written requests had been refused. Dietrich was much too busy to waste time with a bellyaching subaltern who thought himself misplaced.

"I am fed up with this kind of a posting. Secretly, I follow the panzers." Being CO of a tank hunter company was for Kurt a personal disaster. Only once, on the road beyond Wieuroszov, had he been allowed out front of the main column. He had visions of himself condemned forever to hunting tanks. "I was quite worried . . . and reapplied for a transfer." This time he stressed his years of motorcycle training and mental attitude toward being a panzerman, a leader not a follower in the field of battle. Good dramatic stuff designed to catch Dietrich's attention. He crossed his fingers.

The Leibstandarte received orders transferring it to Prague. There were parades, bands, movie cameras and speeches of welcome and congratulations. Time was needed for a refit, for replacements of those men who had been lost, a period for retraining and—best of all—leave. Kurt left at once by car to Offleben.

As always, his first stop was a brief visit to his father's grave. If only Otto had lived. How proud he would have been. The townspeople waved when he drove past. He belonged to them too. A real battle-scarred warrior home on leave after a victorious campaign with an Iron Cross on his chest. Someone ran to tell Kate that he was back.

She was standing in the kitchen nursing the baby. Quite suddenly she felt his eyes upon her. She turned and saw him leaning in the doorway, a smile tugging at his lips.

"How long have you been standing there?"

"Long enough to know what a beautiful woman I married." He kissed her and took the baby. Alma nodded approvingly. Tiny fingers clutched his thumb, then howls of red-faced outrage for having been interrupted at mealtime. He passed the bundle back to Kate.

"The unit has been transferred to Prague for rest and a refit, Mutti. We'll be there several months, I imagine. Too long to be without you. I want you with me."

Kate shook her head. "Quite impossible."

"Why?"

"How would I manage? I've just had a baby. We must try to be practical."

Over the next days Alma watched them together. Her son's return was like a tonic to the household. However, the excitement of his sudden reappearance had upset Kate emotionally and she could no longer breastfeed the baby. Wisely, Alma took her daughter-in-law aside for a talk.

"Spend every available hour with him, Kate. Of course you must go to Prague. The future is so uncertain. There will be another war and who knows how long he will survive?"

Kate agreed. Alma made arrangements for a wet nurse and promised to look after the children. Kurt and Kate left for Czechoslovakia. It was like a second honeymoon.

When they arrived at the base in Prague his troops were horrified. Every man in the company knew that his wife had just given birth to a baby girl. So who was this beautiful bit of fluff he had riding with him in the car? Shameful! Then she stepped out and they saw it was Kate. Red faces all around. "Welcome to Prague, Frau Meyer."

Kurt's transfer approval was waiting for him when he reported in. Command of a motorcycle company. The mobile spearhead for the new Leibstandarte reinforced regiment. First into battle. Motto: "The motor is our best weapon." Brimming with enthusiasm, he went to work with the men on a training program designed to make theirs the best tactical unit in the German army.

While Kurt worked with his boys, Kate spent her holidays shopping and sightseeing. Evenings and weekends they spent together, still very much in love. Which made everything worthwhile.

Himmler's RUSHA, VOMI and RKF branches of the SS had moved into Poland upon conclusion of hostilities.* With 88,000 square kilometres of new territories incorporated into the Reich, there was much to be done. Resettlement plans were already drawn up and ready to be put into action.

These new acquisitions included Eastern Pomerania, Poznania and Slask provinces, plus large portions of Cracow, Lodz, Warsaw and Bialystok provinces not already taken over by the Russians under the Hitler-Stalin agreement. A reign of terror began, aimed at exterminating the Polish nation. People were driven out of entire cities, their property confiscated by the SS. Five hundred thousand Poles were shipped to Germany to work as agricultural labourers, 100,000 for employment in German factories, while thousands of others either died en route or were executed as a danger to the New Order. To fill the empty spaces, Germans were brought in from the Baltic states, Czechoslovakia and Germany.

---

*See Appendix C, "Principal Organizations within the SS."

The contents of the Warsaw University library were burned. All textbooks of Polish language, literature, history and religion were destroyed to prevent private continuation of such studies. Any opposition was met with swift reprisals. Designated as an "inferior race," the Poles were to be allowed to exist only as serfs and beasts of burden for their Aryan masters.

Jews from Germany, Austria and Czechoslovakia were deported to a new "Jewish Reservation"' set up in Lublin Province. Already inhabited by 2.5 million Poles crammed into its 23,300 square kilometres, the area became a nightmare of overcrowding, hunger, filth, disease and death.

In the country's eastern territories, Russia preferred a less blatant form of occupation. It held a plebiscite to determine the percentage of Polish citizens in favour of annexation by Russia. To no one's surprise the results turned out to be unanimously behind the Russian occupation. Mass deportations followed. Over 2 million Poles and Jews were shipped to Siberia.

On 8 November Winnipeg turned cold and windy. Thin swirls of "snow devils" danced across the parade square where the Princess Pats and Royal Canadian Horse Artillery were drawn up for inspection by General McNaughton and Brigadier Pearkes, VC. It was much too cold for long speeches.

"After the General had taken the salute everyone retired indoors to get warm. . . . Colonel Sansom* advised that I am promoted to Brigade Major of the 1st Infantry Brigade now assembling in Toronto . . . finally I am to be involved. War is a young man's game and at 37 I was beginning to worry that someone in Ottawa might think me too old to be of use."

Proudly, Margo affixed the shiny new major's "crowns" to all his uniforms. The bumbling Major Ross shook his hand "for the first time as an equal, he told me . . . poor chap is obviously going crackers." Five days later orders arrived for him to report at once to Col. Armand Smith† in Toronto. The rumour mill claimed the 1st Division would be sailing within the month. He decided to take Margo with him for what little time he had left in Canada.

Robert Muir, Major Ross and the children went to the station to see them off on the evening train. The boys wanted to go along too. They were having a rough time at school with their English accents and strange manners. Harry assured them their mother would be back in a couple of weeks and that in the meantime "Granddad Bob" was in command.

Hugs and kisses for the children. Last feel of masculine stubble chin, last taste of cigarette and whisky lips. The mammoth engine shusshed and hissed. Last moments of self-conscious conversation. The train was already moving

---

*Later Lieut.-Gen. E.W. Sansom, commander of II Canadian Corps at its inception. Sansom served in World War I as a lieutenant-colonel. In 1939 he was director of training.
†Chairman of the Board of E.D. Smith & Sons, Winona, Ontario, his family's business interest.

when Harry jumped onto the bottom step of the sleeping car. "Be good, you two," he called to his sons and with a wave was gone.

Two days later he reported in to his brigadier, Colonel Smith, whose confirmation of brigade command had thus far not been accompanied by a corresponding promotion in rank. Harry liked him immediately as "the sort of fellow who makes you feel at once you could never let him down." During the first war Smith had served as a major, earning an MC for bravery in France. After 1919 he had devoted his time and energy to the family business while remaining in the Active Militia. He was 11 years older than Harry.

After introducing Harry to the rest of his staff and giving him a quick tour through the Canadian National Exhibition grounds where the thousands of troops were being processed, Smith treated Harry and Margo to a sumptuous dinner at the Royal York Hotel. The hotel's fashionable dining room was the best Toronto had to offer.

The days that followed were packed with feverish activity, rushing from one meeting to another, ensuring that the newly activated regiments would be ready to move when the order was given to board the trains for Halifax.

"Went with Brig. and Gen. McNaughton to inspect the Hastings and Prince Edward Regiment in Picton. 'Hasty Pees' they call themselves. Lovely drive. McNaughton talked incessantly about some gadget he'd designed for use by the new anti-tank company that's to be formed. I couldn't make head nor tail out of it. . . . The Hasty Pees seem a really good outfit. . . . Back to Toronto for dinner. . . . The advance parties of Toronto Scottish leaving tonight for Montreal embarkation."

Meanwhile, at Canada House in London, Brig. H.D.G. Crerar* set up a liaison with the British War Office and made arrangements for billeting and supplying the arriving Canadian troops. Space was rented for Canadian Military Headquarters (CMHQ) to be housed in the Sun Life Assurance building adjoining Canada House. By mid-November an advance party under Col. P.J. Montague† had arrived in England to staff the new CMHQ. Unlike 1914 when the entire 1st Division had been shipped overseas in one mighty convoy, it was decided to lessen the risk of German torpedos by sending the men in batches of seven to eight thousand. At the end of November everything had been arranged for the voyage.

"Brig. threw a spectacular luncheon at the University Club for everyone. . . . Phone call from Ottawa ordering Brig. and self onto midnight train to join Divisional Commander in flight to Valcartier. Balls up somewhere. . . . Spent morning at Div. HQ discussing equipment supply arrangements

---

*Later General Crerar, commander of the First Canadian Army. He was commandant at RMC at the outbreak of war. A former director of military operations and intelligence, he played a large part in drafting Canadian war plans.
†Later Lieut.-Gen. the Hon. Percival Montague, chief of staff at CMHQ in London and judge advocate-general of the Canadian Army Overseas.

with McNaughton and Sansom. Both are worried about our preparedness to fight. . . . If they're worrying where does that leave the rest of us? Midway through the meeting McNaughton had another attack of 'the gadgets' and stopped to demonstrate with several paper clips. Very clever idea for loading vehicles on board ship without subsequent damage during rough weather."

Finally, Lord Tweedsmuir, the governor-general, arrived in Toronto to inspect the 1st Division, now up to strength and ready for departure.

"Said farewell to Margo who took it like a soldier. . . . Left Toronto amid much cheers, tears and alcohol set to the tune of bagpipes. The heat of the train is terrific and the troops have smashed out about 50 windows for fresh air." They ran through the night, pausing only for crew changes and to take on coal and water. Next morning was bright and very cold, the snow piled high under the lines of telegraph poles that paralleled the track. The men settled down, especially those nursing hangovers. Blankets were stuffed into the broken windows.

A vast armada of ships lay at anchor in Bedford Basin as the train rumbled into Halifax. Besides merchant vessels awaiting convoy assignments, there were a number of capital ships from the Royal Navy: HMS *Eagle* and *Resolute* along with several cruisers and numerous destroyers. The outer harbour was crowded with more naval vessels: HMS *Repulse*, two French battleships and a score of Canadian and British escorts. Tied dockside were the five passenger liners detailed to carry the troops: *Aquitania, Monarch of Bermuda, Duchess of Bedford, Empress of Britain* and *Empress of Australia*. The men piled out of their trains and were marched aboard.

"We got established on the *Empress of Australia*. The Brig. occupies the Royal Suite while I share a large double room with tiled bathroom done in apple green. The NCOs have the First Class accommodation but our Brigade HQ troops are down forward where conditions are lousy. . . . I hope it's only cockroaches."

The ships were all still fitted out for peacetime travelling. An unbelievable luxury for the men and not one to be repeated for subsequent troop movements when the vessels were converted to pack in five times the number. For three days they remained alongside the dock, boarding troops from the trains still arriving from across the country. The weather turned cold with a damp biting northwest wind. There was a series of shipboard conferences among staffs, with 2nd Brigade on the *Duchess of Bedford* and 3rd Brigade and Divisional Staff sharing the luxury of the *Aquitania*, a four-stacker Cunard liner.

Harry had hoped to find a few hours to slip away to Wolfville to visit his father. But it was impossible. He settled for a phone call.

"I could have Agnes drive me into Halifax," Laffy suggested. Harry said no. He couldn't promise they'd be able to meet even then. Laffy sighed with disappointment. Harry "felt like a heel for having called him in the first place. . . . He is terribly down. His last words were to ask me to keep an eye out for Gil."

A succession of church parades for the religious denominations on board filled the morning of 10 December. Then a British cruiser appeared passing down the line, her crew standing smartly on deck. In her wake sailed the French submarine *Achilles*. A round of cheers went out to the Frenchmen. Four Canadian destroyers followed as the convoy set sail.

"The day is dull, the sea glassy and the weather sharp. At noon the battleship HMS *Resolute* appeared from behind the skirts of George's Island and moved slowly out. Simultaneously the *Duchess of Bedford* backed out with tugs. She departed twenty minutes later. We swung away, turned and followed. Then, as fast as the tugs could handle them the others were underway. . . . We were roundly hooted by hundreds of cars packed all along the shore of Point Pleasant Park. The troops cheered and waved . . . the pipers of the Toronto Scottish marched around the promenade deck playing 'Road to the Isles' and their regimental march, 'Blue Bonnets over the Border'. . . . Passed through the double submarine net that swung in behind each ship. It stretches from York Redoubt fort across to the McNab Island light. . . . The aircraft carrier *Eagle* and HMS *Repulse* are about ten hours ahead of us. By 1430 hours the whole convoy was marshalled off Cape Sambro and headed northeast on an oily sea. A formation of RCAF* patrol aircraft escorted us until dark."

Next morning in mild showery weather four French navy submarines were observed through the thin fog. They were looking for the German warship *Deutschland*, believed to be cruising the area. Overnight their destroyer escort had been increased to six ships. Later they lost sight of the convoy and for four days sailed alone. But as dawn came up on 16 December, two destroyers were again riding herd on them. A great cheer of relief went up all over the vessel. During the morning a Southampton Class cruiser joined them. The *Empress of Australia* altered course to the southeast and came up on the rest of the convoy.

"Throughout the day we had in view the *Repulse, Resolute*, an aircraft carrier, a cruiser and ten destroyers. Overhead several Sunderland flying boats patrolled the convoy's perimeter. . . . It is a sight never to be forgotten."

At 12 noon next day they passed through the submarine net on the River Clyde below Greenoch, Scotland. A marker buoy bobbed over the spot where a German U-boat lay after trying to force entry. Twenty minutes later the ship dropped anchor amidst an imposing array of naval craft. "Besides our own escort there were HMS *Hood*, several Ramillies Class battleships, County Class cruisers, innumerable merchant cruisers of Cunard A boat class and smaller P & O liners. . . . At 1400 hours we parted reluctantly with the *Empress*. Hated to leave—the luxury, the good food and above all her superb crew. I saw the second officer shake every one of our 1,250 men by the hand.

---

*Royal Canadian Air Force.

Even the dour first officer, a Scot, embraced and kissed the Brig. goodbye! Captain Purt beamed down from his bridge and waved. We were all disembarked onto a single tender which was a bit of a jam. Then at 1515 hours Brig. Smith stepped ashore at Gourock, followed by me—the first Canadians of the 1st Division. We are ready to go to war."

4

Kurt's new 15th Kradschützen Company had been handpicked. Given authority to choose the men he wanted, he selected only the best. Many came from his old 14th Company, including Obersturmführer Hugo Kraas, his second-in-command. None of the transferees complained. Meyer was regarded as a stern but not inflexible commanding officer who went out of his way to ensure his boys were happy and to lend an ear when any of them needed help.

His rigid unbending Prussian image had been created by a stiff-back posture. Always self-conscious about his height, he had developed the habit of standing or walking very erect, like a man wearing a back brace or cast. Others might slouch during off-duty hours, but as one of the shortest men in the entire regiment next to Dietrich, Kurt refused to make himself a spectacle for comment. Years later, the injuries from his fall still bothered him, especially when the weather turned cold and damp. At meals on those days when the pain in his hips was bad, he remained seated until the others left the table so that no one would notice the difficulty he had getting to his feet. Stern-faced and ramrod straight, he walked like a man in constant pain, which most of the time he was. Yet no one heard him complain.

He had a direct no-nonsense manner of speaking that many found unnerving. A diplomat he would never be, but he commanded respect. He spoke High German without a regional accent, which gave him a slight advantage over others who had never been able to shake their Upper German dialects, such as the men from Swabia or Bavaria. "A martinet with a warm heart," one of his soldiers described him.

After the reorganization and training period at Prague the Leibstandarte moved to Koblenz during November for a month of tough tactical exercises with General Guderian, originator of the panzer *Blitzkrieg* in Poland. Kate kissed Kurt goodbye and went home to Berlin with the children.

Guderian had a passion for catchphrases. His HQ was peppered with plaques and signs that stated the obvious: SWEAT SAVES BLOOD—BETTER TO DIG 60 FEET THAN BE 6 FEET UNDER—THE TANK MOTOR IS AS USEFUL A WEAPON AS ITS CANNON—and other assorted bromides. The new training program stressed rapid movement of men and equipment supported by minimum supply lines. In each of their field exercises speed became the criterion for success. Speed above all else! Detailed emphasis was placed on the swiftest method for seizing and holding bridges in enemy territory, although no one suggested who the enemy might be.

That winter was unseasonably cold. Deep snow and constant winds streamed down from the North Sea. *Engländer* weather they called it and bundled comfortably into their winter clothing issue. In December Hitler visited their winter quarters. After congratulating them on their turnout, he stated obliquely that there were other battles still to be fought in order to vindicate German honour: "Soon you will be fighting in lands upon which the blood of your fathers has been shed."

Battle hardened, superbly trained and convinced of their own invincibility, the men of the Leibstandarte were ready to go back to war.

In England things were in a frightful mess as the country shifted frantically into a wartime economy and troops from the dominions and colonies started arriving from all parts of the Empire. For the Canadians, used to dry indoor heat in midwinter, the damp, cold English climate came as a physical shock. Accommodations at Camp Aldershot were primitive and badly overcrowded. Beds were folding cots with biscuit mattresses. Heating came from open-grate fires in each barracks; those near the fire roasted while the men at the ends froze. The troops complained loudly and often. The Brits were not amused.

Hoare Belisha, British secretary for war, arrived on 21 December for an inspection of the Toronto Scottish Regiment. Several purse-lipped generals from the War Office were in attendance.

"I think they expected to see something close to bow and arrows. But the regiment bowled them over with a superb showing. The men are in the dog house with Northern Area Command over food and accommodation. The 'Jolly Boys' put them in with the Saskatchewan Light Infantry. 1,500 men in a barracks designed for 850. They're already in serious trouble with their own troops by cramming 1,200 into the same sized units. The local accommodation and cookery 'expert' was shown quickly off the premises."

For Christmas Harry went up to London to meet Gil. His brother's professed "cure" in Wolfville turned out to be a fake. By Christmas Eve he was too drunk to stand. Alarmed, Harry called in the house physician at the Cumberland Hotel where they were staying. The doctor divulged that he'd already treated the patient for one toot after his arrival in England. Together they put him into bed. "Christmas dinner with Gil cancelled. He's feeling too rough. Only four days to straighten himself out before going to the Medical Board which means so much to him."

The second "flight" of troops from Canada arrived at Aldershot New Year's Eve. They had crossed in a convoy of small P & O and Royal Mail packets, badly heated and terribly crowded. The group already had casualties. At Amherst, Nova Scotia, a yard shunter had sideswiped their train, killing one man and injuring several others.

The Hasty Pees arrived two days later. "Tired and very much buggered about, somehow they managed to preserve their stolid Ontario farmer attitudes. They're backward in every respect but they have good men and the right spirit. Now, if we can only sparkle up their officers." But the situation did not improve and by early February the regiment's colonel was sacked for incompetence. A similar situation existed in the West Nova Scotia Regiment and was likewise corrected. Replacements for both units were taken from the RCRs.

"14 Jan. . . . Cold miserable. Fog all day. Brig. returned from France—speechless. Has a hell of a cold and hell of a trip. He went to Lille and Arras on a Cook's Tour to visit the British 1st Guards Brigade. Troops were cold and miserable. No excitement, officers bored to death. No comfort or entertainment. Morale is a worry."

The pipes froze on the sides of the barracks. For three days there was no running water or flushable toilets. "A large overseas mail delivery. Four letters from Margo. She is thinking of taking the boys and going to live in Picton when school ends. Why Picton, I wonder?"

On 17 January an enormous parade assembled on the Standhope Lines parade ground. The 4th and 5th Battalions of the Gordons held a rehearsal for an inspection by the honorary colonel-in-chief, Maj.-Gen. Sir James Burnett. The Canadian 48th Highlanders and Toronto Scottish were invited as sister units to participate.

"To see four battalions at War strength in one lump was a marvelous sight. I thought the Canadians had a bit of an edge over the Gordons. At 1500 hours the King and Queen walked along Pennyfathers Road between lines of cheering troops. They were down to witness the departure of part of the 51st Highland Division for France."

"19 Jan. . . . Attended dinner given to officers of 4th and 5th Gordons. Wow, what a party! Brig. Burney says 153 Brigade will take no prisoners . . . but best news is that General Pearkes has gone sick. He's been chucking his weight around and making people very annoyed."

A letter arrived from Gil. He had passed his medical exam and had been posted to the "Buffs" regimental depot at Canterbury. "I can't afford to buy anything more than beer, brother dear. How about a loan of five quid?" Harry ignored the request. Another of the family drunks turned up the following week while he was in bed with the flu. "Private Harry P. Wickwire visited me in quarters and I had a most entertaining evening listening to his improbable adventures. Before leaving he touched me for ten bob until pay day. He was worth it for cheering me up. . . . Two depressing letters from

Margo. She's not getting mine and her imagination is working; either I've been cashiered or am mixed up with a blonde and dying of remorse. What a hope!"

"1 Feb. . . . Brig. got a little tight last night after dinner at Hog's Back Hotel and came into my room as I was going to bed to inform me that he had the best Brigade Major in the Division and that I was a hell of a fellow and placed the greatest trust in my judgement and military knowledge. And what's more he liked me! Attended a Divisional conference at Sask. Light Inf. lecture hut. Pearkes was unnecessarily devastating when invited by the G2 to criticize Armand's appreciation. But his own solution to the problem was identical. Armand was livid and has not forgotten it. Pearkes, the silly ass, made matters worse by apologizing and saying he was only kidding! Boy, was the Brig. mad."

Operational orders for the Leibstandarte arrived in February. They were to be transferred to the 227th Infantry Division. The division formed part of the German Eighteenth Army in Gen. Fedor von Bock's Army Group B. Von Bock, who had won the *Pour le mérite* for valour in the first war, was the skilful commander of Army Group North during the Polish campaign. His next venture would be the invasion of Holland and France, code-named "Danzig."

Eighteenth Army's role in the operation was to protect the German army's northern flank during the attack. Its job would be to break through the soft defences along the Dutch frontier and capture intact the river and road bridges along the axis of the German advance to the Ijssel River.

Much had happened within the Waffen-SS, as the SS-VT came to be known, since the war with Poland. Himmler had been unhappy about his armed SS units being used in a piecemeal fashion by the Wehrmacht. The Deutschland Regiment, an artillery unit and armoured reconnaissance battalion, had been merged with army forces. Germania Regiment had been attached to the Fourteenth Army in East Prussia, while the Leibstandarte was operating in Silesia. The Der Führer Regiment did not even participate. Of greater concern to Himmler were the casualties. The Wehrmacht considered these to be out of all proportion to Waffen-SS accomplishments in the field, which the army attributed to lack of leadership. Himmler regarded them as an illustration of the Wehrmacht's lack of support.

With Hitler's permission, Himmler was allowed to increase the Waffen-SS to three divisions. But having the Führer's permission was one thing, finding trained men to fill the vacancies quite another. Himmler's ability to recruit was limited by his own strict standards of selection and those imposed by the Reich conscription laws. Standards of recruitment could be waived but the conscription laws were sacrosanct. Every man wishing to enlist in the armed forces had to obtain clearance from his local military registrar.

Manpower requirements for each of the three services took precedence over an applicant's wishes. The army's allotment from the manpower pool came to roughly 66 percent of the draft, and the navy and air force got the remainder. No provision had been made for the Waffen-SS. Consequently, volunteers could not be given assurances that they would be admitted into its ranks even if they met its exacting physical standards. Entry to the SS depended on Wehrmacht generosity, but the Wehrmacht consistently refused to allow the Waffen-SS more men than were needed to bring its units up to divisional strength.

With Hitler's permission to raise two more divisions, however, the army was compelled to release the required numbers from its manpower pool. Himmler still wasn't satisfied. He was in a hurry. With the campaign in the west only months away, he needed trained soldiers ready to go into action, not teenage inductees. To solve the problem and at the same time circumvent Wehrmacht control of future Waffen-SS recruitment, several approaches were taken.

In each division a replacement cadre was organized that could hold new recruits until they had been trained. Thus, each of the divisions would always have reserves to draw upon. Next, he replaced three regiments of Totenkopf concentration camp guards with a call-up of older men, an action the Führer's decree of 1938 allowed him to do in time of war, even if he had to bend the rules a little. The younger camp guards became the nucleus of the new Totenkopf Division.

Incorporation of the civil police into the SS produced enough men for the Polizei Division. Filled with many middle-aged officers in no condition to face the rigours of training and war, the Polizei Division remained a second-rate unit until late in 1941.

The most unique source of Waffen-SS recruits arranged by Himmler came from the 3 million German nationals (*Volksdeutsche*) in Poland, and later in Hungary, Rumania and Yugoslavia. Although Nazi policy recognized the *Volksdeutsche* as German, the German State did not. Therefore, no official way existed for drafting them into the Wehrmacht. Between 1939 and 1942 young men in these *Volksdeutsche* communities regarded German rule as a blessing and one that provided career opportunities within the German war machine. Later, however, Nazi racial policies and resettlement programs destroyed whatever illusions these young men held about their loyalty to the Reich.[1] But by then they could only continue to fight for a lost cause, hoping to save themselves and their families from extermination.

By spring 1940 the Waffen-SS Division, which later became known as "Das Reich," was fully equipped with men, motorized vehicles and the very latest of weapons. As the Führer's favourite, the Leibstandarte was—to no one's surprise—oversupplied with everything but for the time being it remained a reinforced motorized regiment. Totenkopf Division had to make do with arms and vehicles from the Skoda works in Czechoslovakia, while Polizei Division evolved into an infantry unit whose supply and artillery transport were horse-drawn, like most of the German army.

In March, after months of prodding from Himmler, Hausser and Dietrich, Hitler announced that henceforth service in the Waffen-ss would count as military time. This produced a substantial increase in Himmler's manpower reserves. Simultaneously, the designation ss-Verfügungstruppe (ss-VT) fell by the wayside, and the collective title of Waffen-ss, applicable to the armed branches of the ss, cadet schools, reserves, administration and training units, became firmly established. The political chrysalis had shed its cocoon and emerged as a full-fledged military butterfly.

Throughout the winter the British Expeditionary Force (BEF) under General Lord Gort remained idle. French forces had made a few desultory attacks into Germany during the Polish invasion, mainly in the Saarbrücken area, only to be quickly beaten back to the French frontier. Across the Channel the British dubbed it the "phony war," or *Sitzkrieg*.*

The BEF had taken over a section of the Franco-Belgian frontier with Arras as its HQ and spent the winter improving fortifications north of the Maginot Line. Only three corps totalling nine divisions were involved. As Brigadier Smith had observed on his visit with General McNaughton, boredom became the greatest enemy facing the British force. That situation was about to change with Hitler's invasion of Denmark and Norway on 9 April.

Hitler had been prepared to leave the Scandinavian countries alone as long as they posed no threat to his plans or Germany's commerce. However, intelligence reports indicated that the Allies were planning to halt the vital iron ore traffic upon which German industry depended. During winter months iron ore was loaded at Narvik and shipped south along the Norwegian coast to German ports.

By coincidence, Royal Navy mine-laying operations had started the day before Norway and Denmark were attacked simultaneously. German troops advanced from Schleswig across Denmark's undefended border while others came ashore from warships and transports in the harbours of Copenhagen, Korsor and elsewhere. The country's capture was completed in a few hours, with little armed opposition. The Danish government accepted the Germans' presence "under protest" and, together with King Christian, called upon citizens "to adopt a calm and controlled conduct." It was everyone's duty

---

*Literally, "sitting war."

to refrain from resistance and to "show dignified and correct demeanour to the Germans."

The Norwegians were made of sterner stuff and refused the ultimatum for surrender. They ordered a general mobilization. But German troops were already landing in Oslo Fjord, Bergen, Stavanger, Trondheim and Narvik. During the afternoon Oslo was captured with a surprise airborne attack. King Haakon and the Norwegian Parliament fled the capital for the north.

After overcoming fierce resistance from two old Norwegian warships, the Germans landed at Narvik. British naval and air forces promptly counter-attacked, sinking ten German destroyers and one U-boat together with a number of transports. British losses were two destroyers sunk and two damaged. Throughout April, land and sea battles continued up and down the Norwegian coast. German sea losses were catastrophic. In addition to the vessels already mentioned, three cruisers were sunk and two battle cruisers, one pocket-battleship, two light cruisers and one destroyer were severely damaged, reducing the the German Home Fleet to four cruisers and seven destroyers.

"16 Apr. . . . There are persistent press reports that the Canadians have gone into Norway. Well—we're still in Aldershot. . . . Addressed by General Ironsides today. A very good pep talk. We're for France all right. . . . A day of rumour: PPCLI and Edmonton Regiment left Aldershot tonight. Their mortar strength has been doubled. Just the sort of thing needed for mountainous country—is it Norway?"

As one of the most combat-ready divisions on the British Isles in men and equipment, the Canadians were asked by the War Office for assistance in a frontal attack against the Germans in Norway. Eight hundred Canadians were asked to take out the forts guarding Trondheim Fjord, clearing the way for two battalions of Guards and French Chasseurs Alpins to proceed inland and capture the airport. General McNaughton placed Colonel Sansom in command of the Canadian contingent.

But after reaching Dunfermline, the bleak Scottish port from which they were to embark on the destroyers taking them to Norway, they learned the operation had been cancelled. Intelligence reports of German air strength and ground forces at Trondheim made the venture impractical.

Initially, Sansom ordered the operation to proceed anyway, even though intelligence reports showed that the Germans were waiting in battalion machine-gun strength. After an O [Orders] Group briefing the night before the force was due to sail, everyone had his tail between his legs. "We were all scared," John Proctor, 2nd Brigade's staff captain, admitted. As he and Rod Keller, the brigade major, left the briefing tent, the Anglican chaplain appeared. He intended to hold an evening holy communion service for the officers. Would they be interested in attending? Keller glared: "No, I wouldn't.

It's too fucking late to be suckholing now, Padre!" Fortunately, common sense prevailed, the operation was cancelled at the last minute, and the group went back to Aldershot on 26 April.

"10 May. . . . At 0630 this morning we heard that Germany had entered Holland and Belgium. It's come at last."

5

During April the German plan of attack on France and the Low Countries reached the last stages of preparation. Vast armies of men and equipment were moving up to their jump-off points with the same well-oiled efficiency that had been shown in the Polish and Scandinavian campaigns. Not every senior officer was in favour of the plan, despite the proven successes of *Blitzkrieg* strategy. Attacking the combined armies of France and Britain was an entirely different proposition than attacking the poorly equipped and undermanned Polish army or the virtually defenceless Scandinavians. Mutterings of postponing the attack for a year were quickly squelched by Hitler on the correct premise that the Allies would never be weaker or riper for plucking.

The attack called for a two-pronged offensive: a northern diversionary thrust against Holland and Belgium by von Bock's army group, while the major armoured offensive drilled deep into the Allied front where the Maginot Line of forts dissolved at the southern end of the Ardennes forests. The objective was to arrive at the English Channel between Calais and Le Havre, slicing the defending armies neatly in two and thereafter encircling and destroying them.

Colonel-General von Rundstedt's Army Group A would be the spearhead, using 44 divisions, including nine panzer and three motorized. In the north Colonel-General von Bock's Army Group B had 28 divisions, including three panzer and one motorized. Colonel-General von Leeb's Army Group C in the south was given 17 infantry divisions to breach or at least contain the Maginot Line.

The Leibstandarte and Der Führer Regiments were attached to Army Group B. The two remaining regiments of the future "Das Reich" Division were to be held in reserve; Polizei went with Army Group C in front of the Maginot Line; Totenkopf, held by OKH at the Rhine, was to be thrown into the fight when required.

Initially, it was to have been von Bock's Army Group B that would lead the spearhead. But von Rundstedt's brilliant chief of staff, Maj.-Gen. Erich von Manstein, thought an attack through the Low Countries would be too obvious. Unsuitable for tanks, its terrain of canal-studded pasturelands and polders could easily be flooded by the defenders. Additionally, the attackers would be confronted by the British army instead of the more pliable French. Von Manstein advocated attacking through the Ardennes to Sedan, but his lobbying fell on deaf ears. General Halder, the army's chief of staff, did not like von Manstein. Colonel-General von Brauchitsch, his commander-in-chief, likewise showed no interest in the idea.

However, in a private breakfast arranged by Hitler's adjutant, von Manstein explained his concept to the Führer. But what about the terrain problems in the Sedan and Ardennes district? Hitler wanted to know. Von Manstein explained he had already discussed the matter with General Guderian, Germany's acknowledged tank expert. Guderian seemed satisfied that once the initial terrain obstacles had been negotiated, the tanks would break out into the open rolling farmlands of northern France. Hitler was convinced. Operational orders were drawn up to reflect the change.

On 9 May the code word "Danzig" went out to all Wehrmacht units. The Leibstandarte, waiting patiently for weeks at its quarters in Salzbergen, north of Koblenz, was galvanized into action. By 0100 hours next morning the battalions were on the road, driving for the Dutch border.

They paused briefly at the frontier while the assault companies moved to the head of the parked columns of men and machines awaiting the dawn. This time Kurt and his men would be ahead of the tanks. First men into Holland. What an honour! Every fibre tingled with excitement at the prospect of battle. Already Junkers transports were winging across the Dutch and Belgian borders to drop airborne troops onto those strategic areas that needed to be held until the main ground forces arrived. German bombers were pasting the main airports and rail junctions in Holland, Belgium, Luxembourg and a number of French towns along the lines of advance.

At 0530 hours a small ss force slipped over the border and seized the bridge that opened the road to Holland to Army Group B. German tanks clanked across the frontier and the 15th Motorcycle Company raced off to secure the next bridges.

The Royal Dutch Army wasn't much of a foe. Its available forces amounted to 11 divisions, one equipped with bicycles and a few motorcycles, a cavalry unit and 14 regiments outfitted with obsolete artillery pieces. Anti-tank and anti-aircraft guns were practically nonexistent. The country's long irregular frontiers enclosed an indefensible terrain.

For the first few kilometres after crossing the initial bridge, Kurt encountered little opposition. Roads were first class and, except for a few farm wagons, wide open and inviting. In some of the villages people waved. "In the beginning it was more of an outing than an attack. The few roadblocks we encountered were unmanned. What demolitions had been set were quickly defused."

At Bornbroek, 32 kilometres inland, they found the canal bridge had been blown by troops from one of the frontier battalions defending the area.

Waiting for the Pioneers to bring up equipment for a pontoon bridge would take several hours. Kurt decided to improvise. Men were sent out to scour the district for barn doors. An hour later, under badly directed fire from the opposite bank, they made the canal crossing on barn-door rafts. After establishing a bridgehead and clearing the Dutch defenders, the motorcycles were ferried over and the advance resumed.

A few minutes before noon 15th Company roared into Zwolle. The regiment followed close behind. An astonished citizenry gaped at them from the sidewalks and windows. There was no resistance. All Dutch troops in the town and its suburbs surrendered. At one encampment Dutch soldiers were just sitting down for lunch when the Germans arrived. A Dutch officer in charge of the group asked Kurt politely to join him and said, "We weren't expecting you for at least another three days."

"Three days! My dear Captain, we're already running 90 minutes behind schedule."

In less than six hours the Leibstandarte had covered close to 80 kilometres, a stunning accomplishment to enemy soldiers who had been trained to anticipate and fight a static type of war.

From Zwolle they raced south to rejoin the division's main body preparing an assault over the Ijssel. So far none of their units had managed any crossings of the Ijssel-Maas rivers line defences. Alert demolition teams had blown the main spans at Deventer, but an alternate crossing at Zutphen was captured intact. The men forged across.

By 1400 hours the town of Hoven and its main north-south rail line were in the hands of 3rd Battalion, completing the day's objectives planned by OKH. Obersturmführer Hugo Kraas, Kurt's second-in-command, covered himself with glory by leading his platoon 64 kilometres beyond the Ijssel and capturing 117 enemy soldiers in the process.*

As darkness descended, the advance halted for the night. The men had covered 215 kilometres of defended territory in a single day. An extraordinary feat by any measurement of any war, it provided a disquieting foretaste of what the Allied armies could expect when they collided with the new motorized Wehrmacht.

In the air the situation facing the Allies wasn't much better. All day long Luftwaffe bombers and fighter aircraft pounded targets throughout the Low Countries. Junkers 87 dive-bombers with siren screamers attached to their wheel spats were particularly effective both in terrifying the civilian population and hitting their targets with near pinpoint accuracy and devastating effect.

---

*For this action Kraas won the Iron Cross First Class.

Across the Channel, indecision reigned at the War Office. Luxembourg had been expected to fall, but the Dutch and Belgians were predicted to hold the German advance long enough for French and British forces to reach the front. But where exactly was the front? No one seemed to know. It changed from hour to hour. Orders were issued, then countermanded, then reissued again.

"10 May. . . . In the midst of packing our gear to move to Imber on Salisbury Plain orders were changed. By 1230 hours we were told to plan on moving across the Channel. Then at 1400 hours the G1 called at the mess to say that Imber was on after all. . . . What a day! Chamberlain resigned. Churchill is Britain's new Prime Minister."

"11 May. . . . While the BEF marched across Belgium to assist Holland we moved by road and rail to Imber and went into camp at Warminster and Tilshead. Brigade settled in by 1700 hours. A strenuous week ahead. We're to prepare a Brigade defensive position for open country in the face of an enemy already firmly established . . . isn't that just lovely!"

Next day the Leibstandarte transferred to the 9th Panzer Division as a back-up for that unit's northern flank. The regiment swung south to Kleve and took the main road through Nijmegen and 's-Hertogenbosch to Moerdijk where a 1.2-kilometre bridge spanned the Maas River. Until they arrived outside Moerdijk, opposition remained light, more of a nuisance than organized attacks.

"Our next task was to relieve the paratroops who had captured the bridge. Once over the bridge it was into Rotterdam then on to The Hague."

As the von Manstein plan anticipated, the French and British armies on the Belgian frontier had wheeled northeast on the first day and headed toward the river Dyle. Three days later, with the bulk of Allied forces out of the way, von Rundstedt unleashed his 1,000 tanks into the Belgian Ardennes. By the following evening they had reached the Meuse River on a front extending from Sedan to Liège. The Allied armies had never before seen anything like the German juggernaut.

By 14 May, after holding up von Bock's Eighteenth Army for three days, the tiny armies of Holland were completely cut off from any Allied help. Battered and exhausted, they lay behind their main defensive line between Rotterdam and Rossum waiting for the end. An ultimatum went out to the Dutch from OKH: surrender or the cities of Utrecht and Rotterdam would be levelled with air and artillery bombardments. The Dutch accepted at once. Orders were sent to all Wehrmacht artillery units cancelling the bombardment. Unfortunately a foul-up in the Luftwaffe orders resulted in a heavy bombing attack that reduced the centre of Rotterdam to a mass of fires and rubble. Dutch troops defending the perimeters immediately laid down their arms.

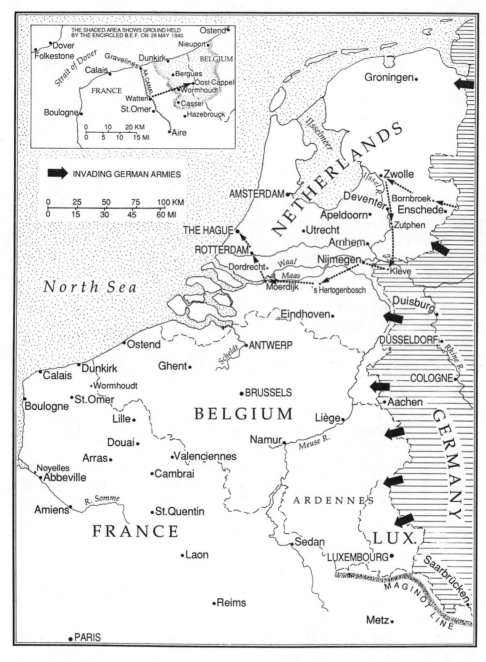

The invasion of the Low Countries, and (inset) Dunkirk, showing the movements of the Leibstandarte.

With his company, Kurt raced into the blazing city to link up with the parachute unit that had been dropped in and cut off on the first day of the campaign.

"It was like a ride through hell. Wrecked aircraft lay scattered in fields outside the city. Some had crashed on the road. The city was in flames. Civilians screaming. Buildings collapsing in fireballs of smoke and plaster."

Several times they had to stop and fight with pockets of spirited defenders who had not received the surrender order. Beyond the flaming city centre they ran into several hundred Dutch soldiers armed to the teeth and grouped near a small park. The street led onto the main highway to The Hague. The motorcyclists swerved for cover and opened fire while the surprised Dutchmen scattered. A white flag went up. "Cease firing!"

Cautiously the men of the 15th Company advanced on foot. To their horror they saw German paratroopers among the enemy soldiers. A few had been hit by the hail of bullets. Lieut.-Gen. Kurt Student, the airborne commander, lay on the pavement with a severe head wound. The ss men were appalled at what they had done. A weary airborne officer explained that the General had been in the midst of surrender negotiations with the Dutch commander when the motorcyclists appeared.

Later, an investigation concluded that no one was to blame for the incident. But the event marred what otherwise would have been a completely successful campaign by the Leibstandarte in Holland.

Laffy died in Wolfville during the early hours of 17 May. His passing was peaceful. Agnes telephoned Margo a day later with the news. "The army insists on looking after all the funeral arrangements. Do you think Harry and Gil would approve?" Margo was positive they would.

She had moved to Picton, Ontario, with the boys, driving from Winnipeg over the Easter holidays in a second-hand Plymouth. She needed a change from the constant carping by her father and Major Ross, a place of her own far away from the crackling winter cold of the prairies. The boys needed a change too. They seemed to spend most of their time at school fighting for survival, a holdover when everyone picked on them because of their English accents. Now that the accents had faded, the bullying continued from force of habit.

She decided to settle in Picton, a small farming community in Prince Edward County—home of the Hasty Pees. The county jutted out into Lake Ontario and came with an enormous sandy beach where the water was always warm for swimming in the summer. She bought an old farmhouse, hip-barn, chicken coop—with chickens and a rammy rooster—together with five acres of cleared cropland that had lain fallow for several years. She had visions of herself as a gentlewoman farmer. The children were enrolled at the local country school—ironically called ss No. 4—a two-mile walk from the farm.

Eight grades in one room with a pot-bellied stove for heat during winter.

To attend Laffy's funeral meant 1,200 miles of solo driving night and day. She packed the children and luggage in the car, arranged for the neighbours to feed the chickens and dog, and left for Nova Scotia. They arrived late the night before the funeral and found Laffy laid out in the front parlour in a beautifully polished casket.

"All the excitement in my life happens in May," he had written shortly after Gil sailed for England. "My birth, graduation from medical school, meeting Janie, our wedding, her birthday, the start of my army career and Janie's passing. It would only be proper for me to join her in May."

Next morning 500 troops from Camp Aldershot marched behind the gun carriage carrying his remains to the Kentville cemetery. The day shone sunny and warm, sweet with the smells of damp earth. Growing things burst forth from every field and garden. As the casket was lowered into the family plot next to Janie, field guns boomed out across the town. An honour guard of six riflemen at graveside timed their volleys to match the bigger guns. Urchins in short pants scrambled for the empty cartridges. Margo kept a tight rein on her two who wanted a share of the bright brass trophies.

"Why can't I?" Tony whispered. The aunts and uncles and assorted cousins frowned. Margo glared down at her son.

"Because it wouldn't be proper."

"19 May. . . . At about midnight I got a cable from Margo in Montreal. She's going to a funeral. The rest was garbled. I can only surmise something has happened to poor old dad. I do hope it was swift and painless."

"20 May. . . . Carried out a dawn attack with tanks at Imber. The tanks failed us badly. Moved the Brigade back to Aldershot by road. Phone call from Gil. Dad died on the 17th. It hurts. Gil has been promoted to corporal and about to go to France."

6

In France the Allied forces were in retreat. Brussels and Antwerp were abandoned, and the Belgian government moved to Ostend. The Germans entered Antwerp on 18 May, but the British-Belgian line remained firm and threw back all attacks. Next day General Weygand succeeded Gamelin as commander-in-chief of Allied forces. Fifteen French generals were sacked for incompetence.

At the start the French had fought bravely and well, but their entire defence posture had been predicated on the Maginot Line of forts that von Rundstedt's armoured columns had already bypassed. Mechanized armour and rapid mobility of infantry had never been accepted by the French High Command as a serious threat. Changing their generals in the midst of an impending defeat accomplished nothing. Morale among France's front-line troops was already fading.

On 19 May von Rundstedt's drive from the Meuse River pierced the French line between Sedan and Valenciennes, then swung westward for the Channel ports. Two days later Laon fell, then Abbeville, Amiens and Arras. An enormous bridgehead had been established by German forces across the Somme. The British counterattacked between Arras and Douai with heavy casualties. Fierce fighting in the sectors of Valenciennes and Cambrai slowed the German advance momentarily.

But the BEF, the French First Army and the Belgians were cut off, although the southern flank remained reasonably intact along the canals between Escaut and La Bassée, and to St. Omer along the Aa River. Main communications had been lost between the armies. Only the Channel ports remained. The Allied forces began to withdraw into a semicircle around Dunkirk.

On 24 May the Leibstandarte arrived at the Aa Canal along the southern and eastern perimeters of the Dunkirk evacuation area. The regiment had been transferred to the 1st Panzer Division as part of Gen. Ewald von Kleist's panzer group. Although they had been all night on the road, they were ordered into battle immediately. Their first objective was the capture of Wattenbourg hill, to the east of the Aa Canal. It held a commanding view of the generally flat surrounding country.

But strangely, just as the troops were assembling for the assault, orders were received forbidding any further advance across the canal toward Dunkirk. General Guderian, commander of von Kleist's XIX Panzer Corps, fumed at the delay. The order made no sense to the men at the front. As the regimental commander, Dietrich decided to ignore it and ordered his men into battle.

Under a heavy supporting artillery barrage one company pressed across the canal, fighting its way into Watten. The Allies made several swift counterattacks but were held off by the SS until the 3rd Battalion arrived in the town. With a sharp determined thrust the battalion smashed through the defence lines and captured the hill.

The OKH "stop" order deserves further explanation, for without doubt it gave the evacuating Allied forces that breathing time needed to produce the "Miracle of Dunkirk." Both Hitler and von Rundstedt, each for his own reasons, had a hand in the creation of this order. Von Rundstedt, after a vicious counterattack by the Royal Tank Regiment near Arras on 21 May, had begun worrying about his tactical position. The British tanks had attacked Maj.-Gen. Erwin Rommel's 7th Panzer Division, bluffing the Germans into believing that they were part of a much larger force. For a few hours von Rundstedt had the uncomfortable feeling his armoured divisions might be cut off before any of his infantry divisions could be brought up for support.

Under the circumstances his sensitivity to the possibility of disaster was not misplaced. He commanded four armies and two large panzer groups strung out across the French countryside. Mechanical breakdowns and troop casualties among some of the armoured divisions were running as high as 50 percent. Many of his infantry divisions were already fighting flanking attacks by both French and British forces kilometres behind the panzer spearheads. In fact, Guderian's leading panzers were closer to Dunkirk on 22 May than the retreating British.

Von Kleist, who was Guderian's superior, related to British historian Liddell Hart after the war that Guderian's lead tanks had reached the Aire-St. Omer Canal when the stop order arrived. "I decided to ignore it, and push across the canal. My tanks had actually entered Hazebrouck and cut across the British lines of retreat. I heard later that Lord Gort, the British Commander-in-Chief, had been in Hazebrouck at the time. But then a more emphatic order came that I was to withdraw behind the canal. For three days my tanks remained halted."

Von Rundstedt expected General Gamelin to counterattack in force somewhere along the exposed German flanks and for the British to make a stand along the Canal Line. On the evening of 23 May he decided to allow time for his armour to close up before continuing the attack. There seemed to be no rush. Von Bock's Army Group B, nearly 65 kilometres east, was driving the Allied left wing back to where inevitably it would be caught between the two German army groups. Von Rundstedt discussed the matter with Gen. Hans von Kluge, whose Fourth Army controlled both Generals Hoth's and von Kleist's panzer groups. The Fourth Army War Diary recorded that it would "in the main, halt tomorrow in accordance with Colonel-General von Rundstedt's order."

The only sensible viewpoint came from Gen. Walther von Brauchitsch, the army's commander-in-chief. If von Rundstedt wasn't up to pressing home the attack to finish off the enemy forces, then von Bock should be given control of the Fourth Army for the final encircling movements. He issued the necessary orders.

The next day, when Hitler visited von Rundstedt and heard his explanation that the stop orders were only temporary while the divisions regrouped, von Brauchitsch's orders were countermanded. On 25 May, when OKH authorized the armour to cross the Canal Line, von Rundstedt ignored it. Von Brauchitsch next proposed a renewed armoured attack. Hitler was not in favour and left the final decision to von Rundstedt. But von Rundstedt was more interested in rest and refit for his tanks and men than in finishing off the Allied armies. Two more days passed in which nothing concrete was decided. Finally, on 27 May, Hitler—not von Rundstedt—ordered the attack to proceed. Those four crucial days of inactivity by the panzers, combined with the loss of German naval ships in Norwegian waters the month before, allowed the bulk of the BEF to escape across the Channel to England.

"23 May. . . . We move by train sometime this evening for Dover. At 1400 hours GOC* held a conference. BEF line of communications has been cut through Arras. Gen. McNaughton with a mixed force of British and Canadians is to establish a protected line of communications from either Calais or Dunkirk. Our Brigade is forming the advanced Party. . . . The GOC said: 'This is our opportunity to show the stuff we are made of. It's going to be a sticky business. You must be absolutely ruthless and in dealing with refugees remember the Fifth Column. Tell the men we are not particularly interested in prisoners.'"

"24 May. . . . Commencing at 0205 hours the Brigade left the Government siding in 5 trains. Too excited to sleep. Arrived at Dover Marine Terminal 0630 hours but were unable to detrain for 45 minutes. The place was congested by thousands of refugee civilians and French soldiers rescued from Boulogne during the night by the 20th Guards Brigade and a destroyer.

"The refugees were enough to make my blood boil. The few Welsh Guards I saw entraining looked like sleepwalkers, all with two and three days growth of beard. 600 of them had been left on the quay at Boulogne fighting off German tanks when all ships had to leave under a terrific air raid. At 0200 hours a destroyer ran in alongside, engaged the tanks and took off 400 guardsmen. The rest were embarked later.

"We were given a filthy breakfast at the customs shed and then embarked on the *Canterbury*. Spent all day loading stores and ammunition. Again everything badly organized. Rail cars with stores for units on the *Canterbury* were spotted opposite the *Moanas Queen* and vice versa. They then proceeded to unload all at once. Meantime a motor convoy of ammunition was unable to approach the quay for congestion. Destroyers came in at intervals throughout the afternoon, unloaded wounded and departed. Hospital trains loaded and left. Plenty of blood curdling tales of Fifth Column activities in Boulogne. Obviously Calais is now out of the question. Why don't we get going for Dunkirk while it's still free?

"At 1800 hours our suspicions were justified. A Divisional liaison officer arrived to tell us to entrain for Aldershot in two hours! How to tell the troops? Their blood is up. At 1930 hours G1 turned up and explained the change in strategic situation. Back in Aldershot at 0130 hours thoroughly weary. If 3 days ago anyone had said it was possible to move, embark, disembark and move a Brigade on verbal orders only I'd have said he was crazy. But we've done it even if all our transport and stores are still at Dover or Southampton.

"26 May. . . . At 0230 hours received a warning order to be prepared to

*General officer commanding (General McNaughton.)

move overseas from the same ports as before and under the same arrangements. Whole force to embark at Southampton we were told at 1130 hours, first trains leaving Aldershot in ninety minutes. At 1215 hours the move was cancelled. We slept the balance of the day. The staff is exhausted. This is getting to be too much of a good thing.

"27 May. . . . Vehicles loaded, everyone standing by ready to move again. The Brigadier and I know once again we are for either France or defence of England. A decision will be taken at a Cabinet meeting this morning. The news in the papers is not so hot but not nearly as serious as the intelligence summaries indicate. We've been beaten. Badly beaten. General Ironsides has been appointed C.-in-C.* Home Defences and General Dill takes over as CIGS.† At 1545 hours received warning order. We do not go to France but will be the mobile reserve for the defence of Great Britain and will move from Aldershot by motor transport on the night of 30/31 May.

"We are to reorganize our grouping on lines similar to the German *Einheit*‡ system. Much more suitable for meeting his current tactics. At last we know where we stand and can now plan ahead. Here's hoping there will be no further changes."

On that same day across the Channel Guderian had ordered his 1st Panzer Division to attack toward the Wormhoudt-Bergues road, running south from Dunkirk. The Leibstandarte, under command of the 20th Motorized Infantry Division, was to form the centre thrust with the 76th and Grossdeutschland Regiments on either flank. Kurt's motorized rifle company formed the spearhead. Their attack got under way shortly after eight in the morning, the motorbikes tearing down the road from Watten to Bollezeele under heavy fire.

Enemy opposition at Bollezeele was fierce and furious. As usual the *Kradschützen* outran their supporting flanks and came under fire from the left rear, a point that should have been captured by the Grossdeutschland. A see-saw battle developed at the edge of town with its British defenders, who seemed far from discouraged by their circumstances. Impatient at the delay, Kurt decided to take a motorbike for a personal reconnoitre. Away he charged like a medieval knight, head down over the handlebars, weaving and twisting past the rubble and shell holes. The British machine-gunners opened up. He raced the motor, skidding from their fire. To stop would have been suicide.

"Suddenly, I felt something like a punch and I was flying past a tree. Then everything went very black and quiet."

A rescue patrol brought him back to the German lines during the next

---

*Commander-in-chief.
†Chief of the Imperial General Staff of the British Army.
‡Fighting units that were highly mobile, swiftly responsive, compact and self-contained.

counterattack. Regimental headquarters, and a dressing station, had been set up temporarily in a farm house. Kurt awakened to hear Dietrich shouting in his ear.

"You're a fool, Meyer! Did you know that?"

"Yes, Gruppenführer."

"Your place is with your men, not in front of them. When you cross their line of fire they stop shooting. I don't like that. We're here to kill British not Germans." Sepp stamped out, leaving him with the doctor. The diagnosis was a concussion, although they wouldn't know how serious for 48 hours. Meantime he had to stay in bed and rest.

Next day, 28 May, it was Dietrich's turn to be caught in an enemy crossfire. Platoon leader Obersturmführer Max Wünsche, who would take over as OC (officer commanding) of 15th Company during Kurt's convalescence, dropped by to wish the regimental commander a happy birthday. It was his 48th. Flattered that the 26-year-old Wünsche would take the trouble to remember the occasion, Dietrich invited him along on a reconnaissance trip in his staff car. They set off at 0600 hours to find out what was happening with 1st and 2nd Battalions deployed west of the main Bergues-Cassel road. An assortment of stragglers and supply trucks looking for their units joined them along the way. They saw no sign of the enemy, and the small convoy moved down the road at a leisurely pace, Sepp chatting amiably with Wünsche on how well things were progressing. He took an avuncular interest in Wünsche. It had been on Dietrich's recommendation that the tall, handsome officer had been appointed Hitler's aide-de-camp (ADC) and had accompanied him to Poland. Despite this honour, Wünsche had transferred back to front-line duty as quickly and as tactfully as possible. He considered himself a soldier, not a Nordic clotheshorse.

Halfway between Esquelbecq and Wormhoudt the convoy came to a roadblock. The men scrambled from the trucks to remove it and immediately came under fire from the 5th Battalion of the Gloucestershire Regiment, of which Cpl. Gil Foster was a member. Machine guns had been set up on either side of the road, with two anti-tank guns firing down the road from Wormhoudt. They were trapped. At once Dietrich and Wünsche bailed out of their staff car. Wünsche related: "I went into a ditch and tried to crawl through a pipe laying there. An anti-tank shell set the trucks on fire. The smoke and petrol fumes caused me to lose consciousness."

Over three-quarters of the men were killed or wounded. Suffering from burns and smoke inhalation, Dietrich and the other survivors hugged the ditch and awaited rescue. But 15th Company together with 2nd Company failed to get through. Nor was the tank brigade's 6th Company able to push past the enemy defences. One attack after another was beaten back. The Gloucestershires were the toughest encountered thus far in the campaign. Convinced they had been up against elite fighting men, the Waffen-ss commanders were startled to discover once the battle subsided that these were only British territorials.

By three in the afternoon 3rd Battalion managed to fight its way into the southwestern part of Wormhoudt, bypassing Esquelbecq and forcing the British to transfer a part of their force over to Wormhoudt to meet the new threat. With the pressure gone, a patrol from 1st Battalion went forward and brought Dietrich and Wünsche back to the lines.

In the courtyard outside his window Kurt heard the sounds of BMW motorcycle engines revving. Cries that the enemy was crumbling brought him off his stretcher and outdoors. He signalled one of the passing grenadiers to slow down and hopped on back.

"Are you all right, Hauptsturmführer?"

"Never better. Let's go!"

Later in the afternoon after furious house-to-house fighting, 2nd Battalion reached the Wormhoudt town square. A steady rain began falling, and the troops donned their rain capes. British forces counterattacked again and again with bayonets, supporting tanks and heavy mortars. But the SS stood firm while more men were brought up during the night to organize a final assault on the Oost-Cappel road.

Slowly the British fell back, their fighting fury subsiding. Then, at first light, the Leibstandarte realized the main force had escaped toward Dunkirk, leaving only a determined rearguard to contest the German advance.

Privates Robert Wildsmith and Alfred Tombs of the Royal Warwickshire Regiment were captured during the battle of Wormhoudt. Tombs, a mortarman in the 2nd Battalion, had been holding a line in front of the village when he and his company were overrun by tanks. The nine survivors, led by Capt. Lynn Allen and the remnants of D Company Headquarters, tried to reach their Battalion HQ by crawling along the ditches. A tank caught up to them and, after forcing their surrender, handed them over to the German infantry. Along with a few other prisoners they were marched to the rear.

Tombs remembered: "We were taken to a field and on the way I saw Private Gould, who had been wounded previously, shot dead by one of our guards as he lay on the ground. Another wounded man was shot as he lay on the road. Three of our trucks were damaged each with a body laying alongside dressed in khaki. Two had been completely burned and one was still burning.

"When we arrived at the field we were joined by about 40 other soldiers . . . all members of my regiment with the exception of a Royal Artillery Dispatch rider who was already wounded. We were taken to a large barn and left in charge of two guards. These, as well as the ones who had originally escorted us, were wearing camouflage capes covering their uniforms but I could see that they had collar badges which resembled forked lightning.

"One of the guards called four men out of the barn and shot them dead outside. Then the other guard called four more out, took them around to the other end of the barn and shot them. Captain Allen went outside to protest and was shot dead. I saw his body laying on his face outside. He had been shot in the back."

Wildsmith continued the story: "We were driven to the rear of the barn. I was one of the last in. Two German guards came forward and each threw a grenade among us. The grenades caused many casualties. The Germans then opened fire on us with Tommy-guns, two firing from the front of the barn, two from the side and one from the rear. I heard a scream from outside . . . through a crack in the side I saw that the German who had been firing from the back had been wounded. While the Germans went to attend the wounded guard I escaped out the front, crossing the field and into a ditch."

Tombs, who had been wounded in the leg, escaped too. Eventually both were recaptured by German artillery soldiers who treated them decently. Neither man mentioned the incident to their captors and both were interned for the duration in a prisoner-of-war (POW) camp. Only five of the 45 men in the barn survived.

With the capture of Oost-Cappel, the Dunkirk perimeter from the Aa Canal to the Belgian border was firmly in German hands. The Leibstandarte transferred to 3rd Panzer Division to prepare for the Allied offensive that von Rundstedt felt certain the British would launch before throwing in the towel. Plans were made for a spoiling attack by four German divisions before the enemy could develop any forward momentum. It was launched on 8 June and stopped the British in their tracks. With the British evacuating Dunkirk and the demoralized French army in disarray, it was no longer a question of if, but when, the government of France would capitulate.

Disquieting information on activities by the Totenkopf began circulating among some of the Waffen-SS units. On 26 May, in an action around the town of Béthune, 80 kilometres from Dunkirk, a mass murder of prisoners had taken place. A battalion of the Royal Norfolks surrendered to the 3rd Company of the 2nd Totenkopf Regiment. The Norfolks had been given orders to hold the village and farms around Le Paradis to the last man. By late afternoon, after hours of savage fighting, the battalion had been reduced to 98 men. Those left alive were nearly out of ammunition. They decided to surrender. Hauptsturmführer Fritz Knöchlein accepted their white flag.

After laying down their arms, the survivors, many of them badly wounded, were marched into an adjacent field, placed in line and machine-gunned. Anyone still alive was bayoneted or shot in the head.[2] "Just what you might expect from concentration camp guards," Dietrich observed in disgust when hearing the news.

An official inquiry into the affair was dropped by the SS because it refused to accept the Wehrmacht's investigative competence in the matter.

7

Luxembourg had fallen on the first day of the attack; Holland on 14 May. Belgium's King Leopold capitulated on 28 May. Surrounded by German armoured forces in Flanders, the British and French troops were now in a very grave situation. One small corridor to the sea at Dunkirk remained, and this was being subjected to continuous aerial bombardment.

A few days earlier a British brigade had been sent from England to join an equal number of French troops to try to hold Calais and reopen lines of communication with the main BEF body. Both tasks proved impossible. Only 165 survivors from an original force of 4,000 were brought out by the Royal Navy on 26 May. However, this incredibly brave sacrifice was not in vain. By keeping two German armoured divisions tied up at Calais, precious time had been gained, allowing the main BEF body to withdraw to Dunkirk and the French to flood the Gravelines water courses that provided a natural defence barrier at the western perimeter of the beaches.

Miraculously, the Channel remained calm. The German tanks had halted and the perimeter defences held. A vast armada of warships, merchant vessels and pleasure craft of all types and sizes crossed and recrossed the Channel, bringing home what remained of the British army in northern France. By 4 June, close to 337,000 men had been taken off the beaches at Dunkirk. All guns, transport, armoured vehicles, field equipment and ammunition supplies were lost. It had been one of the greatest military disasters in British history. Planners at the War Office were already convinced a German invasion on England's south coast to be imminent. The Canadian 1st Division moved north to Northamptonshire to form a strategic reserve, centrally located to meet amphibious assaults on the south and east coasts or to repel parachute troops landing anywhere in southern England.

"30 May. . . . Left Aldershot at dusk and drove steadily all night. Great confusion in the vicinity of Oxford. The bypass we were to take did not in fact exist. All road signs in England were removed yesterday. . . . Arrived at reveille and got the Brigade distributed in Battalion *Einheit* groups in the Wellingborough vicinity. Division and 3rd Brigade are in Northampton while 2nd Brigade is in the Kettering area. Our Brigade HQ is distributed about the estate of Mr. Gilbey—of Gilbey's Gin—at Great Harrowden. I have a gorgeous room at the Hall but the bloody place is like the inside of a convent. Ornate dogan (Catholic) pictures everywhere and 4 nuns, refugees, billeted on the Gilbey's too. Seem to spend all their time praying and bead-rattling. . . .

"10 June. . . . Italy declared war on us today. We are to sail for France and join the reorganized 2nd Corps under Lieutenant-General Alan Brooke. Thank heaven we'll be just another British Division and not a fancy bunch of pampered colonials. I believe we have Gen. McNaughton to thank for that. . . . Today the King and Queen visited us informally. They had tea at the 48th Highlanders mess. They were both charming and full of fun and I believe thoroughly enjoyed themselves. . . .

"13 June. . . . Arrived in Plymouth at 0830 hours and were received by Nancy Astor and many ladies issuing cigarettes and chocolates. Troops fed dockside by the Devons. A very good breakfast. Embarked on the French ship *El Mansur*. Terrific congestion on board. The crew very friendly but the captain turned difficult. For 'les matelots space is desirable. For les soldâts hommes 40 cheveaux 8 is the rule.' We sent for the French admiral. 1,600 troops on board and lifeboats for only 700. Boat drill and emergency practice were too much trouble for the captain. He explained that if we were hit everyone was to stand fast. After throwing the rafts overboard the crew would take to the boats. On the order 'abandon ship' we were to jump overboard and swim. Fine old French naval tradition. . . . Pulled into the stream and sailed for Brest at about 2000 hours. . . .

"14 June. . . . Docked at Brest near dawn. By 0730 hours heard the most alarming stories of our transport drivers beating up the town. Some bloody fool paymaster gave them over 150 francs each and turned them loose on the local estaminets* where they—very naturally—got tight. And very naturally too could not be handled by either the French police or British APMs. A bad show and there will be hell to pay for someone.

"We hid under the trees on 'the ramparts' until noon when the first train left for the Assembly Area. Brigade HQ first, then RCRs, followed by the Hasty Pees. Wine is forbidden to the troops. But at every stop small boys and girls run and fetch it. . . . Glorious weather. Mile after mile of beautiful French countryside. Truly La Belle France and impossible to realize there's a war on.

"At Rennes there are thousands of refugees evacuated from the Paris suburbs. A maddening sight—women, children, old folks and mongrel dogs herded into cattle trucks. Thousands upon thousands of bicycles and prams. God Damn the Germans for creating such misery! . . . Everywhere the people cheer us. 'Vive les Cánadiens—Vive la France—La bas les Boche!' Even the nuns and little children make the RAF thumbs up sign. Our lads are puffed up like a load of dynamite. . . . We continue east. At Laval darkness descends but still we see the long lines of motorists and farm carts loaded with bedding parked beside the road or heading west.

"15 June. . . . Dawn broke at 0430 hours as we arrived two hours late at our destination, Sable. We were greeted by a rather upset RTO† who announced that the French were folding everywhere. Their government had left Tours for Bordeaux and the Boche had already entered Paris. The enemy

---

*Small French cafés.
†Travel officer—a member of the Army Service Corps Railway.

was only 25 kilometres away last night. He told us to return to Brest and was off the train immediately, disappearing into the throng. Doubts at once. Was he Fifth Column? What to do? A few minutes later a reconnaissance aircraft flew over. Too high for identification.

"The engineer refused to move the train. Said he'd been on duty for 28 hours and insisted on having his breakfast. I put an NCO with a Thompson gun in the cab, a locomotive driver in Canada. We soon got up steam and started out. . . . It's hard to know what's been happening. The French railwaymen say: 'La guerre est fini.' I remember the bottlenecks at Laval and Rennes. If only we can get ourselves west of Rennes we might make it.

"At Laval the troops were told to prepare to abandon the train, taking only their essentials. Our plan is to stand and fight until out of ammunition. Each surviving platoon will set out across country for St. Raphael on the Bay of Biscay to find a way home to England. We reassemble our kits, set the compasses, treble the AA defence of the train and cross our fingers.

"We reach Rennes where some stupid RTO routed us to St. Malo instead of Brest. Where do they dig up these people? Didn't discover the error until we were within 10 kilometres of St. Malo. Detrained in St. Malo at 1700 hours and embarked on the SS *Biarritz*—a British ship, thank God!

"On board was a mix of Royal Engineers, Naval Expeditionary Force and odds and sods, all still full of fight. The French have let us down badly. It seems they have agreed to a German ultimatum for all British troops to be out of the country within 48 hours. Yet the French we met—even evacuees—were full of fight. I refuse to believe it's happening. Subalterns with very parochial points of view are spreading alarming stories in the most authoritative manner. An imagination is one thing a soldier can easily do without.

"We are packed aboard like tinned sardines. If they ever bomb us it will be just too bad. But we're all cheerful, We've got a tough job ahead but there's no doubt we can take him. From now on we'll fight our own battle. . . . This of course all based on no news and never having met a single German. . . .

"16 June. . . . Calm sea and clear weather. We're running a zig zag course, north all morning. We passed some of the Channel Islands at about 0800 hours. We're loaded to the gunwales with neither naval nor air escort. Arrived Southampton 1700 hours. Back to Farnborough/Aldershot much to the surprise of our Division. Everyone exhausted. An exciting 3 days. Although a bit unproductive. No word yet of RCR, Hasty Pees or our transport from Brest. . . .

"17 June. . . . France has quit. Still no word on our missing men.

"18 June. . . . Hasty Pees arrived back after shooting down one Boche machine with light artillery fire over Brest.

"19 June. . . . RCR arrived very weary in the small hours of the morning. The whole of our precious new transport was wrecked at Brest and all our kits burned. We must begin again rebuilding from scratch. . . . Thus ended the Bust of Brest."

The battle for France had turned into a general pursuit of demoralized French forces. "A beaten army doesn't fight—it wilts and crumbles like a dry autumn leaf." The Leibstandarte drove on for the Aisne River, through Soissons and Villers-Cotterets, meeting indifferent opposition from the French 11th Division.

Once the Weygand Line of defence had been pierced, the thrust to the river Marne went virtually unopposed. The 2nd Battalion forced a crossing near St. Avige on 12 June, cutting the main railway line that evening. Near midnight, Dietrich received orders pulling the regiment out of action and into billets at Entrepilly for a rest. Two days later the news came that the German army had entered Paris.

"We're all sorry to have missed seeing it. The troops celebrated anyway by ringing the village church bells in spite of opposition from the priest who thought the men were drunk . . . which only added to the general sense of elation. I don't think the local civilians know exactly how to regard us yet. They will learn that we mean them no harm."

Brig.-Gen. Charles de Gaulle, the newly promoted commander of the French 4th Armoured Division, begged Prime Minister Reynaud and General Weygand to allow him to make a stand at the Marne, the Seine or Paris. But the government had already decided to capitulate. De Gaulle realized the only place to continue the struggle was from London. Disgusted by his country's lack of political courage and military leadership, he departed for England.

In its drive southwest the freshly rested Leibstandarte banged into the first contested river crossing at the Allier, a small tributary of the Oise, during late morning on 19 June. Swiftly, a bridgehead was forced near the town of Moulins and reconnaissance units sent off ahead of the main body to grab the bridge crossing at St. Pourçain over the river Sioule. They reached the bridge in time to see French soldiers working frantically on a barricade.

"We were badly outnumbered. Obersturmführer Knittel received orders to rush the French defences in a surprise assault before they destroyed the structure. With covering fire by our mortar teams and the two reconnaissance vehicles the men opened the attack. We made it through the barricades. But they blew the bridge. Several of the men were injured, two seriously."

Regimental objectives were switched immediately to the other side of St. Pourçain where a second bridge remained intact. Hauptsturmführer Jochen Peiper's company forced a crossing, and the French troops at St. Pourçain surrendered. The drive toward the famous spa town of Vichy continued and a French artillery column captured along the way. Forward reconnaissance units entered the town near dusk.

Next day 2nd Battalion overran the airport at Clermont-Ferrand and seized a squadron of aircraft, including a number of French fighter aircraft from a Polish squadron that had been based in France. Thousands of prisoners and eight fully operational tanks were caught in the bag at the same time.

After another two-day rest the regiment joined the attack on St. Étienne. Heavy artillery was called up to help. "Why are they still fighting us? Don't they know it's all over for France. . . . Why prolong the inevitable?" No one apparently had told the French because it took until 24 June before the Germans could enter the town.

As early as 11 June, France had asked Britain for more fighter aircraft. The request had been refused, resulting in great bitterness by the French government. But Churchill knew France was finished and every fighter aircraft in the RAF would be needed for the defence of England.

The French government that had fled to Bordeaux under Reynaud resigned to be replaced by a new government under old Marshal Pétain, the hero of World War I. Pétain asked Hitler for an armistice. In one final attempt to restore French morale, Churchill offered to arrange a solemn Act of Union between the two nations, involving a single war cabinet and common citizenship, but Pétain's new government rejected the concept.

De Gaulle disowned the Pétain regime and appealed to all French soldiers and skilled workers in England and elsewhere to join him in continuing the fight. But most of the nation followed Pétain. Organized fighting ended on 19 June. Two days later the Germans took Brest and reached the lower river Loire between Tours and Nantes. In the forest of Compiègne, inside the same rail car in which the armistice of World War I had been signed, Hitler handed the French plenipotentiaries his armistice terms. German dishonour in World War I had finally been avenged.

On the same day that the French government in Bordeaux accepted the German terms, Churchill moved immediately to prevent Hitler from capturing French naval ships in North Africa by destroying the fleet. Simultaneously, de Gaulle announced the formation of a French National Committee in London, with himself in command, which would carry on the war alongside the British army.

The signing of the armistice divided France into two sectors: German-occupied in the north, Vichy France in the south. A proposed victory march through Paris was cancelled out of consideration for the populace and fear that such a humiliation might provoke reaction among the few ardent nationalists remaining in the city.

The Leibstandarte was ordered to move north into German-occupied territory, where it garrisoned at the ancient city of Metz,* capital of France's Moselle Department.

It had been another successful campaign for Kurt. His courage in the hell-for-leather charge into Bollezeele, together with the general example of leadership given to his men, won him another Iron Cross—First Class, this time—and the nickname "Schneller-Meyer" (like "Speedy Gonzales" in English). And, according to Dietrich, a recommendation had been forwarded to ss Headquarters for his promotion to Sturmbannführer.† Best of all, he was still alive.

His days in Metz passed pleasantly. For the second time in less than ten months the regiment underwent a refit and replacement of its equipment and manpower. There were rumours of an invasion across the Channel, but they were still only rumours. The summer weather was hot. Most of the citizens of Metz were eager to call themselves German—by and large they seemed just as pleased with the new Vichy government and the ignominious defeat of their army as they were with the German presence at Fort Alvensleben.

Once the men had settled into their new garrison, Kurt sent for Kate.

"Can I bring the children?"

"No. There isn't room."

But no sooner did she arrive than she began worrying about them. His billet wouldn't accommodate three young girls so he decided on a compromise without telling Kate. He sent his adjutant off to Berlin to bring back Inge. As the eldest, she would be the least trouble, he reasoned. But three days later when he went to meet them, a scheduling officer at the station told him that the train had been involved in an accident. For an hour he tried frantically to locate someone in authority down the line who might know where the accident had taken place, the number of dead and where the living had gone. The French telephone system defeated him. No one knew anything. He went back to quarters. How to tell Kate the news? He drank several cups of coffee and smoked a dozen cigarettes, trying to screw up enough courage.

"Vati, what's wrong?"

"Nothing—nothing."

"Then come to bed."

"Can't. I have to check the guard."

Long after midnight there was a knock at the door. Kurt sprang to answer it. "Sorry for the delay. We ran into a bit of trouble," his adjutant explained with understatement.

---

*Not only was Metz occupied, but it was annexed as a part of Germany.
†Major.

Minutes later, Kate was hugging Inge. Her five-year-old appeared more annoyed than excited by the experience.

"Just look at this, Mutti. My skirt is dirty!"

8

Kurt organized a visit to Paris for 15th Company and later, during July, a tour of the historic battlefields of Verdun. The men marched up to the monolith of Fort Douaumont. Skies were grey and foreboding, matching the temper of the maimed and moonlike landscape. The men's excitement and laughter faded as he explained what had happened to the hundreds of thousands of French and German soldiers who had died during the eight months of terrible fighting that had raged back in 1916. "I told them of the poor Frenchmen who had died of thirst as our troops attacked with flamethrowers." White crosses stretched endlessly, marking the burial grounds not of platoons and companies, but of entire regiments and divisions. The men gazed silently across the blasted pockmarked desolation.

His history lesson was not lost on the men. They departed white-faced and shaken. Dying in battle for one's country was something every soldier had been taught to accept. During a company assault ten or 20 might be killed. In a prolonged fight against a particularly stubborn enemy, 50 or 60 comrades could die. But to lose entire brigades or divisions? A hundred thousand men? It seemed inconceivable, but at Verdun it had happened. They had seen the evidence. Pray that it would never happen again—to Frenchmen, to Germans or even to the British.

At home, Goebbels's propaganda people were having a field day creating instant heroes for the German press. Youthful Luftwaffe fighter pilots and panzer generals made especially good feature stories. Heroes were expected to have easily distinguishable idiosyncrasies that would endear them to the public. Crumpled field caps, open-necked flight jackets, flying boots, pet rabbits and lion cubs were especially in vogue. As a Leibstandarte member Kurt had never gone short on PR photographs of himself and his men. This special treatment given Hitler's and Göring's favourite units became a constant source of irritation to the less flamboyant members of the Wehrmacht, who carried the lion's share of battle and considered the Leibstandarte and Luftwaffe officer corps to be little better than spoiled brats with political connections.

Kurt chose a low-profile mascot—a German shepherd that developed an instant affection for him and rarely left his side. After a few weeks, when the canine's company became too much of a good thing, he had a sturdy doghouse built to give himself some free time. But the dog dug a hole under his cage during the night and at four in the morning was outside the window howling to be let in. Even worse, the dog was jealous of Kate. He would snuggle in on the bed between them and drape his head accusingly over Kurt's chest. Or if Kate fell behind on a Sunday walk, the dog did his best to keep her from catching up by grabbing at her skirt and coat. Inge he considered a special responsibility and slept at the foot of her bed. Kate was not allowed to approach her daughter. The final straw. "I'll not be victimized by a dog, Vati! Either he goes or I do." Thereafter, banished from quarters, he resided outdoors.

On Sunday mornings Kurt enjoyed a spin on his motorbike, loading Kate, Inge and any other children he could squeeze into his sidecar for a trip around the French countryside. They spent an idyllic summer.

In August his promotion was confirmed together with orders to create a new armoured reconnaissance battalion. The Leibstandarte amoeba was subdividing again. For cadre he took his experienced officers and NCOs from 15th Company; the rank and file he collected from the SS training barracks at Ellwangen where he had been given carte blanche to handpick his grenadiers from among the graduating classes.

News of his arrival spread through the training establishment like wildfire. He had already gained a name for himself throughout the SS as a fearless leader and daredevil. Some of his contemporaries were even jealous of his exploits and rising public popularity.

"I can think of no greater recognition than the envy of my peers. . . . If I provide them with a standard now when I have done nothing to deserve their envy think of how much more envious they will become when I accomplish something worthwhile."

To be a member of "Panzermeyer's" new battalion was a guarantee of excitement, adventure, comradeship and the unique respect awarded every member of the Führer's personal elite guards.

"I selected them carefully. Not so much for their height and appearance than for the strength, stamina and personal initiative they had shown during their training. . . . I'm sure I got the best of the lot."

Those chosen were transferred to Metz and began an intensive program of field exercises and practising swift cross-country deployment against a stationary enemy. He made it very clear what was expected of them. "A reconnaissance group is by definition the first into battle. . . . Where we lead the army follows. We must therefore be better than anybody else . . . stronger, braver, smarter and faster." "Schneller-Meyer" had spoken.

Average age for his new grenadiers was 19, their NCOs and officers only four and five years older. At 29 Kurt was the old man of the battalion.

Reichsführer Himmler arrived in Metz during August to present the regiment with its new standard. It was a solemn occasion. The standard— a red, gold, white and black swastika banner attached to a guidon surmounted by a metallic SS shield—was dutifully accepted by Dietrich on behalf of the

Leibstandarte. Himmler gave a polite little speech, inspected the immaculate troop formations, then retired to quarters to relieve another of his recurring stomach cramps.

The rumours of an impending invasion of England remained strong during the summer of 1940. Göring had promised Hitler that he could reduce the numbers of RAF aircraft to a point where a seaborne invasion force would be safe from air attack during the Channel crossing. If Churchill had not put out peace feelers by then, the Luftwaffe would reduce London and England's major centres to rubble until the British caved in and asked for terms.

The way the Reichsmarschall described it, the plan sounded plausible enough. Hitler deferred to Göring's expert optimism in all aviation matters. "If the threat appears real enough then the English will believe it." A small invasion force of transport vessels began to gather at several Channel ports, mainly coastal ships of under 5,000 tons and flat-bottomed commercial barges from the rivers of France, Germany and Holland. In anything less than ideal weather conditions the barges would be no more than floating coffins looking for burial. Nonetheless, plans were made, troops assembled, and English-speaking intelligence officers transferred to those regiments designated as the first wave of the invasion force.

But the admirals and generals knew better. Without sufficient capital ships and escorts, the Kriegsmarine couldn't guarantee the Wehrmacht free and unmolested passage for its troop transports. And without that guarantee the army wasn't going anywhere. It already knew the mauling the Royal Navy had given the Kriegsmarine during the past 12 months. The ball was back in the Luftwaffe's court. Göring moved his private rail car up to the French coast in order to supervise personally the airborne destruction of England.

Across the Channel the threat of a German invasion felt very real indeed.

"1 August. . . . Gen. McNaughton and his staff moved up to 7th Corps, consisting of 1st Canadian Division, 2nd New Zealand Division* and 1st Army Tank Brigade. Gen. Pearkes takes over our Division. Our role is as GHQ† reserve to counterattack and destroy any German force that succeeds in effecting a landing in Kent, Sussex or Hampshire. This role, which suits our people, has made constant reconnaissance necessary by staffs and Brigade Commands in order to be familiar with the whole area and prepare plans and orders to meet a half dozen possible courses of action. Each time a route is changed or a Brigade Group altered or speed or spacing modified the unfortunate staff has to get out a new set of orders. I am sick of reconnaissance

---

*Actually two brigades and some artillery.
†General Headquarters.

and sick of movement tables and moves that don't take place. . . .

"15 August. . . . The whole Brigade was out on a practice move in the Tunbridge Wells area when the Blitzkrieg started today. At about 1700 hours in a cloudless sky wave upon wave of German aircraft thundered overhead at about 25,000 feet, too high to see our convoy. Many bombs were dropped quite close to us in several places but no one was hurt.

"In the Smallfields vicinity the Messerschmitts were literally falling like driven birds at the rate of one a minute. One Spitfire I saw knocked down a flight of three. Croydon* was their main target. The midnight news gave the tally as 169 for 37. Even allowing for exaggerations that's not too bad. . . .

"16 August. . . . At noon today and again at 1700 hours large numbers of Germans came over above the clouds. We could hear the machine-gun fire above us and many heavy bombs exploded. The clouds were thick and low so we saw nothing of the battle. The thunder of aircraft engines actually made the ground vibrate at one point. Today's score was 69 for 18.

"We are informed by Lord Haw Haw† that southeast England is in ruins and the morale of our people completely shot. Well there are a lot of large holes in many fields and some buildings have been destroyed. But there are German bombers and fighters strewn all across the countryside from Maidstone to Guildford. As for our moral—it's going up—and up—and up!

"17 August. . . . Boche must be licking his wounds. No air raids.

"18 August. . . . Informed that every bomber that attacked Croydon on Thursday was destroyed. I can believe it from the rate they kept dropping from the sky. At about 1700 hours again another terrific raid was delivered. They passed over us but the air battle was fought above our heads. The RAF turned them back from London. I saw one German squadron completely broken up by our fighters. In many cases their three plane flights were down to one machine, and legging it for France."

A brigade field exercise scheduled for the next day was cancelled when dive-bombers hit the division's supply point. With nothing to do, Harry took a three-day leave and went up to London. No sooner had he got off the train than he was sorry he'd come. "London is terribly dull. As one walks along Piccadilly after dark it's quite evident that all the whores of Paris were safely evacuated. I suppose they prefer us because they know an Englishman always pays. . . . Went to see *Black Velvet*, got out after the pubs had closed. Air raid at 0300 hours. Had a hell of a time trying to prevent hotel authorities making me go to their air raid shelter in the basement. Not much sleep. . . . Picked up something for Margo's birthday. Saw *Shepherd's Pie* in the

---

*A centrally located airfield.[3]
†Real name William Joyce, an American-born British citizen employed by Goebbels for propaganda broadcasts to England from Berlin. His nickname by the British press did much to neutralize his effectiveness. He was tried as a traitor after the war at the Old Bailey and hanged in 1946.

evening and then another sleepless night of air raid warnings, bombs and excitement. . . .

"25 August. . . . Returned to duty. The Blitz has started again. Like clockwork at noon and as it gets dark they come over in waves. They dropped 12 at midnight on the RCRs. Two men killed and four seriously wounded. . . .

"26 August. . . . They bombed the RCRs in exactly the same spot as yesterday, injuring two more who required amputations. Left at 1400 hours for Brigade attack exercise. Spent the night in the open watching air battles. Never saw such a display of lights. . . .

"30 August. . . . A day of continuous air battles overhead, so high you could only hear them except when the sunlight flashed on the wings of the steeply turning fighters. We watched a squadron of Hurricanes dash head on into a squadron of German bombers. One Hurricane smashed into a Heinkel, tearing off a wing. It dropped spinning from 16,000 feet. The Heinkel came down in flames. Both machines landed about a mile away. Then a Junkers exploded in midair. Five parachutes came floating down. I ordered out the 48th Highlanders to round them up. After hitting the ground the Heinkel's bomb load exploded and caught the 48th's ammunition truck which promptly blew up. Fortunately, no one was hurt except for the three well cooked Nazis who were blown to bits.

"The Hurricane pilot dropped into C Battery's area and was sent over to our HQ along with an injured German pilot. The Hun and his gear went off under escort to Advance Divisional HQ while P/O [Pilot Officer] Morris stayed for lunch. He turned out to be a South African teenager and quite unruffled by his first parachute drop. I sent him off in my car to his aerodrome at Biggin Hill. His squadron bagged 17 this morning for the loss only of his machine. . . .

"7 September. . . . Everyone confined to barracks. The invasion is expected tomorrow. We're ready to move at an hour's notice. Air battles high overhead all afternoon. At one time I counted 24 parachutes descending. . . .

"8 September. . . . All last night waves of Germans passed overhead and bombed East London. From the night sky the whole east end looked to be ablaze. Actually, the damage, although considerable, is not really vital. We heard that 400 civilians were killed. It was the biggest raid of the war and we're waiting on tip toe for the invasion. Today's score 88 Nazis to 21 of ours."

Throughout the rest of September the armies in England waited for the Germans to arrive. But the Luftwaffe never managed the air supremacy required to guarantee invasion forces a safe passage across the Channel. Instead of bleeding the RAF into oblivion as Göring had promised, the Luftwaffe itself became the biggest loser. RAF pilots and aircraft that were shot down over England could be recycled, the pilots placed in other aircraft, the wrecked machines cannibalized for parts. But every Luftwaffe machine and crew that went down was lost forever.

"27 September. . . . At about 0930 hours a terrific air battle towards Dorking. Three Messerschmitts and one Spitfire went down. We carried out a practice move to the Maidstone area and again in the afternoon watched another big battle over Tunbridge Wells. Today's score: 133 for 34."

It was to be the last of the big air battles over England. The Reichsmarschall's private rail car returned to Berlin. The pressure eased in southeast England, and those divisions on full alert were ordered to stand down and return to their training exercises. Harry found a new amusement.

"I have started riding a motorcycle and am surprised to find it almost as much exercise and fun as riding a horse. . . . The Brig. threw another of his parties—at the Aldershot Club this time—to which all the really big shots were invited. After the GOC left it was a good party. By evening's end Divisional Signals was distinguishedly plastered."

In mid-October Brig. Armand Smith's staff car was hit head-on by a truck belonging to the East Surrey Regiment. His driver sustained a skull fracture and several cracked ribs. Armand's injuries were more severe. After X-rays at the Bramshott hospital the diagnosis was a dislocated hip and broken pelvis. Privately, the doctors agreed he would be partially crippled for the rest of his life. Officially, he was placed on four months sick leave. Col. Bill Southam* took temporary command of the brigade. Harry drove over to Bramshott to try and cheer Armand up.

"He's more comfortable now but very very down. It's a dingy damn hospital. The dear man has recommended me for promotion and an OBE†—which I am not supposed to know about. It seems there are plans afoot to place the reconnaissance squadrons into a Divisional Reconnaissance Regiment. I'm to command it if they ever get things sorted out in Ottawa. Meantime I am to be offered G2 of 1st Division as a filler. Much as I loathe staff work I'll accept. . . . Poor Armand, what an unlucky break."

Grudgingly, the Wehrmacht Command accepted the need to put every rising young SS commander through a proper junior staff officer training program. Sturmbannführer and below were sent to a hastily arranged staff course at Mühlheim. Kurt spent the fall months attending lectures and demonstrations. Detailed staff work and planning were not at all to his liking. "Paper-pushing-training," he called it, gritting his teeth. He was a man of action, not paperwork.

His Wehrmacht instructors were impressed enough to recommend him for future promotion. Their only criticism was that he "prefers to operate independently on his own initiative rather than adhering to prearranged staff

---

*Later Brig. W.W. Southam, DSO, commander of 6th Infantry Brigade during the Dieppe landings in 1942.
†Order of the British Empire—he didn't get it.

planning." Which meant that his personal initiative required careful scrutiny by his superiors.

Dietrich's assessment was much kinder. "Sturmbannführer Meyer possesses an unusually high degree of maturity in relation to his years. A severe taskmaster even with himself, he places his personal welfare behind the care of his subordinates. This was particularly noticeable during operations in the West. Meyer showed unbelievable courage and valour. A role model for his men, he contributed substantially to the success of the Leibstandarte as leader of its advance guard.

"As Battalion Commander, Meyer has executed the tasks given to him for planning and development with great organizational talent, much circumspection and persistence. Meyer is fulfilling his job as Battalion Commander well."

A ten-year Mutual Assistance Pact had been signed in Berlin during the last week of September by Germany, Italy and Japan. By entering the "Axis" sphere, Japan's leadership of the New Order in Eastern Asia was recognized by Hitler and Mussolini as a *quid pro quo* for Japanese recognition of the New Order in Europe under German and Italian leadership. The pact divided the signatories' interests into clearly defined global segments and provided promises of mutual support where and when required.

Thus, with assurances of German help should he find himself in trouble, Mussolini was ready to embark on his own version of *Blitzkrieg*. The focus of military activity now shifted to the Mediterranean. Adding Mussolini's treachery to France's defection, Britain found itself in a very awkward situation. Certain that Hitler had virtually won the war, Mussolini ordered 300,000 Italian troops based in Benghazi, Libya, to invade Egypt. The vastly outnumbered British forces fell back slowly to Mersa Matruh. From bases in Albania—which the Italians had occupied in April 1939—Italian forces attacked Greece on 28 October 1940. The Greeks not only counterattacked but by the end of November had driven back the Italians deep into Albania. British help was refused on the grounds that the greater the Greek success, the more likely a German intervention.

At sea, Mussolini's dreams of using the Mediterranean as his private pond were shattered on 11 November when torpedo bombers crippled the Italian fleet with a surprise attack as it lay in Taranto. Three battleships were hit, of which one sank, for the loss of two Royal Navy planes. Next day, lighter forces of Adm. Andrew Cunningham's Mediterranean fleet sank three transports and damaged a destroyer in the Straits of Otranto.

On the night of 15 November, Henkel 111 bombers struck the city of Coventry. The Germans claimed it was in retaliation for the bombing of Munich. The British press trumpeted the resulting devastation and loss of life as a prime example of German ruthlessness against unarmed civilians.

As much as 503 tons of explosives were dropped, 60,000 buildings destroyed or damaged—three out of every four at the city's centre, including 28 hotels. Of the 238,000 population, 1,400 people were either killed or injured.

Yet the city and its surrounding district were an important manufacturing centre vital to Britain's aircraft industry in much the same way the peaceful cities of Munich or Essen were to Germany's. In September Sir Charles Portal, then AOC* Bomber Command, considered "such a town as Essen, the whole of which can for practical purposes be regarded as a military target," to be fair pickings. It all depended on whose city was being bombed.

For the Leibstandarte the year ended on an upbeat note with the Führer's visit to Metz the day after Christmas. In a mood of wry humour Hitler toasted his guards with mineral water. It wasn't exactly stand-up comedy off the Tiergarten, but the troops loved him. Later, when the celebrations were over and the extra rations gone, Dietrich said that he couldn't recall another time the Führer had laughed and enjoyed himself as much.

Harry took 48 hours leave over Christmas and went to Aldershot for dinner at Mr. Wotherspoon's in one of the stately homes of England. "A grand old Scot. I'm afraid his third wife was a little fed up with 'Road to the Isles.' I offered an old RMC ditty to break the deadlock. It was well received. Colonial humour is still very much in vogue:

> *T'was Christmas Eve in the harem and a voice shouted down the halls:*
> *What d'y'want for presents, lads? And the eunuchs responded: Balls!"*

9

Mussolini's naval and military disasters soon forced him to ask Hitler for help. In the western desert of North Africa British forces suddenly struck back. Between 9 December and 7 February British XIII Corps, numbering 31,000 men, advanced 500 miles across the desert, capturing 150,000 prisoners, 850 guns, 400 tanks, thousands of trucks and cars. Over 22,000 Italians died in the battles that ranged from Sidi Barrani to Benghazi and Beda Fomm. British casualties for the same period were less than 2,000. It was one of the most spectacular defeats in modern history. Italian Field Marshal Rodolpho Graziani[4] fled the field to resign in disgrace.

A plan was prepared by OKH to assist its Italian ally both in North Africa and the Balkans. On 12 February, the formidable and battle-wise Gen. Erwin Rommel arrived in the port of Tripoli where the remnants of Graziani's dispirited forces sat waiting for direction. The Afrika Corps, composed of

---

*Air officer commanding.

the 15th Panzer and 5th Light Motorized Divisions, arrived by sea a few days later. Using his Germans as a nucleus, Rommel reorganized and revitalized the fainthearted Italians and was soon on the offensive.* The days of easy victories for the British were over.

The OKH plan for the Balkans called for the destruction of the Greek army while at the same time denying British forces an advance base in Greece. The Greek government decided to accept the offer of British aid late in February, and a force of 58,000 Polish, New Zealand, Australian and British troops under Lieut.-Gen. Sir Henry Maitland Wilson arrived in Greece on 7 March. They moved north at once to bolster the Greek army and prepare to meet the anticipated German offensive.

Two German armies were handed the job of subduing the Balkans: the Second, under Gen. Maximilian von Weichs, and the Twelfth, under Field Marshal Wilhelm List. It was to List's force that the Leibstandarte was attached.

An oversized Bavarian, List was an unpleasant, sour-faced man with a wedge moustache; yet he was regarded as a cool and sound strategist who detested military gambles. He had made a name for himself in Poland under von Rundstedt in Army Group South, and again under von Rundstedt in France. For his personal fearlessness in outflanking the Maginot Line he had been promoted from colonel-general to field marshal by Hitler in July 1940.

Early in February List concluded a secret agreement with King Boris of Bulgaria's government that allowed German troops free passage through the country to Greece. The King believed in an ultimate German victory and his war minister, General Dascaloff, was hungry for the slice of Greek territory that would provide Bulgaria with access† to the Aegean Sea. Public notification of their agreement was to be made on 1 March.

Once Bulgaria's agreement had been secured, the Leibstandarte and other elements of the Twelfth Army were moved from France via Rumania and across the Danube into Bulgaria at midnight, 28 February. The following morning Bulgaria formally announced its membership in the Axis Pact.

The Yugoslavs were not as amenable to the idea of their country being used as a German thoroughfare to Greece, but the young king's regent was persuaded by Hitler's offer of the Greek port of Salonika, which would give Yugoslavia access to the Aegean. And why not? Hitler could afford to be magnanimous. This bribery agreement was signed in Vienna on 25 March. The next night the regency was overthrown in a popular uprising that placed 22-year-old King Peter II on the throne.

---

*Rommel first went on to the attack with only parts of the 5th Light Infantry Division and remnants of the Italian 132nd Armoured Division.
†This access territory of western Thrace had been part of Bulgaria until the end of 1918.

The young king spared no words in describing his distaste for Hitler and the German armies bivouacked on his northern borders. Furious, Hitler ordered Belgrade destroyed by waves of bombers. "So! The Slavs have decided to fight me, have they? Are they insane or dreaming?" he demanded across the dinner table of his intimates. "I will awaken them to the reality of their madness." Within days the Luftwaffe had reduced the city to a blazing shambles.

Twelfth Army would strike south toward Skopje, the ancient Macedonian capital. It meant complex operations in a rugged mountainous terrain where there were few roads and even fewer railroads. Supplies were rafted down the Danube to the army's depots and within a week all was in readiness.

The Leibstandarte, forming part of XL Corps, received orders to follow the 9th Panzer Division on an inland thrust from the Bulgarian border town of Kustendil. The corps had been divided into two assault columns: on the north, the Leibstandarte with the 9th Panzers; as the southern attacking probe, the 73rd Infantry Division. This southern column was to attack the town of Prilep and then send out patrols to link up with the Italian forces farther west. The panzer forces, meanwhile, would smash their way through the Kriva Pass and capture Skopje.

The attack began on 6 April, under a chilly new moon. Kurt addressed his men the evening before, preparing them for what lay ahead. As he spoke, an odd sensation came over him. "During my words I sensed for the first time the limitless trust that binds me to my soldiers. I believe I could lead them into hell and they would follow."

The day remained overcast with a cold drizzle that curtained the mountains in mist. The fury of the onslaught caught the Yugoslav army by surprise. The German advance smashed through their primary defence line at the Vardar River by midafternoon. Early next evening the Leibstandarte with the 9th Panzers were in Skopje. Less than 48 hours had elapsed and the troops were already 105 kilometres inland and outrunning their supply columns. A day was taken to secure their gains and regroup before plunging south for the towns of Prilep and Bitola.

Beyond Prilep, combat patrols from 73rd Division struck west. On 9 April they linked forces with the Italians near Lake Orchride at the Albanian border. "They seemed overjoyed by our arrival. There was much singing and shouting. Their commander gave a long-winded speech, pausing occasionally to wipe a tear with what looked like a large soiled dinner napkin. . . . No one had the least idea what he'd said. . . . One foul smelling gunner tried embracing me but I soon put a stop to that."

Kurt's battalion, now spearheading the corps' advance, ran into fierce opposition on the outskirts of Bitola. Serbian troops had dug in behind the railroad embankment leading into town, but instead of waiting until the German motorcyclists were within range and gaining the initiative of surprise, they started shooting wildly as the first machines came into sight. The men swerved for cover. Kurt came forward. A light machine gun was set up covering the embankment to encourage the enemy to keep their heads down while men of the point company dashed across the road and stormed the Serbian command post in a railway guard's hut. The Yugoslavs fled into the adjoining fields to pop up and down like grasshoppers, taking snap shots at their attackers. The German force responded with incendiary and small-arms fire. Several haystacks were set on fire. Gradually, the firing subsided as the Serbians fell back on the town.

The battalion advanced cautiously down the road. One final bend around the side of a mountain and they faced the ancient monastery of Bitola guarding the gateway into town. Kurt split his advancing columns into single attack lines covering both sides of every street. "I had no map of the place but assumed that since it was a railroad town the main streets paralleled the tracks. It turned out to be a good guess."

The Serbs had no stomach for a house-by-house, street-by-street battle. Their sharpshooters and artillery observers posted high in the minarets were quickly silenced with a few well-placed anti-tank shells. Heavy machine guns cleared the fire from second- and third-storey buildings while an engineering troop cleaned out the Serbs defending the railway station. Four hours later the Yugoslav commander gave up. "Our bag from the scrap was a good functional battery and a hundred prisoners."

Beyond the town one of the motorcycle support companies engaged another Serbian company trying to slip away to the south. After a sharp 30-minute battle, they too surrendered. It had been a good afternoon's effort. The rain and low scudding clouds that dogged their advance through the mountains finally thinned, and through the patches of fibrous mist a watery sun shone down. Farther east, German forces entered the port of Salonika and, in the process, cut off the Greek divisions that had been isolated in the provinces of Thrace and Macedonia.

The next objective was to secure the 900-metre-high Javat Pass, 32 kilometres west of Monastir, and make a second link with the Italians. Strategically, the Monastir "Gap" provided the gateway to Greece. Kurt's reconnaissance battalion took up the lead, followed by Sturmbannführer Fritz Witt's 1st Battalion. In addition to Witt's motorized infantry, 1st Battalion had been reinforced by two troops of anti-tank guns, a troop of field howitzers, a battery of 88 mm guns, two troops of infantry guns and an engineering company. Air support provided by General von Richthofen's* VIII Air Corps Stuka dive-bombers was available wherever required and as weather conditions permitted.

---

*A younger cousin of the famous Red Baron, Gen. Wolfram Freiherr (Baron) von Richthofen served in the Red Baron's squadron during World War 1.

The terrain through which they travelled made any massed attack against enemy strongholds virtually impossible. Adapting to their new restrictions, the battalions shredded their forces into smaller self-sufficient units, leaving the responsibility for direct action to the junior commander on the scene. The tactic worked well.

Past Monastir Kurt's lightly armed forward reconnaissance units collided with a heavily armed Yugoslav force of battalion strength. Outgunned and outnumbered, he elected prudently to wait for reinforcements. But to his astonishment the Yugoslavs surrendered. He asked their commander why they had given up so easily. With an apathetic shrug the man explained: "When my men heard that your troops were already in Monastir they panicked. The thought of having to fight Germans put them into shock."

During the night the battle groups crossed the Greek-Serbian border and pushed up to the entrance of the Javat Pass. A mixed Australian brigade group positioned on the heights above barred their way. Kurt decided to wait until dark before mounting an attack along with Witt's 1st Battalion. As the night shadows purpled the mountains, the men moved forward, scrambling over the rocky foothills like mountain goats. By midnight all resistance had been overcome. Two batteries and 700 prisoners were taken. Early next morning a second contact with Italian forces was established.

Beyond the Javat Pass the battalions broke through to the entrance of the Klidi Pass. Kurt's reconnaissance patrols reported heavy enemy concentrations guarding the approaches. Its defenders appeared to be British. Remembering the ferocity of the British defenders at the Dunkirk perimeter, they decided to withdraw and regroup, particularly since their reconnaissance force consisted of only two heavy scout cars, a pair of motorcycle carriers and a pioneer company.

The men spent the night huddled under blankets trying to keep warm and out of the fierce snowsqualls sweeping down from the grim mountains. In the morning a German artillery barrage provided the cover needed for sappers to clear the minefields and the tanks to get through. The Leibstandarte, in furious hand-to-hand fighting, gradually gained the edge. Throughout that day the northern Greek mountains reverberated with the rumble of big guns and the sounds of battle. By noon on 12 April the first of some 600 prisoners were in German hands. Leibstandarte's 1st Company led by Obersturmführer Gerd Pleiss finally stormed the heights and in intense fighting at close quarters captured the enemy high ground to find Australians, and not the British, as the foe.*

The Australians were the first colonial troops the Leibstandarte had met. The Germans were not impressed. "They do not behave like the cold English,

---

*For which Pleiss received the Knight's Cross and 14 members of Witt's group the Iron Cross First Class.

except in their arrogance which is more external than real. They don't seem to be as well disciplined as the English nor wear their uniform as a soldier should. They have all just arrived from Egypt and were complaining of the cold."

Next day Witt's men outflanked the defenders by swinging through the hills to emerge at the southeastern exit of the pass. Total German losses were 37 killed and 98 wounded. The heart of Greece lay open before them. Witt's battle group was relieved by the 9th Panzers, who took up the chase after the retreating enemy.[5]

Kurt's reconnaissance battalion meanwhile crossed the open plain toward the next range of mountains and the Klisura Pass. The pass led through to Lake Kastoria then being used by the Greek army as the centre for its withdrawal from Albania. Elements of the Greek 21st Division guarded the pass, and a narrow mountain road provided the only access. The Greeks had placed huge craters along its length, together with mines and barricades to stop tanks.

The farther into the mountains the motorcyclists went, the heavier the Greek barrage. Finally, Kurt called a halt. A frontal attack up the heavily defended road, he realized, would result in a terrible loss of lives. "I know my opponent has learned his lessons at the War Academy. He knows what actions to take if I appear coming out of the ravine. I must therefore surprise him, attacking his flanks." He opted for a flanking action involving a climb of the 1,400-metre mountains.

Small assault groups were quickly organized and began the tortuous assent, carrying only mortars and small arms up the narrow goat paths. A dark overcast blotted out the sky. The advance parties lost contact with each other, and there were delays while the forces reassembled.

Kurt ordered a halt. Doubts crept over him. "I don't dare go any further. The peaks look like ghosts. I want to wait until morning. It's become bitterly cold. We are soaked in sweat and have brought up neither blankets nor coats. We shiver. No thought of sleep. If I could just smoke a cigarette! A communications vehicle drives cautiously toward me. It gives me protection for a smoke and to study the map again. The more I look at the map the more I shiver.

"At first I think it's the cold making my teeth rattle but then realize it's anxiety that's giving me the shakes. The more time that passes the greater the tension. I can't sit in the car any longer. The beep . . . beep . . . beep . . . of the radio gets on my nerves. Standing outside I don't dare talk to the men for fear they'll see my fear. Everybody squats in silence on the mountain rocks and stares off into the darkness. Are my young comrades frightened too?"

By early morning the German 88 guns were brought up to support positions on the surrounding ledges. With each round their crews risked going over

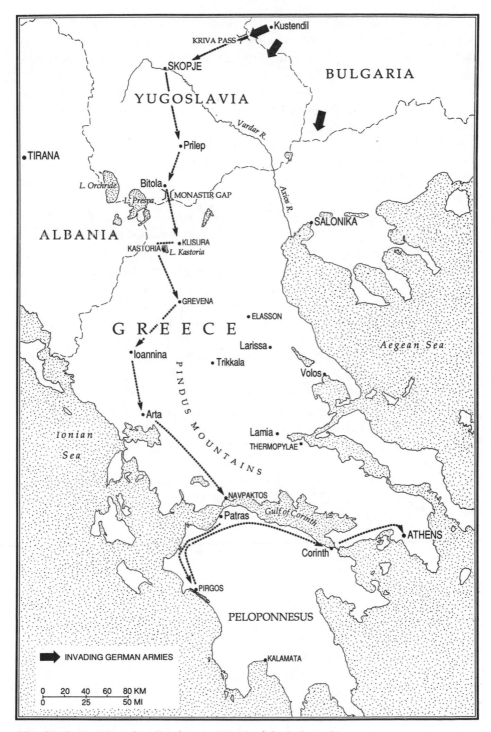

The Greek campaign, showing the movements of the Leibstandarte.

the precipices and into the ravines. The attackers scrambled forward at dawn, running into well-entrenched enemy forces in and around the village of Werjes. The defenders were under orders to contest every fold of the rugged ground.

Kurt arranged his men into three assault groups, leading one himself. "Rolling thunder from the guns echoes these inaccessible mountains. Machine guns bring our attack to a halt. Damn! We can't get stuck here. Although I'm under full cover I too fear for my life. In desperation I grab a grenade and yell to the men. Hey! See this? They look in horror as I pull the pin and lob it behind the last grenadier. Never have I seen them move faster. The spell is broken."

Near noon they slashed through the outer defences. Greek defences began crumbling. The battle was over. Among the 600 prisoners were a brigadier and three battalion commanders. Kurt's losses were seven dead and 18 wounded. They spent the rest of the day mopping up. On the morning of 15 April the road to Kastoria lay open.

But as Kurt's reconnaissance patrols neared the hills ringing the lake, they met stubborn opposition from the Greek 12th Infantry and Cavalry Divisions. The attack halted in a pouring rain that had been drenching them throughout the day. Kurt ordered up a Stuka strike—weather conditions permitting— then sat back to wait.

At 4:30 p.m. 32 Junkers 87 descended through the rain over Hill 800 and in a display of pinpoint bombing hit the Greek positions in each of their defensive vitals. Less than an hour and a half later the peaks were in German hands and the advance rolled forward into the darkness to take the town of Kastoria.

By midnight 12,000 prisoners had been captured along with 36 guns and enormous quantities of vehicles and supplies. Dietrich decided to recommend Kurt for the Knight's Cross.

Approval for a new Canadian reconnaissance battalion came finally from Ottawa on 28 January. General McNaughton strolled into the mess at Aldershot to tell Harry the good news of his promotion and that he was issuing an order for the battalion's formation that afternoon. McNaughton even stood him a drink. The unit was to be known as the 4th Canadian Reconnaissance Battalion (4th Princess Louise Dragoon Guards)—less impressively as the "Plugs."*

Although his new rank of lieutenant-colonel brought him even with Chris Vokes and Guy Simonds, both other men still outranked him in seniority. Vokes had been the 1st Division's assistant quartermaster general and then GSO1 for many months, while Harry had remained a brigade major. Simonds

---

*Cavalry term of derision for old, worn-out horses.

had already commanded the 1st Regiment of the RCHA and had now been appointed to organize the new Canadian Staff College. As far as Harry was concerned, both jobs were "heavy on the paperwork and light on action . . . not my cup of tea." Putting together a new reconnaissance battalion was much more to his liking.

He threw himself into the project with his customary enthusiasm. To fill the new battalion's ranks, an order went out from Division for each unit to supply a quota of NCOs and ORs (other ranks). Naturally, unit commanders used such heaven-sent opportunities to unload their troublemakers, barrack-room lawyers and general incompetents onto someone else. Billeting had to be arranged for the new arrivals, as well as storage parks and maintenance facilities for the motorized equipment. And then the officers and men had to be trained. Ten days after taking command, Harry took his men out on their first field exercise with the division. It lasted three days and to everybody's astonishment the Plugs performed well.

"The outstanding thing to me about the whole exercise is the wonderful spirit and initiative of my lads. They took a tough beating and it never fizzed them. The young dragoons are absolutely marvellous. It's the officers and NCOs who need the training. But above all I'm delighted."

Over the ensuing weeks of practice the unit developed a pride in itself. These successive field exercises became increasingly more cohesive and proficient. There were problems with the Indian motorbikes and shortages of spare parts, and a few recalcitrants had to be disciplined, but nothing that Harry wasn't able to sort out. By mid-April the Plugs had reached a level of competence where even the dour McNaughton felt compelled to say something nice.

"15 April. . . . Today the Corps exercise 'Hare' was conferenced. Only Brigadiers and COs were present. In front of all of them the GOC handed our Recce Group a great big strawberry—the only people he did compliment. The lads deserve it. . . . Acquired the first of our armoured recce cars. Nine were received from Bordon.* Let's hope the Indian combinations† disappear soon. These 'Beverettes'‡ at least look like armoured cars so let's hope the troops have a little more faith in them and take some pride in their maintenance. . . .

"17 April. . . . Last night we watched them give London the worst blitz yet. It was terrifying. This war is all cockeyed. Troops live in the stately homes of England in comparative comfort and safety while the civilians get slaughtered in the towns and cities. Our casualties only occur when people go on leave."

---

*Bordon, Hampshire, not to be confused with Camp Borden, Ontario.
†Indian motorcycles with attached sidecars.
‡Also known as "Humberettes," these were basically civilian trucks, armour-plated and armed with a machine gun.

10

In Greece, Lieutenant-General Wilson's British Expeditionary Force was in the process of being outflanked by the Leibstandarte, which had been ordered by XL Corps to strike south from Kastoria toward Elasson. But the fierce rearguard and rotten weather conditions encountered en route slowed its advance. Realizing the danger to his flank, Wilson ordered a withdrawal in the nick of time. He instructed his force to fall back on Thermopylae in the south and prepare for a general evacuation from the Greek mainland. By 18 April the British withdrawal was well under way and XL Corps in full pursuit.

The Leibstandarte next shifted direction southwest from Grevena to Ioannina and cut off the army of Greece. The Greeks had been squeezed into a funnel between the Pindus Mountains and the Ionian Sea. Once across the Pindus Mountains the Germans would be in a position to strike the enemy at both flank and rear. When the Greeks realized their line of retreat was being blocked, they panicked.

At midmorning, 20 April, one of 2nd Battalion's forward patrols stood in the Katarra Pass, the only entrance through the Pindus Mountains into the Greek province of Epirus. After a short exchange of fire with the enemy, a motorcyclist holding a white flag and leading two staff cars appeared on the road. The SS men held their fire as a group of Greek staff officers climbed out of the cars and came forward. In broken German a Greek lieutenant explained to an incredulous Unterscharführer that the entire Greek army in Epirus of 16 divisions was prepared to surrender. A radio message went out at once to Dietrich to join 2nd Battalion and arrange the final details.

Heavy traffic on the single mountain road kept the ebullient Leibstandarte commander from reaching the pass until late afternoon. He arrived with his adjutant, Max Wünsche, to see a German flag waving proudly over the troops who lined the road cheering him. After a short congratulatory speech he set out with the Greek delegation to discuss terms.

The day also happened to be Hitler's 52nd birthday. Dietrich decided not to inform his Wehrmacht superiors until after accepting the surrender. Then, as a *fait accompli*, he would give the victory to his Führer as a birthday present. Hitler's orders prior to the start of the Greek campaign authorized local commanders to accept every enemy offer of surrender on the spot.

Dietrich's chivalrous terms were from another era and hardly in keeping with the ruthlessness that became so commonplace during this war. Greek officers were allowed to keep their weapons, enlisted men permitted to depart for their homes after handing in their arms. Both commanders drove back to the Katarra Pass for the actual signing ceremony. The surrender was completed under the flags of the two nations.

When the official announcement came out next day, Mussolini flew into a rage over Dietrich's lenient terms and the fact that the surrender had been concluded without Italian participation. A second surrender document had to be signed, this time with Lieut.-Gen. Hans von Greiffenberg, List's chief of staff. It provided much harsher terms. Greek officers were still permitted to retain their side arms, but enlisted men had to be placed temporarily in prison camps. Mussolini was pacified.

Hitler gave Dietrich a mild scolding over the affair. "You are a good, brave soldier, but no diplomat, and still less a politician. You forget that we still have a friend called Mussolini, and he is angry."

The Germans and Greeks held a mutual admiration for each other's fighting abilities and shared an equal contempt for the undisciplined and ineffectual Italian army. After the surrender, 2nd Battalion was ordered north through the Greek lines to join the Italian forces in southern Albania and to protect the defeated Greeks from any acts of vindictiveness by Mussolini's frustrated and inept soldiers.

Surrender of the Greek army ended any chance for Wilson's BEF holding the defence line at Thermopylae. Total evacuation from Greece was ordered on the morning of 21 April. Yet strangely, five days elapsed before the Leibstandarte took up the pursuit.

Kurt's reconnaissance battalion moved south from Ioannina and Arta. In nearly a nonstop drive of over 285 kilometres across the Pindus Mountains they arrived at the Gulf of Corinth to find the British already on the other side. Under a warm afternoon sun the sweating men stared out glumly across the 1.5-kilometre expanse of sky-blue water.

"Four hundred kilometres by road to the other side. What do we do now?" Hugo Kraas inquired, staring through his binoculars at the opposite shoreline.

"Simple," Kurt replied. "We go by boat."

Scouting patrols were sent off to look for suitable water craft. In Holland he had used barn doors. On the road to Kastoria he had used logs to ferry a platoon of men across a river where a bridge had been blown. This time they would travel first class in real boats. After some hours of searching, two reasonably seaworthy fishing craft were commandeered in the small harbour of Navpaktos and, with their owners, pressed into service. Men, motorcycles, ammunition and supplies were loaded aboard and in a succession of ferry trips crossed the gulf near the town of Patras. Scouting patrols were sent out in both directions along the coastal road to find any sign of the enemy. One group surprised a British scouting party of 50 men who had been looking for suitable harbours to evacuate their main force. They appeared perplexed by the speed of the German advance, assuming the men had come around the gulf through the Isthmus of Corinth.

"Tell them we came by fishing boats from Navpaktos." The words were translated to the British officers. "Well?"

"They don't believe you."

"Bah! Stupid Englishmen."

In the afternoon a single platoon took the town of Patras. The Balkan campaign was nearly over. On 27 April, the division motored down the Peloponnesian west coast to the town of Pirgos where troops of the 3rd Battalion captured a rearguard of the British 3rd Royal Tank Regiment. A unit of the reconnaissance battalion cleared the southern coastal road along the gulf to the Corinth Canal. There it linked up with men of the parachute regiment who had been dropped on 21 April in a valiant attempt to cut off the British escape route.

But the bulk of Wilson's Imperial forces had been successfully evacuated. Even so, the cost of helping Greece had been high. To the Germans' 5,000 casualties, British and Commonwealth casualties were close to 16,000, including the loss of 8,000 vehicles plus most of the heavy equipment and guns. In addition, two Royal Navy destroyers and four transports had been sunk and 209 RAF aircraft shot down.

German troops entered Athens on 27 April. Kurt led his men in the victory parade past the Royal Palace. King George was not in residence. He and his family had fled to the island of Crete, less than 120 kilometres away. When the festivities and speeches were over, the Leibstandarte moved out to barracks in Czechoslovakia for replacements and refit.

With the Greek mainland secured, Luftwaffe planners set to work organizing an invasion of Crete.

Mollie Cross had married well. In her youth she had been a redheaded beauty with china doll features, a creamy complexion and a spirited personality. Her husband, a wealthy industrialist from the north of England, had died in early life leaving her with three sons, a "horsey" daughter, a fortune in trust and an enormous home in the village of Fleet, near Aldershot. When the first contingent of Canadians arrived in England, Mollie immediately notified Canada House that her home, "The Poplars," was available for billeting to any senior Canadian officers who were unaccompanied by their wives. "Senior," to Mollie, meant lieutenant-colonels and above.

As Armand Smith's brigade major, Harry didn't quite qualify; yet Mollie couldn't very well deny him her hospitality when the Brigadier brought him along for tea. When news of Harry's promotion reached The Poplars during an after-dinner discussion, her attitude changed. She quizzed her guests on the new lieutenant-colonel's future potential, and after firm assurances by two brigadiers and a major-general that he would in due course reach senior rank, she decided to have him over for her next soirée. When the invitation arrived, Harry accepted.

Eighteen months had passed since he had last seen Margo. He was lonely and badly in need of feminine company. Somebody to talk to besides the men with whom he worked. Margo's four letters per week had dropped to three, then two. Lately he had been getting only one. For months she had chided him for failing to make the promotion list. "You simply must be more assertive, darling. . . . I'm sure you've missed the boat. . . . Much as you may dislike it the fact remains that to get anywhere you have to play politics."

Her letters, for the most part, were filled with chatty inconsequential trivia. Invariably the aerogrammes ended with a passionless perfunctory "love and kisses, Margo." It was like hearing from an old pen pal for whom an obligatory weekly letter had become a habit. About the only item of interest, according to Margo, was the new airport being built just up the hill from the house as part of the British Commonwealth Air Training Plan. "According to Bert Biddle, Picton's Chief of Police, it will be occupied soon with young Englishmen practising bombing and gunnery out over Lake Ontario. . . . I only hope that the noise of the airplane motors won't scare the chickens."

Margo's problems seemed remote. Irrelevant to the reality of the war over England with its air raids, anti-aircraft guns blossoming the skies with flak, and the twisting vapour trails from fighter aircraft locked in a life-and-death struggle every afternoon around tea time. England was real. Canada had faded into a fantasy.

Mollie Cross was part of reality. It would be difficult to say who seduced whom. Perhaps they seduced each other. In any event, within the week Harry was asked to move in at The Poplars. For the sake of propriety they occupied separate bedrooms, but with connecting double doors. They made an odd couple. Harry, ten years her junior, tall, handsome with a quiet sense of humour and natural reticence, appeared misplaced in his new role. She might have been a dotty aunt or an old friend of the family—anything but his paramour. "A forthright charmer although a bit outspoken," he observed tactfully.

In many ways she reminded him of Margo. Certainly not by her appearance, but she did have the same type of dominant personality that made her the centre of attention at any social gathering. He wasn't in love with her. She fulfilled a need. "Besides, there was a war on and I have no intention of turning myself into a monk because of it." Privately, there were those who predicted that the war could go on for years.

With the arrival of spring weather and settling Channel conditions, renewed fears of a German invasion surfaced. Britain's possession of the secret "Enigma" code machine at the outbreak of war had already provided advance warning of Hitler's intentions the previous year. Code-named Operation "Sea Lion," the invasion's D-day had, after much hesitancy, been set for 21 September 1940.

Two armies were to have landed on the south coast from Portsmouth to Margate, establishing bridgeheads between Worthing and Folkestone for their advance north. If required, a third army would be landed in the district of Lyme Regis. But on 17 September Hitler decided to postpone the operation indefinitely. A formal directive followed early in October, cancelling an invasion until spring. But by January 1941 he was still undecided. He confided in Mussolini and Count Ciano, the Duce's son-in-law, on 19 January: "We are in the position of a man with only one round left in his rifle; if he misses, the situation is worse than before."

When the Germans' Balkan campaign began, members of the War Office in London heaved a collective sigh of relief. Thus far in his para-military-political career Hitler had scrupulously avoided committing his main forces to fighting simultaneously on separate fronts.* Then, as the war in Greece wound down and the two great armies of List and von Weichs began withdrawing, rumours of a cross-Channel invasion resurfaced.

On 10 May Hitler's deputy, Rudolf Hess, fled Germany and landed near Glasgow by parachute. In Germany, Hess's precipitous flight as a self-appointed negotiator to arrange a compromise peace proposal was regarded as the action of a mentally unstable member of the Nazi leadership. Goebbels saw to it that the story was treated accordingly. Hitler, shaken at first, was furious at his deputy's defection.

He had only himself to blame. In private he had confided to Hess on a number of occasions the desire for a negotiated peace with England. The reasoning was far from altruistic. Without the Imperial armies opposing his flanks and rear he would have a clear run at Russia. Bolshevik Russia was the common enemy of both England and Germany. Couldn't the stubborn British understand that? Hess had taken his seer's musings to heart and decided to try turning wishful thinking into reality.

Kurt returned home to find himself a hero. On 8 May the magazine *Illustrierter Beobachter* used his picture on its front cover. A photographer had caught him in the middle of roaring out an order during the Greek campaign. "Heavy Artillery Up Front!" the caption read. For several weeks wherever he went, people recognized him. The sudden attention was both pleasurable and annoying. Fame, he discovered, brought with it all sorts of unexpected complications. For one thing, he sensed a feeling of resentment from a few of his brother officers. They had gone through the same war, fought the same enemy, achieved the same objectives.

Dietrich's recommendation that he be given the Knight's Cross had been confirmed, and on 19 May, wearing his plain Waffen-SS uniform for the occasion, Kurt turned up to receive his award from the Führer himself at a brief private ceremony. It was a proud moment for a shopkeeper's apprentice.

---

*Rommel's North African campaign was never more than a miniscule part of the total Wehrmacht war effort.

Hitler remembered him from Schwerin and from his time as the duty officer of the Chancellery guard. He took Kurt warmly by the hand, offering congratulations and thanks on behalf of the German people while flash cameras recorded every nuance of the moment. Then it was over. Outside on the terrace there were more pictures and a clamouring from reporters wanting to hear exact details of the Knight's Cross holder's brave deeds.

Modestly, Kurt told them what had transpired at the Klidi Pass and later at the Gulf of Corinth. The lion's share of the credit he gave to his men. The newsmen ate it up. Next day his photograph and exploits appeared in all the major dailies. Some of his own lads, with straight faces, started asking for his autograph. "I had no idea I was serving under a real hero," one of the Obersturmführers told him facetiously.

A Knight's Cross hanging from his collar and a few days leave to celebrate the event were all he needed for an excuse to visit Offleben. He borrowed a six-passenger heavy-service vehicle from the motor pool and headed out of Berlin. He made reservations at the best restaurant in the district, then took Kate, Melanie and his mother out for an evening on the town. After six hours of eating, drinking, dancing and general merrymaking he realized he was too drunk to drive the ladies home.

The big awkward vehicle was beyond his driving ability. Neither Kate nor his sister had ever learned to drive. Reluctantly, he took the wheel, blinked his eyes and started the motor.

He drove cautiously through the town, easing slowly into the open countryside. He speeded up a little. Maybe he wasn't as drunk as he thought. The night was bright with stars. Good visibility, too late for any traffic, what more could he ask? He accelerated again, a little more than he'd intended. At the next bend of the road he missed the turn, jumped the ditch, knocked out a fence, uprooted a tree and came to rest in a field of turnips.

Kate and Melanie were only shaken, but his mother had broken her front teeth. Very calmly she climbed out of the car and walked around to the driver's side. She opened the door.

"Come here, Herr Sturmbannführer!" Kurt climbed out obediently. Whereupon she lashed out with an open hand, smacking him across the face a half-dozen times. "I'll teach you to jeopardize us all by driving into the turnips!" Groggily he replied, "Not turnips, that's the *Lappwald*."*

The car was a write-off. He phoned Berlin next day and explained sheepishly to Dietrich what had happened. To his surprise Sepp wasn't angry. "Never mind the car. I'll send a crew down to bring it in. The main thing is that you're alive. Fine thing for a military hero . . . drunk in a turnip field!"

---

*A local forest.

Oddly, during the same week, Harry had a car accident in England. A heavy evening rain shower had prompted Mollie to suggest he leave his motorbike at The Poplars and borrow "Black Bess," her Singer convertible, for the drive back to base. Harry agreed. A few miles beyond Fleet he ran into a hidden roadblock set up by members of the local Home Guard out on manoeuvres. The roadblock, a single strand of steel wire anchored between two trees, was designed to decapitate German motorcyclists who might have landed by parachute. "Gives my lads a chance to practise the real thing," the elderly Colonel Blimp in charge of the exercise informed him enthusiastically. The wire tore out Black Bess's windshield and canvas roof. Harry collected a few cuts from the flying glass. Had he been driving his motorbike he would have lost his head in addition to his sense of humour and patience with the irresponsible Home Guard.

PART 6

FORTUNE'S FATE

To conquer Russia, one must first be prepared to die.

NAPOLEON BONAPARTE

HITLER had started operational planning to attack Russia as far back as July 1940. His Directive No. 21, code-named "Barbarossa," set the results of that planning into motion. Like his war with Poland he viewed a German attack on Russia as nothing short of a sacred trust to ensure the survival of European civilization from an inferior Asiatic society. At least this is what he wanted the German people to believe.

But where his conquest of Poland could be seen—at least in part—as legitimate recovery of German territory, war with Russia was justified by a political ideology formulated to coincide with economic and military aims. Germany wanted Russia's oil and vast grain production, plus that warm sense of security on its eastern flanks that a subjugated Russia would provide.

For years one of the main planks of the Nazi party platform had been Hitler's insistence on the need for German *Lebensraum* (living space) and the final "coming struggle with bolshevism." Anti-bolshevism had become a doctrine of German racial superiority, and nowhere was it more profoundly taught than in Himmler's ss. Human nature has demonstrated since the dawn of time that any lie trumpeted long and loudly enough by those in authority will eventually be embraced as gospel by those who must obey. Thus, the majority of Germany's fighting men, particularly those of the SS, believed in the righteousness of their cause against the Slavic and Asiatic subhumans of Soviet Russia.

Three German army groups were to be used for the campaign. Army Group North, under Field Marshal Ritter von Leeb, would strike toward Leningrad. Army Group Centre, under Field Marshal Fedor von Bock, was to advance on Moscow, while Army Group South, under Field Marshal Gerd von Rundstedt, made its way to Kiev and the rich agricultural lands of the Ukraine. The Leibstandarte was attached to Army Group South.

The logistics in assembling such enormous numbers of men, weapons, transport, supplies and equipment were mind-boggling. Besides the millions of men involved who had to be clothed, housed and fed, there were 750,000 horses, 7,000 artillery pieces, 3,000 tanks and over 600,000 vehicles. The original plan called for 147 divisions, including 24 panzer and 12 motorized. It was to be a lightning war beginning in May and finishing before the winter snows brushed the Russian landscape. In February 1941 the first of Army Group South's forces began concentrating along the Soviet frontier. But it took until June before its divisions were positioned.

Yet even using the most optimistic projections, Greater Germany with its population of 90 million was no match for the 205 million citizens of the U.S.S.R. During the conflict's initial stages this disparity was not so much one of men and equipment as of attitude.

Without question the German army of 1941 was the best equipped, best trained, best led and best organized military force the world had ever seen. Theoretically, it should have been able to slice through the Red Army like a hot knife through butter. But what OKH intelligence overlooked was the average Soviet citizen's incredible passion and love for Mother Russia. Political ideology had little to do with it. The fact that an ogre ruled behind the Kremlin walls was immaterial. OKH and Hitler underestimated that strangely oriental capacity in the Russian people to endure and thrive against enormous hardships and, in the end, to prevail.

To this day Western Europeans and North Americans have only the vaguest notion of Germany's war with Russia. By comparison, the battles of North Africa, Burma, Italy and later on the Western Front were little more than a series of compact, hard-fought regional conflicts. The battle lines during the eastern campaign at one point extended over 3,200 kilometres, from the forests of Finland to the subtropics of the Caucasus—roughly the distance from the Canadian-U.S. border to Mexico City or from the toe of Italy to the Arctic Circle in Norway.

At its peak in September 1943, 2.5 million German soldiers were battling against 6 million Russian troops; the former included Finnish, Rumanian, Hungarian, Italian, Croatian, Slovak and volunteer troops from nearly every country in Europe—including a handful from Britain—and over 900,000 Soviet citizens. Von Bock, with his Army Group Centre of over one million,[1] had the distinction of commanding the largest body of men ever to go into battle.

For Germany the war in the east began inauspiciously. The Balkan war had deprived von Rundstedt's Army Group South of one-third of its tank strength. The German air attack on Crete in late May had delayed the return of the decimated VIII Air Corps to Poland (due to the enormous airborne casualties over Crete, Hitler vetoed any large-scale parachute operations during the early stages of the Russian attack). Finally, the 35,000-ton battleship *Bismarck*, pride of the German navy, had been sunk by the Royal Navy on 27 May. The loss ended all hope of German surface raiders being able to intercept and destroy the vital Atlantic convoys supplying England and later Russia.

The Soviet High Command concentrated its forces in the south, believing this area to be the decisive battlefront. The region of flat agricultural lands with few trees was ideally suited to fast mechanized deployment of tanks and motorized infantry. The Russians held a 3 to 1 numerical superiority over the Germans in tanks and, with only partial mobilization, were able to muster 130 rifle divisions. Facing Army Group South were 45 rifle, 20 tank, six cavalry and ten mechanized divisions. The Pruth, San, Bug and Dnieper rivers formed natural defensive blocks against the invaders. The strongest defence line was at Kiev where the Dnieper was 1.2 kilometres wide.

Although the Leibstandarte had been attached to III Corps for the assault on 22 June, because of a shortage of spares for its tracked vehicles it was unable to join the initial attack. Finally, on 27 June, the unit's movement orders arrived from 1st Panzer Group. On the morning of 1 July the main body of men and equipment crossed the Vistula River and joined the battle.

In ten days of fighting the Wehrmacht had already achieved some spectacular successes. The two arms of the 1st Panzer Group's pincer movement had knocked aside the Russian armour and were driving for Kiev and Kasatin. The weather was idyllic: skies nearly cloudless, the breezes warm and inviting. "I could feel myself fill with excitement and enthusiasm for what lay ahead," wrote Ernst Böhm. "No one had the least doubt that we could beat the Ivans. It was only a question of how long it would take us to do it."

Within hours of their arrival on the scene the men of the Leibstandarte were battling Russian tanks attempting to cut the northern highway at Dubno. Waffen-SS gunners drove them back in confusion from the flanks. "Their counterattack was launched while we were still getting our breath. Their infantry came in mounted on open trucks that swayed from side to side with the speed. It looked as if every Ivan on the trucks was standing and firing at us. All quite primitive. Their trucks just drove straight at our positions. . . . A shell hit one and killed many of the infantry riding on it, but the others leaped over the sides and charged us on foot. There was no cover anywhere. They had no hope of reaching our positions, but still they came on."

Heavy rains that evening turned the battlefield into mud. But nothing could dampen the enthusiasm of the young grenadiers after this first taste of combat against the Red Army. Early next morning they were back on the offensive.

Kurt had a sense of foreboding about the war with Russia. His knowledge of history had taught him the danger of fighting on two fronts. Then there were the Russians themselves—strange, fanatical soldiers who seemed to have no regard for their personal safety or survival. The idea of it made him uneasy.

During late morning from his command car at the front of the battalion he saw a pillar of smoke on the horizon. The mushy surfaced road from Klewan to Bronki cut through broad fields of green corn. Patches of clover bordered the shallow ditches on either side. By the road lay an abandoned German artillery piece. The sight shook him badly. "For the first time we find a German weapon left alone on a battlefield. A few paces away from the gun stands a looted ambulance, its bloodstained doors open. We examine the spectacle in silence. Neither dead nor living soldiers can be seen. A slow drive up the hill. Through field glasses I can make out a few bright spots. I lower the glasses, rub my eyes and try again. My God! I can't believe what I'm seeing. . . .

"We cover the last few hundred metres quickly and jump down. Our steps become slower. We stop. No one dares go further. Helmets are bowed as if in prayer. Not a word profanes this place. Even the birds are silent. Before us lie the naked bodies of a company of German soldiers. They have been horribly slaughtered. Their hands are tied with wire. Dead eyes stare up at us.

"Their officers have met an even worse end. Their bodies lie in green clover some yards from their comrades. They have been mutilated and are in pieces. No one speaks. Here, only the Majesty of death talks. We walk along the rows of murdered dead. My soldiers regard me ashen-faced. They expect some explanation or order from me concerning their future conduct in Russia. We regard each other. I look each man in the eye. Then, without a word, I turn away and we continue our advance toward an unknown fate."

Later, Kurt learned that the men were part of a group of 200 soldiers from the 6th and 7th Companies of the 35th Infantry Regiment. A hundred and nineteen of them had been captured by the Russians and were executed on the spot. It was to be a war with no quarter asked or given by either side.

Supporting the Red Army were guerrilla fighters behind the German advance. These partisan activities forced combat units—sometimes whole divisions of troops—to be detached from the main forces at the front in order to deal with them. As the German advance rolled eastward, partisan activities increased to alarming proportions. "The front is everywhere," Kurt observed uneasily. In districts where local populations appeared to be accepting the invaders—some even as liberators—partisan forces savaged the region by sabotage and atrocities to provoke German retaliation against the blameless local residents. Such actions naturally resulted in the recruitment of new partisans.

A vicious retaliatory cycle of brutality developed swiftly between the invaders and defenders during the first weeks of the campaign. Waffen-SS units, spearheading the advance in all three army groups,[2] were especially hated by the Red Army, none more so than the Leibstandarte, who proudly wore the cuff-band of "Adolf Hitler" on their uniforms. (Leibstandarte and Wiking Divisions were attached to Army Group South; Das Reich with Army Group Centre; Totenkopf and Polizei with Army Group North.) To escape torture and mutilation at the hands of the Russians, it became standard practice for Waffen-SS officers to administer a bullet to the brain of those men too badly wounded to be moved; evacuating those who could be moved became a point of honour for every officer in the field. Life became cheap and Waffen-SS units often summarily executed partisans, commissars, Communists or anyone else they considered to be a threat. The Russians retaliated in kind. Thus the hatred grew.

Russian attempts to cut the northern highway continued unsuccessfully for several days. A period of bad weather turned fields and roads into rivers of mud. For a day or two the Leibstandarte bogged down. Seventeenth Army, meanwhile, was busy fighting its way through the defences of the Stalin Line in order to create the opening needed to unleash 1st Panzer Group into the open country beyond. Once the line was breached, the German armour raced ahead across the vast empty Russian steppes, outstripping its infantry support and supply lines by as much as 80 kilometres. It was an intoxicating experience when viewed from a command car at the front of an advancing column.

"Our situation map shows that we are fighting in a sort of vacuum. We cannot stop and wait for them [the infantry] to catch up. We must push ahead. . . . We are like a storm wind."

With the German flanks exposed from the speed of their advance the Soviets attacked, attempting to drive a wedge between the armoured spearhead and trailing infantry columns. Leibstandarte was sent toward Ostrog to plug one of these gaps on the northern flank of the 11th Panzer Division. At noon on 7 July, as part of the advance guard, Kurt led his battalion across the Sluczk River, smashed through the Stalin Line at Miropol, then continued driving up the road toward Zhitomir and Romanovka.

Two days later he received orders to attack the Russians in the heavily forested area north of Romanovka. On a beautiful summer morning he set out from the bivouac area in his command car. Enemy resistance along the route remained light and spasmodic. Where was the enemy's main force? Quite suddenly, he passed a Russian anti-tank gun with its crew set up at the side of the road. He was past before the gunners had time to react. Coolly, he ordered his driver to stop a few hundred metres down the road. Taking the three others who were with him in the car, he crept back through the woods to eliminate the gun and its crew. Without realizing it, he was leading his men into a trap. A company of Russian soldiers were bivouacked in the forest. They had seen the German command car stop and its occupants slip away into the trees. The Russians hugged the ground, waiting. When the quartet had crawled Indian fashion into the midst of them, they stood up grinning, their weapons levelled. Kurt's blood went cold. Somehow he managed to keep his wits about him.

Nonchalantly carrying his own weapon, he walked over to a tall, good-looking man, obviously the unit's commanding officer. Politely, he introduced himself and shook hands with the Russian. Both bowed simultaneously, each declaring the other a prisoner of war. The Russian's blue eyes twinkled in delight at Kurt's joke. He accepted a German "Attica" cigarette and lit a match. Cigarettes were then offered to the rest of the Russians. Everyone lit up. Kurt summoned Drescher, his interpreter. A heated discussion followed on who exactly had to surrender to whom. It was all a desperate stall for time. Kurt figured that if he could keep the man occupied in argument until the rest of the battalion arrived he might stand a chance of living to fight another day. His lead detachments were due along the road any moment. Just as the conversation started turning ugly, the Russian anti-tank gun opened fire. The battalion had arrived. The Russian wasted no more time. Angrily, he signalled that the Germans were to place their weapons on the ground.

Kurt feigned a lack of understanding. He told Drescher to ask the officer if he'd be good enough to demonstrate exactly what it was he wanted. Drescher rolled his eyes and translated. The man blinked angrily at such stupidity and incredibly placed his beautiful automatic rifle with the telescopic sight on the ground at his feet. Kurt promptly stood on it.

Russian voices began shouting from the depths of the forest. German tanks and infantry were approaching. Everyone dived for cover. Kurt used the officer as a living shield. For one of them it would be his last minute on earth.

"A last look into my opponent's eyes. He knows what is going to happen. He seems calm."

Kurt yelled, "Fire!" and dove for cover. The air filled with explosions and the dry crackling of rifle fire. The Russian officer lay dead.

2

While the German advance rolled eastward across Russia, the Canadian army in England played war games and trained. The news from every front was bad, and the frustration of being confined to an endless series of lectures and make-believe battles was beginning to take its toll on the patience of the volunteer army that had come to fight Germans. A steady stream of recruits flowed from the basic training camps in Canada. As the numbers of Canadians in England grew, so did their grumbling. Harry's mood too had changed from its earlier enthusiasm.

"7 Aug. . . . Together with Churchill Mann I am back at Staff College Camberley. This time as an 'expert' on Rcccc Battalions. It seems very strange to be free to walk into the rooms marked 'DS Only.' Actually we find ourselves here under false pretenses. Corps ordered our presence for a conference— some conference! We are simply assisting the D.S.* in an ordinary approach march exercise.

"9 Aug. . . . Returned to Limpsfield in the pouring rain, still unimpressed by the bilge of Staff College. Even now they can't seem to be really practical and although the present Commandant does his best to pin them down, the jolly boy attempt to be theatrical and waffle is still as pronounced as in my time.

"12 Aug. . . . I am ordered to send one Captain, one subaltern and two Sergeants back to Canada as instructors at the Armoured Corps training centre. What a headache. Who will I send? The ones who can do the job I refuse to part with, the ones I could spare are not suitable. No one will volunteer.

"13 Aug. . . . Today we are on 'Action Stations,' for exercise ROFT. It's being staged by Division as a dress rehearsal for an Army show at the end of the month. We begin with an indifferent frame of mind. Same old invasion, same old line of country, same shortages of equipment."

Margo's letters about life "on the farm" were beginning to pall even more. The warmth and chattiness had faded from her prose. Harry assumed it was his fault for not being more outgoing in his own correspondence. He had never been able to accept the idea of military censorship of personal letters. Inscribing his emotions for some enlisted man to read was unthinkable. He also harboured feelings of guilt over his liaison with Mollie Cross. He might have saved himself the worry. Margo was involved with her own "affair."

Flying Officer Jimmy Shields came from Devon. He had flown Sopwith Camels in "that last bit of nonsense with Germany," as he put it. Between wars he had married, raised two children and become a respectable house-

---

*Department staff.

master in a second-rate school. When war was declared, he re-enlisted in
the air force. Because of his age he made ground school instructor and
eventually transferred to RCAF Station, Picton, as part of the cadre at the
new airport. The airport, one of dozens being constructed across Canada
under the British Commonwealth Air Training Plan, sat atop a broad plateau
less than a mile from town. Margo's small farm and house were even closer.
They met on a hot summer weekend at the beach. She felt sorry for him.
He was older than the rest of the young airmen who cavorted about the
sand—grey haired, rakishly handsome, trim physique and smoking a pipe.
It was lust at first sight. She invited him home for supper.

In the weeks that followed, the children came to accept "Uncle Jimmy"
as a permanent houseguest who came and left at odd hours of the day and
night and slept in their mother's bedroom. There was no sense of outrage
or betrayal. It was the way things were and they accepted it. Besides, the
memory of their father had dimmed considerably during his two-year absence.

In the East the Russians went briefly on the offensive. The Leibstandarte
fought back. "These Ivans must have been elite troops . . . nearly as good
as us. We did close combat training back in the golden days but always thought
it somewhat superfluous. We don't now. . . . They use their entrenching tools
like Storm Troops of the Great War. These are the best fighters we have
ever met . . . better even than the Poles. How long ago that all seems."

This particular July attack began at 0100 hours. It developed quickly into
hand-to-hand fighting, with Germans and Russians lunging and hacking at
each other in the dark forests. Exploding mortars set the treetops alight
and showered the combatants with shrapnel. "Losses suffered during this
two-day battle exceeded our total casualties of all the other campaigns," Kurt
reported.

Every thrust met a Russian counterthrust, every pincer movement found
itself outflanked by a wider Soviet sweep. The succession of battles became
confusing. "Are the Russians outflanking us or are we outflanking them?"

But the biggest surprise was the quality of the new Russian T34 tanks
that had begun to replace the earlier Russian losses. Their hardened armour
and sloping sides made them immune to infantry weapons. Even the normally
reliable 88 mm field guns had difficulty piercing the T34's armour at ranges
of more than 900 metres. A discouraging discovery.

Just when it became apparent that the Red Army was in full retreat and
von Rundstedt's Army Group South in a position to seize Kiev, its first
strategic objective, Hitler changed his mind. He decided to shift the main
advance from Kiev to Uman. With new orders the bulk of the Sixth Army
wheeled southeast to cut off the Russian units fighting against the German
Eleventh and Seventeenth Armies.

By 23 July OKH intelligence sources placed Russian losses at 50 percent;

German losses at 20 percent for infantry and 50 percent in armour. The figures were wildly optimistic. In reality many of the panzer divisions were down to 20 percent of their establishment strength. The Russians, on the other hand, were now more numerous and better equipped than when the campaign started. Their massive reserves of manpower were finally coming into the battle lines.

Near the end of July panzer spearheads were approaching Uman. The capture of Nova Arkhangel'sk hastened the ring of the German troops closing around the Soviet Sixth and Twelfth Armies. Fighting remained bitter and continuous. Yet, instead of pulling back to a new defensive line as military logic dictated, the inexperienced—and probably frightened—Russian generals obeyed Stalin's directive to stand and fight. With pistol-waving commissars urging them forward, the defenders fought to the last round, many to the last man. The Germans were astonished by the ferocity of their resistance and such pointless expenditure of human life.

Russian tanks were hurled against the Leibstandarte battalions and succeeded briefly in breaching their lines to re-enter Uman. But the exhausted Waffen-SS soldiers beat them back. First Panzer Group's armoured pincer struck southeast from Kasalin to join up with the Magyar Infantry Division and seal off 25 Soviet divisions. One hundred thousand Russian soldiers were taken prisoner.

Panzer Gen. Werner Kempf, commander of the corps to which the Leibstandarte was attached, wrote afterwards: "Committed to the focus of the battle for the seizure of the key enemy position at Nova Arkhangel'sk, the Leibstandarte . . . with incomparable dash, took the city and the heights on its south. In the spirit of the most devoted brotherhood of arms, they intervened on their own initiative in the arduous struggle of the 16th Infantry Division (motorized) on their left flank and routed the enemy, destroying numerous tanks. Today, at the conclusion of the battle of annihilation around Uman, I want to recognize and express my special thanks to the Leibstandarte SS Adolf Hitler for their exemplary effort and bravery." High praise indeed from a Wehrmacht general.

After the fall of Uman the panzer group's headlong thrust east continued. During the second week of August the Leibstandarte occupied a salient in the crossroads town of Sasselje, captured from a Russian cavalry and infantry division. It was a district of beautiful woods and small lakes. Unaware that the town was already occupied, Russian troops entered it from the west, intending to use it as an escape route. German artillery turned the advancing column of trucks into a line of blazing wreckage.

The Russians counterattacked simultaneously from east and west of the Leibstandarte positions. An infantry attack swarmed in from the fields of corn and sunflowers that lay to the east of town. Their soldiers came in a human wave toward the lines of Waffen-SS and were driven back with terrible losses. An infantry-supported tank assault appeared from the west. The German artillery smashed it to a halt. Kurt's armoured reconnaissance vehicles drove into the mass of Soviet infantry, driving it back in confusion. The fighting subsided.

An old man in Sasselje begged an audience with the German commander. He was brought to Kurt. Through Drescher he introduced himself as a priest of the Russian Orthodox church.

"What do you want?"

"Your permission to conduct a church service, Commander. It has been many years since our town has had one."

"You have it," Kurt replied. "What else?"

The priest hesitated. "My church was turned into a movie theatre by the government. Do I have your permission to turn it back into a house of worship?"

"Permission granted. Anything else?"

"Yes, Commander. Allow me to pray for you."

The war moved on, destructive and bloody. Through the towns where the Russians decided to make a stand, there was street fighting, frantic house-to-house battles, men locked in desperate combat, sometimes within a single room. Sleepless nights, exhausting days, always on the move, thrusting eastward into the heartland of Soviet Russia.

As Kurt's battalion drove along the road, an enemy shell incinerated one of the armoured cars. Kurt stopped but could do nothing. The agonizing screams from his men trapped inside shook him. Finally, on 20 August, the Leibstandarte handed over its sector to a reserve replacement force and moved back from the front for a few days' rest.

On 8 September a small Canadian raiding force of 527 men commanded by Brig. Arthur Potts returned to England from the arctic archipelago of Spitzbergen. The force, consisting of a Norwegian infantry party and a detachment of British engineers, had sailed with the Canadians on board the *Empress of Canada* to remove 2,000 Russian inhabitants and take them to the Russian port of Archangel. Two British cruisers and three destroyers under Rear Adm. Philip Vian accompanied the *Empress*. The handsome Vian belonged to an era of cutlasses and buccaneers. The Spitzbergen venture was tailor-made for him. Although the island was Norwegian territory, the Russians occupied part of it under an agreement that both nations could share its natural resources.

The original plan had been for the Royal Navy to occupy the place and use it as a coaling station for the Russian convoys. But after further consideration they abandoned this idea as impractical. Lying 600 miles inside the Arctic Circle, Spitzbergen was just too far away. Instead, the Admiralty decided that Vian's naval force would send troops ashore and destroy everything of value to prevent it falling into German hands.

The force sailed via Iceland and arrived at Spitzbergen without incident. A signals detachment landed at the island's main wireless station where Norwegian radio operators agreed to begin forwarding false weather reports during their regular transmissions to Trondheim, in German-occupied Norway, thus keeping German reconnaissance aircraft away from the island.

While the Russian contingent was being transported to Archangel, Potts's demolition troops went ashore and systematically destroyed all mining machinery and stores and set alight the vast coal dumps and oil reserves. Over 450,000 tons of coal went up in flames.

The *Empress* returned from Archangel with a surprising collection of 50 bedraggled Free French officers on board. Captured by the Germans and imprisoned in eastern Poland, they had managed to escape to Russia, believing passage would be arranged for them to join de Gaulle's forces in England. Instead, they were imprisoned. The Russians had treated them worse than the Germans had. Potts's brigade major, Scott Murdoch, took a group of them ashore for some exercise and had a tour of the Russian mining settlement. An enormous picture of Joseph Stalin hung in the village's central dining hall. The Frenchmen stopped and glared. "One of them, Billotte—who later became a general—asked to borrow my pistol. I handed it over. Whereupon he began shooting at old Joe. The others cheered and demanded a turn. Fortunately, I had a couple of extra ammo clips. . . . They certainly hated the Russians."

The *Empress* took Spitzbergen's 800 Norwegian residents on board and re-embarked Potts's force. Men and ships headed for home. It wasn't much of an action, but it gave the Canadians a sense of having done something useful instead of lounging around the training areas of Sussex playing war games.

"9 Sept. . . . The raiding force under Brig. Potts returned today. We get our Padre Smith back again. We were rather disappointed to lose him. Now we know why. . . .

"11 Sept. . . . This morning one of our six remaining English armoured carriers threw a track down Wych Cross way. It swung out of control into a deep ditch and somersaulted. Troopers Moriarty and Brouse were killed instantly. From preliminary investigation it appears that the track had a cracked link. It remains to be seen if the fault could have been detected in the course of weekly maintenance. When in God's name will we ever go to war? To die in battle is one thing. To be killed in a stupid training accident is such a pointless waste of life."

The Leibstandarte went back into the line during the first week of September. Its orders were to cross the 1.2-kilometre-wide Dnieper River and advance over the Nogai steppe, a bleak expanse of emptiness between the Dnieper and the Black Sea. Although the steppe was in flower, not a tree or a hill could be seen. Crimson dawns came early with a wide and boundless view that lost itself in the misty horizon. During summer months the streams and creeks dried up under the baking sun, leaving 31,000 square kilometres of parched flat desert. It was ideal country for heavy armour, but the Eleventh Army, to which the Leibstandarte was attached, had no armour other than the lightly armoured scout cars of its reconnaissance battalions.

Kurt led the column's spearhead. Earlier, he had organized his motorcycle units to attack using standard cavalry formations. The results were a great success. Kilometre after empty kilometre they raced across the steppe. Living conditions in the region were abominable.

"There is very little water and what there is, is salty. Coffee is salt flavoured, the soup is oversalted . . . but we are pleased to get even this tepid liquid, for this is true desert country. Movement is visible for kilometres; clouds of choking red brown dust hang over the columns and pinpoint our exact positions. Paradoxically, the only sign of life is the dead tree trunks of telegraph poles. Without them it would be difficult to orientate oneself. . . . Sometimes we find a melon and gorge, but the unripe ones have unhappy effects."

The advance continued across the steppe to Kalantchuk. Orders for a night attack against the town were countermanded. Hitler had changed his mind. An immediate thrust toward the Crimea was now ordered. The Leibstandarte motorized columns turned south.

On the afternoon of 3 September, the XXIV Panzer Corps commander, Gen. Geyr von Schweppenburg, received a charred bundle of papers from one of his intelligence officers. The documents had come from the pouch of a downed Soviet courier aircraft. After reading the translation and studying his maps, the General smiled. The papers revealed a weak link between the Soviet Thirteenth and Twenty-first Armies. Geyr sent General Model's 3rd Panzer Division at top speed toward the Russian gap. Next morning, after a four and a half hour drive covering less than 80 kilometres, Guderian arrived at Geyr's headquarters. Baron Geyr had good news. Model's tanks had already driven through the gap, tearing open the flanks of two Soviet armies. Like a bursting dam, German infantry and artillery units were pouring through the breach toward the south. The delighted Guderian drove on to Model's headquarters.

So began the greatest single battle of encirclement in military history. To the south, von Kleist's XLVIII Panzer Corps, commanded by Gen. Werner Kempf, turned and struck out toward the advancing Model. The Soviet commander, Marshal Budenny, very sensibly issued orders on 9 September to prepare for a general withdrawal while there was still time to escape the closing ring. He asked Stalin's permission to abandon Kiev and the

Dnieper River bend. Stalin, in a raging tantrum, refused. Budenny was ordered to turn back and "stand fast, hold out, and if need be die." Budenny obeyed. His withdrawal orders were cancelled.

At 1820 hours on 14 September, forward elements of the 1st and 2nd Panzer Groups connected near a small lake. The trap had closed around 50 Russian divisions. For 12 days the encircled armies fought to break through the German ring, both from within and without, using counterattacking forces rushed to the scene by Soviet High Command. But they were too late. Stalin's order had sealed their doom.

The Russian attacks were diffuse and uncoordinated. Near Putivl, cadets from the Kharkov academy charged the German positions singing patriotic songs. They were killed to the last man. At no point along the 250 kilometres of Guderian's deep flank did the Soviets manage even a dent. Finally, on 19 September, divisions of xxiv Corps captured Kiev. By the 26th it was all over. Five Russian armies had been smashed and two more badly mauled. One million men had been killed, wounded or taken prisoner.

Marshal Budenny, ex-sergeant in the old Tsarist army and hero of the Revolution, was flown to safety by Stalin's order. Colonel-General Kirponos took over command, but he and his chief of staff were killed trying to break out of the German ring. The final tally of Soviet losses, not including those killed and wounded, came to 665,000 prisoners, 884 armoured vehicles, 3,718 guns and vast quantities of supplies. Kempf's xLviii Corps alone took 109,097 prisoners—more than the total captured in the Battle of Tannenberg during World War i.

Hitler was jubilant. He convinced himself that after such enormous losses the Russian armies in the south could no longer maintain a serious line of defence. He issued new orders: "The Donets Basin and the Don are to be reached before the onset of winter. The blow at the Soviet Union's industrial heart must be struck swiftly." Why he decided to ignore a final thrust toward Moscow that could well have toppled the country's reeling leadership in favour of this side trip remains a mystery.

As it moved toward the Crimea in mid-September, the Leibstandarte began meeting heavy resistance. The Russian armies that had retreated into the Crimean Peninsula might have been held and destroyed had not Hitler dissipated Army Group South's efforts by ordering the front extended and then directing it to capture the Crimea.

The Perekop Isthmus, a slender neck of land only 8 kilometres wide, provided one of the entrances onto the peninsula. It sat heavily fortified and without cover. The task of forcing its passage was handed to the Leibstandarte. The motorized reconnaissance group spearheaded the advance in front of the 73rd Infantry Division. From his command car at the head of the column during the early morning of 12 September, Kurt caught sight

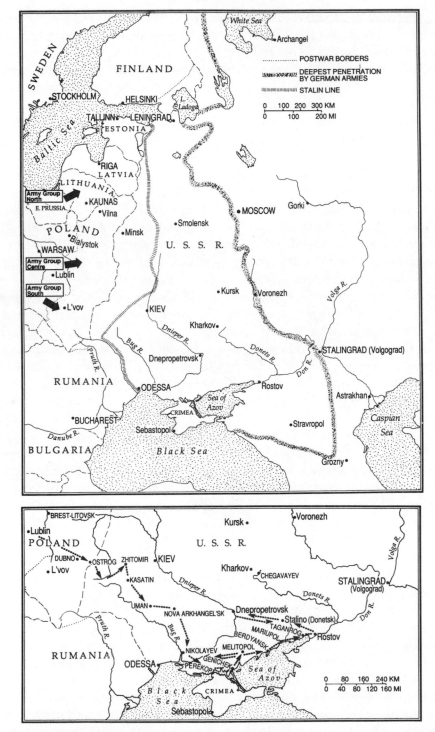

(Above) The Eastern Front and (below) the southern Ukraine, showing the movements of the Leibstandarte.

of several horsemen on the horizon. They appeared like ghosts, then vanished.

The situation called for a cautious approach. "Soviet scouts. Drive in open order!"

Slowly the vehicles advanced, the motorcycle infantry riders poised to leap from their machines and take up defensive positions at the first sign of trouble. A little after 0600 hours a motorcycle detachment under Gruppenführer Westphal reached the outskirts of Preobrazhenka. A flock of sheep barred their way into the village.

"Get your animals off the road, man!" Westphal roared. "We're in a hurry." The Tartar shepherd shrugged his indifference. Angrily Westphal charged the flock, which scampered off the road and straight into a minefield. Exploding mines and the screams of disintegrating sheep filled the leaden morning air. Then, within moments, came the more authoritative sound of artillery from beyond the village. The motorcyclists dismounted and continued their advance on foot.

First attempts to force a passage came to a standstill in front of a defence line tightly secured behind more minefields and backed by an armoured train on the other side of the village. The train's guns shelled the advancing companies with devastating results.

Machine-gun fire swept above their heads. It came both from the train and from concealed foxholes and trenches less than 45 metres in front of them. Kurt gave the order to withdraw. Using their 20 mm guns, the armoured scout cars engaged the train, laying a cover of smoke to shield the running men. An anti-tank gun was quickly brought up by 2nd Company. It managed to get off a few rounds before receiving a direct hit. The gun crew's screams were drowned out by the sound of whistling steel.

Taking a dozen runners with them in case they didn't make it and keeping low, Kurt and Westphal dodged through to the other side of the village for a first-hand inspection of what they were up against. What they saw didn't look promising. Beyond the village were the intricately laid Perekop defences—trenches, barbed wire, minefields, concrete pillboxes and artillery placements. A frontal attack would be suicide.

Suddenly, Westphal yelled for a medic. A shell had taken off his right arm, exploding among the rest of the patrol. Those standing nearby were either killed or wounded.

"We're getting out of here!" Kurt shouted. "Pass the order."

Motorcycles roared in through the smoke screen laid down by the scout cars. Without stopping, they flung the wounded and dead into the sidecars and spun away to the rear. Three times the cyclists raced into the smoke and bullets to bring back wounded. Kurt carried out the last man, whose back had been torn open from a shell splinter. He died in Kurt's arms.

With Westphal out of the fight his second-in-command ordered the attack renewed at noon. Kurt was aghast. To continue an assault against such impregnable positions would assure the battalion's annihilation. He had brought his men through too many battles to allow their lives to be squandered in one final suicidal charge. For the first time in his life he refused to obey a direct order.

Within the hour Lieutenant-General Bieler, 73rd Infantry's divisional commander, received a signal from Kurt and Major Stiefvater, who headed the 73rd's advance unit, stating: "Coup against Perekop impossible." Their assessment was accurate. Not only were Russian defences firmly established along the width of the Perekop Isthmus but they were sitting behind the "Tartar Ditch," 15 metres in depth, which had been built by the Turks during the 15th century to protect the peninsula from the mainland. It provided a secure barrier to modern mechanized armour. Impossible to bypass, the defence line stretched from the salty swamps of the Sea of Azov on one side to the Black Sea on the other. Passage into the Crimea for the moment was effectively barred. The Meyer-Stiefvater refusal to continue the attack was accepted with good grace, and the main thrust shifted to the Crimea's eastern passage at Balykov.

The attack started at dawn under cover of thick fog. By 0900 hours defence lines had crumbled and the Waffen-SS captured Sliakov station together with the town of Nova Aleskova. Beyond lay Genichek and the Sea of Azov. Genichek sat on a plateau with a commanding view of the surrounding countryside. Russian preparations for a counterattack were under continuous observation. When it came, the Leibstandarte stood ready. The hapless Soviet troops were cut down before managing to get within range of the German lines.

The columns pushed along the northern shore of the Sea of Azov toward Melitopol, their next major objective. The land's texture changed to a loose, sandy soil that bogged down the wheeled vehicles and clogged their motors. Four days were needed to cover the distance. Then, on 21 September, just when the objective was within reach, recall orders arrived sending the force racing back to the Crimea's western entrance. Once more the Leibstandarte was asked to force passage through the Perekop Isthmus.

"We are being used like a fire brigade. Always on call to put out brush fires that keep erupting along every part of the front line. . . . We are pleased by the recognition of our value but wish it wasn't quite so repetitious."

One of these brush fires erupted on 27 September when the Ninth and Eighteenth Red Armies counterattacked in the north. The poorly trained and badly equipped Rumanian troops facing them cracked, and the Soviets were able to thrust deep behind the German lines in the rear. Swiftly, the Leibstandarte was rushed from the south to Gavrilovka by General von Manstein to act as linchpin where the 170th Rumanian Infantry Division joined the left flank of xxx Corps. A Russian breakthrough was expected.

After two months of nearly continuous fighting, the Russian war had begun

On horseback, Kurt leads his company into the Sudetenland in 1938.

Standing before grim-faced Czechs
in the marketplace of Krickerhau,
Czechoslovakia, on 22 March 1939.

Snapshots from the Polish
campaign, September 1939: "The
first Polish pillbox" and
"Motorized troops overtake us."

On the Russian front during the winter of 1943.

Leibstandarte commanders before the battle of Karkov. (From left) Kurt Meyer, Tank Regiment Company Commander Wilhelm Beck, the divisional physician, Dr. Besuden, 1st Regiment Commander Fritz Witt and Tank Regiment Commander Max Wünsche.

Hitler presents Oak Leaves for Kurt's Iron Cross in February 1943.
(Below) Celebrating the decoration with Wilhelm Mohnke.
(Bundesarchiv/73-90-10)

Commanders prepare for the assault on Kiska. (From left) Brig. Sherwood Lett, Gen. Pearkes, Lieut.-Gen. Simon Bolivar Buckner, Jr., and Harry.

Winnipeg Grenadiers embark on the *Chirikoff*.

Harry wades ashore.
(Canadian Army photo)

Bulldozers and
materiel are unloaded
at Kiska harbour.

Abandoned Japanese
miniature submarines.
(Canadian Army
photo)

Maj.-Gen. George Kitching (left), Lieut.-Gen. Guy Simonds and Canadian II Corps troops listen to a speech by Montgomery in England, 21 February 1944. (Lieut. F.L. Dubervill/DND/PAC/PA-132650)

Maj.-Gen. Chris Vokes, acting commander I Canadian Corps, in Riccione, Italy, 13 November 1944. (C.E. "Bud" Nye/DND/PAC/PA-140573)

Harry introduces King George VI to 3rd Canadian Infantry Division on 25 April 1944 as Gen. H.D.G. Crerar (far right) looks on. (J.H. Smith/DND/PAC/PA-141624)

Harry and Prime Minister Mackenzie King inspect equipment in England on 18 May 1944. (L.J.G./DND/PAC/PA-140570)

12 April 1944. Taking part in Exercise "Trousers" are (from left) Harry, Admiral Sir Philip Vian, Gen. Sir Bernard Montgomery and Gen. Sir Miles Dempsey. (DND/PAC/ PA-140708)

12 April 1944. Inspecting the troops at Beverloo, Belgium, are (from left) Kurt, Fritz Witt, Sepp Dietrich, Hubert Meyer and Field Marshal Gerd von Rundstedt. (Bundesarchiv)

to take on its own format and identity. In every sector a German thrust would be followed by successive Russian counterattacks, then Soviet capitulation and withdrawal farther inland to new defensive positions where the ritual would be repeated. Occasionally, a Russian counterattack broke through German lines and for a time created havoc, but these were quickly contained and Soviet forces either broken up or captured.

On the evening of 30 September at Gavrilovka, the Leibstandarte, together with crack Alpine troops, repelled a night attack. The German line held. Quickly Dietrich opened a counteroffensive. In short order the enemy's overextended flanks were sliced off. The Russian drive ran out of steam and once more the panzers were rolling forward. By 5 October the entire Russian front had been torn apart.

"We were in among them like Hussars cutting down broken infantry . . . nothing could stop our advance. We passed whole batteries of guns and columns of Russian troops marching east. No time to disarm them; a quick 'hands up,' a gesture toward the west and we roared on. Numbers? Who knows how many we took."

At the town of Terepinye a single bridge spanned the Dnieper River. Masses of retreating Soviet vehicles and troops were struggling across when Kurt's reconnaissance battalion appeared unexpectedly on the river's western banks. The Russians immediately blew the bridge, sending hundreds of their own men to death in the river. Such casual disregard for life never ceased to astonish the Germans.

Four hundred kilometres beyond the Dnieper lay Stalino, the Leibstandarte and Alpine unit's next objective on the road east. Its defence had been given to fresh Siberian troops equipped for winter warfare. Already the nights were cold and the air brittle in the lungs. The Germans, still dressed in light summer uniforms, shivered and pressed forward, fighting a succession of running battles.

The stress of combat leadership began to take its toll on Kurt's emotions. Personal courage on the battlefield was like a bank account. Some had more on deposit than others. No one ever knew the day when his account might suddenly become overdrawn and his courage crumble. He had seen it happen. A man had only so much to give, and when that was gone, he was finished.

"As always when I have to decide to give orders which may mean the life or death of my men, my whole body trembles and I smoke one cigarette after another. Those moments before an encounter, before the first shot is fired, are a burden. But this paralyzing pressure evaporates the minute the battle begins and I'm in the middle of the fighting."

Harry was still playing war games. Exercise BUMPER placed ten British and two Canadian divisions in the Chiltern Hills northwest of London to subdue a "German" force that supposedly had landed from the seaports in East Anglia.

The "war" lasted nine days over late September and early October. The Canadian 1st Division managed to capture the entire British 56th Division, much to the surprise of Lieut.-Gen. Harold Alexander, GOC-in-C. Southern Command.

"Great sense of satisfaction, but hardly the real thing," Harry observed sourly. "Most of the officers still can't understand the basics of leading a company of men in the field. . . . They'd better learn quickly or a lot of good lads are going to die."

After a day's rest he went on leave to London. It was as big a letdown as his earlier trip had been. "Here less than 12 hours and already wishing I was 'home.' Wasted the afternoon hunting for china which is unobtainable. Mollie will have to wait until after the war. Went on to the Windmill Theatre. Boring. Motionless nudes aren't my cup of tea. On to a news theatre which was damn good. Had dinner at the Café Royal. Indifferent meal. Novel experience but no place for a senior officer. Place filled with scruffy Jews and foreigners.

"Returned early to the Cavalry Club and over a nightcap listened to the Old School Tie contingent hold forth. It's an amazing place. I have quite a nice room but the old soldier help is very slow and Victorian. Every request produces a ritual. I have a personal valet—all for 12/6 per night! . . . Walking along Piccadilly tonight I detected a new London Cry. No longer is it: 'Ullow Dahling, can I interest you in a good time?' Now it's: 'Ello, voulez-vous coucher?' What chance for a knee-trembler in the blackout? Still, I suppose there are a fair number of fools that fall for it."

3

At Romanovka and again at the port of Berdyansk Kurt just missed capturing a Red Army general. What a coup that would have been!

His tank destroyers had designed a new weapon for fighting the T34s. He joined in their experiments enthusiastically. Using a bottle of gasoline to ignite an explosive charge, a single soldier could destroy a tank. Tactics for the new weapon were perfected to such a degree that "tank stalking" developed into a recognized sport among the troops, with prizes awarded to the best scorers.

The battalion's next objective was Mariupol. Its capture would pin the Russians against the Sea of Azov. The Leibstandarte rolled forward over arrow-straight roads, through undulating treeless country. At the town's outskirts they paused. "My comrades are waiting for my orders to pursue the enemy. Like always in moments of decision I listen to my officers' counsel. If a planned action looks dicey then they look dull, toying absentmindedly with their weapons. But if there is the least chance of success I can sense their eagerness and feel the indescribable trust they have in me. It gives me the strength to order an attack. . . . Then the fear of being a coward chases me forward."

Attack!

They burst upon the town's defenders. Bitter street fighting ensued. Finally, bloodied and beaten, the Soviets withdrew. The battle of the Sea of Azov had been won.

The battle of Taganrog began on 11 October. Kurt's driver was killed the next day when the lightly armoured command car received a direct hit from a Russian shell, the first of seven of his drivers to be killed during the war. Peter had been more than just his chauffeur. He had been his friend. At the graveside Kurt broke down. "I can't say a single word. Tears are running down my cheeks. Some field flowers fall into the dark grave. I salute Peter and turn away. Later I write his mother."

It took five days before 1st Battalion could establish a bridgehead across the Mius River through which the rest of the Leibstandarte passed, fighting its way toward Taganrog. The town fell to German forces on 17 October, and Stalino surrendered three days later. Then it began raining, a heavy incessant rain that slowed, then halted, the German advance on Rostov.

Icy winds roared down on the exhausted troops. Engines froze. Supply columns from the west could no longer make it over the dissolving muddy roads. Major bridges along the route were destroyed. The rivers they had spanned were now swollen and impassable. German trains could not run on the wider-gauge Russian tracks, so there was no rail service to bring supplies from the west. The Soviet railway system was useless. The Red Army had destroyed nearly all of its rolling stock during the retreat. Using armies of labourers, German engineers set to work readjusting the Russian tracks east of the Polish border, a job that would take two years to complete. Meantime troops at the front did without sufficient winter clothing, food and fuel.

As the fury of the weather increased, the men, already weakened by lack of food, proper clothing and rest, started coming down with bronchitis, lung infections and dysentery. One after another, regiments already decimated by battlefield casualties were reduced further, in some cases to less than 20 percent of their normal combat strength.

Kurt himself fell seriously ill, suffering from double vision, nausea, hepatitis and dysentery. He continued working until he collapsed and had to be removed to a field hospital in the rear. Hauptsturmführer Kraas took over command of the battalion.

On 21 October Harry attended an impressive demonstration of close troop support by the RAF at Warminster on Salisbury Plain. "Ground strafing by 12 gun Hurricanes and Spitfires with cannon, using live ammunition. I hope the Hun hasn't pilots like those. Their flying was incredible and their accuracy terrifying. Believe me, when 36 machine-guns come spitting at you at 400 mph you aren't going to stand up and shoot back at them with a rifle. . . .

"24 Oct. . . . Attended presentation of colours by the Queen to the Saskatchewan Light Infantry at the Guards Depot. It was a good show, somewhat marred by a poor band borrowed from 2nd Division and a shower just at the finish. Was invited to a sherry party with the Queen at Divisional Headquarters but got the message too late to do anything about it. . . .

"13 Nov. . . . For a long time we have feared the promotion of General McNaughton. General Odlum is next in seniority. Today Odlum was removed to become Canadian High Commissioner to Australia. That's where a bloody politician should be—sitting on his arse with his wife in some government sponsored rose garden far enough away that he can do no harm. We all breathe a collective sigh of relief. George Pearkes is now where he should be: senior Divisional Commander."

Two days later the situation changed when McNaughton went on sick leave. "Pearkes takes the Corps; Ham Roberts gets 2nd Division, Potts has 1st Division and Bill Southam gets 2nd Infantry Brigade. I wonder if anyone really understands what is going on?"

Sickness and casualties were wasting away the German army faster than replacements could reach the front lines. A thousand horses were being lost each day from the frightful weather and lack of fodder. Motorized panzer units resorted to cannibalizing their equipment because there were no spare parts. The infantry was in a pitiful state; some men had marched over 1,600 kilometres during the first weeks of the campaign and now were without boots or socks. Frozen toes and gangrenous feet reached epidemic proportions. By contrast, the Russians seemed to gain new strength with the approach of winter. Their counterattacks intensified in ferocity.

On 17 November Cavalry Gen. Eberhard von Mackensen's III Corps, with the Leibstandarte under his command, opened the assault against the city of Rostov on the river Don. Battle conditions were appalling. A near blizzard blotted out the landscape, covering minefields and the Soviet's well-prepared defensive positions. A numbing cold kept the men moving forward. Some units lost their bearings in the blinding, wind-whipped snow.

Russian armour and fresh, well-equipped soldiers—each in turn was subdued. The reconnaissance battalion captured the railway bridge across the Don intact, and by the 20th the city had fallen to III Corps. Two armoured trains, 56 tanks, 159 field guns and 10,000 prisoners were taken. But German jubilation was short-lived. The Soviet army commander, Marshal S.K. Timoshenko, spotted a gap between Col.-Gen. Paul von Kleist's panzers and the German Seventeenth Army. His forces counterattacked in strength, sweeping past the German line with waves of tanks and suicidal infantry to strike at the rear of Mackensen's III Panzer Corps. Through the black smoke and falling snow warmly dressed Russian soldiers appeared like phantoms on all sides. The Germans fought furiously to hold their ground.

"It is not possible to describe with words winter on this front. There is no main battle line, no outposts, no reserves. Just small groups depending on each other to hold defensive positions. . . . We're in the 'sunny South.' How frightful it must be for our comrades up North! Here life is paralyzed. . . . We live on a sort of thick soup made from ground buckwheat and millet. We have to strip the fallen—theirs and ours—for warm clothing. I don't think I will ever be warm again and our tame Ivans say that this winter is mild! God preserve us."

Mackensen could not hold his 110-kilometre front with the forces available. He explained his problem to von Rundstedt, who then asked permission to abandon Rostov. Hitler refused. Von Rundstedt was replaced by Field Marshal Walther von Reichenau, and on 1 December, he too informed Hitler that the front could not be held. Reluctantly, Hitler agreed to a withdrawal behind the Mius River, but not before sending von Kleist a shirty telegram stating that "further cowardly retreats are forbidden." The Führer had apparently forgotten that the Russian breakout had come through positions held by his beloved Leibstandarte.

Tanks, guns and vehicles became unusable from the cold. Troops were left with only their infantry weapons for defence. Isolated, outnumbered and with no chance of relief, the Waffen-SS held fast, facing wave after wave of Soviet assaults from across the Don. The "Buran" became as dangerous an enemy as the Russians; its deadly icy wind could kill a man as easily as a bullet. Soldiers forced from defensive positions by a counterattack had to find new shelter quickly before the Buran killed them. "They came in . . . masses so great as to numb the senses. They had to pick their way through the dead of the other assaults. We drove them off—how easy it seems to write this . . . and when they had gone back across the ice the entire area in front of our positions and on both flanks was carpeted with dead. They were dead all right. . . . The wounded die quickly; blood freezes as it leaves the body and a sort of shock sets in which kills. Light wounds that heal in three days during summer kill you in winter."

For the first time during the campaign Kurt had not been with his men. Illness reduced him to the euphemistic status of a "commander-in-reserve" while he recovered.

The Führer's order to hold Rostov came to him as a terrible shock. Like all officers in the Waffen-SS and most at the junior and middle levels within the Wehrmacht, he considered Hitler a political and military genius. In three swiftly fought wars he had made no major mistakes. To stand and fight to the last man was the sort of idiotic order Stalin had given during the early days of the campaign. It seemed unworthy of Hitler. Even the Russians had finally realized the futility of attempting to stop massed tank forces using fixed lines of fortifications and suicidal infantry charges. Their strategy had shifted to an "elastic defence"—stand and fight, then retreat to stand and fight again, rolling with the German punch, separating the panzers from their infantry support and leaving guerilla operations and a scorched earth behind the invader's lines. Simple tactics known to every German staff officer.

Yet this order to hold Rostov had come from the Führer. Kurt knew it was impossible to obey. Uneasily, he realized how out of touch Army Headquarters was with the situation at the front. Did OKH know that in some sections of the line there were now more Russians than Germans fighting the Soviets, volunteers from the Ukraine and Caucasus Mountains who despised the Georgian beast inside the Kremlin? "They fight willingly on the German side and are the equal of our soldiers and fully respected by them."

During the battles around Rostov numbers of Soviet soldiers deserted to the German lines. A diminutive Cossack named Michel turned himself over to men of the reconnaissance battalion. He could speak enough broken German to make himself understood and he hated the Communists. Kurt took a liking to him. He gave Michel a German uniform and appointed him his unofficial batman for the duration. It proved a wise choice.

The exhausted army withdrew from Rostov and took up positions west of the Mius River. Despite successive waves of exultant Siberian troops flinging themselves across the frozen river, the weakened companies of Waffen-ss held their ground. As winter's frozen grip tightened over the land, operations on either side of the battle lines were reduced to patrol activities.

The English winter was relatively mild. Harry's brigade had moved to its winter quarters at Worthing on the Sussex coast. The men lived luxuriously in requisitioned hotels and expensive houses.

On 8 December one of Harry's men, on his way home from the movies, was accidentally shot by a trigger-happy sentry of the West Nova Scotia Regiment guarding the bridge at Shoreham. A stupid accident. "None of the four in the truck saw any signal light nor heard any challenge—just the two shots which blew half of John Beveridge's head off in the back of the truck, splashing his brains all over Douglas Lough. Poor John was one of my most promising young officers. . . . Tonight we hear that Japan has attacked Pearl Harbor.

"10 December. . . . The Japs have sunk HMS *Repulse* and *Prince of Wales*, our best capital ships in the Pacific. Pretty gloomy news. . . .

"11 December. . . . We buried John Beveridge at Brookwood today. The escort and firing party caused a number of compliments from representatives of the other units attending. John would have been pleased with his send

off. . . . The U.S.A. declared war against the Axis today. Now the world
is well and truly at war.

"22 December. . . . Everyone worrying. Although our 8th Army is doing
well in Libya, now virtually at Benghazi, elsewhere things are not so hot.
It's becoming evident that the Japanese attack on Pearl Harbor was much
more serious than has generally been allowed to come out. The U.S. Pacific
Fleet seems incapable of interfering with Japanese operations against the
Philippines. And our own loss of the *Repulse* and *Prince of Wales* means
that the invasion of Malaya and Sarawak cannot be prevented.

"23 December. . . . Churchill is in Washington. Let's hope he can get the
American fleet to quit the U.S. coast and go to Singapore. This evening
we heard that J.K. Lawson and Pat Hennessy have been killed in Hong Kong.
What a forlorn hope it was to try and defend the place. Thank God we
are not there. . . .

"24 December. . . . Today I had to parade Max Stroud before the GOC
for a reprimand. Potts was damn kind about it. . . . It's Christmas Eve. . . .
How bloody dull. . . . Gave the local Home Guard Commander a bottle of
good port before inspecting his beach defences. . . . Jock C. has brought a
very common local in and introduced her as his fiancée. . . . Midnight news
blocked out by a bunch of Holy Romans chanting their pre-historic Latin
incantations. . . . Christ! What a lousy Christmas Eve. I have a whole parcel
of hates tonight. . . .

"25 December. . . . Last night damned if the beach patrol didn't kill my
best wireless operator, Chamberlain! Contrary to their orders they were
stopping people on the front and the inevitable rifle accidentally went off.
. . . Merry Bloody Christmas."

On the day before Christmas Joseph Stalin summoned one of his best field
commanders, Colonel-General Yeremenko, to his headquarters beneath the
Kremlin. Yeremenko described the interview:

"'Tell me, Comrade Yeremenko, are you very touchy?' Stalin asked.

"'Not particularly,' I replied.

"'You won't be offended if I put you temporarily under Comrades who
until recently were your subordinates?'

"I replied that I was prepared to take over a Corps or any other post
if the Party considered this necessary in order to solve a most important
task. He considered me the right man for the job."

Stalin outlined his plan. Yeremenko was to take command of the newly
raised Fourth Striking Army. This crack outfit would enjoy the same privileges
as the Guards Army units—its officers would receive 50 percent higher pay,
its men double the normal rate plus better rations. Yeremenko was given
complete power for equipping and supplying the new force. Stalin left no

doubt in his mind that the Fourth Striking Army would become the "culmination of the Russian winter offensive."

A few days earlier Kurt returned home for a brief leave. The trip west was a sleepless nightmare. He arrived in Berlin in his ragged, foul-smelling uniform after 18 hours of nonstop travelling. The city lay in the grip of one of the coldest winters in living memory. But there was heat in the houses and food in the shops. To someone fresh from the front it felt like entering another world. Wartime shortages were giving people some cause to grumble, although everyone seemed optimistic that the war with Russia would be over by the following summer. The Führer could then turn his attention to England and the Americans. Kurt wasn't so sure.

He spent an idyllic week with Kate and the girls, relaxing and enjoying the feeling of doing absolutely nothing of military importance. Near the end of his leave, he received orders to report to Hitler's headquarters on 1 January.

"It is bitterly cold in Germany. I say goodbye to my wife and climb into an unheated train. My travelling companion is the Japanese ambassador, General Oshima. After previous bad experiences like this he has supplied himself with large quantities of brandy. Together we fight the cold using his 'fire water.'"

Upon arrival at the Führer's headquarters he was quickly ushered in to see Hitler, who wanted a first-hand report of the fighting on the Russian front. "He makes a fresh and simple impression on me. I'm astounded by his excellent knowledge of weaponry, how he knows the advantages and disadvantages of certain types of tanks. He is even informed about the actions of my unit. . . . I tell him of the superhuman expectations the armies in Russia are expected to fulfil while outnumbered by the enemy and without sufficient supplies. I get the impression that Adolf Hitler is very concerned about the plight of his armies of the east."

Hitler had every reason to be concerned. He had badly misjudged his Russian enemy. There was little sign of the predicted disintegration within the Red Army or the political disaffection upon which he had counted so strongly. Even the populations of those "buffer" states west of Russia who had welcomed the invaders as liberators during the first weeks of the campaign soon became disillusioned by the harsh treatment they received after the main German forces moved on. Himmler's and Heydrich's resettlement programs and the murderous ruthlessness of regular SS and *Einsatzgruppen*[3] thugs toward these unfortunate civilians killed any chance of amicable relations between conqueror and conquered. One dictator had simply been replaced by another. Better the devil they knew; he at least spoke the same language.

The Wehrmacht had not been properly prepared to fight a mobile winter campaign across vast distances of devastated hostile country. Mechanized armies required well-constructed highways, like those in Europe, to operate effectively. The Soviet Union had none. Ground that should have been taken in weeks by a lightning advance took months over rutted dirt roads that turned to mud each time it rained. German lines of supply and communication were stretched to the breaking point, and mastery of the air remained unattained. The flower of German youth lay spent.

The OKW chief, Field Marshal Wilhelm Keitel, explained how crucial the manpower problem had become for the Wehrmacht: "I needed to force upon Speer* a program that would enable me to call up for active service the 250,000 servicemen exempted for armament production. What would these men have meant to the Eastern armies? . . . With 150 divisions of 3,000 men each, they would have meant a reinforcement of their combat strength by half their nominal establishment. Instead, the shrunken units were replenished with grooms and farriers and suchlike, and these in turn replaced by willing Russian prisoners of war." The total number of men who remained exempt from active service Keitel estimated at 500,000.

He tried explaining the law of diminishing returns to Speer and Hitler, but neither would listen. "The monthly losses of land forces alone in normal conditions and excluding major battles, averaged 150,000 to 160,000 men. Of these only 90,000 to 100,000 could be replaced. Thus the army in the field was reduced by 60,000 to 70,000 men each month. It was a piece of simple arithmetic to work out when the German front would be exhausted."

It had not been the Mongolian and Siberian divisions that had stopped von Bock's Army Group B with Guderian's panzer army at the outskirts of Moscow on 5 and 6 December. They were defeated by a combination of irreparable losses of manpower and of mechanized equipment that had not been designed to operate in daytime temperatures of –25 degrees Centigrade. Total German casualties on the Eastern Front as of 5 December were 750,000 men—23 percent of the 3,500,000 troops in the field. Nearly one man in every four had been killed, wounded or reported missing. Despite his intuitive powers, which were considerable, Hitler was not suited to military leadership. His inability to trust his senior staff officers or to delegate authority, his increasing interference in the chain of command—at times down to the battalion level—and the summary dismissal of commanders who displeased him had all contributed to the Russian disaster.[4]

4

During early January Yeremenko's Fourth Striking Army went into action against Army Group Centre. His training methods to prepare the soldiers

---

*Albert Speer—Hitler's newly appointed minister of armaments and ammunition.

for winter battle had been ruthless. Entire divisions, including all senior officers, were ordered to spend four days out in the forests in temperatures from –30 to –40 degrees, without shelter, field kitchens, food supplies or fires. Each man was allowed two handfuls of dried millet mixed with melted snow for daily rations. Daylight hours were spent in combat exercises; the evenings, attending tactical and propaganda lectures.

However fired up with party slogans the men may have been, entire divisions went into battle on empty stomachs. The 360th Rifle Division recorded in its War Diary for 8 January: "Division has no rations." The next day, as Yeremenko's offensive opened, the 332nd Rifle Division recorded the same frightening state of affairs. Some dry bread destined for 358th Division was diverted to the 360th so that its men might have at least a mouthful of food after their first day of battle.

Yeremenko's novel solution: "Get your rations from the Germans," he ordered. Thereafter, finding German supply dumps, food warehouses and field kitchens became the number one priority in his strategic planning.

In Toropets, a major supply base of Army Group Centre, the 249th Rifle Division seized the supply dumps undamaged by a swift encircling action. "We captured approximately 40 food stores containing butter and other fats, canned meat and fish, various concentrates, flour, groats, sugar, dried fruit, chocolate and much else . . . only the personnel changed. These supplies fed our Army throughout a whole month. I felt very proud when I reported it to General Headquarters."

Soviet Army HQ believed that behind their front the Germans had prepared a second heavily fortified defence line with strongpoints placed in deep echelons, covering the flanks. Yeremenko doubted the information and sent the 249th Rifle Division "to carry out reconnaissance in strength and bring in prisoners. Within 5 days I possessed the enemy's system of defences and his units. . . . No second line of defence was found to exist over a depth of 8 to 12 miles."

He realized immediately that once his army, keeping both its flanks protected, smashed through the German front line it would be into open undefended country. Russian country.

In late January Harry attended a "Corps Study Week" in Brighton given by Gen. Bernard Montgomery, the army commander. "Montgomery said he had attended many such sessions but never such a successful one. His closing remarks were frightfully flattering and coming from a hard-bitten martinet like him those of us who took leading parts felt frightfully important."

Harry was in the middle of the line of officers introduced to the Army Commander at the end of the exercise.

Montgomery paused after they shook hands. "Foster, did you say?"

"Yes, sir."

"There was a Canadian named Foster at Quetta when I was there. Any relation?"

"My brother, sir."

"Drank rather a lot, as I remember."

"Yes, sir."

"Hmm. Pity."

Gil's rise through the noncommissioned ranks of the "Buffs" had been spectacular. In just over two years he had gone from private to sergeant-major. His commanding officer confided to Harry that having Gil as an NCO was an embarrassment to the regiment. "I mean, dash it all, the chap knows more about the army than any of my officers. I'd even venture to say he knows more than I do! I must make him an officer. Start him off as a captain. What d'y'say?"

"I say you'll lose him. Change his beer diet at the sergeants' mess to the hard liquor in the officers' mess and you'll end up with a drunk instead of a soldier."

The Colonel appeared sceptical. "I'll take your recommendation under advisement."

Sadly, he didn't. A few weeks later Gil was promoted to captain. He lasted 43 days before being dishonourably discharged for drunkenness. With his money gone, he came out from his alcoholic fog and turned to Harry for help. Arrangements were made for him to work his way home on an empty merchant ship returning in convoy to Halifax.

"4 February.... Out on anti-invasion exercise BEAVER TWO. Not very much to do. Plenty of hanging around. During a lull at Divisional HQ, General Pearkes informed me that I was on the selection list for command of either an infantry or armoured Brigade. He explained that there were a few others on the list and that naturally Chris Vokes was ahead of me. Later, on congratulating Worthy* on his promotion, he said that he hoped to see me again soon ... which might be interpreted as something already teed up. I keep my fingers crossed and my mouth shut. I do however hope for a Brigade under Worthy and a trip—even a short one—back to Canada and Margo....

"4 March. . . . General Pearkes paid us a visit today. Arrived like a thundercloud—car trouble. Left just before lunch wreathed in smiles. Apparently he liked what he saw and again announced to me that Chris, Howard Graham and I are on the selection list for Brigades. When, he couldn't say. At about 1930 hours masses of bombers passed overhead bound for France.

"5 March. . . . Apparently at long last they have smashed the Renault works. About time.

"13 March. . . . Sgt. Edelman, a veteran of the last war, and our expert

*F.F. Worthington, promoted to major general, commanding 4th Armoured Division.

on grenades, allowed one to go off in his hand tonight. He died instantly.

"14 March. . . . Counted seven fighter squadrons out over the Channel this evening escorting a convoy of 24 ships. How different from a year ago!"

As the size and scope of the RAF's bombing offensive over Germany and the occupied territories increased without concentrated Luftwaffe response, fears began to grow that the Germans might be planning a large-scale air attack, possibly in conjunction with an airborne invasion. With hindsight, such an undertaking was clearly preposterous. Yet it didn't seem so at the time. On 3 April Harry confined his regiment to barracks and placed everyone on 30 minutes notice.

"10 April. . . . Nothing has happened. I'm beginning to believe these 'imminent invasion' warnings are hooey designed by the War Office to keep everyone's interest from flagging while we're between exercises.

"21–25 April. . . . Exercise BEAVER THREE. We, as a German invading force, attacked 2nd Division. Our aim was to grab Horsham. We did. The Division, on reduced scale transport and hard rations, was practising for its role as spearhead for the BEF that will one day land on the continent—an optimistic thought. The Regiment did damn well as usual but we still find it difficult to produce the goods without the requisite number of Armoured Reconnaissance Carriers [ARCs]. For the first time we carried out a rearguard by night without lights. Many exciting clashes."

On 25 January 1942 Military Judge Fuchs was ordered to investigate a reported Soviet atrocity in the town of Feodosia. The incident began in late December when strong Soviet forces appeared near the Kertsch Peninsula and Feodosia. Lieut.-Gen. Hans von Sponeck, the XLII Corps commander, ordered his 46th Infantry Division to withdraw from the peninsula because of Russian landings there. Some 160 wounded men, too sick to be moved, were left behind in a military hospital at Feodosia. Their fate was unknown until 18 January when the town was retaken by German troops. Some of the wounded had been shot, some horribly maimed and mutilated, others placed in water along the beach until they were covered by ice. All 160 men had been murdered.

Judge Fuchs reported his findings: "On December 29, Russian Marines and infantrymen entered the town. The Marines were drunk. They went straight to the military hospital opposite the castle and shot approximately 30 to 35 wounded German soldiers. Then, on 1 January, a general order stated that all Germans in the recaptured areas were to be executed. Commissars and the NKVD* then instructed their men to kill any German wounded remaining in the town's other makeshift hospitals."

---

*State Political Administration—the Soviet security service.

Throughout that bitterly cold winter the Russian generals went on the offensive, keeping pressure on the Germans all up and down the line. During January, after a breakthrough west of Moscow, the reinforced Red Army moved to encircle the rear of Army Group Centre. General Model, commanding the German Ninth Army, moved the Waffen-ss Der Führer Regiment under Obersturmbannführer Otto Kumm to a bend of the Volga River near Rzhev. The regiment's job was to form a thin protective screen linking the front with army formations farther west. Kumm's orders were to hold until Model could gather enough troops in the south to smash the Russian forces.

For the rest of that month and into February, fighting in temperatures that at times dropped to –25 degrees Centigrade, Kumm's men held on. Day in and day out, week after week, they fought off persistent Russian attacks. By 18 February Model had won his victory and Der Führer was pulled out of the line. Model went to visit Kumm.

"I know what your regiment must have been through. But I still can't do without it. How strong is it now?"

Wearily, Kumm took him to the window and pointed."They are on parade outside, Herr General. See for yourself."

Model counted 35 men—all that remained of the original 2,000.

Another breakthrough in the line near Dnieperpetrovsk during February forced the German III Corps into the field to prevent a deeper penetration. This time the Leibstandarte was given a section of the line to hold. They fought the swarming Soviets at close quarters.

Behind the lines on both sides, murder and mayhem continued unabated. Captured Russian records showed that disposing of German prisoners had become so widespread that Order No. 0068, dated 2 December 1941, was issued by the Chief of Staff, Soviet Coastal Army, Sebastopol, to clear up any misunderstanding: "As a rule troop formations exterminate prisoners without interrogation and without transferring them to divisional staff. Prisoners may only be exterminated in the case of resistance or escape. Besides, shooting prisoners at the place of capture or at the front line as is now being done so extensively, acts as a deterrent to enemy soldiers wanting to desert to us."

The new order produced little effect within the Russian rank and file. On 29 March a Leibstandarte war graves officer reported that in the courtyard of what had been the local Soviet GPU* Headquarters at Taganrog, six men of the Leibstandarte's 3rd Company had been found murdered. According to civilian prisoners who had witnessed the incident, the six had been taken into the courtyard by security police where, after being beaten with rifle butts, they were hacked to pieces with bayonets and axes. Their dismembered bodies were then thrown down a well shaft.

---

*The predecessor of the Soviet NKVD.

Throughout the Russian campaign, retribution for Russian atrocities taken by soldiers of the Waffen-SS was out of all proportion to those inflicted by the Red Army. Yet, with a few exceptions, senior Waffen-SS commanders— including Dietrich—tried to prevent reprisals against prisoners. "We owe it to the title on our sleeve," Dietrich said.

But during the fury of battle, senior commanders had very little control over how their men in the front line conducted themselves. To show compassion or mercy for an enemy responsible for the deaths of comrades and friends was sometimes asking for more than a fighting soldier could give.

With the April thaw came mud, a thick, oozing and seemingly bottomless gumbo that bogged down everything. The first large-scale operations were to begin in early May. "During winter we had covered our tanks with haystacks. Only one tank started after the hay was removed. Inside the others field mice had gnawed the insulation off every wire. Our mighty panzer divisions had finally been brought to a halt by Russian mice."

Hitler decided that the south was now the critical area for attack. Army Group South moved to break the enemy's defences along the Don, cross the Caucasus and seize the region's rich oil-producing centres. A Soviet spoiling attack on 12 May delayed the advance for a week while the panzers cleared away an enemy bridgehead south of Kharkov.

The Leibstandarte, which had suffered nearly 40 percent casualties to its effective battle strength, pulled out of the line and moved back to Stalino for replacements and retraining. Kurt set to work rebuilding his shattered battalion.

On the other side of Europe, on 28 March, a Combined Operations naval force and a group of Royal Marine Commandos attacked the French port of St. Nazaire. It came as a complete surprise to the Germans. The port operated the only drydock on the Atlantic seaboard capable of handling a battleship. A British destroyer, the *Campbelltown*, rammed the drydock's lock gates, blowing itself up. Ashore, commandos destroyed the drydock's valuable pumping machinery.

The success and impunity with which the attack had been carried out worried the German High Command, even more so because *Abwehr** intelligence sources in the British Isles reported the Allies were planning a major cross-Channel assault sometime during the summer. So far their information remained sketchy.

Near the beginning of June, German agents in England suggested that an invasion in force against the French coast was planned for late June or

---

*Literally, "Defence"—the Espionage, Counterespionage and Sabotage Service of the German High Command—Amt Ausland/Abwehr, headed by Adm. Wilhelm Canaris.

early July. Its exact size and extent were unknown. As a precautionary measure the Leibstandarte was transferred during June from Army Group South to the district around the city of Caen in Normandy.

Harry's war games continued in England. Whatever his frustrations, he seemed to be playing the games well.

"2 June. . . . We have just returned from exercise TIGER, General Montgomery's endurance test against 12 Corps. Constantly on the go for seven days and nights—covered 750 miles. Both men and vehicles came through well. Collected another lovely strawberry from both the Corps commander and Monty.

"25 June. . . . Unit was inspected today by the Army Commander. It wasn't much fun explaining to two Lieut.-Generals how I ran my unit. However, old Monty left me wreathed in smiles and was almost complimentary. Pearkes obviously pleased."

Combined Operations, under Lord Louis Mountbatten, started planning for a raid on Dieppe in mid-April. It was to be a much larger undertaking than St. Nazaire. As no sizeable invasion force had landed from the sea since the ill-fated attack on Gallipoli in 1915, Combined Operations anticipated that a Dieppe raid in force would provide an ideal testbed for the new assault techniques and equipment developed since World War I. New infantry and tank landing craft designs could be evaluated under combat conditions in conjunction with the problems of handling a large naval fleet close inshore to a well-defended enemy coastline.

The Canadians were not involved until 30 April when Montgomery visited General McNaughton and explained the project. The troops were to be drawn from Southeastern Command. General Crerar, whose corps was under Montgomery's command, had suggested that the Canadian 2nd Division be used for the assault. McNaughton gave his approval, subject to confirmation from Ottawa and to the "Outline Plan" prepared by Mountbatten's Combined Operations being militarily sound. Two weeks later the Chiefs of Staff approved mounting the raid. The brilliant, and newly promoted brigadier, Churchill Mann, was placed in charge of the Canadian planning group.

Mann discovered quickly that it was *not* a militarily sound operation and went against the most basic tactical teachings at Staff College. The Canadians were being asked, without naval artillery or air support, to make a daylight frontal assault from the sea across a beach commanded by high cliffs. Machine-gun emplacements in caves along the cliff facings would be able to traverse the entire landing area. In Mann's opinion, the planners would have been hard-pressed to pick a worse place anywhere along the French coast. Realizing it was madness, he tried pointing out the obvious and was reminded that McNaughton and the Chiefs of Staff had already approved the plan. Mann's job was to "put the nuts and bolts together." Reluctantly, he and his staff went to work.

A dress rehearsal held along a section of the Dorset coast in early June ended in a fiasco. Units were sent ashore miles from their proper beaching points, the tank landing craft arrived an hour late, several of the tanks broke down, and once ashore, the men treated the whole affair as a summer outing. More training was needed. Mountbatten postponed the attack date. Twelve days later they tried again, with much better results. A new attack date was set for between 4 and 8 July. The men went aboard their transports on 3 July.

German agents and reconnaissance aircraft had observed the sudden increase of vessels and activity around the Isle of Wight. At 0615 hours on 7 July, while the raiding force sat at anchor waiting for weather conditions to improve, the Luftwaffe struck. Two landing ships filled with men from the Royal Regiment of Canada were hit, but damage was slight. In both cases the bombs passed through the vessels' hulls before detonating. Although the men could easily have been transferred to other ships, the navy decided on 8 July to cancel the operation because of weather. Bitterly disappointed, the men were disembarked and sent back to their bases.

"5 July. . . . Caught the 1640 train from Euston. Am on my way to attend U.S. Armored Division manoeuvres in Northern Ireland. I am the only member of the party with a sleeper. The others—all staff officers—never thought to make reservations. So much for the brilliance of staff planning. It's very luxurious but rather lonely. We detrain somewhere in the wilds of Scotland tomorrow at 0500 hours.

"10 July. . . . Returned this evening from four sleepless days and nights with the 81st Recce Battalion of the 1st American Armored Division. Never had my boots off the entire time in Ulster. Impressions: ten minutes rain every hour—wonderful food—magnificent equipment—grand troops with keen officers, every one a real Kentucky Colonel—poor staff work—no wise guys—a grand keen bunch.

"5 August. . . . Moved my whole regiment from West Grinstead Park to the northern outskirts of Hastings. One of the best night moves we have ever done. Regimental HQ is now located at Langley Place; a luxurious boys school, complete with swimming pool. Drew the balance of our ARCs. At long last we are a complete fighting unit in men and equipment. Hallelujah!

"7 August. . . . The worst has happened. I have been appointed G1, 1st Canadian Division. A staff officer desk job! Godallmighty. The boredom will kill me. Had a very touching farewell parade by the unit and left with a heavy heart to take up my new job."

After much discussion, Combined Operations and the General Staff decided to remount the raid on Dieppe. Under strictest secrecy the men were brought to their embarkation points on 18 August. The main force consisted of two brigades: the 6th, under Brig. Bill Southam, and the 4th, led by Brig. Sherwood Lett. Armoured support was provided by the 14th Tank Regiment of Calgary, with the raid scheduled to commence at 0450 hours on the following morning with five attacks. Lieut.-Col. Lord Lovat's No. 4 British Commandos were to land on the extreme right and silence the coastal battery near Varengeville while Major Young's No. 3 Commandos came ashore on the far left, knocking out the battery near Berneval. Canadians made up the other three flanks. Fifty men from the 1st U.S. Ranger Battalion were dispersed among the group as observers. In all, the embarking force consisted of 6,100 men, of whom 4,963 were Canadians.

As daylight faded, the first ships of a flotilla of 253 vessels sailed from Southampton and Portsmouth, setting course for Dieppe.

"19 August. . . . 2nd Canadian Division's raid on Dieppe this morning. I was at Newhaven when they returned. Casualties were heavy. Air support was terrific—65 squadrons of fighters. Rumour has it that Brigadier Lett is the only survivor from his Brigade HQ. Ben Cunningham was reported captured. . . . What the raid was for no one seems to know yet. They are still streaming back through Newhaven. I went down to check on our anti-aircraft defence—just in case.

"20 August. . . . Latest reports indicate that only 2,400 returned last night. Many of those were bodies. Bill Southam was captured. Also Merritt. Gosling was blown to bits. Johnnie Andrews last seen wounded on the back of a tank in the water and under fire from the coastal defence guns. None of our tanks got off the beaches.* Of the Essex Scottish, one officer returned. No sign of any survivors from the Fusiliers Mont-Royal Regiment. Four officers returned from the South Saskatchewans. It seems it was a massacre in which the Canadians all 'died splendidly.' The Germans were waiting for us."

Of the approximately 5,000 Canadian troops sent on the raid, 3,372 were killed, wounded or missing. The Commandos lost 550, the RAF 190. One destroyer was sunk, together with 33 landing craft and 30 tanks. German losses were 600 men.

"24 August. . . . Today the General informed me that I am at the top of the selection list for Brigadier. He said he thought that I would be getting Bill Southam's 6th Brigade."

5

The policy of general conscription had been a traumatic experience for the Borden government during World War I. Mackenzie King's government faced

---

*About half a dozen actually did, but they could not enter the town.

the same problem in 1942. A national plebiscite had given it the power to "enforce conscription if necessary." But no one knew exactly what the term "if necessary" meant. As expected, citizens in the province of Quebec had voted "*Non*."

King promised the Quebec electorate that any overseas service would be strictly voluntary. Accordingly, the Canadian army evolved into two groups: overseas volunteers and those who were to be used strictly for purposes of home defence. The latter group became known derogatorily as "Zoldiers" or "Zombies." English-speaking Canadians liked to believe that all Zombies were French Canadians from Quebec; yet as the war dragged on, it became apparent there were almost as many Zombies per capita from the English-speaking provinces. In 1942 the conscription issue existed only as a festering political sore to French- and English-speaking citizens alike—although for different reasons. Later, it was to have calamitous consequences.

Margo Foster, meantime, became bored with her country gentlewoman lifestyle. Her lover, Jimmy Shields, had been transferred to Winnipeg. Tony, her eldest and always unmanageable son, had been sent off to a French boarding school in Montreal when he turned nine, the minimum age acceptable for young hellions whose parents wished to shuck them off. The idea was Harry's. Always suspicious about the quality of public education, he thought both boys should be sent to boarding school as soon as they reached the age of acceptance.

Margo felt lonely. The rich ripe smells of chickens, horses and dung no longer held her interest. She longed to be a part of the nation's war machine. The country's newspapers and illustrated magazines carried weekly articles and pictures about the contribution being made by women. She resolved to join them. The house and farm were sold at a good profit in late August, and after placing both boys in Montreal boarding schools—David with the nuns at Mount Holy Names, Tony back at Mount St. Louis—she went to work at the shipyards in Sorel, Quebec.

Her job of inspecting the proper thickness of newly manufactured shell casings turned out to be worse than the boredom of Picton. "But I intend to see it through," she wrote Harry. "Martyrdom suits me and besides, the pay is good. I have a lovely little one-bedroom apartment just ten minutes from work. The only problem is that everyone speaks French. But I am learning that too. They seem to be generally a friendly lot, though suffer from a terrible inferiority complex about 'les maudit anglais.' For some reason they seem to think we're smarter, richer, and much better than they are. What an odd lot! . . .

"Gil came to see me last week, on his way up to the Yukon. He managed to borrow some money from Uncle Fred for a train ticket and expenses. It seems he tried joining the Navy, the Air Force as well as the Merchant

Navy. He even volunteered for tankers. But was turned down flat due to 'medical reasons.' No one, it appears, wants to take a chance. He looked fine. I treated him to a dinner at Sorel's best—which is Chinese and terrible— after which he spent the night on my sofa. He left next morning brimming with good humour, a good breakfast and a bottle of rye that he explained had to carry him through on the train ride to Montreal. Poor Gil. What a waste."

Kate Meyer had never been much interested in her husband's career beyond the fact that it brought the family a degree of respect and a steady income. A passive woman, for whom life seldom presented any real problems beyond the mundane, she would have been just as happy if Kurt had been a factory worker or farmer. Farming she understood. Politics, social intriguing and the war held scant interest, except when it took away her husband. But she accepted his long absences with the placid equanimity of a dutiful wife.

She remained a very private person, living comfortably in her own little world, caring for the children and later trying to protect them from the *Götterdämmerung* that Hitler brought down on Germany. Her "Mother's Cross" award for bearing the children—regarded as new little Nazis under the government's crackpot racial breeding program—was a distinction she could just as easily have done without. Her reasons for having children had nothing to do with politics. She had them because she loved them.

She was the rock upon which the foundation of Kurt's personal life had been built. During one of his brief leaves he told her: "All my victories I owe to you. Do you know why? Believe me I am frightened too. And when I sit in my dugout and the order comes to attack, then I look at your picture. Your eyes tell me: 'Come on, Vati, come on!' and my courage returns."

During June 1942 while the division was being reorganized, Kate visited him at Conches in Normandy. The picturesque tenth-century town, with its mainstreet promenade and beautiful gardens, seemed like a peaceful oasis. They lived in a splendid villa adjacent to the officers' mess. Once more they had time to talk, take a leisurely walk, laugh and love.

In August, Dietrich again recommended Kurt for promotion. The shortage of experienced field commanders had become acute, as had the quality of recruits coming into the Waffen-ss. Most of the best and the bravest were gone, either buried in Russia or invalided home. By Wehrmacht standards, Kurt, at 31, was much too young for regimental command, but in a formal submission Dietrich wrote: "Meyer is a surpassingly, uncommonly mature, responsible and conscientious personality. He combines the highest personal bravery with outstanding tactical knowledge of military leadership. The successes achieved by his battle group—especially in the fight against bolshevism—are uniquely and solely due to his fanatical battle spirit and circumspect leadership. Without consideration to his age and rank, and in consideration of his exceptional soldierly and personal qualities, I recommend that Meyer be promoted."

With the arrival of fall, Kurt asked Kate to come back to Normandy, this time to Bretteville, where part of the division had taken up quarters. Their accommodations were not nearly so luxurious as those at Conches—a soldier's standard living quarters, nothing more. But at least they could be together. Arrangements were made to bring one of the girls along too. Such visits were against regulations; children of serving soldiers were not permitted to leave the Reich. Accordingly, six-year-old Ursula had to be smuggled across the border crouched between the legs of her father's driver, who had volunteered to make the return trip to Berlin.

Tragedy struck a member of the battalion. Hauptsturmführer Montag had gone home on leave to Schwerin and taken his three children for a Sunday morning walk near the lake. Without thinking, he left them unattended for a few minutes. His youngest, a girl, ventured out on the thin ice and fell through. The other two tried to save her and all three drowned. When Kate and Ursula arrived, Kurt told them about Montag's loss, adding, "I know something that will make him smile again, if you agree."

He proposed "lending" Ursula to the soldier as a temporary daughter. Kate and Ursula agreed. When the introductions were made the Hauptsturmführer's eyes filled with tears. He took Ursula in his arms. Discreetly, Kurt and Kate withdrew. Montag poured himself a drink—plus a small one for Ursula—then sat down to tell her stories. Several hours—and many drinks— later Kurt and Kate returned to find both the surrogate parent and their daughter plastered.

On 11 November Kurt received official notification of his promotion to Obersturmbannführer* and special task force commander. He received a special gift also. In recognition of his Knight's Cross and hearing of Kurt's fondness for dogs, Hitler had promised a puppy from the next litter of his specially bred German shepherds. Receiving any sort of gift from the Führer was a singular honour. The dog was delivered to him in Normandy. He named her Patras—Pat for short—in honour of the gulf crossing during the Greek campaign that had helped win him his Knight's Cross. When the re-equipped division transferred back to the Russian front in early January 1943, he took Pat with him.

The shuffleboard game of senior Canadian officers continued in England. Once again Harry was bypassed for promotion to brigade command. He wasn't pushy enough and refused to play internal politics.

"31 August. . . . General Pearkes left by air this morning for Washington.

---

*Wehrmacht equivalent of lieutenant-colonel.

Something is up. We all feel lost without him. Who his successor will be is a deep secret. Many names are being mentioned.

"8 September. . . . It's now settled. Harry Salmon gets 1st Division, Rod Keller the 3rd. Guy Simonds comes here to take over 1st Infantry Brigade, Howard Graham gets the 7th Infantry Brigade under Rod. It would appear that I have missed the boat again.

"9 September. . . . Maj.-Gen. H.L.M. Salmon arrived and assumed command. He's very much the new broom and is right up to the bit. I think we will get along. Lord Lovat visited and told us about Dieppe. What an extraordinary man!

"10 September. . . . Guy Simonds reported in to me. He has just completed a two way Atlantic crossing by air. He looked tired but as full of optimism as ever."

The war news had brightened considerably on all fronts. American men and equipment were pouring into the British Isles. In North Africa, General Montgomery had gone on the offensive against Marshal Rommel's Afrika Corps. By 4 November, after the Battle of El Alamein, Rommel's forces were in full retreat. They took all available motorized equipment and abandoned their Italian allies, who promptly surrendered to the Eighth Army. Then, only four days later, combined British and American forces under General Eisenhower landed in French North Africa at Casablanca, Oran and Algiers, the largest amphibious operation of the war thus far. Their objectives were to strike east and link up with the British Eighth Army.

To the east, the Germans no longer had the manpower or equipment to attack all along the front. Instead, they concentrated maximum strength on narrow fronts, taking defensive positions elsewhere. This strategy, they hoped, would allow them to outflank Moscow from the east, cutting it off from the Urals, then to strike again directly at the capital. However, it was not Moscow but Stalingrad* that became the dominant issue between the combatants. After three months of stubborn resistance against 20 German divisions the besieged city still had not been taken. In the north, the city of Leningrad, cut off from the rest of Russia for 16 months, had against all odds held the Germans at bay.

"2 December. . . . General Salmon and I just can't get along. We both rub each other the wrong way. At times the atmosphere almost crackles. He annoys me with his distrust of all subordinates, his dictatorial manner and complete disregard of other people's ordinary human privileges and frailties. I annoy him by my casual manner and lack of enthusiasm for some of his harebrained ideas which to me are unworthy of a divisional commander. We must part. I have been loyal to him—at considerable expense to my self-control. Today we finally had it out and I have asked for other employment.

---

*Its name was changed to Volgograd in 1961 as an act of de-Stalinization.

"14 December. . . . I am appointed to command the Highland Light Infantry of Canada in 3rd Division with Rod Keller. It's a demotion, but it's miles away from Salmon and the 1st Div. which no longer resembles that wonderful group of which we were all so proud. George Kitching gets my job—poor devil.

"16 December. . . . I reported to Brigadier Haldenby, 9th Infantry Brigade, at Horsham. My unit—less a rear party—is in Scotland undergoing special training. I went into London and, feeling like a terrible fraud, got myself rigged out as a Highlander. As usual Miss Miller at 'Hobsons' came to the rescue and produced the right Balmoral badges, shoulder flashes and ties. It will take some time to get a jacket and trews cut by 'Jones, Chalk & Dawson' where miraculously I still have a £13 credit. The regiment's camp is a quagmire of red clay in an estate known as Strood Park—about 3 miles West of Horsham.

"20 December. . . . Left Horsham for the West coast of Scotland to join the unit on its special training."

On the morning of 22 December Harry began a tour of his new regiment's companies. They were scattered up and down the coast. To reach them he travelled by boat, jeep and shoe leather, mostly the latter. Next day he sailed around the Moidart Peninsula to inspect D Company, which was scheduled for an invasion landing exercise at Roshnen. But the seas off Roshnen were too heavy for the small navy craft to operate safely.

"24 December. . . . I have two blistered heels and an introduction to a bunch of muscles I never knew I owned. However, without a murmur I did another 6 miles today across the hills in new boots—not pleasant. Colonel Macklin of the Scots Fusiliers of Kitchener arrived for a three month attachment. I'll send him on to Roshnen tomorrow by drifter. D Company is the only place with any accommodation. Drinks tonight before dinner with Major Rose and the House Staff. A very quiet and circumspect Christmas Eve. Lonely and missing Margo mightily. God, I'll be glad when this do-nothing war is over. Everyone I know seems to be in line for something worthwhile soon except me. If that sounds like self-pity it is."

6

The pendulum of battle had swung again on the Eastern Front. With the arrival of winter the Wehrmacht's summer territorial gains were being systematically retaken in the Red Army's offensive. Relief forces had broken through the German line at Stalingrad, then pushed on across the Don, cutting off von Paulus's Sixth Army. In the Caucasus the Germans were being cleared from the valuable Maikop oil fields. What had been a confident and victorious military machine was suddenly transformed into a defensive force desperately fighting a series of rearguard actions simply to avoid being captured.

On 9 January 1943, in a frantic attempt to stabilize this deteriorating situation, the newly equipped ss Panzer Corps was ordered to Russia at top speed. The corps, consisting of the Leibstandarte, Das Reich and Totenkopf Divisions, was given complete rail and road priority. Within the week the troops were back in the front lines east of Kharkov.

To achieve maximum effectiveness, the divisions were broken up into a collection of independent battalion-sized *Panzer-Kampfgruppe** units. The sectors they were expected to hold were ridiculously strung out. The Leibstandarte's bridgehead at Chegavayev along the Donets River stretched for more than 110 kilometres. When Fritz Witt's panzer grenadier regiment went off to take part in a corps attack southeast of Alkatavka, the line holding the front became even slimmer. Yet despite the fury of Soviet attacks and the bumbling confusion of retreating Italian, Hungarian and German units pouring westward through their bridgehead, the Leibstandarte held fast and died magnificently.

By late January, disease, famine and Russian shells at Stalingrad had reduced von Paulus's proud army of 300,000 to 90,000 men. His 11th-hour promotion to field marshal by Hitler changed nothing. On the last day of the month he surrendered the remains of his exhausted forces to the Russians. Quite apart from the loss of men, the catastrophic losses in equipment and prestige shook the Wehrmacht to its foundations. Responsibility for the Stalingrad debacle belonged to Hitler, who had ordered the fatal stand while the way still remained open for von Paulus to escape encirclement. After the first flush of German victories in the East, Hitler's battle plans were simply too grandiose for the limited resources of manpower and equipment he had left.

Early in February, during a week of blinding snowstorms, the Leibstandarte's forward outposts were driven back by the Russian tide with appalling losses on both sides. But by the following morning the positions had been retaken after a bitterly cold night of furious fighting. Kurt spoke with one of the captured Soviet officers. Their dread of German invincibility had passed. The Russian's sincerity impressed him.

"We will win this war," the man said confidently. "Because of help from the United States. You'll lose. But one day we'll be friends again. Then we will fight together and win."

By 10 February the Soviet army, relieved from the pressures of Stalingrad, threatened the entire Donets Basin and western Caucasus in the south. During the three winter months it had recaptured all the territory taken by the Germans during the previous five summer months. Although few realized it at the time, the turning point of World War II had arrived.

On 13 February, while the battle for Kharkov raged, Kurt's tank reconnaissance battalion was surrounded by Russian forces in the nearby town

---

*Literally, "fighting group."

of Alexeyevka. Fuel and ammunition were running low. Heavy snowstorms and bitterly cold weather prevented a supply drop by the Luftwaffe. Witt's regiment tried desperately to smash its way through the Russian forces for a rescue. Kurt wondered who would reach his beleaguered position first.

"I am with my wounded comrades in a school building. They know exactly their situation and implore me not to let them fall into Russian hands. Dr. Gatternigg and I both know the fate of captured German soldiers. The doctor shrugs his shoulders, shakes his head and turns away. My men's voices tear at my heart. What can I do except give the order to supply the wounded with pistols. Relieved, the boys thank me. I'd rather be in close combat than have to go through this again. . . . My men are wearing four and five suits of underwear and still we are freezing. We defecate in our clothes with no discomfort because it freezes. Of the transport horses only the females remain. The males died when their urine froze during passage. One of my officers asks: What can we do? I think a moment. Take ten good men and burn the village. Begin with houses on the perimeter, I tell him, and work toward us. At least we'll arrive in hell warm."

Fortunately, an armoured unit from the 1st Battalion of Witt's battle group, led by Max Wünsche, broke through the encirclement and the wounded were evacuated. For this action and the destruction of 54 Russian guns and other Soviet equipment, Wünsche received the Knight's Cross. The fighting raged for several days with see-saw battles in and around small towns and villages, which soon became littered with burned-out vehicles, blasted artillery pieces and piles of frozen dead. Alexeyevka changed hands several times.

"It is a merciless godless war. We have become no better than wolves snapping at the smell of food . . . life or death is now all the same. To kill means nothing. Anything that moves we kill before it kills us. All war is madness," Grenadier Koppel wrote. "In every village the Ivans hide inside their houses until our comrades are nearly upon them before they shoot. Then our tanks move in. Most of their houses have thatched roofs and go up like bonfires. . . . We kill them as they run outside."

Kurt called it "an inhuman war fought without mercy." In the desperate fight for survival both sides came to accept murder as a natural adjunct to war. Even his dog, Pat, became a casualty when she ran out and caught a live grenade that her master had hurled against the enemy.

While the Russians flung themselves against the thinning lines, aiming for Kharkov, weary German field commanders realized that the time had come for a general withdrawal before the town was taken and their panzer corps trapped and destroyed. Hausser, the corps commander, asked for permission to pull out. Hitler refused. His orders were to hold the town. Hausser, Dietrich and the other ss leaders were caught between a rock and a hard place. They had sworn an oath of allegiance to Hitler of unconditional obedience. Were they to obey him or save their men? Time was running out. The escape corridor to the west of Kharkov was already less than 1.5 kilometres wide. Sensibly, Hausser decided to ignore the order and evacuate.

Soviet forces entered Kharkov on the morning of 15 February. A day earlier they had recaptured Rostov, but before they arrived, the retreating Germans blew up all stores of food, fuel, utilities and military installations.

Later in the week Kurt received a signal that he had been awarded the Oak Leaves to his Knight's Cross. The news arrived during a pause in the fighting. It gave him little joy.

"I leave my comrades and their congratulations and go out into the biting cold to visit the graves of the men killed in action. The front is silent. Snow covers every sound. Flashes of light flicker on the horizon. The graves are barely visible. Neither crosses nor gravestones mark these last resting places. It is done purposely because sometimes the Russians open up our graves and make a mess. A few snowflakes fall. . . . More demoralizing than the cold is the wave after wave after wave of Russian attacks. The men shoot and shoot and shoot. Yet they come, rising like ghosts over their own dead. That is the worst part. There is no end to them."

Once again he was ordered to report to the Führer's headquarters in East Prussia. He turned over his command to Kraas and caught the Luftwaffe's first available westbound flight. He found Hitler's mood much subdued since their last encounter. After he had received his decoration, the news photographers were dismissed and he was asked to join the German leader for a private discussion. For an hour they spoke together without interruption.

"His voice is calm. His thoughts keep returning to the tragedy of Stalingrad. He places no blame on individual officers. It is war; like the ceaseless Allied bombing raids. They worry him because of the suffering they are bringing to the homeland. He thinks now that the war will last quite a while longer. He considers Churchill to be his worst enemy."

There wasn't time to see Kate and the children. He had to settle for a phone call. They needed him back at the front.

Harry returned from Scotland in early January to take over command of the regiment's new quartering at Strood Park. The next weeks were occupied organizing the unit to his satisfaction. Finally his promotion came through.

"17 February. . . . Was called to Division very suddenly this afternoon to be informed that I have been a Brigadier for the past two days. Rod Keller presented me with my red tabs, offered congratulations, then said to take over the 7th Infantry Brigade as soon as possible. . . .

"15 March. . . . Returned from exercise SPARTAN. Two weeks of tough slogging. This really *is* a wonderful Brigade. Smooth and efficient. At Muswell Hill we captured the Brigadier and practically the whole of the British 147th Brigade. Compliments from the Corps Commander no less. . . . Letter from Margo about Tony running away from school. Apparently he walked 45 miles from Montreal to Sorel. Quite a hike for an eleven year old at this time of the year! The school doesn't want him back. He's too unmanageable for them. Bloody French priests. She has decided on an apartment in Montreal where she can put both boys into day schools and keep an eye on them— particularly Tony to whom I give full marks for his show of independence— along with a damn good hiding if I could get my hands on him."

But Margo's reason for moving to Montreal was much more serious than a rebellious son. Her time between menstrual periods had been getting shorter until finally she was experiencing a slow but continuous bleeding. Alarmed, she had visited a Sorel doctor who recommended that she see a Montreal specialist at once. For a few days she hesitated. After all, what did a French Canadian GP know about internal medicine? Her prejudices were as fully developed as Harry's. Then, for awhile, the bleeding stopped. But on the day the school phoned to say that her son had run away it started again. When Tony arrived next morning, she had already decided to leave Sorel and get proper medical attention. It was too late. After a hysterectomy at Montreal's Royal Victoria Hospital her doctor delivered the grim news. She had cancer. How far it had spread he didn't know.

She needed to talk to someone. She telephoned her father in Winnipeg. Major Ross had died the year before, leaving Robert Muir alone with his birds and the big house. Since Ross's death his letters had become strangely disjointed, and on the phone he sounded very peculiar indeed. For the moment she forgot her own problems. She promised to take the train out to see him when the Easter holidays were over and the boys back in school.

A few days later the Montreal police called to say that Robert Muir had been arrested that morning after creating a disturbance in Windsor Station. He had climbed off the train from Winnipeg and started scattering hundred-dollar bills like confetti around the main concourse. In the resulting riot several people were injured, one seriously. Aghast, Margo went to the police station. Only vaguely did her father recognize her. Because he kept lapsing into long periods of silence, it took several hours to piece the story together.

The week before, after their telephone conversation, he had cleaned out his bank accounts, cashed his bonds, stocks and securities, then caught the first train to Montreal. He intended spending every cent he had in finding a cancer cure to save his "Duchess" from death. When she was not at the station to meet him, he assumed the worst. Of what value then was his money? Better to give it to others who might need it. She realized that he was going mad. A medical examination confirmed it. For some time he had been suffering from presenile dementia.* Sorrowfully and reluctantly, she had him committed to the asylum for the insane at St. Anne de Bellevue.

---

*Alzheimer's Disease. He died three years later.

On the Southeastern Front, von Manstein began a counteroffensive to
recapture Kharkov. As a prelude to his main assault a series of small-scale
encirclements were conducted to snip off various Russian salients. These
attacks, coming first on one flank and then the other, threw the Soviet
commanders off balance. Von Manstein's plan was to fall back in front of
selected enemy forces, trapping them in a pocket for a swift counterattack.
By 25 February, after three days of vicious fighting by the First and Fourth
Panzer Armies, most of the Soviet First Guards Army and General Popov's
armoured corps were encircled and destroyed.

Quickly, the Russians reorganized. Their Third Guards Tank Army was
brought up for a new assault. But on the last day of February, before it could
be deployed, the Leibstandarte launched a spoiling attack. The three-day battle
ended with the encirclement of the Soviet XV Guards Armoured Corps. Von
Manstein's counteroffensive could now commence.

It was brilliantly executed. During the first days 634 Russian tanks and
1,081 guns were destroyed. Within the week Soviet forces were being cut
off and systematically wiped out. The enemy's lines of defence were ripped
apart, and the men of the Leibstandarte poured through the gap, heading
for Valki and Kharkov. A motorcycle company of the reconnaissance battalion
led the advance into Valki. The German thrust rolled forward, forcing the
Russians back across the Donets.

For Lieut.-Gen. Paul Hausser, blinded in one eye in 1941, retaking Kharkov
was to be a sweet revenge and absolution for his disobeying Hitler's orders
to hold the city. He launched his attacks from the north and west. On 10
March, supported by batteries of *Nebelwerfer** and Stuka dive-bombers, the
grenadiers advanced. Soviet forces inside the city were trapped. Kurt's
battalion took the city's eastern outskirts next day to cut the Staryi escape
road. But three more days of house-to-house and room-to-room fighting were
needed before the Russians capitulated. By late afternoon on 15 March the
last resistance ended at the city's tractor factory. The third battle of Kharkov
was over.

"How pleased we all are with our success. . . . We have thrown them
back and once again Kharkov is German. We have shown the Ivans that
we can endure their terrible winters. It can hold no fear for us again."

The four-week offensive had indeed been a spectacular feat of arms by
any standard. The Germans, outnumbered in infantry by 8 to 1 and in tanks
by 5 to 1, had fought against a determined and well-entrenched enemy. The
cost to the SS Corps over the period had been high, however: 365 officers
and 11,154 other ranks were dead, wounded or missing.

Russian losses were appalling. Every available man, woman and child had
been used in the defence of the city. Fritz Richter—Kurt's old friend from

---

*A concentrated battery of smoke mortars fired from mobile transporters.

the Schwerin Police School—was in charge of organizing convalescent hospitals for both Russian and German casualties, but it took several weeks before any of the captured Russian nurses were able to help out. All were suffering from badly infected fingers. During the battle for Kharkov they had been put to work digging anti-tank ditches in the frozen ground with their bare hands.

Yet the victorious German army remained in very serious trouble. There were no longer sufficient reserves at home to replace its losses. A call-up for three-quarters of a million men produced only 185,000. It meant, as Keitel had warned, that future losses would never be replaced. The Wehrmacht's establishment after the spring of 1943 would begin steadily to decrease. Nor could the nation's industrial output of armoured vehicles needed to re-equip its panzer divisions come anywhere near matching the monthly Russian production of 1,000 tanks. The great German war machine was having difficulty keeping pace with its opponents.

A long-term decision had to be made. Should future military operations on the Eastern Front become strictly defensive or should a military initiative be maintained through carefully planned local attacks designed to bleed the Red Army slowly to death? While Hitler and his generals pondered their problem, the Leibstandarte was assigned to the relative calm of security duties in and around Kharkov.

In London during the last week of April, Gen. Sir Alan Brooke, chief of the Imperial General Staff, invited Lieutenant-General McNaughton over to the War Office for a chat. The War Cabinet, he informed McNaughton, had decided to undertake special operations in the Mediterranean area based in Tunis. The plan had come about as a direct result of the Casablanca Conference between Prime Minister Churchill and President Roosevelt three months earlier. McNaughton was asked if Canadian forces would be interested in participating in the affair by supplying one infantry division and a tank brigade together with necessary support troops. It was made clear that the Canadians would not be operating as an independent command but would be under British control and direction.

Finally, after nearly four years of dashed hopes and mounting frustrations, a substantial force of Canadian soldiers was being given the chance to fight in a proper war. Ottawa's reply to McNaughton's signal was not long in coming. Within 48 hours General Brooke had authorization to use the troops. Eleven weeks later these men would be landing on the beaches of Sicily on their long, long road to victory.

While Harry received orders to turn over his sector of the coastal defence to British forces and move his 7th Brigade back to Lower Beeding, 1st Division began scrambling at once to ready itself in time for the embarkation date. Raiding parties descended on the other divisions, including Harry's, to make up shortages of men and equipment. Rumours of the division's impending departure into action didn't make things any easier for Harry to accept.

"Due to Harry Salmon's death Guy is now Maj. Gen. and takes over 1st Division. Chris will be taking 2nd Brigade—lucky devils! It appears I am destined to rot forever in England."

He needn't have worried. On 8 June a call came in from Canadian Corps Headquarters to pack immediately for the next draft back to Canada. Mystified, he rushed to London. Maj. Scott Murdoch, brigade major on the Spitzbergen expedition, also received a call to report to London from his job at I Corps HQ. Harry recorded the results: "Got an outline of a hush hush assignment from Bunny Weeks, the BGS at CMHQ.* Scott Murdoch, G2 of 1st Canadian Corps, and I are going out, having been elected by Army Command. It looks like our big chance . . . finally."

The draft leaving next afternoon included a sorry collection of military misfits: "a drunken Brigadier, a cashiered Captain, a bigamist, several crooks and other naughty boys being sent home in disgrace. Not altogether an inspiring party. . . . Still rather dazed next morning. Had breakfast with Scott at the Central Hotel in Glasgow. Nearly wrecked the place by asking for water at the table *to drink*—damned if they were going to produce it for us. . . . Went aboard a tender at Gourock which carried us out through a maze of aircraft carriers, battleships, cruisers and destroyers to the *Queen Mary*. Spent the afternoon settling into a very cozy private suite on the sundeck. . . .

"Later, for amusement, I watched some 4,000 POWs from Rommel's Afrika Korps file aboard into the bowels of the ship. They struck me as a very hard but subdued lot, no sign of any Nazi arrogance. . . . One of the ship's officers said later that both the Germans and their Italian allies on board are terrified of the crossing. German propagandists have convinced them that as every Allied vessel puts to sea it is immediately torpedoed by a U boat."

Without escort, the *Queen Mary* slipped down the Clyde and out to sea. The first two days were stormy, mountainous seas and a gale blowing. Maindeck cabins were flooded under three feet of water. Then the weather moderated. Harry spent the days walking the sundeck: "Twelve miles this morning, another twelve this afternoon. I finally had to forbid other ranks from saluting me during each circuit. My arm was getting tired. . . .

"16 June. . . . Passed the Statue of Liberty at 0900 hours. Very stately, very green and surprisingly dignified. Famous Manhattan skyline rather disappointing but impressive. Saw the New Yorkers in the millions being carried to work on jammed ferry boats from the New Jersey side. . . . Docked at 1000 hours beside the partially submerged hulk of the *Normandy*—the

---

*Ernest J. Weeks, brigadier of the General Staff at Canadian Military Headquarters.

pathetic victim of New York's Fire Department and American hysteria.

"Prisoners off first. But before they can go ashore we were invaded by what appears to be half the U.S. Army carrying typewriters! As the Americans have no available Civil Service the army has to do all the fingerprinting and recording of each prisoner. They're so bloody efficient that they're falling all over each other. The ship's company and British personnel are mildly amused. The Greek naval party are definitely impressed; the Herrenfolk definitely delighted.

"We disembark at 1300 hours and Scott and I are rushed by staff car with sirens screaming to La Guardia airport to catch a plane for Toronto—so I don't get to see Margo after all this anticipation. . . . On to Toronto and the Royal York Hotel where we had a sumptuous dinner for a dollar. . . . Phoned Margo in Montreal—out. Tony proved very amusing. . . . Left Toronto for Winnipeg near midnight . . . arrived hungry, sleepy and bored—half a continent to go. The prairies look very green and wet for this time of year. Touched down at Regina, again at Lethbridge. A bumpy breakfast over the Crow's Nest Pass at 14,000 feet in thick cloud. Saw nothing of the Rockies the entire way. We arrived at Vancouver 'spot on' at 1230 hours with sore arses and ready to go to work."

His new job—still top secret—was command of the 13th Canadian Infantry Brigade being assembled on Vancouver Island for an amphibious invasion of the Japanese-held Aleutian island of Kiska.

7

The Aleutian Island chain is all that remains of what was once a land bridge joining Alaska to the Kamchatka Peninsula of Asia. These barren mountainous islands have absolutely nothing of value to attract commerce, mineral exploration, tourists or conquest. The weather is unpredictable, the islands at times smothered in violent storms or blinding fog.

But they are a part of America's Alaskan territories, and in 1942 Japan decided to invade them. Three Japanese naval task forces, including two aircraft carriers, were involved in the operation. The plan called for an assault force to be put ashore on the island of Adak, destroy all American installations,* then withdraw. Farther west, the islands of Kiska and Attu were to be taken and held.

The invasion was a feint in the Japanese Midway plan. The first air attack came in over Dutch Harbor on the island of Unalaska on 3 June 1942, with a more successful second strike the following day—the same day the Battle

---

*There were none. Japanese intelligence about American forces on the Aleutians was woefully inadequate.

of Midway was being fought in the South Pacific, where the Japanese navy lost four of its aircraft carriers. For a few hours Admiral Yamamoto's nerve failed him. He cancelled the rest of the Aleutian campaign but then quickly reversed himself. Japanese forces were landed on Kiska during the afternoon of 6 June and on Attu early the following morning. Adak was bypassed after American fighters from the new airfield on Umnak Island gave the invasion fleet a mauling.

By spring of 1943 the Japanese garrison on Attu had 2,500 men; Kiska slightly under 6,000, including civilians. The captured islands were like festering sores for the military psyche in Washington. Plans to retake them began. Forward air bases were built on the islands of Adak and Amchitka—only 80 miles from Kiska.

Over the winter months American and Canadian fighters and bombers launched periodic attacks against the Japanese garrisons. Results were less than spectacular. The enemy had spent his time on the islands to good purpose, building a scattering of impregnable defensive positions among the hills and mountains. Yet for Allied aircrews the unpredictable Aleutian weather seemed far more dangerous than any Japanese anti-aircraft fire they encountered.

American troops landed on Attu on 11 May 1943 in one of the bloodiest assaults of the war up until that time. Although outnumbered 10 to 1, it took two weeks before the remains of the Japanese garrison made its final *banzai* charge. Thirty prisoners were taken. The rest were either killed or committed suicide. Only the island of Kiska remained in Japanese hands.

Canadian military participation in the American invasion of Kiska came about as the result of an inquiry made on 12 May by Maj.-Gen. M.A. Pope, Canada's Washington liaison officer, to Gen. George Marshall, chief of staff of the U.S. Army. Pope had been instructed by the Canadian chief of the General Staff in Ottawa, Lieut.-Gen. Kenneth Stuart, to sound out Marshall on a contribution by Canadian troops. Marshall appeared receptive to the idea and, after conferring with Lieut.-Gen. J.L. DeWitt, his Fourth Army commander on the Pacific Coast, wrote Pope that both DeWitt and "Major-General Simon B. Buckner, Commanding General, Alaska Defence Command, were delighted at the prospect of having units of the Canadian forces associated with his Command in present and future operations in the Aleutian area."

On 31 May the Canadian War Cabinet Committee gave its approval for the use of a Canadian brigade group. The 13th Brigade and three infantry battalions on the Pacific Coast were selected, and for political reasons a French-speaking unit added later. The operation was given the code name "Cottage." A signal went out immediately to First Canadian Army HQ in England asking for the nomination of a brigadier to command the new force. Harry was selected.

"20 June. . . . Having got myself completely in the picture from Bill Bostock, the BGS at Pacific Command, I flew to Nanaimo to look over my new job. First impressions: for conscripts who form the majority, the troops look pretty good material to me. But there are altogether too many old soft officers to my liking and I feel uneasy about the 24th Field Regiment. For the job in hand I would have preferred to have younger and more adaptable officers. However, time will not permit—here are the tools, get on with the job. I am a little staggered at what has to be accomplished in a matter of weeks. And we are to use all American equipment!

"21 June. . . . Flew with CGS, Lieut.-Gen. Stuart and Maj.-Gen. Potts to Courtney to visit No. 15 (Winnipeg Grenadiers) Combat Team undergoing assault landing training. The CGS promised to help Menard replace the bulk of the useless French officers in Le Regiment de Hull. Returned to find Morgue Morrison, the gunnery expert, there to discuss our artillery set up. He was most informative. We can't use American optical instruments with British guns nor British optical instruments with American guns. How are the Battery Commanders with their teams to control the fire of one 25 pounder troop and one 75 mm troop? Have they considered this in drafting their firing support plans and load tables? Good God! I don't know nor do the gunners. I'm off to Vancouver tomorrow to find out. Cheerful guy, Morgue. . . .

"23 June. . . . Gen. Pearkes returned from Alaska this morning. I outlined to him and Gen. Stuart that I was a little dubious about the officers I had seen in 13th Brigade. I was told to fire whoever I saw fit and ask for anyone in Canada that I wanted. . . .

"It was intimated by the CGS that if I hadn't confidence in the troops under my command it was unfair to ask me to do the job and that they would have to appoint someone who did have that confidence. . . . I got Scott Murdoch made Lt. Col., stopped the removal of Stephen and got authority to reorganize the Brigade Headquarters along American lines. I asked also for the removal of Brigadier Roy Sargeant. This was implemented immediately."

The principal problem for the Canadian force was that while its officers and most of the NCOs in the brigade were Canadian Active Service (CAS) volunteers, the enlisted men were all Zombies to whom the government had promised military service "solely for the purposes of home defence." Explaining how participation in the recovery of an American island had suddenly become an obligation of the Canadian home defence force would require very fancy footwork indeed, even if it could be explained to the anxious Zombies. Which of course it couldn't for security reasons.

Throughout the rest of the war and particularly when the shortage of overseas replacements reached a critical state after June 1944, the masses of uniformed Zombies sitting safely at home in Canada brought the blood of the country's fighting troops in Europe to a boil. But, to be fair, there was another side to the story. Scott Murdoch asked one of the young "home defence only" soldiers why he had refused to volunteer for overseas duty.

The lad, a farm boy from the prairies, shook his head vehemently. "I'll go wherever I'm ordered by the government because I'm a loyal Canadian, sir. But I'm volunteering for nothing. Last war my dad volunteered. He was gassed at Ypres. When he came home he couldn't work. His pension was nothing. My mum had to run the farm by herself. We grew up poor. My dad was only 34 when he died. I'm all my mum's got now to look after her in her old age. If you had gone through what I did growing up you wouldn't volunteer either."

Harry's second problem with the operation was more personal. He was a bigot. "I dislike Americans, French-Canadians, Jews and discrimination—and in that order." In a patronizing sort of way he found Americans amusing, "but most of the time they are insufferable ill-mannered louts with only the barest sense of diplomacy or historical perspective."

As an arch imperialist, brought up in the rich Edwardian traditions of King, Empire and Country, his prejudices were understandable. Yet he remained flexible enough to revise any opinion—however disagreeable. The first revision came at a staff briefing for officers in Nanaimo. A group of American marines had been sent up to explain the finer points of loading the ships and landing craft that were to be used on the expedition. The lieutenant-colonel in charge of the group bounded up onto the lecture platform and announced to everyone that he was an "expert." Harry, sitting in the front row, turned to Murdoch and glared his disgust.

"I assume that everyone here knows the definition of an expert?" the American continued.

"I don't," Harry growled.

The Lieutenant-Colonel nodded. "An expert, sir, is any sonofabitch with a briefcase who is more than 50 miles from home. And here's mine!" He held it aloft.

Harry laughed. The ice was broken.

"9 July. . . . Flew across to Vancouver and phoned Margo. ($17.25). She sounded sick and tired and very depressed. She's not telling me everything so I'm powerless to help. The boys were out on their bikes. . . .

"Plenty of grief had piled up during my brief absence. Winnipeg Grenadiers, Canadian Fusiliers and Rocky Mountain Rangers all having trouble with A.W.L.s* reaching alarming proportions. One company of Winnipegs on the verge of mutiny. Their grievances chiefly concern leave which some damn fool—now fired—promised them. They share the belief they are being railroaded into the U.S. Army for employment in the South Pacific, and a general distrust of the unknown. I went in turn to each Combat Team and gave them a fatherly talk, explaining the necessity for security and their position as Canadian soldiers. I then told them of conditions in England

---

*Absent without leave—AWOL in the U.S. Armed Forces.

and made them realize that they were not at all hard done by. It worked! The tension eased, absentees dropped and everyone got down to work."

On the Eastern Front a powerful Russian salient left over from the winter campaign threatened the right flank of Army Group Centre and the left wing of Army Group South. This huge bulge on the plains of Kursk stretched over 640 kilometres wide and in places 240 kilometres deep. It would have to be pinched off. Planning began for Operation "Citadel," based on an attack by two armoured forces, one provided by Army Group Centre swinging down from the north, the other furnished by Army Group South. The two pincers would meet to encircle the Soviet armies within the salient and destroy them— a classic armoured manoeuvre at which the German army had always excelled throughout the Russian campaign. The Fourth Panzer Army, assembled west of Belgorod, was given responsibility for the southern attack. Its job: to break through the Russian lines on both sides of Konarovka and, slashing through Oboyan, roll on to capture the city of Kursk.

There were, however, those within the Supreme Command who disagreed with risking Germany's entire military future on one massive and strategically questionable operation. Even the Führer admitted that "my stomach turns over whenever I think of it." While Hitler wrestled with indecision and continued postponing the D-day for "Citadel" through May and June, valuable time was being given to the Red Army to prepare its killing ground. German plans for the attack had already been betrayed to the Russians by the spy ring symbolized by the name Rudolf Rössler, code name "Lucy."

A deep, well-fortified defence system, extensively protected by minefields, was being constructed. Equally as important, by the end of June 6,000 new armoured fighting vehicles were delivered to the Soviet armies. The Russian High Command had decided that Kursk was to be the battlefield on which the Red Army would break the back of German military power.

Finally, Hitler set D-day for 5 July. The Germans were confident of success. Their mobile armoured tactics had never failed them. The magnificent Fourth Panzer Army with its ten divisions consisting of 1,137 tanks and self-propelled guns appeared unstoppable. The men of the Waffen-ss Corps, guarding the left flank with the 167th Infantry Division, were brimming with enthusiasm as they moved up to their jump-off positions.

At precisely 0345 hours Stuka dive-bombers howled down through the rosy dawn on Belgorod, taking over from an artillery barrage. Fifteen minutes later Tiger tanks of the armoured spearhead led the Fourth Panzer Army's death ride into the battle of Kursk.

Tens of thousands of mines had been laid across the plain. Mine-lifting teams marked the locations with their bodies by lying down beside them. The tank squadrons rumbled past. In a practised rhythm the tanks cut off, then encircled, the Soviet positions while the grenadiers shot them to pieces.

The first defence line was overrun with ease. But before reaching the second, the Leibstandarte's advance slowed in the face of massed Russian artillery and checkerboards of minefields.

Furiously, the Russians counterattacked, hurling in willy-nilly entire squadrons of their tanks against individual German positions. Near Stalinsk Kolkhos, 40 Soviet armoured vehicles went in against a German platoon of only four anti-tank guns. Before they backed off, allowing a two-battalion infantry assault to be brought in against the platoon, 24 of their armoured vehicles had been destroyed. The platoon fought to its last round of anti-tank ammunition and then charged the Russians in hand-to-hand combat. By day's end the Leibstandarte losses were 97 killed and 522 wounded.

Heavy rains next day delayed the advance until later in the afternoon. Meanwhile, the Red Army had pressed every available citizen into service. Some battalions were made up of civilians without uniforms, boots or weapons, others only of women, who fought just as bravely and ferociously as the men. The Russians planned to smother the thin German line by sheer weight of numbers. At the end of the second day, with only a 19-kilometre penetration to show for the effort, the division lost another 84 killed and 384 wounded.

By the end of the third day the corps had only 40 Panther tanks still operational from its original 200. Russian tank losses, on the other hand, were staggering. By 8 July over 400 had been destroyed. The Red Army literally threw its armour away.

"We had some of their tank crews bale out in front of our trenches. Then, with their hands up, run in to us for safety. . . . They say that their tanks go up like torches from a single incendiary bullet. Most of their crews are very young and very inexperienced."

But the Geman tankers were experiencing their share of problems too. The Tiger Ferdinands, heavy tank destroyers with enormously thick armour, were prone to serious suspension failures that immobilized them suddenly on the battlefield; without machine guns, they were helpless against infantry. The new remote-controlled "Goliath" demolition tanks turned out to be nearly as useless when sent against Soviet fortifications.

For the next two days, supported by Luftwaffe bombers, the division flung itself against the Russian defences. A few cracks appeared in the line but none wide enough or left open long enough for tactical exploitation. The incomparable Michael Wittman smashed one opening by destroying seven T34s and 19 guns belonging to the Soviets' 29th Anti-Tank Brigade. A Leibstandarte motorcycle company immediately plunged through the gap and captured a Russian brigade headquarters intact. At Psyolknee an enemy counterattack came against the 1st Waffen-SS Panzer Regiment's 13th Company. For over two hours, the German tank crews knocked out nearly half of the 50 T34s that came against them. The rest withdrew.

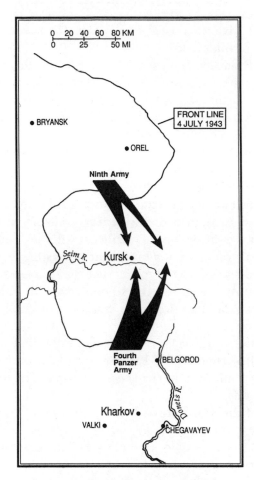

The German assault on the Kursk salient,
showing the planned pincer movement
(after Natkiel *Atlas of World War II*).

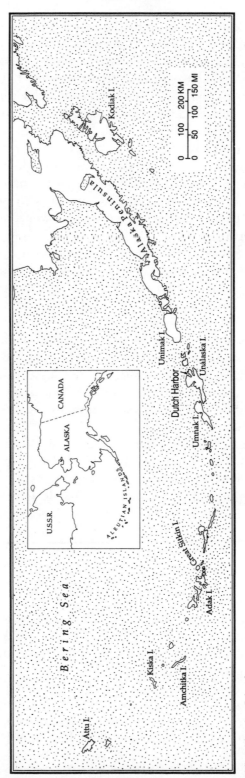

The Aleutian Islands.

Waffen-ss tank kills claimed on the Eastern Front always sound a bit far-fetched to Western ears. Yet these claims were no more excessive than those by regular Wehrmacht units or by Luftwaffe pilots during the same period. In the latter case, individual scores often exceeded 100 aircraft. The top German ace was Erich Hartmann, with 352 confirmed kills. In the nine days of battle at Kursk the Leibstandarte was responsible for destroying over 500 tanks.

Such astonishing figures were the direct result of Soviet willingness to waste prodigious numbers of machines and lives to hold or gain an objective. This combination of blind obedience and indifference to human life so indelibly stamped over the centuries into the Russian people by its rulers should give pause to modern-day strategists who would subdue the U.S.S.R. through force of arms.

On 12 July the Soviets went on the offensive with a force of about 850 tanks against Army Group South. Two of the world's mightiest tank armies clashed in a final decisive battle. The Waffen-ss and III Corps took the brunt of the attack. Sky and ground shook for kilometres from the thunder of tank engines, aircraft, guns and screaming men. As the late summer darkness dimmed the plains of Kursk, blasted, burning and smouldering tanks littered the landscape as far as the eye could see. The enormous Russian losses could be replaced; the proportionately smaller German losses could not. For another week the battle dragged on until it became obvious that Operation "Citadel" had failed. By 19 July it was all over. Withdrawal orders went out to the units to shorten the lines.

Hitler's last major Russian offensive had been an unmitigated disaster. Army Group South lost 20,700 men. The Ninth Army—part of Army Group Centre—lost 10,340 men in two days. Entire divisions of infantry and panzers had shrunk to regimental or battalion size. On 16 July the only remaining armour in the Waffen-ss Panzer Corps consisted of 183 tanks, 20 command vehicles, 11 captured T34s and 64 self-propelled guns.

But the price for Soviet military ascendancy came high. In the two weeks of battle the Russians lost 2,108 tanks, 190 guns and 33,000 prisoners. No accurate accounting was ever made of their dead.

On 3 August Hitler ordered the Leibstandarte withdrawn from Russia and posted to Italy as an occupation force to stiffen the back of his Italian ally. Since the Allied invasion of Sicily on 10 July, Mussolini's modern Roman Empire had been coming apart at the seams.

Kurt, however, did not go to Italy with the division. Early in July he had been selected together with a few other of the Leibstandarte's more experienced officers to attend a senior command staff training course at Döberitz-Kampnitz back in Germany. It had an added bonus: a few days leave at home with Kate and the children. He brought Michel, the Cossack, with him.

As Allied air power grew, so too did its bombing offensive against the German homeland. In the beginning the bombers—British and American—concentrated on strategic targets such as factories, bridges, power plants, warehouses, railyards and shipyards. But when subsequent low-level reconnaissance photographs after each major raid illustrated the impossibility of achieving pinpoint accuracy over the targets, tactics were quickly revised.

"Saturation" and later "carpet" bombing became standard procedure for the Allied air forces. Instead of pinpointing strategic objectives, entire manufacturing and city areas—sometimes as much as a square mile—were saturated with bombs. It was the London blitz multiplied at first by 10, then by 100, finally, beyond comparison. During July and August Allied bombers dropped 8,600 tons of explosives on the city of Hamburg; 275,000 apartments, 2,632 shops, 277 schools, 24 hospitals, 58 churches and the zoo were either destroyed or damaged. Most of the 42,000 casualties were civilians. Berlin became a regular target. On Kurt's first evening home the air raid sirens sounded. "Come along, Vati," Kate told him. "Time to go down to the bunker." In the preceding weeks she had spent many nights with the children in the cellar.

"You go ahead. I'll stay here."

Kate was adamant. "No! You come with us or we won't go."

Reluctantly, he followed them down the steps. Then the staccato roar of anti-aircraft guns and exploding bombs began. His eyes widened in wonder. "My God! This is worse than a battle."

Later, while he was away on the staff course, Kate returned from a brief holiday at her parents' farm to find the house in a shambles. Shards of glass lay scattered across the beds, blinds were torn off their mountings, the walls were cracked and much of the family's linen and clothing shredded beyond repair. A bomb had landed across the road destroying several homes. The Meyers had been lucky. She wrote to Kurt, telling him what had happened.

Mindful of the fact that she was expecting their fourth child, he replied at once: "You can't stay there. We'll have to make arrangements to get you away. All this excitement might affect the baby." He appealed to his old friend, *Gauleiter* Hildebrandt: "I have a premonition that if they remain in Berlin I shall lose them."

Hildebrandt knew of an empty villa at Ludwigslust in Mecklenburg.* Its previous owner, Count Schulenberg, had led a strange, solitary existence. His

---

*Now a part of East Germany.

housekeeper discovered him one morning lying in front of the kitchen stove. The gas valves had been turned on full. An inert mouse lay on the floor beside him. Both man and mouse were quite dead. Kate came up from Berlin to inspect the premises. It was such a dark, bleak-looking place and seemingly so filled with misery that she wept. But Hildebrandt, through the local party administration, offered to make arrangements to renovate the premises. A few weeks later Kate and the girls moved in.

On 11 August Gerhild, her fourth child, was born at Ludwigslust. The villa became their family home until it was overrun and they were forced to flee from the Russians in 1945.

8

Embarkation of the Canadian Kiska force began at Nanaimo on 10 July. There were a few embarrassing moments when a battalion of the Winnipeg Grenadiers marched smartly onto the dock, halted and then refused to go up the gangway to their ship. Three or four rifles were thrown into the sea to the delight of news reporters covering the event. The battalion's commanding officer was furious. Before matters got out of hand, a detachment of Provost was summoned from Nanaimo to assist and the troops were marched back to camp.

Officers and senior NCOs then divided the men into groups and in short order sorted everything out. A few ringleaders and barrackroom lawyers were cut from the boarding roster, and the battalion marched back next day ready to board its ship. Other Zombies who headed for the hills once the embarkation date had been announced began trickling back into camp. By 11 July Harry was able to report the following: "Absentee situation completely under control. Some returning voluntarily, others being rounded up by the Provost and in custody. . . . One Sergeant and a Corporal of the Winnipegs caught with a large store of supplies in bivouac on Mt. Benson! Had the Deputy Minister of National Defence, Lt.-Col. G.S. Currie, on my hands all day. I've explained what has been going on and told him I was confident that I can count on them from now on. . . . Gen. Pearkes, the Deputy Minister and I dined on board U.S.A.T.* *David W. Branch* with all the Seattle Port officials. Everything running quite smoothly. I took up official residence aboard at 2230 hours."

Two days later, under balmy summer skies and several RCAF patrol aircraft, the convoy set sail.

"14 July. . . . Moderate seas, weather cloudy and warm. One corvette escort

---

*United States Army Transport.

replaced by the cruiser U.S.S. *Charleston* during the night. Air cover still in evidence. I spent most of the day working up a lecture on the American Attu operation for the officers in the saloon after dinner. . . . Received a coded message from Pacific Command via H.M.S. *Chignecto*. Quite unintelligible. I sent back for checking. Apparently the bloody politicians are still playing it safe and tying my hands as much as possible on where I commit this force. Hell, I don't stand to lose votes, I stand to lose my life and that of 5,000 men. Stupid Bastards!

"The food on board is so good and so plentiful that I am ordering Capt. Fray to serve only two meals a day for fear the officers and troops won't be able to move on reaching Adak. . . . Today's Sunday dinner was roast turkey, cranberry sauce and asparagus followed by mince pie and ice cream—three flavours and all you could eat. For supper: tenderloin steak followed by plum pudding. The troops can't believe it's true. I saw one little French lad from the Gaspé coming from the messroom crossing himself as he staggered off to his bunk."

A week later, sliding through fog and occasional rain squalls, the convoy neared the island. Schools of giant whales broke and sounded around the ships in the flat oily sea. Once ashore the troops were put to work with the mix of American marines and army personnel on a series of training exercises designed to harden them. Marine Maj.-Gen. Holland M. Smith, commander of the training program, seemed mightily impressed by the quality of the Canadian troops. They reminded him more of his own marines than soldiers. Accustomed to the American army's casual dress, discipline and poorly trained soldiers, Smith turned to Harry during one inspection and inquired, "Say, General, how do you get these men of yours to shave every day?"

"Well, General, I tell them that I don't want them looking like a bunch of bloody Americans."

Smith gave a grim smile. "Iszzatso?"

The American navy, "dry" at sea, had built the longest bar in the world for themselves on Adak. Harry wrote in awe: "It is really an engineering marvel. Two Quonset huts laid end to end. It's so long that it is impossible to see through the cigarette smoke to the other end. Army officers are not allowed inside the place, the exception being my Canadian contingent. This VIP treatment doesn't seem to bother their Army types who, for some reason, think that we are all trained commandos. In their eyes this apparently warrants the VIP treatment . . . odd bunch but friendly as hell. . . .

"31 July. . . . Met our Force Commander, Maj.-Gen. C.H. Corlett, this afternoon and received our copy of 'The Plan.' I was impressed by him. He's a soldier not a stuffed shirt."

"The Plan" that Corlett handed him consisted of a ten-inch pile of paper. Harry turned it over to Scott Murdoch to read. Next day Murdoch delivered his appraisal. "It's unworkable, Boss. You're going to have to speak to General Corlett or we're in trouble."

"What's the matter with it?"

"Force headquarters intend detailing what everyone does right down to individual sections. It isn't realistic. Apparently our American friends don't believe in passing orders through a chain-of-command system. They want everything in writing and idiot-proof. If we do things their way, we might just as well send our officers and senior NCOs home because no one will be in command of anything except Force Headquarters."

Harry went off to talk again with Corlett. A couple of hours later he returned rubbing his hands. "You can trash all that crap, Scott. I have my orders and you'll issue them to our men in the regular form . . . but for God's sake don't let the other American commanders find out what we're doing. They're mad enough at us already."

A three-day landing exercise was organized on the nearby island of Great Sitkin as a dress rehearsal for Kiska. The force returned to Adak to find four loaded transports, six new destroyers and a couple of battleships in the harbour. D-day had been set for 15 August.

"11 August. . . . The past three days have been a constant procession of last minute changes, visiting publicity blokes, distinguished visitors and finally, a very fine party given jointly by Lt.-Gen. Simon Bolivar Buckner, Maj.-Gen. Pearkes and Admiral Kincaid, our naval force commander. Gens. DeWitt and Buckner, Gen. Pearkes and Brig. Lett saw us off amid a barrage of movie cameras and flash shots. We don't lack for publicity. . . . 'Corlett's Widow Makers' are on their way . . . pulled out to anchor among the other transports in Kuluk Bay."

The force sailed from Adak on Friday the 13th: 29,126 American soldiers and marines along with 5,300 Canadians. Over the preceding two weeks RCAF No. 14 Fighter Squadron had made 33 individual sorties over Kiska. One pilot in a seven-plane sortie reported having seen bursts of anti-aircraft fire from the island. However, low-level aerial reconnaissance on 10 and 11 August reported: "No signs of life seen anywhere. . . . No AA or MG fire received."

But in 1943 the Japanese talent for treachery and deceit came as an unpleasant fact of life. Knowing the fanaticism shown by the enemy on Attu, the larger Kiska garrison was expected to be a far tougher nut to crack. Thirty percent casualties were anticipated among the invasion forces.

"I feel strangely excited. It's just another exercise. We've been through it all so many times before. Our plan is good. It's well rehearsed. Our equipment is the best any force ever had. We have the strength in numbers and our troops' morale is good . . . and the Japs know we are coming. I would be much more excited if I was going to meet Margo tomorrow."

Kincaid's naval bombardment opened at dawn on 15 August, while the troop ships carrying the Canadian force steamed in slow circles through the fog off Vega Bay. The first wave of American assault troops went in to the beaches.

On board the *David W. Branch* Harry waited impatiently on the bridge for news. "1200 hours. . . . I am about to go into the saloon to be served a good meal by white coated Philippino waiters while somewhere over there in the murk the American Southern Forces are fighting for the beaches— or are they? We can't hear any firing. Where are the capital ships? They too should be firing. . . . At last an intercepted message: 3rd Battalion 87 Combat Team has secured its initial objective. Allowing for encoding and decoding and all that damned nonsense, they were probably there by 1000 hours. . . . Another intercepted message from Force HQ to the South Sector. Apparently the MTBs* were within 300 yards of the shoreline in Vega Bay and saw no fire—and no Japs."

The entire operation turned out to be a fiasco. Under cover of fog the last Japanese had been taken off the island a week before—and just as well. Several of the American landing beaches were so strewn with gigantic boulders that the troop assault craft couldn't make it ashore and instead had to use the beach assigned to the Canadian force.

"Unbelievable chaos at sea with American landing craft circling while somebody decides what to do next. . . . If it's not in the 'Plan' they're lost. . . . One landing craft came in carrying only a brass band playing 'California Here I Come!' The Japs would have loved that."

Once ashore, the invasion force's only combat casualties came from a few trigger-happy Americans exchanging fire with their own troops and from booby traps left by the enemy. While climbing the hills above the landing beach with a patrol, Harry and Scott Murdoch were fired on by some enthusiastic Americans from the landing force that had come in on the other side of the island. Murdoch ran toward them waving his arms and cursing their stupidity. The firing stopped.

Satisfied that the landings were unopposed, Kincaid withdrew his capital ships. They were needed elsewhere in the Pacific. In the days that followed, enormous mounds of equipment and supplies were dumped on the beaches from the departing supply vessels. Working parties were organized, camp sites set up, supplies placed under cover out of the weather. Gradually order was brought out of the chaos.

Harry and Murdoch climbed the heights above the beach where the Canadian force had landed. They found the mountainside peppered with small caves. At the mouth of each, one or more machine guns had been positioned. Boxes of food and ammunition were stacked inside, enough to last several days. Every well-oiled gun had an ammunition belt loaded and waiting to

---

*Motor Torpedo Boats.

be fired. From one cave, Harry squinted down the gun-sight and traversed the weapon's field of fire. It covered the entire landing beach.

"Well, Boss, what do you think?"

"I think we're lucky to be alive."

"Amen."

In spite of the enormous relief at finding the Japanese gone, there remained among the troops a sense of having somehow been cheated of the only chance for action most of them were ever likely to see. All their heartaches and training had been for nothing. Harry's sentiments were no different.

"I feel bloody silly coming all this way for nothing. . . . How the Japs must be laughing at us. . . . Received a long congratulatory parliamentary telegram today (for what?) from the Minister of National Defence. I hope that after all the eulogy he doesn't forget we're up here. It's a morale destroying country and no place for soldiers with any sort of fighting spirit. Too much muck, murk and working parties and no women to make them take pride in being men. The Americans go in for construction gang dress and mannerisms. I won't tolerate it. A British soldier is a soldier, regardless of where and under what circumstances."

While the American soldiers lounged around the island, Harry set the Canadian force to work on combat exercises to keep them fit and out of trouble. One of the American generals seemed surprised by the activity in the hills above the Canadian camp and dropped by to inquire what the Canadians were doing.

"Training exercises," Harry explained.

"Really?" The General looked genuinely puzzled. "Our troops are already trained."

At the Château Frontenac Hotel in Quebec City, Prime Minister King hosted the "Quadrant Conference" between President Roosevelt, Prime Minister Churchill and their assorted chiefs of staff and advisors. Now that their common enemies had gone on the defensive, the time had come for Allied agreement on retaking the rest of the Japanese-held islands in the South Pacific and Hitler's Fortress Europe. The European invasion, known as the COSSAC[5] plan, was approved and given the code name "Overlord." May 1944 was selected as a tentative invasion date.

On Kiska, masses of supplies continued coming ashore from the transports. By 4 September the Canadians had created an all time record by unloading 90,000 tons of stores by hand in two weeks. Harry's feelings about remaining on the island were ambivalent.

"Gen. Corlett phoned this evening to say goodbye. He's off by air to command the 7th U.S. Division in Hawaii. He informed me that he'd put my name in for the U.S. Distinguished Service Cross* . . . which is a bit of an embarrassment because I haven't done anything. . . . The Commander is now Col. Frye of the U.S. Artillery. It creates an odd situation. I am the senior officer on the island but since it's U.S. territory, he commands. As Kiska rapidly develops from a Task Force to just another Post under Alaska Command, there is less and less reason for Murdoch and me to remain. It's an old gentleman's command from now on. However, if there is any promotion in it I wouldn't mind staying. . . .

"8 September. . . . It was officially announced today from Algiers Radio that Italy had surrendered unconditionally. Don't imagine that will make a hell of a lot of difference so long as the Germans are in control. . . . The weather continues fine, but noticeably cooler."

A week later he was ordered to report by air to Canadian Pacific Command in Vancouver for a conference. But the weather grounded all flights. He decided to take the sea route. The U.S. destroyer *Beale*, travelling at a circumspect six knots through mountainous seas, brought them to Adak. He went ashore to arrange air transport at Alaska Defense Command and was greeted by a telegram "from Margo asking my legal authority for a Dr. Powell to perform a serious operation! On whom I don't know—not Margo, I hope. This is a hell of a position to be in. If the weather continues improving a PBY† will take me to Umnak in the morning, from there a Flying Fortress will fly me on to Seattle. I'm billeted with General Post for the night. After a tent on Kiska the heat of this oil fired hut is unbearable." A week later he was with Margo in a Montreal hospital.

In mid-June, when her weight suddenly started dropping, she had gone back into hospital for a checkup. The doctor recommended exploratory surgery. Ever practical, she waited until the boys were on summer holidays, then arranged for an apartment with a housekeeper. She knew now that she was dying. Late at night, during the last days before she went into hospital, the boys lay awake listening to her cries of sorrow, pain and frustration. To hear their invincible pillar of support crumbling frightened them. Yet when they crept into her bedroom, asking how they could help, she ordered them out in a rage. Bewildered, they returned to their beds and lay listening as she cried herself to sleep.

The "exploratory surgery" resulted in the removal of a kidney and a recommendation for more radical surgery, but only with Harry's written approval. She resisted. Not through heroics but because she wanted to spend the little time left to her with the children. By the third week of July she was well enough to go home. But the remission turned out to be short-lived. The boys were placed in boarding school at Lower Canada College (LCC),

*Instead, he received the U.S. Legion of Merit medal.
†Long-range Navy Catalina Flying Boat.

and she checked herself back into hospital.

The doctors told Harry she hadn't a chance. He refused to believe it. "If there is a God in heaven he couldn't be this unfair after four years separation and just when the future looks so promising." Cruelly, they handed him a straw of hope to clutch. A specialist on the West Coast—Dr. Shinbine at the Vancouver General Hospital—if anyone could help Margo he was the man.

Harry arranged transport on Trans-Canada Airlines. He explained to the boys that he was taking their mother on a holiday. They would all be together again for Christmas. It sounded reasonable. The trip west turned into a nightmare of weather delays and aircraft mechanical breakdowns, and Margo racked by continual pain. Two days after their arrival Harry moved into the hospital room to be with her.

"Dr. Shinbine operated today. The cancer had spread everywhere. He gives her 30 days."

Near the end she told Harry that he must remarry "for the sake of the children. . . . My only regret is that I won't be around to see how they turn out." Then she asked him to take a few photographs "so that they'll remember that they did have a mother and that she loved them very, very much." In tears, Harry complied.

"1 December. . . . It is finished. She died at 2315 hours tonight. Oh my poor darling, your courage will be an inspiration for the rest of my life."

With Margo gone, he realized uncomfortably that if anything happened to him his sons would be orphaned. It didn't need to be a German or Japanese bullet that killed him; an air crash would do it, a training exercise, a motor accident. Who to turn to? Hastily, he dashed off a telegram to Mollie Cross in England, giving her the news of Margo's passing and a terse request that if anything should happen to him in the meantime would she please take care of his sons. Their mailing address and name of the headmaster at Lower Canada College were included.

Mollie, with four grown sons of her own, sat down and wrote a long letter of condolence to the boys, signing it "Aunt Mollie." Which was how they learned of their mother's death a week before the school's Christmas holidays. Harry telephoned LCC's headmaster, Mr. Pendelton, instructing him to put both boys on the train for British Columbia when the term ended.

His private rail car was attached to the CPR's transcontinental outside of Kamloops. Past midnight the children were awakened in one of the regular sleeping cars and brought by the conductor to join their father. How do you tell an 11- and nine-year-old that their mother is dead? He had fretted over it all the way from Vancouver. He sat them in the car's comfortable dining room. A uniformed waiter brought them hot chocolate and a huge glass bowl filled to overflowing with freshly sliced fruit.

"Well boys . . . I'm afraid your Mummy is gone." He waited for a reaction.

They lowered their eyes. "You knew?" They nodded.

"A letter from England," Tony explained. "Who is Aunt Mollie?"

Harry swore under his breath. "A friend. A good friend," he added as an afterthought.

They were enrolled in "Mackie's," a prep school operated by two elderly brothers near Vernon in British Columbia's Okanagan Valley. The school took boys from grades 3 to 8, with preference given to those with fathers overseas. The gentle Mackie brothers provided free schooling, room and board to any boy whose father died while serving overseas. Their financial shortfall from this arrangement was made up by charging surviving parents a little extra in fees, which Harry thought "a very sensible form of insurance."

He paid the extra gladly, then rejoined the war.

9

Spring, 1943: manpower losses among the various Waffen-ss divisions had become critical. Worse, the quality of replacements provided by the ss Hauptamt* was now so low that the force's basic fighting abilities were in question. Most of the idealists who had gone off to war brimming with enthusiasm and desire to serve their Führer and Reich were dead. Their lonely graves lay scattered across the vastness of Russia. One-third of the original Waffen-ss divisions had fallen, enough to break the back of any other military force.

The "volunteers" that replaced them were realists. Many had joined reluctantly or had been press-ganged into service. They were badly trained, indifferent to political ideology and sceptical of their leaders. The *Führungs-hauptamt*[6] reported: "Morale is bad. Unmistakable signs of home and church influences. General attitude: if I am conscripted I can do nothing about it, but I will not volunteer." The German people, horrified by the towering casualty figures from the Russian front and the savagery of the conflict, were becoming anti-military, particularly in the Catholic areas of the nation. Not unexpectedly, the reservoir of volunteers for both the Wehrmacht and the Waffen-ss dried up.

In mid-May, Gottlob Berger, the unscrupulous Swabian who had been in charge of ss recruitment since 1938, lamented to Himmler: "In my view the overall conclusion is that the youth of our people has clearly and deliberately been poisoned by Christian education. We have obviously not countered it by sufficiently positive ideological education, particularly now in wartime." The anti-Christian propaganda, so long a part of ss ideology, had begun to boomerang. From recruiting centres across the Reich, similar

---

*The ss Directorate.

reports flowed in to Berger's office: "Influence of parents and church negative . . . Parents generally anti–Waffen-SS . . . Church influences very strong." One potential recruit reported: "The priest told us that the SS was atheist and if we joined it we would all go to hell." As a lad from Hannover put it succinctly: "We didn't want war. We had enough to eat and still have. Let those who haven't enough to eat carry on with this war."

The ever-resourceful Berger refused to accept that all recruiting had evaporated. He cast his covetous eyes on the pre-military training camps of the Labour Service and Hitler Youth. Both organizations, composed of young men approaching the legal age for military service, held enormous untapped reserves of manpower. To make sure the Waffen-SS got the jump over the Wehrmacht's mustering commissions, Berger had his own recruiting officers institute "preliminary mustering" sessions at which the young Labour Service prospects were ordered to attend. The SS recruiters used a combination of promises, intimidation and outright threats to get the recruits to sign up.

Berger had much less trouble recruiting from the Hitler Youth. Its leader, German *Reichsjugendführer** Axmann, had offered to supply Hitler with enough volunteers to form a complete SS division. Responsibility for making it all happen was given to the SS *Führungshauptamt*. The first problem: finding a cadre of experienced officers and senior NCOs for the new division. The Waffen-SS, already critically short of both, had none to spare. Berger discussed the situation with Sepp Dietrich. With his agreement, the new division's senior NCO and officer corps would be taken from the Leibstandarte Division.

The decision made sense for two reasons. The Leibstandarte had always been strong in officers and NCOs. And, since the Hitler Youth Division was to become a part of the new I Panzer Corps being made up of both divisions, the corps could anticipate a harmonious collaboration between the officers and men of both divisional units. This new divison was designated as the 12th SS "Hitlerjugend." Most of its officers and NCOs had been Hitler Youth leaders. Its cadre included a sprinkling of Wehrmacht and Luftwaffe officers and NCOs.

To cement this relationship between the 12th SS, the Leibstandarte and I Panzer Corps, new divisional and corps emblems were created. For the 12th SS, the *Dietrich* (skeleton key) of the Leibstandarte was crossed with the Sigrune symbol of the *Deutsches Jungvolk* of the Hitler Youth, the whole framed by the Oak Leaves decorations of its newly promoted commander, 35-year-old SS Standartenführer Fritz Witt. The new corps emblem became a blend of both divisional logos: two crossed *Dietrichs* in a wreath of Oak Leaves and Swords.

---

*Youth Leader.

Early in August the new division's young recruits started arriving in the Turnhout area near Beverloo, Belgium. None had ever been in battle. Ninety percent were volunteers. They ranged from 16½ to 18 years of age. Training supervision came under General of Panzer Troops West, the elegant and eminently practical Baron Leo Geyr von Schweppenburg. Kurt, who had been promoted to ss Standartenführer, joined the division the following month after finishing his senior officers' staff course. He was appointed to command the division's 25th Panzer Grenadier Regiment.

But before going to Belgium he took a few days' leave at the family's new home in Ludwigslust. The Cossack, Michel, went with him. Alma came to visit. Gerhild, the new baby, was just six weeks old. A large lawn and fenced garden surrounded the villa. On the other side of the fence lay an apple orchard, its trees laden with ripening fruit. After dinner, on his first day home, the family went out to the garden for conversation and coffee. The latter, a vile ersatz liquid, bore little resemblance to the real thing. While his children played and amused themselves exploring the property, Kurt sat contentedly enjoying the pastoral surroundings. High overhead, Allied bombers droned across the peaceful afternoon sky, heading for Berlin.

"Vati! The apple orchard next door. Does it belong to us too?" the children asked.

"Of course it belongs to you," Kurt told them expansively. "Off you go and help yourselves."

They found an opening in the fence and climbed through. Michel joined them to supervise. Within minutes of their foray the orchard's owner appeared on the scene and began yelling at the trespassers. His property was fenced. The apples belonged to him. They were trespassing. Kurt cooled him down. "Fence or no fence, a few apples more or less; what difference does it make?"

Near midnight, as the evening sorties of Allied bombers started passing over Ludwigslust and the rest of the house was asleep, Alma caught the Cossack coming from the maid's room tucking in his pants.

"Michel!" she spoke sharply. "What were you doing in there?"

"Ah, the poor girl was moonstruck. I had to cure her."

In the quiet of early morning the children crept into their parents' bedroom and snuggled in under the blankets next to their father. It was a ritual whenever he came home on leave.

"Shh!" he told them with a sleepy smile. "Don't wake your mother."

A few days later the little Russian and his master arrived in Belgium. One of the officers returning from leave in Berlin told Kurt that the street of Leibstandarte houses where he lived had caught the brunt of a bombing pattern. The Meyer house received a direct hit. Everyone inside had been killed. Silently, Kurt thanked whatever gods had given him that premonition of disaster in time to move Kate and the girls to the safety of Ludwigslust.

From the outset he had misgivings about the sort of training his officers and NCOs would be giving the regiment's youngsters. Their military service had been limited to the Russian front, where European rules of military conduct between enemies did not apply. On the Eastern Front no quarter had been asked or given by either side. He was one of the few who had fought on the Western Front and knew the difference. His concerns were voiced to the Corps Commander. Baron Geyr listened thoughtfully, then suggested that as regimental commander it was Kurt's responsibility to make sure the men understood the difference between "fighting barbarians and civilized soldiers."

At 32, Kurt was the regiment's oldest man. He took an almost parental interest in the men's discipline and welfare. "Because of their youth the cadre had to adopt a new way of teaching. Their only knowledge of discipline was based on family foundations, fundamentally different from the discipline of a young soldier. . . . Beyond the normal military relationships a brotherly relationship was established between officers and men. . . . I issued orders prohibiting smoking, the use of alcohol and visiting any Belgian brothel. Female relationships were forbidden for all soldiers up to the age of 18."

He selected his officers carefully on the basis of character and past performance. Those found unsuitable or caught brutalizing the soldiers were transferred back to Germany within the first few weeks of training. Despite his own abandonment of formal religious beliefs, he gave the men freedom to choose whatever belief they wished, explaining: "God cannot be proved but he is to be believed. Man only becomes man when, through his conscience, he feels himself responsible to his God. A soldier who does not believe in God cannot fight."

He instilled in them a respect for motherhood with the dictum "The mother fights, lives, sacrifices and dies for her family and her children." Over one three-month training period he persuaded them to give up their wages voluntarily and send them to the poor and bombed-out people at home.

But where their military training was concerned all gentleness left him. "I tried to approximate war conditions. All exercises were conducted with live ammunition using fighting, not training, weapons. The injuries and loss of lives that resulted had to be accepted in order to avoid losses during action. . . . For their fighting motto I gave them a soldierly idealistic point of view: 'I am nothing. *We* are everything.' The entire troop was regarded as a single unit. . . . The unit represented a cross-section of the best German youth from all social strata. In all my years of military service I had never had a troop of men as good as this one."

Throughout the fall and winter months their training continued. Slowly, his boys were turned into fighting men.

On the Eastern Front the German army went on the defensive. No longer the hammer, it became the anvil. Strategic towns and rivers that had been triumphant milestones along the victorious road to conquest in '41 and '42 became treacherous stepping stones on the pathway to defeat. Army Group South's imposing strength of 42 divisions looked good on paper, but in reality most of the infantry divisions were down to less than one-sixth of their establishment and only a thousand rifles. Eighty-three tanks and 98 self-propelled guns were all that remained of the proud panzer juggernaut that had hurled itself into battle only two years before.

Facing them was a new, revitalized and re-equipped Red Army lacking nothing in men, tanks, guns and motorized equipment. It outnumbered the German forces 7 to 1—in some locations by as much as 40 to 1. In a series of rapid advances the Soviets had recaptured the cities of Kharkov, Saporzhe and Melitopol and finally, in the last months of 1943, had retaken Kiev. Army Group South appeared about to be cut off. The Leibstandarte, together with several other divisions, was called to this cauldron of chaos. After a period of confusion resulting from conflicting and countermanded orders, the division took up a position early in November south of Kiev. Their third and final disastrous Russian campaign was about to begin.

After the loss of Margo, Harry was assigned to give a two-week lecture course on the Kiska operation to the U.S. Infantry Combat Training School in Orlando, Florida. After weeks of agony watching Margo waste away, he needed time for quiet reflection. He crossed the American continent by train in leisurely comfort, staring out the window as the miles clicked past.

In Orlando, the base commander assigned him a private car with the one-star fender flag of a brigadier-general and an enthusiastic young major to act as his official tour guide. Harry was overwhelmed by all the attention.

Two weeks later he was back in Canada with orders to report overseas and take command once again of the 7th Infantry Brigade. He left in a Ferry Command bomber from Montreal on 21 January, arrived at Prestwick at noon the next day, flew on to Hendon in an American DC3, then was driven to 3rd Division HQ at Brockenhurst in Hampshire. Maj.-Gen. Rod Keller put him in the picture.

Much had happened to the Canadian army during the eight months he had been away. In the Mediterranean area, Operation "Husky" had paid rich dividends by producing qualified battlefield commanders, something Harry had missed with the Kiska fiasco. In a little over three months Sicily had been captured, Italy had capitulated, the vital Foggia airfields and the port of Naples were in Allied hands. Led by Guy Simonds, the 1st Canadian Division had played an important part in the campaigns. Even Montgomery, rarely given to praising the individual performance of his commanders, had been impressed by Simonds's tactical and organizational abilities during the advance from the Sicilian beaches to the German defence line at the Sangro River.

Early in October the British and Canadian governments ambitiously agreed to create a Canadian corps in the Mediterranean theatre. Lieut.-Gen. Harry Crerar's I Canadian Corps HQ, together with the I Canadian Corps Troops and the 5th Canadian Armoured Division, would be sent to Italy to join Simonds's 1st Division and 1st Army Tank Brigade. It resulted in splitting the army's two corps between theatres while Canadian Army HQ remained in England—not the brightest of arrangements for running an army. A flurry of transfers, new appointments and promotions from the most senior officers down had resulted.

General McNaughton handed his army command to Lieut.-Gen. Ken Stuart, who took over on an acting basis while at the same time becoming chief of staff, Canadian Military HQ, London, with Brig. Churchill Mann as his chief of staff.* After a short stint as commander of the 5th Armoured Division, which arrived and began unloading at Naples in early November, Simonds returned to England to be promoted to lieutenant-general in command of II Corps. Chris Vokes was promoted to major-general and given command of the 1st Division, while Bert Hoffmeister, former CO of the Seaforth Highlanders of Canada, became a brigadier and took over Vokes's 2nd Brigade.

It seemed everyone was moving up the ladder except Harry. Militia officers he had helped train were now battle-scarred veterans, experienced regimental commanders in the field slated for command of their own brigades. They had earned the right. Harry realized that in eight months he hadn't earned a thing. Thirty-three-year-old George Kitching, 1st Division's GSO1 in Italy, had been promoted to a major-general. He had been brought back to England to command the 4th Canadian Armoured Division, replacing the venerable Frank Worthington, founder of the nation's armoured establishment. Even Brig. Charles Foulkes, the politically astute opportunist and staff officer at Canadian Army HQ—Harry's nemesis from Wolseley Barracks in London, Ontario—was now a major-general and commander of the 2nd Infantry Division.

For the impending assault on Europe every first-class experienced officer who could be spared from the Italian front was being transferred back to England. Senior Permanent Force officers with no battle experience were used to make up the shortfall.

After offering his condolences over Margo, Keller explained as much as he knew of the invasion plan. The Canadian sector of the beach had been given the code name "Juno." The 3rd Infantry Division would be the attacking force. The battle planners anticipated that by D-Day plus 21 the division would be written off. Those that survived were to be used as replacements for the fresh units coming in behind.

"Going ashore we'll have the British 6th Airborne and 3rd Infantry Division

---

*The former BGS (brigadier of General Staff) title had now been changed to chief of staff.

on our left, the British 50th Infantry Division on our right. The 6th Airborne will be dropping in after midnight. The rest of us at dawn, God willing. Seventh and 8th Brigades go in first, the 9th will be our reserve. We're expecting up to 20 percent casualties on the beaches. The plan is for late May or early June. It all depends on the weather."

He found the 7th Infantry Brigade stationed at Newport on the Isle of Wight preparing for exercise "Cordage," one of several pre-invasion drills that were to take place over the next three and a half months. But before joining the brigade, Harry drove to Fleet to see Mollie Cross. He had a business proposition to discuss with her, something he'd been tossing over in his mind since Florida. He told his driver to wait, then dashed into the house. He gave her a perfunctory kiss and came straight to the point.

"Here's the situation: the big show will probably go this summer. I'm in it. I may be killed. If that happens my sons are going to need a responsible guardian. I want you to marry me. As my executor you'll be in a position to collect whatever financial benefits are due for a wife and two children. If I survive I'll probably make major-general. Being a general's wife isn't such a bad deal. It has its compensations. And the boys aren't all that bad from what I've seen of them. Well, what do you say?"

"Is there time to discuss it?"

"No. I have a car waiting."

"In that case, I accept."

"Good." Another perfunctory kiss. "You make the wedding arrangements. I'll call you in a week." With a wave he was gone.

They were married in Fleet on 12 February in one of Hampshire's more bizarre weddings of the season. For a wedding present his officers presented them with a sterling silver tray inscribed with the crests of the brigade's three regiments: the Regina Rifles, the Winnipeg Rifles and the Canadian Scottish. There wasn't time for a honeymoon. Harry had to get back to work.

Mollie wrote to her stepsons, introducing herself as their new mother and promising a letter every week. She signed it "Mum." She offered no explanation as to why their father had felt compelled to marry again so quickly. Had Harry taken a few minutes to explain matters in a letter much of his sons' subsequent animosity toward Mollie might have been avoided. Her intentions were always the best, but it was too soon after their mother's death for her to be an acceptable replacement.

Weeks later, when her letter arrived at Vernon Prep School, they discussed this strange turn of events, finding it difficult to put into words. They felt that somehow their father had betrayed them.

PART 7
NORMANDY

*Here dead we lie because we did not
  choose*
*To shame the land from which we
  sprung.*
Life to be sure is nothing much to lose,
*But young men think it is, and we were
  young.*

A.E. HOUSMAN

IN KURT'S OPINION, 15th Company was the best choice for his regiment's reconnaissance unit. It had the best officers and that devil-may-care attitude so important to the élan of any reconnaissance group. At a formal dinner given by 15th Company to which he and Kate were invited, he made sure his men understood what made them different. As an old motorcycle reconnaissance rider, he found the subject dear to his heart.

"There are in our regiment many companies of one sort or another. But there is only one recce company. You have been selected from the entire regiment because you are the best I've got. I expect you to be the model for the regiment. . . . In battle you will never have comrades on your left and right. Your unit will push far into enemy lines and fight alone. . . . You must give me the openings for my battle leadership. If you are good then the regiment can fight well. If you are no good then the regiment will pay a high price in blood. . . . Your strongest weapon is not the machine gun or cannon. It is speed—your vehicle's motor."

After explaining that a reconnaissance unit was the safest place to be in battle ("Throughout the entire battle of France in 1940 I lost only seven men; in Greece only three"), he then proceeded to give his views on prisoners.

"There is nothing honourable in being taken prisoner. . . . At the end of each war every prisoner should be able to prove that he was honourably captured. Our battle experiences in 1941, 1942 and 1943 have taught that capture is not for us. Between 1939 and 1943 not one man in my troop was ever taken prisoner. Those comrades who had the bad luck to be seriously injured or could not get back to our lines used the last bullet in their weapons on themselves. I have sworn to myself, my family and my wife that I would not go on living if I was imprisoned. I mean that. Let your comrades tell you—listen to our volunteer Cossacks. They will tell you why we must act this way. . . . My boys, I wish no imprisonment for you. I wish no prisons for anyone in this company. Remember, the last shot always belongs to you."

In April Field Marshal von Rundstedt and Sepp Dietrich arrived to inspect the new division. Von Rundstedt liked what he saw. To the credit of the training cadre, close to 20,000 boys had been turned into professional soldiers. Using a map of the Beverloo combat training range, Kurt explained to the Field Marshal how the war games had been conducted. An army photographer recorded the scene.

That same afternoon along the Devonshire coast, an enormous invasion exercise code-named "Trousers" was under way at Slapton Sands. Army photographers recorded the event. Standing near the beach when Harry came ashore behind the Regina Rifles stood a group of senior British army and naval officers—Adm. Sir Bertram Ramsay, the naval commander-in-chief of "Overlord"; Rear-Adm. Sir Philip Vian, commander of "Overlord's" Eastern Task Force on the Channel crossing; Lieut.-Gen. Sir Miles Dempsey, commander of the British Second Army—of which the Canadian 3rd Division was a part; and Monty, now Gen. Sir Bernard Law Montgomery, commander of 21st Army Group.

"Well, Foster, how are things going?" Montgomery inquired.

"I don't know, sir," Harry answered. He produced his map of the beaches. "I was put into a landing craft three miles offshore and I've had no communications with my troops from that point on."

Monty raised his eyebrows. Quickly Admiral Vian explained that landing craft were not being put at risk inshore during exercises. "At this juncture we can't afford to lose any. A safety precaution, you understand."

Monty shook his head. "Not good enough. How do you expect Foster to handle his reserves when he's commanding an assault for us if he doesn't know what's going on onshore?"

"One thing more, sir?" Harry offered.

"Well?"

"I think we're carrying too much personal equipment. If the sea is rough, a lot of troops will drown simply trying to wade ashore. Then, once on the beach, they have to run for cover. It's hard enough to run on sand without being weighted down with nonessentials."

"Good point. Give me an appreciation in writing of what you consider to be nonessentials."

"Yes, sir." Harry saluted and trotted off to rejoin the brigade.

By mid-April the 20,540 officers and men of the 12th SS "Hitlerjugend" Division were ready for combat. Composed of the 25th and 26th SS Panzer Grenadier Regiments, two armoured battalions of the 12th SS Panzer Regiment, plus flak, engineer and reconnaissance battalions, it presented a formidable fighting force. The division moved into Normandy, taking up position around the town of Lisieux, 18 miles from the coast.

On an inspection tour in early April, Gen. Heinrich Eberbach, then inspector of tank troops, noted that there were some equipment shortages. By 1 June only 148 of 186 tanks had been delivered; only 333 of 390 armoured carriers; and 923 of 1,007 jeep-type vehicles. And only, 1,834 of the promised 2,114 lorries had arrived, many of them an Italian make and of questionable serviceability. Eberbach praised the division's excellent officers and NCOs for "training these young boys to become extraordinary soldiers not by giving them hell but rather by fatherly methods. The division paraded—not goose-stepping—but singing as they marched."

The division's positioning concerned General Geyr. He discussed with Field Marshal von Rundstedt the advisability of shifting the 12th SS further inland on the theory that mobile forces would need more manoeuvring room during the first critical hours of any Allied assault. Accordingly, with the Field Marshal's agreement, the 12th SS moved another 30 miles inland. Kurt set up his 25th Panzer Regimental HQ at LeSap. The Germans waited.

As D-Day approached, a series of Canadian and British VIPs made the rounds of 3rd Division. Harry observed, "Most are a pain in the ass but it is an honour to greet some."

"25 April. . . . His Majesty arrived today with Gen. Crerar on an inspection tour. The troops were lined up three deep on both sides of the road for over a mile. They put on a good showing. I heard later that HM and the brass were mightily pleased. He is such a charming and courteous man. . . .

"18 May. . . . The PM [Mackenzie King] arrived today in a banker's suit to shake hands with a few of the men. He tried very hard to be pleasant but wound up instead being political. It is hard to imagine him leading anybody anywhere. Even more strange that anyone would want to follow. . . . After everybody left I reprimanded two officers for giving him a horse laugh during his talk. . . . He may not look or sound like much but he is our Prime Minister and I will not tolerate disrespect."

At East Grinstead the 4th Armoured Division put on a splendid show for the Prime Minister. As the hundreds of tanks and motor battalions streamed past the reviewing stand, King was moved to tears. He was escorted back to the division's mess for a small sherry and to compose himself. "I've seen the cream of Canada," he wept. "I know most of these boys will never see their homes again." His words came as such a surprise that even the most cynical officers were moved.

For the next three weeks tight security enveloped the entire south of England as gigantic convoys of tanks, armoured vehicles, guns, men and equipment lined the country roads. All leave was cancelled. The huge troop-assembly areas were cordoned off and no one allowed in or out. At seaports from Harwich, northeast of London, to Falmouth, near the southwestern tip of England, fleets of warships and transports lay berthed and at anchor. The waiting began.

Five landing sites had been selected for the "Overlord" invasion assault on Normandy. To the west the Americans would land on beaches designated as Utah and Omaha. On the east, British forces would storm ashore on beaches Gold and Sword, while the Canadians came in between them at Juno. One hundred and thirty thousand men were to be landed from the sea with an additional 23,000 airborne troops dropping inland ahead of the assault forces. Taking part in "Neptune," the naval part of the operation, were over 190,000 men and 7,000 surface vessels. On the evening before and during the D-Day landings, more than 14,000 sorties by Allied aircraft of all types were planned. It would be the largest invasion force in the history of mankind.

Finally, on 3 June, embarkation orders were issued. D-Day was announced as 5 June. The Canadian three-brigade divisional group, together with 400 Royal Marine Commandos, was assigned as part of assault Force J, boarding at Portsmouth. Throughout the breadth of southern England men and machines began closing up on the coastal seaports. Harry went aboard the troopship *Prince David*, a medium-sized converted CPR passenger boat.

"3 June. . . . I could feel the tension coiled inside everyone like an electrical charge waiting to explode . . . troops all frantically writing letters home . . . a few already seasick. . . . Outside a heavy blow and a rising sea. . . . I remember thinking 'Thank God this isn't an airborne division' . . . and since there was nothing more for me to do I went to sleep."

As darkness descended, the ships began casting off from their jetties to join the assembling convoys. Steadily, the wind and rain increased until the white wave crests were scattered into a frothy foam. At sea the tightly packed vessels pitched and rolled and creaked. Shortly past 0400 hours, Sunday morning, 4 June, Supreme Allied Commander Dwight Eisenhower decided that weather conditions would make air and airborne operations impossible. He postponed the invasion by 24 hours.

Convoys already at sea were ordered to anchorages along the coast, while those that had not yet sailed were to remain in port. Troops on board ships still tied to the jetties were to be allowed on shore to stretch their legs, but those on vessels lying at anchor were to remain where they were. At 2300 hours the Commander-in-Chief Portsmouth reported that all convoys, with the exception of units from assault Force U, were safely at anchor. The Force U convoy of 138 ships had missed the postponement signal. Hurriedly, a naval aircraft flew out to direct it to anchor and refuel in Weymouth Bay, but strong westerlies and roiling seas prevented any ships from reaching port until well after midnight.

Just east of Sword, where the Orne River flowed into the Channel, mud flats stretched seaward more than a mile. The low shoreline had few distinguishable landmarks, and even a small navigational error while making landfall could be a disaster. Numbers of rocky outcrops lay offshore, any one of which could gut the frail landing craft.

Two Royal Navy midget submarines—X20 and X23—had sailed from Portsmouth on the evening of 2 June and were already submerged in position off the French coast. Before dawn, D-Day morning, they were to surface showing identity lights to seaward for the assault craft heading in to shore. Both submarines surfaced in the darkness on the morning of 5 June to hear the postponement signal. Imprisoned in their cramped quarters the five-man crews settled back on the bottom to wait.

Throughout Sunday the unsettled weather intensified. By late morning, gale warnings were issued by the Admiralty to all shipping in the Irish Sea. Near dark the storm peaked. Washtubs filled with tinned peaches and urns of lukewarm tea were set up on the docks for men in the transports that had tied alongside. Those who weren't still seasick chatted quietly among themselves, smoked or slept.

On board the troopships anchored out in the harbour, conditions were far from pleasant. Ventilation systems had been designed to operate while the vessels were under way, not riding at anchor. Battened down against the weather and with strict blackout conditions in case of enemy air attacks, the troops remained crammed together in an atmosphere foul with sweating bodies, vomit, sterno fumes and mock turtle soup. The tinned soup, part of every man's rations, had been designed with a striker and fusee on the bottom of each can so that it could be self-heating.

For Stan Dudka, a six-foot five-inch, 235-pound sergeant of the North Nova Scotia Regiment, the smell was overpowering. "Fortunately I had a strong stomach. But there were some who never did recover until after they went ashore in Normandy. By then we were all too busy to be sick."

But the weather was changing. A northwest Atlantic depression had started pushing a cold front much farther south than expected. The prognosis was that Portsmouth and the entire English side of the Channel would clear during Sunday night and that a period of fair weather would follow, lasting until early Tuesday. At 0430 hours on the morning of 5 June Eisenhower gave the order to launch the invasion at dawn of the following day.

All up and down the English coast, ships and small craft again began pouring out into the Channel, heading for the Spout.* Once past the Portsmouth buoy, the Canadians aboard the vessels in Force J opened their sealed orders. New up-to-date maps were issued with actual names, replacing the coded designation maps that had been used on the practice invasion exercises. Weapons were checked and rechecked. Carefully, with a sense of anticipation and mounting excitement, the men studied their unit assignments.

Juno beach assumed an identity. From the town of St. Aubin-sur-Mer on the east it extended 4.5 miles to beyond the town of Courseulles-sur-Mer on the west. Bernières-sur-Mer lay between the two. Once the troops were ashore, Bernières would be used by General Keller as the division's HQ. The battle plan called for Harry's 7th Brigade to come in on the right with the Regina Rifle Regiment landing between Bernières and Courseulles. The Royal Winnipeg Rifles and C Company of the 1st Canadian Scottish Regiment were to come ashore between Courseulles and opposite the village of Vaux, a quarter of a mile inland. The brigade's tank and armour support was being provided by the 6th Canadian Armoured Regiment (1st Hussars).

Brig. Ken Blackader's 8th Brigade, supported by the 10th Armoured Regiment (the Fort Garry Horse), would land the North Shore Regiment opposite St. Aubin, the Queen's Own Rifles of Canada in front of Bernières, and Régiment de la Chaudière as the brigade's reserve. Brig. D.G. Cunningham's 9th Brigade was designated as the division's reserve and scheduled to land two hours after the main force.

As darkness closed on the evening of 5 June, the lead ships of the armada were already entering the Spout. Shortly after midnight long lines of troop transport aircraft and glider trains of the British 6th Airborne Division roared through the black sky overhead.

"We began boarding the landing craft shortly after 0400 hours. The sea had moderated but there were still five foot waves. . . . It wasn't anything like Kiska. . . . The troops boarded quietly but were all wide awake, probably from the benzedrine tablets they had been issued."[1]

The paratroops were already on French soil and fighting Germans when a green light appeared to seaward off Sword beach from X23. Moments later, three miles off Juno, a second light was visible from X20. Seventy-six hours had elapsed since the midget submarines had left Portsmouth, 64 had been spent underwater.

The log entry read: "0500. Surfaced and checked position by shore fix in

---

*A geographical area of the Channel cleared by minesweepers and designated for funnelling the ships across the Channel in ten lanes to the various assault areas.

dawn light. Rigged mast with lamp and radar beacon. 0508. Commenced flashing green light."

The Allied invasion had begun.

ss Brigadeführer Witt's 12th ss Panzer Division sat waiting south of Lisieux. At 0300 hours Witt received a signal from the commander of the 711th Division, Lieut.-Gen. Reichardt, stating: "Enemy airborne landing behind our left wing."* A report had been forwarded by a Luftwaffe sentry position on the coast that Allied airborne troops had landed at several sectors east and west of the Orne River. Witt placed the division on full alert. Kurt was awakened by his communications officer with the news. "I ordered out the regiment and was ready to move within the hour."

German meteorologists, unable to obtain a weather watch on the northwestern Atlantic, were unaware of the shifting frontal conditions that had prompted Eisenhower to release his invasion forces. OKW had been assured that any invasion after 4 June would be impracticable for several days. Accordingly, naval patrols scheduled for the night of 5 June were cancelled on account of weather. Officers were permitted local leave throughout the coastal areas. So certain was Field Marshal Rommel of Allied intentions that he left his Army Group B Headquarters in France to attend his wife's birthday party at her home in Herrlingen near Ulm on the upper Danube before continuing on for a meeting with Hitler.

Overall command of the German western armies had been given to Field Marshal von Rundstedt, whom Hitler had brought out of retirement for a second time in March 1942. Von Rundstedt, now 66, was still respected as a strategist and gentleman. He held no illusions on the army's ability to repel a massive coastal attack by an enemy whose main point of assault could not be determined in advance with any degree of certainty. He believed the best chance for repelling the invaders lay in holding strong mobile forces in reserve, available for use as and where the situation required.

Hitler disagreed.

Field Marshal Rommel, the younger ardent tactician, shared Hitler's viewpoint: create an interlocking fortified coastal defence network that would halt and defeat the invading forces on the beaches before they had a chance of gaining a toehold. The basic problem with this philosophy lay in the number of troops required to cover the enormous distance from the Netherlands to the Breton Peninsula. In early 1944 Germany had over 300 divisions operating outside its borders, but only 53 were stationed in France and the Low Countries. All Hitler's huge land forces had been committed. There were no reserves left in Germany. Any increase for the western armies would have to be taken from other battlefronts.

---

*From the 12th ss Division's records covering 6 June 1944.

To overcome this handicap, Rommel, with Hitler's agreement, decided on positioning the bulk of his defence forces at those points along the coast where he believed the attack would come. In March he asked that the armoured divisions von Rundstedt had intended forming into a mobile reserve be placed under his command. Additionally, he wanted control over the armies allotted to defend the entire French coast, including the Mediterranean sectors. Sensibly, he believed that the coastal battle should be fought by a single commander who had all available forces under his direct control.

Although Hitler agreed with Rommel's coastal defence plans and considered the "Desert Fox" one of his ablest generals, he could hardly retain von Rundstedt as C.-in-C. West if Rommel held command not only of Seventh and Fifteenth Armies assigned to defend the most threatened portions of the coast, but also command of the reserves and a degree of control over the old field marshal's other two armies—the First and Nineteenth.

By applying his favourite "divide and rule" policy, Hitler settled the matter with a compromise unsatisfactory to both commanders. Neither Rommel nor von Rundstedt would have control of the reserves. Rommel was handed three armoured divisions—the 2nd, 21st and 116th—as a reserve for his Army Group B. The remaining three divisions stationed in the north were designated as OKW reserves under Hitler's orders. These were the 1st SS Leibstandarte, the Panzer Lehr and the 12th SS. Von Rundstedt was left with no reserves under his command, and Hitler, by retaining personal control of these reserves, would sooner or later have to become involved with any battle plans in which they were to be committed. The organization and chain of command of the major commands in the West was, in the words of Rommel's chief of staff, Lieut.-Gen. Hans Speidel, "somewhere between confusion and chaos."

Unlike the type of unified command adopted by the Allied armies, the German Wehrmacht operated on a horizontal rather than vertical plane of responsibility. Close cooperation among the three services was virtually nonexistent, with each service jealously guarding its area of command. In consequence, a host of absurdities developed. Coastal shore batteries set up by the Luftwaffe were under naval control while pointed toward the sea. If these same guns traversed to fire at land-based objectives, then they came under military orders. Occupation troops, Waffen-SS units and divisions were under von Rundstedt's control for operational purposes but not for commitment to battle. Even his chief transportation officer, inspectors general of infantry, armoured forces, engineers and a few of his headquarters staff members in OB West* were subject to OKW direction or that of some political authority.

The Field Marshal complained: "The only forces I actually commanded

---

*Oberbefehlshaber: literally, "the senior command holder"—Commander-in-Chief West.

were those guarding the entrance to my headquarters" at St. Germain, outside Paris.

On the stormy evening of 5 June Lieutenant-General Speidel had been left in command of Army Group B during Rommel's absence. Although as senior staff officer the brilliant Speidel knew exactly what measures needed to be taken in the event of an attack, he could not speak with the same authority as Rommel. At the next lower command echelon two more officers were also absent from their posts—Col.-Gen. Friedrich Dollmann, chief of the Seventh Army in Normandy, was away in Rennes conducting war games, while Sepp Dietrich, commander of I Panzer Corps, had gone to Brussels. As the first streams of Allied paratroop aircraft flew toward their drop zones at either end of what on the following morning would be the invasion front, Speidel was in the middle of a dinner party at Rommel's La Roche Guyon castle headquarters. News of the first parachute landings arrived while the party was still in progress.

Over the next few hours confusing and often contradictory reports continued coming in to Army Group B and were dutifully passed along to OB West for evaluation. First reactions from OB West, and later from OKW once it had been advised, were that the airborne landings were localized feints designed to distract attention from the real invasion point. Hitler had already been convinced by his OKW staff that the main thrust would come across the Channel from Dover to the Pas-de-Calais area.

2

Maj.-Gen. Edgar Feuchtinger's 21st Panzer Division had the mobile force nearest the Orne where the British 6th Airborne was dropping. His panzers lay spread through a dozen villages and hamlets in a 25-square-mile area southeast of Caen. Most of the division's 16,000 troops were combat veterans from campaigns in Crete, Russia and Rommel's Afrika Korps. They had 120 tanks as well as artillery and infantry units.

Coastal defences in the Caen area were manned by the 716th Infantry Division under Lieut.-Gen. Wilhelm Richter. Standing orders allowed Richter to commit the 21st Panzer Division's guns and infantry into battle but not its armour; the armour remained part of Rommel's mobile reserves. At 0120 hours Richter ordered Feuchtinger by telephone to send his units nearest the British drop zone to attack. Forty minutes later he revised his order, telling Feuchtinger: "Commit the entire 21st Panzer Division in an area east of the Orne!"

Feuchtinger hesitated. Although Richter was his immediate superior, in the event of an invasion he was also responsible to General Geyr's Panzer Group West, a part of Rommel's reserves. And Rommel was away. Richter might command the coastal defences but he couldn't speak for the Field Marshal. Feuchtinger decided to wait until things became clearer. Meantime, Richter's 716th Infantry Division would have to manage on its own. As a precaution, Feuchtinger placed the entire 21st Panzer Division on full alert.

The 716th was one of several *bodenständig* units designed as static formations to fight from fixed positions. Its soldiers were under 18 or over 35. Many had been recruited from the occupied Eastern countries. Some were third-degree frostbite victims from the winter carnage in Russia or suffered other partial disabilities from battle zones of the Reich. These second-rate defence divisions were equipped with older and often foreign-made weapons captured in earlier campaigns. Their transport consisted of horses to pull the artillery and supply wagons. As a token gesture for rapid deployment, one battalion operated with bicycles. Usually the only motorized vehicle possessed by a *bodenständig* unit was the divisional commander's staff car. Everyone else marched.

Richter's division comprised only two infantry regiments: the 726th and 736th. Unfortunately, most of the 726th was absent from the area, although its second battalion had been stationed as a reserve four miles inland for counterattack in case of a breakthrough. Four reserve companies from the 736th were two miles inland. Neither formation could reach the beaches faster than they could march. In essence, Richter had four battalions defending a front 19 miles wide, with each of the 736th's 12 companies expected to hold over a mile of front during the initial invasion assault until reserves could be brought forward.

Consequently, at dawn on 6 June only three companies of second-rate troops—400 men in all—were covering Juno beach. Coming in against them after devastating air and naval bombardments were 2,400 superbly trained men in the Canadian first wave supported by 76 amphibious tanks.

The defenders were under orders to give no ground. Surrounded by mines and interlocking coils of barbed wire, they were in no position to retreat anyway. Their nearest mechanized reserves were six miles away in Caen, where several self-propelled artillery units from the 21st Panzers were on detached duty with Richter's forces. But these were terribly vulnerable to air attacks once they came out from under their camouflage nettings and began to move. The German air force no longer controlled the skies. In fact, on 4 June the Luftwaffe had exactly 160 operational aircraft in the whole of France. Two days earlier 124 of these had been ordered to leave the coastal area for inland bases closer to the German border. On the morning of 6 June, Col. Joseph Priller's 26th Fighter Wing based at Lille—within striking distance of the Normandy beaches—consisted of two serviceable Focke-Wulf 190 fighters. "You're crazy!" Priller[2] told Luftwaffe Command over the telephone when the orders came in to withdraw the fighters.

The Kriegsmarine was in no better state. At 0300 hours Naval Group

HQ West, in Paris, ordered the 5th E-boat Flotilla in Le Havre to leave port to reconnoitre the Channel. Three boats sped out in darkness and an hour later passed through the smoke screen being laid down by the invasion armada. The British battleships *Warspite* amd *Ramillies* spotted them and opened fire, but the E-boats pressed home their attack and launched 18 torpedoes. A Norwegian destroyer was hit amidships and blew up, but the capital ships managed to sheer away in time. The E-boats vanished into the smoke screen. Flotillas from Cherbourg also attempted sorties against the Allied Fleet but failed to penetrate the defence screen. Like the Luftwaffe, the Kriegsmarine had become a toothless tiger.

Although weak in infantry, the 716th Division was supposedly strong in artillery. Besides its normal complement of eight field guns and four medium batteries, plus the self-propelled artillery from the 21st Panzers, there were three 155 mm guns and two coastal artillery pieces, as well as a variety of Czech, Polish, Hungarian and French batteries. On paper the division supposedly had 83 guns of various calibre. The real total came to 67 because a number of pieces had been lent to other units. Still others were unserviceable.

All of the heavy guns were supposed to be sitting under concrete, but Rommel's hurried construction program for coastal defences in the Caen area was not yet complete and only two gun emplacements were finished. These mounted 100 mm Czech guns. Elsewhere, unroofed bunkers, many dug into pits among the open fields, provided little protection for the artillerymen.

The infantry companies were much better placed. They had been organized into four *Widerstandsnester* (resistance nests) along Juno beach in front of Vaux, Courseulles, Bernières and St. Aubin. Each nest contained one or more heavy-gun emplacements set in concrete and supported by trenches and gun pits for the machine-gunners and mortarmen. Interlocking firing zones had been carefully calculated to cover the obstacles planted along the shoreline just below high-water tide. These included iron "hedgehogs," concrete tetrahedrons, and massive iron brackets from Belgium's prewar anti-tank defences set out in the sand to tear the bottoms from landing craft making for the beach on a falling tide. Rows of concrete stakes pointed seaward, backed by wooden ramps raised six feet on the landward side built to impale approaching vessels. Teller anti-tank mines were scattered throughout the structures and set to explode on contact.

Although the defenders had been assured their positions were impregnable, Richter knew the reality of their plight. None of the nests were manned by more than a platoon of men, and each had been placed roughly 2,000 yards apart from each other—the extreme limit of automatic weapons fire. On the morning of 6 June the 400 men of the 716th Division at Juno beach stared out between the grey seas and overcast skies and waited for death to arrive.

The first phase of the Allied bombardment had been given to RAF Bomber Command for a midnight attack by four-engined Lancasters. This was to be followed by a dawn raid with Flying Fortresses of the U.S. Eighth Air Force. Due to thick low cloud the results of both raids were described as "spotty." In fact, not one of the German beach defences was hit at all.

At 0530 hours the next bombardment phase opened when the British cruiser *Belfast*, followed 22 minutes later by the *Diadem*, began shelling the heavy-gun positions at Ver-sur-Mer and Beny-sur-Mer. A half hour later the accompanying destroyers opened fire as they moved closer inshore. Shortly after seven they were joined by the Landing Craft Gun (LCG) and creeping barrage of the self-propelled artillery that had already embarked into the four-foot waves. In the final moments of the barrage, rocket ships delivered thundering broadsides equal to a hundred Diadem Class cruisers. Inside the bunkers the Germans crouched, stunned by the shock waves and the noise of the screaming shells; yet the Royal Navy estimated later that less than 15 percent of the bunkers had been destroyed by the bombardment, although nearly every one of the summer houses lining the beach was flattened to rubble.

Courseulles-sur-Mer was the most heavily fortified strongpoint at Juno. One 88 mm gun, a 75 mm gun and three 50 mm anti-tank guns, plus 12 machine-gun pillboxes and two 50 mm mortar emplacements, faced the sea. Two more 75 mm guns at either side of the town protected the flanks. Most of the gun positions were protected by concrete.

"The plan called for a frontal attack if the air and sea bombardment hadn't knocked them out already. A bloody business. But we had no choice. The guns had to be taken quickly or the landing craft and men coming in behind would be in trouble."

Lying off Juno in a patch of sea five miles wide and ten miles deep were 365 ships of various types and sizes. At 0530 hours the slowest of these vessels headed for shore. These were the LCT—Landing Craft Tank—carrying the amphibious squadrons of the armoured regiments. An hour later and flanked by destroyers, the heavier support craft followed. Next came the LCA—Landing Craft Assault (Hedgerow)—carrying bombs and explosives to breach the beach obstacles. Following close behind were landing craft containing the companies of infantry battalions of the first wave. After a 15-minute interval the second wave followed.

Enemy fire turned out to be much less than expected over the last 2,000 yards of the run-in. Coastal batteries had been silenced temporarily by the cruisers, and although the inland field guns made a few desultory attempts to reach the ships at sea, the incoming smaller craft were ignored because the fall of shot could not be calculated. All beach guns were silent. Their embrasures had been designed to engage an enemy on the beach, not out at sea. This left only the mortars and small-arms fire to contend with. It was not particularly effective.

Only after the landings did the really fierce opposition begin. The greatest losses during the run-in had nothing to do with enemy fire. They were caused by the sea and tides.

"Touchdown for our first wave had been set for 0735 hours on the rising tide. This was changed to 0745 hours because of sea conditions that prevented orderly groupings of assault craft. This ten-minute change turned out to be critical, resulting in the craft beaching among the obstacles instead of short of them." The obstructions and the mines attached to them were to take a heavy toll.

On board the LCTs, amphibious DD[3] tanks of the 6th Armoured Regiment were supposed to roll into the sea at the 7,000-yard point from the beach, proceeding under their own power to arrive at exactly 0730 hours, five minutes ahead of the infantry. Launching these awkward-looking machines had always been a breathtaking experience during the repeated practice exercises. "The LCT slowed until it was dead in the water then the bow ramp was lowered into the sea by thick chains flooding the tank deck. With their motors running, the DDs rolled off the ramp and into the water where they all but vanished from view. Most of the machine hung below the surface, buoyed by a canvas flotation collar that kept part of its gun turret above the waterline."

In calm water the DDs had a two-foot freeboard. To contemplate launching them into Force 6 winds[4] and four-foot waves required very stout hearts indeed. "Since the sea was still too rough for launching I decided on disembarking them ashore. However, on the way in one of the troopers got into an argument with his CO, Major Duncan. He said that his men preferred to take their chances in the sea rather than end up impaled on the shoreline defences. His argument prevailed."

At about 3,000 yards out one of the LCTs lost headway, the "doors down" bell rang, and its four DDs were launched in direct disobedience to orders from craft HQ. Once the other LCT commanders saw that the DDs remained afloat, they signalled craft HQ to launch their own. Duncan's own tank sank when its flotation collar collapsed. Nevertheless, 14 of the Sherman DDs made it to the beach at their proper point and well ahead of the AVREs (Armoured Vehicle Royal Engineers) and infantry. It was the only sector where the tanks arrived ahead of the infantry as planned.

"Tanks, obstacle clearance groups, flail tanks, assault engineers and infantry were all timed to arrive within minutes of each other. That was the plan. That wasn't how things worked out. Everyone seemed to be arriving at the same time or in the wrong sequence or at the wrong time in the wrong place. It had nothing to do with the Germans. The fault lay with the bloody weather."

Numbers of the DDs foundered among the waves. One sank when mortar fire shredded its canvas collar. Fortunately, most of its crew survived. As the tiny assault craft of the first wave, each carrying up to 40 troops, approached the beach on the rising tide, they ran into the obstacles. Many exploded and sank after Teller mines blew out their bottoms, others were hung up on the concrete stakes or gutted by the hedgehogs. "One in four of the LCIs [Landing Craft Infantry] were lost. Through binoculars I could see the shoreline beginning to look like a Nova Scotian junkyard."

Navy frogmen worked frantically underwater setting explosive charges to blow 30-yard gaps through the obstacles for the approaching assault craft. Sappers cleared the mines affixed to the obstructions now rapidly disappearing beneath the rising tide. Along the beach, flail tanks began beating lanes across the sand, detonating mines as they went.[5] Overhead, the sky rolled with the thunder of low-flying, rocket-equipped Typhoon aircraft of the RAF sweeping inland to their targets.

The infantry came scrambling from their disabled craft only to be cut down by German machine-gunners as they waded chest-high through the last 300 yards of water. Those who made it ashore were soaked and in many cases still seasick. They went to their rehearsed positions quickly and began deflecting the German fire from the working parties who were trying to clear the beach obstacles and were far too busy to take up weapons and defend themselves. Casualties were very heavy during the first few minutes after landing. The air smelled of cordite and seawater.

While the Regina Rifles with the tanks of the 1st Hussars were fighting their way into Courseulles to the east of the river dividing the town, the Royal Winnipeg Rifles and Canadian Scottish battled through the beach defences on the west side of the river. The Winnipegs' landing craft arrived well ahead of their DDs and AVREs and came under heavy fire from one of the strongpoints even before reaching shore. But there was no hesitation. Holding their weapons aloft, the men waded into the sea, then raced across the sand to engage the mortar and machine-gun emplacements. The Winnipegs' B Company, and the Royal Canadian Engineers 6th Field Company assault team working with them, had one of the highest beach casualties for the day. Their courageous company commander, Captain Gower, was left with only 26 men.

"Engineers in the AVREs were intended to skim obstacles off the beach as the tide rose; another party was to prepare the landing for exits. . . . Sappers were not able to land in time and arrived, in some cases, an hour and a half late to find the beach crowded with milling men, tanks and recce cars . . . unable to proceed further inland."

The LCA carrying Harry and his staff narrowly missed striking a mine suspended from a post. It became impossible to manoeuvre the craft without running into it. Everyone on board climbed over the stern into a foundering LCT and leaped from its bow into the waist-deep surf to get ashore.

"Dozens of bodies sloshed against the beach on the incoming tide from

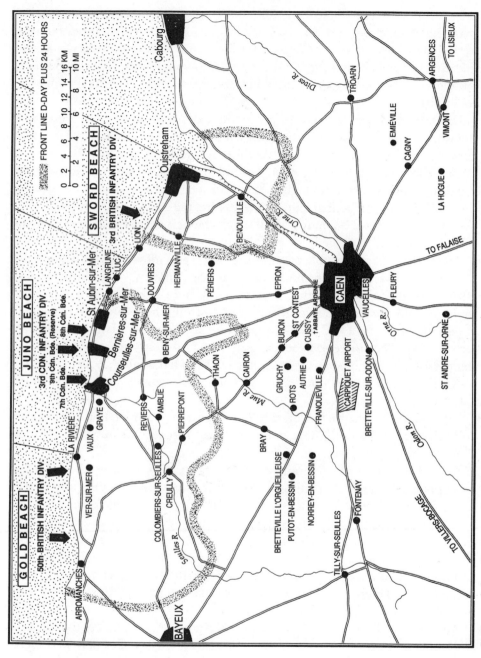

D-Day and the advance on Caen.

the poor devils of the first wave. The sandy high ground beyond lay littered with the dead, dying and wounded. The dead looked like disjointed bundles of wet clothing. . . . Battles flared and died up and down the beach as the infantry systematically reduced the German strongpoints. They had to be winkled out of their lines of pillboxes and network of trenches before we could push on."

Fully two hours were spent in preparing exits from the beach. Men from the Royal Winnipeg Rifles with their own sappers, and later assisted by AVRE personnel, after much digging, sweating and ducking managed to prepare a road through the boggy ground beyond the dunes, even making use of a paling flung across a tank that had sunk far into the muck. By driving their vehicles over it, a firm foundation was created and a primitive but usable exit obtained. In two hours it was all over. The defenders had either escaped inland, surrendered or died.

"Once the tanks were able to leave the beach and move inland they fought fiercely and were of enormous help to the infantry. The tank crews' performance was gallant rather than brilliant, but their sheer courage made them formidable and they profited quickly from their bitter hard-gained experiences. . . . As I had always expected, the timing as planned had been far too fast. The immediate beachhead took D-4 hours to secure. Most of the personnel assault equipment could have been left behind. A steel helmet, mess tin, weapon and ammunition bandoliers would have been quite sufficient."

The troops fought their way through Courselles-sur-Mer house by house and street by street until, near noon, they had reached the outskirts. "From then on things got a bit easier."

Behind the narrow front, more men, tanks, artillery, vehicles and supplies were pouring ashore. Beachmasters sorted out the chaos, keeping the newly constructed roadways clear, the equipment and supply columns moving inland.

A few prisoners waited dejectedly for interrogation and transport back to England. They sat in small clusters on the dunes near the sea wall, staring silently at the Allied colossus sweeping in from the sea. A pall of smoke and haze drifted above the beaches. Recovery parties began picking up splayed bodies and limbless torsos from along the shoreline and laying them out in orderly rows for identification and burial.

Able Seaman Edward Ashworth, Royal Navy, off one of the LCTs that landed at Courseulles, saw some Canadian soldiers march six German prisoners behind a dune some distance away and decided to follow. He wanted a German helmet to take home for a souvenir. He ran up the beach after them. Among the dunes he came upon the six Germans "all lying crumpled up." Still determined to get his helmet, he bent over one of the bodies, but "the man's throat was cut—every one of them had had his throat cut," and Ashworth "turned away, sick as a parrot. I didn't get my tin hat."[6]

Meanwhile the ships carrying the 9th Brigade circled offshore waiting their turn to land. Shortly before 11 o'clock Keller's divisional HQ on board HMS *Hilary*, ordered them ashore, landing through the 8th Brigade who were already moving off their beaches. Since assault craft casualties and opposition from the St. Aubin strongpoint were still a matter of concern, Brigadier Cunningham was instructed to land the entire brigade opposite Bernières before moving south on a single road to the assembly area at Beny-sur-Mer, two miles inland. Sergeant Dudka saw that "there was terrible congestion on the beach and fighting still going on in the town. I knew we were running late."

The delays were to prove costly as the day wore on, making it impossible for the 9th Brigade to reach its objective. At 1200 hours Harry reported that the beach was secure and his troops were moving inland.

General Keller left *Hilary* and by early afternoon had set up his divisional HQ with part of his staff in a small orchard at Bernières. He summoned the commanders of the 2nd Armoured, 8th and 9th Brigades to a conference. Harry was too far forward to attend. The Winnipegs had pushed well beyond the first line of their D-Day objectives and were now driving for the village of Columbiers-sur-Seulles. In spite of the delays by 8th and 9th Brigades, Keller decided to hold to the original plan. Near three in the afternoon a company of Winnipegs made contact with the Green Howards Regiment of the British 50th Division, which had landed on the right. It was the first linkup of the day between Allied forces.

Not until after 1600 hours did the traffic around Bernières thin sufficiently for Lieut.-Col. C. Petch to lead his North Nova Scotia Highlanders toward Beny. Tanks of the 27th Armoured Regiment (the Sherbrooke Fusiliers Regiment) accompanied them. The rest of the brigade's battalion followed.

Dudka and his men were near the front. "We passed Gen. Keller standing on the side of the road directing fire at one of the huge concrete bunkers. The Germans had knocked off three of our four self-propelled guns. Their one gun had been holding up the whole division. In Beny we waited again. Patrols went out to flush Germans from the underground bunkers in the area. Some had women and children hiding along with the enemy. I saw one of our men toss a grenade into a bunker without first checking. 'How do you know it's not full of civilians?' I yelled. He gave me a funny look and went inside. He came out holding a German officer's Luger. 'No civilians in that one, Sergeant. Just dead Germans,' he said."

At 1820 hours the North Novies, along with the 27th Armoured as the brigade's advance guard, moved out from their assembly area, passing through the Queen's Own Rifles and Chaudière Regiments. Dudka was part of a 300-man special force. They carried rations, ammunition and supplies to last eight days. A platoon of heavy mortars from the Cameron Highlanders of Ottawa was attached to the group to provide the critical firepower against tanks and enemy counterattacks. Their objective was Carpiquet airport, lying 6.5 miles to the south. By the time they bivouacked for the night, "our tanks surrounding us—like a wagon train from out of the old west," they were only three miles from the outskirts of Caen but still 4.5 away from their objective.

During the afternoon in the 7th Brigade's sector, Sgt. Léo Gariépy, a tank commander with a squadron of the 1st Hussars, was supporting an infantry attack against the village of Pierrepont. Of the squadron's 18 tanks that had landed that morning only nine remained.

"Swerving off the road on the attack, the force lost five more. . . . I saw Lieut. McLeod's tank burst high in flame. The troop corporal's tanks suffered the same fate, and I saw several other tanks knocked out." Filled with fuel and ammunition reserves, the vulnerable Shermans went up like Roman candles. Gariépy spied a German 88 mm gun barrel rising 30 yards ahead from its camouflaged position.

"I gave rapid evasive orders to my driver and told my gunner to blast him. He fired two rounds; the second scored a direct hit. I moved up on the gun emplacement and shot all the crew of 14 cowering in the trench." The squadron now had only four tanks left.

"I was called by an infantry officer who told me a sniper had shot the commanders of three DD tanks. The sniper had not shot at the infantry; he was after tank commanders. I moved slowly toward where the other crew commanders had got hit, wrapped my beret over my earphones and waved it above the turret. The shot, when it came, was from an attic window, but the infantry were unaware of it and they were all around the house making it impossible for me to fire into it. So I and my loader operator jumped out, hugging close against the wall, and bashed the door open. We found an old man and woman, imploring us in German, but we could not understand what they were trying to tell us. We rushed up the stairs and there in front of the attic window, holding a Mauser low but pointed at us, was the sniper. A girl of 19. I cut her down with the Sten. Angry, irritated, probably scared, I could not hesitate. We learned from the old people that the girl's fiancé had been shot by a Canadian tank that morning and she had sworn she would liquidate all crew commanders."[7]

By day's end Cunningham's 9th and Harry's 7th Brigades' spearheads had penetrated deeper into France than any other division of Montgomery's army. Although casualties were far lower than planning estimates, they were painful nonetheless: 574 men had been wounded, 340 had died on the beaches and during the fighting inland. During the day Allied bombers and fighters had flown 10,585 sorties in addition to the 1,730 flown by the airborne troop transports. No aircraft were lost in combat with the Luftwaffe. Near dark, four Heinkel IIIs slipped past the fighter cover to scatter their bombloads near Juno beach. Like angry hornets, Spitfires knifed down and destroyed them all.

Of the German 716th Division little remained. From its original six battalions only one survived and that had 20 percent casualties; 80 percent of the division's artillery was gone. As a fighting unit, Richter's 716th Division ceased to exist.

At 2115 hours Keller sent out his orders for the night to each of his brigade commanders. Harry, who had established his HQ in the village of Columbiers-sur-Seulles, was to occupy and hold the area around the villages of Cainet and le Fresne-Camilly. The entire division was ordered to active patrolling and "utmost preparation" to meet a counterattack at first light.

Near midnight several German scout cars blundered into the 9th Brigade's bivouac area. They were advance patrols from the 21st Panzer Division, finally released from Hitler's hoarded reserves to explore the gap between the Canadian and British advance columns for a counterattack. The Sherman tanks knocked out the cars, and 19 Germans were taken prisoner. The rest fled into the darkness.

3

Hitler was not an early riser. An insomniac, he usually stayed up late and slept late, requiring a drug to sleep at all. Waking him before the effects of his sleeping draught had worn off was pointless. As dawn broke on the Bavarian Obersalzberg, 6 June, the Führer slept.

Nearby at the *Führerhauptquartier*,* OKW Chief of Staff Field Marshal Keitel was also asleep. But his chief of operations, Col.-Gen. Alfred Jodl, had been up since six and after a frugal breakfast sat down to study the night's situation reports. The Russian front appeared to be quiet. One million, five hundred thousand German troops were massed, waiting for the spring offensive to begin. Several reports from von Rundstedt's headquarters indicated an Allied attack in Normandy, but that situation needed further clarification. His immediate concern lay with the Italian front. Rome had fallen the day before, and he feared an Allied breakthrough before the retreating German troops could be consolidated into a new defensive line farther north.

Jodl's deputy, General Warlimont, had received a message from OB West asking for release of the reserve Panzer Lehr and 12th SS Divisions to advance at once toward the Normandy coast. Warlimont had been monitoring events

---

*Führer Headquarters had been installed temporarily at the Berghof before being moved back to Rastenburg, East Prussia, on 14 July.

since 0300 hours and had discussed the situation with von Rundstedt's chief of staff, Maj.-Gen. Günther Blumentritt. The Allies appeared to be starting their long-expected invasion of the French coast. Shortly before 0700 hours Warlimont called Jodl with OB West's request for the OKW reserves. Jodl wasn't convinced. He still believed the invasion to be a diversionary attack ahead of the main thrust intended at the Pas-de-Calais. Italy was his problem for the day, not France.

Warlimont reported back to an incredulous Blumentritt that the panzers were to be held until Allied intentions became clear. Von Rundstedt turned nearly apoplectic with rage; yet the stiff-backed aristocrat refused to call the man he referred to as "that Bohemian Corporal" either then or at any time during the day. Had he done so, Hitler in all probability would have released his panzers and the outcome on the invasion front might have been quite different.

While Allied forces poured ashore on the five landing beaches throughout the morning, junior and senior officers from the embattled front pleaded for reserves. Finally, at 0630 hours, after a series of arguments first with the desperate Richter and then with Richter's immediate superior, Gen. Erich Marcks, LXXXIV Corps commander, Feuchtinger decided to act on his own initiative and ordered the 21st Panzer Division into battle.

The tanks that could have moved under cover of darkness four hours earlier now became targets of opportunity for low-flying fighter-bombers of the Allied air forces. Worse, instead of aiming his columns directly at the beaches, he ordered them to cross inland and engage the British 6th Airborne east of the Orne River, where Richter still believed the greatest danger lay. Thus, the only mobile force capable of containing a breakout from the beaches was squandered on a piecemeal cross-country expedition.

Meanwhile, the two OKW reserves closest to the invasion front had already been alerted. At 0230 hours General Warlimont phoned from OKW to Lieut.-Gen. Fritz Bayerlein's divisional HQ at Nogent le Rotrou, 95 miles southwest of Paris: "The Panzer Lehr Division is alerted for an advance in the direction of Caen. You will receive further orders from Army Group B."

Only a few hours earlier OKW had ordered the division to send its best tank battalion to the Eastern Front. Hurriedly, Bayerlein cancelled those transfer orders and sent his new Panther and Royal Tiger tank companies back to their stations to draw ammunition preparatory to moving out. Had the Panzer Lehr and 12th SS Divisions left at once, both could have been in action along the invasion front before noon in spite of Allied fighter-bombers. The inland weather remained hazy with low overcast skies and drizzle throughout the early part of the day, giving road convoys a degree of cover from air attacks.

At 0800 hours, while the panzer reserves waited inland, 80 tanks from the 1st Battalion of Feuchtinger's 22nd Panzer Regiment—part of the 21st

Panzer Division—were bypassing the blazing town of Caen on their way to meet the British 6th Airborne at the Orne. The regiment's 2nd Battalion with another 40 tanks received its movement orders from Feuchtinger's dispatch riders at 0900 hours. It too turned northeast toward the British 6th Airborne. By keeping 100 yards between tanks in case of air attack the columns reached the Orne area without loss, but before a shot had been fired against the enemy, new orders arrived from General Marcks's Corps HQ: "About turn. Head for Caen. Maintain radio silence until enemy contact."

Deprived of the OKW reserves, Marcks decided to use the 21st Panzers against the British 3rd Infantry Division, which had been coming ashore on Sword beach since dawn. What had been the battalion's rearguard now became its spearhead, while the spearhead became the rearguard with the unit's commander positioned at the wrong end of his column. The tanks spun around and clanked their way back to Marcks's new assembly area north of Caen. By early afternoon they were in position to launch the only counterattack of the day, striking for the beach through a gap in the British and Canadian 3rd Divisions, which had not as yet joined forces.

By early afternoon both battalions of the 22nd Panzer Regiment were ready. Marcks arrived from his HQ at St. Lô to lead the 98-tank formation. He held no illusions of the importance of his task. Grimly, he went over to Colonel von Oppeln-Bronikowski, the regimental commander, and said: "Oppeln, if you don't succeed in throwing the British back into the sea, we shall have lost the war."

At the same time that Marcks climbed into his armoured scout car to lead the tanks into battle, Hitler decided at last to release the OKW reserves. The Panzer Lehr and 12th SS were ordered to aid the peripatetic 21st Panzer Division. Bayerlein had his units on the road by 1700 hours, too late to be of any value for the day's fighting.

The 12th SS had better luck. Witt's first movement orders came at 0700 hours from the commander of I SS Armoured Corps, placing his unit under LXXXI Corps in Rouen. His orders were to assemble around Lisieux, the same place from which General Geyr had moved the division during April. He issued his marching orders and by late morning had the 12th SS on the road with time enough to strike a counterattack on the coastal area before dark. Kurt, at the head of the 25th Panzer Grenadier Regiment, led the division's vanguard.

But by midafternoon Witt received a message from Army Group B changing the Lisieux assembly point to a new area west of Caen where Marcks's LXXXIV Corps was organizing a counterattack. Witt's units were moving in the wrong direction. Furious at such stupidity, he sent dispatch riders tearing through the lines of tanks, trucks, men and armour to deliver the revised orders.

By the time word reached Kurt at the front of the column, it was well past 1600 hours and the regiment was already in the area west of Lisieux. He now had to take his men and equipment another 44 miles to reach an assembly area that was only half the distance from their initial departure point that morning.

"We old soldiers are somewhat worried about the future. We can feel in our blood what is going to happen"—not surprisingly, in view of the paralysis within the decision-making apparatus at OKW. "The handsome young Grenadiers look at us and laugh. They don't care. They are all cheerful."

As they neared the coastal district, the ceilings lifted, bringing swarms of Spitfires and Typhoons buzzing down for low-level attacks across the column. Trucks laden with troops and ammunition exploded. The grenadiers of the 15th Reconnaissance Company leaped into the ditches or scattered screaming like living torches among the fields as screeching rockets and winking scarlet cannon fire flashed overhead and in seconds were gone. Smoking vehicles and shattered tanks with drooping guns blocked the road in both directions. Drivers picked their way carefully around the wreckage and pressed forward. His teenage soldiers were no longer laughing.

At last the summer afternoon faded into the safety of darkness. Kurt sped ahead of the main body and arrived at Richter's 716th Division HQ on the outskirts of Caen near midnight. Its streets lay littered with debris, and fires started by Allied shelling cast an eerie glow over the city. Civilians huddled in their basements and shelters. In the weeks ahead, Caen would be all but destroyed from this constant bombardment.

Kurt was conducted through a series of underground tunnels and corridors to Richter's command post. The dead and dying from two divisions lay on stretchers lining the passageways. He reported to Richter, explaining that it had taken eight hours to reach him, "four of them spent lying in roadside ditches due to air attacks. The division's marching columns are suffering serious losses in men and materials."

Richter had no news for him. None of the dispatch riders had reported back. Everything remained in a state of confusion. Marcks's counterattack at the head of von Oppeln's tanks had failed, although troops in his forward element had managed to make it through the gap between British and Canadian lines to the sea. By early afternoon they had reached the last few remaining strongpoints still held by 716th Division. But it was to no avail. The tanks, following behind the infantry, were unable to pass the well-concealed British anti-tank gunners who held the high ground. One after another they were hit. Outside the village of Bièville, five were blown up within minutes. The rest withdrew. In all, von Oppeln's 22nd Panzer Regiment lost 16 tanks.

Near 2100 hours, as Feuchtinger assembled his division for another race to the beach in relief of the vanguard, a roar of aircraft engines swept in low from the Channel. Using the setting sun to shield them from flak gunners stationed at Le Havre, 250 gliders with their tow planes arrived overhead. Supported by swarms of Mustang and Spitfire fighters, they were bringing in the reinforcements of the British 6th Airborne. As the sounds of motors faded, the evening air filled with the whispering of wind on wood and canvas. The Germans watched in disbelief, wondering what sort of enemy could order up an airfleet of gliders in less than half a day to repel a counterattack.[8] Unnerved, they fired wildly at the Horsas and Hamilcars sliding down—literally—on top of their positions. The 21st Panzers' planned thrust for the coast died in its tracks.

In Richter's command post, Witt, Feuchtinger, Kurt and a liaison officer from the Panzer Lehr Division began planning their counterattack for the next day. A telephone, silent for most of the afternoon and evening, suddenly started to ring. Richter picked it up. The caller, Oberst* Krug, spoke from the headquarters of his 736th Grenadier Regiment buried deep beneath one of the domed concrete heavy-gun emplacements. He had been surrounded by the British Suffolk Regiment. Richter could hear the chaos of gunfire and shouting men in the background. "The enemy is on top of my bunker! I have no means of resisting them and no communications with my men. What shall I do?"

Richter's face paled in the harsh yellow light. For a moment he hesitated, then said very slowly: "I can give you no more orders. You must make your own decision now." With infinite regret he added softly: *"Auf Wiedersehen."*

Harry's 7th Brigade linked up with the British 50th Infantry Division, which had come ashore on his right and was established at Creully, giving a common front 12 miles wide and six miles deep.

"All in all I thought it had been a pretty good day. The outstanding features of the assault were, first, the admirable spirit of the men, and second, the excellent fire support of the artillery. No request for support went unanswered and many infantry professed to understand for the first time that the gunner's role was something other than to block traffic. . . . Years later the wise guys and armchair strategists comparing our D-Day losses to Dieppe would say it had all been easy. Well, it was not easy. It was hard. And a lot of good men died. . . .

"We were now holding a very thin line with a number of gaps. If the Germans organized a counterattack during the night we'd have been in serious trouble. The men were bushed. Some hadn't slept in three days. They were stuffed with wake-up pills and just about dead on their feet. Div. HQ said that aerial reconnaissance had spotted the 12th SS moving up and for us to expect counterattacks during the early morning. . . . I called an O Group for regimental commanders for 0130 hours to lay out the next day's drill."

---

*Colonel.

The brigade's final objectives were two villages on the other side of the Caen-Bayeux highway. "Once we reached them we were supposed to consolidate our front and await reinforcements. I wanted the Winnipeg Rifles on the right, the Reginas on the left and the Canadian Scottish to stay put, but ready to lend a hand once we found out what we were up against. Then I stretched out for some shut-eye because it looked as though we were going to have an interesting day."

Over the years he had trained himself to remain alert for days at a time on 20-minute catnaps taken at odd hours of the day or night. "The problem with wars," he observed many years later, "is that they operate on a 24-hour basis and those intending to make the decisions necessary for fighting them either learn to adapt or are swiftly replaced. Too many lives are at stake for it to be otherwise. . . . It is not his opponent but mental fatigue and muzzy-mindedness that will always be a commanding officer's greatest enemies in battle."

Shortly past 0600 hours his lead battalions moved out, cautiously probing for German resistance. What little they met was scattered and ineffective. Three hours later when it became obvious there was nothing to impede their progress, Harry ordered all three battalions to go flat out for their objectives. The Winnipegs made it first and checked their advance by the railway tracks at the village of Putot-en-Bessin, becoming in the process the first battalion from either Canadian, British or American armies to reach its final D-Day objective.

"I was proud of them. The easy part was over. So far we still held the advantage because the Germans had fumbled the ball. Now it became a matter of hanging on to what we'd captured while both sides brought in their reserves. Ours were still coming ashore as fast as ships could bring them from England; theirs were racing to reach the coast. But even matching the Germans division for division, man for man, they still held an enormous advantage: experienced front-line leaders. . . .

"Our superiority lay in ships, aircraft weapons and supplies. But in war that's not enough because in the end it all comes down to a few men at the front who do the actual fighting and the even fewer who lead them. Our front-line leaders—myself included—from sergeants through to divisional generals were greenhorns. Our battle experiences for the most part consisted of war games played along the English coast or on the moors and downs. Our instructors were professionals who'd seen action in the First War or learned their trade in North Africa, Sicily and Italy. We could listen and try following their advice. Yet battle conditions are never quite what one expects. A senior officer might get top marks on exercises leading his troops at the divisional, brigade or regimental level yet wind up as a disaster when it came to the real thing. During those first days in Normandy our troops fought superbly but their leaders left a hell of a lot to be desired."

On the eastern sector of the Canadian front, Cunningham's 9th Brigade resumed its advance on Carpiquet airport. Using the same formations of tanks from the 27th Armoured Regiment and four companies of North Nova Scotia Highlanders that had spearheaded the previous day's advance, the tanks and men moved off at 0745 hours. The morning was cool and hazy under a warming sun.

Sergeant Dudka rode one of the tanks. "There wasn't much resistance until we reached Buron. Then the mortaring started to get heavy and we began collecting casualties among those riding the tanks."

They worked their way through Buron, knocking out two German 88 mm guns, and by noon, after bitter fighting, had occupied the village. C Company was left behind to search for German holdouts while B Company rolled through on their Shermans heading for Authie, the next village on the road to Carpiquet.

"Just beyond Buron we ran into a heavy mortar barrage. Our tanks deployed and started firing at Authie while the men on foot spread out and worked their way forward trying to keep low and under cover. . . . The German tanks were dug into a 'V' formation directly in front of us along either side of the road with only their gun turrets sticking out. Behind them, on higher ground, were their anti-tank gunners. We had walked into a beautifully laid trap. . . . Within minutes most of our tanks had been knocked out. Everything happened so fast that the crews never had a chance. . . . The Shermans went up like torches . . . explosions, fire, smoke and screaming men. The bulk of A and C Companies were either wiped out or captured."

The "trap" had been set by Kurt Meyer.

4

Witt's battle plans on 7 June for his 12th ss were to be carefully coordinated with Feuchtinger. Despite the lack of Bayerlein's Panzer Lehr, still moving toward the front, the two divisional generals felt reasonably optimistic about their chances for a successful counterattack. Most of the 12th ss had arrived or were close to Caen, and Feuchtinger's depleted 21st Panzers still represented a sizeable fighting force.

It was decided that Colonel von Oppeln's 22nd Panzer Regiment would join Witt's northward thrust the moment their battle lines converged. From there they would go forward together to the sea. Meanwhile, Kurt's reinforced regiment would take up positions northwest of Caen and await the attack that Witt and Feuchtinger had scheduled for noon. Witt's orders were explicit: "The Division will attack the disembarked enemy in conjunction with the 21st Panzer Division and throw the enemy back into the sea. . . . Objective: the beach."[9]

Leading units of Kurt's 25th Panzer Grenadiers reached the western edge of Caen near dawn. The town still lay in flames fed by the constant artillery shelling from behind the Allied lines. With first light the fighter-bombers returned in force from across the Channel, swooping down to pick off the column's tanker trucks. Without their precious fuel supplies the tanks would be immobilized. Quickly, Kurt organized deliveries, using his small, nimble Volkswagen to outfox the Allied aircraft that were searching for more worthwhile targets.

With his regimental HQ set up on the outskirts of Caen and his battle units deployed, he drove to an advance lookout post he had selected at the ancient Abbaye Ardenne located in the fields northwest of town. The abbey towered in isolated magnificence over the entire Canadian and British front. He made the long climb to one of the turrets and gazed out at the panorama of villages, orchards, ripening fields and criss-cross hedgerows. Except for scattered puffs of cumulus, skies were clear in summer blue. Every few minutes an echelon of low-level Allied aircraft darted across the fields and villages, engines snarling, searching for targets. A light haze obscured parts of the coastal activity where the armada of ships continued unloading along the beaches. Dozens of silver-sausage barrage balloons floated serenely above the fleet as protection against Luftwaffe air attacks, had there been a Luftwaffe to attack.

Kurt rested his elbows on the stone parapet in the abbey's bell tower, steadying his glasses. "I could see the coast. Not the water, actually, but the barrage balloons of the ships. I could see movement from the motorized columns moving in a southwesterly direction. . . . I knew the invading troops intended pushing through between Caen and Rots in order to reach the main Caen-Villers Bocage highway."

He decided to place his three grenadier battalions in the front line: the 1st on his right between the villages of Epron and St. Contest next to units of the 21st Panzer Division and facing the British infantry; the 2nd Battalion in the centre between St. Contest and Buron and facing the advancing Canadian 9th Brigade with its North Novies vanguard and Sherman tanks; his 3rd Battalion to cover the left flank from Buron past Authie up to the Caen-Bayeux highway where Harry's 7th Brigade was now advancing.

Two tank companies would be positioning behind the 1st and 3rd Battalions and artillery support pieces set up on the south side of Caen to cover his entire front. It was a standard textbook disposition of regimental forces and provided the option of using the units in an infantry-led counterattack supported by tanks or in a defensive line where the tanks and infantry could dig in and rely on artillery coverage to discourage an advancing enemy.

Witt was having problems deploying the rest of the division in time for his 12-noon attack deadline. The 12th SS rearguard units were still arriving at the assembly areas. As a result, his midday attack was postponed. He ordered

Kurt to tell his young grenadiers to dig in and await the arrival of reinforcements. They were to hold their positions at all costs.

But in view of the impending threat to his front, Kurt decided "not to await further reinforcements but to attack after the troops were in position. . . . When I came down from the tower I met two officers of the Coastal Division who had arrived with an assortment of troops. They intended a retreat further south. I forbade any further withdrawal and gave them orders to accompany the attack of my troops with their men and reconquer the territory which they had lost."

He left the abbey to check the disposition of his men, then drove back to the village of St. Germain, where he arranged to set up his headquarters in a gas station at a fork in the road. He heard a discussion between two headquarters runners and some displaced soldiers from 21st Panzer Division. "The runners said they had heard that the Canadians took no prisoners. Soldiers coming from Rots said that they had seen some prisoners who had been shot. I then prohibited the men from spreading this rumour and told my DRs, Orderly Officer and Adjutant who were present that a report should be made to Divisional HQ. I told the Adjutant: 'I can only believe it when I see it myself.'"

A few minutes later Witt arrived to discuss troop dispositions. Witt had no exact information about the movement of the 26th Panzer Regiment, which was supposed to be on Kurt's left facing Harry's 7th Brigade. Neither had Kurt. Witt drove off to check while Kurt returned to his forward observation point in the abbey tower. "I gave orders to bring over a small Tactical HQ staff and then outlined my battle plans with the commander of the 2nd Battalion."

Günter Fromm, an NCO attached to the Volkswagen and motorcycle company protecting Witt and his staff, was ordered to occupy the bridge over the narrow Mué River at the village of Rots. "Panzermeyer had attacked Buron exposing his left flank to a counterattack. Bronay and Bretteville had been occupied at dawn by the Regina Rifles and the Fort Garry Horse. Their tanks had retreated to Secqueville. Meyer saw their dust cloud as they moved into positions near Secqueville and Bray. A Canadian attack through Rots would have outflanked Meyer's 25th Panzers. . . .

"We were to occupy the Rots bridge at noon. Another platoon led by a Company Commander with a 2 cm AA gun mounted on a *Horch** were to approach Rots from the east along the main Caen-Bayeux road while our group of eight men with a motorcycle-sidecar and two Volkswagen were to join them from the Carpiquet airport road. As we approached the railroad bridge between Caen and Bayeux we were stopped within 20 yards by a platoon of Canadian soldiers who were digging in. They shot three of our men and

_____
*A small command vehicle.

blew up the first Volkswagen with a hand grenade. After making a hurried U turn I escaped in the second vw." The flank remained exposed at Rots.

Peering out from the abbey tower, Kurt detected some movement through his glasses beyond Authie. Suddenly, a single enemy tank came nosing through an orchard. It paused while the tank commander checked his field of view. It advanced slowly from the orchard and past a tangled hedgerow behind which grenadiers of the 2nd Battalion lay hidden. No shots were fired. Two hundred yards from the grenadiers the tank stopped. Again its commander checked his range of view with binoculars.

Kurt swung his own glasses toward the Canadian front. This lone tank, he realized, was the flank guard for an armoured column now emerging from the village of Buron and making for the Caen-Bayeux highway and the Carpiquet airport beyond. He knew the airfield had already been abandoned by its Luftwaffe defenders. Incredibly, the entire column appeared intent on moving directly across his 2nd Battalion's front and exposing one long unprotected flank. Such stupidity was difficult to understand—just the sort of opportunity regimental panzer commanders only dream about.

He sent off dispatch riders to notify 21st and 12th ss Division HQ that he intended launching an immediate attack once the enemy had stretched out across his front.

Below, in the abbey garden, Obersturmbannführer Max Wünsche, commander of the 12th ss Panzer Regiment, stood in his turret listening to Kurt's orders through a field telephone and passing the information on by radio to his tank commanders. One company lay inside the abbey grounds; the other, also supporting the 2nd Battalion, sat camouflaged near the Authie-Buron road on a reverse slope. The tension was electric. Wünsche spoke to his commanders almost in a whisper. Slowly, cautiously, the Canadians approached. Finally, the moment arrived.

"Attack!" Kurt roared in Wünsche's ear.

As their anti-tank gunners opened fire, the waiting tanks clanked to the top of the slope, then stopped and began firing down on the Shermans. The first tank blew up. Then a second and a third were engulfed in flames. The crews bailed out, rolling wildly across the ground in an attempt to douse their fiery clothing. Two more tanks exploded.

Tank after tank was hit. "I noticed two of my own tanks being blown into the air. Of the Canadian tanks I didn't see any escape. . . . The two frontal companies and the tanks bypassed the town on either side, making for Buron. As soon as they were beyond Authie and the flanks were sealed 3rd Company began its frontal attack. The battle lasted no longer than 15 or 20 minutes."

His grenadiers swarmed after the retreating enemy before they had time to dig a defensive line at Authie. Through the haze of smoke he saw the first prisoners coming out of the village toward the abbey, hands above their heads. The time was 1635 hours.

In his rush to reach Carpiquet airport Lieutenant-Colonel Petch had moved his regiment too quickly and with inadequate forward reconnaissance. Without artillery support he had no alternative but to fall back and regroup, holding his line until the brigade's guns could be brought to bear on the German attack.

Sergeant Dudka and his men were ordered to retreat behind an anti-tank ditch that had been dug on the seaward side of Buron. On their way into the village they met the regimental commander. "Petch took our PIATs* and told us to go back and dig in to give the other fellows a chance of getting out. He sent off a Bren gun carrier to collect the rest of our anti-tank weapons then ordered Maj. Learment, Sgt.-Maj. Mackie, Fifer, Shoemaker and anyone else he could find to go along."

Cautiously, they worked their way forward through the tall, grassy hay fields bordering the main road, keeping low and out of sight of the German gunners. At the front, the two dozen men that remained from A and C Companies dug in amid the ripening hay to await their artillery support. D Company, still intact, lay behind them in ditches bordering the road.

By late afternoon German tanks and infantry had filtered into the fields around them. Neither side could see the other in the tall grass. One of the German tanks passed Dudka's position and started firing only 30 feet away. They were surrounded.

"I had two wounds, one in the face—a bullet passed through one cheek and came out the other—and another in my right arm. The German tanks were almost on top of where I was dug in. I could hear them talking to each other. One of them hollered in English to come out. I had no choice. I raised my hands and stood up very slowly. . . .

"The fellow that took me had on a camouflage suit. I was marched back to Authie. In the village I saw seven men from C Company with Corporal Davidson sitting across the street at the side of the road with three Germans guarding them. . . . When I first looked they were just sitting there. Later, I saw two of them remove their steel helmets. . . . Then I heard firing and saw some of the boys tipping over towards the road and a couple tipped over backwards. . . . I could see the guards standing on the road firing at them. . . . After that they pushed the bodies toward the centre of the road."

His own guard escorted him another few hundred yards to where a large group of captured Canadians was assembled. "The soldiers guarding us were youngsters, no more than 16 or 17. We were lined up against a low stone wall and searched. . . . Private Metcalfe must have had something interesting

---

*Acronym for "Projector Infantry Anti-Tank" weapon.

in his pocket because suddenly one of the Germans gave him a burst with his Schmeisser. Metcalfe dropped."

While they stood waiting, a furious mortar barrage began falling around them. Then, from the sea, heavy guns of a British cruiser zeroed in on the enemy's advance. The Germans crouched as the ground shook. "The firepower from our side was tremendous. They were suffering one hell of a lot of casualties. Truckload after truckload were gathered up and taken to the rear. I could hear them hollering and crying. They were beaten. They kept us exposed in front of the wall—hoping one of our artillery shells would finish us. . . . I saw portions of the wall exploding on either side from hits and Germans screaming in pain from their wounds. But somehow we escaped a direct hit. . . . They held us there about 20 minutes. Then the lad who had shot Metcalfe kicked him to see if he was still alive. Metcalfe moved a little. The German gave him another burst and finished him off."

An officer appeared and although none of the prisoners understood what he said, there was little doubt what he meant. Most of their captors were ordered immediately up to the front and an escort chosen to deliver the prisoners to the rear.

"I saw German troops going about the area shooting at our wounded who were lying on the ground. . . . On the way back one of our shells burst in amongst us. Private Hargraves was hit. I tried picking him up but the Germans wouldn't allow it. They shot him. . . . Farther along we came across more bodies lying on the side of the road without helmets, shot in the back of the head. . . . One man was run over by a German tank while still alive— another bayoneted. . . . I saw one of our men, a medic, giving help to a wounded tanker. The Germans shot him, then shot the wounded man as well."

The group paused on a sunken road, waiting for a break in the shelling. Suddenly, without slowing, a truckload of troops roared through the column, scattering bodies in its wake. Two of the prisoners, Tobin and MacRae, were killed instantly. Others suffered broken backs and legs. Those who attempted to climb the roadbank were shot. A half hour later the 20 men remaining reached the Abbaye Ardenne and were locked into one of the storage sheds bordering the courtyard. Dudka received morphine for his wounds from one of the German stretcher-bearers. He recognized a few of the other North Novies who had been captured earlier. They were locked up and under guard on the opposite side of the courtyard.

"There appeared to be four groups of prisoners in each lockup. We were given no food or water and there were no toilet facilities. I didn't blame the Germans for that. They already had their hands full."

German losses among the young soldiers and their battle-hardened NCOs had been heavy. A few, seeking revenge, turned on their Canadian prisoners.

Authie stonemasons, Constance Raymond Guilbert and Louis Marie Alaper-
rine, witnessed the Canadian capture and German recapture of their village.
Guilbert's house faced the main square. He saw the Germans leave and the
Canadians arrive, advancing beyond the village.

Then "at five o'clock . . . I heard the sound of firing come closer. I went
upstairs and looked from a window. I saw a Canadian soldier giving himself
up. As he was crossing Madame Godet's garden and was within three or
four metres of the Germans he was shot. He had his hands up."

A few minutes later, from the front window Guilbert watched a wounded
Canadian being butchered. "There were several Germans under the trees
who were machine-gunning the church. A wounded man who was under
the tree moved his left arm and leg a little. . . . One of the German soldiers
took a bayonet and hit him, opening his head. . . . He gave three or four
bayonet thrusts into the middle of the body and a burst from a machine-
carbine."

The Germans refused to allow burial of any of the Canadian bodies. Those
that Guilbert and his friends dragged from the road were ordered returned
so that vehicles could run over them. Burial permission was eventually given
by the Kommandantur in Caen. In all, he and his friends buried 37 Canadian
dead.

"We were obliged to take two of them up with a shovel because they had
been reduced to jelly. Three others were in a hole and had been shoved down
hard into that hole. You could still see the trace of heels on their shoulders."

Louis Alaperrine of Authie saw three Canadian soldiers outside his house
near the kitchen shortly before seven that evening. "The Germans sent a
shell into the kitchen. Two soldiers were killed outright, the third was
wounded in the foot and kidneys. I had just left my shelter trench and began
bandaging the soldier's foot when a German officer and another rank arrived
and looked at the two bodies. Then they turned towards the wounded man.
The officer took out his revolver and fired two shots into the Canadian soldier's
head. . . . Later in the evening I saw in the back of Mrs. Godet's yard, six
or seven dead Canadians of which a few had their arms raised above their
heads."

Before any of the prisoners arrived, Kurt came down from his perch in
the tower. The planned 12th ss divisional attack, supported by 21st Panzer
Division, had apparently been aborted. It was critical that his battalion
commanders be notified not to advance north of Buron in case they were
cut off. He took a motorcycle and roared off to see the 2nd Battalion's
commander. They met at the Cussy village crossroads.

"On my way through Cussy I noticed a group of prisoners in a fruit garden.
Artillery fire was quite heavy. I left my motorcycle and proceeded on foot.
The motorcycle was shot to pieces behind me. After a brief conversation
with the Battalion commander I headed back towards Cussy . . . but had

to crawl on my stomach to the 3rd Battalion because their flank company began shooting at the prisoners and myself, in spite of my signalling with a map."

The men were expecting a counterattack. He caught a vehicle back to the abbey and climbed the tower to oversee the battle. "When I came down next, I saw prisoners sitting and smoking in front of the chapel. They were poorly guarded. Someone had brought them water. Straw bedding was being carried into the chapel. A few shells landed in the area. I told the G3: 'We'll soon be under artillery fire here. It's time you were leaving with your prisoners.'"

He arrived back at the 2nd Battalion area in time to watch its commander being decapitated by a direct hit from a tank shell. He appointed a replacement at once, Hauptsturmführer Schrott. While the battle and the shelling raged around them, he put his new battalion commander in the picture. The regiment was to change from attack to defensive positions and hold the line. Then he drove off to deliver the same instructions to the other two battalion commanders. Past 2300 hours he returned to the abbey. He had been awake and on his feet continuously for 44 hours. Yet there was still work to be done: the day's events entered into the War Diary, his daily situation report to Division, casualty figures and the next day's orders to be dictated.

The division's situation report showed problems with the 26th Regiment's sector and a serious gap in the line that the Panzer Lehr Division had not yet filled. Near midnight, while Dudka and the other prisoners slept fitfully, Kurt summoned his company commanders to a meeting in the abbey.

"I gave the Commander of the 15th Reconnaissance Company orders for the morning. He was to go towards Carpiquet into 26th Regiment's sector. I wanted to know what was going on in the Regiment's northwest flank. Where were the enemy troops in relation to the 26th? Where was the Regiment's right wing? . . . The second reconnaissance order was to advance in the direction of Rots on the main Caen-Bayeux highway. I wanted to know how far enemy troops had advanced along that road."

Near 0300 hours the conference adjourned.

5

By early afternoon of D-Day plus 1 Harry's 7th Brigade was comfortably astride the Caen-Bayeux highway. Four companies of the Royal Winnipegs occupied Putot-en-Bessin, with a flank guard north of Bronay maintaining contact with the British 50th Division's Green Howards. The main body of Reginas had taken up positions at Bretteville l'Orgueilleuse. Its C Company was across the railway tracks at Norrey-en-Bessin. Harry had moved his Brigade HQ up to Le Haut de Bretteville, now the geographic centre of his area.

"I was feeling very pleased with myself until news of 9th Brigade's problems reached me." His left flank was seriously exposed. He sent a company of the Canadian Scottish along with a tank squadron of the 1st Hussars and an anti-tank troop to plug the gap. Artillery, mortars and medium machine-gun units were set in place to repel any attack. A German probing attack against the Reginas that came in shortly after dark was quickly beaten back.

Eight June dawned under clear skies with a light mist rising from the fields. It was to be a bloody day. Lacking detailed intelligence on the exact Canadian positions, SS Obersturmbannführer Wilhelm Mohnke's 26th Panzer Grenadier Regiment had set up its HQ in the village of Cheux and then proceeded to place its three battalions directly in front of 7th Brigade's main forces instead of its exposed left flank. The German attack on Norrey and Putot opened at first light. The Reginas' C Company beat off the first Norrey attack while the Royal Winnipegs' A Company scattered a German force trying to cross the railway tracks into Putot. Throughout the morning the pressure increased.

"I ordered Matheson* to withdraw. He protested vigorously, reminding me that pulling out now meant that we'd only have to go back and take it again later. I agreed he could stay and crossed my fingers."

By midafternoon A, B and C Companies of the Winnipegs had been encircled and were nearly out of ammunition. Putot was lost. Under cover of smoke they began withdrawing. Only a handful made it back to join D Company and set up defensive positions at the battalion's HQ, east of Putot. It was a bitter blow. Forward units of the British 8th Armoured Brigade halted the left wing of the German advance.

Quickly, Harry began organizing a counterattack with his reserves to be led by Lieutenant-Colonel Cabeldu's Canadian Scottish. At 1700 hours he called his commanders to an O Group at Brigade HQ to map out plans. A creeping artillery barrage carpeted the attack in front of the advancing troops and armour.

The Canadian Scottish War Diary recorded the action: "The country was mainly flat wheatfields with orchards giving excellent concealment for the enemy. The men advanced without falter into a veritable wall of fire. Their courage was magnificent. . . . Cpl. Bob Mayfield of 8 Platoon, turned grinning to his section as they swung into the advance: 'Boy! This is going to be one hell of a good scrap!' . . . This spirit was maintained throughout.

"The casualties were naturally heavy but never a wounded man whimpered—the opposite in fact was the case . . . time and again badly wounded men had to be ordered back. . . . As the objective was neared A Company more or less merged with D who had been slowed by the enemy defence and . . . lost their Company Commander, wounded 2 i/c and CSM killed. . . .

---

*Lieut.-Col. Foster Matheson, commanding officer of the Regina Rifles Regiment.

"It was questionable whether the men were more human or devil at this stage . . . men like Cpls. Dodd and Jebes and Pte. Mulcahy . . . took turns jumping to the top of the bridge with a Bren gun at the hip and spraying the enemy, laughing gleefully as they did so."

By 2130 hours, after furious fighting, all of Putot except the railway line was back in Canadian hands.

The Royal Winnipegs had 256 casualties of which 105* were dead. What men were left from the decimated regiment were transferred to the brigade's reserve, replacing the Canadian Scottish. Harry defended the losses. "They had been overrun chiefly because one of their assault companies had been practically obliterated on the beach and the gaps in the ranks had to be replaced by reinforcements of all sorts, some not even infantry. There had been no time for reorganization."

By noon of the same day, after scouting his forward lines, Kurt realized that Canadian 9th Brigade forces had no immediate plans for a counterattack in the Buron area. After their beating the day before they needed time to regroup. He decided to lend a hand to his sister regiment, the 26th, moving up on his left. Reports from his 15th Reconnaissance Company, probing the Caen-Bayeux highway, indicated that in conjunction with the 26th Regiment the way was open for a lateral advance along the road toward Bayeux. After a hurried planning session at his HQ in the abbey with Max Wünsche over lunch, the Divisional Commander was notified. Witt told him to proceed. While Wünsche organized his tanks, Kurt delivered attack orders to his subordinates and then took a nap, his first in over 60 hours.

At the Abbaye Ardenne, shortly after lunch, 19-year-old SS Sturmmann Jan Jesionek, a German-Pole from Upper Silesia, waited for someone to give him another motorcycle. A reconnaissance driver and dispatch rider with 15th Company, he had parked his unserviceable bike along the road in front of regimental HQ and was waiting for orders. He watched as a group of Canadian prisoners arrived under escort and were taken into one of the stable lockups. "One of the guards asked: 'Where is the Regimental Commander?' As I wanted to wash myself and my washing gear was in one of the cars inside the chapel, I said: 'Come along with me, perhaps he is in the chapel.'"

On Kurt's orders the reconnaissance company's *Schwimmwagen* (amphibious cars) and other small vehicles had been parked inside the chapel 20 minutes earlier to escape air attacks.

"The guard saw Standartenführer Meyer and announced to him the seven Canadian prisoners of war. Whereupon Meyer said: 'What should we do with these prisoners; they only eat up our rations?' Thereafter, he spoke to one

---

*These included a number of men executed at the Abbaye Ardenne after capture.

of the officers who stood with him. . . . He spoke in half-tones to this officer and afterwards said for all those who were in the chapel: 'In future no more prisoners are to be taken.'"

Jesionek went out to the courtyard pump to wash his hands. He saw the same officer interrogating individual Canadians in English. Some were weeping. The officer, an Obersturmführer, laughed at them. After their personal papers were collected, each soldier was taken separately through a passageway into the abbey's garden as his name was called. Each shook hands with the others as he left.

"When they entered . . . there stood the Unterscharführer. After the prisoners had been shot I saw him as he reloaded and put the safety catch on his pistol."*

Kurt's adjutant awakened him in time for a wash, shave and an early supper. Then, brimming with enthusiasm, he climbed on a motorbike and headed off to join his Bayeux highway assault group.

"When the tanks had filled up with petrol I had them taken forward to the Flak position at Franqueville . . . shortly before dusk. I had 15th Company get on the tank tops. This was 15th Company's first attack. I had promised that I would participate with them in their first attack. I led the entire attack on my motorcycle up to Rots."

During the evening Günter Fromm returned to the scene of his narrow escape at Rots. The town and bridge had been captured by 1st Company of the 26th Panzer Regiment. He looked around for the remains of his companions. "The motorcyclist's body was gone. That of the Platoon Commander, who had been riding in the sidecar, was torn in two from a grenade. The driver of one of the Volkswagen had burned to death beneath the car, his machine-gunner shot through the forehead. The sergeant also had a bullet through his head." In retrospect he felt they should have been given a chance to surrender. "The Canadians saw our dust cloud coming at 40 mph from 1,000 yards away. Apparently they had orders to take no prisoners. . . . The soldiers were dog tired and high on 'bennies' and apparently too shaky for proper aim because they missed me and my two friends at a distance of less than 20 yards."

He saw the motorcycles, scout cars and Panther tanks of Meyer's battle groups approaching. "The Standartenführer had already been informed of the Canadian ambush earlier in the day."

As the force neared Bretteville and the shooting started, Kurt sent a few of the tanks ahead to smash through the Canadian lines. Sectors of the Regina Rifles were overrun in the first collision of combat. A few Panthers pushed to within 300 yards of the Battalion HQ in Bretteville. But the Reginas held.

---

*This was to be Jesionek's evidence at Kurt's trial in 1945.

Unknowingly, he had led his force directly into the strongest part of the Canadian line. German casualties mounted quickly.

"Hauptsturmführer von Buettner, CO of the 15th Company, was shot off the top of his tank. He fell on the road to the edge of the ditch. . . . I was in close combat with a machine gun which lay in position behind a small tank. My driver, Behlke, was shot through the stomach. I was on fire because of leaking petrol. My comrades of the 15th Company quenched the fire."

Fighting raged throughout the hours of darkness. Near midnight, two Panthers entered the village. One made it as far as the headquarters where it was promptly knocked out by three successive anti-tank shells. Lieutenant-Colonel Matheson reported: "22 Panthers circled about Battalion HQ and A Company's position during the night. . . . It is hard to picture the confusion which existed. Contact with all but D Company was lost. Fires and flares lit up the area and the enemy several times appeared to be convinced that opposition had ceased. A foolhardy German dispatch rider rode through Bretteville on a captured Canadian motorcycle, only to be brought down by the CO's Sten gun. Some time later a German officer drove his Volkswagen up before Battalion HQ, dismounted and gazed about for a few seconds until an excited PIAT gunner let fly with a bomb which hit him squarely."[10]

Kurt attributed his defeat to the failure of 27th Regiment's 3rd Battalion to link up with his own forces because they had split their own. "The village of Norrey had been heavily occupied and in spite of 3rd Battalion of the 27th Regiment pushing on both sides of the railway up to Norrey and the adjacent Battalion reaching a point west of Bretteville . . . my own group was too weak to hold on for the next day. . . . I resolved to pull back my troops to the heights at Rots in the early morning hours. . . . The young soldiers don't hate their enemies. They are filled with respect for his fighting spirit."

Harry's observation of both the commander of the 26th Regiment and Kurt's battle sense was blunt: "The attacks were launched without any semblance of tactical sense. The flanks of the battalion were exposed and the position almost isolated. In such a case where a carefully conceived flank attack might have been deadly, the enemy flung himself straight against the strongest points and utterly failed to exploit the weaknesses of my positions. . . . It wasn't very bright."

6

The rumour of Canadian troops killing German prisoners that Kurt had heard two days earlier was confirmed with an on-site inspection by motorcycle. Dr. Gatternigg rode in the sidecar with him.

"After the Bretteville attack I drove back to Authie. Wünsche reported that the attacking troops on the west side of Rots had dug in and that by now Kraas's 3rd Battalion of the 26th Panzer Grenadier Regiment had made contact with my left wing. Whereupon I drove from Ardenne to Kraas's Battalion HQ at Rots and discussed the situation with Hugo personally. After leaving Rots I drove south, under the railway viaduct."

A few hundred yards beyond the viaduct he came across a burned-out armoured troop carrier of the 21st Panzer Division and a radio car belonging to the 12th SS. On the opposite side of the road he saw ten bodies lying in a semicircle, one a medic still holding a field dressing who had apparently been in the middle of giving aid to a wounded comrade when he was gunned down.

"They were all shot through the chest or head. Their weapons were still on the burned vehicle. Within the semicircle of bodies there were no weapons. In all my battles I have very rarely found a whole group of infantrymen dead in one bunch. That sort of thing happens in street or house fighting or on roads, but never in open countryside. . . . After I returned to the Abbaye I spoke to the Divisional Commander on the telephone about the tactical situation and after . . . made this report. . . .

"On 7 June, a notebook was taken from the body of a dead Canadian captain. In it were notes written apparently a few hours before the invasion. In addition to tactical orders the handwritten notes stated that 'prisoners are not to be taken.' Some Canadian prisoners were asked to verify these instructions. They confirmed that their orders were to take no prisoners if they were a hindrance to their advance."*

A day earlier, a commando raid had captured Port-en-Bessin. With the port of Courseulles, Montgomery now had two secure areas available for building up supplies and reinforcements for 21st Army Group. Contact had been made between the U.S. 1st and British 50th Divisions west of Bayeux. The Allies now held an unbroken strip of coast 35 miles long.

Over the next several days while both sides regrouped, the front remained static, with action limited to sniping, shelling and mortaring, plus intensive patrol activities. Kurt felt uncomfortable seeing his armoured strike force reduced to a defensive role. The *blitzkrieg* days were over. From the east, the west and the south of Europe, Allied armies were advancing on the German homeland. Final defeat was now just a question of time.

On 8 June the 12th SS came under command of I SS Panzer Corps. The following day 26th Regiment moved in to take over the division's left flank up to Tilly-sur-Seulles. The German line, although badly in need of replacements, remained for the moment secure behind a deep artillery

---

*Quoted from the petition of Hubert Meyer given before the Hamburg court in 1948 during the trial of SS Obersturmbannführer Bernhard Siebken.

defence. On that same day General Geyr, commander of Panzer Group West, arrived at the front for an inspection tour and strategy conference. Kurt attended.

"It was agreed to put forward to OKW in the strongest terms that further resistance in Normandy against the overwhelming mass of Allied strength both on land and in the air could only end in disaster. . . . They would advise that steps should be taken at once to retire, using their armoured formations to get the infantry out, thereby giving the infantry the chance to get back behind the Seine." As usual with recommendations to OKW from senior officers at the battlefront, the advice was ignored.

Throughout the night of 8 to 9 June, while Kurt's and Harry's troops were battling, Caen was subjected to heavy naval shelling. The church steeple of Saint-Pierre received a direct hit and came crashing to the street. In the morning a massive exodus of the population began, seeking refuge at nearby Fleury. By late evening on Friday, 9 June, the Allies' four eastern beachheads were linked and the American gap between Omaha and Utah was closing.

Another gap that needed closing lay between the 7th and 9th Brigades in the little wooded Mué Valley between Cairon and Rots. Seventh Brigade's artillery units near Bray were enticingly exposed. Accordingly, the Queen's Own Rifles from 8th Brigade were transferred over to Harry and moved into Bray preparatory to clearing the Mué Valley.

While Geyr visited Kurt's HQ at the Abbaye Ardenne on the morning of 9 June, two of his regimental officers approached Kurt as he left the tower and requested permission to file a report on the group of Canadian bodies lying unburied in the abbey's garden. The officers, Sturmbannführer Gatternigg and Obersturmführer Stift, were both regimental doctors.

"They were under the impression that the Canadians there had been shot. Thereupon I laughed and said: 'You must be crazy.' . . . I went with my Adjutant, Obersturmführer Schuemann and the two doctors to the garden entrance. . . . I was incensed . . . and had a heated argument with my Adjutant. I asked him: 'How does it happen that you were not informed of such a deed here at Regimental HQ? It is out of the question that activities here at HQ should be reported to me by other officers. Only the fact that you were not here at all times during the 7th and 8th keeps me from handing you over to the Divisional Commander.' I ordered him to find a replacement for himself after which he would be returned to the front.

"I told him that he would not receive a company but be placed into the 1st Battalion as a platoon commander. Simultaneously, I gave the order to ascertain who had done the deed and ordered the Canadians buried. Shortly past noon I went to the 2nd Battalion to inform the Regiment's judicial officer, Doctor of Law, Tiray. On the way I met the Divisional Commander, Witt. . . .

"I said: 'I have an unpleasant report. This morning in the area of Ardenne

(Abbaye) shot Canadians have been found. I have the impression they were shot there.'

"'Well,' Witt said excitedly, 'we'll have to put a halt to that sort of swinishness. This taking the law into one's own hand must be stopped.'

"'This could only have been men who heard about the shooting of our own comrades,' I said. 'I do not think it was my young soldiers.'"

Witt agreed that it was unlikely that the 17- and 18-year-olds were responsible. He ordered Kurt to find those guilty and command them to the division for punishment together with a full report of the incident. A divisional order appeared next day concerning the treatment of prisoners. But subsequent internal regimental investigation into the killings failed to produce a scrap of evidence against anyone.

The original invasion plan for General Bradley's U.S. First Army, after linking its two bridgeheads, was to cut the Cherbourg Peninsula in half, then wheel to capture Cherbourg itself. General Dempsey's forces were to hold their flank at the Dives River and take Caen and Bayeux. But by the 9th, when it became obvious Caen was not going to be taken by the initial assault momentum, Montgomery decided to modify the plan in Dempsey's sector. He proposed a pincer thrust around Caen, with the British 1st Airborne landing behind the city to close the circle. A right-wing assault by the British 7th Armoured, supported by the 50th Division, would wheel around the German positions and capture the highway junction at Villers-Bocage. The Canadians were ordered to prepare a limited strike force at Le Mesnil-Patry to "assist" with the 50th's attack.

It sounded plausible. But it was too early in the game for an elaborate tactical assault. What should have been an effectively organized spearhead to penetrate the German defences turned into an unmitigated disaster. Instead of taking a day to clear the Mué Valley before starting the main attack, both ventures went ahead simultaneously without proper reconnaissance, preparation or adequate artillery support.

German attacks on the east of Caen across the Orne doomed the left wing of the pincer to failure. On the right wing, British and Canadian forces were badly bloodied by the 26th Panzer and 2nd Battalion of the 12th ss Panzer Regiments based at Le Mesnil-Patry. The Queen's Own Rifles and 1st Hussars who led the charge had 114 men killed. Nearly an entire company of the British 5th Black Watch Regiment was annihilated.

After this debacle Montgomery decided to wait and build up his forces before launching another attack. "Be on the defensive . . . but aggressively so," he ordered his commanders. Almost immediately murmurings began among senior British and American officers that he had allowed his eastern flank to become bogged down by a miasma of indecision. In Britain and America, editorial strategists of the popular press joined the clamour for action at the British front. National pride was as much to blame as anything else for the furor. "Does General Montgomery plan on leaving General Bradley to finish off the war for him?" the *Washington Post* inquired indignantly.

Monty did indeed have a plan, the same one his HQ outlined on 7 May— a month before the assault—entitled "An Appreciation on Possible Developments of Operations to Secure a Lodgement Area," and delivered on 18 May to Bradley's 1st U.S. Army Group and Dempsey's Second British Army. The summary of its conclusions provided ample vindication for his subsequent tactical conduct once the troops were ashore.

"The type of country immediately south of the initial bridgehead does not favour a rapid advance. The Allied build-up relative to the estimated German build-up indicates that a period may supervene round about D + 14, when there will be a grave risk of operations stabilizing on a line which gives the Germans advantages in defence. The greatest energy and initiative will be required at this period to ensure the enemy is not allowed to stabilize his defence.

"Once through the difficult *bocage** country, greater possibilities for manoeuvre and for the use of armour begin to appear. Our aim during this period should be to contain the maximum enemy forces facing the eastern flank of the bridgehead. . . . By alternate thrusts towards the east and towards the southwest, we should be able to retain the initiative, reap the benefit of interior lines, and keep the enemy moving his reserves from one flank to the other."

As long as the Germans continued believing in the strategic importance of Caen and bringing up their precious armoured units to prevent the perceived threat of a breakout by the British and Canadians, there would be less pressure on Bradley's American front. OKW no longer had the armoured reserves to cover both sectors of the Western Front. The First U.S. Army, confined to the tortuous *bocage* country of the Cherbourg Peninsula and fighting its way toward St. Lô, Hitler tended to dismiss as a collection of inexperienced amateurs.

In the 7th Brigade sector, activity was limited to "a cat and mouse game of heavy shelling and nightly patrols gathering up whatever intelligence and prisoners that came our way," Harry reported.

"12 June. . . . Heard that Churchill arrived on the beach at Courseulles today, greeted by Monty and usual bevy of VIPs. He apparently enjoyed himself and spoke to the troops. . . . A series of truly frightening air raids on Caen tonight. I can't see how anyone could survive such devastation. Fires lit up the entire sector."

Sergeant Dudka, meanwhile, had been subjected to the ruthlessness of his

---

*Cultivated fields surrounded by a tangle of underwood and hedges.

captors. After spending one night in the Abbaye Ardenne stable, his group was marched to Bretteville-sur-Odon* beyond Carpiquet airfield where they remained until 11 June. Eighty men of the Regina and Royal Winnipeg Rifles captured at Norrey and Putot were herded in and joined them.

"Next morning we were turned over to the *Feldgendarmerie*† and ordered to march to Stalag 221, a French concentration camp at Rennes used during World War I.... During the march anyone caught stepping out of the column was shot. . . . On the way we were strafed by three American Mustangs. They killed 15 and wounded 45. I was hit twice in the arm and knee. . . . Our guards scattered."

A number of the wounded managed to sneak away while the *Feldgendarmerie* were busy rounding up everyone. French civilians hid them. Dudka was brought to an old-age home that had been evacuated. Nuns visited the men daily, dressing their wounds. The tenth day after their escape they were betrayed.

"The Germans came and took me to one of their military hospitals in Le Mans where I was treated identical to their own wounded. Those of us who were walking wounded were put to work emptying bedpans. They didn't want their nurses emptying Allied bedpans."

When he was fit enough to walk, the march to Rennes continued. "I was put into a prisoner of war hospital when we arrived, filled with hundreds of wounded Americans, many of them dying. . . . One American Jewish officer complained loudly about conditions, citing Rules from the Geneva Convention. The next morning he disappeared. We knew he'd been shot. . . . The Germans were mighty quick to shoot Jews. The first thing they did with anyone they captured was to examine his paybook and find out if he was Jewish. If he was, then they shot him. Even the *Feldgendarmerie* were watching for Jews."

After discharge from hospital Dudka went over to the concentration camp. "But I knew we wouldn't be there long once our troops started advancing inland."

Early on 14 June Kurt took the Divisional Commander on a tour of his front line in a motorcycle sidecar. Witt inquired how the investigations into the shooting deaths at the Abbaye Ardenne were proceeding. Kurt admitted "that up to now I had no information about the culprits. The Divisional Commander once again asked me to give a written report about this matter."

On the same day, north of Caen, a German counterattack was broken up by naval guns supported by heavy land-based artillery. During the course of the shelling Fritz Witt was killed. Upon hearing of his old comrade's

---

*Not to be confused with 7th Brigade HQ at Bretteville l'Orgueilleuse.
†Literally, "Field Police"—German Provost who wore chained disc insignia on their chests.

death, Dietrich exclaimed: "That's one of the best gone. He was too good a soldier to stay alive for long."

Friday morning, 16 June: the Royal yacht *Arethusa*, accompanied by two destroyers, dropped anchor off Juno beach. King George VI, wearing his uniform as Admiral of the Fleet, climbed down into one of the launches from the cruiser, HMS *Scylla*, then transferred to a DUKW* for the trip ashore. After spending a few hours on French soil, he returned to England.

During the night of 17 June—one of the shortest of the year—Ken Blackader's 8th Brigade moved up to occupy positions at Putot, Bretteville and Norrey, relieving men of the depleted 7th Brigade, who moved to the rear for a rest and refit. Harry observed that the two units "exchanged areas in the face of the enemy, without incident."

On the German side of the line, Kurt was appointed to command of the 12th SS. He was, at 33, the youngest divisional commander in the German armed forces.

7

On 17 June during a flying visit to the Western Front, Hitler met with Field Marshals von Rundstedt and Rommel at Margival, near Soissons. Ironically, the concrete bunker at Margival had been set up as a Führer Headquarters in 1940. From there Hitler had intended directing the invasion of England. Discussions centred around the Allies' long-term plans for breaking through the perilously thin ring of German defences.

Despite linkup of all five Allied beachheads and the enemy's secure inland hold of a line running roughly from north of Caen to Caumont and from there to just short of St. Lô, Hitler still clung to his belief that a further Allied assault was yet to come from across the Channel at the Pas-de-Calais. Conditioned to the numerical superiority of their enemy on the Eastern Front and familiar with Montgomery's hesitancy about committing troops until he held the tactical advantage of surprise, equipment and numbers, German intelligence had wildly overestimated the strength of Allied reserves sitting in England.

Hitler refused to believe that the Allied armies were so firmly entrenched that they could not be driven out. Suggestions from his two field marshals of pulling back beyond range of Allied naval gunfire to consolidate the German lines went unheeded. Instead, he changed the subject to his new Victory Weapons offensive. Pilotless rocket-powered "Doodlebug" bombs had been

---

*An American-designed amphibious vehicle (also known as DUK).

Royal Winnipeg Rifles and support troops head for Courseulles. (DND/PAC/PA-132651)

North Nova Scotia Highlanders and the Highland Light Infantry of Canada land at Bernières-sur-Mer on 6 June 1944. (DND/PAC/PA-122765)

The Abbaye Ardenne, Kurt's HQ on 7
June 1944.

Max Wünsche. (Bundesarchiv)

Les Fusiliers Mont-Royal enter Moy-sur-Orne, 9 August 1944. (Ken Bell/DND/PAC/
PA-135962)

Canada's Fighting Generals. Seated (from left): Guy Simonds, H.D.G. Crerar, Charles Foulkes. Standing (from left): B.M. Hoffmeister, R.H. Keefler, Chris Vokes, A.B. Matthews, Harry Foster.

Harry with the City Fathers of liberated Bruges and (bottom) Rotterdam.

Kurt arrives in Aurich for the war crimes trial, 31 October 1945. (B.J. Gloster/ DND/PAC/PA-140574)

Harry is sworn in as court president. (From left) Brig. J.A. Roberts, Brig. H.A. Sparling, Lieut. Col. W.B. Bredin, Harry and Brig. Ian S. Johnston. (B.J. Gloster/ DND/PAC/PA-140576)

Kurt stands before the court. (B.J. Gloster/DND/PAC/PA-140575)

Flanked by Maj. Arthur Russell (left) and Capt. Elton
McPhail, Kurt awaits sentencing. At the table behind
him are Lieut.-Col. Bruce Macdonald (left) and Clarence
Campbell. (B.J. Gloster/DND/PAC/PA-141890)

Meyer in handcuffs after
the death sentence was
passed at Aurich, 28
December 1945, and
(below) at Dorchester in
1946.

Kate Meyer in January 1946, after Kurt's sentence was
commuted.

(Top left) The Meyer family in 1950. (From left) Irmtraud, Ursula, Kate, Kurt, Inge and Gerhild.

(Above) Kate and Kurt in 1954.

(Left) In Mainz in 1954 with "Uncle Fritz" (right).

(Below left) Meeting with old comrades, including Sepp Dietrich (right), and (below right) addressing the HIAG in 1958.

As GOC Eastern Command, Harry addresses troops (above) and attends the opening of the Nova Scotia House of Assembly in 1948. (NS Bureau of Information Services-3519)

(Below left) With Premier Angus L. Macdonald (right) and Lieut.-Gov J.A.D. McCurdy, and (below right) with Mollie at Fleet.

Fifteen thousand people attended Kurt Meyer's funeral in Hagen. A cushion-bearer (left) holds his medals.

Following the military procession through the streets of Halifax, David, Mona and Tony stand by Harry's grave.

crashing blindly on London and the Home Counties since 13 June.

He had convinced himself that these V1 rockets, developed at Peenemünde on the Baltic coast, would soon have the Allies on their knees and begging for peace. He had other "surprises" in store for the enemy. There were new mines to be dropped at sea, a newer rocket, the V2, was nearing completion, and a new twin-engined fighter powered by jet engines would soon be able to run rings around the fastest Allied aircraft. It all sounded good. The field marshals and their staff were unimpressed.

The Americans, their armour floundering through the *bocage* country, had managed to cut the Cotentin Peninsula by the night of 18 June, isolating the badly needed port city of Cherbourg. On the same day the Canadian army commander, Gen. Harry Crerar, arrived in France aboard HMCS *Algonquin*. He set up a small tactical headquarters in the village of Amblie, east of Creully, where General Montgomery had his headquarters.

A Channel storm, building since 16 June, reached its peak on 19 June with hurricane-force winds. Cross-Channel operations were suspended. Up and down the French coast, ships and small craft crowded into the shelter of Mulberry harbours and Gooseberry breakwaters. The Gooseberries—made up of sunken ships—and the Mulberry harbours were not large enough to hold all the vessels. Huge waves breaking across the shallow water near the beaches drove hundreds of craft ashore, where they broke their backs or were severely damaged.

Finally, on 22 June, the storm abated. Nearly 800 vessels of all sizes had been either stranded, damaged or destroyed. On some beaches wrecked craft were piled on top of each other. The worst damage had been to the Mulberry harbour at St. Laurent, off Omaha beach. It was nearly destroyed. Many of the Gooseberry breakwaters had broken open to the sea. Frantic repairs were started.

On the day the storm ended, General Crerar attended a conference of army, corps and divisional commanders at Montgomery's HQ. To his disappointment he learned that Monty had decided "that owing to the delay caused by the weather in the 'build-up' and in the capture of Caen" there simply wasn't enough elbow room to bring the rest of the First Canadian Army from England. This was a politically sensitive issue. The original plan called for Canadian forces to be commanded by the Canadian Army Commander.

But Crerar was assured that as soon as the Canadian 2nd Division arrived early in July together with corps and headquarters troops, both Canadian divisions would be placed under the unified command of Lieut.-Gen. Guy Simonds, II Canadian Corps commander.* Until then General Dempsey would continue to command five corps. Once Caen had been taken and the Dives

---

*He had been promoted to corps commander in January 1944.

River line secured, however, the British I and Canadian II Corps would be grouped under the Canadian Army Commander. Crerar's army would then be responsible for the army group's left sector. Satisfied, Crerar returned to his headquarters to await developments.

Caen. The bone that continued to stick in everybody's throat. Montgomery couldn't advance until it was taken; von Rundstedt and Rommel couldn't afford to lose it. Day after day the shelling and bombing of the city continued. Casualties on both sides mounted.

"25 June. . . . I'm beginning to worry about our replacements. Most of the men we're getting are soft. They have been trained to cook, bake, drive, type and shuffle papers. Everything but kill Germans. I have organized intensive training sessions for all units. The Winnipegs are in especially poor shape. I have told Rod. He has promised to talk to Gen. Crerar. . . . Attended a Divisional conference. General Crocker outlined the plan for Operation 'Epsom.' He said British 8th Corps would go through the Hun like a dose of salts. . . . I'll believe that when it happens. Afterwards we all went outside and had our picture taken."

The Odon River ran southwest from Caen. The plan of attack visualized an encircling movement of the city, with the newly arrived and unblooded 15th (Scottish) Division capturing the Odon bridges five miles to the south, thus enabling the 11th Armoured Division to then pass through them and go on to seize the next set of bridges over the Orne, opening the way to the high ground south of Caen. As the attack proceeded, the Canadian 3rd Division would advance on Buron, Authie and Carpiquet airport.

At 0800 hours on the morning of 26 June, under teeming rain and low, scudding cloud that had grounded all aircraft, the enthusiastic Scotsmen moved out, supported by their own artillery and that of the Canadian 3rd Division, plus naval gunfire. At first, progress behind the barrage although slow remained steady. However, once the barrage moved on and the enemy emerged from his dugouts to find his positions being overrun by "furious Scotsmen throwing grenades," the advance deteriorated into hand-to-hand fighting. By the end of the first day the Odon River had not been reached, nor did the Germans appear to be weakening.

German Army Group B recorded the day as a "complete defensive success" achieved only by I SS Panzer Corps "employing its last reserves" together "with all the forces of the 12th SS Panzer Division and Panzer Lehr Division taxed to their utmost."

Next morning at 0500 hours the British advance resumed. By late evening a shallow bridgehead had been established across the river. Furiously, the Germans counterattacked. But the line held. On the following day II SS Panzer Corps, with the 9th SS Panzer and others, arrived from the Eastern Front from where they had been rushed at top speed. By late afternoon the Germans had succeeded in reducing some of the bridgehead, but losses from the incessant Allied air strikes and pounding from land- and sea-based artillery had taken its toll. The fury of the counterattack faded, then dissolved.

Although German losses were heavy, the attackers had suffered too. Casualties for the Scottish 15th Division alone were 2,720 during the Odon battles. When it was obvious the British offensive had failed in its objectives, the plan—code-named "Ottawa"—for the Canadian 3rd Division to move on Carpiquet was cancelled.

The port of Cherbourg fell to the Americans during the evening of 26 June after vicious street fighting. Lieut.-Gen. Karl von Schlieben surrendered what was left of the Fort du Roule garrison. The fort, at the end of the half-mile-long Cherbourg jetty, was the last point of German resistance on the peninsula. Furious about this loss and a general lack of progress in the West, Hitler summoned von Rundstedt and Rommel to his fantasyland at Berchtesgaden for 29 June. Forbidden to travel by train or aircraft, both men set out by separate cars for the 600-mile journey. They arrived shortly after six in the evening.

For losing Cherbourg, he wanted the Seventh Army commander, beefy Col.-Gen. Friedrich Dollmann, courtmartialed. Von Rundstedt refused to listen to such nonsense. Hitler then demanded that at the very least the man should be dismissed for incompetence. But Rommel stood up for the ailing Dollmann and changed the subject. As before, the Führer refused to accept the opinions of his field marshals that the existing battle lines could no longer be held. He did agree, albeit reluctantly, to abandon his absurd idea of a major offensive against Cherbourg to split the Allied armies and retake the port. Von Rundstedt and Rommel returned to France despairing over Hitler's intractability.

A week earlier, on the third anniversary of the German invasion, the Red Army's summer offensive had opened like a whirlwind. Backed by 6 million troops, the Russians fell upon their invaders. Within days the German army reeled in full retreat. At times it appeared touch and go whether or not the entire German centre would collapse.

Next day the commander of Panzer Group West, directing operations on the British front, sent a detailed list of suggestions to Seventh Army HQ. In it General Geyr stated, "The situation at Caen and east of it demands basically new decisions." He recommended the army evacuate that part of the city lying north and west of the Orne to a new line six miles south of Caen. The proposed withdrawal would be followed by a "renewed transition to offensive thrusts beyond the most effective range of naval artillery."[11]

It made sense. The Seventh Army commander, ss General Hausser,*

---

*ss Obergruppenführer und General der Waffen-ss Hausser replaced Col.-Gen. Friedrich Dollmann, who committed suicide a day earlier.

Rommel and von Rundstedt all agreed, although Rommel questioned the logic of giving up as much territory as Geyr suggested. He regarded Caen as the critical anchor point against the Allied thrust toward Paris. At 0300 hours on 1 July von Rundstedt asked permission from OKW to begin the planned withdrawals.

Hitler's blunt reply arrived later that afternoon: "The present positions are to be held. Any further enemy breakthrough must be prevented by obstinate defence or local counterattacks."[12]

While discussing the hopelessness of the situation by telephone with Field Marshal Keitel, von Rundstedt was asked plaintively by Hitler's chief of staff: "What shall we do?"

"Make peace, you idiots!" von Rundstedt snapped. "What else can you do?"[13]

Hitler would not accept any form of defeatism from his senior officers. Next day von Rundstedt received notification that he would be replaced by Field Marshal Günther von Kluge. Two days later the axe fell on General Geyr. He was ordered to turn over his command to General of Panzer Troops Heinrich Eberbach. Rommel met him in a forest near St. Pierre-sur-Dives and broke the news. "I come to tell you that you have been relieved," he told Geyr cheerfully. "Rundstedt has been too; I'm the next on the list!"

Eberbach immediately studied his predecessor's recommendations and wrote a letter at once to von Kluge stating that he agreed with General Geyr entirely. Von Kluge didn't—or wouldn't—pass this endorsement on to OKW.

On the last day of June, Montgomery issued a lengthy directive to Generals Omar Bradley and Sir Miles Dempsey giving his battle plan and orders. The plan in outline: "to hold the maximum number of enemy divisions on our eastern flank between Caen and Villers-Bocage, and to swing the western flank of the Army Group southwards and eastwards in a wide sweep so as to threaten the line of withdrawal of such enemy divisions to the south of Paris."

Montgomery's policy of drawing in the bulk of German forces against the British sector had succeeded beyond expectation. Confronting the British Second Army at the end of June, Panzer Group West had seven and a half of the eight panzer divisions in Normandy plus a further six divisions or remnants of divisions. Facing the American front the German Seventh Army had only six divisions—one a SS Panzer, three of the others divisional remnants.

Bradley's First U.S. Army, with seven armoured, two airborne and 14 infantry divisions, was ordered to open an offensive southwards on the Allied right flank beginning Monday, 3 July. Simultaneously, on the British front, plans were made for the capture of Carpiquet airport and Caen. The job of capturing the airport, Operation "Windsor," went to the Canadian 3rd Division.

The Allied armies had now landed over one million men in Normandy together with 600,000 tons of supplies and 171,000 vehicles.

At Harry's 7th Brigade HQ in the village of Bray, 2 July—a Sunday—dawned cloudy and cool. General Keller arrived during the morning for preliminary discussions on "Windsor." Blackader's 8th Brigade, with the Royal Winnipeg Rifles temporarily attached, was to take Carpiquet village and the airport.

"I spoke with Rod again about the quality of our replacements. Particularly in view of what the Winnipegs were being asked to do now. He said Guy was already working on it. It seems the problem is with the bloody politicians in Ottawa who don't realize that in war men are wounded and die and have to be replaced. . . . Charles Foulkes* arrived this afternoon and after sniffing round for awhile left. Wonder what he is up to?"

On the next day the Royal Winnipegs were taken up to the Marcelet assembly area in the rain where they joined the Queen's Own Rifles, the North Shore Regiment and Le Régiment de la Chaudière. Twelfth SS artillery spotters observed the activity around Marcelet. Throughout the rest of that day and night, enemy artillery and mortar shells whistled down on the men. At 0500 hours, 4 July, they moved off from their start line behind a creeping artillery barrage and the heavy 16-inch guns of the battleship HMS *Rodney*. At once the Germans replied with a counterbarrage, catching the lead companies as they moved out of cover and across the mile of ripening wheat fields. In that last instant before death the attackers must have thought it was their own shells that were falling among them. As men fell, comrades marked their locations with bayoneted rifles rammed upright into the ground for the stretcher-bearers to see.

The plan called for the brigade's three regiments to advance on the village, hangars and control buildings located at the north side of the airfield while the Royal Winnipegs on the right flank thrust toward the south-side hangars. Defending the airfield were 150 grenadiers of the 12th SS. Within two hours leading sections of the North Shores and the Chaudières had reached the village and were proceeding to clear it. Only 50 youngsters of the 25th Panzer Grenadier Regiment[14] defended the village garrison. They put up a furious fight. "No one took any prisoners that day," the Chaudières' captain, Michel Gauvin, admitted. Once the village had been cleared of Germans, the men quickly dug in.

The Royal Winnipegs ran into problems almost from the start line. Although they reached the hangars, they were unable to dig in because of

---

*GOC 2nd Canadian Division arriving from England.

heavy artillery fire. Interconnecting concrete pillboxes and bunkers built by the Luftwaffe covered the approaches. From these and the hangars themselves heavy machine guns erupted against the attackers.

Lieut.-Col. J.M. Meldram, the Royal Winnipegs' CO, dashed back to 8th Brigade HQ and asked for help. A squadron of tanks from the Fort Garrys moved forward, but when they reached the edge of the airfield, German 88 mm guns cremated two of them. The Royal Winnipegs withdrew to Marcelet and reorganized a second attack later in the afternoon. It was no more successful than the first. By early evening Blackader ordered Meldram to pull his men off the airfield. Two squadrons of Typhoons were brought in for a rocket attack on the enemy tanks and self-propelled guns dug in around the airport perimeter.

A communications link had been set up between Harry's HQ and 8th Brigade so that the battle could be monitored. Throughout the day a succession of war correspondents and visitors came and went. By midday Harry had heard enough. Finally, he told his brigade major, P.W. Bennett: "Call me if anyone higher than a brigadier shows up. . . . I'm going to have a snooze."

Three prisoners captured by the Royal Winnipeg Rifles were brought in for interrogation that evening. "All were filthy, poorly clad youngsters of eighteen . . . or so—sullen, but a little more than thankful to be out of the war."[15] In spite of thundering German artillery and mortar fire during the night and into the following day, the 8th Brigade managed to hang on to Carpiquet village. Kurt no longer had sufficient reserves to mount a successful counterattack, although one company of the Chaudières was overrun, with only a few of its men managing to escape. The rest of the French Canadians refused to budge.

A few days later, the London *Daily Telegraph*'s special correspondent wrote: "It is no wonder the German troops believe Nazi propaganda about Canadian soldiers being savages with scalping knives." His report was precipitated by an incident that took place during one of the counterattacks. Sgt. Léo Gariépy of the 10th Armoured Regiment (the Fort Garry Horse) supporting the Chaudières witnessed the resulting carnage: "The Germans had succeeded in infiltrating the advance post of the . . . Chaudières, tough rugged French-Canadians who brawl at home on weekends for *divertissement*. We were very close by when the alarm sounded at 0400 hours. The . . . Chaudières scurried in the semi-darkness and actually slit the throats of most soldiers they found, wounded as well as dead. This horrible carnage I . . . saw from the turret of my tank at first light. These boys were actually crazed by some frenzy at being caught napping; the officers of the Regiment had to draw their pistols against their own men to make them come back to reason. This was shortly before the so-called massacre of some Canadian prisoners by the ss. Are you surprised?"

In retaliation the 12th ss machine-gunned a group of Canadian prisoners who had been captured on patrol outside Caen. Their bodies were found in a farm near St. Germain-la-Blanche-Herbe.

Although the narrow salient at Carpiquet managed to hold, Operation "Windsor" had been a failure. Montgomery and the British corps commander, General Crocker, openly criticized General Keller and his forces. There were angry mutterings among the generals in England that after D-Day the Canadians had lost their heart and their leadership.

By the end of June accumulative 12th SS losses were becoming serious. There were no replacements and no reinforcements. His eyes red-rimmed from lack of sleep, Kurt rushed from one killing ground to the next, exhorting the shrinking numbers of troops to maintain their élan, their pride, their courage. But beneath his external enthusiasm he knew the situation to be desperate.

"For the first time I feel a burning emptiness in my heart and curse the murder which now has lasted for years. What I see now is no longer war but naked murder. I know every one of my young grenadiers. The oldest is hardly 18. They have not yet learned to live, but God knows they have learned how to die."

Near midnight he was surprised by the faithful Michel arriving at his HQ. Somehow the Cossack had managed to make his way out of Germany and across France to bring him news of Kate's latest pregnancy. He apologized for taking so long. He had been arrested, but escaped.

Hitler's orders for Caen to be defended to the last shot "means the end of the division. The men are prepared to fight. Prepared to give their lives. But there must be some sense to the fight. I don't like to let my young soldiers die in the city's streets."

He decided to take the unusual step of telling his corps commander, and later Field Marshal Rommel, that Caen could no longer be defended. Four years earlier this would have been tantamount to treason and grounds for instant dismissal. Now his superiors merely shrugged and repeated Hitler's orders that the city must be held under all circumstances.

"I am filled with rage when I think of my brave grenadiers who have been fighting day and night for four weeks and who are now to be senselessly sacrificed."

Rommel, already involved in a plan to arrest Hitler, put him on trial and enter into negotiations with Montgomery to end the war in the West, told Kurt astutely: "Something must happen. The war must finally come to an end. But what will happen in the East?"

Kurt was urged to make do with what he had and continue the fight. On 6 July Field Marshal von Kluge formally relieved von Rundstedt as C.-in-C. of the German armies in the West.

On the same date the Royal Winnipeg Rifles were returned to 7th Brigade command. Next day Harry attended a divisional O Group on the final battle for Caen. Senior and junior field commanders who had been complaining about Montgomery's habit of sending a regiment instead of a brigade, a brigade instead of a division, a division instead of a corps, against the enemy, found little to criticize in Operation "Charnwood." Three infantry divisions were to advance on the city in a semicircle: the 3rd Canadian Division on the right, the British 3rd Division on the left, and the British 59th (Staffordshire) Division in the centre. A bomber attack, heavy artillery and naval gunfire from the battleship *Rodney*, the monitor *Roberts* and cruisers *Belfast* and *Emerald* would open the attack.

There were few Germans or French left in Caen. Most of the city's population had been evacuated the previous week. Under the weight of 2,500 tons of high explosive whole sections of the city were needlessly destroyed, including the university. Civilian casualties were between three and four hundred. Unfortunately, the Lancasters never touched the surrounding towns and villages of the German defence perimeter beyond depressing the morale of its defenders. The raid had been a huge and tragic fiasco.

Kurt had moved his HQ from Venoix into an army barracks on the north side of Caen next to the old garrison church at the edge of the target area. He watched the raid with his GSO1. The church was destroyed but his headquarters escaped without casualties. "The troops themselves were entirely unaffected by this attack," Kurt reported.

After the bombers left, long-range artillery harassed the southern roads leading into Caen. An hour before midnight 656 guns of the British I Corps opened up on the towns and villages behind the German lines. Finally, on 8 July at 4:20 a.m. a gigantic artillery barrage using every gun in the British Second Army, plus offshore naval guns, thundered down across the start lines of the British 3rd and 59th Divisions as the troops took up their positions. Then the men moved out.

The day dawned cloudy and cool with scattered showers. On the Canadian 3rd Division's front Dan Cunningham's 9th Brigade opened its attack at 0730 hours. Confidently, the troops moved forward against the exhausted troops of the 12th SS. Once the villages of Gruchy, Buron, Authie and Franqueville had been taken, Harry's 7th Brigade was to push through the 9th, taking out Cussy and the Abbaye Ardenne.

"First contact was made with the enemy by 9th Infantry Brigade at 0750 hours in opposition . . . of heavy mortaring and shelling and machine-gun fire. The advance continued and Gruchy was reported as taken—in the meantime troops advancing on Buron were having a sticky time and under constant shellfire, both from artillery and tanks."

Buron was held by the depleted 3rd Battalion of Kurt's 25th SS Panzer Grenadiers who had withdrawn from Gruchy. They fought like madmen against the troops of the Highland Light Infantry of Canada. All day the

Germans battled among the rubble, losing 14 tanks in one counterattack that was beaten off. When it was over, the Highland Regiment had lost 262 men and its CO, Lieut.-Col. F.M. Griffiths.

At 1030 hours Harry ordered the 7th Brigade forward to its assembly area behind Gruchy.

"At approximately 1300 hours . . . Brigade was in position—the two forward battalions of Regina Rifles and Canadian Scottish were being heavily mortared and shelled—moaning minnies by the cartload, 88 mm High Explosive, armour piercing and larger shells, 150 mm . . . they were throwing everything."

By midafternoon the North Nova Scotia Regiment, waiting outside Buron and taking heavy casualties, passed through the Canadian Scottish to take Authie—the village where so many of the Novies had been captured, wounded or had died on D-Day plus 1. Outside of Marcelet and in the Carpiquet salient men of the 8th Brigade watched German troops withdrawing in disorder as the Novies drove on toward Franqueville and the airport beyond.

At five that afternoon it was Harry's turn.

"I set zero hour for 1730. The Reginas and Canadian Scottish crossed the start line on time under heavy shelling. The depleted Winnipegs were held as a reserve. . . . Within ninety minutes Cabeldu* had run into trouble at Cussy."

The village had been taken but the Germans counterattacked with tanks and infantry. Although Cabeldu's men held, knocking out six tanks, he feared a second attack might overwhelm their positions. Harry sent up two companies of Royal Winnipegs with a pair of anti-tank guns and plenty of ammunition. But there were no more counterattacks.

"By 2300 hours Cussy was firmly in our hands. The Reginas, meanwhile, attacking the Abbaye had run into heavy machine-gun fire, mortars, shelling and tanks."

Since Kurt's departure to take over the division, the abbey had remained the 25th SS Panzer Grenadiers' command post. Realizing it was now threatened, he drove over at once to direct its defence, bringing with him a Panther tank company and what remained of the Leibstandarte's 3rd Battalion of the 1st Panzer Grenadier Regiment, now attached to the 12th SS. For a time these reinforcements brought the Reginas' attack to a standstill.

But the 12th SS position holding the German centre and west flank became untenable. The inexperienced 16th Luftwaffe Field Division, which had taken over from the 21st Panzer Division northeast of Caen three days earlier, broke apart before the solid advance of the British 3rd Division. As these raw Luftwaffe troops fell back on Caen, the men of the 12th SS were in danger of being cut off.

---

*Lieut.-Col. F.N. Cabeldu, CO of the Canadian Scottish Regiment.

Doggedly, the Reginas pressed forward into the cauldron of darkness and flames. Burning Canadian and German tanks scattered the landscape like huge Halloween bonfires. Fifteen minutes before midnight Harry received a message from the Reginas that the lead companies had reached the Abbaye Ardenne. Kurt Meyer and his men were gone.

The Battle of Caen ended next day. A victory that came 33 days too late. Total Canadian casualties were 1,194, of which 330 were killed—a loss heavier than on D-Day.

8

The German forces that withdrew south across the Orne to take up positions in the suburb city of Vaucelles were but shadows of their former strength. The 16th Luftwaffe Division had suffered more than 75 percent casualties. Every one of its battalion commanders had either been killed or wounded. On three separate occasions during the bitter fighting Kurt had seen his grenadiers jump onto Allied tanks with explosives tied to their bodies.

A single battalion was all that remained of the 12th ss Division's infantry. Most of the unit's anti-tank guns were gone, along with 65 tanks. The 25th ss Panzer Grenadier Regiment had suffered most. Only 485 men remained. These were hollow-eyed and weary.

Kurt noted: "The losses were caused not by the Allied bomber attacks but mainly by flame throwers that attacked immediately after the bombing ceased, catching many of the men in a dazed condition. . . . Officers and men know that the struggle is hopeless. Silent but willing to do their duty to the bitter end, they wait for their orders."

Their orders arrived on 11 July. The 12th ss was to hand over the Caen sector to the 1st ss Panzer Division (Leibstandarte Adolf Hitler) and withdraw behind the lines for a rest and refit.

On the same day Harry set up his headquarters in Caen. Intermittently, German 88 mm shells whistled in from across the river, grinding down what was left of the city's gutted buildings into clouds of plaster and stone.

"Surprisingly, there were still citizens living in the town. Even more surprising that they were happy to see us in spite of what we had put them through. . . . Moving the rubble will take months. The REs [Royal Engineers] are already hard at work clearing the streets. . . . Guy Simonds has now officially taken over 2nd Canadian Corps and a section of the Caen front . . . 2nd and 3rd Divisions, 2nd Armoured Brigade and 2nd Group Royal Artillery. . . . It still gives me an odd feeling whenever we meet. If Gil had behaved himself I am certain that he and not Guy would have been the Corps commander. Guy certainly knows his job, but will never understand his men. Gil understood. That is the difference between leadership and command.

. . . The Corps is still under Dempsey and not quite yet an army. Gen. Crerar and the politicians must be chewing their nails."

They weren't the only ones.

American generals back in Washington were nervously urging Eisenhower to order Montgomery to begin his breakout. As Air Chief Marshal Leigh-Mallory acidly pointed out, the capture of Caen did nothing to provide the RAF with forward airfields in the flat country southeast of the city.

Over on the American front General Bradley was in trouble. After 10,000 casualties his offensive had bogged down at St. Lô for the same reasons as before: *bocage* country and flooded marshlands that could only be crossed on narrow causeways and on which it was impossible to mount an armoured attack. However, Bradley found the arrogant little British general easier to blame than the terrain. Four days earlier, von Kluge and Rommel had decided to shift the Panzer Lehr Division to the American front. It came into action against Bradley's troops on 11 July. Bradley called on Montgomery for help. He needed a ten-day respite to rebuild and supply his forces for the American breakout. Montgomery agreed to a British attack; code-named Operation "Goodwood," it would cross the Orne and smash the German line.

A day before Operation "Goodwood," Rommel visited the headquarters of I SS Panzer Corps and met with Sepp Dietrich and Kurt Meyer. Rommel expected a British attack within 24 hours. When it came, he wanted Kurt's 12th SS to support the 272nd Infantry Division.

Dietrich complained bitterly: "I'm being bled white and I'm getting nowhere!"

Two days earlier Rommel had reported to von Kluge that his army group had lost 97,000 men since D-Day and received only 6,000 replacements. Only 17 new tanks had arrived to replace the 225 that had been destroyed. During the discussions with Dietrich and Meyer it became apparent that he held out little hope of preventing enemy armoured units from smashing through the German line.

Over the weeks of battle Rommel had been shaken by the mounting casualties. "It was one terrible blood letting. Sometimes we had as many casualties on one day as during the whole of the summer fighting in Africa in 1942. My nerves are pretty good, but sometimes I was near collapse. It was casualty reports, casualty reports, casualty reports, wherever you went. I have never fought with such losses. If I hadn't gone to the front nearly every day I couldn't have stood it, having to write off literally one more regiment every day."

On the way back to his own headquarters at La Roche Guyon, his open staff car was attacked by a pair of cruising Spitfires near the village of St. Foy de Montgommery. During the brief splatter of machine-gun bullets and

20 mm cannon shells, he was seriously wounded when his car crashed.* Captain Lang and aircraft spotter Holke, who had been riding with him, pulled him unconscious from the car. Field Marshal von Kluge was ordered to take over temporary command of Army Group B.

"Atlantic" became the code designation for the Canadian participation in Operation "Goodwood." Simonds's II Corps was ordered to support the British VIII Corps' right flank by capturing the various suburbs and villages along the east bank of the Orne. Eighth Brigade would lead off the Canadian attack behind an intensely concentrated barrage 45 minutes after the British armour had started to roll. Harry's 7th Brigade would follow later, crossing the river from the centre of Caen and occupying the twin city of Vaucelles. The 2nd Division would wait as a follow-up reserve, with specific tasks given by the flint-eyed Simonds to Foulkes's various brigade commanders.

Guy Simonds, in Harry's view, was "the brightest tactical army commander Canada had produced in any war. Where others fell asleep after two or three days on their feet, Guy could keep going, his brain still working at top speed. He had that amazing ability of being able to analyze any given situation swiftly and accurately, cutting through irrelevancies to the heart of the problem, then making up his mind. His orders were always clear, concise— straight to the point. But he was a hard man to work for.

"The performance standards and expectations he set for his subordinate commanders were so high it was impossible ever to satisfy him. Later, after he had promoted me, I tried talking to him privately as a friend about the way he ran roughshod over one of my own brigadiers and a regimental commander. He seemed genuinely surprised. 'Somebody had to speak to them, Harry. I did it because you didn't.' After that I kept my mouth shut.

"He mistrusted and detested Foulkes. But then we all detested Foulkes, so that was to his credit. Unfortunately, he didn't have much time for poor old Harry Crerar either. General Crerar was a good solid soul, part soldier, part politician. He could never understand how Simonds's mind worked. I know he thought Guy a little mad. But no one could ever replace him. Guy was the best we had."

On 18 July, as the first Americans entered St. Lô in the west, the 8th and 9th Canadian Infantry Brigades were carrying the 3rd Division assault across the Orne. Both were soon bogged down in heavy fighting. Harry waited.

"18 July. . . . One battalion ready to cross the Orne on order from the Divisional Commander. . . . Patrols were pushed over the river just after 1300 hours. . . . Assistance given by a member of the FFI† who was unfortunately killed. . . . By 2030 hours the battalion was across . . . quite

---

*A fractured skull, brain concussion and an eye injury.
†French Resistance.

a feat as very few boats were available—the majority swam or waded. . . .
A German bomb dropped 20 yards from the paymaster's vehicle during
twilight which rather shook him."

Things had not been quite that easy on the other fronts. At dawn, after
bombers dropped the heaviest tonnage of the war,[16] the first of the three
crack British armoured divisions that had squeezed onto the narrow bridgehead over the Orne rumbled up the slopes against the enemy line. German
troops in the forward positions offered little resistance. Most were still dazed
from the effects of the bombing and heavy shelling that preceded the attack.
But farther inland British losses began to mount as enemy troops in each
of the villages recovered their equilibrium and started fighting back.

The Leibstandarte Division, well dug in, sat waiting in five defence lines.
Out of range of the British guns and beyond the bomb pattern, rows of field
artillery, 88s and *Nebelwerfer* multibarrelled mortars straddled Bourguébus
Ridge. Gunners waited for the British to come into view. Under their
concentrated fire the Shermans began exploding like huge fireballs. The 11th
Armoured Division lost 126 of its tanks; the Guards Armoured Division
lost 60. Sepp Dietrich ordered out his Tigers and Panthers. By evening the
British attack had been halted. The tanks backed off and the troops dug in
for the night.

Meanwhile, in Caen, 2nd Division troops began moving forward in the
early evening to take up their battle positions. Divisional engineers were
bridging the Orne. It was the division's first exposure to fighting since the
disaster of Dieppe. The troops were green but eager. In their enthusiasm
next day, 2nd Division's artillery began shelling Harry's positions.

"19 July. . . . The Brigade moved across the Orne to the vicinity of Vaucelles-
Cormelles without incident. Capt. Baker acted as traffic control officer at
the bridge. It took all day to get everyone across. 2nd Division spent most
of the day splattering our new position with artillery fire. Try as we would
we could not stop it."

As the British VIII Corps armour began to withdraw, the army commander,
General Dempsey, ordered Simonds's II Canadian Corps to take over. Keller's
3rd Division was sent up to relieve the badly depleted British 11th Armoured
Division. Foulkes was instructed to advance his 2nd Division three miles
south of Caen and establish itself astride the kidney-shaped Verrières Ridge.
Foulkes handed the job to Brig. Hugh Young's 6th Infantry Brigade* bolstered
by the Essex Scottish Regiment detached from the 5th Brigade.

On the morning of 20 July, as the 6th Brigade crossed the Orne heading
toward the ridge, British troops of the 7th Armoured Division were

---

*Consisting of the South Saskatchewan Regiment, the Queen's Own Cameron Highlanders
of Canada and Les Fusiliers Mont-Royal.

approaching it from the east side of the arrow-straight road running from Caen to Falaise. British tanks and a company of the rifle brigade, supported by VIII Corps artillery, managed to smash their way across the road in the face of heavy opposition from I Panzer Corps. However, they failed to scale the ridge's 300-foot heights. After a hurried conference between the British and Canadian corps commanders, it was decided that the British tanks would withdraw east of the road and provide additional fire support to Young's brigade, which would then take the ridge with infantry.

The attack began in midafternoon. Les Fusiliers on the left flank made it forward to the Beauvoir and Troteval farms. Two companies were sent ahead to seize the village of Verrières. On the right, the Cameron Highlanders entered St. André-sur-Orne against light opposition and later managed to hold out against steady German shelling and several counterattacks. It was in the centre where the problems developed.

The South Saskatchewans moved quickly over the first thousand yards through the German forward positions. Then, from the low leaden overcast that had filled the skies all day, a heavy rain enveloped the battlefield. Further rocket attacks by the 24 Typhoons assigned to the operation were suspended. Blinded by the rain, artillery observation and supporting shellfire stopped.

Then the Germans struck.

Tanks of the Leibstandarte lumbered out of the rain directly into the path of the South Saskatchewans, who were advancing through the tall, wet grass. A furious battle exploded—men against tanks. During the course of the action the regiment's acting CO, Maj. G. R. Matthews, was killed together with 65 of his men. Another 142 were wounded or taken prisoner. Those who remained from the forward companies crawled or stumbled back through the rain and mud, pursued by German tanks and infantry.

The Essex Scottish, from southwestern Ontario, held the line behind the Saskatchewans. Commanded by Lieut.-Col. Bruce J. Macdonald, the men had been awake for 26 hours during their march to the front. Due to a mix-up of messing arrangements, most had had nothing to eat since dawn that day. On empty stomachs they waited anxiously to go into their first battle.

Macdonald explained: "We were in exposed static positions. It was nearly impossible to dig into the rock-hard soil. Fields of waist-high wheat stretched out to the base of Verrières Ridge. Any man sticking up his head was liable to be plugged by German marksmen. . . . Earlier, I had asked Brigadier Young to allow me to move in behind the Saskatchewan Regiment while we had artillery coverage. He refused. He was very snappy about it all."

The sight of the Saskatchewans streaming toward their lines in disorder followed by a fierce German counterattack unnerved them. In a panic, two of the regiment's lead companies took to their heels. Fortunately, the remainder held their ground and stopped the German advance. Throughout the night the men waited for brigade support. It never came.

"When I heard that some of my men had gone back to the rear area, I took a carrier and went to gather them up. When I found they were without weapons I marched them over to Brigade Headquarters where we were told that nothing could be issued until morning. I then instructed my 2IC [second-in-command] that as soon as the men were armed they were to be brought back into the line."

Early next morning Young summoned Macdonald back to Brigade HQ. Macdonald left at once only to find that the Brigadier had left to visit the Divisional Commander. "Word arrived that he had changed his mind and wanted me up at the front. Neither Brig. Young nor Gen. Foulkes seemed able to decide what exactly they wanted me to do with the battalion. On my way back to the line I ran into what was left of the battalion coming out."

As a result of the Verrières Ridge action, Brigadier Young sacked Macdonald later the same day for—as he reported to General Foulkes—"mishandling the Regiment."

Next morning the rain continued. Dietrich's panzers struck again, fracturing the Essex Scottish front and overrunning the two lead companies of Les Fusiliers who had spent the night holding Troteval Farm. If Young had not arrived in the nick of time with the Black Watch,[17] the 6th Brigade might have been destroyed. When the dust settled, Verrières Ridge remained in enemy hands. In the four days of fighting, 2nd Division suffered 1,149 casualties, of which 254 were fatal. The more experienced 3rd Division's losses were 386, with 89 of that number losing their lives.

9

Predictably, Eisenhower found the results of "Goodwood" and "Atlantic" disappointing. His deputy, Air Chief Marshal Tedder, a long-time critic of Montgomery's leadership, wrote the Supreme Commander on 20 July: "An overwhelming air bombardment opened the door, but there was no immediate determined deep penetration whilst the door remained open and we are now little beyond the farthest bomb craters. It is clear that there was no intention of making this operation the decisive one which you so clearly indicated."

According to U.S. Navy Capt. Harry C. Butcher, Eisenhower's naval aide, Tedder remarked somewhat callously that he "would support any recommendation" that the Supreme Commander might make toward the commander of 21st Army Group.

Eisenhower flew to France to meet with Montgomery. This was followed next day with a letter covering the substance of their conversations. The letter concluded with the observation that "eventually the American ground strength will necessarily be much greater than the British. But while we have equality in size we must go forward shoulder to shoulder with honors and sacrifices equally shared." In other words, British and Canadian forces were not doing their fair share of the fighting.

Both Eisenhower and Tedder were wrong. Neither seemed capable of understanding Montgomery's strategy. They had only to re-examine the "Ultra"* classified intelligence, the daily reports from the French Underground, and aerial reconnaissance photographs to appreciate the disaster facing the Germans. Operations "Goodwood" and "Atlantic" *had* produced positive results. German armoured units destined for the American front were quickly switched back to the British-Canadian sector in anticipation of Montgomery's breakout for Paris. The unsupported German front was now thin enough for Bradley's Operation "Cobra," his sweeping attack and breakout from the west designed to encircle the German forces and capture Paris.

The senior German commanders were demoralized. Army Group B reported on 20 July: "The extraordinary vigour and the colossal material superiority of the enemy in the fighting east of Caen on 18 and 19 July are indicated by the fact that he fired 103,000 artillery shells on the left flank of the 86th Corps and 1st ss Panzer Corps alone, and according to his own reports dropped in our positions 7,800 tons of bombs from 2,200 two and four-engined bombers."

Next day, von Kluge wrote a letter to Hitler, attaching one from Rommel that he had been sitting on for a week, hesitating to forward it because of its outspokenness. The Rommel letter, dated 15 July, was his personal appraisal of existing realities. In it he cited the German losses, lack of equipment and reinforcements, supply problems and mounting Allied air strength. "In these circumstances," he concluded, "we must expect that in the foreseeable future the enemy will succeed in breaking through our thinly held front, especially that of the 7th Army, and so thrust deep into France. . . . The unequal struggle is nearing its end. It is in my opinion necessary to draw the proper conclusion from the situation."

According to Lieutenant-General Speidel, his chief of staff, Rommel considered the letter a warning, a last chance for the German leader to come to his senses. If Hitler did not act, Rommel intended to take independent action to bring hostilities in France to an end.

After "Goodwood," von Kluge decided that Rommel's appreciation of the situation was correct: "The psychological effect on the fighting forces, especially the infantry, of such a mass of bombs, raining down on them with

---

*This intelligence was the result of breaking the German codes produced by the "Enigma" enciphering machine.

all the force of elemental nature, is a factor which must be given serious consideration. . . .

"I am able to report that the front has been held intact until now. . . . However . . . the moment is fast approaching when this overtaxed front line is bound to break up. . . . When the enemy once reaches the open country a properly coordinated command will be almost impossible, because of the insufficient mobility of our troops. I consider it my duty as the responsible commander on this front, to bring these developments to your notice in good time, my Führer.

"My last words at the Staff Conference south of Caen were: 'We must hold our ground, or if nothing happens to improve conditions, then we must die an honourable death on the battlefield.'"[18]

A day earlier, shortly past noon at Hitler's Rastenburg headquarters in East Prussia, a colonel on the General Staff, Count Klaus von Stauffenberg, placed a briefcase filled with a plastic explosive under the conference table during one of Hitler's planning sessions. The strikingly handsome 37-year-old von Stauffenberg, minus one eye and an arm from war wounds, waited outside the conference centre when the explosion occurred. Convinced that Hitler was dead, he left immediately by air for Berlin. The army conspirators intended making immediate overtures to the British and Americans for a separate peace to prevent Germany from being overrun by the Russians.

Then, to everyone's astonishment, while Wehrmacht generals prepared to issue orders to round up every Nazi official and Gestapo man in the major cities and place them behind bars, word came that Hitler had survived. Those involved in the plot hesitated, unwilling to act prematurely, while those not involved hesitated in view of the contradictory orders they were receiving. Orders coming from Berlin in the names of Generals Fromm and Hoepner and Field Marshal Witzleben were to be disregarded, according to the Hitlerites.

Von Kluge, who had taken over Rommel's old headquarters to be closer to the front, heard the news from Lieutenant-General Speidel upon his arrival at La Roche Guyon in late afternoon. First he telephoned Berlin and spoke to General Beck, who confirmed the Führer's death. Next, he telephoned Rastenburg and was told that Hitler was alive and to pay no attention to orders from the plotters. He called Berlin again, speaking to von Stauffenberg.

At 2000 hours teletyped orders arrived from Berlin stating Hitler was dead and that the army was now the only governmental authority. Who were the army commanders to believe? Even if Hitler wasn't dead, there was still time for a coup provided the C.-in-C. West (OB West) would join the plotters. Everything now depended on von Kluge.

The trim military governor of France, Gen. Count Karl-Heinrich von Stülpnagel, and other members of the conspiracy arrived during the early evening at La Roche Guyon to ask for his endorsement. But the Field Marshal was not prepared to dive into the scheme just yet. Instead, he invited them all to dinner. Late in the meal, the agitated von Stülpnagel pressed for a decision, telling his host that he had already issued orders back in Paris for the arrest of all Nazi officials, SS and Gestapo personnel. Von Kluge was furious and ordered his chief of staff to telephone Paris and cancel the orders. Too late. The army, without bloodshed, had already taken control. All potential Nazi party troublemakers were safely under lock and key.

Von Kluge suggested von Stülpnagel return to Paris, change into civilian clothes and hide. But von Stülpnagel was made of stouter stuff. With a heavy heart he arrived in the city at the same time General Blumentritt, von Kluge's chief of staff, turned up. Blumentritt informed von Stülpnagel that on von Kluge's orders he had been relieved of his command. Blumentritt then arranged immediate release of SS Lieutenant-General Oberg. To save face for both the Gestapo and the Wehrmacht, the C.-in-C. West War Diary recorded: "In the ensuing discussions it was decided that the whole affair should be publicly described as an alarm exercise carried out by two parties."

Von Stülpnagel received orders to report to Field Marshal Keitel at OKW. Instead of obeying, he drove off to visit some of the old French battlefields where he had fought as a young subaltern during World War I. Along the way he left the car and stepped into a canal, where he put a pistol to his head, but succeeded only in blinding himself. Next he threw himself into the water, hoping to drown, but soldiers found him and rushed him to hospital where in delirium he mentioned Rommel's name, thereby implicating him as one of the conspirators. For his part in the conspiracy von Stülpnagel was hanged in Berlin on 30 August 1944.

Stunned, deafened and with an injured arm and scores of wood splinters in his body from the conference blast, Hitler exacted his revenge. Some of the leading conspirators took their own lives, but the majority, together with their wives, children and relatives, were turned over to the Gestapo. The chief conspirators were either shot or hung on meathooks with piano wire while newsreel cameramen recorded their death throes. The hunt for conspirators continued to widen until the German collapse. Relations, friends, even friends of friends, were drawn into Himmler's net. In the early morning hours of 24 April 1945, with Russian troops already in the Berlin suburbs, the last 25 "conspirators" were executed.*

A few days after the attempt, von Kluge spoke to the man who on 21 March 1943 had tried blowing up Hitler and himself and failed. The man, Col. Freiherr von Gersdorff, later General Hausser's chief of staff, urged the Field Marshal to make peace with the Allies and "become the greatest man in German history."

---

*More than 153 conspirators of the July plot died from suicide and outright murder. Their wives and children survived.

Von Kluge placed his hand on Gersdorff's shoulder and told him with a sad smile: "Gersdorff, Field Marshal von Kluge is not a great man."

Like most men of the Waffen-SS, Kurt disapproved of the Hitler plot. The whole business outraged his sense of honour. Regardless of his private thoughts or misgivings on how the German leader had been conducting the war, he had, like everyone else who wore the double lightning flash of the SS on his tunic, given his oath of loyalty to the Führer. Months later, when he and General Eberbach were prisoners of war in the Kensington Cage in England and had become good friends, Eberbach told him about discussions with Rommel and his part in the conspiracy, reminding him that as far back as 1925 Hitler had authorized his own overthrow in *Mein Kampf* when he wrote: "If a government is using its apparatus of power to lead a nation to destruction, rebellion is not merely right, but the duty of each and every citizen."

Kurt was shocked. "If I had known that I would have shot you from across the table."

SS loyalties died hard.

Results of the plot on the Wehrmacht were not long in coming. Himmler, already in control of all security forces, became C.-in-C. of the Home Army, which supplied all field commanders at the front with reinforcements. The Waffen-SS was given equal status with the other three services, and soldiers were no longer permitted the traditional army salute. Henceforth the Nazi salute was to be used exclusively.

Finally, and most demeaning of all to the once-proud officer corps, General Guderian, acting as army chief of the General Staff, ordered that "every General Staff officer must be a National Socialist Political Officer . . . cooperating in the political indoctrination of younger commanders in accordance with the tenets of the Führer."

Like von Rundstedt, Guderian had known some of their fellow officers who had discussed plans to overthrow Hitler but refused to join, realizing that it would lead to civil war, since nearly all younger Wehrmacht and Waffen-SS officers were opposed to the idea. As long as the Allies insisted on unconditional surrender of Germany's eastern and western armies, the younger German officers intended to fight to the last. Even an unconditional surrender with a promised caveat of a fair peace to a German anti-Hitler government would not have ended the war. The conspirators asked for such a declaration, but their request had been ignored. Allied aims appeared to German military eyes to be not only the destruction of national socialism but of Germany itself. As such, there could be no point to an unconditional surrender. The war was lost, but the Allies would be made to pay a heavy price for their intransigence.

After the war Churchill admitted the error when he observed: "It seems we've killed the wrong pig!"

Lieut.-Col. Bruce Macdonald of the Essex Scottish was a bitterly unhappy man after the battle of Verrières Ridge. To be sacked for "mishandling the Regiment" on his second day at the front was a blemish a man took with him to his grave. He considered himself a victim of circumstances. Any blame attached to him for the regiment's conduct in the face of the enemy he felt should be shared equally by Brigadier Young and the Divisional Commander, General Foulkes. As Macdonald saw it, the only "mishandling" done by him had been under orders from his brigade and divisional commanders.

Like other regiments in the 6th Brigade, the Essex Scottish were promised artillery and air support for the attack. When heavy rain suspended that support, Macdonald felt that the Brigadier should either have withdrawn the South Saskatchewans to the Essex Scottish line or brought forward the Essex Scottish to bolster the Saskatchewans' attack. Young did neither. As noted earlier, the Saskatchewans' acting commander had died along with many of his men and those that survived death or capture had retreated in disorder.

Over the next few days Macdonald waited in limbo for final disposition of his army career. Angrily, he complained to Young about the incident report he had written to Foulkes. Much of what the Brigadier had stated as fact was patently untrue. Grudgingly, Young withdrew and rewrote his report but only after Macdonald had written Foulkes a long, detailed outline of the actual events.

At first Foulkes agreed to transferring him to a new command but, after further discussion with Young, changed his mind. The sacking and regimental disgrace would stand. If a scapegoat was needed for 6th Brigade's failure in Foulkes's report to Corps HQ, Macdonald was going to be it. Young notified him that he would be returned to Canada for "Adjutant General's disposition"—a polite way of sending him home in disgrace.

So strongly did Macdonald feel that he was being victimized, he sat down and wrote an appeal to the Corps Commander, fully prepared to take the matter all the way up to the Minister of National Defence if necessary. While he awaited a reply from General Simonds, new orders arrived transferring him to SHAEF* as Canadian army representative in the newly formed standing Courts of Inquiry investigating war crimes.

Disquieting reports about suspected shootings of unarmed British and Canadian prisoners of war in Normandy had been filtering back to SHAEF in London for several weeks. They came from French eyewitnesses and several Canadian soldiers who had escaped after capture. The Courts of Inquiry were given the job of finding the facts.

The army couldn't have picked a better man for the job than Bruce Macdonald. Born in Lunenburg County, Nova Scotia, Macdonald had grown up in Medicine Hat, graduated from the University of Alberta with a law

---

*Supreme Headquarters Allied Expeditionary Force.

degree and taken postgraduate studies at Harvard. He worked as a junior with an established law practice in Windsor, Ontario, until 1929, when he was appointed city solicitor and joined the militia. By the late 1930s he had become a militia captain and met Permanent Force officers Captains Charles Foulkes and Harry Foster at Wolseley Barracks in London, Ontario, during the regular summer training exercises. Foulkes had made no impression on him, but Harry had. At their first meeting in the officers' mess Harry had picked out his Nova Scotian origins after listening to his pronunciation[19] of several words. Fifty years later Macdonald remained impressed by that feat.

He went overseas as a major with the 2nd Division during the summer of 1940 and, like Harry, spent his next years training in England. After a brief stint as an instructor back in Canada in 1942—by which luckily he missed Dieppe—he returned to England to be appointed commander of the Battle School set up at Goodwood Park racetrack in Sussex. Promoted to lieutenant-colonel, he took over the Essex Scottish in May 1943. At 41, he was the oldest man in the regiment and one of its toughest. Within weeks he had his men marching 40 miles in under 18 hours, specified by General Montgomery as the ideal criterion of troop performance. "Even office and administration staff were ordered to complete the first 25 miles. The marches were great morale boosters because there wasn't another regiment in the division that could match us. The men liked to brag about that."

The Essex Scottish arrived in Normandy in July as part of Brig. Sherwood Lett's 4th Infantry Brigade. Lett, a Rhodes scholar and lawyer who had been wounded at Dieppe, was Macdonald's idea of the perfect army officer, "highly intelligent, always courteous, willing to listen to any sensible idea and prepared to change his opinion if a suggestion was proved to his satisfaction." The two lawyers got on well. Unfortunately, during Operation "Atlantic," the Essex Scottish were switched to Young's 6th Brigade.

Brigadier Young, a Permanent Force officer, had served in the ranks during World War I. He had little patience with self-appointed militia "experts"—particularly lawyers—who had never heard a shot fired in anger but began offering gratuitous advice on the eve of a major battle. The fact that Macdonald's suggestions might merit consideration apparently never entered his mind. The Essex Scottish were moved into a reserve position behind the centre of his front. Within 48 hours this mutual antagonism finished Macdonald's career as a battlefield commander.

Still smarting from the loss of his command, he faced his new job with a combination of curiosity and anticipation. He knew little about what constituted a battlefield atrocity and even less about war crimes. But he was willing to learn.

"In 1941, I attended a meeting called by Maj.-Gen. Victor Odlum of all 2nd Division officers at Brighton. He stated categorically that 'the Canadians will take no prisoners.' Everyone accepted it. What did we know? We assumed those were the rules. We were never told anything else. Later, at the Battle School, I taught everyone to go in with guns blazing. If something was booby-trapped then you pushed a German at it to try it out. Prisoners were never mentioned. . . .

"Two officers of the Essex Scottish served under Major-General Vokes in Italy and had read Vokes's bulletin stating: 'We will take no prisoners.' Once the senior British commander, General Sir Oliver Leese, got wind of the affair he ordered all bulletins and evidence of them destroyed."

Long after the war ended, Harry observed that "battlefield atrocities are generally only uncovered by advancing armies. Russian atrocities against German and Polish[20] troops were discovered during the first days of the Russian campaign when the Germans were advancing. German atrocities only came to light as the Russians began retaking their lost territories. Similarly, the knowledge of how the Germans conducted themselves in Normandy was not completely understood until we started advancing inland. What we discovered was not pleasant. When a soldier sees or hears about his pals being butchered he gets mad. He swears to get even on the first opportunity that presents itself—and usually does.

"It may be gunning down a single Hun who tries surrendering, or bayoneting a wounded German teenager whimpering for water in a ditch. Then again it may be more serious, like frying an entire platoon with a Crocodile [flame-thrower tank] as they come out of their bunker with a white flag and their hands up. At one time or another most front-line troops lose their tempers and take it out on the enemy that they have learned to hate. We are all guilty. But the enemy appears more guilty than we because any evidence of our excesses remains buried safely behind our advance."

What exactly constituted an atrocity? Or a war crime? Macdonald was about to find out.

10

First investigations by the SHAEF standing Courts of Inquiry concerned shootings near the villages of Pavie and Mouen.

It was learned that on 8 June the headquarters and headquarters company of the reconnaissance battalion of the 12th SS had established itself on the grounds of the Château d'Audrieu, near the village of Pavie. The command post had been set up under a large sycamore tree behind the château. Three Canadian soldiers were observed leaving the CP under escort and ordered into the woods by an officer where they were summarily shot. Their unburied bodies were discovered later by British troops who overran the position.

A short time later three more prisoners were marched into the woods and executed. The three, Riflemen D.S. Gold, J.D. MacIntosh and W. Thomas, were all members of the Royal Winnipeg Rifles. Gold's body, when found, still wore the Red Cross armband of a stretcher-bearer. Seven other Canadian bodies were uncovered nearby. Although there were no eyewitnesses to these killings, it was assumed that they had died like their comrades from heavy small-arms fire. During late afternoon on the same day, 13 more Royal Winnipegs from A Company's No. 9 Platoon were executed within 100 yards of the CP with German officers and NCOs in attendance.

There had been no fighting in the vicinity of the château, nor had any Canadian troops ever been in action in that area. The investigators determined that the unit's commander, Sturmbannführer Gerhard Bremer, had been wounded earlier in the day and that the battalion's second-in-command, Hauptsturmführer von Reitzenstein, probably ordered the prisoners to be executed in reprisal. Obersturmführer Hansman, the escort officer, and Oberscharführer Stun, who commanded the firing squads, simply followed those orders.

The second incident concerned seven prisoners—six from the Queen's Own and one from the 1st Hussars—who had been taken back to headquarters of the 12th SS Engineering Battalion in the village of Mouen, some distance from the front on 17 June. The men had been reported missing after the battle at Le Mesnil-Patry on 11 June.

After several hours interrogation, the Canadians were marched to the village outskirts and executed by a firing party composed of 14 grenadiers under the command of a senior NCO. Local French civilians were ordered to dig a grave for the bodies. Sturmbannführer Mueller, the battalion commander, had been heard ordering his company commanders to take no prisoners.

The executions at the Abbaye Ardenne and elsewhere had yet to be investigated.

By the time Macdonald's request to see General Simonds was granted, he was already hard at work on the SHAEF investigations and receiving better pay and allowances than any regimental commander. Nevertheless, he remained annoyed over his dismissal by Brigadier Young.

"It's your right to pursue the matter, if you wish," Simonds informed him cryptically after hearing his side of the story. "However, my advice is to drop the matter. These things have a way of sorting out themselves.[21] You're much better placed and qualified for the job you have now."

Macdonald accepted his advice.

The 12th SS took over a sector of the German line between La Hogue and Emiéville on 20 July, with the 21st Panzer Division on its right and Kurt's old unit, the 1st SS Panzer Leibstandarte Division on its left. Twelfth SS divisional strength had been reduced to approximately 2,000 fighting men and 50 tanks. With so much equipment and the best and bravest of its men gone, it was no longer a division but a collection of decimated units. Kurt reorganized what remained into three battle groups, each named after its unit commander: Waldmüller, Olboetter and the redoubtable Hugo Kraas.

A two-week period of comparative peace and quiet followed. "Although the men were rested and the equipment overhauled, no refits came and the overall weakness was not rectified."

The division's main task, like its sister divisions', was construction of three defence lines to maintain the grip south of Caen. Realizing that enemy patrols would be out searching for information on German strength and positions, Kurt ordered his companies to post a few sentries and sleep by day. At sundown, every company would stand-to and maintain an alert throughout the hours of darkness.

"In this way I was able to neutralize the enemy patrols and prevent them from taking back information. . . . All tank and artillery companies were employed on the construction of the defence lines. The first was a series of battle outposts. Along the second I had assembled approximately 40 dummy tanks backed up by five real ones. The tanks, made of wood, were assembled with the idea of concealing the true location of the tank regiment which at this time was down to about 50 runners. The tanks were located south of Vimont where they were camouflaged and ready to move should a breakthrough occur."

An anxious Field Marshal von Kluge arrived unannounced one night on an inspection tour. At 0400 hours Kurt accompanied him on foot to his front lines.

"When the British attack comes, how long can you hold?"

"Until there is no one left, Herr Feldmarschall," Kurt replied.

Von Kluge nodded morosely and departed.

To Kurt's delight, 22 new Mk IV tanks arrived. But before going into action they needed complete overhauls and their guns calibrated. On 5 August the 12th SS was relieved by the 272nd Infantry Division and moved back to an area near the Laison River to act as a mobile armoured reserve.

"In order that the Allies should believe 12th SS was still in its old area, I left behind, near Vimont, a wireless set in a Volkswagen with orders to transmit on the tank regiment's frequency." His signals were in fact picked up by Canadian army special wireless units and relayed to Corps HQ as proof of 12th SS presence in the area.

"I realized that this period of rest north of Falaise could only be as a drop in the ocean. While in the Vimont area I had noticed great activity going on in the Allied lines. With the situation deteriorating so rapidly on the Orne front, an attempt to break the German defences around Caen was overdue."

Reports of Allied atrocities were coming to light through the rigid German chain of command. On 8 June Colonel Luxenburger, regimental commander of the 130th Artillery Regiment of the Panzer Lehr Division, had been captured by a reconnaissance unit of the Inns of Court Regiment. Taken with him was Battalion Commander Major Zeissler, Captain Count Clary-Aldringen, his adjutant, and six other ranks. After the German officers refused to serve as shields on the reconnaissance cars, two British officers tied up Luxenburger and beat him into unconsciousness. Dripping with blood, he was then bound to the front of the lead vehicle. The others were executed, with the exception of Count Clary, who was severely wounded. Shortly thereafter the reconnaissance cars were hit by German shellfire. Luxenburger, who had lost an arm in World War I, was freed but died later in a German hospital. Count Clary managed to escape back to German lines, where his wounds were treated. In retaliation three Canadian prisoners were executed the following day by Sturmbannführer Siebken, Untersturmführer Schnabel and others.[22]

On 17 June a French civilian reported: "Four German soldiers, two of them wounded, were in a cellar with us. . . . An English patrol came . . . and threw a smoke shell into the cellar window. We shouted 'Civilians! French civilians!' Shivering, we went outside. But when the two young German soldiers came: 'Rarrr-Rarrr!' They fell down dead. Then the two wounded ones were led away. I got the impression that the English didn't take many prisoners."

After overrunning a German position south of Caen during the battle for Verrières Ridge, a German-speaking Canadian officer invited a group of Leibstandarte troops to surrender, promising that nothing would happen to them. Thirty-five men came forward with their hands raised. As they approached, the Canadians suddenly opened fire. In the resulting melée a few managed to escape and made their way back to the German lines. An incident report was filed to OB West by the tank group involved, with a copy forwarded to the International Red Cross, witnessed by General Gausse, Lieutenant-General Speidel and SS Gruppenführer und Generalleutnant der Waffen-SS Fritz Kraemer.

Due to wet weather, Bradley's Operation "Cobra" in the American sector could not begin until 25 July. The British and Canadians were asked to hold the bulk of the German forces from slipping away westwards to the American front. Operation "Spring" was designed to do what "Goodwood" had already failed to do with armour and infantry a few days earlier. Brigades from both the 2nd and 3rd Divisions participated. The 7th Brigade was not part of the attacking force but positioned as reserve behind Cunningham's 9th. A fortunate circumstance, since everything imaginable that could go wrong did go wrong.

The ambitious attack, to be completed in two phases, was never properly controlled or directed from the start. By the time it ended on the evening of 25 July, the two-day action had cost 450 lives with 1,000 wounded or taken prisoner. The Fort Garrys lost 11 tanks in addition to self-propelled anti-tank guns and carriers. The Black Watch Regiment from Montreal lost its CO, Lieut.-Col. Steven Cantlie, and later Maj. F.P. Griffin, who took over when Cantlie had been hit. Of the 300 men who had started the attack in that sector, less than 50 made it back. Only the Dieppe raid had been a worse disaster for the Canadian army.

Simonds, sitting back at Corps HQ, believed until late afternoon of the second day that the operation was proceeding according to plan. Keller and Foulkes were equally out of touch with the reality of the situation on their divisional fronts. When everything appeared hopeless, Brigadier Cunningham, Lieutenant-Colonel Petch of the North Novies and Lieutenant-Colonel Christiansen of the Stormont, Dundas and Glengarry Highlanders confronted Keller with the scope of their disaster and the futility of continuing the attack. Harsh words were exchanged.

Brigadier Young delivered the same information to General Foulkes— although without the same degree of forcefulness used by the 3rd Division's battlefield commanders. Foulkes agreed. Once Simonds possessed all the facts, he went to the Army Commander and recommended that the operation be called off. The debacle came as a bitter blow to his prestige, and he blamed himself for not keeping closer tabs on the battle as it developed.

In the wake of the operation's failure, Cunningham, Petch and Christiansen were sacked. Simonds wanted leaders the troops would follow, not commanders who simply issued orders expecting them to be obeyed.

Harry said: "I felt sorry for Dan Cunningham. It had been his bad luck to come up against the best and most experienced German division in the line.* But Guy was as much to blame for the 'Spring' mess as anyone. He hadn't done his homework.[23] I suppose if he had used the 7th instead of the 9th Brigade, then in all likelihood I would have been the one he'd have sacked."

After a month of practising infantry and tank tactics, Operation "Cobra" began on 25 July with a carpet-bombing of the German line by 1,500 Flying Fortresses. Facing Bradley's awesome force of 19 divisions and 750 tanks were only 110 German tanks—most of them obsolete—and nine divisions, of which half were merely remnants. The great breakout battle for the conquest of Europe began.

Four days later, after furious fighting through hedgerow country, Bradley's forces had reached the coast at Avranches. Here, by prearrangement, the armies split. Lieut.-Gen. George S. Patton's Third U.S. Army[24] began a pell-

---

*1st SS Panzer Division Leibstandarte.

mell drive through Brittany, while Lieut.-Gen. Courtney Hodges's First U.S. Army* maintained its pressure against Paul Hausser's Seventh German Army.

As the enemy front began crumbling, Montgomery and Bradley expected the Germans would fall back before the Allied thrust and make a stand at the Seine. With the bridges gone, any crossing would have to be done at night over temporary bridges that would certainly be destroyed by Allied aircraft at first light. For the Allied generals it was an enticing thought: two German armies trapped with their backs to the river. Even von Kluge, Hausser and Eberbach agreed that the sooner they got their armies moving inland the more men could be saved.

Hitler, however, had different ideas. He decided to counterattack, with the 3rd Panzer Division, elements of the 4th, and a panzer grenadier division smashing through the American front at Avranches and Mortain. But to assemble what was left of the depleted armoured panzer divisions for a concentrated thrust would bring down the wrath of Allied air attacks. Ultimately, as von Kluge knew, two German armies would be lost. In light of his involvement in the Hitler plot, however, the Field Marshal was afraid to argue. His generals, including Sepp Dietrich, agreed that for anyone to question the Führer now would be suicidal.

On 3 August, Eberbach and Dietrich met with Gen. Walter Warlimont, Colonel-General Jodl's deputy chief of operations, who had been sent by air to deliver Hitler's lunatic plan of attack in person. A record of their meeting went into the Fifth Panzer Army War Diary (Eberbach's Panzer Group West had been rechristened Fifth Panzer Army).

Dietrich: If the ss divisions are pulled out south of Caen the enemy will attack there and break through.

Warlimont: However, the ss divisions are not in their proper place there; they are employed in an immobile role not at the focal point of the enemy's effort.

Eberbach: The infantry divisions now approaching will be committed there as soon as possible, but the ss divisions must be held ready in the rear to support the front. The main question remains how the front can be held in the long run against an enemy so far superior in material.

Warlimont: Two ss brigades can be moved from Denmark; the homeland and occupied France are being combed through for all available material.

Eberbach: Moving in the ss brigades will take from eight to ten days; that is too long. Pulling out the ss divisions and launching them in the direction of Avranches takes at least three or four days. And we do not know what the situation will be there then.

---

*Hodges took over the U.S. First Army from Bradley on 1 August when Bradley became commander of the expanded 12th Army Group directly under Eisenhower.

Later, Dietrich recalled: "There was only one person to blame for this stupid, impossible operation. That madman Adolf Hitler. It was a Führer Order. What else could we do?"

Montgomery and Bradley learned of the impending attack on the evening of 6 August. Countermeasures were organized to deal with it. Both generals realized very quickly the enormity of Hitler's blunder. The Germans intended thrusting themselves into a dangerous salient. By pinching it off at its base between the towns of Falaise and Alençon, von Kluge's two armies would be trapped. It was almost too good to be true.

As promised by Montgomery, the First Canadian Army under Lieutenant-General Crerar came into existence on 25 July. A proud moment for Canada. However, the reason for its creation was more practical than one of political pride. By agreeing to replace 1 Canadian Corps in Italy with one of their own, the British had made Crerar's army possible. It ensured that Canada would supply the thousands of support troops behind the front lines so necessary for any modern army to function. While Mackenzie King and his cabinet colleagues might worry over the conscription issue and lack of volunteers back in Canada, their problems paled beside those of Churchill and his cabinet. Britain simply had no more men to send.

Lieutenant-General Crocker's 1 British Corps now came under Crerar, a cosmetic arrangement, since Montgomery decided the issues, leaving his two army commanders—Dempsey and Crerar—to pass the orders on to their respective corps commanders, who would then handle details at the divisional level. But Crocker balked at the idea of serving under an inexperienced "colonial" army commander. Jarred by his attitude at their first meeting, Crerar asked for Crocker's objections in writing and then turned to Montgomery for advice. In a private meeting Monty lectured both men on the need for cooperation. Harmony was restored.

The last two divisions of Crerar's army arrived from England in July: the 4th Armoured Division under its youthful commander, 33-year-old Maj.-Gen. George Kitching, recently returned from Italy, and Maj.-Gen. Stanislaw Maczek's 1st Polish Armoured Division. Both units were made up of raw inexperienced troops.

To Harry, the Poles "were a tight-lipped glum-looking lot with shaven heads and a grim determination to kill as many Germans as they could get their hands on. . . . At O Group meetings Maczek usually prefixed every sentence with 'Ze focking Gairman bastards' before getting to his point."

After 55 continuous days on the front line, Keller's 3rd Division was relieved by the fresh, eager troops of Kitching's 4th Armoured Division. "They arrived wearing incredibly clean uniforms in their new tanks with pennants flying. Our filthy lot were not impressed."

"2 August. . . . Inspection of the Brigade by Rod Keller at 1000 hours. It went off well. Afterwards I asked Bennett to hold an informal O Group with the men and give them the larger picture plus answer any questions. I think they all have a right to know what is going on. It's their lives we're playing with. . . . Had a talk later with Rod. He sounded worried. Apparently Guy is putting the heat on everyone after our 'Spring' fiasco. . . .

"4 August. . . . Conference at Army HQ. Gen. Crerar put us in the picture for Operation 'Totalize.' Guy then took over. This sounds like the big one. I hope so. The troops are getting restless with nothing to occupy them except smelly . . . women and too much wine. . . . Bashed my knee against the dashboard on the way back. . . . It hurts like hell. . . . Several amusing letters waiting for me from the boys and Mollie. . . . Doc says I'll be down at least two days with this knee. Damn! . . . Bennett is off to Corps HQ tomorrow. Rumour that he is to be new CO of the Essex Scottish. Jack Stevens takes over officially as my new Brigade Major. . . . I hope he has managed to retain his 'Kiska' sense of humour. . . .

"5 August. . . . Genls. Simonds and Keller arrived for an inspection this afternoon. Meldram handled the parade that included the Canadian Scottish band decked out in kilts. . . . It was Guy's turn to give the troops a pep talk à la Monty—but not quite with the same flair. . . . I'll give him credit, he does try. . . .

"6 August. . . . Knee is much better. Attended Div. O Group in the afternoon on 'Totalize.' It will be strictly a 2nd Div., 4th Armd. Div. and 51st Highland Div. show under Guy's direction. 3rd Div. will be the reserve. . . . The Brigade is to move from the rest area to the Fleury-sur-Orne area south of Caen. . . . Held my own O Group when we got back."

11

This time Simonds left nothing to chance. Since it was obvious to the Germans from which direction the attack would come, any plan had to rely on a combination of surprise and innovation. On both counts he rose splendidly to the occasion.

For the infantry to overcome the German anti-tank and mortar positions that had so devastated the armour in the "Goodwood" battles, Simonds invented the forerunner of the modern Armoured Personnel Carrier (APC) to carry the troops into battle (nicknamed "Holyrollers"). He outlined his ideas to divisional commanders for the first phase of Operation "Totalize."

"The infantry accompanying the armour to first objectives in Phase One must go straight through with the armour. Arrangements have been made for about 30 stripped 'Priest' chassis[25] to be available to each of the infantry divisions. . . . The balance of personnel required to be carried through to the first or any intermediate objectives must be mounted under divisional arrangements. The essentials are that the infantry shall be carried in bullet- and splinter-proof vehicles to their actual objectives."

The advance started in the early evening and continued throughout the night. At one hour before midnight on 7 August a massive air attack by over 1,000 of Air Marshal Harris's heavy bombers hit the enemy defences on the flanks. Close tactical bombing support for advancing troops had never been attempted before at night. Target drops for the master bombers were defined by radio-directed pathfinders and illuminated coloured artillery star shells.

Thirty minutes later the tightly packed assault columns of tanks and infantry crossed the start line toward the bursting bombs and artillery barrage. Navigating tanks with gapping teams of flail tanks and AVREs to clear mines led each column. To maintain direction, drivers followed the steady tracer fire from the Bofors guns on the flanks and the reflective glow from searchlights beaming at the low clouds.

The dense lines, each only 16 yards wide—four vehicles abreast—rumbled forward slowly into the darkness, the dust and bombglow. A few feet—no more—separated the successive columns. Sherman tanks and Simonds's Holy- rollers carrying in the main assault force followed behind the leaders. Coming in behind them were the infantry's support weapons, armoured recovery vehicles, ambulances and bulldozers. Reserve tanks brought up the rear.

In six parallel columns they moved down either side of the Falaise road behind a barrage of 360 field and medium guns. Artillery fire straddled the road across the assault front, lifting 200 yards every two minutes to keep pace with the advancing columns until eventually reaching the limit of their range. The bombers departed. The guns fell silent. Then through the swirling dust and smoke the fighting began.

The German 89th Infantry Division faced the attack. Four days earlier it had relieved the Leibstandarte so that it could join the absurd operation against the Americans at Avranches. The fresh 10,500 men of the 89th, detached from Fifteenth Army, were mostly inexperienced troops of German and non-German extraction over 40 and under 18 years of age. In reserve, some distance behind them at the Laison River, lay the 12th ss.

On the airless afternoon of 7 August, as the Canadian forces for "Totalize" moved up into position under huge clouds of dust outside of Caen, Kurt received an appeal for help from the 271st Infantry Division. The unit was struggling to hold off a British assault across the Orne near Grimbosq forest. The 12th ss liaison officers had been sent up to the 271st and 89th Divisions to keep him informed on trouble spots as they appeared. He wanted no last- minute surprises. Quickly, Kraas rushed off with 20 tanks and 200 men to help out.

That night by candlelight Kurt wrote a birthday letter to Gerhild, his youngest, who would be a year old in a few days. In reality the letter was to Kate. "In the last weeks we have often spoken about the hopelessness of our situation in the fight and cursed war with all its terror. But why don't we end it? Why go on with this crazy fighting? Desperately, we search for an answer. Officers and grenadiers see the defeat coming but yet nobody thinks of putting down his arms and saving his own life. The political aim of the Allied powers—unconditional surrender—is considered more cruel than the cruelest death."

Earlier he had courtmartialed one of his young grenadiers for the rape of a French girl and with heavy heart sentenced him to death. There was no excuse for troops under his command to act like Russian barbarians. He attended the execution. The girl's father, the mayor of the village and the curé were brought in as witnesses.

When news of the Canadian attack reached him in the early hours of 8 August, the Canadians were already beyond their first objectives. He jumped on a motorbike and raced up to 89th Division's HQ at Urville to find out exactly what was happening. Due to bombing and incessant fighter attacks the 89th's divisional commander hadn't the slightest idea of the situation. Before Kurt left, he recalled Kraas at once from the 271st Division and ordered Waldmüller to take his battle group with about 20 tanks and head north to Cintheaux and block the Falaise road. Kraas, when he arrived, was to join Waldmüller in a counterattack.

Kurt borrowed a scout car and went out to the Falaise road to see the situation for himself. He arrived in the midst of a bombing attack. "I got out of my car and my knees were trembling, the sweat was pouring down my face and my clothes were soaked with perspiration. It was not that I was particularly anxious for myself because my experiences of the last five years had inured me against fear of death, but I realized that if I failed now and if I did not deploy my division correctly, the Allies would be through to Falaise and the German armies in the west completely trapped. I knew how weak my division was and the double task which confronted me at that time gave me some of the worst moments I have ever had in my life."

The Canadians were having their troubles too. Although Phase I objectives had been reached, the momentum of Simonds's advance had slowed. The areas behind the lines were packed with men, vehicles and equipment. The Polish and Canadian armoured divisions, despite a stream of impatient urgings to keep moving, were having great difficulty getting themselves up to the start line through the masses of men, equipment and choking dust.

A bombing sortie by 492 Fortresses of the U.S. Eighth Air Force opened Phase II shortly past noon. The bombing run from the coast led to a rail- and road-crossing target. Unfortunately, there were two identical crossings along the route and the master bomber dropped his target marker of yellow smoke on the wrong one. The rest followed. Troops and equipment were uncovered and in the open preparing to move off as the bombs began falling on their positions. Quickly, identification flares were lit to show the American pilots their error. Either no one had told the Americans that the Canadians were using yellow smoke to signify their front line or Simonds's HQ had not been advised that the Americans would be using yellow smoke as target indicators. The more yellow smoke the frantic Canadians put up the more bombs fell. Close to 1,500 tons were dropped on both the Germans and Canadians through what the U.S. Air Force historians termed "gross errors on the part of two twelve-plane groups."

The 3rd Division TAC HQ (Tactical Headquarters) received several direct hits. General Keller, wounded in the hand, arm and leg and in great pain, was loaded onto a stretcher. "Roberts!" he yelled to his batman. "Give me my revolver. I'm going to shoot the first goddam American I see."

Brigadier Blackader took over temporary command of the division.

The Polish armoured division had over 300 killed and wounded; the North Shore Regiment, in convoy and bombed as it moved through the village of Faubourg-de-Vaucelles, lost 100 officers and men. Fortunately, most of the bombs dropped where they should—on the German 89th Division. Ten of the Fortresses were brought down by flak.

As an aftermath to this tragedy the popular Keller arrived back at a Canadian general field hospital close to death. Possibly because of his rank, the normal procedure of marking a black cross on the forehead of a wounded man given morphine had not been followed. During his trip to the rear a succession of sympathetic medics had given him injections until his heart stopped. Luckily, the doctors were able to revive him. But it took a week for him to recover consciousness. He was invalided back to England. Keller's war was over.*

When the bombing attack ended, Kurt saw a disorderly mob of panicky troops from the 89th rushing toward him through the fields and along the road. It was the first time he had ever seen German soldiers running from the enemy. Before their retreat turned into a rout, he lit a cigar and stepped forward confidently.

"Where are you all heading?" he shouted. Those nearest slowed and stopped. "You're not going to leave me here alone to face the Allied attack, are you?"

---

*Eight years after the war Keller's weakened heart gave out during a memorial visit to the Normandy battlefields.

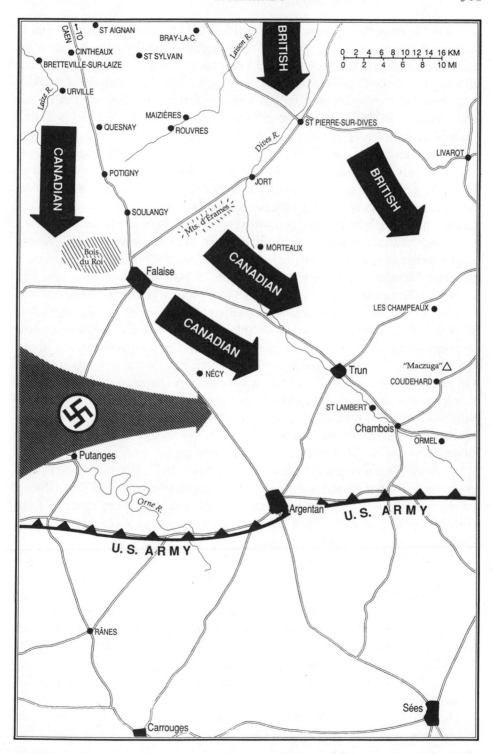

The Falaise Gap.

Someone laughed and their panic subsided. He got them organized building defensive positions on either side of the highway. Sheepishly, the men set to work. Kraas and his tanks arrived two hours later and joined Waldmüller in a combined tank and infantry attack. Later, Waldmüller's enthusiasm nearly cost him his unit when the Polish armoured division came within an ace of encircling his entire battle group. The Poles beat off the attack, inflicting heavy German losses.

By day's end the German line had been forced back nearly five miles, yet the lead Canadian troops were still 12 miles from Falaise. Kurt decided to organize a new defence line in the Laison Valley. He ordered Waldmüller to pull out and make for the village of Maizières beyond St. Sylvain; Kraas, to take up position in the Quesnay Wood and protect the left flank. Wünsche's battle group would hold the centre. The entire front was covered by divisional artillery that included a Luftwaffe flak regiment with 37 valuable dual-purpose 88s and *Nebelwerfer*. The change of 12th SS positions was duly noted by Allied aerial reconnaissance and resulted in a prompt attack by the Canadians.

The 12th SS position at the front remained precarious. Its strength had sunk to 500 fighting men and a few tanks along a divisional sector extending approximately nine miles. The only help available was the remains of the 89th Infantry Division, which, as Kurt admitted, "were worth very little. On the other hand 85th Division was on the point of coming in, and in fact, cyclists companies were already arriving." He advised General Eberbach "that if help is not forthcoming in the immediate future I cannot hold myself responsible for the future defence of Falaise. My troops have been in action practically continuously since D-Day and are in urgent need of rest and refit."

As 85th Division came slowly into the line, the 12th SS infantry were replaced, leaving their tanks and artillery to support the 85th and 89th. "Never in my life have I seen infantry so completely tired out. They came in from the lines asleep and slept solidly for two days. To these soldiers rest was more important than food. They were completely out."

Hitler's Avranches offensive had already run out of steam. Late that night von Kluge reported to OKW: "The idea of the thrust to Avranches is now scarcely feasible. In the north the English [sic] have achieved a very deep penetration astride the Caen-Falaise road. . . . Field Marshal Sperrle* told us again today . . . that he cannot even get his 110 fighters into the area where the 1,000 fighter-bombers are drumming down on us. The cover provided by enemy fighters is such that our fighters cannot get into the danger zone at all. . . . For the most part . . . aircraft were caught on the airfields as they were taking off."

He added that he would, of course, continue carrying out his orders. Von Kluge was under the impression that the day's carpet-bombing attacks had

---

*Field Marshal Hugo Sperrle commanded what remained of the Luftwaffe's Third Air Fleet.

wiped out most of the 89th and 12th ss Divisions. The two divisions had suffered severe casualties but were far from destroyed as far as the hesitant, slow-moving Canadian and Polish armoured forces were concerned. Like Hausser's advance on Avranches, Simonds's attack was also running out of steam.

Instead of continuing to advance, with the approach of darkness Kitching's 4th Division's armoured units packed it in for the night, "harbouring" their tanks as they had been taught during exercises in England. An exception was the 28th Tank Regiment of British Columbia. Commanded by Lieut.-Col. D.G. Worthington, the British Columbia Regiment, together with the Algonquin Regiment infantry riding on its tanks, moved off at 0300 hours, 9 August, making for the high ground across the Falaise road southwest of Quesnay Wood.

In the dawn mists and separated from part of his unit during the night, Worthington arrived in an open field surrounded by a scattering of trees. He was in sight of what he believed to be his objective. He ordered the regiment to park and wait for reinforcements. Their arrival was reported to 4th Brigade HQ: "Objective 0650 hrs. No evidence of enemy occupation—but recent signs. . . . We are holding until our friends come forward to consolidate." In fact, they were lost and well over three miles from where they should have been.

Worthington's arrival in the midst of enemy-held territory had not gone unobserved. Kurt noted: "Of great help to us was the lack of wireless security among the Allied forces. Not only within units was it bad but frequently orders were given over the air by senior commanders who should have known better. We were able to pick these up and immediately initiate counter-measures before the orders were implemented. . . .

"Astonishing amounts of valuable material were carried in the enemy's tanks. Code signs, simple map codes, cover names for places—not just for one day but sometimes three or four—could be found in captured tanks. So valuable did this prove from the start of the invasion that it was always an accepted practice to let an Allied tank into the German lines before knocking it out so that these valuable items could be obtained."

Lieut. Bernhard Georg Meitzel, an English-speaking officer from Kurt's divisional HQ, had been out with a radio reconnoitring the area in a scout car when he stumbled upon Worthington's tanks. Meitzel and the two soldiers riding with him were captured but not before getting a message off to Battle Group Wünsche lying nearby under camouflage netting. Wünsche's tankers fired up their motors and rumbled toward the unsuspecting quarry, the Tigers attacking from the west, the Panthers from the east. Within the hour Worthington's force was surrounded, under fire and urgently asking Brigade for artillery support. Unfortunately, the map coordinates given to the artillery were nowhere near the regiment's position.

Caught in the open, they started digging in and, without hope of reinforcements, fought throughout the day. A pair of stray Typhoons helped at one point by rocketing Wünsche's forces. Yet in spite of making several sorties, neither pilot reported the regiment's position nor did any air support unit receive instructions during the day from either Brigade or Division to keep an eye out for Worthington and his missing tanks. Hours after eight of the force's tanks broke out of the encirclement, no attempt was made by anyone to obtain an accurate position report of the unknown hill where the rest of the force were still fighting for their lives from hastily dug six-foot trenches.

Although Worthington and his officers may have lacked judgment, no one could fault them on their courage. By late afternoon even the wounded were fighting Germans. Near 1800 hours an unruffled Worthington brought his four surviving officers together for a conference. Burning Shermans littered the area, sending up palls of black smoke. German mortar and gunfire rained down on them. The regiment's War Diary recorded that "he informed them that due to loss of command tanks, radio communication was impossible and it was unlikely that any support would be given us. . . . The regiment's task was to hold this ground as long as possible and to engage as large a force of enemy as possible, thus enabling the brigade and division to gain their objectives." The conference came to an abrupt end by a warning that a strong counterattack had been launched from the southeast edge of the perimeter.

"The colonel wished us luck and headed for that sector to direct the battle. . . . Four tanks fit to fight remained; these tanks immediately took on the German infantry who were advancing in waves, and inflicted heavy loses. This attack coincided with very heavy and accurate mortar concentrations which accounted for a large proportion of our infantry around the perimeter. . . . A direct hit set fire to one of the tanks. The attacking force . . . judged to be two companies in strength, suffered heavy casualties . . . Lt. Col. Worthington at this time returned with some wounded infantrymen and gave them First Aid in a dugout position under one of the tanks. . . . The counterattack was renewed, led by a mixed force of Tiger and Panther tanks. As the tank the colonel was under had been hit and was in an extremely vulnerable position, he ordered it forward to a covered position with complete disregard for his own personal safety. He evacuated the wounded to the slight shelter of the hedgerow and was killed at this point by a mortar bomb. The remaining tanks continued to engage the enemy until all were knocked out or out of ammunition."

The battle effectively wiped out the B.C. Regiment as a fighting force; 47 tanks were gone along with 112 officers and men either dead, wounded or captured. The Algonquins lost 128 men together with their commanding officer. Those who survived escaped into the darkness on foot. Lieutenant

Meitzel, who had remained a prisoner throughout the day, led the walking wounded into the German lines for medical attention.

Kurt, who appeared as the battle ended to congratulate Wünsche, visited the Canadian wounded. "Among the prisoners is Capt. G.A. Renwick of the 28th Tank Regiment of B.C. I have a half hour's conversation with Renwick about this crazy war. I got a very good impression of him."

First SS Panzer Corps Commander Sepp Dietrich's recommendation for the award of Swords to Kurt's Knight's Cross with Oak Leaves was dazzling. It included a capsulized account of 12th SS Division's battles since Caen; while three Canadian divisions had been fighting the depleted 12th SS, it was—incredibly—fighting three British divisions at the same time!

> After taking over the 12th SS Division, the enemy began to attack on the left sector with the British 11th Armoured, the 49th and 15th Infantry Divisions, with the goal of winning a bridgehead over the Orne near St. André. After two days of hard fighting, the division succeeded in preventing a breakthrough by the enemy and bringing him to a standstill at the Odon. In this battle 117 tanks were destroyed. . . .
>
> On 8 July, the enemy attacked Caen with the British 3rd and 59th and the Canadian 3rd Divisions. In hard, crisis-filled fighting, heavy casualties were inflicted on the enemy. Although the enemy was successful in breaking through to the eastern edge of Caen, until noon of 8 July the Division held its position and prevented the breakthrough, thereby enabling a new defence line to be built. Enemy losses were 103 tanks in this combat. . . .
>
> On 8 August, the enemy began an attack on the 89th Infantry Division's sector using the 1st Polish Tank Division. Its goal was a peak 4 kilometres northwest of Potigny. While one battalion of the 12th SS was fighting with units of the 271st Infantry Division over the Orne, another battalion was successfully fighting to the east of Vire, while a third battalion caught the badly split enemy at the St. Aignan-Bretteville-sur-Laize line. In the heavy fighting the 1st Polish Armoured Division was heavily beaten and 90 tanks destroyed. . . .
>
> Despite high casualties from fighting on 7 and 8 August, the 12th SS attacked the 4th Canadian Armoured Division northwest of Rouvres-Quesnay-Bray en Cinglais and destroyed 103 enemy tanks. The building of a new line northwest of the Laison was made possible. . . . That the enemy did not succeed in breaking through to the tank lands south of Caen we owe only to the unprecedented brave actions of Meyer who always led his men from the front even in the most desperate of situations. . . .
>
> Despite over 6,000 casualties the successes and achievements of the 12th SS speak of the outstandingly brave and decisive leadership of their commander. . . . He was the soul of fanatical resistance.

But war is a matter of personal perceptions. Kurt, the "fanatic," was under no illusions on how it would be resolved.

"We all know that this fight can only end with death or becoming prisoners but nobody is willing to end the fight. The Casablanca formula for Germany's unconditional surrender makes us fight on. Sure, the war is lost for Germany

but the front must be held. . . . The Allied powers must see that the decision
for unconditional surrender is not worth fighting for. There must be a
negotiated peace. There is no fanaticism in the ranks of my men. They want
to live. And they want to return in health to their homes. No, there is no
fanaticism as our enemies say and we are not fanatics to go on fighting.
We do not put down our arms because we must go on fighting for our country."

12

Operation "Totalize" came to a halt in the early hours of 11 August when
a frustrated Simonds cancelled any further attacks. Besides the appalling losses
of men and tanks by the Polish division, the B.C. Regiment and the
Algonquins, the battle-hardened Queen's Own Rifles of 8th Brigade lost 85
killed and wounded during an attack in Quesnay Wood. Every officer and
senior NCO of the regiment's lead company became casualties when the
Germans, who had been waiting patiently for them to come within range,
suddenly opened fire.

The North Shore Regiment, with only three rifle companies remaining
after the bombing accident two days earlier, made its way into the wood
under heavy mortar fire. It was then forced to withdraw when it came under
Canadian artillery fire and their battalion communication broke down. The
regiment's casualties were 22 killed and 58 wounded, including Lieut.-Col.
D.B. Buell, the commanding officer.

Harry observed that "'Totalize' was to all intents and purposes a failure.
Once more—and with some embarrassment—we had to face facts. We were
no match for the Germans once they were dug in. It could be argued that
everything being equal, defenders always hold an advantage over attackers.
But in Normandy everything wasn't equal. We held the advantage; in the
air, at sea and on the ground. Yet every time our troops got beyond range
of supporting artillery or sour weather grounded our fighter-bomber cover,
the Germans stopped us cold. . . .

"Seeing 12th SS POWs brought back to my HQ or Div. HQ for interrogation
was always an uncomfortable surprise. They were so young compared to our
own troops—too young to have had more than a year or two of training.
Some weren't even old enough to shave. But my God could they ever fight!
Sometimes they hid in trees and orchards, individual snipers with telescopic
sights tying themselves to the branches, waiting for anyone wearing a rank
badge or someone silly enough to stick his head up. Their snipers never
surrendered. Each had to be flushed out."

Simonds's disappointment paled beside von Kluge's with the Avranches
offensive, which ended in chaos the day after it began. Instead of assembling

eight panzer divisions for his attack against the Americans, he managed to muster four. The fresh divisions arriving from southern France had been mauled along the route by Allied aircraft. Outside Mortain the Americans brought the Germans to a standstill. By the evening of 11 August, German forces were under heavy attack and most of the salient between Mortain and St. Barthélémy had been lost. By next morning both places were in American hands. Orders and counterorders kept coming from Hitler for the conduct of the battle.

Von Kluge's next problem: obtaining Hitler's permission for a general withdrawal before what remained of his two armies was trapped. By late afternoon of 12 August, long convoys of horse-drawn wagons, vehicles and men were streaming east, into what was shortly to become the blazing cauldron of the Falaise Gap. As they moved, Allied aircraft smothered them with rockets, bombs and bullets.

On the same day, at the 7th Brigade front: "The big thorn in our sides is the Quesnay Wood—here the enemy has formed a battle group consisting of ss troops and Wehrmacht with quite a few 88 mm guns—time after time we've bombed and shelled them but they hold on with fanatical grimness. So during the evening we decided to try new tactics . . . and if possible to burn them out. The method . . . 4.2″ fire phosphorus bombs. . . .

"The Regina Rifles who were closest to the woods were requested to report results. The Reginas reported our bombs on target but no immediate results could be indicated. Towards the early hours of morning 1st Canadian Scottish reported they were being counterattacked by a sizeable force. Artillery fire was called and received—what actually happened was that the Germans sent out a fighting patrol and, when they bumped into our forward defence lines, laid down a lot of fire, leaving us to believe they were a stronger force than was the case. The attack was beaten off and once more a semi-quiet reigned in our area. . . .

"13 August. . . . A patrol from the Reginas tried to work their way down to the River Laize early this morning in order to find suitable places for crossings—but unfortunately just as they left their battalion positions and moved out several hundred yards, they ran into two enemy positions and were forced to turn back. Patrols from the Winnipeg Rifles contacted 1st Canadian Scottish and the Regina Rifles without incident. Our acting mortar officer decided to make the trip with one of the Winnipeg patrols and got as far as an abandoned six barrelled *Nebelwerfer* which he thought to be of more interest so disengaged himself from the patrol and brought the *Nebelwerfer* back to HQ including an assortment of maintenance and firing gear. . . . Attended a Div. O Group at 1600 hours."

At the divisional O Group Harry was informed of final details for Operation

"Tallulah,"* which he described as "certainly one of the strangest attack formations anyone ever dreamed up and without a hope in hell of succeeding as planned. What looked good to Guy's precise engineering mind on paper seldom worked in practice once the human element was added. A simple plan was always the best. But you couldn't argue with Guy; not and keep your job."

Simonds's new plan called for a surprise attack in broad daylight by two solid armoured phalanxes charging across the country against the German line, as usual preceded by heavy artillery and RAF bomber support. To maintain secrecy he issued no written orders. Unfortunately, one of the officers attending the O Group blundered into German lines on the way back to his unit. Pencilled notes and map tracings found on the dead body gave the Germans time to rearrange their positions to meet the attack. Simonds admitted later that the adjustments "undoubtedly resulted in casualties to our troops the following day which otherwise would not have occurred and delayed the capture of Falaise for over 24 hours."†

Twenty-four hours were needed to assemble the assault forces of the 4th Armoured, 3rd Canadian and 51st British Infantry Divisions. Shortly before noon on 14 August the order came to move out. Typhoons roared low overhead, plastering the enemy's forward positions. The copper sun vanished behind a cloud of rising dust, smoke and haze. As the blocks of men and armour advanced toward the enemy line, chaos ensued. Drivers worked frantically trying to hold direction in the choking dust and tangle of vehicles. Harry was nearly killed through another bombing error.

"Operation 'Tallulah' began today with Bomber Command leading off. Due to the close proximity of the Reginas to the target, which was Quesnay Wood, they were told to keep well underground and issued with absorbent cotton to plug their ears. The first wave of bombers swept over the target and scored direct hits—but the next waves somehow got off the track and dropped their eggs to the left and rear of Brigade HQ in our own guns area. Wave after wave did the same thing—Brigade HQ was fairly well ringed with bombs. Frantic calls were put in . . . to try and correct the bombers errors. . . . Capt. Eckenfelder and Sgt. Briscoe stood out in the open with a beacon lamp signalling that we were friendly—yellow smoke thrown out in all directions but to no avail. Finally, around 1545 hours when the situation seemed desperate our flying Artillery Observation Posts sized up the situation and at great risk to themselves soared into the blue and guided the last wave of bombers in to the target. . . .

---

*The name changed later to "Tractable."
†Hubert Meyer's divisional history of the 12th SS disputes this; although he admitted the documents were captured, no alterations to dispositions were made.

"It was a balls up. Bomber Command still didn't know yellow flares were army standard recognition signals to friendly aircraft. Bomber Command used yellow markers for their targets."

The error resulted in nearly 400 casualties; 65 Canadian and Polish lives were lost. During the raid two bombers were shot down, one apparently by Canadian anti-aircraft fire. For the Poles, already battered by the USAF Fortress bombing on 8 August, the event had a depressing effect on morale. Unlike other Allied units, Maczek's division had no reserves to replace the men it lost. To make good his losses, Maczek combed the ranks of all German prisoners taken in Normandy. Any Polish national who had been inducted into the Wehrmacht or SS was promptly drafted by the Polish armoured division.

When RAF bombs hit the 4th Armoured Division's artillery, they ceased firing. Without smoke shells covering the advance across the plain, the densely packed armoured columns were in the clear. The German screen of 88 mm guns blasted them. A shell hit the command tank of the 4th Armoured Brigade, instantly severing all communications between Brigade and Division HQ and the regiments in the field. Bleeding to death, Brigadier Booth climbed out of his burning tank with one leg gone. Brigade Maj. Jerry Chubb tied a tourniquet on the stump, threw Booth on the back of his own tank, and took off down the road to find a casualty nest where the Brigadier could be unloaded onto a jeep ambulance for evacuation to a field hospital.

At the Laison River the importance of accurate intelligence was once again demonstrated. Simonds's planning staff had ignored the importance of this little creek with its quagmires and steep muddy banks. In minutes two squadrons of the 1st Hussars were bogged down and vulnerable to enemy fire. Troops clambered from their armoured personnel carriers and waded across the stream while the tankers jumped out and began swivelling trees felled by the German 88s down to the stream, forming them into crude corduroy bridges for the tanks to cross. Once over the Laison, German resistance began collapsing. Wehrmacht soldiers came out in the hundreds with their hands up.

"Our job was to come in behind the 8th and 9th Brigades at the Laison River line then follow it along to the objectives at Soulangy and beyond on the Falaise road. Facing us was a mixed bag of Wehrmacht and 12th SS still fighting like tigers. . . . We moved off shortly before six . . . relatively easy going through the path cleared by the other brigades. By ten that night with resistance stiffening we were halfway to our objectives. . . . I moved up my HQ and ordered the troops to dig in."

At 4th Division HQ, Major-General Kitching went forward to find out what had happened to Booth's armoured brigade and its regiments who hadn't "netted in" to the divisional radio centre. For 12 hours, contact had been lost. Montgomery and Simonds arrived to check the division's progress. Lieut.-

Col. John Proctor, the division's AA (assistant adjutant) and QMG (quartermaster-general), met them.

"What's going on, Colonel?" Simonds demanded.

"I don't know, sir. Things are rather confused."

"Where's General Kitching?"

"I don't know exactly, sir. He's gone off to try and sort things out."

Montgomery snorted at Simonds: "Get rid of him. He's obviously lost control of the situation. Why, he isn't even at his own headquarters!"

Kitching's days as a divisional commander were numbered.

Although progress had been slow on the Canadian front, it had been even slower on the British sector. Montgomery decided now that the capture of Falaise should be completed by II Corps. Simonds's orders for 15 August were for the Polish division to seize a bridgehead at Jort while 3rd and 4th Divisions continued the battle for the heights above Falaise. Foulkes's 2nd Division was to take the town. Impatiently, he insisted that his commanders show a great deal more enthusiasm and tenacity than had thus far been evidenced in the battle.

Next day Brigadier Blackader, the 3rd Division's temporary GOC, made 7th Brigade the spearhead for the attack on Soulangy. Harry held an O Group at his new HQ to outline the plan of attack.

"I ordered the 7th Recce followed by the Winnipegs to advance on the right down the main road while 2nd Armoured Brigade followed by the Reginas were to attack through where the Canadian Scottish were dug in."

The Royal Winnipeg Rifles and 7th Reconnaissance Regiment fought their way into the village where they found German tanks waiting for them. The resulting casualties together with a strong enemy counterattack forced them to withdraw. A single Tiger in the space of a few minutes knocked out six of the ten tanks lost by the Fort Garry Horse.

Beyond the village on the left the Canadian Scottish were badly mauled when supporting tanks from the 2nd Armoured were held up by German tanks and anti-tank gunners. The Canadian Scottish made a stand in what turned out to be their most costly fight of the entire campaign, 37 dead and 93 wounded during a day-long battle.

For Harry the day ended disappointingly. "Our objectives had not been reached, although we were closer to Falaise. . . . The Regina Rifles not having married up with the tanks and as darkness was falling, we decided to form up. Accordingly, the Reginas withdrew slightly and took up position between and in line with the Canadian Scottish and Winnipeg Rifles. The tanks were ordered to rally and refuel. . . . During the night the Reginas reported being bombed and strafed by our own aircraft."

Kitching's 4th Armoured Division had a bad day as well. Once more the exhausted remains of Kurt's 12th ss made the difference. With only the remnants of Battle Group Wünsche and Kraas left[26] to him, he had dug in his remaining Tiger and Panther tanks on high ground well supported by self-propelled and anti-tank guns. Once beyond range of its own artillery, the now leaderless* 4th Armoured Brigade found it impossible to advance across the exposed rising ground. By dusk the Governor-General's Foot Guards and the Canadian Grenadier Guards were down to about 50 serviceable tanks. Supported by units of the Lincoln and Welland Regiment, men and tanks hunkered down in hastily prepared defence positions for the night.

Operation "Tallulah" had ended.

Much has been written about the four-day delay in closing the Falaise Gap and where the responsibility or blame for that failure lay. It is still worth repeating—however briefly—if only to illustrate the shortsighted and inept planning by Montgomery and Bradley, who, after agreeing to a bold imaginative course of action, failed to follow it through to the best tactical advantage.

The German retreat began 8 August after the Avranches offensive failed to penetrate the American lines. Except for continuous aerial attacks and the resulting loss of men and equipment, it was an orderly withdrawal aimed at bringing the Seventh and Fifth Panzer Armies out of the dangerous pocket into which Hitler had placed them. Pushing from the bottom of the pocket was Bradley's First Army under Lieut.-Gen. Courtney Hodges. Squeezing from the flanks were Lieut.-Gen. George Patton's Third Army with the French on the south and the two British and Canadian armies descending from the north. The pocket's 14-mile opening lay between the towns of Argentan and Falaise. Through this gap von Kluge's two armies would have to pass.

On 8 August Bradley and Montgomery—with Eisenhower's approval—had decided to take advantage of the opportunity presented by German withdrawal from the Mortain salient for a double envelopment. The U.S. First Army would swing north to meet the British Second Army south of Condé while the U.S. Third Army would join the Canadian First Army south of Falaise.

At the time, Montgomery still hoped that between 8 and 10 August "Totalize" would capture the high ground outside Falaise. When the Canadian operation foundered, he issued a new directive to his five army commanders on 11 August. Simonds's II Corps was to capture Falaise, then continue on into the British Second Army's sector, and with its armoured forces take Argentan.

Harry felt that "either Monty's mind wasn't on the job or he hadn't studied a map of the area. Instead of an eight-mile advance into Falaise the Corps was now being asked to cover 20 miles and take Argentan as well. We were already having a hard enough time trying to reach Falaise."

---

*Lieut.-Col. M.J. Scott took over command after Brigadier Booth's death the previous day. Scott was replaced by Lieut.-Col. W.W. Halpenny after being wounded at 1800 hours on 15 August.

No arrangements were made to reinforce the four Canadian divisions that had just finished an exhausting three days of battle. Yet on the American side of the Falaise Gap, Gen. Wade Haislip, Patton's XV Corps commander, had two fresh armoured and two infantry divisions at his disposal, with most of the U.S. Third Army to call upon if he got into trouble. Why Montgomery didn't use Patton's forces led by Haislip to charge across the gap remains one of the great mysteries of the Normandy campaign.

On 12 August Haislip captured Carrouges and Sées and could have thrust at once for Argentan had not the bloodyminded French 2nd Armoured Brigade, in direct disobedience to orders, caused his armour a six-hour delay by using the Alençon-Sées highway. Patton ordered an attack on Argentan the next morning. Thereafter, Haislip was told to advance "slowly" to meet the Canadians.

These critical hours gave Eberbach time to reach Argentan and organize a defence with the 116th Panzer Division. During the night his forces were bolstered with 60 tanks from the Leibstandarte and 2nd Panzer Divisions. It was enough to bring Haislip's armoured spearheads to a full stop next day five miles from the town. Before Haislip had time to regroup his forces, Bradley ordered a halt to the advance. American troops were already beyond the Carrouges-Sées stop line set by Montgomery in his directive of 11 August in order to prevent an accidental clash between Allied forces.

Angrily, the flamboyant Patton pressed his former junior commander to call Montgomery and ask for a boundary change. Only Montgomery had the authority to change boundaries. "Let me go on to Falaise and we'll drive the British into the sea for another Dunkirk!" Patton pleaded, correctly assessing the need for swift action. One assumes the anglophobic American general spoke facetiously.

Bradley refused and Eisenhower agreed. Montgomery appeared satisfied that Simonds's Canadian II Corps could close the gap. An exasperated Patton was forced to acquiesce. He left enough men and equipment to hold the southern line of the open pocket outside Argentan, then raced away to the east, toward the Seine and Paris. Five days later, when Montgomery finally did change the boundaries, it was too late.

In his postwar memoirs, *A Soldier's Story*, General Bradley wrote:

> The decision to stop Patton was mine alone. . . . Monty had never prohibited and I never proposed that US forces close the gap. . . . Already the vanguard of panzers and ss troops were sluicing back through it towards the Seine . . . stampeding to escape the trap. Although Patton might have spun a line across the narrow neck, I doubted his ability to hold it. . . . The enemy could not only have broken through, but he might have trampled Patton's position in the onrush. I much preferred a solid shoulder at Argentan to the possibility of a broken neck at Falaise.

Either the years had dimmed his memory or he had been badly misinformed on 13 August 1944. "Panzer and ss troops" were not "sluicing back" toward the Seine at all but were moving back under Eberbach's direction to defend Argentan. Neither were German divisions "stampeding to escape the trap," but rather were fighting determinedly to prevent reduction of the pocket into which their armies were being squeezed.

13

For Hitler, "the 15th of August was the worst day of my life." Every bit of news coming into OKW was bad. Allied forces had begun landing on the French Mediterranean coast. The Red Army had halted momentarily[27] outside Warsaw, while within the city an uprising against the German garrison had resulted in the loss of several key sectors in the city. Elsewhere the Russian steamroller threatened the Ploesti oil fields in Rumania. Falaise was on the verge of being lost; between it and the sea the British were attacking LXXXVI Corps, which was withdrawing across the Dives River. The I Panzer Corps at Falaise was exhausted, 85th Division nearly wiped out. The 12th ss was down to a handful of tanks. The LXXXIV Corps near Condé was running out of ammunition and could no longer hold without further supplies. The French at Ecouché, southwest of Argentan, were only ten miles from closing the gap with British forces. Eberbach's troops at Alençon had gone on the defensive. As if this wasn't enough to upset the Führer, von Kluge had gone missing—probably to negotiate terms with the enemy, Hitler decided. Since the 20 July plot, he trusted no one except the sycophants of his inner circle.

Far from deserting his post, the hapless von Kluge at first light had left Eberbach's Fifth Panzer Army Headquarters at Nécy, halfway between Falaise and Argentan, to visit Hausser. When Falaise fell, the main east-west highway to escape would be lost and what remained of his two armies would be encircled. He wanted support from both of his army commanders in asking Hitler permission for an immediate withdrawal. Hausser had already left when he arrived at the agreed rendezvous point south of Falaise. Von Kluge followed. En route his small convoy came under air attack. His car ditched and the escorting communications truck was destroyed. Immobilized and out of radio contact, von Kluge "vanished" inside the pocket until late that evening.

General Blumentritt, von Kluge's chief of staff, notified OKW that the situation required immediate action. Colonel-General Jodl informed Hitler, who made Hausser temporary C.-in-C. West (OB West). Hitler ordered Army Group HQ to report to OKW every hour until von Kluge was located. By the time he did appear at Hausser's HQ, the deeply suspicious Hitler had already set the wheels in motion to replace him with Field Marshal Walter Model. Known as the Führer's "fireman," he had just stopped the Russian drive against Army Group Centre on the Eastern Front where earlier he had replaced Field Marshal Busch.

By next morning the pocket had shrunk to about 35 miles in depth, with only 12 miles left at the Falaise opening where the Canadians were already on the outskirts of town. Still inside the pocket were Seventh Army and most of Eberbach's Fifth Panzer Army, comprised of four panzer corps, two army corps and one parachute corps—what remained of 21 divisions. There was no more time to argue counterattacks with OKW. Von Kluge told Jodl that the withdrawal order had to be issued at once. Then, without waiting for an official directive, he ordered the retreat to begin.

Late the same morning Harry held an O Group with his commanders to outline his own plans. The battered Canadian Scottish were to hold their position, leaving the Royal Winnipegs and Reginas to forge ahead. The Royal Winnipegs were to advance down the main road to Falaise and, backed by some excellent artillery ranging, reach their crossroads objective before dark.

"During the attack . . . the Regina Rifles with two squadrons of 2nd Armoured Brigade were attacking parallel on the high ground to the left. The enemy confronting them seemed a little more determined than on the Winnipeg Rifles sector, pinning their sub-units down time and again with machine-gun fire. However, with the use of our supporting tanks and their own smoke the opposition was overcome.

"Unfortunately, just at the height of the attack our friends on the left, the 4th Armoured Division, decided the Regina Rifles were enemy and promptly started to mortar and shell them. The situation cleared up in due course—quite an understandable mistake . . . when three divisions converge on one spot [Falaise] confusion is bound to reign—it did! All during this attack the Reginas and the tanks especially were having trouble with enemy anti-tank guns—a screen of 88 mms was so well situated that whenever one of our tanks so much as showed itself on the crest line it was either knocked out or the near miss took the tank crews' breath away. By 2200 hours two companies of the Reginas were astride the main east road leading out of Falaise and looking down on the town. . . . As the clock struck midnight the Reginas sent us a hurried flash to say their forward companies were being attacked by tanks but when the excitement died down the report was cancelled to read: 'Heard movements thought to be tanks.'

"Prisoners identified today from 1st SS Panzer . . . 89th Infantry . . . and 85th Infantry Divisions which merely confirm what we already knew that the enemy is grabbing troops from anywhere and forming them into battle groups in a desperate last effort to hold up our advance. SITREP from 2nd Canadian Infantry Division attacking Falaise from the Northwest reported they had completely surrounded the town and were sending in a battalion to mop up. . . .

"17 August. . . . Cloudy and cool. . . . As is usual come daylight the general Brigade situation looked more reassuring than . . . during the hours of darkness. The Reginas found no enemy in their objectives and both the other two battalions were in a happy state of mind. Patrols were sent out during the day to recce as far forward as the river running slightly north of Falaise. No enemy was contacted. The Brigade Major and Intelligence Officer visited all three battalions in the morning, passing on the latest information as we had it and generally putting them in the picture. They were all warned to take advantage of a one-day lull, after that we expected to push on rapidly.

"Coming back from the area of the Winnipeg Rifles and approaching the Canadian Scottish position the Intelligence Officer made a chance remark that he had a sneaking suspicion that the Luftwaffe would be out today. Speaking of the devil! Nine of them almost at that moment came wheeling out of the clouds bent on some mischief. . . . They didn't get very far. . . . Our A/A guns without a moment's hesitation opened up and nailed one plane so fast that it was a tremendous surprise to both the Luftwaffe and us. The Hun was so impressed that . . . immediately all eight of them turned tail and fled."

The mystery of Brigadier Booth's whereabouts was finally solved. The jeep ambulance on which he had been loaded had stopped at another nest of casualties on its way back to the dressing station. Seeing that Booth was already dead, the driver placed his body in the ditch, loaded a live casualty and continued on his way. Booth had gone into battle without rank badges, so it was not until a burial detail checked his identification tags three days later that the legless body could be given a name.

During the nights of 16 and 17 August, the Germans withdrew the bulk of their forces in orderly fashion across the Orne. Inside the pocket, shrunk now to an area no more than six by seven miles, tens of thousands of exhausted German fighting men along with six army and corps headquarters and 12 divisional headquarters were still trying to escape. Convoys of men and vehicles moved under a steady artillery bombardment from the closing ring of Allied forces on the ground and fighter-bombers from the air. Wrecked tanks, abandoned guns, smoking vehicles and splintered wagons littered every road. Flies swarmed across the bloated bodies of blasted horses and the German dead. The dull, windless air filled with dust and the sweet sickening scent of rotting flesh.

On the evening of the 17th, Field Marshal Model arrived at OB West HQ with written orders from Hitler to take over command. Von Kluge was ordered to report back to Berlin. It was as good as a death sentence. "Der Kluge Hans"* wrote a last pathetic and undignified letter to his master.

---

*"Clever Hans"—a German play on words.

My Führer. When you receive these lines I shall be no more. I cannot bear the accusation of having brought about the fate of our armies in the West by mistaken measures, and I have no means of defending myself. I am therefore taking the only action I can, and shall go where thousands of my companions have preceded me. . . .

My Führer, make up your mind to end the war. The German people have borne such untold suffering that it is time to put an end to this frightfulness. . . .

My Führer, I have always admired your greatness, your conduct in the gigantic struggle, and your iron will to maintain yourself and National Socialism. If Fate is stronger than your will and your genius, so is Providence. You have fought an honourable and great fight. History will prove that for you. Show yourself now also great enough to put an end to a hopeless struggle when necessary.

For von Kluge, who had stood fifth on the Army List as one of the nation's foremost senior officers, to write such fawning rubbish to the man most responsible for the disaster that had befallen him shows an incredible degree of naivety. He concluded by writing: "I depart from you, my Führer, as one who stood nearer to you than you perhaps realized, in the consciousness that I did my duty to the utmost."

On his way home to Germany he committed suicide by taking poison. He was 62. Hitler read the suicide letter next day and handed it over to Jodl without comment. Unforgiving to the last, he denied von Kluge any military honours at his funeral.

Next morning—the 18th—Model ordered Panzer Group Eberbach and Hausser's Seventh Army to be brought out of the pocket as quickly as possible. What remained of the 12th ss, 9th ss and 2nd ss Panzer Divisions in II Panzer Corps were to hold open the Falaise Gap at the north shoulder of the pocket while 2nd and 116th Panzer Divisions held open the gap's southern wall of the escape corridor.

On the afternoon of the 18th, Harry's 7th Brigade was ordered to hold a line at the Dives River from the village of Trun north to where troops of the 9th Brigade were positioned on their left flank. Trun formed the apex of a triangle between Falaise and Argentan. "Our task was to seal the gap and so contain enemy forces trying to break out from the Falaise area to reach the Seine River, and to prevent the enemy from sending forces from the east to relieve the troops caught in the Falaise mantrap."

The gap was now less than five miles wide.

With the fall of the Laison Valley defence line, the 12th ss had been reduced to 300 fighting men and 11 tanks. Kurt reorganized what remained for a final battle at Falaise. "Eighty men were sent into Falaise to hold the Post Office. One hundred more held the northern outskirts of the Bois-du-Roi to the Caen-Falaise road; 50 in Les Monts d'Erames and 40 more scattered

in between. Olboetter still remained with 89th Division with his two tanks.
. . . Kraas made his stand on the Caen-Falaise road with two heavy infantry
guns and fought to the end."

Falaise fell on 18 August. The remains of the 12th ss—120 men and six
tanks—took new positions on the high ground south of town.

"At this stage Waldmüller came back on the scene with some 300 refits
and what he had been able to procure from the administration troops who
had left the area ten days before. I was given the task of keeping the 'Cauldron'
open." Kurt told his men: "Those who have no personal weapons are cowards.
We don't want anything to do with them. Only those with weapons may
join our group for the breakout. Those without weapons better find some
soon."

He made one last stand with 60 men inside the pocket near the village
of Vignates.

While units of Foulkes's 2nd Infantry Division cleared the last Germans from
the devastation of Falaise, Simonds ordered Trun and Chambois to be taken
by the 4th Canadian and 1st Polish Armoured Divisions. Unfortunately, one
column of the force that General Maczek assigned to capture Chambois took
off in the wrong direction toward Les Champeaux, a village due east of the
start line. As the convoy of Polish tanks rumbled into the midst of the enemy,
German traffic controllers obligingly stopped the flow to let it pass.

A mile or two down the road they caught up with part of a panzer division
and immediately opened fire. Cruising Spitfires and Typhoons, their pilots
unaware of the Polish error, swooped down on the vanguard, blasting Pole
and German alike. Once more Maczek's men suffered horribly at the hands
of their allies. Throughout the day over 3,000 sorties by Allied aircraft were
made.

During the morning Kitching's 4th Armoured Division fought its way
onto the pockmarked crossroads at Trun. Newly promoted Brigadier Robert
Moncel arrived to take command of the luckless Booth's 4th Armoured
Brigade. Moncel, at 26, became the youngest brigadier in the Canadian army.
A protégé of Simonds, he had commanded the 18th Armoured Car Regiment
(12th Manitoba Dragoons) attached to Simonds's II Corps Troops. Quickly,
Moncel positioned his armoured regiments to control the Vimoutiers road
and area around Trun.

The Poles, however, were still short of their objectives. Argentan was being
defended furiously and Chambois was beyond reach. Any further movement
south took them across the path of Germans retreating toward Vimoutiers.
After three days of heavy fighting, the division was running low on supplies
and ammunition. Throughout the night the Germans battled to hold open
the gap. By morning its width had shrunk to 3.5 miles.

On Harry's sector, troops maintained position as part of the "plug."

"19 August. . . . Cloudy and cool with rain in the afternoon. . . . Both the Regina Rifles and Winnipeg Rifles patrols contacted the enemy during the day. A one-man patrol captured 42 of the enemy. . . . C Company of the Winnipeg Rifles attacked the enemy on the other side of the river, bringing the score to 150 prisoners. The enemy in turn counterattacked but only succeeded in having two of his tanks knocked out with PIAT bombs and one platoon annihilated—the remainder then withdrew."

Maczek split his division, sending a third of his forces cross-country to take Chambois. The lead squadron smashed its way into town that evening. Then, in the midst of a street battle, the enemy firing stopped. White flags were raised. A few khaki-uniformed soldiers of the 90th U.S. Infantry Division waved their distinctive steel helmets at the Poles. Someone cheered. The Falaise Gap had been closed. It was a loosely held line of closure, more sieve than barricade. German troops continued to pour through.

The rest of the Polish division had made for a wooded ridge that overlooked the Trun-Vimoutiers highway and most of the surrounding countryside. Maczek named it "Maczuga"—the Polish word for a medieval mace. For the next two days Maczuga became the fragile cork in the bottleneck of retreating Germans.

When his Vignates position was finally overrun, Kurt reported to Hausser for further orders. He was told to collect what remained of his troops and service personnel and attempt a breakout south of Trun together with Generals Meindl of the II Parachute Corps and Schimpf of the 3rd Parachute Division. Accompanied by 200 men "determined to use their weapons," together with General Elfeldt, Obersturmführer Köln and Michel, the Cossack, Kurt's task was to cover the breakout's northern flank, then cross the Dives River behind Meindl's parachutists.

The march began in the middle of the night. He split his escort into independent commando units. Two columns were sent off: a motorized to Chambois, the infantry to St. Lambert. Guns and heavy ammunition carriers were abandoned. Every road and pathway leading out was hopelessly blocked. They struck off diagonally across country. Fires, burning trucks, exploding shells, and rockets lit the night. The bombardment was continuous and "registering bull's-eyes every time. The Canadian and Polish guns found our range and could not miss." Where were Meindl and his parachutists? Crouching in a ditch or already dead? They never made contact.

But the resourceful Meindl had made it through the gap. With 20 handpicked parachutists, he crawled through cornfields to the Trun-Argentan road. Slithering past gunfire from the Canadian positions, they reached the Dives and struggled across in water up to their chests. By dawn Meindl made contact with men of the German 353rd Division.

Throughout the night Kurt struggled on. He had been without sleep for days. "I am exhausted. I can't go on anymore. Hubert Meyer takes the lead. The others are all ahead. I am left behind. Only Michel the Cossack remains. Tears are running down his cheeks. He tries to keep me moving. He is like a mother with her child. Time and again he says: 'Commander come. Commander come. Only 200 metres. Please come.'"

Sweat stung his eyes. His old head wound had opened and throbbed painfully. The only route out, he knew, lay in the valley between Coudehard Ridge and Mont Ormel. In the first light of dawn Mont Ormel appeared like a jagged tooth. What he did not know was that 1,900 Polish soldiers backed by 87 tanks held the high ground in front of them. Allied artillery spotter aircraft took to the air, directing fire on top of the teeming masses of men, animals and machines struggling up the western slopes. "The whole country was saturated with dead or wounded German soldiers."

West of Chambois, Kurt jumped onto the back of a Leibstandarte tank, clutching one of the other riders. He lost his balance and fell to the ground. The man he had been holding was blown to pieces by an anti-tank shell. Kurt collapsed into a ditch filled with dead soldiers crushed by tank treads.

Meindl and Hausser held a conference in a shell hole. Arriving forces were quickly organized for an assault against the Poles. By midmorning the enemy was surrounded. At 1630 hours Meindl began his attack against Coudehard Ridge with everything and everyone he could collect. Dismounted tank crews, mortar crews, artillerymen and riflemen were launched against the Polish line. When the men ran out of ammunition, they fought with knives.

At 1900 hours Meindl arranged for a column of assorted vehicles flying Red Cross flags to remove his wounded. He stopped all traffic for a quarter of an hour in front of and behind the column of wounded. Moving slowly, the vehicles set out under the eyes of the Polish gunners on Mont Ormel and at Boisjos. Meindl crossed his fingers. For more than an hour the guns remained silent. Meindl wrote after the war: "Not a shot was fired at my column and I can only express my gratitude to the chivalry of the enemy."

Meindl's breakout spurred those troops still wandering the plain to try their luck over the same route. A river of assorted uniformed men and vehicles flooded onto the escape road. Kurt joined them. "As if rocket-propelled, we rushed through the astonished infantry in a few seconds and in a silence broken only by the bursting of a few shells," the last remnants of the once-mighty 12th ss went through the Falaise Gap.[28]

On the high ground before crossing the ridge, he paused with Köln and Michel to look back at the chaotic scene below. The sun had begun to set over the smoking battlefield. "We can see dead comrades everywhere. We dodge across the roads cursing the men who have so senselessly sacrificed two great German armies for nothing."

The fearless 64-year-old Hausser, marching in the maelstrom with his troops, was badly wounded in the face by shrapnel. He managed to escape the cauldron on the back of a tank. Eberbach took over the Seventh Army, while Sepp Dietrich assumed command of the Fifth Panzer Army.

"20 August. . . . Cloudy with rain. . . . Activity on the 7th Brigade front today was confined mostly to sitting tight and waiting for the enemy to try and make a breakthrough. On our left flank 9th Brigade was busy handling a never-ending stream of POW—all fight taken out of them by our constant artillery barrage and air activities. Enemy tanks did try a breakthrough to the Seine from south of Trun but 4th Armoured Div. handled them with an iron fist. Those that did get away were nailed by our Typhoons."

On Maczuga Hill, down to 80 tanks and less than 1,600 men, Col. Stanislaw Koszutski and his exhausted Poles spent their day fighting off the full fury of Eberbach's panzers and Meindl's paratroops. By evening almost a third of the Polish force were either dead or wounded. Koszutski summoned his remaining officers to an O Group. After explaining the hopelessness of their position he announced: "Gentlemen. Tonight, we die."

The next day—21 August—Simonds sent Moncel's 4th Armoured Brigade to relieve the beleaguered Poles. A squadron of the 22nd Armoured Regiment (Canadian Grenadier Guards) made first contact. The regiment's War Diary recorded the encounter: "All the Germans in the area were either killed or ran away. . . . The picture . . . the grimmest the regiment has so far come up against. The Poles had no supplies for three days; they had several hundred wounded who had not been evacuated, about 700 prisoners of war lay loosely guarded in a field. The road was blocked by burned out vehicles both our own and the enemy. Unburied dead and parts of them were strewn about by the score. . . . The Poles cried with joy when we arrived and from what they said I doubt if they will ever forget this day and the help we gave them."

At St. Lambert, on the road between Trun and Chambois, Maj. David Currie's tiny force of 175 men, 15 tanks and four self-propelled guns from the 29th Canadian Regiment (SAR) held back the German tide in their sector for three days. With all his officers killed or wounded, Currie calmly took control of the battle. He was everywhere, directing everything—even knocking out a Tiger tank singlehandedly. When it was over, he and his men had destroyed seven enemy tanks, twelve 88 mm guns and 40 vehicles and had killed or wounded 800 Germans and taken 1,100 prisoners.

Lieutenant-Colonel Proctor had kept Currie's tiny force supplied with food and ammunition throughout the three-day battle. After one ammo delivery the laconic Currie asked Proctor to escort 500 of his prisoners back from the front with his scout car.

"Supposing they decide to bolt?"

"If they're as tired as I am, they haven't got the energy. If it will make you feel any better, I can send my driver and batman in another scout car for company."

Proctor accepted. "Currie was right. They marched along as meek as lambs. We fired a burst every so often to remind them we were still there."

Currie's citation for the Victoria Cross concluded:

When his force was finally relieved and he was satisfied that the turnover was complete he fell asleep on his feet and collapsed. . . . The courage and complete disregard for personal safety shown by Major Currie will forever be an inspiration to his regiment; his conspicuous bravery and extreme devotion to duty in the presence of the enemy an example to the Canadian Army for all time.

So strong was the sweet, sickening stench of rotting flesh lifted aloft under the scorching sun that its smell filled the cockpits of the low-flying Allied aircraft thundering over the retreating Germans.

Lieutenant-Colonel Proctor's War Diary described the finale: "The German escape route . . . has been aptly termed 'Dead Horse Alley.' The road is in very bad condition. . . . The sights and smells . . . are even more frightful than those of last night. Bulldozers have made a pretty good job of clearing wreckage, dead horses and dead Germans to the sides. Both sides for miles are lined with smashed or burnt-out Tiger and Panther tanks, trucks, guns, half-track vehicles, buses, wagons and all sorts of dead horses, now badly swollen and some in the most grotesque positions. In among it all, German bodies add to the scene of utter annihilation. The stench is terrific and a constant stream of cigarettes is the only thing that saves one's fifth sense. . . . The destruction was not solely confined to the road, for every field and wood along it has its quota of smashed vehicles and dead horses. It seems as though death and destruction reached out for the Germans no matter how hard they tried to avoid it being there. Close along the edges of the road are deep slit trenches at regular intervals as though dug there before the collapse in preparation for the withdrawal. Civilians are moving along the wreckage, eagerly filling bags with the spilt German belongings."

In the end, it had been Kitching's and Maczek's armoured divisions that had plugged the gap after all, and Kitching's armour under Moncel that had rescued the Poles. But Montgomery had already expressed his thoughts about Kitching to Simonds—so Kitching had to go. Nor was he the only one Simonds sacked; two brigadiers lost their commands—including Bruce Macdonald's nemesis, Brig. Hugh A. Young—as well as two armoured regiment colonels and five infantry and machine-gun battalion commanders who hadn't measured up to expectations. Yet it does seem illogical that Eisenhower, Montgomery, Bradley and Simonds expected two worn-out armoured divisions to close the gap while three fresh but immobilized American divisions were left guarding their side of the pocket only a few miles down the road.

"21 August. . . . Cloudy with rain. . . . I was called back to Corps HQ after lunch. Guy handed over a pair of crossed swords and scabbards, congratulated me and said I am to take over command of the 4th Armoured Div. tomorrow. He grumbled a few minutes about the division's lack of performance to date and of Booth's colossal gall getting himself killed at the head of his Brigade instead of staying back where he belonged. I feel sorry for poor George Kitching. He is just too nice a man for this sort of treatment. Guy said that if I got into any trouble I could always rely on Moncel. I came away with the distinct impression that if young Moncel had been 10 years older Guy would have given him the division and left me with the Brigade. . . . A Major-General at last! My only regret is that Margo and Dad did not live to see it. . . . I am beginning to think now that I may even survive this war."

Von Paulus's Sixth German Army died at Stalingrad with 260,000 dead, wounded and taken prisoner. Hausser's—later Eberbach's—Seventh Army died on the Dives River after losing over 300,000. Having gained the initiative, the Allied forces began the pursuit to the Seine. Compared to that at Falaise and the gap, opposition seemed light. American and French troops entered Paris on 24 August.

On the same day Eisenhower decided—over Montgomery's objections—to split the Allied forces into two army groups. The 21st Army Group would advance northeast, seizing the Pas-de-Calais area, Channel ports, Belgian airfields and the badly needed Belgian seaport of Antwerp. From there it was to swing eastward into Germany's industrial heartland. On the advance up the coast, Crerar's Canadian army would hold the 21st Army Group's left flank.

Bradley's 12th Army Group would support Montgomery's force initially, while cleaning up the Brittany Peninsula and "begin building up, out of incoming forces, the necessary strength to advance eastward from Paris towards Metz." Eisenhower advised that he would be taking over personal command of both army groups on 1 September.

The Normandy campaign had lasted 88 days. By late August, on the Eastern Front the Red Army reached the border of East Prussia in the north; Rumania and the Ploesti oil fields were already in Russian hands in the south. Soviet troops in the centre were within 300 miles of Berlin. However, despite these spectacular successes and the apparent crumbling of German resistance, the war in Europe still had 243 days left to run.

PART 8

VICTOR AND VANQUISHED

"You will observe the Rules of Battle, of course?" the White Knight remarked, putting on his helmet too. "I always do," said the Red Knight, and they began banging away at each other with such fury that Alice got behind a tree to be out of the way of the blows. "I wonder, now, what the Rules of Battle are," she said to herself.

LEWIS CARROLL

HARRY TOOK OVER command of the 4th Armoured Division at 1800 hours on 21 August. "Kitching was still in his caravan at his Montreuil la Combe HQ when I arrived. He was brokenhearted and in tears. I felt like a shit and sent for Wigle, his GSO1 and John Proctor, the division's QM, trying to make things as painless as possible for him. It was an awkward moment."

Proctor, who had been out all day supervising supply deliveries, arrived to find Kitching still in tears. "Well, John, they've fired me, goddammit! I've done my best. But there it is."

Harry sat uncomfortably while Kitching pulled himself together. As Worthington's successor, great things had been expected of Kitching and the division. In spite of errors he had turned the division into a formidable fighting force and felt that if Simonds had given him a few weeks longer he could have straightened things out to everyone's satisfaction. But Simonds had to appease his army commander. Montgomery had fired Major-General Pearkes in England when they didn't see eye to eye and Lieutenant-General Sansom after Exercise Spartan while he was still in hospital recuperating from illness. Simonds had replaced Sansom and knew only too well what would happen if he failed to follow Montgomery's instructions on Kitching.

"Kitching introduced me to the rest of his HQ staff. We had a drink, I wished him godspeed and he was gone."

Next day Harry visited his brigade commanders.

"What's the situation?" he asked Brigadier Moncel the moment he reached 4th Armoured Brigade's TAC HQ. Hurriedly, Moncel produced a clipboard and went over a map of the area, outlining the disposition of his various units. "When I finished, General Foster asked a couple of questions, then immediately called General Simonds on the radio and to my surprise repeated verbatim what I had just finished telling him. . . . I resolved then and there that no matter how bad things got I would never shade the truth or lie to such a man. . . . I never did."

Harry discussed his ideas on regrouping units along the lines of independent battle groups similar to those being used by the Germans and Americans. "I made it clear to everyone that as long as I was kept informed and no one let me down, each brigade group would be operating on its own. . . . Moncel seems to know his business. . . . If only he didn't look so damn young!"

He brought the Quartermaster into his newly acquired caravan. "I understand you know what you're doing?"

Proctor shrugged. "During the day I'm up at the front. Whenever the tanks begin shooting, my ammo trucks drop their loads and head to the rear for more supplies. If we have a breakout, then they drop their ammo and go back for petrol."

Harry smiled at the Quartermaster's oversimplification. "I hate paperwork and administration. I'm not worth a shit at it. It's up to you to run it. I won't interfere—I'll keep you in the picture but you run it. Understood?"

"Yes, sir."

"Good. Well, that's settled. We start our pursuit to the Seine in the morning. Get a good night's sleep."

Spearheaded by the Staghound armoured cars of Lieut.-Col. J.A. Roberts's 12th Manitoba Dragoons one hour ahead of the main force, Moncel's 4th Armoured Brigade led the advance. Troops of Brig. J.C. Jefferson's 10th Infantry Brigade followed. The main 4th Division HQ brought up the rear.

Jefferson, former CO of the Loyal Edmonton Regiment, had distinguished himself in the Mediterranean campaign from Sicily to Ortona, Italy, until recalled to England and appointed brigade commander.

"I was a bit envious of Jefferson. A steady, plodding, fearless sort of militia officer without much sense of humour or imagination, Jeff had had one hell of a war in Italy and experienced that thrill of commanding his own regiment in battle. Something that I would never know. I regarded a battalion major or regimental colonel leading his troops into battle to be the highest goal to which any officer could aspire. Unfortunately, the higher one climbed in rank the farther back he was placed from the front on the theory that commanders are supposed to command battles—not fight in them.

"At Army HQ and corps levels, far removed from the shouts of men and the crash and thunder of guns, there existed a tendency by senior staff officers to regard front-line units simply as coloured flags and plaques on a wall map or sand table. When troop performance didn't measure up to expectations, then somebody had to shoulder the blame—but never the Corps or Army Commander's staff. Their plans were always considered sound. . . .

"Battlefield commanders have a very limited appreciation or understanding about details of the full tactical picture in the war being waged. Nor do they have much say in how it is conducted. Our system wasn't as bad as the German method, which tolerated very little independence among its fighting units below the regimental level. Neither were our armies burdened by self-styled military geniuses like Adolf Hitler. Our politicians, fortunately, left the job to professionals and hoped for the best. On the whole, I don't think we let them down.

"A front-line soldier has only the foggiest idea about what's happening beyond his immediate front. Nor does he care. His job is to stay alive and alert and follow orders. He places his trust and chances of survival in the hands of the men with whom he serves, his platoon leader and the company commander. There is a bond between them difficult to put into words.

"Troops in the army's various militia units come from the same district or county. They train together, live together, fight together and sometimes die together. Despite the contention of novelists and wartime romantics, a soldier never fights for king and country, democratic ideals, his wife and family, medals or glorified political concepts. He fights for his regiment, the men in it, and because he is there. And for no other reason.

"When troops cross the start line and the battle begins, a soldier's range of vision narrows to himself, the few friends advancing with him, and the enemy whom he must kill. In the fury of hand-to-hand fighting between individual soldiers of opposing armies this viewpoint shrinks even further. Then the fight is for one reason only: survival.

"A platoon leader at the front concerns himself with the 30-odd men in his charge; how they are dug in, supplied with food, ammunition and medical attention when the battle begins. His range of interest is limited to the platoons positioned on his left and right and the enemy that faces him. He knows that they are all part of a grand plan somebody with red tabs on his collar produced for them to follow. He doesn't know if it's a good plan or a bad one. Naturally, he hopes it will succeed. But even if it is suicidal, as a soldier he has no choice except to follow his orders.

"Company, battalion and regimental commanders share the same sense of tunnel vision and rely on the occasional information gem from their brigade, divisional or visiting corps commander for a glimpse of their unit's place in the scheme of things. Only upon reaching brigade and divisional command can a soldier grasp some perspective of the overall action planned by the politicians and army commanders and its chances of success or failure."

Stan Dudka, the giant North Nova Scotia Highlander sergeant captured and taken to the Abbaye Ardenne on D-Day plus 1, reported back to his regiment in late August. He had lost 45 pounds and had an interesting story to tell Lieut.-Col. D.F. Forbes, the regiment's new commanding officer.

"After leaving Rennes in early July, I was put in Stalag 221 nearby. I figured we wouldn't be there very long. Every day American planes flew over strafing and bombing the city and railway station. Finally, after two or three weeks we could hear American artillery fire from the outskirts. The Germans decided to evacuate us. That night we were crammed into boxcars so tightly that only a third of us could sit."

For two weeks Dudka and his fellow prisoners were shunted around France in the sweltering boxcars attached to various military trains also hauling damaged tanks and weaponry back to Germany for repair. Food consisted of 20 loaves of black bread and several buckets of water thrown into each car once a day. The train paused briefly at St. Nazaire and Nantes, slowly moving inland.

"Twenty miles from Tours we stopped. A nun opened the car door and began handing in plums. Suddenly, a dozen American P47 Thunderbolts started strafing the train. She died along with some of the prisoners. One lad had his head blown off. I scooped up some of his blood in my hands and wiped it over my feet to make it look like I had been wounded. Then, while the Germans were shouting and firing at the aircraft, I climbed out of the boxcar and hobbled away."

He hid the rest of the day and that night made contact with the Underground. Eight days later, following the river Loire he crossed into the American lines near St. Nazaire. Instead of accepting three months rest and leave in England to regain his strength he was back with his regiment by the last week of August.[1]

Dudka became the first eyewitness to events at the Abbaye Ardenne to return to his unit. Lieutenant-Colonel Forbes was understandably fascinated to hear what he had to say. He reported their interview to SHAEF Headquarters in Paris where the war crimes investigating team had opened its offices. After reading Forbes's report, Bruce Macdonald requested that Dudka be sent to Paris immediately.

A week later Macdonald, his deputy, Lieut.-Col. Clarence S. Campbell, the British representative, Lieut.-Col. J.H. Boraston, and Sergeant Dudka drove to Caen. Although much had changed since early June, the big sergeant was able to pinpoint the locations where the killings had occurred and where some of the bodies were buried. The Germans had forced him and a few of the other prisoners to participate in a propaganda news film of a military funeral for some of the murdered Canadians. The bodies were still where they had been buried. Macdonald made arrangements for exhumation, identification and—if possible—determination of the means by which each man died.

Sergeant Dudka went back to war.

During the euphoria of late August with the Germans in full retreat, a few optimists were predicting the war would be over by the New Year. The troops were enjoying the adulation of the French citizenry. In every hamlet, village and town, men, women, children and dogs turned out to welcome the clattering carrier convoys of tired and dusty soldiers. The startled liberators were engulfed with cries of welcome, garlands of flowers, bottles of wine and sweet kisses from the ladies.

Mile after mile the story repeated itself. Forty years later one soldier remembered: "I felt like Jack the Giant Killer . . . part of a whirlwind against which nothing could stand. . . . Their happiness became so infectious that we spent the days grinning foolishly at each other or choking back our tears for having been able to help. It was like Moses leading the Israelites out of bondage—like Wellington's armies at Waterloo—and I was a part of it. . . . and I thanked God that I was still alive to see it all happen."

While Allied columns pursued the stream of shattered German units across France, Field Marshal Model worked frantically to organize his forces into a stable defensive line, first at the Seine, then at the river Somme. But the best his retreating forces could manage was a few sharp and bloody rearguard actions that did little to slow the advance. The 4th Armoured Division reached the Seine near the resort town of Elbeuf on 27 August.

"We have covered 50 miles in the last week, nearly twice the distance from Juno beach to Falaise. A few pockets of German opposition along the way. Only 70 miles to the Somme. However, a general lack of assault equipment has slowed things considerably. . . . Sent Wigle to 3rd Div. to see if we could use their bridges to move Moncel's Brigade across the river. . . . Proctor is off looking for some water transport."

Although his orders stated "4 Canadian Armd. Div. will by *coup-de-main* seize a bridgehead on the north bank of the Seine," Harry had been cautioned by Corps against crossing until sufficient boats and equipment were brought forward and the size of German forces on the opposite bank determined, in case of a counterattack. Unknown to Harry, Kurt Meyer and a scratch force had taken up positions on the other side.

Nearby, at Criquebeuf-sur-Seine, a patrol from the Lincoln and Welland Regiment paddled across the river in a small boat. They returned to report no sign of the enemy. Lieutenant-Colonel Cromb decided such an opportunity was too good to pass up. Quickly, he ordered a larger force to cross and occupy the village of Freneuse. By dark, D Company was dug in on the opposite bank, the first Canadians to cross the Seine. Cromb then reported to Brigade, Brigade to Division, and Division to Corps. Meanwhile, Proctor located a few rafts and amphibious DUKWs to ferry some light armour across to support Cromb's force, which by this time had grown to three companies.

Near noon the Germans counterattacked but were beaten off. Harry decided to keep pouring men and equipment of 10th Brigade to the other side, using anything that would float. He had half of Jefferson's men across when Simonds and Montgomery arrived at his TAC HQ scowling like a pair of thunderclouds.

"What th'hell do you think you're doing?" Simonds demanded. "You were supposed to wait!"

"My orders were to seize a bridgehead by *coup-de-main*, sir. I decided to exploit an opportunity that presented itself as any good cavalryman would."

"Elbeuf is our crossing point, not Criquebeuf! An armoured division is not a cavalry squadron, goddammit!"

"The tactics and principle are the same," Harry replied evenly. "Give my men 48 hours and they'll be dug in and ready again to move for you."

Montgomery nodded. "Quite right, Foster. Carry on."

He heaved a sigh of relief as they drove off. The situation on the other side of the river was not as cut and dried as he had indicated to Simonds. Jefferson's brigade had been ordered to take up the positions held by the Lincoln and Wellands, then carry forward an attack through the villages of Sotteville and Igoville. The high ground covering the crossings was occupied by men of the 17th Luftwaffe Field Division, part of what was left of Dietrich's Fifth Panzer Army. They intended blocking any advance toward Rouen from this direction. There was much lighter opposition across the curving river at Elbeuf. "By late afternoon I decided to abandon the idea of putting 4th Brigade's armour across at Criquebeuf and ordered Moncel to use rafts and the Bailey Bridge at Elbeuf when it was finished."

The 8th GHQ Troops, Royal Engineers, worked throughout the night. At first light on the 28th a Bailey pontoon bridge capable of carrying the tanks was completed. By the time the rest of the corps' heavy armour reached the far bank, Proctor had all his supply dumps moved across the river and was providing the Polish armoured division with ammunition, petrol and spares until their own supplies were brought over. By dawn of 30 August the entire division was on the north side of the Seine and ready to move.

Once more Roberts and his Staghounds took up the lead, but this time enemy rearguard became more active as they advanced. By midafternoon *Panzerfäuste** had knocked out three of the armoured cars. The Germans waited until the lead vehicles entered a village, then caught them in the narrow streets at minimum range with devastating results.

---

*A shoulder-held short-range anti-tank weapon.

At Bierville, troop leader Sgt. Ross Bell, unable to reverse his Staghound to escape the frontal fire, decided to charge the German positions at full speed. Bursting out the other side of the village, he and his men collided with 60 German infantrymen and three anti-tank guns. Guns blazing, Bell knocked the anti-tank guns off the road and killed most of their crews. Half of the infantrymen died from bullets or under the wheels of Bell's Staghound. A few miles farther along the road Bell encountered a Tiger tank.

"Hold your fire!" Bell ordered his men.

The commander of the German Tiger obligingly moved to the ditch to allow the Staghound passage. Bell waved a thank you and raced on. Next, they encountered a horse-drawn convoy of 300 troops with a few anti-tank guns in tow. The column marched along a sunken road between two high banks. The Staghound leaped forward, its machine guns slaughtering men and animals, its heavy wheels chewing through the screaming mass of scrambling, terrified animals and men. Out of 300 troops in the column, Bell and his men estimated that they had killed or wounded 200.

Out of ammunition and lost, the crew fortunately made contact with the FFI. They were led into a thick wood by the Underground where the Staghound was carefully camouflaged and guarded until able to rejoin the regiment. Bell was awarded the Military Medal for his exploits.

Simonds promised that troops would be given a five-day rest once the next objective, St. Croix-de-Buchy, had been captured. Spurred by this carrot the men drove forward in driving rain. By early the following day Buchy had been taken.

"No sooner had I got everyone organized for our rest than orders arrived from Guy to move immediately on Abbeville (at the Somme). Apparently British Second Army reached the Somme today. U.S. First Army is almost to the Belgian border and still going flat out. We're being left behind. Guy wants us to catch up by tomorrow morning. I delivered this cheerful news at my divisional O Group this evening. Much wailing and gnashing of teeth. Poor old Wigle blanched at the thought of organizing a divisional movement on such short notice. . . . Thank God I am not my own GSO1. . . . A night movement for the Division covering 30 kilometres. It should be interesting."

It was. In pitch blackness and led by Roberts's Staghounds, the division crossed the start line at 30 minutes past midnight on 1 September. They were moving on a single road through unreconnoitred country without proper maps.[2] For 90 minutes the column proceeded without incident, the lead squadron signalling "Nothing to report" at ten-minute intervals.

Then the column halted. The long line of vehicles and crews waited, motors idling. Radio reports from the lead squadron grew fainter and fainter until they faded completely. A half hour passed. Harry borrowed a motorcycle from one of his dispatch riders and raced up to find out what had happened. A few hundred yards from the head of the column he stopped.

Lieutenant-Colonel Roberts appeared out of the darkness on foot. "Good evening, sir."

"Why are we stopped?"

"I don't know."

"Find out will you?"

Roberts continued on foot. Up and down the column cigarette ends glowed from hatch tops as vehicle commanders waited patiently. Roberts reached the lead vehicle—a medical lorry. When the commander of the lead Staghound had stopped to check his navigation before proceeding, the entire column had come to a halt. During the wait the medical lorry driver fell asleep at the wheel. The rest of the column had then moved off without him—and the division. Roberts woke him up.

"1 September. . . . Flew back to Corps HQ to see Guy. Discussed our present traffic problems with British 7th Armoured Division who are on our right and the German opposition at Allery. . . . When I returned Moncel had solved the problem of who would be responsible for taking Allery. After a long fruitless discussion with the commander of the British 4th Armoured Brigade, he simply bypassed the town and harboured his brigade northeast of Airaines."

Proctor was having his own problems with the British 7th Armoured Division. For some unexplained reason Simonds and the British Corps Commander had given both divisions the same highway centre line. Proctor had been the first to station his Provost along the route for traffic direction. When the British appeared, they were asked politely by Canadian Provost— most of whom were peacetime RCMP officers—to take themselves off the road until the 4th Armoured Division had passed through. The British response was to arrest and replace the Canadians with their own Provost, and lock them in assorted town and village jails along the route. As the 4th Armoured moved down its centre line, it was directed off along side roads by the haughty British Provost.

Furious, Proctor stormed over to the British 7th Division and demanded an explanation from his opposite number. The Quartermaster, also a lieutenant-colonel, called him several rude names, whereupon Proctor, a roughneck diamond driller in civilian life, invited the supercilious Englishman to join him behind a hedgerow where he promptly knocked him cold with a solid left hook. When the man recovered, he ran whining to his divisional commander. In due course Harry took up Proctor's cause.

"Maj.-Gen. Verney, GOC of the British 7th Div., came to see me. He was not happy. . . . I got the feeling that as far as he and his staff are concerned we're just a bunch of ill-mannered damn Colonials. . . . A lot of ruffled feathers on the British side. . . . Christ, you'd think we were at war with each other instead of the Germans."

Divisional HQ harboured that night near a gravel quarry. Sentries were posted. At first light hell broke loose. A squadron of German Panthers had decided to harbour on the other side of the quarry. Both sides opened fire simultaneously. The Divisional HQ Company was a battleworthy unit with 16 tanks plus armoured scout cars under Lieut.-Col. Clarence Campbell. In the exchange of fire Campbell's gunners knocked out six Panthers for the loss of four Shermans before the Germans withdrew.

2

The brief but sharp resistance now being put up by enemy forces along the coastal flanks of the Northern Army Group came from rearguard units of the German Fifteenth Army that had been waiting patiently for the Allied landings at the Pas-de-Calais. Unlike the chaotic retreat from the Falaise Gap by Eberbach's and Dietrich's forces, the withdrawal of the Fifteenth Army under General of the Infantry Gustav-Adolf von Zangen was completed in orderly fashion. Von Zangen had assumed command on 27 August with the responsibility of defending the Channel coast from the Seine to the Scheldt estuaries, including the Dutch island of Walcheren and North Beveland.

By 2 September, with the British across the Somme and with what remained of the German Fifth Panzer and Seventh Armies unable to stop the Allied advance, Model ordered von Zangen to extend his front inland, taking over the sector occupied by the Fifth Panzer Army.

Von Zangen observed dryly: "Additional forces for carrying out this order were not placed at our disposal. . . . As a result of a representation . . . made by telephone to Model giving a description of our own situation the order was withdrawn."

That evening Montgomery sent Crerar a sharply worded message about the general lack of Canadian progress: "SECOND ARMY are now positioned near the BELGIAN frontier and will go through towards BRUSSELS tomorrow. It is VERY necessary that your two Armd. Divs. should push forward with all speed towards ST. OMER and beyond. NOT rpt NOT consider this the time for any div. to halt for maintenance. Push on quickly."

Montgomery's use of the "not, repeat, not" hyperbole in orders and signals was well understood. It was about as close as he ever got to swearing at a subordinate.

Crerar replied tartly and in the same vein, offering his congratulations on Second Army's achievement but at the same time pointing out that until late that afternoon none of Second Army's units had been within five miles of the Canadian position at Abbeville. There, on the Somme, all bridges had been blown and the Germans were holding the north side of the river in considerable strength. There was a big difference between fighting

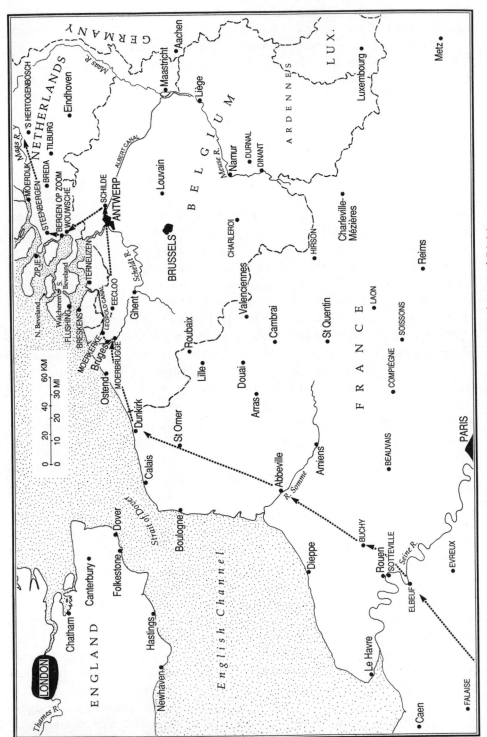

From Falaise to the Scheldt, showing the movements of Harry Foster's 4th Canadian Armoured Division.

German resistance and motoring over a first-class highway into Brussels with only the wind in your face.

The following day Crerar missed a conference at Montgomery's headquarters. Instead, he drove to Dieppe to take part in ceremonies with the 2nd Division, who had been given the satisfaction of taking the town and beaches where so many of them had died in 1942. Later, arriving at Army Group HQ, Montgomery blasted Crerar for his attitude and performance. Monty stated darkly that "our ways must part." To his credit, Crerar refused to be intimidated. He told the newly appointed field marshal (as of 1 September) that "he could not accept his attitude and judgment . . . [and would] never consent to being pushed about by anyone." He then suggested they air their grievances "through official channels."

The sparks of Montgomery's anger sputtered and died. Although he had no use for Crerar as an army commander, he was acutely conscious of the political implications of fighting with him.

Harry's perception of his superior officers came from watching their performance in the field and back at headquarters.

"As the Allied 'political' military supreme commander, General Eisenhower was a fortunate choice. He might not have been a great soldier but he was probably the only man capable of handling the considerable egos of the men who commanded the British, Canadian and American armies.

"General Montgomery, on the other hand, was the strategist. Probably the best we had. But he was a bastard to deal with. I never ran into anyone who really liked him. He was invariably sharp, short on compliments and always free with criticism. Yet we had to admire him. He had that phenomenal ability of being able to organize and plan the timing of every movement for an entire army group during a two-week campaign and be out by only six hours when it was over.

"His relationships with most senior officers were more like an English housemaster with his sixth-form prefects than that of an army commander. The British troops adored him, particularly when he came down off his perch to exude his version of the 'common touch.' It was fascinating to watch one of these casual but carefully orchestrated 'impromptu gatherings.'

"Monty, dressed as always in his sheepskin jacket and black beret with the dual cap badges, stood in his jeep, one hand resting on the windshield, urging the men to move closer so he could speak to them man-to-man. There would be a brief introductory joke about the Germans or Adolf, a few compliments on how well they had done—or were going to do—with a short outline of what to expect and how it was impossible to lose battles when he had men like them to lead. Then with a wave he was off to the next unit where the process was repeated. He was like a prairie politician on the hustings. How his men ate it up!

"The Canadians, on the other hand, thought he was a horse's ass and hated his guts. When he stood up to make a speech, there were always a number of uncomplimentary mutterings from our troops: 'Listen to that silly old Limey sonofabitch!' or 'Aw, what a crock of bullshit!' To his credit, Monty never indicated he heard a thing.

"Generals Crerar and Dempsey, Monty's army commanders, were as different as chalk and cheese. Both had served in the First War but there the similarity ended. Prior to his appointment in October 1943 as Canadian Corps commander in Italy, Harry Crerar had never commanded a field formation. Like Eisenhower—but without his warmth or personality—he was more suited to the art of peacetime military politics than leading men into battle. Dempsey, on the other hand, had commanded the rearguard action during the Dunkirk evacuation and later the British Eighth Army's XIII Corps in North Africa. He was a precise energetic fellow who knew his business.

"At Corps and Army HQ O Groups I got the feeling that Crerar relied on his corps commanders, Guy and General Crocker, to make the decisions on how Monty's orders were to be carried out. I never heard of Crerar coming up with an idea of his own, yet it was due to him as much as anyone that the British were prepared to accept a 'Canadian' army. Probably because he posed no threat to outshining his Sandhurst-trained rivals.

"On the surface he appeared a gentlemanly inoffensive sort of chap. But there was an unpleasant mean streak in him. At times he treated his subordinates in a shabby manner, holding some of the brightest officers at his headquarters back from promotion and in the process destroying what might otherwise have been spectacular army careers. He never grasped the fundamental difference between operating a peacetime Permanent Force and a wartime army of civilian militiamen. He believed the same set of rules and regulations were applicable, irrespective of how absurd they might be.

"In Italy, when Guy refused to conform to his ideas during the Italian campaign, Crerar became convinced that Simonds had gone mad and ordered the army's chief psychiatric advisor, Dr. Fred Van Nostrand, flown out to examine him. Simonds had just come out of hospital to take over command of the 5th Division near Caserta, under Montgomery. Fortunately, Van Nostrand was intercepted before reaching Guy's HQ or there would have been hell to pay.

"In comparison to Crerar, both corps commanders were a pair of brightly lit dynamos. Guy was always respectful but it was no secret that he felt himself better qualified to be the army commander. Yet even without the title, it was Guy and not Crerar who called the shots and made things work. Everyone knew and accepted that fact.

"I think General Montgomery realized this early in the game. Whenever a planning conference was held at Army Group HQ, Crerar and Dempsey were expected to bring their corps commanders along to the briefing. Later, when Crerar held his own O Group covering Montgomery's plan, corps, divisional and sometimes brigade commanders were in attendance. Thus, Guy knew exactly what Montgomery wanted and, as corps commander, made it his business to see the job got done. Crerar might take the credit or handle a press conference with war correspondents after we'd won or lost a battle, but it was Guy who did the actual planning and saw to its execution. Uncle Harry was smart enough to leave him alone and let him get on with it.

"Except for conducting O Groups, Guy spent little time back at his Corps HQ. His chief of staff, Brig. Norman Rodger, ran the day-to-day business. Guy was up at dawn and on the road with his TAC HQ, always on the move, checking on everything and everyone, the way a field commander should. By day's end he knew the troop dispositions on every sector of the front right down to regimental and sometimes even the battalion level.

"This example was not lost on the rest of us. Whenever his Staghound command car arrived at someone's TAC HQ or command post and Guy raised his goggles and climbed down, the senior officer present was expected to deliver a concise situation report on his sector of the line. Heaven help him if he couldn't! The result of these unannounced visits was that colonels, brigadiers and major-generals made it a habit of keeping themselves informed about their various units by making a daily habit of visiting their front lines.

"Guy had an excellent philosophy: 'Never hold anyone back from promotion; always promote a man when he leaves you. That way there will never be any hard feelings if you have to sack him. Always award medals or citations as soon as practical after they have been earned. In this way everyone sees evidence of the reward and your appreciation for a job well done.' It was these little considerations that made Guy a great general.

"Unless there was a lull in the fighting, my time each day was spent continuously on the move between Army and Corps HQ on the one hand, and my brigades and various regimental HQ on the other. I made it my business to know what was going on. With the exception of two or three short breaks I had been maintaining a ferocious work pace since D-Day. Without the ability of taking 20-minute catnaps during odd times of the day or night I would never have made it. Those who have never fought in a series of lengthy battles find it hard to understand how fatigue can be as great a threat to a commanding officer's survival as enemy shells or bullets.

"When not fighting the enemy, front-line troops have little to do. They can sunbathe, write a few letters home, relax, read or sleep. Their commanders, on the other hand, never relax. They're on the job around the clock and those that don't learn to delegate authority and acquire an ability to catnap soon run themselves straight into the ground. As days pass and they stay awake nights worrying and becoming more and more fatigued, their ability for rational decisions is impaired. Finally, a battalion or regimental commander reports to Brigade or Divisional HQ that enemy resistance has stiffened, that his troops are exhausted and need a rest. In reality it is he and not the troops who are exhausted.

"A brigade or divisional commander who fails to go up to the front regularly and check things for himself can end up passing misinformation back to Corps and Army HQ. At least two instances of reported troop fatigue brought Guy up to the line to investigate. He arrived during midafternoon. Everything appeared quiet. The men were playing games or sunbathing between swims in a nearby river. Their exhausted commanding officer was asleep in his command post. In both cases the COs were sacked."

From Brussels, Dempsey's Second Army made a spectacular 60-mile dash to capture the great inland seaport of Antwerp on 4 September. Thanks to the Belgian Resistance, the huge docks and warehouse facilities were virtually intact. However, capturing Antwerp was one thing, being able to use its harbour facilities quite another. Until both banks of the 50-mile Scheldt Estuary leading out to the Channel were in Allied hands, the magnificent seaport would be useless. The Scheldt was to become one of the worst battlefields of the war.

On the same day, General von Zangen commented: "The news of the fall of Antwerp . . . and envelopment of the Fifteenth Army—seemed now to be completed. . . . To the army, still comparatively strong numerically, but seriously impeded by their low fighting qualities and lack of combat experience . . . the following possibilities remained: (1) withdrawal to the Channel coast . . . to reinforce the garrisons of the fortresses and defence areas; (2) withdrawal to the Scheldt Estuary in order to cross the river there with the main body . . . to . . . the mainland over Walcheren and South Beveland; [and] (3) breakthrough to the east."

Hitler's orders next day to Model for transmission to von Zangen were to abandon any breakout attempt and move the Fifteenth Army across the Scheldt to the mainland from where it was to defend the Albert Canal line just north of Antwerp. The Scheldt Estuary and Channel fortresses were to be "held perseveringly."

Evacuating an army of 90,000 men, 600 guns and over 6,200 vehicles and horses by sea was a formidable undertaking. It required a 3.5-mile crossing by boat from Breskens—13 miles from Terneuzen—to Flushing on Walcheren Island. From Flushing, an unprotected narrow causeway connected Walcheren to South Beveland, and a single road led from there to the mainland, 15 miles north of Antwerp. Throughout the withdrawal von Zangen's forces would be in the open and subject to Allied air attacks. Nevertheless, on 6 September, while a determined rearguard held back the Canadian and British advance, the evacuation began.

Allied forces in the west now stretched 400 miles from Holland and the

German border in the north to the Vosges and Swiss frontier in the south. Once again, von Rundstedt was called out of retirement to take command of the Führer's western armies. Since presiding over a number of "Courts of Honour"[3] of senior officers involved in the July plot, he was considered a trustworthy choice. Model, Hitler's energetic "fireman," would continue to command Army Group B and direct the battle for Belgium and Holland.

The wily von Rundstedt realized at once that without a continuous flow of supplies the Allied advance must eventually come to a halt. Until late August everything brought ashore had to come by truck from the beaches and wharfs of Normandy. The roads from Falaise to Caen and beyond to Courseulles and Cherbourg had developed into an endless traffic jam. In stifling heat under a canopy of grey, gritty dust that stretched to the horizons, lines of slow-moving trucks rumbled to and from the front.

While the French Channel ports of Le Havre, Boulogne, Calais and Dunkirk remained in German hands, the Allied supply lines from the Normandy beaches would continue to stretch. Sooner or later they would have to snap, at least in theory. Every day that the German forces could hold the ports, the better the chances were for rebuilding a strong defensive West Wall along the Rhine to protect the Fatherland. But once the prize—the great inland port of Antwerp—at the end of the thrust up the Channel coast fell, the Allied supply problems would be solved and Germany doomed.

Since von Rundstedt's departure in July when 62 German divisions faced a 100-mile Allied front in Normandy, the situation had changed considerably. To defend a front four times larger, Model advised him that total German fighting strength amounted to no more than 25 divisions. In a single week Allied armies had crossed the Somme and the Marne and had swept through Flanders and the Argonne Forests, the same battlefields over which their fathers had fought so valiantly nearly 30 years before. It was the Schlieffen Plan in reverse. After three months of hesitant fighting in Normandy the Allied armies were now showing themselves to be just as effective at *Blitzkrieg* as the Wehrmacht.

Von Rundstedt was not optimistic. "As far as I was concerned," he stated later, "the war ended in September."

For Eberbach it ended at Amiens on 31 August when he was captured along with his headquarters staff by the British 3rd Royal Tank Regiment. For Kurt it ended six days later near Namur in southeast Belgium. Both had been fighting almost continuously since escaping through the Falaise Gap.

Kurt had joined what was left of the I Panzer Corps on 20 August. So few of the original Leibstandarte remained that he barely recognized the unit. "I couldn't help the tears from running down my face. Thousands of my comrades lay dead in the Norman earth. . . . Our expulsion proves that west of the Seine there remains no stable front. Nor to the east of the Seine is any defence available. The prospects are catastrophic. We can hope now only for the West Wall."

Near Rouen he joined Model's OB West. The Field Marshal tried frantically to organize a holding action. Under no illusions, he told his senior officers during a briefing that "35 to 40 divisions were required if the situation on the Western Front is to be strengthened. Since we all know that 40 divisions are no longer available, we return to the hope of the West Wall."

Kurt was placed in command of one of Model's improvised divisional fighting groups and sent to Elbeuf to delay the Allied advance as long as possible. From Elbeuf his unit was pushed two miles back from the Seine to the Forêt de la Londe. There, from 26 to 28 August, Meyer's tiny battle group under Mohnke's command met the Canadians for the last time. They held them three days and inflicted considerable losses before withdrawing in good order.

The 3rd and 4th Canadian Divisions were already across the river. It was difficult to understand why General Foulkes found it necessary to order five of his division's battalions* to continue a piecemeal attack that resulted in 577 casualties. The German pocket in the Forêt de la Londe could just as easily have been bypassed with a rearguard left to mop up.

Kurt's battle group continued its retreat. "After a two-day stop in the area around Beauvais the division is transferred to Hirson. . . . We march under cover of darkness across the bloodsoaked fields of the First World War and over the same streets where we raced westwards in 1940. Our marching band looks miserable. Escort convoys roll by throughout the night . . . General Stumpf personally brings news of the award of Swords to the Oak Leaves of my Knight's Cross."

Two days later his tiny force was on the move, making for the river Meuse in northeastern France. During the withdrawal his long-time friend, Erich Olboetter, commander of the 26th SS Regiment and Knight's Cross winner, drove over a mine laid by partisans in a village street. "Both his legs were blown off. He died the same night near Charleville. . . . I lost an old fighting companion who had been by my side since 1939."

As they continued their withdrawal, partisans appeared from everywhere to harass, kill and hurry them on their way.

---

*The 2nd Division's Royal Hamilton Light Infantry, Royal Regiment of Canada, Essex and Scottish, South Saskatchewan, the Cameron Highlanders, the Fusiliers Mont Royal and the Calgary Highlanders all took part in this somewhat pointless three-day battle.

3

At the Meuse in southern Belgium Kurt made his last stand against the Allied steamroller. During the night of 5 September, American forces crossed the river at Namur. Near 2300 hours a lone reconnaissance trooper reported that the enemy was advancing down the main road on the north side of the river, the last defence line before the West Wall. The German border lay only 55 miles to the east.

"It seemed unbelievable to me but at 2315 hours the information was reconfirmed. . . . The units were immediately alerted with orders to retreat behind the Ourthe."

The retreat could only be made in darkness. Speed was essential. The Americans were heading for Durnal. Once that town's crossroads had been taken the column would be trapped. They raced through the night and reached Durnal by dawn. Kurt sped ahead past the headquarters' vehicles to join Hauptsturmführer Heinzelmann at the point.

"I wave to Heinzelmann as we encounter the first houses in Durnal. The place lies in a densely wooded hollow. A five-foot wall curves along the left side of the street. . . . I stay in the truck. . . . I cry out to warn Heinzelmann, but it is too late. A shot . . . tears into the first truck. An American tank rolls around the curve, firing. The picture changes quickly. . . . A few Volkswagen against a column of tanks is not very amusing."

There wasn't room to turn around. The Americans were looking for targets, not prisoners. Quickly, he jumped from his vehicle, vaulted a garden gate, then a wire fence, and after a short run found sanctuary in a chicken coop behind one of the houses.

"A body comes flying over the wire. Max Bornhöft catches up to me. Now we are both in the soup. The shed hides us. We hope to find the way back to our comrades when it's dark. Loud cries come from the street. The people are welcoming the Americans . . . tanks are rolling by. . . .

"2400 hours and a light drizzle is falling on the roof of the shed. I can't stand it any more. I have to know what is happening on the street. . . . I crawl out to the wire fence . . . barely reach the corner of the shed when I experience one of the most frightening seconds of the war! A few partisans come to the fence and ask an old farmer something . . . probably wanting to know if the farmer has noticed any German soldiers. . . . The farmer shakes his head. With my teeth pressed together I lie only a few metres from the partisans. . . . My hand is tightly holding the grip of my pistol. They don't see me. A stinging nettle bush is my cover. . . .

"Cries and shouts draw them to the neighbouring yard. The life of a comrade has ended. We feel safer because the yard has been searched. We also hope—curiously—that the rain will keep up. Minutes turn into hours. The rain falls harder. . . . The chickens are making a commotion outside and want to get into the building. The old farmer stays inquisitively at the wire, trying to chase the poultry into the shed. The soft-headed beasts want their empire to themselves. . . .

"Curious, the farmer sticks his head into the shed. . . . Before he can open his mouth he is sitting on an old barrel in the darkest corner . . . playing third man in our bond. He looks anxiously at our pistols. The situation is becoming complicated because if we allow for good intentions the farmer's wife will be joining us shortly, looking for her lord and master. We decide to let the old man go. He promises to keep his mouth shut and not to go to the partisans. He slinks away. . . .

"Of course we don't take his promise at face value. The old man has barely disappeared before we climb the wall and start running . . . straight up to the front of the partisan headquarters . . . located in the furnace cellar of the church. A young lad is standing by the door smoking his first American cigarette. Heavily armed partisans come down the steps. Like weasels, we jump, creep, scurry and run for cover in the cemetery. We land in a compost heap at the corner of the cemetery. Further flight is impossible. I cover Max with old wreaths and tell him to watch the exit to the church. I am intent on creeping up behind a few of these fellows. . . .

"A cry rings out . . . I turn around and see two policemen on the porch. I look into the muzzles of their weapons. For a minute they are confused. They haven't discovered Max yet. Instantaneously, I fire my pistol at them and run . . . to the southern wall of the cemetery—straight into the muzzle of a carbine. The marksman . . . scrambles away when I run straight at him, threatening him with my own gun. We are surrounded. The old man has given the alarm. I jump over the centre wall and land on the village road 12 feet below. Max lands behind me. . . .

"My God, you can be brisk when your life depends on it! The road goes up the slope. My lungs are bursting. Shots ring out around my ears. I hear Max cry. I turn and shoot down the street. Max is lying on the ground. He has been hit. My shots have forced the freedom fighters under cover. . . . My glance falls on a small door hidden in the wall by a big boulder. I take cover behind it. Through a crack I watch the enraged partisans. Every bush is searched. They cannot explain my disappearance and blame each other. . . . One of them orders me loudly to come out and give up the fight. He promises to respect the law and turn me over to the Americans. . . .

"My gun is becoming heavier. There was a time when we swore never to be taken alive. The cruel Russian experiences moved us to it. Now that is all so far away. One bullet gone on the run and another in the magazine. Should I honour the oath? Or does it only apply to the Eastern Front? Minutes pass. My eyes are drawn repeatedly to the metal object in my hand. I think of my family and our coming child. It is difficult, so difficult to make a decision.

The partisans are standing a few metres from my hiding place. I study their faces. A few are bitter and brutal while others seem to be no more than harmless burghers into whose hands someone pressed weapons a few minutes earlier. . . .

"Their leader orders me to give up. A boy of about 14 stands beside him. Father and son. The boy holds a carbine. Suddenly, with excitement he points to my door and the stone that was rolled away. Where the stone had lain the earth is dry. . . . Again, the father orders my surrender. A shot goes through the door. Hand grenades are brought out. More shots split the wood, forcing me into the corner. I scream at the father: 'My weapon is pointing at your son. Will you keep your promise?' Immediately, he pulls his son to him and repeats his promise. . . .

"Now it is over. My only hope is a counterattack by my comrades. I toss the magazine in the corner, the gun next to it. What a pathetic feeling it is to be captured. Slowly, I open the door and go to the partisan leader. A few of them want to fall on me straightaway. . . . I look into the father's eyes. With a movement of his hand he forces his companions to lower their weapons. Grumbling, they obey. . . . The leader tells me that he was a worker during the war in Germany and experienced only good; he has no intention of leading a band of murderers. . . .

"Max Bornhöft is still lying on the road. He has been shot in the upper shoulder. We carry him to the police station where he gets a tetanus shot from the village doctor. . . . Two police take out handcuffs . . . and put them on me. My knees buckle from the pain. They muzzle me in the joint. The chains cut into my flesh. They look at my face intently, sneering. They have tried this torture many times before. It is obvious they are waiting for my howls of pain. Max looks on and cries: 'Oh, these dogs!' . . .

"The leader returns and I am led off across the cemetery to their headquarters in the furnace cellar. Max is laid on a straw mattress . . . in great pain. He asks me over and over to greet his father if I should survive. He himself has little hope. . . . The leader brings us some bread. He is unsure of himself. German troops are still to the west and will probably pass by tonight. . . .

"Tensely, I listen to each noise. . . . From partisan conversation I assume that the Americans have gone on toward Dinant and in a short time there will be no Americans left in Durnal. A very taciturn partisan guards us. If only he wouldn't fumble so carelessly with his gun. The young man is terribly frightened. . . . At midnight everyone suddenly disappears, leaving only the man guarding us. . . .

"Vehicles drive through the village. American or German? After an hour I hear shots followed later by exploding shells. Cartridges shatter in the air. A German vehicle is probably burning. At dawn everything is shaking from German and American machine-gun fire. Our guard is . . . more restless.

He flat out refuses to let me give Max some water. . . .

"Suddenly, the window panes are flying around our ears. . . . Americans are ordering us to surrender. . . . Things are looking up! The guard stands frightened in the corner threatening me with his gun. I roar at him to open the door, to stop the Americans from their bloody senseless firing. . . . The Americans fire even harder. . . . Our partisan finally opens the door and calls the Americans. Machine-gun fire hits the church wall as the first American comes down. To my surprise our guard steps softly into the background and runs to the nearest corner. He turns out to be a deserter from Lothringen* and is confused by the way the Americans treat him as a cad. . . .

"The muzzle of a machine-pistol is pointed at my stomach. 'Don't move!' the American yells. 'My buddy wants your decorations as souvenirs.' Faint with rage, I must allow my Knight's Cross, which I have had since April 1941, to be stolen. The second American speaks good German. His mother was born in Germany. After a short time he tells me: 'For God's sake, don't say who you are. Your troops are receiving terrible treatment.' Twenty-four hours later I understood the meaning of his words."

While Foulkes's 2nd Division moved against fortress Dunkirk on 6 September and Spry's 3rd Division came to an abrupt halt before the high ground of German defences outside Boulogne, Harry divided the 4th Armoured Division into two spearheads—"Moncel Force" and "Stewart Force"†—and pushed forward. But their easy-motoring days were over. Moncel collided with determined German resistance at Bergues near the Dunkirk perimeter. When the garrison refused to surrender, Harry ordered Moncel to bypass it and head into Belgium, with the ultimate objective being an area around Eecloo.

The rolling French countryside with its protective folds of ground and commanding features gave way to the undulating terrain of Belgium. The cities of Bruges and Ghent were Simonds's next objectives. The 4th Armoured was ordered to take Bruges, while the Polish division was sent toward Ghent, 50 miles to the east.

Both 4th Division battle groups reached the Ghent Canal a few miles south of Bruges early the following day. They found the enemy sitting snugly in well-prepared positions across the narrow expanse of water. Von Zangen had ordered the canal line to be held during the Fifteenth Army's evacuation across the Scheldt from Terneuzen and Breskens.

Harry set up his divisional headquarters at the community of Rolleweg in an old stone farm house three miles south of Bruges. He considered his

---

*The French province of Lorraine, which provided many unwilling German-French troops to the German army.

†Lieut.-Col. J.D. Stewart held temporary command of the 10th Brigade during Brigadier Jefferson's absence due to illness.

options: "I didn't want to lay on an air raid or shell the city. It was filled with civilians and Flemish art treasures too beautiful to destroy. Taking it by force would have cost lives—ours and theirs. Narrow city streets are no place for tank operations. If I sent them in, we might have lost half our armour and the Belgians would have lost Bruges. It wasn't worth risking. Nor was I keen on an infantry attack house to house. A flanking movement across the Ghent Canal struck me as the best approach . . . 10th Brigade to establish a bridgehead across south of the city; Moncel to slip in from the southwest."

Near midday a young woman arrived on a bicycle claiming to be an Allied agent and head of the Underground. The Rolleweg farm belonged to her grandparents. The Germans allowed her to leave the city daily for fresh produce. She introduced herself as "Renée" and demanded to speak to the "general in charge." Lieutenant-Colonel Wigle turned her over to his intelligence officer with strict orders that she was not to see any operational maps. A hasty interrogation followed, during which she demonstrated an astonishing amount of knowledge about every German strongpoint in and outside the city, including a weak point in their line near the village of Moerbrugge on the other side of the canal. She explained that the city was being held by what the Germans called "The Stomach Division"—20,000 soldiers from the Eastern Front who had developed ulcers, dysentery and other stomach complaints. Belgium, with its availability of fresh vegetables, milk and eggs was awarded as a recuperative posting to the battle-hardened veterans inside the city. Counting Germans, refugees and citizens, over 75,000 people were inside Bruges.

She claimed to have been trained at Camp X near Bowmanville, Ontario, by "Intrepid"—spymaster William Stephenson. To prove her bona fides she gave an identification number to be checked by radio with London. After promising to return with more information next morning, she collected a few eggs and pedalled back to the city. Later in the day London confirmed Renée's identity. Harry ordered Stewart Force to make a crossing at the village of Moerbrugge later that evening.

"My first serious tactical mistake of the war was in trying to rush the crossing without proper planning or artillery support. Since Falaise I had allowed myself to be lulled into a dangerous sense of invincibility. I anticipated the same sort of short sharp fight we had experienced at earlier river crossings, followed by a general enemy withdrawal. . . . It didn't work out that way and, sorrowfully, the casualties were heavy."

A battalion of the Argyll and Sutherland Highlanders of Canada Regiment went over in two large punts taken from a mooring nearby. Fortunately, the landing was made at Renée's weak juncture point between two German divisions or the heavy casualties from the mortar and 88 mm guns that rained down on the men might have been much more serious. Under heavy fire from both flanks a battalion of the Lincoln and Welland Regiment joined the Argylls before dawn on the 9th. Then, cut off from the main force, they held their precarious toehold along the north bank against repeated German attempts to dislodge them.

That morning Harry flew back to Corps HQ to discuss the situation with Simonds, who was smarting from Montgomery's continual complaints that the Canadian corps wasn't moving fast enough. The British had been in Antwerp since the 4th. Simonds wanted an aircraft, artillery and tank bombardment of Bruges, followed by a tank-supported infantry assault. Harry disagreed. They argued. Finally, Simonds agreed to give him two days. Harry flew back to Rolleweg.

At the canal, sappers toiled gallantly under heavy and concentrated fire to throw a bridge across during daylight, but it was too dangerous and the work had to be abandoned until dark. By morning it was complete, and units of the 29th Armoured Recce Regiment started moving across. The main body of German troops began withdrawing behind the next water barrier—the Leopold Canal.

"By day's end the bridgehead at Moerbrugge had been extended with two battalions, one company of infantry and three squadrons of tanks. Six hundred prisoners were estimated to have been taken but the advance is still slow. . . . During the afternoon, Main Division HQ assumed the appearance of a market place or a world's fair information booth. The Intelligence office was besieged by civilians of all shapes, sizes and varieties who wanted to impart 'THE' piece of vital information which would end the battle for Bruges. . . . At 2130 hours relief from this struggle arrived in the person of two Belgian and two Dutch liaison officers."

Approaching Bruges, the tanks and vehicles of Moncel Force funnelled into a road junction with the British 4th Armoured Brigade. Smoothly, Canadian and British tanks merged into a single column and proceeded toward the city. On the outskirts they halted and harboured together for the night. In the darkness Brigadier Moncel returned to his TAC HQ command vehicle to find it occupied by a young English brigadier. He protested the intrusion. The officer apologized and introduced himself as Mike Carver.* In the darkness one command vehicle looked much like another.

A Belgian priest, suitably blindfolded, arrived from Bruges as emissary from the Mayor to plead for the city and its treasures. He advised that the German garrison commander was willing to cooperate if the Canadians would allow him and his troops 24 hours to vacate the city. As a precaution, the priest was treated to a carefully orchestrated tour of Moncel's forces and told to report what he had seen to the Germans. After viewing the tank squadrons

---

*Later Field Marshal Lord Carver, chief of the Imperial General Staff.

from several different angles between blindfoldings, he returned to the city convinced that most of the Canadian army was waiting outside the city's gates.

Harry agreed to wait 24 hours and ordered Moncel Force to bypass the city and cross the canal at the Moerbrugge bridgehead.

Renée brought news for the division's medical officer (MO). A German field hospital in one of the country homes at the edge of the city held a number of Canadian wounded. This was too much for Col. Charles Gossage, the chief MO. Carrying a white flag, with a bright red cross painted on his jeep, he went off to collect the Canadian wounded. The Germans allowed him through their lines.[4] He drove up to the field hospital and demanded to see the CO. By one of those strange coincidences that make readers of popular fiction wince, the German senior medical officer turned out to be a classmate of Gossage's during his postgraduate days at Heidelberg University. They shared a bottle of champagne and discussed the situation. The country house had a cellar filled with vintage wines and spirits; the hospital was short of medical supplies. They worked out an amicable arrangement: boxes of Canadian army penicillin would be exchanged for cases of wine plus all the Allied wounded. Gossage went back to the Canadian lines and returned with ambulances and the penicillin. Besides Canadian wounded, he brought out a number of British and South Africans, together with a truck filled with assorted wines.

The Germans kept to the bargain. After blowing only the main bridge, they withdrew leaving Bruges intact. Moncel and his staff, as the first senior officers into the city, were treated to a sumptuous dinner at the Golden Basket Restaurant. Harry drove in with his aide-de-camp, Capt. Ken Scott, Proctor and Wigle on the afternoon of the 12th to a tumultuous reception at the Town Hall.

"I made a short speech which I'm sure no one understood, signed the guest book and was presented with an autographed set of reproductions by a Flemish artist named Muerling of whom I had never heard. But then I don't suppose any of them had ever heard of Cornelius Krieghoff or the Group of Seven. . . . We were all made honorary citizens and inducted as life members into the ancient Guild of Archers of the Society of San Sebastian. . . . What a celebration!"

The division's next objective was to cross the double canal line at Moerkerke, six miles beyond Bruges. Separated by a single 60-foot dike, the Canal de Dérivation de la Lys and the Leopold ran side by side for 13 miles to the North Sea near Zeebrugge. The waterways were no more than a stone's throw in width yet too deep to wade and too wide to jump. Intelligence reports indicated that the Germans were in full retreat and opposition for the crossing would be light.

"The plan was to cross the canals and hustle the enemy into Holland and off the Scheldt Islands.* We would then hold fast until the Channel ports had been cleared when 2nd and 3rd Divisions could join us to finish the job. Once again without double-checking on German strength in the area I made the mistake of believing the intelligence 'experts.'"

Bridging equipment and 40 assault boats were brought up for the crossing. Near midnight on the 13th, all four companies of the Algonquin Regiment, part of Moncel's brigade, were ferried across under fire.

"Instead of establishing a bridgehead they ran into concentrated German resistance and found themselves trapped in three separate pockets. As with the crossing at Ghent, enemy fire prevented engineers from building their bridges. By dawn the situation became critical. Enemy shelling made it impossible to bring over ammunition and food supplies. No aircraft were available for a supply drop on such short notice and there were simply no reinforcements to beef up the bridgehead. . . . The only sensible alternative was to withdraw before any more good men were killed."

To mask the withdrawal the division's artillery laid down a thunderous barrage and smoke screen that the enemy would interpret as the prelude to a concentrated Canadian effort to expand their precarious toehold. Instead, and while German corps reserves were being rushed forward, the Algonquins withdrew, fighting their way back across the canals. Most of the boats had been sunk, forcing the men to shed equipment and clothing and swim to safety. Of those who had crossed the previous evening, 28 had been killed, 40 wounded and 66 taken prisoner—over half the original force.†

"It was a case of faulty intelligence on both sides of the line," Harry admitted. "I went forward to visit the casualties. . . . A terrible feeling to see wounded men on stretchers and know that the reason for their suffering was because I gave the order. I offered one man a cigarette and lit it. His grey face reflected the imminence of death. A huge bloodstained bandage covered his midriff.

"'How are you feeling, Sergeant?' A stupid question.

"'Lousy, sir!'

"I gave his arm a pat. 'You'll make it.'

"'Don't shit me, General. Jerry blew away most of my stomach. I'm finished. From now on it's your fight. . . . Win it for me, will you?'

"I promised to do my best. Such courage brought tears to my eyes. But generals aren't supposed to cry. It sets a bad example for the troops."

---

*Walcheren, North and South Beveland.
†The narrow road lined by tall trees that runs beside the canal near Moerkerke still carries the name "Algonquinstraat" in memory of those who fell.

4

Kurt was led from the church cellar in Durnal straight into German machine-gun fire from across the cemetery where he and Max Bornhöft had hidden. His American escort pushed him to the ground. While they lay waiting for a break, the GIs took his wrist watch and SS ring.

"I have fallen into the hands of gangsters! Behind the church I am parted from my money and another GI takes over. Angry because he can't steal anything he hits me a couple of times in the small of my back with his rifle butt. . . . We pass a few frightened women standing in their doorways. I collect another smash in my back, stumble forward a few steps and slowly turn around. Enraged, he hits my head with the rifle butt. . . . As I fall to the street I hear the Belgian women protesting. I get up dazed and stumble on. The gangster pushes me into a small garden. Blood covers my eyes and splashes into my ear. I have no more time to think. He pushes me against a berry bush. . . .

"So this is how my life ends! In a flash I see my family before me. 'Missing' will be the official notice—murdered, unknown and wiped out will be my real end. I look at this bastard with burning contempt as he lifts his carbine. I close my mind. I am already in the other world. Shocked, I realize suddenly he has lowered the carbine and moved away. My saviour is the young lieutenant with the German mother. He tries excusing the soldier and tells me a propaganda story about his cause and the secret war. I sit on the fender of his car so as not to stain it. But the wind blows my blood across its windshield."

His captor drove him to an American advance column where he was loaded into another car. More mobile than the Leibstandarte had ever been, the Americans seemed to use vehicles for everything. Surprised and envious, he watched the well-equipped, well-clothed and well-fed troops going casually about the business of war, oblivious to air attack. A tank division sat parked in a large expanse of open country.

Ruefully he observed: "Five Tigers breaking out of the forest could not hurt the assembled division. Between the Meuse and the Reich border there are no more Tigers, only worn-out men wandering around defeated by fate. The Americans will be impossible to stop. There are no more combat units. The West Wall is only a cracked and neglected skeleton. The Ruhr lies undefended and nothing can stop Montgomery from occupying the German weapons factories. A strong push by ten to 25 Allied divisions in the northwest and the backbone of German defence will break. . . . The fight in Europe is lost."

During late afternoon the prisoners were divided and loaded into trucks for the drive back to Namur. Each truck was covered by a machine gun from the truck behind to discourage escape attempts, while armed Military Police (MPs) rode inside. At Namur the prisoners were unloaded in front of the prison. Bornhöft, still bleeding badly, was lifted down on a stretcher. Mobs of civilians, some armed, pressed in from all sides. A shot ripped out. The crowd gave an enthusiastic roar. Max was dead. The Americans shook their heads and shooed them away.

The 60 prisoners were marched across the road to the police station and into a yard guarded by cherubic teenage partisans. They were lined up with a flurry of kicks and rifle butts. About 20 men wearing paratroop and Waffen-ss uniforms were taken away and executed. Some were only 18 and had joined their units fresh from basic training just two weeks earlier. The intervention of an American sergeant and the mistaking of Kurt's camouflage smock for a tanker's uniform saved his life. The bloodthirsty young Belgians were told that orders had been given by an officer to treat Kurt's skull fracture.

At the Catholic hospital he begged to use the toilet. Permission granted. A partisan accompanied him, then waited outside the door. Quickly, he shredded his paybook only to discover that the plumbing was broken. The toilet would not flush. Certain that it would only be a matter of hours before someone found the pieces of incriminating evidence, he lowered the lid and staggered out. A Belgian doctor ordered the partisans to strip his clothes and put him to bed.

"I notice them searching the pockets. . . . They were looking for my papers. . . . I will be asked about my paybook. . . . 'Where is it?' Very slowly I open my eyes and in a strong voice say a single word: 'Americans.' Satisfied, they wave and depart. In the middle of the night someone brings me a new pillow. . . . Exhausted from the loss of blood I sleep and think of my home."

Hindsight—always the clearest form of critical analysis—proved the seriousness of Montgomery's tactical error in allowing the Germans to escape across the Scheldt River from the Breskens pocket. After taking Antwerp on 4 September, Lieut.-Gen. Sir Brian Horrocks's xxx Corps had sufficient fuel to carry his forces another 15 miles across the Albert Canal and close off the South Beveland exit from the Scheldt. Had they done so, the German Fifteenth Army would have been trapped and forced to evacuate by sea 50 miles north through Rotterdam. Instead, Horrocks's forces were ordered to thrust east toward Louvain.

His army commander, General Dempsey, estimated that the maximum force capable of being maintained beyond the Louvain-Brussels line without opening an operational seaport was a single corps of three divisions plus airborne forces. By 8 September the Germans were dug in on the north side of the Albert Canal outside Antwerp and putting up a determined fight. As a supply port Antwerp was lost until the Scheldt could be cleared.

Montgomery turned his attention to the Channel ports. He planned a single concentrated lightning thrust into the Ruhr. Without the industrialized Ruhr Valley Germany was finished. The war would be over in a matter of weeks. It was a bold idea. But to make it work required the Supreme Commander's support and sufficient dock space to keep such an attack supplied with the materials required to sustain its momentum.

On 9 September, he calculated that with the ports of Dieppe, Boulogne, Dunkirk, Calais and Le Havre, he could get his armies to Berlin. With "one good Pas-de-Calais port" plus 1,000 tons airlifted a day and additional motor transport, he could make it across the Rhine and into the "Münster Triangle."* He selected Boulogne as the "good" Pas-de-Calais port because it was far enough north for a cross-Channel fuel pipeline to be laid. Eisenhower agreed to provide the logistical support needed for the plan by reining in Bradley's American armies in the southeast.

The plan, Operation "Market Garden," was scheduled for 17 September. With a combination of ground and airborne troops, an Allied corridor was to be driven across canals and rivers through to the Dutch city of Arnhem at the junction of the Rhine and Ijssel.

The Germans withdrew from the Canal de Dérivation de la Lys on Harry's front during the darkness of 15 September. Next day the division crossed the canal and moved northeast toward Eecloo. Vehicles reached the town in the early hours of 17 September and parked nose-to-tailboard in the streets until first light. Divisional HQ set up southeast of town on the carefully tended lawns of a fashionable château. Throughout the morning of the 17th, while the division arranged its HQ, formations of allied aircraft passed overhead on their way to Arnhem.

"First news was not good. Part of the German II Panzer Corps had harboured nearby and were in action against our troops almost at once. . . . Faulty intelligence on our part. . . . The operation turned into an unqualified disaster."

A week later Montgomery decided to withdraw from Arnhem. Canadian engineers using stormboats joined the assault boats† of the Royal Engineers in a cold pouring rain during the night of 25 September to ferry the exhausted airborne troops who escaped back across the Neder Rijn. Throughout the darkness the tiny outboards sped back and forth under continuous mortar and machine-gun fire. The Canadians brought out most of the 2,400 men who were rescued, including Maj.-Gen. R.E. Urquhart, GOC of the British 1st Airborne whose division suffered 7,500 casualties of the 10,300 who had jumped at Arnhem.

Canal, dike and polder country were not suitable for armour. Harry was

---

*Münster-Rheine-Osnabrück.

†Canadian stormboats were made of wood and used outboard motors. British assault boats were smaller, made from collapsible canvas and used paddles.

ordered to keep pressure on the retreating enemy but without risking forces to a pitched battle. For the rest of September and into October the division remained headquartered at Eecloo, keeping up the pressure, patrolling for prisoners, and training the new replacements coming from the Manning Depots in England.

Moncel's brigade designed a "milk run" for its motor battalion to keep the German forward positions across the Leopold on their toes. Several times daily a parade of Sherman tanks rolled along the top of the canal bank, all guns blazing, then ducked down behind the embankment until their return run. The sport was not without its risks. One German "dead-eye" armed with a bazooka managed to knock out a tank of the 28th Armoured Regiment from across the canal. His Iron Cross citation for this feat was later captured by the brigade.

Harry's days became routine. Dressed in a heavy duffel coat to keep out the fall chill, he visited the brigade fronts with Ken Scott, preferring his ADC to a regular driver. The tall handsome Scott had a quick wit and deprecating manner that Harry enjoyed.

"I'll give you odds the war will be over by the New Year, sir."

"Done! My bet is early summer."

"That long?"

"Still time enough to get killed, Kenny."

After a long pause: "General?"

"Well?"

"Which side are you betting will win?"

At the end of September Crerar was evacuated to England for medical reasons. Simonds took over temporary command of the First Canadian Army while Foulkes became temporary corps commander. Calais fell to the 3rd Division on 1 October, releasing troops for the battle of the Scheldt. Led by the 7th Brigade, the attack to take the Leopold Canal and clear the Breskens pocket began in the cold dawn of 6 October after a feint some miles away the previous day by the Algonquin Regiment. Progress by the division was slow but steady. During the week infantry and artillery support plus some additional feints were made by the 4th Armoured Division to keep the Germans off balance.

"8 Sept. . . . This afternoon the Minister of National Defence, Col. Ralston, arrived with Guy and Gen. Foulkes. . . . An inspection tour, and to learn about our situation on reinforcements which is still bloody bleak. . . . I hope I wasn't too blunt. Politicians can't seem to get it through their heads that in war there are casualties that must be replaced. More than anyone he* should realize the seriousness of the problem. We need live bodies not wishful

---

*Col. I.L. Ralston, a battalion commander during World War I, had won two DSOs and a CMG.

thinking. . . . My comments on Zombies sitting safely at home defending Canada were not appreciated. . . . Guy wants Moncel's Brigade moved to the Antwerp area, one regiment at a time, beginning on the 11th. The Division to follow. We will be under command of British 1st Corps. Our job will be to protect 2nd Division's flank on the advance into Holland. . . . Finally, on the move again."

Kurt lay two weeks in hospital. Slowly his strength returned. The nuns gave him cigarettes and one of the kitchen staff smuggled extra food to him. As his strength returned so did his optimism. He began formulating escape plans. When he was well enough to walk, the partisans moved him to the Albert Military Barracks in Namur to convalesce. At first he was the only prisoner in the building, in a third-floor locked room.

Later, company arrived. Lieutenant Aumüller had led a group of infantrymen through the forests and fields of northern France and Belgium for three weeks, only to be caught north of Namur, a few miles short of the German border. Wagner, Oberleutnant (first lieutenant) of an infantry company, had been captured with what were left of his men at the Meuse. Wagner had hidden several hundred francs in his uniform. Together, they planned their survival and eventual escape.

They were still wearing summer uniforms. To keep warm they burned every stick of furniture in the barracks they could lay their hands on. For outside news they relied on idle chatter from their partisan guards. A Belgian military cadet released from a German POW camp and a Russian slave labourer who managed to escape from a Belgian factory became the key to their survival. They provided war news, food, homespun philosophy, and arguments on global politics.

Allied bombers flying overhead day and night on their way to northern Germany renewed Kurt's interest in an escape plan. But escape to where and for how long? Eventually he faced the reality of the situation.

"We cannot arrange an incident to make our dash to freedom. We are too heavily guarded. . . . One day a Belgian brings us a few pieces of uniforms from old German stock. I get a field shirt and coat. At last we are protected from the cold. We look more like a band of robbers than German soldiers. . . . In the beginning of October a pair of Americans arrive under the direction of an MP Major and we are bundled into a truck. We are heavily guarded, making escape impossible to contemplate."

They stopped at Rheims for the night and were locked in the city jail.

"The cells are filled with noisy negroes. . . . Next morning we drive further west . . . sitting depressed in the corner of the truck we look at a gigantic Allied supply depot. Inconceivable piles of ammunition, fuel and other supplies lie on either side of the road. Depot follows depot at kilometre distances. In between are airstrips and large reserves of tanks and artillery.

Traffic winds peacefully in and out of the depots. There is no trace of air cover, camouflage or anti-aircraft guns. We are looking at the house of a rich man! Do the Americans really understand what kind of superiority in weapons and equipment they have at the German border?"

In late afternoon they reached a huge POW camp at Compiègne surrounded by barbed wire and patrol dogs and run by bored-looking Americans. They were taken to the Camp Commandant separately, Kurt still as Colonel Meyer of the 2nd Tank Division. The Commandant, an old Berliner who had had a law office on the Kurfüstendamm and emigrated to the U.S. in the Thirties, accepted his lost paybook story. Impressed by Meyer's bearing and obvious qualities of leadership the Commandant appointed him assistant camp manager and asked that he supervise the POW officers. The perks included his own hut—into which he installed Wagner and Aumüller—and the right to visit every part of the compound. The camp held several thousand men and was divided into three divisions for administration purposes.

"My first journey to the NCOs' camp I meet a sergeant from the 1st Parachute Division who warns me to be careful. The place is teeming with informers and traitors. The First Commandment is caution! . . . Before long every position is infiltrated with our own people. Escape provisions are organized and divided systematically among the different barracks. . . . We are lucky owners of a compass. Wagner managed to hold on to his despite all the searches. . . . We live now only to escape."

5

On 16 October the 4th Armoured Division HQ shifted from Eecloo to the village of Schilde, four miles east of Antwerp. General Spry's 3rd Division was already advancing beyond the Leopold Canal to take out the German pocket between Breskens and the floodlands surrounding the coastal town of Zeebrugge. On the north bank of the Scheldt, Foulkes's 2nd Division had started moving across the Beveland Peninsula. The 4th Armoured Division struck north from Calmpthout on 20 October. The British 43rd Division advanced on its right.

"22 Oct. . . . Moncel's Bde. reached the Dutch border today near Wouwsche Plantage. The 10th Bde. is at Esschen. . . . Commander of 1st Corps, Gen. Crocker, dropped in this afternoon. . . .Yesterday the Hun apparently caught him with his pants down during a visit to 49th Div. HQ. . . . Working with the Brits has been an eye opener for our HQ staff rank and file. The habit of using 'Eh'—'yeah'—'uhuhuh'—'shit'—'fuck' and other assorted Canadianisms to provide pause for additional thought is unknown to the British. Their conduct seems aloof by comparison to our own. It is a bit unnerving to the staff. Wigle is certain they're faking it. I'm not so sure."

Wouwsche Plantage lay behind a river and in front of a great anti-tank ditch. The town provided the pivot point for enemy defences in the Bergen-Op-Zoom area. Moncel sent his motor battalion off with a squadron of tanks from the 21st Armoured Regiment to cross the two-mile approach into town. The tanks stayed "road-bound" because of the ten-foot ditches and soft muddy fields. German self-propelled anti-tank guns, cleverly hidden to cover the entire area of the advance, caught the attackers in the open. Ten of the original 11 tanks exploded in flames. The motor battalion carried on alone, pulling up a mile short of Wouwsche Plantage.

Jefferson's 10th Brigade had turned over its position at Esschen to the British 49th Division the day before and now joined Moncel's armour in front of the town. Before first light on 24 October the Argyll and Sutherland Highlanders and a tank squadron of the 22nd Armoured Regiment advanced through heavy opposition to within 200 yards of the outskirts. Next day, coordinated attacks from the east and south by the Lake Superior Regiment, two companies of the Lincoln and Wellands plus tanks of the 21st Armoured Regiment entered the town. For more than 24 hours the Germans held on with savage ferocity. Finally, after fierce hand-to-hand fighting they were crushed.

"23 Oct. . . . A meeting with Gen. Crocker at 1st Corps. . . . Our objective is now Bergen-op-Zoom. . . . Field Marshal Montgomery arrived at 1030 hrs. . . . He held a short O Group, asked Proctor about our winter clothing, then left after restating that he expects me to have Bergen-op-Zoom the day after tomorrow. . . . I'll try."

After a quiet night the advance northwest continued against stiff opposition. Extensive mining, booby traps, roadblocks and obstacles of all types slowed 10th Brigade's progress. Where penetration was made, enemy opposition was so strong that further advance became impossible. North of Wouwsche Plantage, 4th Armoured Brigade finally managed to get a bridgehead across the tank ditch and tried advancing against furious opposition west of the town.

"25th Oct. . . . The past few days have been cloudy, damp and growing cooler. This combination has prevented air cover being flown over the area north of Bergen-op-Zoom. There was a time when the thought of armour operating north of the Leopold Canal drew forth . . . facetious remarks about waterproofing, etc. The country from Bergen-op-Zoom to the Maas River is almost past comment. Only ducks would find the going suitable."

Bergen-op-Zoom was taken on 27 October by the 29th Armoured Recce Regiment. "Reception by the population was as enthusiastic and wild as any yet seen. Evidently the small amount of fire which our gunners sent into the town on the night of 23/24 Oct. did not upset too many."

Steenbergen, six miles north of Bergen-op-Zoom, was to be the last objective before the Maas River. As Moncel's brigade advanced, conditions deteriorated. The countryside became more open. Tanks, road-bound by flood waters, were picked off at leisure by German anti-tank gunners. The brigade's shrunken infantry forces were worn out from lack of rest. On 2 November a half mile from Steenbergen, the 10th Brigade took over to assault the town.

Two days later the Germans withdrew.

"4 Nov. . . . Today all resistance ceased in the lower Scheldt pocket. To 3rd Cdn. Div. and 52nd Div. it wrote 'finis' to a bitter struggle. To 4th Cdn. Armd. Div. the final clearing of the area north of the Leopold Canal was the end of something which this division had begun. From mid Sept. to mid Oct. all or part of our division was engaged along the entire length of this canal. . . . We read of 12,812 POWs being taken . . . which denoted an original force of some 20,000 enemy. . . . No one has pointed out that it has taken over 60,000 Canadian and British troops with a full armoured division to beat an already retreating and battle-weary enemy infantry desperately short on armour, ammunition, food and transport. . . . By God the Hun knows how to put up a fight!

"6 Nov. . . . Attended a mutual admiration society luncheon at First Army HQ in Antwerp. Army and command staffs from all divisions were represented. A veritable sea of red tabs . . . and red faces by the end of the meal. . . . On the front steps after lunch Maj.-Gen. Terry Allen, GOC of the U.S. Army 104th 'Timberwolf' Division, pinned me with a gong [U.S. Legion of Merit] for my part in the Kiska operation."

On the same day in Holland a patrol from the Lake Superior Regiment reached the end of the St. Philipsland Peninsula to find four enemy gunboats lying at anchor across the water in the harbour of Zipje, at the eastern end of Duiveland Island. Moving swiftly, Moncel's brigade moved up some heavy weapons and engaged the vessels. All four were sunk before German 88 mm gunfire inflicted any damage on the Canadians. The sequel came next day when a patrol ventured onto Duiveland in the early morning. They circled cautiously around the back of the harbour and entered the town. After gunning down a few of the departing enemy making for the western end of the island, they arrived at the harbour. Five naval ratings surrendered. The captain of the largest vessel—AF92—lay dead in his wheel house. The CO of the Lake Superiors inserted the final entry into his ship's log: "Gesunken by the Lake Superior Regiment (Motorized) Canadian Army."

With the end of fighting on Walcheren Island on 8 November, the army began a three-month period of relative inactivity. All three Canadian divisions were exhausted. Time was needed to rest, re-equip, train replacements and plan the next campaign—the Battle of the Rhineland. The winter "Watch on the Maas" became a time of continuous patrolling and nasty fights with small enemy forces on both sides of the river.

The 4th Armoured Division moved inland to relieve the British 7th Armoured Division in the area north of Tilburg and 's-Hertogenbosch, 35 miles from the coast. The divisional front on the Maas stretched 27 miles wide—"the Poles are on our left and we are spread very thinly."

But not nearly as thinly as the Canadian army itself. General Crerar, who had reassumed command on 7 November, was now responsible for a 140-mile front that included the priceless Nijmegen bridgehead, seized by the American 82nd Airborne Division in September. The front swept in a great curving arc from Walcheren Island, along the lower Maas and Neder Rijn, to Cuyk.

During the month a shuffle of promotions and commands occurred: Crerar was promoted to full general, the first time such a rank had been held by a Canadian soldier in the field; Simonds returned to his command of II Corps; Foulkes was appointed to command of I Corps in Italy; and Brig. Bruce Matthews took over 2nd Division. The dashing Lieut.-Col. J.A. Roberts of the 12th Manitoba Dragoons had taken over 8th Brigade on 29 October.

During its first week on the Maas, 4th Armoured Division HQ received a call from forward troops of the South Alberta Regiment that they had overrun a concentration camp. The army had already encountered German POW camps and an assortment of prisons on their advance from Normandy, but a concentration camp was something new. Lieut.-Col. Proctor took a jeep and went forward to investigate.

He returned badly shaken and reported: "You'd better see this for yourself, sir."

Harry went with him.

The camp lay at Vught in Brabant province, on the road between Breda and 's-Hertogenbosch. The main gates had been left open. Guards and prisoners were gone.[5] An ashen-faced lieutenant of the South Albertas showed them around.

"It was laid out like an army camp with barn buildings that housed up to 1,500 prisoners. A rail spur ran into workshops at the rear where slave workers rebuilt downed Allied aircraft for use as German spy planes. Several machines were in process of assembly. One, a Spitfire, had 'City of Oshawa' painted on its cowling.

"In the central yard stood eight strangling posts. Eight ropes dangled from a 6x6 overhead beam. Wood blocks, 18 inches square with foot staples, were set out under each gallow. Victims stepped up onto the blocks, received the noose then had the blocks kicked from under their feet by the guards. As they hung slowly strangling ankle arteries were sliced open and their blood collected in a marble catch-basin through a series of connecting gutters. For what purpose the blood was taken we could only guess.

"Close by were two banks of ovens for disposing of the bloodless corpses. Beside this crematory was a pile of human bones 8 feet long and 4 feet wide. Local village officials estimated that the Germans had disposed of over

10,000 victims at this camp; resistance fighters, students, government officials, many of them Jews. . . .

"What sort of people do such things to their fellow humans? Why they are no better than animals . . . no, they are worse."

At the Compiègne POW camp a group of 100 prisoners arrived from the battle of Aachen bringing news from the Fatherland. Among them were some grenadiers from the Leibstandarte who told Kurt what had happened to the division.

"Shocked, I hear about the murder of my dear comrade, Waldmüller . . . a sacrifice to the Maquis on 9 September in the Basse-Bodeux region. . . . They put a cable car rail across the street . . . he and his motorcycle driver were torn apart. Terribly injured, both were subsequently drowned like rats. . . . The brave Obersturmbannführer Hauck drove over a mine in an ambush and was badly burned."

He was told that the 12th SS Panzer Division had last been reported near Plettenburg in the Saarland. At once, he put his escape plans into high gear, trying to arrange a spot on a woodcutting detail that left camp each day. Time was running out.

In the exercise yard during the late afternoon of 7 November the Camp Commandant took him by the arm for a friendly chat. "Herr Oberst, I have a favour to ask. I find myself in a very unpleasant situation. Ach, Herr Oberst, it is crazy. I have received information that a high-ranking SS officer is in this camp. It would be a personal disgrace for me if this is true, you understand?"

Kurt held his tongue, thinking furiously. They continued walking. Finally, he promised to do whatever he could to help.

"Do you have his name, Commandant? Or any idea what he looks like?"

The American sighed. "Not the slightest. I know only that he is greeted respectfully and everyone smiles when he goes through the camp."

Relieved, Kurt promised to get to the bottom of the matter and report back. He made a beeline for his hut to find Wagner and Aumüller to announce with a straight face: "I have just promised to look for me and then deliver myself to the Camp Commandant."

Early the following morning the three friends presented themselves at the camp gate to join the woodcutting detail. No luck. Few cutters were needed that day. Near 1100 hours two enormous MPs arrived at the hut. Kurt was escorted to the Commandant's office. An American intelligence officer glared at him.

"Shirt off! Raise your arms above your head."

The Commandant gasped, swore in English, then demanded an explanation for the blood-group tattoo under his arm. Kurt played dumb, countering with a request for an explanation from the intelligence officer.

The man yelled: "You're that high-ranking ss sonofabitch we've been looking for!"

"You are mistaken," Kurt replied quietly. "Blood-group tattoos proved so successful in the Waffen-ss they were adopted by the Wehrmacht tank divisions. Every tank school graduate had to undergo tattooing."

They accepted this explanation. He put on his shirt and went back to the hut. Shortly thereafter the camp exploded in activity. MPs began a search for radio equipment that American ADF (Automatic Direction Finding equipment) monitors had picked up. The POWs had been on the air to Germany planning an escape for 9 November during a bombing raid they had organized with the Luftwaffe.

"We are ordered into columns for transfer. Within a half hour we are marching through the city and into a freight train. Wagner and Aumüller are in the same car. Cursing, Wagner tries cutting a hole in the floor. It is made of thick plywood. His efforts produce little damage. . . . Just before departure I hear my name called. I am ordered off the train and into a jeep. . . .

"A quick trip back to camp. I'm not terribly surprised to recognize a young German infantry lieutenant in civvies standing in front of the administration building. . . . He looks away, ashamed. I shout: 'Miserable bastard!' The first cowardly creature I have met in German uniform. He is the camp informer.

"The Commandant forces me to stand 4 feet from a wall and lean forward until my fingertips touch the plaster. If I move, a rifle is jammed into my back and I am ordered to 'maintain discipline.' . . . Early next morning we travel to Paris to an airport west of the city. By 1400 hours I am in an aircraft looking down at the old battlegrounds of 1940. We leave the continent over Dunkirk. . . .

"For the first time I give up to fate and abandon all thoughts of escape. For me the war is over. Behind, lies Europe, destroyed and bleeding from countless wounds. Beneath lies the Channel, and in front—England. That England that wanted to free Europe and now, by strange irony, has probably thrown it away to the Communists."

On 14 November Harry was summoned to Corps HQ in Tilburg by Simonds, who explained that he would be returning to England for a time and had decided to appoint Harry acting corps commander during his absence.

It turned out to be a short-lived promotion. A week later Crerar invited him to Canadian First Army HQ and over dinner informed him that he was being transferred to Italy to command the 1st Infantry Division. Its present GOC, Chris Vokes, would be returning to take over the 4th Armoured Division.

"A straight switch?" Harry asked incredulously. Vokes had no training and little practical experience in armoured tactics. He was an engineer by trade and a first-class infantry commander.

Crerar nodded. "A straight switch."

"May I ask why, sir?" He felt crushed. Somewhere he had failed. Hadn't Guy just handed him the corps for safekeeping? It made no sense.

Crerar pursed his lips. "It's rather a complicated story."

6

Since arriving in the Mediterranean area during 1943, Canadian troops had been under command of the British Eighth Army. The Sicilian and Italian campaigns provided the only training in actual combat for Canadian officers and men prior to D-Day. Crerar, Simonds, Kitching, Jefferson and a host of others owed their "blooding" for command to the time spent in the "Spaghetti League." From a single division of Lieut.-Gen. Sir Oliver Leese's xxx Corps in the invasion of Sicily, Canadian forces by August 1944 had grown into a corps of two divisions plus an armoured brigade.

On New Year's Day, 1944, Montgomery handed command of the Eighth Army to General Leese and flew back to England. Three months later, Lieutenant-General Crerar was appointed Canadian army commander and turned over the 76,000 men of the I Canadian Corps to Lieut.-Gen. E.L.M. Burns, commander of the 5th Armoured Division.

Unfortunately, neither Burns nor his staff had had any experience commanding a corps in battle. Within the month Leese and Burns were scornfully critical of each other. Burns, with his brilliant erudite mind and aloof personality, was the antithesis of the charming and extroverted Leese. The introverted Burns didn't fit. He lacked flair. He wasn't part of the "Club."

At an Eighth Army O Group in late April, while Leese outlined, with dramatic hand flourishes and liberal quotations from Shakespeare, his plans for cracking the Hitler line, the stolid Burns turned to Vokes and muttered, "What the hell is he talking about?"

"Our attack on the Hitler Line, sir."

"Then why in hell doesn't he say so instead of prancing about waving his hands like a whore in heat?"

Leese let it be known to CMHQ in London in no uncertain terms that Tommy Burns had to go. In June, Lieut.-Gen. Ken. Stuart, chief of the General Staff at CMHQ, flew out to Italy to investigate. After extracting promises from Vokes and Maj.-Gen. Bert Hoffmeister, the new GOC 5th Armoured Division, that they would remain loyal to Burns, he flew home, leaving Burns with his command. At the end of September Leese became commander-in-chief, Allied Land Forces South-East Asia, and Lieut.-Gen. Sir Richard L. McCreery took over the Eighth Army. He was already aware of the problems with "Laughing Boy."*

An argument developed between Burns and Vokes over a troop movement. Burns considered Vokes insubordinate, and Eighth Army HQ invited Vokes in for an explanation. McCreery sided with Vokes. Burns had to go. At the end of October plans were made at CMHQ to replace Burns with Charles Foulkes from the 2nd Infantry Division in Holland. Burns was sacked and Vokes made temporary corps commander, pending an official CMHQ signal.

In due course CMHQ sent a signal through Eighth Army HQ confirming Lieut.-Gen. C. Foulkes as the new corps commander. The British had never heard of C. Foulkes—only C. Vokes. They assumed a transmission error, made the necessary correction and passed it on to Canadian Corps HQ. Vokes was understandably delighted and immediately put on his new rank insignia. The following week Foulkes arrived to take command, and Vokes was left looking foolish. Signals flew back and forth to London. How to save face for everyone involved? Switch divisional commanders? Never mind that it made no military sense. It was a matter of military politics.

Harry met Chris in London. Over dinner they discussed the vagaries of their profession.

"For one fucking week I was a lieutenant-general and I Corps commander!" Vokes groused. "And then that purse-lipped sonofabitch showed up and took it all away."

"How the hell do you think I feel?" Harry demanded. "I was sitting with command of II Corps when 'Uncle Harry' invited me to dinner. By the end of the evening I had lost the corps, my division and was exiled to Italy to serve under Charles Foulkes!"

Vokes brightened. "Harry, you'll like Italy. It has good food, willing ladies, and pretty country—whenever it stops raining. Too bad it belongs to the Italians."

After a two-week leave with Mollie in Fleet he flew out to Italy at the end of November in an American B17 and reported to General Foulkes. Brigadier Kitching† met him at Corps HQ in Riccione Marina, and "after pumping me for fifteen minutes for news from the Division [4th Armoured] he put me in the picture. . . . No hard feelings. . . . He seems to be enjoying himself. For my money it's not as good as Holland. But what could be?"

Foulkes ordered him to take a week to familiarize himself with the division before taking over from Brig. J.D.B. Smith, its acting GOC.

"The division's three brigades consisted of an armoured car and ten infantry regiments. For the past 18 months they had been in the line more or less continuously. The regiments and battalions were tired, under strength and,

---

*Nickname given to Burns by Canadian troops in Italy because he never smiled.
†After his dismissal from 4th Armoured Division, Acting Maj.-Gen. Kitching reverted to brigadier and was posted to Italy as the BGS of I Corps.

in a few cases, badly led. A clique had developed between senior officers starting with Vokes and Hoffmeister. It carried down to the regimental level. Burns, the perfect staff officer, had lost control—if he had ever had control— and the respect of his battlefield commanders. Foulkes said he intended to straighten the matter out quickly. He wanted my help . . . which seemed to me the beginning of another clique; Foulkes and I against everybody else."

Harry agreed to do whatever was required to get the job done.

The British were tired as well. Their men had been fighting since the North African campaigns of 1940–41. They could see the German collapse coming, and their enthusiasm for battle was gone. No one wanted to stick out his neck or do anything foolish. This "what the hell" attitude had its effect on the Indian, Canadian and New Zealand divisions serving with the Eighth Army.

The battle line stretched across the width of northern Italy from a few miles north of Pisa on the Mediterranean side to south of Ravenna near the Adriatic. Facing the American Fifth and British Eighth Armies under Field Marshal Harold Alexander were the German Fourteenth and Tenth Armies commanded by Luftwaffe Field Marshal Albert Kesselring.

Rimini, the eastern pivot of the German "Gothic Line" and Apennine Mountain defence, had fallen to the Eighth Army on 22 September. The battle for the Gothic Line ended on 4 December when the city of Ravenna, once the capital of the Western Roman Empire, was taken in "a brilliant encircling movement by the Princess Louise Dragoon Guards which out- flanked the city and forced the enemy to withdraw to avoid being trapped."

Further inland, British forces drove over the last foothills of the Apennines to reach the Maraccha River. Beyond lay the Po Valley and the city of Bologna, Field Marshal Alexander's ultimate objective before the full misery of winter arrived. The Germans fell back slowly, fighting all the way. It was a test of endurance. Kesselring, knowing he could never win, was managing to tie down 25 Allied divisions that could have been used in Europe; Alexander, knowing that eventually he would win, was keeping 25 enemy divisions from reinforcing the German homeland.

"It was more of a standoff than a stalemate, each side prepared to do a lot of shooting but without the devotion necessary for serious battle. But then perhaps my opinion had been coloured by the Battle of Normandy. . . . The first thing I had to find was a competent GSO1 to handle the administration and paperwork that I loathed."

He was in luck. Scott Murdoch, his brigade major during the Kiska expedition, had rejoined the Seaforth Highlanders. The regiment's CO, Lieut.- Col. H.P. Bell-Irving, had had him reassigned from Crerar's HQ in October. A signal went out to the Seaforths requesting that Major* Murdoch report

---

*After Kiska he took a reduction in rank to get back overseas.

to the GOC. Word of the change in divisional command had not yet reached the Seaforths. Mystified, Murdoch borrowed a jeep and driver and arrived at Harry's TAC HQ near Russi. He knocked at the door of his caravan.

"Hello Scott, how's the world been treating you?"

"Fine, sir."

"Congratulations. You're my new GSO1. Your caravan is over there under that tree. Now get to work."

Within the week Murdoch regained his former rank.

After 7 October Brigadier Smith was given command of 1st Brigade; Brig. M.P. Bogert the 2nd Brigade; Brigadier Bernatchez remained with 3rd Brigade, a position he had held since April. An organizational shambles during a night attack across the Lamone River in early December by 1st Brigade brought Harry down hard on the officers and NCOs responsible in the RCRs and Hasty Pees. Several officers were sacked, including the RCRs' CO—the first of two RCR COs he had to sack.

In the London detention centre, Kurt was being put through the standard interrogation process: isolation—abuse—abandonment—discussion. After dealing with Germans throughout two world wars, the British had it down to a science.

"Mysterious silence hangs over the complex while I am led through a door and locked in an interrogation room. Heavily armed Englishmen watch. A questionnaire is placed before me which—for the sake of peace—I fill out immediately. A man storms into the room, shouting hysterically. He stands in front of me with his fists raised. Large sunglasses shield his eyes. He shouts at me like a Berserker and, in a fit of rage, fires at my field cap hanging in the corner. The young man is too eager to impress me . . . a terrible actor. I am taken to an isolation cell. . . .

"Next morning some bread is passed in to me. Finally, I am allowed out for 20 minutes in the fresh air. It is impossible to see fellow prisoners during the walk. Big canvas walls separate us. . . . After a few days isolation I am happy to go back for interrogation. . . .

"An American is waiting for me. He begins talking about the military situation . . . prospects for freedom in Europe after German defeat . . . rosy times for Europe under England's leadership. When I try telling him that I disagree, that the Allies are on the path to destruction from Communism, he stops talking. My view of Russian soldiers opposing the Allies angers him. . . .

"In late afternoon I am taken to the 'generals' camp in Enfield. It is surrounded by a high spiked fence. There are a dozen German generals and staff officers on the premises. Gen. of Panzer Troops Ritter von Thoma is the camp senior. He was taken in North Africa and is well respected by the English. After reporting in, I am led to my room and meet Gen. Eberding, commander of the 64th Infantry Div. which so doggedly defended the Scheldt and had to give up the fight at Breskens.

"Thankfully, I shake the hand of my old commander, Gen. Eberbach, and meet Gens. von Schlieben, Ramcke, von Choltitz and Elfeldt, who had been missing since Chambois. . . .

"The first evening we discuss conditions inside the camp and the new political developments in Germany. The latter subject thrown in by Oberst Wildermuth.* Some of the gentlemen present cannot accept the reality of the changes that are happening. They remain steadfast in their beliefs, considering captivity and its attendant symptoms as a passing aberration. Others have lost all illusions. For them the world in which they participated has vanished in ruin and they see nothing to replace it."

In Italy, the battle for the rivers across the Po Valley moved slowly forward; the Lamone, the Vecchio, and the Naviglio Canal were crossed. The weather alternated between cold steady rain and mist and intermittent showers. Low baggy clouds scudded overhead. The thick, rich Italian earth turned to gumbo mud. On rare occasions when the sun did appear, fog rose in smoky tendrils to mask the landscape.

Four days before Christmas the Canadian Corps reached the banks of the Senio. British v and Polish I Corps on the left also had their noses pressed against the Senio. A Christmas pause was declared. Harry pulled 3rd Brigade and half of 1st and 2nd Brigades out of the line for a few days rest.

"24 Dec. . . . The day in the line was quiet. Maybe it is the approach of Christmas that works charms. . . . The G boys went the rounds and wished everybody all sorts of good things and were given all sorts of good things in return. The duty officer was frequently told where everyone was; that was a good thing because we are not sure that everybody knew where they were or where they had been or where they were going."

Yet everyone was certain that next Christmas would be spent at home in Canada. Through the haze of alcohol in A Mess it was decided that when the war ended they would all retire to live out their days in "Sheepshit, Sask.," a mythical prairie town where "the sun always shone, the smiling women were all beautiful, the animals and children well behaved." Public and political patronage appointments were awarded to everyone from garbage inspector to dogcatcher. Harry was to be the mayor, Scott Murdoch the town clerk, and Davie Fulton the city solicitor. A Rhodes scholar, the red-haired Maj. E.D. Fulton of the Seaforths was DAAG† at 1st Division HQ and the butt of every political joke making the rounds.‡ For the rest of his time with

---

*Later a cabinet minister in a postwar German government.
†Deputy assistant adjutant-general.
‡Son of a former B.C. premier, Fulton was elected to the House of Commons in 1945, later serving as minister of justice in the government of John Diefenbaker.

the division he was addressed and referred to as "the City Solicitor of Sheepshit, Sask." Fortunately, he had a good sense of humour.

"25 Dec. . . . Greetings were exchanged across the short no man's line, but this time not with bullets. . . . A Jerry was seen displaying first a white flag then running up to the bank of the Senio and in full view of our troops yelling: 'Why don't you surrender?'"

Harry opened the men's Christmas dinner with an appropriate speech and was roundly cheered. Then, following tradition, the officers served the men their meal.

"Tomorrow we return to the cold reality of war and all its ugliness but we won't forget Christmas 1944, because for 24 hrs. men became human again and war seemed very far away."

7

Field Marshal Alexander decided to abandon the advance on Bologna at the end of December and settle into a defensive line for the winter. The decision left the Germans in possession of two large areas east of the Senio in front of the Canadians and British. Both areas had to be cleared before closing down operations for the winter. General McCreery's plan, suggested by Foulkes, was to launch a British infantry and armoured brigade, supported by one infantry battalion, carried in "kangaroos," from the British sector. Four hours before this attack the Canadian 1st Division would cross the Naviglio Canal above Granarolo in a surprise assault. Harry assigned the task to Pat Bogert's 2nd Brigade.

"The action began on the afternoon of 3 January; Hoffmeister's 5th Armoured on the right, our British cousins on the left. A beautifully coordinated attack. I had to give Foulkes his due. Our experience in Holland outflanking enemy river crossings had not been lost on him. In three days we were across the Naviglio, the Vecchio and Canale di Bonifica and ready to snug in for the winter."

Bogert, who had taken his objectives with only 29 casualties, reported that the action had been "one of the neatest battles this Brigade has ever had." Six hundred miles to the northwest in the Ardennes another "neat" battle was reaching its climax.

Von Rundstedt had refitted eight panzer divisions and received reinforcements from the Eastern Front to bring together two panzer armies equipped with new Tiger and Panther tanks. Hitler's plan was to break through the thinly held American front and drive to the Namur-Liège area of the Meuse. Once this was taken, he would press on to Antwerp, cheating the Allies of their main supply port. Even better, British and American forces in the north would be cut off from American and French forces in the south. It was a bold, imaginative concept.

On 16 December, in a thick fog that would deprive the Allies of air support until the 22nd, von Rundstedt struck with 24 divisions, rolling through the American line. Next day at a road junction, near Malmédy, Belgium, members of an American field artillery battalion surrendered to an advancing tank column. Marching to the rear, they encountered a second tank unit that, not realizing the men were prisoners, opened fire. The Americans fled into the fields. It was over in a matter of seconds. According to official sources, 86 American soldiers lay dead. The German advance rolled on.[6]

Four days later Americans of the 328th Regiment, 26th Infantry Division, received orders to take no German prisoners because of the "Malmédy Massacre." American retribution became widespread. Lieutenant-Colonel Solar, leader of Kampfgruppe Solar, reported that 14 infantrymen of his panzer brigade had been found on 30 December, northwest of Steinbrünn, lying on the road with their hands still raised. "Lieut. Ziemann reported that they had neither arms nor belts. All had been shot in the head at point blank range." Thirty miles southwest of Morehet an American battalion commander, after searching a group of 20 captured Germans, ordered them executed; they were machine-gunned. And on New Year's Day, 60 Germans captured in the Belgian village of Chegnogne were taken into a field by their 11th Armoured Division captors and shot dead.

Montgomery and Patton swung their forces toward each other to contain the shoulders of the German salient that, by 3 January, had breached a 45-mile gap 60 miles westward into the Allied line. Von Rundstedt's forces were finally halted less than four miles from the Meuse. By 10 January they had begun to withdraw from the tip of the salient. At the end of the month they were back at their start line.

Although von Rundstedt conducted a skilful retreat, his losses were catastrophic: 600 tanks and assault guns, 1,624 aircraft and thousands of assorted motor vehicles were gone, and 120,000 men had been killed, wounded or captured. It was Hitler's last major attempt at salvaging an already hopeless situation. The entire effort served only to delay the Allied spring offensive by six weeks and force the strategic air force to neglect its deep penetration targets inside the Reich.

In Italy it snowed and rained. There were patrol clashes along the front and spasmodic shelling, but generally things were quiet. Most days Harry took a jeep and went forward from his Russi HQ to visit the brigades. It was what he enjoyed most, being with the men where the action was and away from the Corps Commander. Foulkes and Harry shared a mutual respect for each other's abilities and an equally mutual dislike.

"I thought Foulkes suffered from a sense of inferiority. He was not liked by any senior British or Canadian officer that I ever saw, including Simonds. To my knowledge he had few friends and in a way I felt sorry for him. He reminded me of someone who, knowing that he has overstepped his abilities, tries to bluff his way through. . . . Our personalities clashed."

Whenever word reached 1st Division HQ that the Corps Commander was on his way up for a visit, Harry took his jeep and fled to the front, leaving Murdoch to make the necessary apologies. The less he saw of Charles Foulkes the better.

"Where's the General?" Murdoch would be asked.

"With the brigades at the front, sir."

"Proper place for him to be."

"I can get him if it's important, sir."

But it never was. And after glancing over the division's operations maps, Foulkes drove back to his Corps HQ. Later, when Harry returned, he would ask what Foulkes wanted.

"It wasn't important, Boss."

"Hmm. It seldom is."

Early in February orders arrived at Canadian Corps HQ in Ravenna that all Canadian units serving in Italy would be transferred to northwest Europe. Officers and men were delighted. It meant they could finish the war under a unified Canadian army command.

"10 Feb. . . . Rain and mist all day. . . . The pullout begins in 3 days with Corps HQ moving in column to Naples for embarkation. . . . We take command of 1st Corps sector today . . . including the Cremona Brigade."

The brigadier commanding the Italian Cremona Brigade had arrived at 1st Division HQ in January "looking like something straight out of a Gilbert and Sullivan opera. He wore a shiny blue tailored uniform cinched with a cummerbund to which a cavalry sabre had been attached. Gold epaulettes and braid covered his shoulders. Medals clanked on his chest. . . . Through his interpreter he asked me for orders. 'Where did the Generale wish that he dispose of his forces?' . . . I managed to keep a straight face."

Assorted partisan, Greek and Jewish brigades, plus Popski's Private Army,[7] had been attached to 1st Division. They were all competent fighters. "The Italians were a joke. I put them into a quiet part of the line on our right. Two days later a German patrol discovered their identity and mounted a small Company-size counterattack. At the first sound of gunfire the Brigade's officers, sitting comfortably ensconced well back of the front line, high-tailed it south. The rest of the Brigade followed. The Germans had a good laugh and withdrew."

Kurt's days in captivity passed slowly. He worried about Kate and the children and the new baby he had never seen. Was it a boy or girl? Chess tournaments were organized to help pass the time and quickly became the central focus of daily life. It was a matter of pride, each general trying to prove himself the best tactician. The British arranged for a library of German books and a regular newspaper delivery. The newspapers were regarded purely as propaganda.

"One paper is particularly obnoxious with its hysterical articles, evil lies and inventions against Germany. . . . We had been so happy until this paper reported on the Ardennes offensive . . . and its amazement at the spirit of German soldiers after their enormous exertions during the last years. The offensive came as a total surprise to all of us. . . . We knew the condition of our troops and the enemy strength. It was incomprehensible to me that my old division was fighting again as a group with only 21 commanders after losing over 10,000 soldiers. . . . The outcome is predictable and can only end in a bloodbath for the German army due to the Allies' huge superiority in material."

Day and night, streams of heavy aircraft rumbled menacingly overhead, heading for Germany. The generals listened and returned to their chess.

On 11 February, after a week of meetings at the Soviet "Riviera" city of Yalta on the Black Sea, the Allied leaders issued a joint declaration. Churchill, Stalin and Roosevelt stated their intention to "destroy German militarism and Nazism and to ensure that Germany will never again be able to disturb the peace of the world." They also declared that they would bring all war criminals to "just and swift punishment . . . [and] . . . exact reparation in kind for the destruction wrought by the Germans."

Lines of demarcation between the Western and Eastern Allied armies were firmly established. Eastern Poland—that part taken by the Soviets with Hitler in 1939—would to be given back to the Russians as compensation. Each of the signatories agreed to assist liberated countries or former Axis satellites in the formation of democratic interim governments through free elections. Finally, after its defeat, Germany would be divided into three* zones of occupation and governed through a central control commission situated in Berlin. That city too would be divided into three zones. Provision was also made for a reparation commission to work in Moscow. Yalta turned out to be the high point of Soviet-Western relations over the next four decades.

Between 14 and 15 February Allied bombers struck at the medieval city of Dresden, the capital of Saxony. The city was crowded with refugees fleeing the advancing Russian army. By the time the raid ended, Dresden lay in ruins and upwards of 25,000 were dead, nearly all of them civilians, mostly old people, women and children. It was one of the largest death tolls from

---

*Later divided into four zones to include the French.

any conventional bombing attack in history.*

Word arrived in Ludwigslust that Kurt had been reported missing. Kate and the children's world seemed to be crashing about them. Later Ursula felt a compulsion to set down, for family posterity, a record of these times, when the family was surrounded by destruction, death and an uncertain future.

"We live in a big house just outside the town in midst of a huge partly wild park. Mother is growing some vegetables in the park. My sister Inge keeps a silver-grey rabbit. I have a golden-brown one. We used to have chickens but one morning they were all dead. A marten had sneaked in and killed them. In the nearby wood that borders the park we can roam freely. In fall we trade cartridges for apples with the soldiers. We get the apples from our neighbour's orchard. For two years we have been living in this freedom. . . .

"Oma [Granny] comes to deliver the baby. Maybe it is just another sister. Granny and Mom talk about Vati. He has been missing for more than six months. Oma says: 'If it is a boy now, he should get his father's name.' Doesn't *missing* mean he is still alive and that you just don't know where he is? They talk about the war. Oma says: 'What will become of you now that the war is nearly over?' But why—there has always been war? How can it come to an end? We can always move to our grandparents on the farm. . . . But Oma says: 'The wagons are coming from the East!' I want to know why but it seems to be a terrible thing. I better not ask. . . .

"After lunch mother gets up and walks around the table. She laughs: 'It's going to happen soon!' Oma says: 'Well, if I shout Inge, then it's a girl. If I call Uschi, it's a boy.' Next morning the cry is 'Uschi! Uschi!' Hurrah, I have a brother! . . .

"Our air-raid shelter in the park is a dugout in an earth mound. It's pretty cold there in February. When there is an alert we usually sit together with neighbours in our big cellar. Gerhild usually sleeps in the arms of our French nursemaid. Again and again the sound of bombers is over our heads. Bright Christmas trees light up the sky. They look so beautiful you want to shout with joy. The adults are silent. . . .

"Next morning Oma says: 'Uschi, I'm leaving and taking you with me. Inge wants to stay.' Why me? But I get dressed, take my backpack and off we go. Oma says: 'Say goodbye to the house, you may not see it again!' But all I see is a woman on the road with two children, same age as me. They are wounded—the bombs. We reach the station but there are only ruins left.

---

*German air raids over Britain took a total of 146,760 lives during the entire war. In the nuclear raid on Hiroshima 85,000 were estimated to have died, 35,000 in Nagasaki. The Tokyo raid with conventional bombs on 9 March 1945 killed nearly 84,000 and wounded another 41,000.

After a long wait a train comes. We squeeze inside. Lots of people are travelling. I fall asleep."

A smooth takeover of the Canadian 1st Division's front by the 8th Indian Division began on 23 February. It was based on verbal arrangements made between the various divisional, brigade and regimental commanders two days earlier. "Not a signature, not a piece of paper, not a signal changed hands."

A few days later three truck convoys spaced 30 minutes apart began moving the men 154 miles south to Fermo, on the Adriatic. The weather was warm, the skies sunny. Villa Vinci became the new divisional HQ.

"A handsome building perched atop a mountain, 363 metres above sea level and from here the view is magnificent, incomparable to anything we have seen. . . . Facing the villa is a large park at the end of which is the Fermo cathedral. No other buildings are situated up here. . . . Down a stiff climb lies the town. . . . Here for the first time in months we know once more what running water is. We hear with strange glee the flushing of a toilet! . . . The villa is owned by Countess Julia Vinci née Valdeschi. The Count, a Capt. in the Italian Artillery but now a prisoner of war . . . was caught by the British at Sidi Barani during Gen. Wavell's campaign. . . .

"28 Feb. . . . Countess Julia . . . is organizing a tea dance for Sunday, 4 Mar. . . . Meanwhile G branch is dead quiet and its members spend the day taking in the sights and sunning themselves. What a life! One should really feel remorseful. . . . But being practical fellows, we haven't a single remorse. . . . Is it our fault we are here? The entire setting is designed to bring out in each one of us that appreciation of the better things which we are so liable to forget in war."

That evening, leaning on the villa's balcony overlooking the town, Harry watched the Fermo fishermen hauling in their boats and nets. They sang as they worked. Beautiful tenor and baritone voices floated in harmony on the soft twilight. He called Scott Murdoch outside to listen. The war seemed far away. For a long time they stood together in silence, smoking and listening to the concert. At length Murdoch sighed: "Marvellous! We'll never hear anything like that at home."

"You're right, Scott. They're bloody fine singers. But they can't fight worth a shit."

Code-named Operation "Goldflake," the embarkation of the division's troops began at Leghorn on 7 March. Leaving Italy, the war diarist wrote that it was "a country we neither loved nor hated, a country so full of history, so beautiful and at the same time so dirty, so modern in its antiquity." The convoy carrying the division sailed for Marseilles.

Harry flew back to England.

8

Chris Vokes was having his share of problems as GOC 4th Armoured Division. His explosive and at times high-handed methods did not sit well with a number of the division's senior officers. One of his brigadiers described him as "likeable enough but an infantryman, pure and simple, who hadn't a clue on how to operate an armoured division."

In planning his fight for Kapelsche Veer, a small silt-filled harbour on the Maas occupied by the enemy, Vokes decided to use war canoes for transporting troops down the river. An attack against this stronghold, a staging point for a planned German assault across the river, had been tried by the Polish 1st Armoured Division on the night of 30-31 December. It had failed. Over protests from his planning staff that the canoes were much too vulnerable to enemy machine-gun fire, Vokes ordered Jefferson's 10th Infantry Brigade to make the attempt on the bitterly cold morning of 26 January.

The attack, Operation "Elephant," was led by Maj. J.F. Swayze. Two complete companies from the Lincoln and Welland Regiment were lost when their war canoes were holed and sunk by enemy fire. Many of the men drowned. Lieutenant-Colonel Proctor felt so strongly about this tragedy that he went to Corps HQ and asked to be transferred from Vokes's command. When asked for an explanation, he told Simonds: "I have backed him up but I can't serve him anymore." Simonds paid Vokes a visit. Proctor was promoted to brigadier and placed in command of all Army Terminals.*

By February, Allied strength on the Western Front had reached 4 million men. Now, only the Rhine lay between the Allies and a final victory. The main effort to close up on the river was to be made by seizing various river crossings north of the Ruhr. While the U.S. First Army advanced beyond the line of the Erft River, northwest of Cologne, the Canadians and the U.S. Ninth Army were to move against the Rhine north of Düsseldorf.

The Canadian First Army, with a large number of British troops under its command, launched its offensive between the Maas and the Rhine on 8 February. Three weeks later it had crossed into Germany to penetrate the last belt of the Siegfried Line defences in the Hochwald area, 20 miles southeast of Nijmegen. Fierce fighting developed east of the Hochwald as the enemy attempted to cover the Rhine bridges at Wesel, 20 miles northwest of Essen. But once the Siegfried defences were overcome, the whole Allied advance closed quickly on the left bank of the Rhine. German forces west of the river were systematically split and destroyed.

---

*Included 15,000 men, all roads, railheads, ports and PLUTO—the underwater pipe line.

On 7 March, the same day that Cologne fell, Lieutenant Burrows, an American platoon commander, made a dash across the river on the Remagen Bridge only ten minutes before the Germans planned to destroy it. Grimly, his platoon held its toehold until units of the U.S. 9th Armoured Division consolidated the position. The Allies were across the Rhine.

Two days later a lodgement area three miles deep had been taken that German reinforcements failed to contain. As it grew, the vital north-south autobahn was cut. By 24 March, when the main attack eastward began in the north, three corps were concentrated in an area ten miles deep by 25 miles inside the Reich. The American grip was extended on the left bank of the Rhine below Koblenz. To the north, the Wesel salient finally succumbed to the Canadians and the American Ninth Army. The Allies now stood along 125 miles of the Rhine from Nijmegen to Koblenz.

As the numbers of senior German military and political prisoners being captured by the advancing armies grew, the process of separating "good" Germans from "bad," and the "tame" Germans from the fanatics, gathered new urgency. Hurried legislation had already been undertaken in Canada, England and the United States to provide a democratic legitimacy for bringing the "war criminals" to trial.

Generally, every member of the SS was considered to be a Nazi and possible war criminal. The Allies still had no clear understanding of Waffen-SS recruiting methods. Additionally, every Wehrmacht and Luftwaffe general, every admiral and Nazi administrator, was regarded as a potential war criminal. Hitler's closest advisors were already doomed, as were the *Reichs-kommissars, Gauleiters* and anyone even remotely responsible for the operation of the concentration camps. Front-line generals who gave the battle orders were likewise considered dogmeat, particularly when incidents of brutality or atrocities by troops under their command might be proved. Kurt fell into this latter category.

To separate the doomed from the merely evil, the Kensington Cage Interrogation Centre had been set up in London under Lieut.-Col. A.P. Scotland. Scotland's army career rivalled that of any fictional hero of the period. Born in England, the trilingual Scotland was much better informed on German military matters than many of the men he was interrogating. Earlier in the war, his interrogation group had garnered immense amounts of valuable information from German POWs through a combination of intimidation, threats and mock trials followed by death sentences and firing squads that used blank ammunition. Any prisoner managing to hold out through his staged "execution" was congratulated by the chivalrous Scotland and shipped off to a life of leisure at a POW camp in Canada or the U.S.

During March, Kurt was taken to London for three days of intensive interrogation. The encounter was chaired by U.S. Maj.-Gen. R.W. Barker.

Lieutenant-Colonels Scotland, J.H. Boraston, Bruce Macdonald and Maj. John Page were also present.

It was Macdonald's first meeting with the man he was to prosecute. "Meyer from the outset denied any knowledge of any killing of prisoners. It was forbidden, he said, and never to his knowledge had it taken place. He had never in the fighting in Western Europe issued orders to deny quarter. . . . However, he was ready to talk of his military career. . . . When asked how he could square his belief in following Hitler and the Nazis with what was happening to Germany because of Hitler he answered: 'You want me to deny the Führer? I have led over 10,000 men to their deaths. You ask me now to betray them? To tell you that it was all a mistake, that it was all for nothing? I cannot. I will not. Do not ask me.'"

The intent of the questioning quickly became clear to Kurt. "My interrogation at first dealt with purely military-political questions then turned to events in Normandy. I soon concluded they wanted to hold me responsible for all that happened on the battlefield and that I should become the scapegoat. During the fighting north of Caen the Allied propaganda machine had made my division out to be a band of young fanatical Nazis. Now proof of this press campaign had to be produced and preparations on the severity of the revenge decided. . . . My troops were still fighting so I answered negatively to any question that could incriminate them."

He was more interested in giving his interrogators his views on the Allied forces. "The Canadian army of 1944 was a high-class force . . . destined to fight an enemy who was, in manpower and equipment, inferior. Every Canadian operation bore the mark of intensive planning and was built on sound tactical principles. Every opening phase was a complete success and the staff work a mathematical masterpiece. The staff always succeeded in burying the enemy under several tons of explosives and transforming the defence position into a cemetery . . . [but] every one of the Canadian attacks lost its push and determination after a few miles. . . . British and Canadian planning was absolutely without risk. Neither army employed its armoured strength for which it was created. Both used the tank more or less as an infantry support weapon. . . . They executed the operations in an inflexible, time-wasting method. Never once did speed, the most powerful weapon of armoured warfare, appear."

Years later he was particularly critical of the Anglo-Canadian forces for sticking to their step-by-step schedule to take Falaise in eight days, as planned, even after air and artillery attacks had obliterated the German defence line and opened the road through to Falaise on the first night of the attack. The time lost allowed the Germans to regroup and bring up reinforcements. The Russians, he said then, would probably have adopted a similar plan but would have fought it through far differently. "They certainly would not have permitted a battle of phases with the first objective only three miles behind the enemy's front line. . . . Their junior officers are a well-trained, fanatical body and brutal commanders. Their armoured force is excellent. Its tanks are the best in the world. The tank men are handpicked, good mechanics and very skilful in improvisation. . . . Russian infantrymen are bad soldiers by Western standards but they are the most ferocious killers. The core of the infantry is composed of Asiatic races of barbaric mentality. Despite their low standards, or because of them, they are masters in defence and in attack the most savage fighters I have ever encountered. Death seemed meaningless to them."

He believed that had the Red Army been in Normandy, at the first sign that the Falaise road was open an armoured column would have struck straight for the town under a "fanatical young Communist who would stop at nothing." It was this dynamic up-front leadership that the Canadians lacked. Instead of bombers the Russians would have used tactical aircraft under the direction of their young leaders. "In a matter of hours instead of days Falaise would have fallen. For Russian leadership knows the value of time."

At the end of the third day he was returned to his cell. News of the great Allied assault across the Rhine filtered through to him in bits and pieces. Two airborne divisions had been dropped on the homeland near Hamminkeln on 24 March. A depressing thought. The Wehrmacht could not even muster sufficient anti-aircraft guns to bring down the nearly 3,000 gliders and paratroop aircraft used in the operation.

The weeks passed. He waited.

After the Allies had crossed the Rhine, the desperate and now apparently quite mad Adolf Hitler, operating from his underground bunker beneath the Reich Chancellery, ordered Field Marshal Kesselring from Italy to replace von Rundstedt. The best Kesselring could do was attempt to hold the German armies together. With the junction of the American First and Ninth Armies near Lippstadt on April Fool's Day, the Ruhr encirclement was complete. Twenty-four divisions were trapped.

Three main avenues for the advance into Germany were now open: across the north German plain to the Baltic and Berlin; from Kassel through Erfurt and Leipzig to Dresden; or via Nuremberg along the Danube River and into Austria. Eisenhower chose the middle course, knifing the country in half, with supporting limited operations by Montgomery in the north and General Devers in the south.

Once this central thrust met the Red Army, Allied forces would then swing north to the Baltic and clear the northern areas before plunging south along the Danube and into the Alpine Redoubt, where it was assumed that all remaining German forces would make a last stand. From Holland to the resort town of Baden on the edge of the Black Forest, 14 armoured divisions thrust deep into the heart of Germany. By the time the attack began,

Montgomery's vanguard was already 80 miles beyond the Rhine and driving furiously inland.

At the end of their voyage from Leghorn to Marseilles the men of the 1st Division were trucked overland up the Rhone Valley to I Corps' assembly area at Itegem, Belgium. The Canadians still occupied 21st Army Group's left flank, the position they were to remain in until the war ended. A week earlier Montgomery had acidly observed to Simonds that "if the words 'left flank' and 'fuck' were removed from the English language the Canadian army would be left immobile and speechless."

Harry returned to the division in late March. Movement orders were received 3 April to join II Corps at the Reichswald [the Imperial Forest] just over the German border southeast of Nijmegen. Under cloudy skies and a cold drizzle the truck convoys moved out. They found the route jammed with every type of military traffic.

That night for the first time the men of 1st Division put up their tents on German soil. Reichswald had been the northern end of the Siegfried Line, but now all that remained were a few scattered pillboxes and an occasional trench.

On 2 April, near the newly constructed Melville Bridge crossing the Rhine at Emmerich, a captain in the Seaforth Highlanders attached to Simonds's HQ, was hailed by the British prime minister. Churchill's entourage of vehicles and staff were visiting the area. The PM left his car and lumbered over to the edge of the river bank. For a moment he stared down thoughtfully at its dark waters, then, with a chuckle, unzipped his boilersuit and glanced at the startled Seaforth officer. "Hello Canada! Do you know I have waited six years to piss in the Rhine?"

Harry too was savouring the *Götterdämmerung*.

"3 April. . . . It is a good feeling to be here for the end. . . . The Boche can't hold out much longer. Everything he has is crumbling. . . . Heard today that I have been awarded two more gongs: the Croix de Guerre avec Palme, and I am now a 'Chevalier de la Legion d'Honneur.' It has a nice ring to it. Preparations now underway for Operation 'Cannonshot' . . . objective is to cross the Ijssel and capture Apeldoorn. It will probably be our last major action of this war."

It was. The division packed up and left the Reichswald for an assembly point near Baaksonemara in Holland on 7 April. The division's diarist recorded his first glimpse of Holland: "We leave the great German forest with no regret. . . . Materborn and then . . . through the city of Cleve. . . . Both are in ruins, but the roads have been cleared and we move easily through the bombed out areas. No civilians to be seen but as we near the Rhine a few are to be seen here and there. They look grave. Some are sullen, others venture a smile but we must not fraternize so we try to look straight ahead.

At the Rhine a 1,280 foot pontoon bridge takes us across . . . to Emmerich, a shell torn devastated city. Only Cassino in Italy looks worse. . . . In Holland . . . the little Dutch villages have hardly been touched by war and the cottages and houses are very pretty and very clean, the villages neat. . . . We reach our area, which is just another wood, at 1815 hrs. This is no better than the Reichswald. At this point we are no farther than 3,600 metres from the front line, and the enemy shells the surrounding area at regular intervals."

Roads from the north of Holland were packed with retreating German troops. Advancing along the Dutch border to capture Nordhorn, Canadian troops crossed the Twenthe Canal, effectively threatening all German supply lines into the Netherlands. In a wide wheeling movement Canadian I Corps pivoted near Arnhem toward the Ijssel River line. Its armoured columns lunged north for the sea. After bitter resistance at the approaches to Deventer, both it and the town of Zwolle fell on 10 April. The entire German army west of the Ijssel was now cut off in a pocket that contained nearly all the principal cities of Holland.

"11 Apr. . . . This afternoon, Guy, Foulkes and Keefler* came to discuss 'Cannonshot' and what must be done to feed the Dutch. The poor buggers are all starving."

At 1600 hours the artillery began in preparation for the attack. A half hour later troops of Bogert's 2nd Brigade under cover of smoke began crossing the Ijssel. By midnight two battalions were on the opposite bank.

"The action went speedily and according to plan. Surprise was definitely achieved. The screening of the bridge site and the bridgehead area by smoke was well done. The 'Buffaloes' did a good job. This was the first occasion the Division had employed 'Buffaloes'; operating . . . conditions in Italy were such that we had no need of nor could use them there."

Once again he found himself placing troops in a position that he had sworn never to allow.

"On the night 13/14 Apr. a change in plan was necessary. The original plan visualized 49 (WR) Infantry Div.† crossing west of Arnhem, but they crossed east of the vicinity and caught the enemy off balance. . . . I received orders to link up with 49 (WR) Div. and to open the road down the west side of the river Ijssel so that a bridge could be built across from Zutphen. This additional job was given to 2 Inf. Bde., though my original intention had been to keep them in reserve, since they would have done enough by making the assault crossing and establishing the bridgehead. . . .

"We were facing three ways at once. 1 Inf. Bde. on the right, with an exposed north flank, was moving on to Apeldoorn; 3 Inf. Bde., in the centre, was moving up to the canal south of the town and linking up with 49 (WR)

---

*Maj.-Gen. R.H. Keefler took command of the Canadian 3rd Infantry Division on 23 March 1945.
†The British 49th West Riding Division.

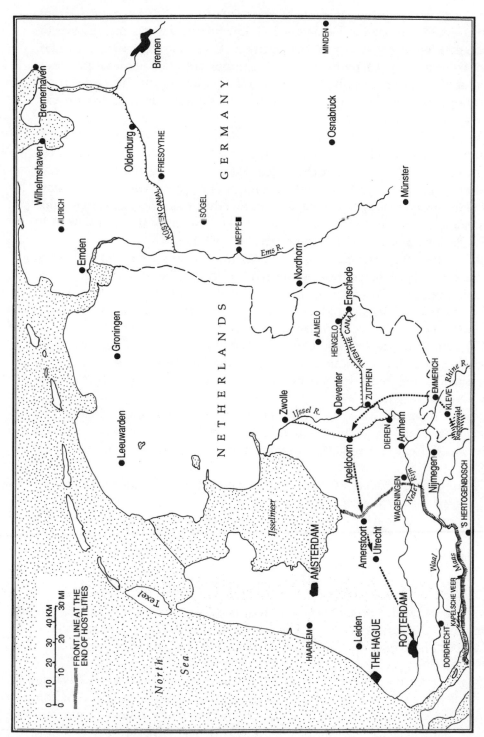

The northern and central Netherlands, showing the movements of the 1st Canadian Division.

Div. I had always been conscious of my northern flank because we did not know where the enemy had jumped. 2 Inf. Bde. had been my reserve in case anything went wrong in this northern flank. Now all three brigades were committed and fully extended. Had things not gone according to plan there was no reserve in sight to restore a bad situation. Fortunately the enemy were equally extended and were not able to exploit our thinness on the ground."

As the end approached, even the most senior politicians and army commanders viewed the imminent German collapse as spectator sport. One morning Prime Minister Churchill, Field Marshals Brooke and Montgomery, Generals Eisenhower, Crerar and Simonds visited 4th Armoured Division HQ and decided to stay for lunch. Crerar, together with Vokes, arranged the postprandial entertainment. A bulge in the line opposite Moncel's 4th Armoured Brigade was to be straightened at 1400 hours.

While the VIPs watched from a hill, Moncel sent his first tank out from under cover. German gunfire promptly blew it up. The VIPs waited. When a second tank failed to appear, an embarrassed and angry Crerar sent Vokes off to investigate. Sensibly, Moncel had cancelled the operation.

"Goddammit, what do I tell Uncle Harry?" Vokes demanded.

"Tell him I've just lost one tank crew and am not about to risk any more lives on something as idiotic as this. If he's that interested in straight lines, tell him I'll straighten this one out tonight when it's dark and the German gunners can't see us."

Vokes reported back to Uncle Harry. Crerar was livid at Moncel's disobedience and quite prepared to sack him on the spot. Cooler heads intervened. Next morning Monty stopped off for a moment at Moncel's TAC HQ.

"Young man, I understand you straightened out the line last night."

"Yes, sir. I did," Moncel replied.

The Field Marshal smiled. "You jolly near went home yesterday!"

9

To the northwest, beyond the river Ems, the Canadian 4th and Polish 1st Armoured Divisions rumbled across the flat and boggy north German plain. In the south, British and American armoured divisions raced eastwards to meet the Russians.

Sögel lay in the path of Vokes's 4th Armoured Division on its advance to the Küsten Canal at Oldenburg. Although the town had been cleared on 9 April, the Germans counterattacked several times the following day and at one point reached the centre of town. The Lake Superiors and Lincoln and Welland Regiments drove them out. The troops reported that German civilians had joined the enemy soldiers and killed a number of Canadians. Furious, Vokes decided that an object lesson was required. The citizens of Sögel were given 24 hours to vacate their town. The division's chief engineering officer, Lieut.-Col. J.R.B. Jones, was then ordered to go in with several truckloads of dynamite and guncotton to flatten the town centre. Any rubble remaining from the stone buildings was to be bulldozed flat. Reluctantly, Jones obeyed. Thereafter he became known as "The Sod of Sögel." The division moved on.

Friesoythe, the next major town along the route, fell on 14 April to the Argyll and Sutherland Highlanders of Jefferson's 10th Infantry Brigade. Its CO, the popular Lieut.-Col. Freddy Wigle, died at his TAC HQ during the action. Wigle had been Harry's GSO1 when he commanded the division. Later, Vokes had given Wigle command of the Argyll and Sutherlands when the vacancy occurred. Like Harry, he had been very fond of Wigle.[8] The first report of his death was that he had been shot in the back by a civilian sniper. Vokes summoned his GSO1, Lieut.-Col. Mackenzie Robinson.

"Mac!" he roared. "I'm going to raze that goddamn town. Get out some proclamations. Tell 'em we're going to level the fucking place. Get the people t'hell out of their houses first."

Robinson hesitated. "All right, sir. But you can't put that in writing!"

The populace cleared out. "The Sod of Sögel" and his engineers went in and levelled then burned what remained of the town. They used the resulting rubble to reinforce district roads for the division's tanks. Later, Vokes discovered that Wigle had in fact been shot in the back with a Schmeisser by a German soldier, one of a group the Argyll and Sutherlands had bypassed earlier in the day. Vokes admitted to "no feeling of great remorse over the elimination of Friesoythe."

Kurt moved to a prison camp at Windermere in Westmorland, bordering the Lake District. Max Wünsche met him. After settling in, he was escorted to see Dr. Otto John, the German inmates' camp commandant,* who had taken part in the anti-Hitler plot of July 1944. He shouted hysterically: "Do not try escaping. If you do, your corpse will be brought back and your family will never see you again."

Kurt held his tongue. "If this pathetic creature, strutting like a peacock, suspected my contempt for him he would have sunk into the earth with shame. I was told that I could no longer join the general exercise periods. Wünsche, Linger and I would now only be allowed to move about under guard. We maintained our dignity despite the rumours flying around the camp. Kapitänleutnant Eck and Dr. Weisspfennig, the camp doctor, advised

*Later, first chief of West Germany's new secret service. He defected to East Germany, returned after some years, and was imprisoned.

that I was considered one of the camp's candidates for death. Neither comrade suspected that they too had been listed as war criminals.*

"On our next walk we were separated like three black sheep and marched like dangerous criminals. Two Tommys marched with us through the gates. Once we were out of sight from the camp they hung their machine pistols around their necks and ignored us. . . . At the start of our next walk Admiral Hüffmeier stepped out of the general ranks and demanded to join us. He was allowed only once. The Tommys did not appreciate such displays of comradeship. . . . I met my old CO, Lieut.-Gen. Pflieger, in whose division I received my first training in 1929. It was both a happy and sad reunion for us. Most of our comrades were gone."

Ursula settled into Alma's second-floor flat in Offleben. "The place has a big brown-coal mine and behind the train station is a mighty carbonizing plant with a huge chimney. A fine brown dust covers everything. I'm surprised to find a well-built bunker. It is for the workers of the plant, which is expected to be destroyed any time now. There are air raids here too. But my 80-year-old great-grandmother cannot be moved to take cover. She stays in her room. My girlfriend Hanna gave me a doll to play with in the bunker. We tell the dolls not to be afraid of the bombs and that we won't leave them alone.

"One day a message comes from Ludwigslust. Mum writes that everybody is well, little Kurt is okay and the house is filled with refugees. Oma says to Aunty: 'They are in the middle of it now—the Russians on one side, the Americans on the other.'

"One day we pack all our important papers and pictures in a box and bury it in the garden. The entrance to the village is barred by a roadblock made of beams. I don't understand this—I once rode in a tank with Dad and know that it can push any obstacle aside. The adults are unnerved. Suddenly, jeeps and little tanks drive past our house. The British arrive! Now it is almost certain that Mum will come. But where is she amongst all the refugees?"

After crossing the Ijssel, the 1st Division, between 16 and 18 April, made one last push to capture the city of Apeldoorn. It was Harry's final combat assault.

"It had never been my intention to assault Apeldoorn frontally. It was a friendly city, filled with refugees and I was not prepared to use artillery on it. . . . The plan was to isolate the place with 1 Inf. Bde. keeping the enemy garrison occupied while 3 Inf. Bde. crossed the canal south of the city and came in from the rear. The plan was modified later because 2 Inf.

---

*Both were executed for war crimes a few months later in Hamburg.

Bde. as usual had done a fine job in the south getting across the canal at Dieren. . . .

"When the enemy resistance crumbled on the west bank of the Apeldoorn canal all three brigades did an excellent pursuit job, considering the distance covered and the thickness of the country, all of which had to be searched. The speed with which this was done was remarkable."

Between 18 and 24 April the division advanced to the enemy's "Grebbe Line," intending to crash through "and take out Amersfoort in much the same way as Apeldoorn. . . . A plan was prepared to pass through the front of the 49 (WR) Div. on our left. It was then that we received an indication that we would probably never be required to carry it out. . . . The officers and men did a first class job in a very professional and business-like manner. They carried out successfully a series of difficult operations and certainly showed that they were no 'bush-leaguers.' A fact commented on by British units who were working under our command. . . . When all the guff is stripped away a general's army is no better than his front-line troops and a handful of brave, tired and dirty company commanders that lead them. Mine were the best in the world. More imaginative than the Germans; more flexible than the British; more sensible than the Russians; better trained and led than the Americans and worth any six of their soldiers when it came to close combat."

A truce had been struck with Seyss-Inquart, German governor of the Netherlands. Provided the Canadians held their positions at the Grebbe Line, convoys and air drops of food for the Dutch would be allowed to enter German-occupied territory unmolested. In exchange the Germans promised to cease all flooding and end repressive measures against the Dutch.

On 24 April Reichsführer Himmler, through the Swedish government, offered to surrender all forces fighting on the Western Front. He was informed that only a simultaneous and unconditional surrender on both fronts would be acceptable.

Next day men of the U.S. 69th Division reached the river Elbe at Torgau to shake hands with battle-weary troops of the Russian 58th Guards Division. Germany had been cut in half.

During the night of 29 April, in the Führerbunker, while Russian artillery shredded Berlin block by block, Hitler married his faithful mistress, Eva Braun. They retired to their honeymoon quarters. During the afternoon of 30 April both committed suicide. The following day, in their apartments underground, Goebbels and his wife gave poison to their children before killing themselves.

The Camp Windermere prisoners heard the war news "with bleeding hearts. . . . It was incomprehensible to us that so many were still fighting. . . . We believed that somehow, after reflecting, the Europeans would prevent the Red Army from taking over Central and Eastern Germany. We were mistaken. Fate ran its course, leading the Asiatics to the Elbe and into the heart of Europe.

"The complete collapse of our homeland struck us in the marrow. Stories about the cruel events in the Russian zone nearly drove us insane. No one knew with certainty where his family was—or even if still alive. Was our fifth child all right? Had my wish for a son been granted or did I have another daughter? Day and night all of us worried about our homes. Despite these broodings there were no answers. Outside camp privileges were withdrawn gradually until our life shrank to confinement behind the barbed wire. Our walks were terminated. The Civil law of the conqueror took over.

"Field Marshals von Kleist and Sperrle arrived. Shocked, we heard the first eyewitness accounts of the torn homeland. There were debates over how the war ended, over the political mistakes and the lack of preparations. There was much bitterness over the failure of leadership. Most officers rejected the 20 July assassination attempt. I knew no one who supported the authors."

The roads in Germany were filled with refugees, everyone trying to escape the advancing Russians. The Red Army was exacting a terrible retribution on the German people for its years of suffering under the Nazi war machine. Reichsmarschall Göring, blushing like a Rhinemaiden and lugging a suitcase filled with codeine pills, surrendered to the Americans. Members of the Gestapo in every town and city changed into Wehrmacht uniforms or civilian clothes and vanished. Behind the battle lines, roaming SS execution squads delivered summary justice by shooting and hanging anyone found in uniform who wasn't wounded and lacked papers or a good explanation for his presence.

One after another the concentration camps were overrun by Allied troops. They found the front gates left open, the watchtowers empty. In most, the SS guards had gone. Hollow-eyed emaciated prisoners in striped rags tottered out to greet the liberators. Most were too far gone to be saved. Battle-hardened front-line soldiers gulped in stupefied disbelief and broke into tears. "How was it possible for a civilized people to become such barbarians?" Later, when the shock passed, they swore through clenched teeth that whoever was responsible must pay.

At the Meyer house in Ludwigslust even the hallways were being used by transients. They talked in low, frightened voices. Everybody had a story to tell about the Russians. "It's not their front-line soldiers—it is the ones who come after that will steal everything, then rape and murder you," an old woman whispered.

A group of doctors and nurses fleeing from Berlin stopped overnight at the house. They were headed north for Flensburg. Kate approached one of the doctors. "May I ask a favour? On his last leave my husband left me a pistol and bullets. He said if the Russians come I was to kill the children and then myself. A police officer gave me instructions on how to do it. But when the time comes I don't think I'll be able to. Do you have any morphine?"

The doctor obliged. Thereafter, she carried the vials with her everywhere.

The British arrived. Two days later they left. An officer explained politely that they were withdrawing because Ludwigslust was in the Russian-occupied zone. Kate became frantic. She had to take the children and leave. But where could they go? Salvation arrived in the form of Fritz Richter, Kurt's old friend from the Schwerin Police School. He had realized that Kate's only chance for survival was to escape to the west. The Russians wanted Kurt Meyer for his part in the destruction of Kharkov, and Richter knew that Kate and the children would make excellent bargaining chips for negotiating Kurt's surrender to the MKVD* by the British.

Despite his own serious wounds, Richter brought a car and obtained travel documents for all of them through *Gauleiter* Hildebrandt, plus enough gasoline for two cars to get them to Heide, in the British zone, 60 miles northwest of Hamburg.

All fighting ceased in Italy on 2 May. But Grand Admiral Karl Doenitz, Hitler's successor, tried to delay surrendering to the Russians to give civilians and the Eastern Front troops time to reach positions in the West. His emissaries, led by Admiral von Friedeburg, met with Montgomery at Lüneburg Heath. At 1830 hours on 4 May they signed the surrender document, according to which effective the following day all German forces in northwestern Germany, Holland, Schleswig-Holstein and Denmark were to lay down their arms.

During the afternoon of 4 May, Capt. A.E. McCreery, Protestant chaplain of the Canadian Grenadier Guards, accompanied by Lieut. N.A. Goldie, went forward to help some German wounded. While attempting to collect them, both men were killed. They were among the last Canadians to die in World War II.

In a battered hotel at Wageningen, Holland, General Foulkes accepted the surrender of the military commander of the western Netherlands, Col.-Gen. Johannes von Blaskowitz. "The terms of surrender were read over by Gen. Foulkes, and Blaskowitz hardly answered a word. Occasionally he would interpose with a demand for more time . . . otherwise nothing was said from the German side. They looked like men in a dream, dazed, stupefied and unable to realize that for them their world was utterly finished."9

Von Friedeburg went to Eisenhower's HQ during the evening of 5 May and was told that only an unconditional surrender would be acceptable. Next day Colonel-General Jodl arrived to discuss the matter. It became clear that the Germans were stalling, trying to give hundreds of thousands of their citizens and soldiers time to reach the British and American lines. Eisenhower

---

*Military intelligence branch of the Russian army.

threatened to seal off the Western Front against any westward movement unless all hostilities on both fronts ceased within 48 hours. At Eisenhower's HQ, at 0241 hours on the morning of 7 May, Jodl signed the act of surrender, to become effective at midnight.

The war with Germany was over.

PART 9

FLAGS ARE
FOLDED

*When you have to kill a man it costs
nothing to be polite.*

WINSTON CHURCHILL

H ARRY FELT NEITHER elated nor depressed when the news arrived from
Corps HQ. "I think we were all a bit numb. Six and a half years is
a long time for any man to be thinking about just trying to stay alive and
hoping to see that day when it's all over. Of course we were pleased. We
smiled. We joked. But I think everyone was just too bloody tired to get excited."

The formal parades, congratulations and honours would come later.
Meanwhile, there were 120,000 former enemies sitting in western Holland
who had to be repatriated and several million Dutch people on the verge
of starvation. Food air drops had started on 29 April, when over half a million
rations were delivered by 253 aircraft of RAF Bomber Command. These were
joined later by planes of the U.S. Eighth Air Force. By 8 May, over 11 million
rations had been dropped. Canadian army food deliveries by road and rail
had been ready to move into occupied Holland as far back as 26 April, but
negotiating delays kept everyone waiting until 2 May. However, once the
truce was arranged, 30 truck convoys were able to cross the German line
every 30 minutes around the clock. A week later this operation was still
delivering 1,000 tons of supplies daily.

"Within 24 hours we received a pretty tall order: to advance 100 miles, seal off four different areas of Western Holland, disarm some 30,000 enemy troops in these areas; then organize the disarming of the remaining Germans. . . . Rotterdam became my new Divisional HQ. Brigade groups were sent off to establish themselves north of Rotterdam, at Haarlem, Leiden, The Hague, Amsterdam and Dordrecht. Each brigade HQ received instructions to position itself near a German Div. HQ. The Germans were to keep their weapons until collected into assembly areas when they would then be disarmed and placed under Canadian guard until their march back to Germany."

Harry, with a staff officer and an interpreter, went through the enemy lines under German escort to meet the commander of the German XXX Corps, Gen. Philipp Kleffel, at his HQ to arrange the mechanics of surrender.

"Much saluting and heel clicking all around. The old boy appeared genuinely cooperative and terribly worried about his family. He was a model train enthusiast and had the largest track layout I'd ever seen. He had placed most of the Gestapo behind bars already, saving us the trouble of rounding them up."

Next day, 8 May—VE Day—at 0700 hours, the 1st Division rolled into Holland. The route lay through Amersfoort, Utrecht and along the autobahn into Rotterdam.

The division's war diarist recorded the triumphant journey: "Every village, street and house was bedecked with red, white and blue Dutch flags and orange streamers which, in the brilliant sunlight, made a gay scene. The Dutch people had heard a rumour of our arrival and were lining the roads, streets in thousands to give us a tumultuous welcome. . . . When the convoy reached the outskirts of Rotterdam it lost all semblance of a military convoy. The dense crowds cut it into pockets; a vehicle would be unable to move because of civilians surrounding it, climbing onto it, throwing flowers— bestowing handshakes, hugs and even kisses. One could not see the vehicle or trailer for legs, arms, heads and bodies draped all over it as it made its precarious way through the last few miles of Rotterdam streets. The enthusiasm of the crowds seemed to have infected the German soldiers of the Wehrmacht, for in some cases they, going the opposite way in wagons or on foot—waved and grinned."

Harry moved into the official residence of the city's traitorous mayor, a magnificent house facing a small park. Divisional officers were quartered in a variety of comfortable hotels and private homes.

"My first problem was with the Dutch underground. They were armed and wanted to shoot every German, Dutch Quisling[1] and collaborator they could lay their hands on. . . . In several towns German soldiers and collaborators were executed before I could put a stop to it. . . . It was hard to blame the Dutch. They had been through hell. . . . God, how they hated the Boche! There was an immediate urgency to get the Germans out of Holland."

What galled the Dutch was to see German officers and men still living in Dutch homes and keeping their weapons, bicycles, motor vehicles and food supplies. Most German food supplies were locked away inside Dutch establishments. In one case, three soldiers in a German truck arrived at a butcher shop, unlocked the door and began loading sides of beef while a group of hollow-eyed and hungry Dutch civilians looked on.

Yet in spite of a few scattered incidents "the Germans showed all the willingness in the world to cooperate, but the rigidity of their system of command made it rather exasperating and . . . slow to our local commanders."

Kleffel was summoned to Harry's TAC HQ for an explanation. He made the German wait outside the caravan. "It suddenly hit me that if he saw our troop disposition maps and realized that all we had containing his corps was one widely scattered division he might get ideas." Hurriedly, he and Murdoch crayoned in another four Canadian divisions before inviting Kleffel inside.

"I . . . explained our system of decentralization. I told him that he must issue orders that his local commanders on the spot . . . obey the orders of my local commanders, and not appeal to him for every mortal thing. This immediately speeded up the whole program."

Once the German troops in Holland were gathered into concentrated areas, they were no longer permitted on the streets. Anything considered loot was confiscated. Canadian troops responsible for the disarming were ordered not to keep any weapons, compasses, binoculars or personal effects taken from their captives. All German MPs on duty at the concentration areas remained armed and German officers continued carrying personal weapons, although they were not permitted to display them.

"13 May. . . . Mandatory church parade so I had to attend. A good turn out—obviously. . . . I read the lesson. 'Lord, now let thy servant depart in peace. . . .' I sanctioned the shooting of a half dozen German deserters that had been tried by their courtmartials. . . . They were executed today. 12 more German deserters have been picked up in Rotterdam jails and are being turned over to the German Commander at the Ijmuiden concentration area for disposition."

The Germans started leaving Holland. Long irregular lines of shabby, bearded soldiers carrying knapsacks, pushing carts or pulling wagons tramped through the villages and towns, beyond the Zuider Zee,* back into Germany.

---

*The Ijsselmeer.

Most were old men and boys. The Dutch watched in grim silence, occasionally breaking into cheers at the sight of a lone Canadian vehicle or armed escort.

On Texel, largest of the Dutch Frisian Islands, troops uncovered a bizarre situation. A few weeks earlier, 900 Russians serving in the Wehrmacht had mutinied in the hope of avoiding "repatriation" to the U.S.S.R. "When told they would have to fight us, they killed their German officers and NCOs and have since been fighting the remaining Germans. 500 Germans and 600 Russians were killed. There are still clashes occurring. There are now some wounded Russians lying in a minefield and neither side will let the other reach them." They were evacuated next day and the Germans rounded up and disarmed.

"21 May. . . . Victory parade in The Hague under a heavy rain . . . a miserable showing by the troops. . . . Uncle Harry, Prince Bernhard and I took the salute. The men looked slovenly and were out of step. Now that the party is nearly over discipline will become a problem. I can't blame the troops. They are not PF. The war is over and they want to go home. . . .

"22 May. . . . A presentation by the orphans of St. Joseph's street in Rotterdam today complete with band turned me to tears. Poor skinny kids without a penny had got together to give me an inscribed paperknife thanking me for liberating them. How does one thank such generosity?"

On 23 May, Reichsführer Heinrich Himmler was captured by the British at the town of Bremervörde near Bremen. He bit into a cyanide vial concealed in his mouth and died immediately. He was 45.

On the last day of May an astonishing letter arrived addressed to a hardtack biscuit maker, "c/o The Canadian Army, Heemraadsingel, Rotterdam." Crayoned coloured flags decorated the outside of the envelope. Inside, attached to the carefully penned letter, was a routine factory inspection slip stating: "Should there be any complaints about the biscuits in this tin please send this slip with full particulars." The letter read:

> Dear Givers,
> We write a letter to you, though we don't have any complaints. On the contrary we are thankful. We all thank you very very much for the biscuits, they were delightful. We were surprised that it was such a lot of biscuits. Our gratitude is great. It has been a nice gift. We enjoyed it very much. We were glad to receive it. We have no words for it. Only: Thanks awfully!!!

Several signatures confirmed these sentiments. In all military history it is doubtful if army hardtack ever received such fulsome praise.

Among the latest arrivals at Camp Windermere was a colonel with a message for Kurt. "For two weeks the Colonel had been stationed with my brother-in-law, a Luftwaffe lieutenant. He brought the latest news of my family. I had had no contact since August and knew nothing about my loved ones.

This perpetual worry about our wives and children was the hardest to bear. Personal needs seldom affected anyone because we had become hardened through war; it was lack of knowledge about our families that almost broke us. His few words made me the happiest man in camp. 'Your brother-in-law says to tell you that your family has fled to West Germany and that your son was born on 15 February.' . . .

"In June, together with a hundred comrades, I was sent to Camp 18 at Featherstone;* a pleasant break from the paralyzing captivity. We were put on buses and driven through England. The new camp, on the river Tyne, had been used by American troops. It was made up of countless barracks divided into compounds and surrounded by barbed wire. A depressing place. Nor were we pleased by our welcome. The bus wheels had barely stopped when a horde of uniformed guards armed with cudgels and shouting and waving wildly, trotted us into the reception barracks. . . .

"Over the next 24 hours we discovered that we were no longer regarded as prisoners of war but criminals. We were divided into three groups; white, grey and black Nazis. I joined the best: paratroopers, U-Boat officers and about 20 officers of the Waffen-ss—all of us classified as Black Nazis. . . . At once we set to work, endeavouring to make our captivity more endurable. Courses and working schools were organized under Colonel von Viebahn. . . .

"In the summer, we received a new decent commandant. . . . The former commander was replaced on the basis of our complaints to representatives of the International Red Cross. Life behind the wire became bearable. Lieut.-Col. Vickers allowed us more freedom, not for humanitarian reasons, but because he understood the need to restrain our restless spirits and nourish the hope that one day soon we would all be returning to the homeland."

Kate's trip north from Ludwigslust to Heide with Richter had been a three-day nightmare. At the last minute, Via von Büttner, a French woman, decided to join them. Via had married one of Kurt's officers. Only 21, she was already a war widow with two children. In all, seven adults and eight children started out in two Volkswagen. Kate, Gerhild and Kurt travelled with Richter; Inge and Irmtraud rode in the second car. All the family's possessions, except what could be carried, were left behind. Within minutes they were under attack from Allied fighters.

They hid in the woods nearby, where Irmtraud lost her knapsack—no more clothes. They scrambled back into the cars. Refugees crowded the roads. Everybody was fleeing from the Russians, hiding from the air attacks, searching for food. The cars broke down, were repaired and broke down again. No one slept. They learned quickly that night was the best time to travel.

---

*In Northumberland County, about 20 miles from the Scottish border.

They were hungry all the time. During one low-level air attack the cars were separated. Kate assumed the others were dead. Her emotions were near the breaking point. Miraculously, they crossed into Schleswig-Holstein and met up again in Heide. Richter turned them over to Frau Wisch, the wife of Sepp Dietrich's successor as commander of the Leibstandarte, who had agreed to help.

Their home in Heide consisted of one room on the ground floor of an abandoned SA office. Its broken windows had been boarded. A small slit provided light and ventilation. Everyone slept on four straw mats on the floor. An enormous wooden "pigeonhole" cabinet, once used for files and letters, covered one wall. Into one of the slots Kate hid the precious morphine vials. She begged food from the soldiers and cut firewood in a forest nearby. It was green, and as it burned, the room filled with smoke.

British occupation forces decided to designate Schleswig-Holstein a "barred area." The district held huge military supply dumps and depots. So that large-scale theft by the impoverished local population might be prevented, no one was to be allowed in or out of the state. But before the border closed, Via decided to take her two children and go to her family in France. Kate grew more and more depressed.

When neighbours told her of a radio broadcast stating that all German generals would probably be shot, she decided the time for her family suicide had arrived. But Inge refused to die. Knowing her grandmother could solve any problem, she insisted that her mother send a postcard to Alma asking for help. "You can kill yourself and Irmtraud. But I want to live! I'll care for the two young ones."

Kate shrugged. What did it matter? What did anything matter?

While her mother withdrew into a paralytic somnolence, Inge got up each morning before dawn. She went out scrounging for milk, food, water, clothing—anything she could get her hands on. She bathed her sisters, did the laundry, kept the place clean and tried bringing her mother back to reality. She arranged for neighbours to talk with Kate and take her out for walks. It helped a little.

Kate's postcard reached Alma in Offleben. She decided to leave for Heide at once. Salt trucks from the nearby town of Schöningen made regular deliveries into the barred zone of Schleswig-Holstein. Next morning, she bribed a driver to let her hide behind the salt sacks and reached Heide early the following afternoon in time to go out with Inge and beg some food for supper. Begging became a daily family ritual. A difficult and demeaning chore because there were few people with food to spare. Nevertheless, Alma, who always thrived in adversity, managed to keep them all from starving. As she assumed the mantle of family responsibility, Kate's spirits rose. If they were to survive, Alma realized that she had to get everybody back to Offleben.

"I found a truck and driver who would take us to the border. When we arrived the British wouldn't let us across. I waited for the appropriate moment and then took out Otto's expensive old pocket watch and pushed it over the counter to the soldier. He said only: 'Okay—go quickly!' We made it across and continued our journey in an open freight train. During the journey I spoke to the engine driver. He was kind enough to warm Kurt's milk bottles . . . and thus we reached Offleben."

2

Canadian forces in Holland started to wind down into a peacetime army. The sweet taste of victory, the parties, the receptions and the accolades were beginning to pall. Willing women, wine and spirits were still plentiful and there for the taking, but the thrill of taking was gone.

"It was like coming out of a hangover. That was what the war had been, one great big goddam hangover. Nobody thinks about the future with a hangover because everyone feels on the edge of death. Then one day it's over and you start feeling better, feeling that there's a future for you after all . . . and you begin to look ahead."

There was still the Pacific war to settle and no shortage of volunteers for it or the newly constituted CAOF—Canadian Army Occupation Force— being drawn from units of the 3rd Division. Then there was to be a grand Allied victory parade through Berlin during July. A composite Canadian battalion, drawn from the 1st, 2nd and 4th Divisions, would march with troops from the other victorious armies, "rubbing the Germans' noses in it just the way they had done in Vienna, Prague and Paris."

The generals and brigadiers settled into comfortable city houses or spectacular country châteaux. Some acquired mistresses—unattached women or other men's wives—others "dabbled" in cameras, cigarettes, petrol and paintings.

"Guy's château was the best. He deserved it. A dozen servants looked after the place. The gardeners used nail scissors to trim the sweeping lawns and flowerbeds. Chris Vokes, appointed to command the CAOF, lived in a mansion at Oldenburg with four senior staff officers and 14 servants. I settled for *Nerlandia*, a 65-foot ocean schooner. She became my all-consuming passion and I took her sailing with a scratch crew at every opportunity."

The end of hostilities also brought out the Ottawa bureaucrats. "They arrived from overseas in droves. Those from the Treasury were the worst. Their job was to recover whatever of value they could lay their hands on. A particularly obnoxious gentleman in a shiny blue serge suit stormed into my office demanding to know what had happened to my divisional and regimental mess funds. If other divisions and regiments could operate their messes to produce substantial profits, why couldn't I?

"'Three reasons,' I said. 'First, a mess—any mess—is not a corporate body or financial institution designed to produce a monthly profit. Its purpose is to provide a civilized and congenial atmosphere for its members. Next, if it produces profit then it is not being run properly. Finally, I gave orders to all divisional mess officers that any profits were to be spent on a party at the end of each month.'

"Mr. Sergesuit was aghast. 'But why, General?'

"'Why? Because the money belonged to the men.'"

Vokes too had problems with authority. A royal summons arrived at his Bad Zwischenahn HQ from Queen Juliana of the Netherlands requesting his presence at the palace. No explanation offered. Mystified, he put on his best dress uniform and took a plane to The Hague. In case something newsworthy resulted, he brought along his PR officer, Capt. Jack Golding. A staff car with motorcycle escort was laid on at the airport and raced them to the palace.

Prince Bernhard, the Queen's Consort, greeted them at the door. "She's furious," he cautioned. "Treat her with kid gloves."

"Furious? About what?" Vokes demanded.

The Prince rolled his eyes. "I'll let her tell you."

Vokes and Golding were ushered into a formal reception room. They saluted the Dutch monarch, who had spent the war with her family in Ottawa as guests of the Canadian people. She asked them to be seated. For 20 minutes they were subjected to verbal fireworks by an angry queen. The problem was Canadian soldiers—his Canadian soldiers—who appeared to be spending their time fornicating with every respectable girl in the Netherlands, leaving them pregnant and unmarried. She was dismayed, shocked and disgusted and had decided finally to do something about it.

"And what did you have in mind, Madam?" Vokes inquired politely.

"I want you and your Canadians out of Holland. All of you. You're a bad influence on the women of this nation. You're to leave now, General, and take all your soldiers with you!"

The audience over, Vokes and Golding came to their feet, saluted and withdrew. At the door Vokes paused. "Madam?"

"Yes, General?"

"Does that include the dead ones?"

Slowly, in shame, Queen Juliana lowered her head.

The troops started for home. Divisions shrank to brigades, the brigades to regiments, the regiments to battalions. The search for war criminals continued. The major ones—Göring, Hess, Ribbentrop, Doenitz, Keitel, Jodl and 16 others—were already in custody and awaiting trial in Luxembourg at the luxurious Palace Hotel in Mondorf-les-Bains.

On 2 August the Allied leaders met for the last time in the Berlin suburb of Potsdam to set the final basis for the way Germany was to be divided and left in legal limbo. Roosevelt had died in April, and the dapper Harry Truman was now president of the United States. Churchill had been replaced halfway through the conference by Clement Atlee when the Labour party won the British election. Stalin looked on amused. The conference ratified an earlier proposal that Germany "in its borders of 1937" should be divided into zones of occupation and administration. These borders were picked— in Stalin's words—"as a point of departure."

It was a legal question whether Germany existed at all. If it did, then it was only within the borders of 1937 before union with Austria, the Sudetenland annexation and the invasion of Poland. The crafty Stalin had already given a large part of Germany's eastern territories—Silesia, Pomerania and half of East Prussia—to Poland as compensation for the disputed areas of east Poland that the Soviets had already claimed for themselves. The Western leaders accepted this, agreeing that those parts of Germany lying east of the Oder and Neisse rivers "should be placed under Polish administration" until the borders of Germany could be determined at a final peace conference. The trouble was that by its unconditional surrender there was no one left in Germany legally entitled to sit down at any conference table to sign anything.

With great fanfare Truman, Atlee and Stalin signed the Potsdam Agreement, which made it effectively impossible for a unified "Germany" to exist.

Shortly after 0800 hours on the morning of 6 August, a B29 Superfortress named *Enola Gay* dropped the first atomic bomb on Hiroshima, a city with a quarter of a million inhabitants. In the blink of an eye four square miles were destroyed and 60,000 people incinerated; another 25,000 died over the following weeks and months. Total casualties reached 140,000.

Two days later Stalin declared war on Japan and the Red Army invaded Manchuria. On 9 August a second atomic bomb was dropped on Nagasaki, destroying 1.5 square miles; 24,000 people were incinerated, and 30,000 injured, many of whom died later. The Japanese government promptly accepted the Allied terms of surrender. World War II was over. Now everyone could concentrate on their war criminals.

In mid-September orders arrived for Kurt's transfer to the Kensington Cage in London. He was told to pack his gear and be ready to leave in a half hour. "Gen. Kroh and Max Wünsche accompanied me to the gate. A beautiful summer day. I travelled in a special compartment with a captain and two junior officers who were soon sleeping like marmots. In London, a sergeant who had once lived in Berlin took my belt and shoelaces then jeered when I stumbled out of my shoes on the stairs. My room was at the end of a corridor on the fourth floor. Inside I found a comrade from Austria. A week before this poor man had been a prisoner in Italy. He was just skin and bones. The treatment in Italian prison camps must have cost the lives of many comrades. . . .

"Next morning during the 20-minute exercise period I met Gen. von Manteuffel and Gen. Schimpf. After Schimpf worked a few days on the wall separating our rooms we were able to converse with ease. . . . One day, while passing an open room, I glanced inside and to my astonishment saw comrades Meitzel and Hauptmann Steger. Both had been reported dead. I was told that the Canadians intended to try me as a war criminal. . . . I prepared myself for the interrogations that followed. . . .

"Lieut.-Col. B.J. Macdonald acted as chief interrogator, supported by C.S. Campbell. Maj. J.J. Stonborough, supposedly from Vienna, acted as interpreter and cleverly built the foundations of their case through the questions he posed. I learned from Meitzel that Stonborough told everyone in the place that I was a dead man. It appeared my death had already been decided before the trial. Since there was now no doubt about my trial I asked permission to confer with Col. von der Heydte and my old Commander-in-Chief, Gen. Eberbach. A few days later the request was granted. . . .

"I continued to avoid every question that might in any way hurt my troops. I saw no reason to give the 'victors' an opportunity to judge German soldiers. No law covers a victor's conduct over the conquered. Can anyone who has survived the reality of a battlefield believe that beasts fought on one side and angels on the other? All men must stand equally in the melting pot of murderous slaughter and will, no matter which side they serve, deny any responsibility for the terrible events. . . . The conquered become scapegoats to be tried by Kangaroo courts. Not because the charge against them is proved but because 'they are proved to have been seen' during the action. Such trials come only from hate and the victor's rage. War Crimes trials were biased. Only we Germans were charged; a contradiction of the basic precept of law."

He had a point. Not a single soldier of any Allied army in any theatre of the war was ever charged with a war crime.* As early as 1944 the British, U.S. and Canadian governments were acutely aware of the legal limitations imposed by Common Law in justifying charges laid against a defeated enemy. How could a fair and impartial verdict be reached in any public war crimes trial where the judges served a dual role as jurors and where prosecutors and defence counsels were appointed by the victors?

To be sure, crimes had been committed. Heinous and unspeakable crimes that for over a decade had plunged the world into misery and swept away tens of millions in a holocaust of madness, destruction and death. Scant attention would have been paid by any of the Allied armies if the 48 hours of criminal immunity given to all troops on the day the war ended had been devoted to butchering the enemy's political and military leaders. If a few

---

*Charges made under civil and criminal laws are not considered war crimes.

innocent heads had rolled in the process, well—tough. How many innocent millions had died already? What would a few thousand more have meant to the final tally if it guaranteed the peace?

But citizens of civilized democratic nations are enslaved by a collective conscience. They make ferocious soldiers in time of war, yet they abhor violence. Rules must be followed, the laws and niceties of convention observed. Without them anarchy would replace civilization. There was the dilemma: how to take revenge against the German and Japanese nations with a clear conscience and execute their leaders together with everyone responsible for what had transpired?

The problem was resolved, as usual, by lawyers. Through a succession of wordy self-serving platitudes, the rules were changed to accommodate the proposed acts of vengeance. The new rules, based solely on the French Code Napoleon, British Common Law and the *Manual of Military Law*, provided for a quasi civilian-military-courtmartial criminal trial. There were obvious advantages in foregoing the annoyance of a jury with its attendant impond-erables.

The Rules of Evidence were amended to allow unsubstantiated second- and third-party hearsay testimony to be presented. Both prosecution and defence were permitted to enter sworn affidavits into evidence if any of their witnesses were unable to appear. Since the prosecution and defence generally shared the same national identity and the accused was forced to rely on them for any witness he might care to call, the temptation existed to fill the proceedings with sworn affidavits that couldn't be contradicted through cross-examination. At the same time defence counsel could plead "difficulty" in rounding up any witnesses for the accused who might cast the prosecution's case in an unfavourable light. Most witnesses were accessible but behind barbed wire in Allied POW camps.

Bruce Macdonald spearheaded the preparations to legalize—and legiti-mize—the procedures for Canadian war crimes trials. Nearly a year had passed since his days as CO of the Essex Scottish Regiment. He decided to follow the route taken by the British. Their procedures for military war crimes trials were created by use of a royal warrant, an order signed by the King on the advice of his minister of war. Starting with what he believed to be *prima facie* cases against Kurt Meyer and Wilhelm Mohnke, Macdonald flew home to Canada on 1 June accompanied by Majors Griffin and Stonborough, his chief intelligence officer and interpreter. After reporting to the war crimes interdepartmental committee in Ottawa, he set off across the country on his interrogation of witnesses.

"We went first to the SS camp at Gravenhurst, Ontario.* . . . We found

---

*Originally a wartime training base for Norwegian pilots, it is now the minimum security prison camp of Beaver Creek, operated by the Canadian Penitentiary Service.

hundreds of bronzed, well-fed and fine looking specimens of the 'master race,' swimming, boating and living the life of Riley at what appeared to be, except for a few fences, an exclusive summer camp on the lake. We got some useful leads from our inquiries."

Over the following weeks he and his team visited POW camps in Quebec, Alberta, Colorado, Kansas and Oklahoma. Sworn depositions were taken and a hundred possible witnesses interviewed, including a number of Canadian soldiers returning home for discharge.

Once back in Ottawa, his group got to work drafting procedures to be followed for the trials. "With some modifications we adopted the British regulations and added some additional ones of our own. . . . Reports from certain military courts and official bodies could be received, provided, in the opinion of the Court, such documents would be of assistance in proving or disproving the charge. Any statements made prior to the trial by the accused or any witness, whether preceded by a caution or not, were admissible evidence. It was specifically provided, however, that the Court was to judge the weight to be attached to such otherwise inadmissible evidence."

In other words, virtually *anything* could be used and it was up to those sitting in judgment to decide on the validity of "evidence." Without such safeguards, Macdonald pointed out, "it would in many cases be completely futile to attempt to convict admitted war criminals and the guilty would escape just retribution."

There was some question whether the Governor-General of Canada had the same royal prerogative as the King in authorizing implementation of the new procedures. Parliament had adjourned for summer recess and there wasn't time to wait for a Supreme Court decision on the matter. What to do to make such trials legal under Canadian law? It was a sticky problem for anyone bedeviled by a conscience and a knowledge of the law. But any concerns were laid to rest by utilizing provisions set forth in the War Measures Act of 1939 authorizing the government to act by orders-in-council for the "speedier and most effective prosecution of the war." The fact that the war was over and that five years imprisonment had been established as the maximum penalty for violations under the act appeared irrelevant. In due course the order was approved by the Liberal cabinet and signed by the Governor-General.

The Prime Minister rose in the House of Commons on 13 September to announce that "Colonel Macdonald and his associates will undertake the prosecution of the accused. . . . Courts will be established in accordance with military law, the procedure will be in accordance with the principles of justice, the accused will have full opportunity for defence and the arrangements for constitution of the court and execution of sentence will follow recognized military practice. . . . The courts will be constituted from military personnel experienced in the laws and usages of war and the proceedings will be conducted with dignity, fairness and justice."

By the time news arrived that he had been appointed to act as chief prosecutor at Canada's first war crimes trial, Macdonald was already back in London at the Kensington Cage interrogating Kurt Meyer, Max Wünsche, Heinrich Eberbach and the other witnesses he intended to call.

3

Once her mother, sisters and baby brother had settled into Alma's house in Offleben, Ursula's attention turned to more immediate concerns.

"We now live in Oma's big flat with lots of room and everybody is healthy. But we have nothing to wear anymore. Most of our remaining clothes were left in Heide. Hunger is also quite a problem. Some people in Offleben who don't like us now control the political scene; they are mainly Communists. We can't get permission to move [officially to Offleben] and thus no food vouchers. Oma has to quit her job because she was a Nazi.* But we have lots of friends here. Oma is loved by everybody as an able midwife. We get food and clothes from those who hardly have enough for themselves. . . .

"Most important is milk for Kurt. Sometimes Inge and I walk three miles to get bottles of milk. We cast lots for the one who has to beg. Mostly it is Inge who says: 'Best wishes from our Oma, Mrs. Meyer. She asks politely if we could get some milk?' While the bottles are being filled we usually get a sandwich and a cup of milk for ourselves. We go always to the same farmers. They are never impolite but it is always a great effort for us to beg. . . .

"The border zone used to go through Offleben but then the Russians withdrew to another village and now Offleben is on the border with a customs checkpoint. Five hundred yards of no-man's-land separate the last houses from the Russian patrols. Trains don't cross the border any more but people still can."

Throughout their zone of occupation the Soviets were busy dismantling businesses, factories and entire industries for shipment and reassembly inside Russia. Municipal, state and national governments were reorganized into one-party systems operating under a chain of command that began in the Kremlin. All political parties, other than those Communist inspired or controlled, were banned. Anyone objecting was shipped to Russia. An estimated 5.5 million dissident Poles, Germans, Rumanians, Yugoslavs, Austrians, Bulgarians, Czechs, Albanians, Hungarians, Latvians, Estonians and Lithuanians disappeared inside the Soviet Union. Several million Ukrainians, no longer

---

*Alma had been the town's local *Frauenschaftsleiterin* (women's leader).

considered trustworthy because of their contact with the Germans, were executed or transported to Siberia. Although fully informed of these outrages by their own intelligence services, the Western Allies turned a blind eye.

Early in October, Macdonald was ready to bring his case to trial. He flew to Vokes's HQ at Bad Zwischenahn to obtain officers to sit on the courtmartial. Meyer must be judged by peers who were at least equal to him in rank. All had to be experienced battlefield commanders. Vokes offered Macdonald a selection of six brigadiers for court members and three major-generals for president, with Harry as his first choice. Macdonald perused the list and then asked for Major-General Keefler and Brigadiers Sparling, Johnston and Bell-Irving as members with Harry as president. When Keefler objected to sitting as a member, he was replaced by Brigadier Roberts.

Kurt, meanwhile, asked to be represented either by an English or German barrister assisted by a legally qualified Canadian officer or by two legally qualified senior Canadian officers. If he was to be tried, it seemed only sensible to enlist some professional representation. The Canadians were spending so much trying to convict him, surely they could afford enough for a token defence?

Macdonald forwarded his request to CMHQ, which decided that private barristers were too costly to consider. Instead, Lieut.-Col. Maurice W. Andrew, CO of the Perth Regiment and a lawyer in civilian life, was assigned as defence counsel, assisted by Capt. Frank Plourde of the North Shore (New Brunswick) Regiment. Since neither spoke German, Macdonald brought in Capt. Wadi Lehmann, one of his unit's best German-speaking intelligence officers, to act as Kurt's personal interpreter.

Despite all the research, travel, witnesses and trial procedures stacked in the prosecution's favour—to say nothing of the expense—Macdonald had by no means an open-and-shut case, as he pointed out in a memorandum of 6 November to CMHQ. "Evidence is so difficult to obtain, and so much depends on its circumstantial character, one would be foolish to make any certain predictions about the outcome. What is . . . completely established, by reason not only of our own evidence, but because of Meyer's own voluntary statements recently obtained, is that 18 prisoners were killed at his Regimental Headquarters during his period of command. That, apart from anything else, calls for a great deal of explaining . . . if he is to escape the almost inevitable conclusion that the murders could not have occurred there in the manner in which they did without at least his tacit approval. I feel that our case is sound and the only real question to be determined is the degree of guilt or responsibility chargeable to the accused."

Early on Wednesday morning, 31 October, Kurt was awakened and ordered to dress immediately. "I was taken in chains to an airport. London was barely awake. We drove in silence and in silence flew over the Channel to Germany.

I had no idea where we were headed. Then landscape appeared below the overcast. We were flying a few hundred metres over East Friesland. Streets straight as twine, shining canals and windmills greeted us. An airport emerged suddenly out of the weather. . . .

"A large group of soldiers, reporters and photographers were waiting for the 'Beast of Caen.' If all of it hadn't been so deadly serious I would have had a hearty laugh. Lieut.-Col. B.J.S. Macdonald was the Chief advertising planner for this circus of security arrangements, journalists and organized hangers-on. I was last out of the airplane under a whir of cameras. At the bottom of the steps two officers awaited me. I saluted them. The greeting was not returned. As my hand sank it was chained instantaneously to the larger officer. Maj. Arthur Russell headed the escort. I climbed into a waiting tank vehicle with Capt. W.H.J. Stutt. . . .

"Accompanied by tank scout trucks and motorcycles the convoy headed into Aurich through roadblocks and sealed streets. There was a quality of comic opera about the entire journey, particularly when I noticed Capt. Stutt's right hand remained deep in the pocket of his trousers where his service revolver lay outlined. . . . In Aurich I was taken to the barracks of the former marine school and immediately subjected to a painful strip search in front of the prosecutor and several officers. . . .

"Special measures were taken with my accommodations. At the end of a long row of jail cells, two cells, divided by an iron door, had been made into a secure compartment: one cell was to be used as an interrogation 'room'; the other to become my 'home.' It had been built especially for me. The heavy beams that framed the bed were impossible to move. Built by a German craftsman, the bed had neither nails nor brackets. It came with a pair of covers. A large square hole had been cut in the door, big enough for the guard to stick his head through. . . .

"No sooner had I settled in than Capt. Stutt appeared. Once again I was chained to him and, together with three guards, conducted to the Regimental Staff HQ of the Royal Winnipegs. The reasons for my arrest were finally explained to me. Lieut.-Col. R.P. Clark* read me the charges through an interpreter. . . .

"Now I knew where I stood. Despite the unpleasantness of the situation I felt a certain relief over the charges. Now I could prepare myself to face them. The handcuffs clicked back on and our steps rang hollowly through the long empty halls of the building. The few Germans and Canadians inside regarded me curiously. . . .

"Sitting in my cell I tried befriending a guard. It worked. The lad had fought against my unit and behaved towards me in a comradely manner. The Canadian soldiers and officers always treated me decently. Not once was

---

*OC of the Royal Winnipeg Rifles Regiment.

I mistreated. But there was an obvious difference between those who had served as front-line soldiers and those who had not. My young guard was quickly replaced in the first days for giving me newspapers. . . .

"Towards evening, Capts. Plourde and Lehmann visited me. The Chief of Defence was not yet established. Lieut.-Col. Peter Wright, who was supposed to defend me, had refused because he was of the opinion that the sentence had been decided already and that there could be no fair defence. . . . I discussed my material witnesses with Plourde and Lehmann . . . when I had concluded neither gentleman believed I would be convicted. . . .

"It was an opinion shared by the guards. Frequently, I heard: 'If they sentence you then they will have to sentence our officers too. The same things happened on our side—it isn't right that only the losers are made responsible.' The front-line soldiers knew what had happened; they endured their guilt and kept their mouths shut. Only the desk strategists, the parasites and better educated spoke now."

A month earlier Harry's status of major-general from "acting" major-general was confirmed. Next day he was appointed to command what remained of the 4th Armoured Division. "I'd had a respectable war: a DSO after Holland and a CBE* when it was all over, five months of partying, two whirlwind romances with a couple of Dutch girls and a trunk full of memorabilia for my old age. As far as I was concerned the fun was over and it was back to the paper shuffle of peacetime soldiering. My appointment to Meyer's courtmartial came as a surprise. And an annoyance. . . .

"Courtmartials are boring affairs and, except in unusual cases, end up with the accused getting his just desserts. I had sat on many, although none as grand as the one being planned for Meyer. From the beginning it had the appearance of a carefully orchestrated three-ring circus complete with barkers and lion tamers. Nevertheless, I packed my kit and proceeded to Aurich."

Comfortable accommodations had been arranged for members of the courtmartial in a fully staffed private home, complete with a well-stocked bar that the Royal Winnipegs had thoughtfully provided.

"A damp miserable place filled with sullen Germans and nothing to do. The others were already there when I arrived and just as anxious as I to get on with it and back to civilization. We spent the first evening drinking and reminiscing about Normandy then Italy. I didn't realize that I'd had such a good time there! . . . Budge Bell-Irving grumbled about the way I had taken Scott Murdoch out from under his nose to be my GSO1. . . . But by the third night everyone had talked themselves out. After dinner and a drink they went to their rooms. I went for a walk, trailed by an MP. . . . There appear to be horses available. Perhaps I can get in some riding."

---

*Commander of the Order of the British Empire.

Lieut.-Col. Maurice Andrew arrived to organize the defence. Through Lehmann, he explained how he proposed to conduct the case. During their first meeting in his cell Kurt demanded irritably: "Why are you wasting your time on all this—why not just shoot me?" Patiently, the soft-spoken Lehmann explained that under Canadian law everyone had a right to a fair trial.

"Isn't the outcome already decided?"

Lehmann and Andrew assured him that it was not.

Kurt shrugged his disbelief. "Go ahead, I'll cooperate—but I still think you're wasting your time." An attitude that he maintained throughout the trial.

Andrew and Lehmann made a strange team. The fatherly CO of the Perth Regiment was considerably older than either his interpreter or client. A small-town Ontario lawyer, he had won his DSO in Italy and still believed in the good of all men. The fact that the SS—any branch of the SS—by popular definition had now come to mean criminal responsibility for "crimes against humanity" appeared irrelevant. Kurt was entitled to his day in court and Andrew intended to provide him with the best possible defence.

Lehmann, on the other hand, seemed more of an internationalist. His father had been born in Moscow. German was only one of the languages spoken at his home in Vancouver where he had grown up. If his parents had wanted to keep something from the children, they spoke Russian. While everyone else in high school took Latin and French, he concentrated on his German. When war came, he was a natural for the Army Intelligence Branch. Trained in England and sent to Canadian I Corps in Italy, he worked first on radio intercepts and later as an interrogation officer at the army's sprawling POW camp north of Rome.

Through hundreds of interrogations with POWs from every branch of the German armed forces he gradually developed an understanding of the Nazi mentality and a "feel" for the truth. "Intimidation was the general method for getting information. It didn't work with the SS or men from the Hermann Göring Parachute Division. Interviews with them became a form of reverse intimidation. All were splendid physical specimens but filled with arrogance and disdain; hard-bitten Nazis who bowed to no one. I enjoyed them."

His next posting involved translating documents as an intelligence staff officer at Corps HQ during General Foulkes's term of command. "Foulkes's only interest in intelligence appeared to be his collection of German pornographic letters, texts and photo captions which he had me translate. He had a large collection of German ribbons and medals. From time to time he turned up with a new one to ask if I could explain its meaning."

He was 28 and a captain when the war ended. CMHQ assigned him to the War Crimes Investigations Branch based in Germany. For six months he had been sifting through war crimes against Canadians, most concerning airmen who had been shot down over Germany. At the end of October he received orders to report to Aurich. Over the next two months through innumerable personal conversations and professional discussions translated on Andrew's behalf, he got to know Kurt as well as any man in the Canadian army. And he believed that he was innocent.

The conviction was shared by Maurice Andrew, who saw Meyer as "a charismatic man with an absolutely unshakeable belief in his personal convictions. Over the weeks I developed a respect for him both as a man and a soldier. I disagreed with his Nazi ideology and couldn't believe that he ordered the executions for which he was charged. He played it too straight. . . . His religious beliefs were straight out of Norse mythology. His attitude towards wife and family was commendably conventional. Man was the protector, his woman designed to be 'mother bountiful.' She was entitled to great respect."

By mid-November Andrew felt sufficiently confident about his chances for winning that he sent Lehmann to Offleben to see if Kate and other family members could be persuaded to come to Aurich. In Canada any testimony by witnesses concerning the sterling character of the accused in a murder trial gave the jury food for thought when considering its verdict. Why not at a courtmartial in Germany? Lehmann requisitioned an HUP* carrier with driver and left at once for Offleben.

Kate heard news of Kurt's impending trial over the radio. She felt a tremendous relief knowing that he was alive and being looked after. But a trial? For what? He was a simple soldier. What remained of Germany's political and military masters were on trial in Nuremberg. One of them, Dr. Robert Ley, had already committed suicide by strangling himself on the water pipe in his cell. But what did Kurt have to do with this sort of man?

One evening there came a knock at the door. Kate answered it and saw a man on the front step. "Frau Meyer, I bring you a message from your husband."

Kate invited him inside. His behaviour seemed most mysterious. "You have come from Aurich?" she asked.

"No, from the Russian zone." He went on to explain that Kurt had escaped and was hiding across the border. He would take her to him.

She became suspicious. Something wasn't right. "Do you have a note from him—something with his signature?"

The man shook his head. "It was too dangerous to carry one through the border crossing."

"You are a liar! My husband would never run away from anything. Get out!"

---

*Heavy utility personnel—an uncomfortable 12-place vehicle.

A few evenings later the doorbell rang again. Kate was up to her elbows boiling sugar beets into syrup. Inge answered it and Wadi Lehmann stepped inside, bearing letters from Kurt.

His arrival made a lasting impression on Ursula. "He is very polite and speaks excellent German. He says that Mother is allowed to visit Father in Aurich. I am to accompany her. The next day before we leave he takes a picture of the family for Father. He makes a detour to the local administration in Helmstedt. 'Let's see if we can straighten out your food voucher problem,' he says. I dread this, because we have spent so many hours waiting there. But in a few minutes he reappears and with a laugh tells us: 'Everything is okay now. You'll get your vouchers immediately and you'll be allowed to live here in peace.' . . .

"In Aurich we are put in a hotel. Mother's and my thoughts are: 'When are we going to see Father?' Finally, a soldier appears and drives us to a big barracks situated on the outskirts. Everybody is very polite. We sit in an office. Some officers stand at the desk. We hear steps in the hall. The door opens and in comes Father handcuffed to two soldiers.

"Father looks over at us. His escort tries to undo the cuffs. The clasps won't open. Father pulls at it, looking at us sad and helplessly, then angrily at the officers. His hands won't come free. It takes ages. We want to go to him, to laugh and enjoy this family reunion but still his hands are not free. We are overcome by tears and anguish. These first minutes suffocate all happy expectations. . . .

"On Father's lap I keep thinking: 'Don't tremble, don't tremble!' But Father is trembling and Mother too. She forces a smile and begins to talk. The tension eases. We have survived the ordeals of war, capture, captivity, bombs, flight, hunger, lost belongings and still remained a family. It gives our parents a new strength and calmness. We still have life. After 20 minutes we have to say goodbye until the next visit. . . .

"For the next few weeks I live only for these 20-minute visits every second day. Nothing else is important."

4

On the morning of 10 December, at exactly 1030 hours, Kurt entered the courtroom at "Maple Leaf" Barracks handcuffed to Major Russell and Captain Stutt. He bowed his head courteously to the bench then took a seat. Kate sat in the first row of the spectators' gallery. He gave her a brief expressionless glance.

"In front of me sat five judges, all generals. I searched until I caught the eye of Gen. H. Foster. My battlefield opponent of 1944 had been elected president of the court that was to condemn me. What a strange meeting of two soldiers! After fighting for months with every fibre of the heart the victor sits in judgment over the vanquished. The choice of president and jurors violated international law. All these gentlemen had fought against me. How could they be impartial? I detected sympathy and understanding in Foster's eyes. At least I had the feeling that here was a genuine soldier and a gentleman. After the usual formalities, the charges against me were read out."*

They were read first in English and then in German. The pauses for translation throughout the trial were an annoyance and seemed to slow the proceedings considerably. However, with the assortment of French-, German- and English-speaking witnesses there was no alternative.

The prosecution's case opened badly. After Major Stonborough took the stand briefly to swear on the authenticity of German documents and military formations, the prosecution's second witness, Grenadier Torbanisch, did not appear in court. Which was just as well in view of his background and the evidence that Macdonald read into the record. A Czech national from Kurt's 15th Reconnaissance Company that had been attached to regimental HQ, Torbanisch had murdered an officer and deserted at L'Aigle, France, in April 1944. He turned himself over to the Belgian Underground and worked with them until his capture. He told a story about "secret orders" he claimed that his sergeant-major had read out to the company during its training at Beverloo, with instructions to commit them to memory.

As no written copy existed, Torbanisch had dictated them from memory to the Underground, which translated his German-Czech version into Flemish, which Macdonald then had translated into English. A photocopy of the orders was offered in evidence with an apology from Macdonald that Torbanisch, a POW, after giving his evidence under oath at a SHAEF court in Chartres, France, "could not be found."

An abbreviated version of the orders is worth examining, if only as an illustration of the extent to which inflammatory third-hand hearsay evidence was permitted to be introduced under the new ground rules.

1. Re attitude to civilian population in occupied countries: anyone acting contemptuously to an SS soldier can be beaten and arrested; if questioning reveals him to be anti-German he is to be secretly executed.
2. Anyone trying to get information re weapons and ammunition is to be arrested and questioned vigorously: if proved to be anti-German he should be executed for espionage. Soldiers passing such information should suffer the same fate.
3. Guards leaving their posts etc. are to be punished by death.
4. The attitude at the front: SS troops shall take no prisoners. Prisoners are to be executed after interrogation. SS soldiers do not surrender but commit

---

*See the introductory section entitled "Prelude."

suicide if no other choice remains. The officers have stated that the British do not take SS prisoners.

5. Re secrecy of communications.
6. Re change of route when reconnaissance parties return from the front.

Kurt fumed. "Item 4 was absurd. It would have undermined troop morale. Units were not authorized to interrogate prisoners, consequently they had no instructions on how it was done. . . . After this incident I had little hope for impartial justice."

Nineteen-year-old Grenadier Alfred Helzel was Macdonald's third witness. Another ethnic German from Czechoslovakia, the tall, well-built Helzel had been a member of 15th Company. He had been wounded in the action at Bretteville in June 1944 and taken prisoner. Macdonald had interviewed him during the summer at the POW camp near Hull, Quebec, where he claimed to have heard Kurt tell the company that his regiment took no prisoners. The company commander, von Büttner, subsequently reaffirmed the order.

Macdonald felt that Helzel had given substantially the same story about the secret orders as Torbanisch, but when he put him on the stand, "he became evasive, ill at ease and slumped down in his chair. He dodged questions, could not remember and eventually denied any knowledge that either Meyer or von Büttner had made the alleged statements. He so qualified the meaning of the orders read by the *Spiess* [sergeant-major] at Montegnée that they had no relevant significance. . . . I was completely mystified. . . . Our case was off to a very rocky beginning. I began to have visions of the other German witnesses going back on their statements in a similar manner. . . .

"I looked around the courtroom in dismay and for the first time realized what had gone wrong. Meyer . . . sitting diagonally across the room from the witness had fixed him with a glare, the equal of which I had never seen and which fairly shot sparks across the room. The unfortunate witness, like the proverbial bird caught in the hypnotic stare of the serpent, was panic stricken. His powerful physique meant nothing and his previous assurance evaporated like dew drops in the fierce heat of the sun. It was an amazing demonstration of the tremendous disciplinary hold this SS officer still had on a former soldier and of the fear inspired by his presence. . . .

"I placed myself between Meyer and the witness so that the latter could no longer see his former regimental commander, but only me. He soon regained his composure."

Macdonald then treated him as a hostile witness under Regulation 10(g), which he had formulated. But the damage had been done. Helzel did not come across as a credible witness. In cross-examination, Andrew got Helzel to admit that the whole purpose of his reconnaissance company was to reconnoitre the enemy lines—not to be out collecting prisoners.

Harry then adjourned for the day. He felt that "Macdonald was putting too much emphasis on the 'no prisoners to be taken' order. Every man jack of us at some point during the war had heard the same sort of nonsense from our own people. Things were always different in a battle. Every soldier made up his own mind about accepting an enemy that surrendered. And then whether to shoot him afterwards."

Next day, Sturmmann Horst Heyer took the stand. He too had been a member of the 25th Regiment, but in Waldmüller's battalion. Although in vague terms he confirmed what the other two had said, he also admitted under cross-examination by Andrew to hearing an order in mid-June that provided up to 24 days' leave for any soldier who brought in a prisoner. This concluded Macdonald's evidence on the first charge. It was patently thin.

Testimony given by Lieut.-Col. Charles Petch, former CO of the North Nova Scotia Highlanders Regiment, to the SHAEF Court of Inquiry was read into evidence and followed by excerpts from the regiment's War Diary. Both described in considerable detail the unit's action on 6 and 7 June 1944. Next, Macdonald produced the transcript of Kurt's testimony taken down in London two months earlier, outlining the activities and dispositions of his battalions during the same battle. Having set the scene of action on both sides of the line, Macdonald then called his next live witness, Constance Raymond Guilbert, the stonemason from Authie who had witnessed the death of several Canadians.

His testimony, although sickening, did little more than illustrate the brutality of the German soldiers during the afternoon in question. Guilbert's credibility became undermined when he admitted to being under sentence for looting. Prompted for an explanation, he replied: "I found 2,000 bottles of wine and brought them home and I drank them. That is all."

"You are not going to ask the court to believe that you drank the whole 2,000 bottles are you?"

"I made a distribution . . . because there were a lot of my friends who were also thirsty."

To their credit, the generals managed to hold straight faces.

Evidence from the next eight witnesses, French civilians and Canadian soldiers, was read into the record in support of Guilbert's testimony. It concluded with testimony from Maj. John G. Learment, who commanded C Company of the North Novies vanguard and had himself been taken prisoner that day.

This ended Macdonald's presentation of the see-saw battle for Authie as viewed from the front lines. His next witness, Sgt. Stan Dudka, was called to explain what happened to the Canadian prisoners that the Germans were moving to the rear. Dudka had already been discharged from the army and now lived in Stellarton, Nova Scotia. Macdonald had him flown over for the trial. Dudka verified everything said by his company commander: the soldiers who captured them wore dapple-brown camouflage clothing, a few wore the

Adolf Hitler sleeve insignia. They were very young, very excited—and in his view completely ruthless.

For the rest of that day and throughout the next, Macdonald slowly and methodically built his case out of the mouths of witnesses and the sworn statements he had collected over a 13-month period on two continents.

By the time Harry adjourned in the late afternoon of 13 December, darkness had fallen outside. "The court had a fairly comprehensive understanding of what had happened to the troops at Authie and later in captivity. The mush of bodies crushed by tank treads, the brutal treatment of the wounded and the slaughter of the living—for no apparent reason—was enough to revolt the stoutest heart. Had Meyer been responsible for all of it, I wondered? It seemed unlikely. . . .

"Yet I recalled an incident in Italy when Scott Murdoch received a call from one of the battalion commanders asking what to do with a collection of German prisoners captured by his unit. Scott told him to 'shoot the buggers!' A day earlier I'd said that we wanted no more prisoners. They were a nuisance to feed and look after. His job was to anticipate my orders. As GSO1 he spoke in my name. How many prisoners did that battalion commander shoot? I never knew, neither did Scott. Was I guilty of a war crime; was Scott; was Meyer? Probably."

Each evening after court Andrew and Lehmann visited Kurt to plan the next day's strategy. Andrew assured him that although the testimony so far put officers and men of the 25th Regiment in a very bad light, there was no evidence to prove Kurt had been directly involved. Macdonald's attitude puzzled both Lehmann and Andrew. Although they were only four days into the proceedings, Lehmann saw a pattern beginning to emerge. "I had a feeling from the start that Macdonald was putting a lot of his own personal feelings into the trial. I don't know whether it was because he had such a hatred of the ss and wanted a spectacular trial for political reasons or simply had a pride in his job. In the temper of the times Meyer, being ss, couldn't be anything else but guilty. But if you accuse someone of a crime then somewhere there has to be a crime. It seemed to me that he was forcing the evidence to suit his own ends."

Every morning after breakfast Kurt went out for exercise. He enjoyed running, but it proved an awkward performance while handcuffed to Major Russell and pursued by two guards toting truncheons. He found Russell irritating and amusing. One morning after exercise Lehmann entered his cell to find him chuckling. It was the first time he had heard Kurt laugh.

"That Major Russell—he's a proper old woman, isn't he? Every day he looks under my bed. Why in God's name would I hide anything under my bed?"

Had it been an NCO he could have accepted this daily routine with good grace, but a field officer—and a major at that—down on his hands and knees looking under a bed struck him as ludicrous. Russell, however, had reason for concern. During the first strip search he discovered a razor blade sewn into an epaulette of the uniform Kurt wore. Kurt's explanation that the tunic had been issued to him by the Americans from a German supply dump after his capture was accepted. Nevertheless, Russell, a charming and conscientious man, resolved to keep a close eye on his charge.

Throughout the trial on alternate days the family visits continued. The Meyers sat together talking quietly, feeling the warmth of each other's presence. Ursula did not attend the trial; only Kate turned up each day.

"Mother attends the trial. During her absence I walk for hours through the bleak grey streets of Aurich. I have many questions to ask her but I can't. Mother is so absentminded. She doesn't hear me. It is ever so sad. The parents are in such a sad mood. The odds for Father seem unfavourable— his comrades are not allowed to be witnesses for him—foreign men accuse him beyond reason. I don't want to hear this. I prefer to walk through the wet and cold streets until it gets dark. I talk to nobody. I prefer to be alone with my dreams and thoughts of Father."

The prosecution's key witness took the stand next morning. Nineteen-year-old Sturmmann Jan Jesionek was the only man Macdonald had found who claimed to have been present at the Abbaye Ardenne and to have heard Kurt give the orders that resulted in the executions. Jesionek's testimony was crucial. Macdonald had interviewed him in Paris, later in London, and as a test had taken him to the Abbaye Ardenne, making him recount everything that had happened. He had passed without difficulty. Macdonald had no doubts on his ability to handle himself on the stand.

Jesionek entered the courtroom wearing Allied battle dress, a matter that elicited several frowns from the bench. This "good guy" image was a tactical blunder. Macdonald should have arranged for a German clothing issue or at least civilian dress. But he wanted to distance his witness, a Silesian Pole, as far as possible from the ss. Realizing the error, he asked Jesionek, after having him identify himself, to explain his dress. Jesionek said that it had been given to him in England by the Red Cross. The frowns subsided.

Carefully, Macdonald took the young German Pole through his involuntary membership in the Hitler Youth, then into the Waffen-ss at the age of 16½ while his father was serving a four-month prison sentence for refusing to use the Nazi salutation. After basic training and driving courses he transferred to 15th Company of Kurt's regiment. He and Torbanisch served together in No. 4 Platoon. The incident about the secret orders was reconfirmed, although Jesionek could no longer remember what the orders said. None of it was particularly damaging. Finally, Macdonald led him to the events that he had seen and heard at the Abbaye Ardenne on 8 June.

He stated that when the seven Canadians were brought to the regimental HQ he had heard Kurt say: "What should we do with these prisoners—they only eat up our rations?" Then, after speaking to a *tall, thin man of athletic build in half tones*, Kurt added loudly to everyone present: "In future, no more prisoners are to be taken." Shortly thereafter the Canadians, one by one, were led out into the adjacent garden and executed.

That was Macdonald's whole case in a nutshell. Believe Jesionek's testimony and Kurt was a murderer, based on a time-worn formula for the acceptance of circumstantial evidence: "It must be consistent with the evidence and inconsistent with any other rational conclusion." Everything depended on Jesionek's credibility.

To Harry he came across to the court as an ingratiating "young smart aleck who possessed a remarkable memory." Macdonald decided to use that strength to convince the court of his witness's sincerity. With maps, photographs, diagrams, and prompting from Macdonald, Jesionek provided a surfeit of minute details of events at the abbey that day. He described the surrounding terrain, the weather, the sense of urgency inside the abbey, naming the officers and NCOs who were present, their ages, what they looked like, where they were standing and how they were dressed, and what everyone was doing at the time. This total recall impressed Harry. He had fought through the area into the Abbaye Ardenne and mentally confirmed portions of Jesionek's descriptions.

Then it was Andrew's turn. He concentrated on the man's weaknesses. He got him to admit that his knowledge of German came only after joining the SS, although he considered himself fluent for purposes of conversation; that he had deserted to the Americans on 30 March 1945; that his statements given at the POW camp in Chartres, France, about events at the abbey contained errors and contradictions and were extracted from him when he had been threatened with hanging by the Americans for being an SS soldier. But in spite of his contradictory testimony and generally objectionable attitude, Jesionek left the stand with his credibility more or less intact. A severe blow to the defence.

That evening in his cell Kurt seemed detached and disinterested in the proceedings when Andrew and Lehmann called. "As though he saw himself as a third party to what was happening instead of principal actor. . . . He insisted that he had never worn the raincoat type of dress Jesionek ascribed to him, that he had never given such an order to anyone and had in fact been away from the Abbaye during the crucial hours when the killings took place. He concluded by saying: 'Sure, I'm a Nazi, but I'm also a soldier and as a soldier what does it benefit me to kill a couple of dozen troops? I haven't got time to run around worrying about prisoners when I'm trying to hold a crumbling front.'"

5

Next morning, Friday, 15 December, was taken up with a discussion on the polemics of Jesionek's contradictory statements given to the Americans at Chartres, to Macdonald in Paris and London, and finally to the court. Originally, he said that Kurt's words were: "Why do you bring prisoners to the rear, those murderers only eat off our rations?" The word "murderers" had been missing from his courtroom testimony. Additionally, his signed statement claimed that "immediately afterwards he gave the order to the Executive Officer to have the prisoners shot." Yet in court he admitted to being unable to hear what was said at the abbey because Kurt had spoken in half tones. Jesionek's credibility once again came into question. If he had been guilty of "assuming" Kurt's words in his Chartres statement, why hadn't he stuck to the story in Aurich?

Harry decided that the embellishment at Chartres was probably done to sensationalize the information, "which it certainly did. But instead of sticking to his original story in court he retracted part of it; an action potentially damaging to the prosecution's case, since it changed instantly Meyer's culpability from giving a clearly audible positive order to only an inaudible and probable one. I concluded, therefore, that everything Jesionek had said in court was, to the best of his memory and ability, the truth."

Had Andrew realized the thinking from the bench he would probably have thrown in the towel. Oddly, he regarded Jesionek's contradictory evidence as another bonus point for the defence.

Corroborating testimony, covering Jesionek's visit and comments during his visit to the Abbaye Ardenne with Macdonald and others, came from Capt. R.J. Pootmans, a German-speaking field intelligence officer formerly attached to 3rd Division HQ. The rest of the day was taken up by the French civilians who had discovered the grisly remains oozing from shallow graves in the abbey garden and by the Canadians who had exhumed and identified the bodies and later had conducted examinations to determine the causes of death. Harry adjourned court for the weekend.

The weekend found the generals bored; Andrew, Lehmann and Kurt plotting defence tactics; Kate and Ursula worrying. "It will soon be Christmas and I want to ask Mother if Santa Claus is coming this year. But after the usual questions like—'hungry?'—'cold?'—Mother's mind wanders away. You can see and almost feel it. I think my questions bring her to the edge of tears. It is better to be silent."

Andrew decided to put Kurt on the stand, followed by Bernhard Meitzel and Max Wünsche, and then rely on recalling other prosecution witnesses to conclude his case. He didn't have much to work with. Every supportive witness Kurt suggested was either unavailable or could not be located. After

Andrew left their strategy session, Lehmann stayed to talk awhile. These frequent personal discussions ranged over every conceivable topic, at times developing into heated argument.

"His life really meant very little to him. His only regret was that he hadn't died in battle. He still idolized Hitler and became vehement in his support of the Führer when I suggested that all he'd done was lead Germany into destruction. Russia was the enemy. Not the Western Allies. Stalin and the Communists were out to destroy the world. . . .

"He said: 'If your armies had continued across the demarcation line into Russia the German nation would have backed you to a man.' When I tried explaining that Russia was an ally and we didn't operate that way towards allies he looked me straight in the eye the way he always did and said: 'Russia is not your ally. One day you will learn that she is your enemy. And you will have to fight her. God help you.'"

Monday was the last full day of the prosecution's case. Macdonald read more affidavits into evidence. Purely overkill, but he seemed determined to account for every murdered soldier and lay the blame for each, directly or indirectly, at the feet of Kurt Meyer.

An affidavit from Pvt. Marcel J. Dagenais of the Sherbrooke Fusiliers stated that he had been in a tank with Lieutenant Windsor and troopers Ball, Lockhead and Philip when it was knocked out on 7 June. The five, along with a private from the North Novies, were escorted to the Abbaye Ardenne. He saw German soldiers kill wounded Canadians who were unable to walk. During interrogation by an SS sergeant-major, Windsor was slapped across the face when he refused to give more than his name, rank and serial number. Dagenais, possibly because he spoke French, was separated and taken to German HQ at Caen by staff car together with several North Novies. In Caen he saw a truck deliberately run down and kill two North Novie prisoners marching at the rear of a column. He never saw Windsor again.

Staff officer Lieut. Bernhard Meitzel, the tall, blond and handsome Obersturmführer, was called as the prosecution's 25th witness. In perfect English, he confirmed that Kurt had taken over command of the 12th SS on 17 June 1944. Obersturmführer Kurt Bergmann, adjutant in Kurt's 3rd Battalion, followed Meitzel. He said that Obersturmbannführer Milius had been his battalion commander until 16 or 17 June, when he took over command of the 25th Panzer Grenadier Regiment from Kurt.

Capt. M. Bluteau of Canadian Records Branch established that the bodies found at the Abbaye Ardenne had been identified as missing in action on 7 June. The body of an officer found in a single grave near Kurt's regimental HQ was that of Lieut. F. Williams of the Stormont, Dundas and Glengarry Highlanders. The unit's War Diary, entered in evidence, showed that on the night of 6-7 June Williams and Lance-Corporal Pollard and a sapper went missing on patrol near Buron. The last Williams was heard to say was: "Carry on, Corporal, and give them hell!" Moaning sounds indicated that he had been wounded. His body was found three miles away within 150 feet of Kurt's HQ.

Bergmann was recalled to confirm that his 3rd Battalion under Milius had captured Buron on 7 June. He saw Kurt, Schueman, the Adjutant and a staff officer in regimental HQ at 1630 hours. Only three prisoners were taken from 10 June until 9 July, when Bergmann himself was captured. However, he testified that in the middle of June two wounded prisoners were brought in around 0300 hours one morning and a third a short time later. The first two were treated for their wounds and escorted to regimental HQ. It was reasonable to conclude that they were the missing Williams and Pollard.

Alfred Helzel's evidence, taken by Macdonald at Hull in July, confirmed that he had seen a wounded prisoner at Battalion HQ on the same night who was later taken to regimental HQ. Later that afternoon, when his job as dispatch rider brought him back to regimental HQ, he heard shots coming from the HQ house. A soldier standing nearby suggested: "Perhaps it is a prisoner who has been shot who would make no statements." It was said in a matter-of-fact manner as if this was an everyday occurrence at regimental HQ. It was in this location that Lieutenant Williams's body was found.

Slowly, inexorably, Macdonald tightened the noose of responsibility around Kurt's neck.

Next morning he put Rottenführer Ewald Wetzel of the *Feldgendarmerie* on the stand. Wetzel confirmed that a prisoner had been shot on the night of 17 or 18 June at regimental HQ. The shots were heard between 0400 and 0600 hours. Upon cross-examination by Andrew he stated that Milius had already taken command of the regiment and that only the regimental commander, his adjutant or staff officers had the authority to order a prisoner shot.

Hauptmann Fritz Steger came next. A Knight's Cross winner, the Wehrmacht captain had commanded 3rd Battalion of the 25th Regiment from 1 July until his capture near Buron nine days later. He finished the war as a POW in Kansas. Macdonald had interviewed him twice in London during October. Steger testified that upon his arrival at regimental HQ, 30 June 1944, he spoke to the administrative officer, Obersturmführer Huffendieck.

> Q. And did you have any conversation with him with relation to the matter of prisoners of war?
> A. Yes sir.
> Q. What did he say to you about it?
> A. He said he heard that the shooting of prisoners at Regimental HQ was reported to have taken place. . . .
> Q. Now, when you joined the 3rd Battalion of the 25th Regiment, did you have any conversation with anyone there with respect to the matter of prisoners of war?

A. I only once spoke with an Oberscharführer whose name I cannot quite precisely give you, it may have been Kneip or Quest, and when I asked whether he had heard anything of shootings, he answered he heard that shootings were reported to have taken place.

Q. Did he say where?

A. At Regimental HQ.

He said also that during the 12th SS training at Beverloo Kurt had told him that in Russia he had frequently had to shoot prisoners. Before Steger withdrew, Harry asked, "As Battalion Commander did you have authority to order the shooting of prisoners of war?"

The Knight's Cross winner shook his head. "No, sir."

To conclude, Macdonald turned to excerpts from Kurt's own statements given during his numerous London interrogations. He covered the critical points one by one. Kurt had agreed that he *had* addressed the troops of 15th Company when von Büttner took command of the company in Beverloo. It was therefore highly probable that he *had* made a statement to his troops at the time about his unit taking no prisoners, just as Helzel and Torbanisch testified. He agreed that it *had* been his 3rd Battalion that made the attack at Authie and Buron.

Schueman, a *tall, thin man of athletic build* who served as Kurt's adjutant until relieved by Milius in mid-June, spoke fluent English. He fitted exactly Jesionek's description of the interrogating officer who dealt with the seven prisoners at the Abbaye Ardenne and the man to whom Kurt spoke in half tones. Bornhöft, one of Kurt's drivers, *was* an Unterscharführer, the same rank as the NCO Jesionek claimed had shot the prisoners on 8 June.

Kurt had said that he was at the abbey on the morning of 8 June at the time of an air attack. Jesionek had stated that it was 15 minutes after an air attack that seven prisoners were brought in and reported to Kurt. Jesionek also said that it was the Adjutant who had supervised the transport of prisoners to divisional HQ the previous day. Kurt had agreed that on 7 June he *did* order a few prisoners sent to Division for interrogation. The inference could be drawn that Lieutenant Windsor's refusal to answer more than the three questions prescribed by international law for prisoners of war explained why he and his group, with the exception of Private Dagenais, never got beyond the abbey and paid for their courage and intransigence with their lives.

Macdonald closed his text and looked up at Harry.

"That is the case, sir." The time was 1155 hours.

Harry nodded. "The accused and escort may withdraw from the court. The court will adjourn for ten minutes."

When they reconvened, he asked Kurt through the interpreter: "Do you wish to give evidence yourself as a witness, make a statement, or do neither?"

"I myself wish to make a statement," Kurt replied. "I request that it be made under oath." Andrew then asked for an adjournment until after lunch.

Kurt took the stand shortly after 1400 hours. He appeared completely at ease, speaking calmly and quietly. Under Andrew's questioning, he told his story as it began in August 1943 when he assumed command of the 25th Panzer Grenadier Regiment.

Q. Of what did the personnel consist?
A. The troops consisted of 90% volunteer young Germans, the youngest sixteen and a half years old, the oldest 18 years old. The remainder consisted of taken over German soldiers, soldiers who were posted to the unit, not volunteers.
Q. Had these men that you had in August 1943 ever been in battle before?
A. No.

Then, he took the court through the regiment's training period at Beverloo, the substance of his speeches to the troops and the fighting in and around Buron, Authie and the abbey from 7 June until Witt's death, when he took over the division.

Harry thought "he spoke simply and eloquently. . . . As the interpreter translated Meyer's description of the frantic fighting, the need for him to be everywhere, looking after everything, I found myself transported back to those first few frantic weeks in Normandy when our green troops faced his green troops—our green officers and NCOs faced his experienced ones . . . and beat them at their own game."

Kurt concluded his testimony next day at noon. After the lunch-time recess, Macdonald rose like a wolf on the scent of succulent quarry to begin his cross-examination. There were troubling contradictions in testimony between what Kurt said in court and what he had signed as the truth during the London interrogations. "Which is the truth?" Macdonald demanded.

If ever there was a case to illustrate why an accused should remain silent in the presence of his accuser, this was it. Many of the discrepancies and contradictions were no worse than those of Helzel and Jesionek, but Macdonald made the most of them. That was his job. He was alternately sarcastic, abusive, disdainful and vicious as he bore down on his prisoner, trying to shake him, force him to alter his testimony, make him look like a fool. Several times Harry interrupted when he thought the prosecutor's enthusiasm went too far. Throughout, Kurt remained calm. When he couldn't remember the exact date he took over command of the 12th SS Division, Macdonald blinked in amazement.

Q. Do you expect all of us here to believe that?
A. Whether it is believed or not is a matter of indifference—that is the way it is.
Q. Now you have beautifully provided alibis and stop-gaps for everything that has been suggested as to your behaviour as a Regimental Commander. You have stopped up some gaps which did not exist so far as the evidence was

concerned anyway. I do not know whether that was due to a conscience with regard to the matter or not but that is a fact. Now. . . .

Andrew was on his feet protesting. "That is not a fact! It has not come out yet."

"It will in just a couple of minutes," Macdonald promised.

For his part he found cross-examining Kurt an unsatisfactory experience. "There was little that he said to the court which had not already been said in prior interrogations. The most that could be accomplished would be to point out and obtain explanations for, or admissions of, contradictory statements. . . . This was complicated by the fact that every question had to be translated . . . before the next question could be asked. I was satisfied, after my many conversations with Meyer, that by this time he could understand and follow the English questions quite well. The interpreting of the questions, therefore, gave him considerable time to decide upon and to formulate his answer. . . .

"Added to this, Meyer chose to be evasive and indirect in his answers on the matters with which we were principally concerned. When faced with any embarrassment, he would launch into long irrelevant speeches and it was with great difficulty that he was brought back again and again to the question until finally a straight answer was obtained. . . .

"On tactical matters he was prepared to talk all day and the court was taken on many tours of the Caen battlefield with expositions on the dispositions of troops. This, while interesting at first, eventually became rather tiresome."

Kurt's statement that before noon on 7 June he had heard about German prisoners being killed by Canadians at Villeneuve, south of Rots, was patently untrue (see page 313). He offered the thesis that this incident triggered retaliation, resulting in the killings at the abbey. The problem was that Canadian troops were nowhere near Villeneuve until the night of 7 June. Further, in his first London statement, he said that he had no reports or information suggesting the mistreatment of any German prisoners.

In a later interrogation, when he referred to this incident, Macdonald arranged to have some of the Canadian troops who had taken part in the ambush present for the trial. But upon reflection he decided to drop the matter as a "side issue," which was just as well in light of the circumstances under which the German bodies had been found. Even if Kurt had been lying about the timing of events in order to provide some justification for what happened at his abbey HQ, the question still remained on how the German soldiers riding the reconnaissance vehicle had met their deaths.

The day ended in a draw.

6

Next morning Macdonald began his cross-examination by insisting on an explanation for Kurt's original denial of any knowledge about the 18 bodies found at his HQ. His original statements made in London on 15 October and signed—with minor alterations—on 17 October had also been made under oath. At the time, even though Macdonald had given him complete details of Jesionek's evidence, telling him that he was going to be put on trial, Kurt stuck to his story.

Later, on 28 October, he sent for Macdonald and, after being advised against making a statement, admitted to discovering the bodies at his HQ on 11 June. He agreed that the first seven soldiers must have been killed at a point less than a 100 yards from the chapel where he was standing at the time but suggested that some of those who died were the wounded. Macdonald grilled him on the semantics of prisoners being buried who had "died" or been "shot." Could the bodies include prisoners who had been shot?

A. Yes, sir. I did not hear that wounded died or that others died. I did, however, hear, as was reported to you, that Canadians had been shot there.
Q. What did you think happened to the Canadians who were shot if they didn't die?
A. I have already said that under "died" I understood a wounded person, who because of loss of blood, died.
Q. Well, don't you suppose that is what happened to these people?
A. I don't regard that as dying, that is not described as dying in Germany, that is murder.
Q. Well, I agree that it was murder but I can hardly see how you can have a murder without somebody dying. Will you tell me how that is accomplished?
A. I cannot give any answer to that question.

Macdonald pressed home the attack, cornering his quarry about the truthfulness of his earlier sworn testimony. "At this point Meyer had lost his composure and was glaring furiously at me. I began to experience the hypnotic sensations that must have overcome the first witness, Alfred Helzel. Whether Meyer had privately practised and perfected the 'out-staring and glaring technique' said to be part of the training of Prussian officers, I do not know; but I do know that under his amazingly fierce and frightening glare I began to feel a little giddy. . . . I was no match for him in a glaring competition but something had to be done right away, if I was to continue my cross-examination. . . .

"He had asked to have part of his evidence re-read and I had suggested that he was stalling to gain time. The glare was at its maximum intensity at this point as he replied: 'I don't need any time to think this over.'

"To this I answered: 'And glaring at me isn't going to answer anything either. You are not going to intimidate me by your glares, I can assure you!'

"With these words the most astonishing transformation occurred in Meyer's countenance. He looked around the courtroom in a sheepish manner, and the glare dropped from his face as if a magic wand had suddenly been passed over it. From that time on I experienced no further difficulties with the witness."

Macdonald harked back to London and Kurt's denying knowledge of the shootings, then two weeks later, when told that he was going to trial, admitting to such knowledge. When Kurt tried explaining the delay had been due in part to Macdonald's absence from London, the prosecutor snapped back: "You mean until you discover that you are for it you keep silent."

Harry interrupted: "This is a military court and sarcastic suggestions and a running commentary is something that we do not have in a military court."

Macdonald apologized. He concluded his cross-examination with a few throwaway questions designed to show the consistency of ruthlessness prevalent throughout the 12th SS. Had Kurt any knowledge of 43 Canadians being executed on 8 and 9 June by Sturmbannführer Bernhard Siebken, commander of the 26th Panzer Grenadier Regiment's 2nd Battalion? Or had he heard that on 11 July 1944, after interrogating three Canadian prisoners at his HQ, Obersturmbannführer Wilhelm Mohnke,[2] regimental commander of the 26th, had stood outside and watched them machine-gunned? To each question Kurt admitted knowing the men but nothing about the incidents.

Harry interrupted for the benefit of the news reporters, who were scribbling furiously: "The accused, incidentally for the record, cannot be held answerable for these incidents which occurred in other regiments, nor can that information which has just been divulged be used to influence the court in this trial here."

Macdonald had no further questions. Kurt's ordeal on the witness stand was almost over. "I was alone. Hundreds of eyes observed each of my movements and facial expressions. Not a moment to relax. A group of men against one—men with all the authority, pushed by decorations and ambitions against an outlaw. Questions after questions: training and educational matters; content and meaning of speeches I'd held years ago; character of conversations in front of French fireplaces and so forth. Fire! Fire without grenades and an even chance—spiteful words—wrong interpretations—questions, confusing allusions—distorted pictures of a distant past. Thus, Macdonald tried defeating me. But I refused to capitulate. In sheer delight he tried denouncing me as a liar because I first denied and then confirmed the finding of the dead Canadians."

Court adjourned until the next morning.

Andrew's second witness was English-speaking Bernhard Meitzel. Kurt asked Harry if he would give Meitzel permission to testify in German so that he could understand what was being said. Harry agreed.

Meitzel had joined the regiment in August 1943 and remained with it throughout its training period. He denied ever hearing Kurt counsel his troops to take no prisoners. He related the incident of a German soldier from the 6th Battalion who had been courtmartialed and executed for raping a young French girl. Kurt had said: "The young soldiers of the division are being brutalized by battle and it is under all circumstances to be prevented, that this leads to crimes of this nature. I order that such occurrences be most strictly punished. This is all."

He remembered that on 10 July, when 150 prisoners had been taken during a storm, Kurt ordered them put inside buildings out of the weather. Andrew then asked:

Q. Do you remember any other incidents where General Meyer was connected with Canadian prisoners?
A. On the 10th August, 1944, I had been captured by the 4th Canadian Armoured Division, as I succeeded in escaping I reported back to Brigadeführer Meyer. He was having supper with three Canadian prisoners of war at his Headquarters.
Q. Did you see anything that should not have been done to the prisoners there?
A. No. . . .

He had seen Kurt, wearing a camouflage uniform, standing in the Abbaye Ardenne's tower with an artillery officer around noon on 8 June. He denied there was any minefield in the area of the abbey as claimed by Jesionek.

Macdonald then cross-examined, rehashing old material, looking for contradictions in Meitzel's testimony from that of earlier witnesses. Had Meitzel, in his capacity as a staff officer at divisional HQ under Witt ever seen any reports of summary executions of prisoners? Was Meitzel aware that 150 soldiers had been executed by men of the 12th SS? The questions were quite pointless. Even if Meitzel did know, he was hardly likely to confess to it now.

When Macdonald finished, Harry kept Meitzel on the stand. He wanted to be clear in his own mind at what time the staff officer had left divisional HQ and reached the abbey. It was a crucial point because it placed Kurt at the scene of the killing at approximately the same time Jesionek had stated.

Meitzel thought a moment and then replied: "I cannot remember exactly but it was around noon because afterwards I was invited for lunch. . . . I had already made the 8 and 10 o'clock SITREPS [situation reports from divisional HQ to Corps HQ] without the information from the Regiment and sent it on, now I was fetching the noon SITREPS. . . . I had Brigadeführer Meyer mark the positions of his battalions onto the map and note down a few facts about the way the morning's battles had gone."

Kurt *had* been there.

For the afternoon session Andrew called Max Wünsche. His appearance startled those on the bench. Harry restrained a smile.

"Wünsche arrived wearing dark trousers topped by a mustard-coloured tunic with high collar. His chest was littered with decorations—including the Knight's Cross. He was young, tall, slender, blond and blue eyed with his hair combed straight back and unbelievably handsome. He should have been a movie star. He stepped up to the witness box in a condescending manner then carefully turned his chair so that he was facing the court—me in particular. He answered each question through the interpreter without looking once at either Andrew or Macdonald, all the while fixing me with a wide-eyed and unblinking insolent stare. The minutes passed. Finally, my eyes started watering and I had to look away. When I glanced back and saw his look of triumph I smiled. One for the weaker side!"

In spite of the histrionics, Wünsche was obviously a competent military professional. Hitler's former ADC answered every question clearly and intelligently. His unsuccessful tank attack against the Regina Rifles of Harry's 7th Brigade at Bretteville on 8 June gave him a healthy respect for the calibre of Canadian troops. His losses on the 7th and 8th severely curtailed the overall German battle plans. He related visiting Kurt at the Abbaye Ardenne around 1400 hours and seeing him with two young staff officers. Witt had just approved an evening attack on Bretteville to be commanded by Wünsche.

Macdonald saw this as "an interesting point because Meyer claimed that earlier in the morning he had gone to reconnoitre the Bretteville area for that same attack; clearly impossible when divisional HQ hadn't decided on proceeding with it until that afternoon."

Obersturmführer Kurt Bergmann, adjutant of the regiment's 3rd Battalion, had already testified for the prosecution. He was Andrew's last witness. He said that three or four days after the invasion Kurt had ordered the burial of dead bodies in Authie. At the same time, orders came from Division reminding troops of the necessity of evacuating prisoners for interrogation to Division as quickly as possible. It had been Bergmann's battalion that captured Lieutenant Williams and Lance-Corp. Pollard on 17 June. He testified that the two had actually arrived back at regimental HQ where Williams's body was discovered. Pollard's body was never found.

Andrew concluded by saying how every effort to obtain additional eyewitnesses from the 25th Regiment for his client had been unsuccessful. Discouraged, he sat down.

Next day, 23 December, was Kurt's birthday and Macdonald's opportunity for rebuttal witnesses. He recalled three, including Jesionek, to clarify earlier testimony. Once again, Jesionek demonstrated his amazing memory. Giving evidence on where his *Schwimmwagen* patrol had hit a mine—a spot where Meitzel had said there were no mines—his finger jabbed the exact location in reference to a burned-out tank on a large map that Harry provided. Harry was impressed "by this feat of memory and map reading. I remembered seeing that burned-out tank on the same rise of land when we finally took the area, exactly as he described it."

Macdonald's final rebuttal testimony was to read a short excerpt from Kurt's testimony given under oath in London on 27 and 28 March. Kurt had said he had never heard of Canadians being shot in retaliation for the shooting of ss prisoners. To this he had added that "during June I received an inquiry as to whether Canadians had been shot in my sector. I made the enquiry and was able to reply that while I had been in command, there had been no such case."

After being shown five volumes of reports of atrocities committed by his regiment and division, he demanded to know: "In which sectors can these things have taken place? I find it impossible to believe. . . . I can only say that I gave no orders in connection with any such thing and have never heard anything of these atrocities nor has any official report been made to me about them."

Q. It is difficult to believe that these things could have been done without knowledge coming to you, at any rate after the event.
A. I have never heard anything about these things.
Q. Can you quote a single example where you took action to restrain any members of your Division from the improper treatment of prisoners of war?
A. I have had no experience, have not been and have had no reports of improper treatment of prisoners of war.

After driving what he hoped were these last nails into Kurt's coffin, Macdonald sat down. That completed the evidence. Harry adjourned court for a three-day Christmas recess.

Christmas and her father's birthday—for Ursula the two were always synonymous. "He is 35 years old. It is rumoured that his sentence is already decided but will not be released before Christmas. Why not? Things can't get gloomier than now. Why do they do this? Why do they condemn him? What is a sentence?"

It had been one of the alternate days for Kurt. No visitors. He stared glumly from his cell window. "After sunset I heard an unscheduled rattling of keys in the corridor. Doors banged. Suddenly some officers were in the cell. In harsh words I was ordered out. I was handcuffed and marched into the darkness, two sergeants with submachine-guns in front and rear of me. We stumbled across the yard and arrived in front of the officers' living quarters. The guards were ordered to watch the doors and windows. I had

no idea what this was all about, only a funny feeling in the pit of my stomach.
. . .

"An officer opened my handcuffs. They fell to the floor with a clatter. Two of the gentlemen asked for my word of honour not to attempt an escape. I complied. Then they opened a door. I thought I was dreaming. In front of me was a beautifully decorated table that could hardly support the abundance of food and drink. Candlelight gave a special air to the room. Hesitatingly, I entered. A half dozen officers started singing a birthday song. They had arranged a birthday party for me! My enemies! . . .

"I stood stunned, watching them and could not prevent the tears from running down my cheeks. The transition from prison to birthday party was just too much. I was even more moved when the officers introduced themselves as unit commanders of the 3rd Canadian Division—men I had been fighting from June until August 1944. . . . We had an open conversation that night about the whole problem of war crimes. They agreed that if I was to be condemned then the Canadian army generals should follow my fate because they too were guilty of exactly the same atrocities. . . .

"It was interesting to hear how my prosecutor went to the bar every day to swallow his anger with whisky. The officer, who had seen active service, had nothing good to say about Macdonald. Our celebration ended at midnight. Shortly after, my cell door closed again and I was a prisoner."

Christmas Eve he met with Kate and Ursula. They talked about family, the hotel, the food, the weather, his birthday—everything except the trial. Ursula had been invited to a Christmas party put on by the Canadians for German children.

"In the evening we sit with the landlord around the Christmas tree. I got out the chess set and we played. At night a rat walks over the end of my bed and frightens me. Mother says: 'Come over to my bed.' I'm so glad. I'm hardly asleep when someone knocks at the door. Mother jumps up, gets dressed and opens the door. Soldier Stadt walks in. He is a little drunk and takes me on his arm and gives me some chocolate. In broken German he says: 'Imagine yourself on your father's arm. You alone here. I alone here. All my loved ones are far away.' . . .

"He leaves before there is trouble. Hardly has he gone than we hear a squeal of tires. Three Military Police appear. They talk to mother. What is going on? One sits on my bed and wants to talk. He gives me a bar of chocolate. I can't understand him and I have to take care of Mum. She is so self-assured and calm, even smiles slightly. They leave as quickly as they came. Next morning Mother asks Capt. Lehmann not to punish Stadt. He said: 'No, he won't be punished but he will be transferred and not allowed back.'"

Christmas. The guards brought a small tree into Kurt's cell and helped him decorate it. Brigadier Bell-Irving went grouse shooting. Brigadier Roberts drove to Doorn and stayed with a friend. Brigadier Johnston took the Royal Suite in the Hotel Amsterdam. The others flew back to England. Harry spent the holiday with Mollie in Fleet. CMHQ advised that he would be leaving for Canada sometime in January. Mollie put The Poplars up for sale and began planning what furniture she wanted shipped overseas. Everyone returned to Aurich on the night of 26 December, anxious "to get the business over and done with."

Next morning, as every other morning during the trial, Kurt was escorted into the room between Russell and Stutt. He bowed politely to Harry and then took his seat, glancing behind him to make sure that Kate was present. She was. No smile, merely a tightening of lips as she acknowledged her husband. His face betrayed not a flicker of emotion.

The morning was taken up with final addresses by counsel. Both Andrew and Macdonald presented brief reviews of their cases and their interpretation of the evidence. They did it clearly, concisely and in a highly responsible manner. Afterwards, Lieut.-Col. W.B. Bredin, the judge-advocate, gave a short address covering the duties of the court. Throughout the proceedings Kurt's expression remained impassive. At exactly 1330 hours Harry adjourned for the court to consider its verdict.

7

"We retired to our meeting room with Bredin. There were still questions of law to be answered before any of us were competent enough to reach a verdict. I think Johnston and Sparling had already made up their minds. Bredin answered the questions. The new laws and regulations governing War Crimes were broad and definite. There was nothing for it. Under these laws Meyer was guilty. Yet I had great sympathy for him. I knew what he must have gone through during those first few frantic days in Normandy. . . .

"We proceeded through the charges one at a time, voting as we went and not always unanimous in our findings. If a tie occurred—as it did because Roberts and Bell-Irving were more inclined to be lenient—I cast the deciding vote. . . .

"On the first charge we were unanimous. Meyer had indeed counselled his men to deny quarter. On the second charge I was not satisfied that he bore full responsibility for the killing of the 23 soldiers at Authie and Buron. It seemed to me that this sort of charge threw open to question the entire area of a field commander's responsibility for every action by his troops. On this one I cast the deciding vote to acquit. . . .

"Likewise on the third charge, I was not satisfied that he had actually given the order for executing the seven at his headquarters. He may have done so but no evidence was offered by anyone to prove that he did. However, we agreed unanimously that he bore a vicarious responsibility for all the killings that took place at the Abbaye.

"It was inconceivable how he, sitting in his headquarters, could have heard a succession of regularly spaced pistol shots less than 150 feet away and not sent someone off to investigate. I would have, as would any commanding officer, particularly so close to the front. Meyer didn't. He didn't because he *knew* what was going on—even if he hadn't given the order."

The court reassembled at 1615 hours. Without preliminaries, Harry addressed Kurt directly: "Brigadeführer Meyer, the Court has found you not guilty of the second and third charges. You will sit down please."

Before the passing of sentence on the other three charges, it was Andrew's right to have character witnesses called on Kurt's behalf. Harry adjourned court until the following morning. Andrew had done his best. He remained convinced of Kurt's innocence. He tried to think of something comforting to say to him, failed and quickly left the room. It was the last time Kurt saw him. That evening, after turning everything over to Capt. Frank Plourde, his assistant, Lieut.-Col. Maurice Andrew left Aurich.

Ursula spent the day in the hotel waiting for news. "After noon Mother comes, accompanied by Capt. Lehmann and another officer. How dreadful she looks! Something terrible must have happened. I tell myself 'Quiet, be quiet, don't say a thing.' But I hear it loud and clear. 'Father is going to be shot!'

"There is a Canadian Christmas party this afternoon. The adults think it is better that I go there and accept the invitation politely. It gives Mother time to organize the things she must do: she has to find a German lawyer and send for Oma and the other sisters. . . .

"Thus I find myself amongst happy foreign children. They sing, shout and laugh—I can think only of Dad. I sit and stare in front of me. A young soldier takes care of me. He is friendly and wants to talk. But I can't understand his language; he offers food but I don't want to eat; I don't want to sing and laugh. I want to be alone. Is one of these soldiers going to shoot my father? . . . I know when I see Father tomorrow everything will be okay again. We'll find new hope then the party is over. Mother asks: 'How was it?' I tell: 'Nice.' They are glad."

At 1000 hours next morning and wearing his full uniform with decorations, Wehrmacht General Heinrich Eberbach appeared as Plourde's first character witness. Although Plourde announced that Eberbach spoke fluent English, Harry asked that he testify in his own language. It was clear that the older general thought very highly of his subordinate. He gave a brief history of the 12th ss.

As inspector of panzer troops he had visited the unit during its training at Beverloo. Instead of goose-stepping fanatics he had found young lads singing as they marched. Kurt appeared to be more of a father figure to the troops than a commander. Eberbach divided the division's officers into two categories: "One category are the young people who from sheer idealism joined the SS and the other category I would like to describe as brawlers and bad mercenaries. I wish to state in conjunction with General von Geyr that the Army itself regarded Divisional Commander Witt as well as Meyer . . . and Wünsche to be numbered among the idealists. In contrast . . . other commanders . . . Mohnke and Bremer were counted among the bullies and brawlers. . . .

"When I took over the Panzer Group West from Gen. Geyr, he and I discussed the Divisions, especially each Divisional Commander's capabilities. I asked whether Meyer, who now had taken Witt's place, was not a bit too young for the job? But Geyr described Meyer as one of his best Divisional Commanders. . . . His record of knocked out enemy tanks, captured enemy prisoners, captured enemy machine-guns, was approximately three times the success figures of the 21st Panzer Division and double the figure of the Panzer Lehr (Tank Instructional) Division. . . .

"Gen. Geyr said that it was frequently due only to the Hitlerjugend that the Normandy Front was held. . . . In spite of these heavy losses it remained the corset-stay of the other Divisions who were less efficient."

Neither he nor Geyr had heard anything about atrocities. Eberbach took out a piece of paper—a brief treatise on Kurt prepared by Geyr and himself. He read it aloud. It described Kurt as a "young, fresh, dashing man of position, quick in resolution, better in attack than defence; ambitious, conscious of his abilities but always eager to learn. An outstanding soldier, who took care of his boy soldiers, brave, good trainer, believer in the revolutionary ideals of training which Geyr taught him, self-made man—as far as Geyr and I know, without hate against Canadians. Murder of prisoners not in his line." Unless he had misjudged him badly, Eberbach said that he refused to believe that Kurt would be stupid enough to order the execution of prisoners.

Kate was Plourde's second character witness. Pale and trembling, she took the stand and was sworn in. Her pathetic appearance was an embarrassment to everyone. Harry burned with indignation "over young Plourde's stupidity in putting the poor woman through such a pointless exercise. Of course she loved her husband and children! And of course they loved him. Naturally, he was a good husband, father and provider. Under the circumstances what else could she possibly say?"

Next to appear was prosecution witness Hauptmann Fritz Steger of the 3rd Battalion, who gave a two-minute glowing account of the accused as a soldier, commander, comrade-in-arms and man. Plourde made sure the court understood that Steger was a Wehrmacht officer and not SS.

Capt. J.A. Renwick* of the British Columbia Regiment (28th Armoured) was the last witness to appear. He had been captured on the evening of 9 August after the destruction of his regiment and conducted 1,000 yards behind the line where he was introduced to Kurt. A short time later Kurt drove him to his divisional HQ where he was interrogated for a half hour through an interpreter.

"At that time they produced to me a copy of *The Maple Leaf* newspaper containing a news item covering an Order of the Day issued by Gen. Crerar regarding the alleged killings of Canadian soldiers on the 8th of June. The officer who interrogated me in the presence of the accused said that they did not wage war that way."

Kurt spoke to him another 15 minutes about the war, Nazi philosophy and his belief in the justice of the German cause. He came across to Renwick as an able and capable officer who behaved in a correct and gentlemanly fashion. At no time had he been subjected to threats or intimidation either by Kurt or any of his officers.

It was nearly over. Harry asked Kurt if he wished to speak.

Kurt nodded and rose. "Yes. Mr. President, for 17 years I have been a soldier. Of these I was in battle for five." He told of his desire at Beverloo to build a first-rate fighting unit and the time and care he took with his young troops to make this possible, to teach them from his own experience. To train them "not only as soldiers, but to give them a backbone for their entire life. The battles in Normandy, the battles of the invasion showed that the spirit of these young troops was good. . . . These young people of 17 and 18 years fought for three months without any relief, without a night of sleep. During the first four weeks of the battle my division had between four and six thousand casualties. . . . This division fought in these months against four well-trained, well-equipped divisions; the 3rd and 4th Canadian Divisions, the 51st British Division and the Polish Tank Division. If a troop can stand a quarter of a year of such attacks and air raids then it must consist of good soldiers. . . .

"I have here, during these proceedings, been given an insight into things which, in the aggregate, were unknown to me up until now. I wish to state to the Court that these deeds were not committed by my young soldiers. I am convinced that there were elements in the Division who, due to the years of battles, due to five years of war, had become brutalized. . . .

"I wish to assure the Court that I lived and fought as a soldier, that I gave no order to annihilate defenceless people, neither orally or in writing. . . . How far a Commander can be held responsible for misdeeds of individual members of his troop the old soldiers of this Court must decide. . . . As a soldier, I have a clean conscience. Here, in front of the German public,

---

*Later a New Democratic party member of the Ontario Legislature.

I wish to say that the Canadian Army treated me as a soldier and that these legal proceedings were conducted fairly."

At 11:20 on 20 December the court adjourned to consider the sentence. Kurt was escorted to the corridor outside where his mother, his sister, Melanie, and Kate were allowed to sit with him. With the news of his conviction, Alma and Melanie had come to Aurich to be with him for the end. They sat in silence. Guards, with weapons drawn, lined the walls.

Kate began weeping quietly. Alma glared: "Stop that! Don't you dare let them see you crying!" Kate stopped.

Kurt asked Melanie to sing for him. She sang Zarah Leander's "I Know One Day There Will Be a Wonder." Her clear soprano voice moved even the stern-faced guards to tears. When she finished, Kurt lowered his head and stared sadly at the floor.

It took exactly 25 minutes to decide. Roberts, Bell-Irving and Harry had had misgivings about the legality of what they were doing. Despite Macdonald's oratory and Bredin's judicial interpretations, the Rules of Evidence—cornerstone of British Common Law—had been suspended and they had conducted a courtmartial cum trial that was without precedent. They sympathized with Meyer.

Bell-Irving, at 32, the second-youngest brigadier in the Canadian army and temporary GOC of the 4th Armoured Division after Vokes's departure, felt a particular kinship to the youthful Kurt. "We all knew that our troops at various times were guilty of similar conduct. Whenever it happened we looked the other way. There was an intensity of relationship and affection for those among us who did the actual fighting. The sort of relationship that was unknown in peacetime. . . . I had been a Company and Regimental Commander and knew how hard it must have been for Meyer trying to run a one-man show with a bunch of green kids and battle-hardened NCOs. . . . But the legal restraints under which we were placed allowed for no other verdict than guilty. And it was a verdict that *required* the death penalty."

Brig. Ian Johnston, the Toronto lawyer, was of the opinion that "if Meyer was any kind of a soldier, instead of being tied up to a wall and executed, he should have taken his own life." Exactly how he was expected to complete this act while under Major Russell's care and custody, Johnston—who had won two DSOs fighting in Italy and northwest Europe—didn't explain.

Harry saw the matter from a soldier's viewpoint also, expressing what he believed would be Meyer's choice. "I would feel better dying before a firing squad than wasting away the rest of my life inside a prison." The others agreed. They butted their cigarettes and returned to the courtroom.

For the last time, Harry addressed the accused: "Brigadeführer Kurt Meyer, the Court has found you guilty of the First, Fourth and Fifth charges. . . . The sentence of this Court is that you suffer death by being shot. The findings of guilt and the sentence are subject to confirmation. These proceedings are now closed."

Kurt showed no emotion. He bowed to Harry one last time and was escorted out. Minutes later, as the Meyer family left, Captain Lehmann warned: "*Achtung*! There are the photographers outside. Don't let them see your grief." Alma straightened her shoulders and nudged Kate. "Don't cry! Laugh into the face of these gangsters!"

That same evening Harry boarded an airplane to England.

Alone with Lehmann in his perpetually lighted* cell Kurt faced the reality of his imminent demise. "Barred windows throw a long shadow on the wall. I look at the pictures of my wife and children. Kate must hear of my feelings. Capt. Lehmann promises to tell her personally. I am in the midst of a battle, comrades about me. A voice calls: 'Don't be afraid, General, we are fighting for your life!' My enemy—my friend. . . .

"This night I am near God. We talk all night. Strong again—I wait for the brightness of morning. It is hard to accept the fact that my life can now be measured in hours. Yet I recognize death as part of Creation. I pray to Him to allow me to meet it as a man unbroken."

In the morning his decorations were returned. He was handcuffed and taken to the visitors' room where Kate was waiting. "I fear this meeting. For years she has worried about my life. Now she greets me on my way to death. Considerately, the Canadian officer removes my handcuffs so I can enter the room as a free man. . . .

"Tearlessly she comes towards me. But, when our hands touch all defences crumble. Her tears fall on my decorations. I give them to her for my little boy. Never was I so proud of my wife as in these minutes. In spite of her grief she sent me back to my cell consoled and invigorated. . . . Before Col. Andrew left he begged me to send a petition to Maj.-Gen. Chris Vokes. . . . I declined. We parted as soldiers. For us the war is only a memory now."

He had told Kate how their boy was to be raised and his sorrow at not seeing him before he died. With that she was determined to bring all the children to Aurich for one last visit. But how? Out of the blue a local Communist offered to pay their transportation costs. Kate was flabbergasted. The Offleben Communists hated the Meyer family, while in Aurich the sympathetic Canadians supported them. Now the sympathetic Canadians were going to shoot her husband, while the hateful Communists spent money to bring the family together. The world had gone mad.

---

*The original bright light was changed to a lower wattage and shaded after his first week.

Elsewhere in Germany other courts were listening to evidence, sentencing, then hanging, war criminals. In Nuremberg, the international trial of the 22 leaders of Nazi Germany entered its sixth week. At Dachau, death by hanging was ordered for 36 of the concentration camp's staff, including the commandant, Martin Weiss, and Dr. Karl Schilling, for atrocities committed against tens of thousands of prisoners.

During the same week Joseph Kramer, "The Beast of Belsen," his blond queen, Irma Grese, and nine others were hanged in the courtyard of the little red prison of Hamelin after conviction by a British military court for mass murders and atrocities at Belsen and Auschwitz concentration camps. Elizabeth Volkenrath and Juana Bormann were among the condemned. Volkenrath, known as "The Dog Woman," had been chief of the ss women at Belsen. Often for sport, she unleashed her huge dog at prisoners' throats. All pleas for clemency were turned down by Field Marshal Montgomery.

8

Neither Kate nor Alma nor Lehmann was prepared to give up. Alma searched the town for a lawyer willing to help. "An ss general convicted of war crimes? Frau, you must be joking!" Finally, she found Dr. Schapp. The tall East Frisian listened sympathetically, accepted her gift of Canadian tea and then went to work at once on a petition for clemency. A judicial purist, Schapp was outraged by the new makeshift war crimes regulations.

He, in turn, enlisted support from the highly respected Clemens August Graf von Galen, Catholic bishop of Münster. Throughout the war the Bishop had been harassed repeatedly by the Gestapo for his firm anti-Nazi stand. In Allied eyes he was a "good" German. Ironically, Graf von Galen and Kurt had met in 1940, a week before the Leibstandarte invaded Holland. The Bishop had given the unit his blessing.

Meanwhile, Lehmann urged Plourde and Kurt to try for an appeal—not on the verdict, but on the sentence. He remembered Kurt's words before the trial: that the arrival of prisoners was a minor incident compared with what was happening elsewhere along his front. Kurt's prediction on the outcome, and his resigned "I told you so" when it was over, stuck in Lehmann's throat.

"Frank Plourde was a little naive on how we should proceed. I suggested using the basis of 'degree of responsibility,' exactly the way Meyer had described it to me; how could everyone in a unit be responsible for the actions of one man? I provided Meyer with writing materials which, reluctantly and after much badgering from me and his wife, he promised to use. It was a longshot but at this juncture anything to save his life was worth trying. . . .

"Early New Year's morning I came to pick up his petition. Without thinking, I wished him a Happy New Year. The words froze on my lips. I apologized immediately. He gave a rueful smile. 'Forget it—I've sent more of my friends to a certain death than I care to think about. My life now is unimportant.' . . . I translated his petition into English, keeping it simple and straightforward. Plourde sent it off with the appeal to Gen. Vokes, forwarding a copy to the Judge Advocate-General at CMHQ in London."

Armed with their petition and letters of support, Kate, Alma and Dr. Schapp started out for Bad Zwischenahn by car in the pouring rain on the morning of 2 January to see Vokes. Suddenly, Schapp, who was driving, swerved to avoid a small boy walking along the side of the road. Too late. With a sickening crunch of fender the youngster's broken body sailed into the ditch. He died instantly.

Kate sat stunned. This on top of everything else! It wasn't fair! Didn't God care about anyone—killing a small boy while she was trying so desperately to save her husband's life? Was that a fair exchange? They were held by police for most of the day while the matter was investigated. The documentation reached Vokes next day.

As convening officer, Vokes had remained aloof from the proceedings throughout the trial. "Most of the crap coming out of the trial via the media had Meyer condemned even before the trial was over." When the Judge Advocate-General reported the results to him as straightforward, recommending confirmation of findings and sentence, Vokes rubber-stamped the warrant. The appeal for clemency he rejected, albeit "somewhat reluctantly. But after making my decision I wanted no time wasted in getting on with the business. A firing party was detailed and rehearsed, a site for the execution and burial arranged, Meyer given an opportunity for last farewells to his family."

Major Russell was summoned to Oldenburg to see the DAQMG* and given map references for the execution and burial ground, together with instructions to provide "Meyer with a hearty breakfast for his last day on earth." The original execution date moved from 4 January to 7 January in order to assist British Intelligence who had a few questions to ask him about Dunkirk. Even allowing for British optimism, why anyone would think that an SS general under sentence of death would be in a cooperative mood remained obscure.

On 5 January, the family gathered for their last visit. Alma, Kate, Melanie, the four girls and baby Kurt crowded into the visiting room. The handcuffs were removed.

"I see my young boy for the first time. Irmtraud sings a Christmas carol. Inge consoles me: 'Father, you can never really die. Not when our boy looks exactly like you! I will always take care of him.' Oh, how my children make me happy. Mother and wife are now responsible for them all. Time rushes

*Division Adjutant and Quartermaster-General.

past. A last word, a quick hug, a contorted smile finish this last meeting. My life has come to an end."

On the following day, the younger Kurt broke out in a severe skin rash. Lehmann drove mother and child to the Canadian hospital where, after an examination, the boy was admitted. In addition to the rash, he had a serious hernia that required surgery. Depressed, Kate returned to the hotel alone. Why did everything keep going wrong? To Frau Snacker, the proprietor's sympathetic wife, who had provided support plus a shoulder to lean on throughout her stay, she said wearily, "Ah, these Canadians—they sentence one of my Kurts to death. Now they are going to operate on the other." That evening the army surgeon arrived to tell her in person that the operation had been a success and that young Kurt was sleeping peacefully.

Since there could be no more visits, Melanie agreed to take the four girls back to Offleben. There were black mourning dresses to be made. Kate and Alma would stay in Aurich until the boy was out of hospital and then see what arrangements could be made after the execution for bringing Kurt's body home for burial in a grave near his father's.

Vokes had second thoughts. "The documentation of the proceedings that had arrived on my desk was over two inches thick. Being a lazy sonofabitch, my first reaction had been to confirm the findings and sentence, and lay on the shooting party. But then I thought if I am to be put in the position of God then I'd better read the goddam evidence. . . . It would be around for everyone to read long after Meyer was gone. So I scratched the original confirming order. . . .

"I took a night to read it, page by bloody page. Then I picked up Meyer's petition for clemency and read and reread that. So eloquently was it done that I could sense the urgency of his battle, smell the fear and cordite around his Abbaye Headquarters. I had gone through that same exercise many times myself. By next morning I concluded Meyer had been convicted on evidence that was sort of second hand and although he had a vicarious guilt there was not a whit of evidence that he had given a direct order to have the soldiers executed.

"I then called Reggie Orde* and asked if he had read the transcript. He said that he had. I told him: 'Then take that pile of bullshit and go and read it through again then tell me what you think.' Orde's opinion turned out to be the same as mine . . . using the corollary of Meyer's actions being more akin to manslaughter than murder. Most of the legal beagles at CMHQ who had cocked up the charges in the first place had never seen a shot fired in anger. So I decided to postpone the execution and ask for advice."

Simonds, the senior Canadian officer in Holland, refused to have anything

---

*Brig. R.J. Orde, judge advocate-general of the Canadian army.

to do with the matter. Vokes took Orde with him and flew to London to see Lieut.-Gen. M.C. Murchie, chief of staff at CMHQ, and Vincent Massey, the Canadian high commissioner.

"I told them about all sorts of things that had gone on during wartime that weren't according to the Rules and Usages of War. Every commanding officer I knew had at one time or another told his troops to take no prisoners. In Sicily and Italy the only way we rid ourselves of Italian camp followers was to shoot the bastards before they robbed us blind. . . .

"I told them of Sögel and Friesoythe and of the prisoners and civilians that my troops had killed in Italy and Northwest Europe. . . . While I could certainly be held responsible for their undisciplined behaviour did they think I should be condemned for their murders? . . .

"I told them that Kurt Meyer meant nothing to me, but that after my examination of the evidence, I had decided to commute his sentence to life imprisonment and that only because I didn't have the guts to let him off entirely. Both 'Murch' and Massey agreed."

In Aurich, Kurt sat waiting to die. "I am astonished that death has lost its terror. Is this the result of the long years of war? Each morning when I hear those voices I throw a quick glance at the pictures of my family. . . . On January 13, the doors seem to clatter more loudly than ever and there is a certain restlessness in the corridors. A group stop in front of my cell.

"No doubt about it—this is it.

"Numbly, I listen to an officer read something to me. . . . I keep looking at the pictures, the men are of no interest. But suddenly the words 'life imprisonment' and 'Canada' are ringing in my ears. I need time to adjust, to comprehend the impact of events. No sooner have they gone than I sag onto my bed, completely baffled. I wasn't expecting this at all. But what a thing to look foward to—the rest of my life behind bars! Hours pass before I can come to grips with this new turn of events. . . .

"Then my life-force begins to reawaken and by afternoon I am making plans for the time after my release. I just can't imagine finishing my life off inside a prison."

Kate was helping Mrs. Snacker in the hotel kitchen when three Canadian officers appeared. She assumed that they had come with word of Kurt's execution, and her heart sank. But one gave her a big beatific smile. "Frau Meyer, your husband will not be shot. He is being sent to Canada!"

It was all she could do to keep from kissing the man. Kurt had asked for a huge photograph of her to take with him. Impossible. She looked a sight. Mrs. Snacker came to the rescue. Wearing Mrs. Snacker's best dress and blouse, Kate drove off in a jeep to have her picture taken by a local photographer. He promised to have it ready next morning in time for Kurt's departure. The officers paid him.

On the way home one of them placed a package on her lap. She assumed it was soap, tea or coffee. The Canadians were continuously handing the family presents. When she opened it back at the hotel, she found a letter inside and a box of chocolates. It read: "My Darling, you can have anything you want. You need only ask." Signed: "A Canadian Admirer."

How embarrassing!

Next day, as Kurt boarded an RCAF Dakota for the trip to England, her picture was delivered. A small one. The photographer had made two, but the larger one disappeared. Lifted, no doubt, by her "Canadian Admirer."

Kate was told that she could stay in Aurich at Canadian army expense while her son remained in hospital; then transport would be provided to carry them home to Offleben. Not exactly a happy ending, but much better than she had expected.

"15 January. . . . I fly in handcuffs to Reading, England. For the first time I enter the crowded confines of a jail, the same jail where Oscar Wilde served time and wrote his ballads. It is now a Canadian military prison and houses some hundred defectors and other offenders. During my first walk I jog along the walls tied to a sergeant. From him I learn that one of the buildings nearby has a gallows inside and that we are jogging over the bodies of the hanged. According to British law the convicted are buried under the prison pathways."

Back in Canada the media screamed for Kurt's blood: "Meyer's Commutation a Betrayal"; "Our Brave Canadian Dead Are Turning in Their Graves." It was an outrage to allow this notorious SS monster to escape the supreme penalty for his crimes. What must the families of the murdered soldiers think of Canadian government resolve? There were even rumours that the Meyer family would be coming to Canada at taxpayers' expense. Everyone knew that "life imprisonment" meant parole eligibility after only seven years. Thousands of outraged telegrams, letters, phone calls and resolutions of protest poured into Ottawa from across the country. Questions were asked in Parliament. Canadian Legion posts, municipal councils and civic groups went on record as opposing the commutation. So great was the volume of mail that the bureaucrats prepared 12 different form letters to provide adequate explanations to the objections being raised.

Frantic TOPSEC* telegrams zipped back and forth across the Atlantic. Ross Munro and Bill Boss, two of Canada's premier war correspondents, were invited to CMHQ in London for a "briefing." Brig. W.H.S. Macklin reported later to Ottawa that both supported the Vokes commutation and, like Vokes, considered the whole business "a nine-day wonder."

---

*Top Secret

Bruce Macdonald was a very unhappy man. He believed the verdict and sentence were just. Yet he had been the one who had drafted the regulations specifying a review of the court's findings by the Theatre Commander as an additional safeguard for the accused. Simonds had been the theatre commander at that time; but Vokes had replaced Simonds, and Vokes was too unconventional.

Wadi Lehmann thought that Macdonald looked angry. "To my embarrassment he kept saying: 'I'd like to know who worded that appeal!'" But Lehmann, happy that he and Plourde had been able to contribute toward saving Kurt's life, held his tongue.

Harry sailed on the *Queen Elizabeth* in early January. Mollie would follow later once he knew his next posting. Brig. Ian Johnston sailed with him. So did Winston Churchill. "He had been thrown out of office by an ungrateful British electorate to the complete bafflement of everybody except—presumably—the bloody English trade union movement who were now running the show. On the third night out I was asked to dine with the great man. I accepted and at the appointed hour presented myself properly dressed outside his suite of cabins on the upper promenade deck. . . .

"He greeted me effusively, bobbing like a jack-in-the-box and ushered me into his lounge. We had a drink. He was remarkably well informed on the Meyer affair and my part in it. Then it dawned on me that I was his only dinner guest. We discussed the postwar army. He believed that future wars would be won and lost through technology. I disagreed and told him so. 'You may have all the atomic bombs, Big Bertha artillery and heavy tanks you need to conquer the world, sir. But in the end it will be the section leader with his seven or eight men who finally decides each issue at the front.' He didn't like that one bit."

Nevertheless, next day Churchill sent a handwritten note thanking him for his ideas.

The ship docked in New York. A day's delay for connections to Ottawa. Harry and Johnston checked into the Astor Hotel and then went to the 21 Club. "During the evening Johnston became quite maudlin and kept telling me how lucky I was to be staying in while he returned to a dull law practice. . . . Judging by what was happening to the army I wasn't so sure he hadn't made the wiser choice."

He reported in at Ottawa to the new chief of the General Staff, Charles Foulkes, at National Defence HQ. "Foulkes was a consummate intriguer. He had managed to jump Guy in rank by coming home early to play Ottawa politics while Guy remained in command of the shrinking overseas army. It was a slick piece of manoeuvring on his part. He'd offered the job of QMG to Vokes in November 'to round out his army career,' as he put it. Chris turned him down flat. Now he offered it to me. I, likewise, declined, although for different reasons. Even if he was a horse's ass I didn't object to serving under him. I had served under worse horses' asses and survived.

"'Why not take the job?' he demanded.

"'Because I'm a field commander, not a paper pusher. I'm not a politician. I hate intrigue and I refuse to kiss any Ottawa asses.'

"'Then you'll go no higher in the army!' he warned.

"'I shall count on that, sir.'

"'But why?' He appeared genuinely surprised that everyone wouldn't want to try and become the goddam CGS or at least the vice-chief.

"'It might go to my head. Then look where I'd be!'"

Foulkes gave him a choice of GOC Central Command in Oakville, Ontario, or Eastern Command in Halifax. He picked Halifax. He wanted to go home.

News of Kurt's commutation brought "reporters down on me like clouds of angry black flies. Did I agree with Vokes's action—was Meyer really guilty—and other such nonsense. Later, when word came that CMHQ and Mr. Massey had approved what Chris had done the press returned. What did I think? I shrugged, 'I suppose they know what they're doing.' Not a very satisfactory reply, but all that I was prepared to give. From then on it was a political matter and out of my hands."

9

Before Harry settled in Halifax, Foulkes ordered him to preside over another trial, this one against a Canadian soldier. Mollie arrived from England and they took the train west to Winnipeg.

The accused, Company Sgt.-Maj. (Warrant Officer Class II) Marcus Charles Tugby of the Winnipeg Grenadiers, had been a member of Brig. J.K. Lawson's unhappy C Force that had arrived for garrison duty in Hong Kong three weeks before the Japanese attacked Pearl Harbor on 7 December 1941. The Japanese attack on Hong Kong began on 8 December.

For 12 days the island garrison held out, but at 1515 hours on Christmas Day, a white flag was raised. Canadian losses were 290 officers and men, who were either killed or died of wounds, including some gunned down while trying to surrender or after surrendering; 493 others were wounded. The victorious Japanese acted like barbarians—prisoners, the wounded, women and children were indiscriminately butchered according to whim. Those who survived went into a barbaric form of captivity. Sergeant-Major Tugby had been one of these. At war's end only 1,480 men of Lawson's original C Force returned to Vancouver. Once ashore, Tugby was arrested for collaborating with the enemy.

His trial got under way on 2 April at the Fort Osborne Barracks. Tugby faced 19 charges, three of stealing from Red Cross parcels belonging to other men, 15 of what amounted to common assault for striking various other prisoners with and without his captors' approval, and one charge of collaborating with the enemy.

"A conviction for collaborating carried the death penalty. But having just sentenced one man to death for murder I had no intentions of sentencing another—and a Canadian at that—simply for stealing chocolate bars out of Red Cross parcels to bribe his captors and socking a few people on the jaw. There was of course more to it than that. . . .

"The difficulty lay in trying to view the circumstances rationally. There is a world of difference between a man's perspective during his years in a Japanese POW camp and his outlook once he is released. Events that seemed terribly important—cried out for justice at the time—shrink to insignificance in the bright lights of freedom and common sense. As the witnesses came forward to testify against him I detected an embarrassed reluctance to press their testimony against the accused. I had no doubt that Tugby was a mean one. The type of clever opportunist who always rises to the top in adversity. He had been appointed by the internal camp administration to act as a go-between with the Japanese. But he had given away no military secrets to the enemy. Nor had he betrayed his fellow prisoners to them. He had entertained, eaten and drunk with them. But in the process he'd managed also to collect a few favours for himself and some of the other prisoners that made their lives more bearable. . . .

"The trial lasted a week. When it was over I decided the most he deserved was a slap on the wrists so I dismissed the major charges, threw out eight and gave him a severe reprimand on the others. A few years later British author, James Clavell, wrote a book called *King Rat*. The principal character was a dead ringer for Tugby."

Harry hadn't seen his sons since 1943. They were still at boarding school outside Vernon, B.C. When the trial ended he telephoned the Headmaster and asked him to put the boys on the next train to Winnipeg. Mollie went with him to the station. For two years she had been writing to them and they to her. Sunday letters to parents, including stepparents, was a school regulation. Theirs had been formal and stilted while hers had been chatty and filled with stories about her own children, domestic problems and social activities—nothing that would interest two young lads who already regarded her with deep suspicion. A chasm existed between them. The first meeting did little to narrow the gap.

"I don't think I'm going to like you!" she told Harry's eldest, who at 13 stood nearly six foot. "You're already a head taller than me."

Their relationship deteriorated rapidly. A week later they were all back in Halifax waiting to move into the 150-year-old, but newly renovated, GOC's residence at Royal Artillery Park. It would be their home for the next five years. After Easter holidays the boys were off again to boarding school, this time to the same King's College School in Windsor, N.S., where Harry and Gil had gone 30 years before.

Back in London and still smarting from Vokes's commutation, Macdonald was handed another senior prosecutor's job by CMHQ, this time against a Canadian officer. Charges had been laid by General Simonds against the head of his HQ Administration Staff, Brig. J.F.A. Lister, for "misappropriation of army goods"—in other words, graft.

Macdonald flew over to Holland for the case. "It was the damnedest thing I ever got myself into. Lister had requisitioned an enormous apartment in Amsterdam, set himself up a full supply of coal and food, a private plane, three cars, three servants and someone else's wife. He was being defended by a pricey British barrister. Brig. Sparling and some noncombatant generals were on the Board. . . . Several immaculate British generals with smart salutes and beautifully tailored uniforms gave evidence on his behalf. The way they talked you would have thought we couldn't have won the war without Lister. Although he'd never seen any action he had managed to cover himself with medals, grabbing at any gong that was going through channels. Finally, Gen. Simonds slouched into the room sneering at everybody. As the most senior officer present he obviously had little use for those at the table, with the exception of Sparling. His testimony was delivered in a patronizing manner which infuriated the Board. . . .

"When it was over the Members took 20 minutes to find Lister 'not guilty.' Dejectedly, I phoned CMHQ in London and told them the verdict. To my astonishment the Duty Officer, a Colonel, replied 'Good show!' I hung up and went across the street to the officers' mess where Lister was celebrating with champagne for everybody. Next day the *London Express* ran a caption: 'Canadian Brigadier Acquitted. Entertains Court at Champagne Party!' . . . The matter was brought up in the House of Commons where I was accused of complicity in the acquittal. . . . That was the final straw. I told CMHQ that I'd had enough. I wanted out before any more bright ideas for prosecuting turned up."

A few weeks later he arrived home in civilian clothes to practise law in Windsor, Ontario.

With Reading Gaol returned to British civilian authority, Kurt moved to a barbed-wire enclosure at Hedley Downs near Aldershot. "I am well housed, even allowed to tend a small garden and sun bathe. The guards are all veterans who fought against me. For the first time I hear the reaction to my pardon by the Canadian public."

Near the end of April orders arrived transferring him to Canada. He was dressed in the uniform of a Canadian private and taken at night to Southampton where he boarded the Cunard liner *Aquitania*. The ship was filled with war brides and their children. He stayed in a cell until the vessel cleared port, then was released and given the run of the ship.

"One day a senior officer approaches while I am playing cards with my guards. He says: 'Hey, boys, don't make such a noise. Let the German general sleep.' We are all silent. He doesn't know he is standing in front of him. . . . Nobody recognizes the Nazi-Beast. . . . Some miles off the Canadian coast I'm put in my cell again. I am told of possible public reaction: a drowning in Halifax Harbour is not the worst of ways to eliminate me. . . . Thousands of people are on hand to welcome the brides. There are speeches. A band plays inside the terminal."

Harry met him as he came down the gangway. "To prevent an incident I gave instructions that Meyer was to depart the ship unescorted and without handcuffs then climb into a waiting car. If he decided to run I was satisfied he wouldn't go far before the Provost Marshal had him collared. . . . He came down the crew gangway and caught sight of me as he stepped ashore. For a moment we stared at each other. I wanted to say something appropriate but couldn't find the right words. Did I detect a tinge of amusement in those milk-blue eyes? He nodded his head to me, as he had done so many times in court, then squared his shoulders and marched to the car. I never saw him again."

He was taken to the Halifax Citadel, fed, then driven on to Dorchester Penitentiary. "We finish our ride across the Nova Scotian peninsula at 0400 hours and reach Dorchester prison. The big building towers over the Bay of Fundy; a depressing mass of stone and steel. Everybody stops talking. I feel that I am attending my own funeral. My guards salute and depart. . . .

"I am handed some old rags and just manage to save my orthopedic shoes. Afterwards, I am led past cell after cell of interlocking cages, until placed in one of my own. There are no cell doors, only bars. Prisoners never know refreshing darkness—there are always lights and a perpetually revolting smell. . . .

"Next day I get my hair cut. The barber is not impressed by my sentence. He got 20 years for murdering his uncle. I'm glad once my beard is off and his razor leaves my throat. I am given a number 2265 on my chest. I fume with rage. From now on I am only a number. My left cell-mate is a criminal, in prison, with the odd interruption, since 1917. He has a life sentence now for burning seven people alive. The one on my right raped his own daughter. . . . I will never forget this shame. This is more a criminal training school for young offenders than a place for rehabilitation. . . .

"After 4 weeks I am made librarian. My boss, J.E.L. Papineau was an Air Force officer. His attitude is excellent. The newspaper is filled with propaganda about me. But I realize that the public's opinion about my sentence and that of the soldiers is different. . . .

"In the summer the first letter from my family arrives. They are existing on only $25 per month welfare. Their sufferings are hard for me to bear. I owe so much to Dr. Schapp, the lawyer. My wife had a complete breakdown and is in hospital with a heart condition. Schapp paid all her expenses. My mother has to support the whole family now. . . .

"The days pass . . . one like the other."

As did Harry's. The duties of a peacetime GOC were mostly ceremonial and illusionary. He managed to persuade Scott Murdoch to stay in the army and join him again as his GSO1, but once the administration and the reams of paperwork were in Murdoch's capable hands, he found little for himself to do of any real value.

He inspected. Oh how he inspected! He visited militia units in every Maritime province, high school cadet corps, bases that were closing or (as in the case of Camp Utopia*) expanding, married quarters, officers' quarters, enlisted men's quarters, abandoned forts and other Department of National Defence buildings. He met civic officials, shook hands with mayors and aldermen, kissed mothers and babies, presented ribbons, plaques and awards, and graciously accepted the same from innumerable admirers of the military.

He stopped at each place long enough to make a short stirring speech, modestly acknowledge the tributes to his "heroic accomplishments" from whoever introduced him, then take a "march past salute." This would be followed by a few stories swapped in the officers' mess before driving on to his next pointless appointment. Everybody regarded him as a hero and that galled him. "There is nothing more useless than a general without a war," he observed ruefully to Murdoch.

Halifax retained the same insular outlook that he remembered as a boy. Its population remained divided equally between Protestants and Catholics, with an invisible but real social barrier between the two. Halifax's social life also was divided between a garrison mentality arising from the navy and military establishments that had existed without interruption since 1749 and a peninsular mentality of the "South End" where the Establishment and its wealth resided. His position permitted him to bridge the two.

Local businessmen invited him to join the prestigious Halifax Club, but unlike his father, he had no head for business and found it "all dreadfully dull." After three visits of listening to "money and business shop-talk" he never went back. The Press Club was more to his liking. Halifax newspapermen were notoriously hard drinkers with the sort of acerbic wit and cynicism he enjoyed. Harry liked to drink and laugh. He began drinking a little too much, although he never staggered or slurred his words. His new life of social indolence took its toll. His weight began climbing. Eventually he had to buy a full set of new uniforms.

---

*Known now as Camp Gagetown, New Brunswick.

He acquired an eclectic circle of friends, oddballs like himself who suffered no delusions about their own grandeur. The provincial premier, Angus L. Macdonald, the lieutenant-governor of Nova Scotia, J.A.D. McCurdy of *Silver Dart* fame, Sidney Oland, head of the brewery family, and wealthy industrialist Jack MacKeen were among the regular dinner guests in the house at Royal Artillery Park.

His cousin, Jim Wickwire, was on his way to becoming deputy minister of highways; a younger cousin, Bill Wickwire, had become one of the city's most prominent lawyers. And there were the cousins, aunts and uncles still living in the Annapolis Valley to remind him of his roots. Mollie found them "a parochial and rather simple-minded lot but pleasant enough on the whole." They in turn tolerated her but only because of Harry.

Then there were the official garrison social activities. He entertained visiting naval squadrons, field marshals and generals in transit, and ministers of the Crown stumping for publicity. And they in turn entertained him. His private life resolved itself gradually into a succession of endless cocktail and dinner parties. He bought himself a 38-foot schooner and named it the "Mollie F." On summer Sundays he played Captain Bligh to his sons and listened to Mollie carp about the smell of canvas, fish and seawater.

Field Marshal Montgomery passed through the city on a whirlwind tour. There was no practical purpose to his visit other than to collect whatever cheers were still available for his spectacular wartime accomplishments. He was another lost general looking for a battle.

"You've grown soft and fat, Foster," he snapped.

Wearily, Harry agreed. At 60 and a teetotaler, Monty still retained his lithe wartime figure, while Harry's new "stout" uniforms were already beginning to bulge. Throughout his three-day stay Monty was alternately bored or rude to nearly everyone with whom he came in contact.

"Fortunately the citizens of Halifax were too enthralled by his presence to notice. After three days of listening to him pontificate on every subject under the sun I finally got a chance to shut him up. A motorcade through downtown Halifax had been laid on for his final day. He insisted on a convertible. I arranged one through a local dealer. The weather was sunny and warm. Halfway along Barrington Street with the crowds screaming in our ears he caught sight of the 'Tattoed Man,' a local character who had had himself ferociously tattooed from head to foot. Monty stopped waving and sat down. 'Foster! Did you see what I saw?'

"'It's a Newfoundland Beothuck,'[3] I told him with a perfectly straight face. 'Very rare. In fact they're practically extinct.'

"'Oh really, why?'

"'We hunt them here in season. They're not allowed on the mainland. This one must have slipped through.'"

Field Marshal, the Viscount Montgomery of Alamein K.G., believed him.

10

During the cold drizzling night of 15/16 October 1946, the condemned leaders of Nazi Germany met their end on the gallows erected in a Nuremberg gymnasium—all save one. Flamboyant and master of his destiny to the end, Göring escaped the unbearable ignominy of the noose by biting the cyanide capsule he had retrieved from his luggage thanks to the magnanimity of an American officer—three hours before he was due to mount the scaffold.

From 0100 hours on 16 October, the remaining ten were taken in handcuffs from their cells, along the corridor . . . the trap sprung.

The former foreign minister, Joachim von Ribbentrop, was the first to be executed, followed by Field Marshal Keitel, and the next to last, Col.-Gen. Alfred Jodl, who exited with a quiet: "I greet you, oh you my Germany.'" They died unrepentant, reaffirming their faith in Germany or angrily denouncing Allied justice.

As a final precaution against any shrines or places for Nazi pilgrimage, the bodies were driven to Dachau that same day and, in a final irony, cremated in the ovens that Himmler and Heydrich had thought so necessary to prevent the corruption of the German people.

The numbers of condemned German leaders who were executed after the war were but a fraction of those who died in the war—936 generals, colonel-generals, field marshals and admirals fell in action or perished in captivity during the conflict. Of that number 96 were suicides who preferred death to falling into enemy hands or a certain slow murder in prison. Only three armed forces generals (Field Marshal Wilhelm Keitel, Col.-Gen. Alfred Jodl and Gen. Anton Dostler) were executed by the Western Allies. Many more generals and senior officers were executed in Russia and what were to become the Eastern Bloc countries under Soviet control.

Guy Simonds accepted an appointment as chief instructor at the Imperial Defence College in London. Chris Vokes returned home with the Canadian occupation forces to become GOC Central Command. The elegant Churchill Mann was posted to National Defence HQ in Ottawa. Always a little strange, he went through a physical fitness craze and ordered a rope ladder installed outside his office window, which he used to enter and leave the building each day.

Mann, a cavalryman at heart, sent Harry a signal through military channels asking support in his application for government fodder to feed his horses at the vast "View Hulloa" farms north of Toronto, owned by his wife. In a national emergency, he explained, the horses would be made available to the government.

Harry replied over the same communications network: "Dear Church. Will support fodder for your horses if you agree to support government mooring for my schooner. 'Mollie F' available to Royal Canadian Navy in event of national emergency. Harry."

Foulkes received copies of both signals. He was not amused.

Kurt settled into the Dorchester routine. He was allowed to write two letters a month home. Like those sent to him from Germany, they were forwarded to Ottawa for translation before delivery.

He wrote Kate: "From my window I can see the adjoining forest, the water and the town of Dorchester. Life on the farm and the trains that are passing make me dream of the future. The treatment here is perfectly correct and conscientious, good food and plentiful. For the time being I am learning the language and Canadian history."

A few weeks later, looking from the same window, he could "watch the men working in the fields and I think often of our walks on which we talked to our children about the great wonders of nature. I yearn for a plow and a horse and the smell of good earth. Do you remember when we helped Fritz bring in the rye crop, the day on which our Inge walked for the first time? Yes, my dear, we have had happy days together. I can scarcely believe that we have been living apart from each other several years now. My dear Kate, continue to be my brave comrade."

He wrote to Colonel Andrew, thanking him for his help, assuring him that he felt no ill will. "I greet you in the certainty that our peoples and our Nations will one day work and agree together against communism."

He sent a long letter to Guy Simonds asking that his case be reopened. He wrote to the Canadian Minister of Justice, the Red Cross, Dr. Schapp and to Harry. It was still too soon to be asking for a reassessment. Passions needed time to cool. The old front-line soldiers understood, but they were only 15 percent of the armed forces. It was the others, the ones who never saw or smelled the smoke of battle, the self-anointed champions of justice, who were still muttering for his blood.

Each month Maj. James R. Millar, the senior Protestant chaplain from Eastern Command, dropped by to see him. It became a ritual. The prison chaplain sat in on these visits. Millar always began by telling Kurt that Harry sent his greetings. Was there anything he needed? Any complaints? Any way the army could be of help? Besides an obvious desire for freedom he worried constantly about his family. Millar promised to keep in touch. Kurt offered to help the Canadian military in any way that he could. He missed being among his own kind. Some project where his talents might be of use, perhaps? Millar promised to pass the request along through channels.

His German-accented English became fluent, but although he got on well with the prison staff and other inmates, he remained a loner with few close associates. Most of the other 400 prisoners looked up to him. Dr. Millen, a dentist from New Glasgow, N.S., became his best friend. In Kurt's opinion the justice of Millen's conviction for performing an abortion seemed as big a travesty of justice as his own. Jack MacLean, a former mayor of Sydney, N.S., was another friend. MacLean had murdered his wife. He worked as prison gardener.

Sitting near one of MacLean's flowerbeds, Kurt discussed his philosophy of mercy killing with them one afternoon. Ralph Seymour, another inmate, sat in on the discussion."Was there ever justification for a killing? That was the question. Meyer stared at the seagulls wheeling back and forth above the prison's stone walls. He said the German people were like gulls, industrious and energetic. In life that was what mattered. 'Have you ever seen a sick or lazy gull?' he asked. Nature planned for the survival of the fittest. He quoted the Bible and Moses leading only the fittest out of Egypt. That same sort of superiority applied to all the races of the earth, he claimed. Germany had been superior because it was prepared to exterminate the misfits, idiots, the handicapped and loafers. 'In Germany we used common criminals to clear minefields instead of risking valuable sheep and dogs,' he told us. He predicted that Canada would one day find itself in the same position as Germany before Hitler came to power, where 20 industrious citizens were forced to support 60 loafers."

Gene Hattie, an ex-RCAF medic, ran the prison hospital. He knew Kurt as well as anyone on staff. The hospital wing, located on the third floor of the central building, consisted of five six-by-nine cells on either side of a corridor which "were larger than the cells used by the rest of the prison population. Each contained a table and chair and a comfortable hospital type bed. In addition to treating illnesses the hospital was used for prisoners whose lives might be in jeopardy for one reason or another. They lived in the hospital until their problem was settled or they were transferred to other prisons. The warden, Col. George Goad,* had wanted Meyer segregated in case of trouble with other prisoners. It turned out to be a non-problem and Meyer, since he had settled in, was allowed to remain in a hospital cell throughout his stay. . . .

"He went about his business quietly, always polite with everyone. If one of the guards gave him a hard time he was courteous but firm, coming to attention 'Boom!' then, speaking reasonably without raising his voice. Only once was there an incident when he bowed very low to a guard that was harassing him. The staff sided with Meyer. The guard received a reprimand. . . . He spent an hour each day in the yard walking. A solitary grey denim figure marching quickstep like a toy soldier, his shoulders and back very erect, head held high. He had a slight build and although was generally very healthy,

---

*Formerly Provost marshal of the Canadian army.

complained periodically of rheumatism from his time on the Russian Front.
. . .

"Most of his free time he spent in his cell writing letters. He was very
proud of his family, especially his son. Their photographs were always on
the table. 'They are what I live for, Mr. Hattie, only them.' His general attitude
seemed rather distant. Yet I enjoyed talking with him. He was a stern
professional soldier, the sort of natural leader who men would follow. I liked
him. . . . It was impossible not to like him."

A new prison chaplain, Lorne Baker, arrived in 1948. He found to his
surprise that Kurt held deep religious beliefs. "Not so much in a personal
God as in the idea of an all Supreme Creator. He didn't attend church every
Sunday but when he did I made certain that the hymn 'Glorious Things
of Thee Are Spoken' was never played. Its tune was the same as the Austrian
Anthem . . . . I didn't think it was fair to him to play that. . . . As a former
army chaplain I found his appraisal of the forces he fought against interesting.
The Russians were the most ferocious; the Germans the best in the world
and the Canadians a close second. The Americans came in at the bottom
of his list . . . no guts and poorly organized. Take away their equipment
and they were nothing. . . .

"We played mind games whenever he dropped into the chapel office for
a talk. He'd come on to me about the Americans' carpet-bombing Germany.
Then I reminded him of London and Coventry. He would become agitated,
'Yes, but when we bombed a railway station or yard we hit the yard and
station. The Americans smashed the whole town.' I agreed. 'Yes, but they
did win the war.' His face would redden and he'd leave. A day or two later
he'd be back with a grin. . . . 'You caught me again!'"

Baker lived in Moncton across the road from Fritz and Ina Lichtenberg.
Fritz came from Niegripp on the river Elbe but had grown up and served
his carpenter's apprenticeship in Magdeburg, 24 miles east of Offleben. He
had emigrated in 1911, married a Canadian and become a successful general
contractor. The Lichtenbergs were comfortably retired with several houses
when the story of Kurt's trial appeared in the *Moncton Transcript*. Always
an active man and stoutly proud of his German heritage, he found the
combination of media hysteria, news photos of Kate, Alma and Ursula in
Aurich, the town of Offleben, and finally Kurt's arrival at Dorchester too
much of an enticement to resist. Fritz resolved to help the Meyer family
in any way he could.

The Lichtenbergs were childless. They decided to adopt the Meyers. First
they tried visiting Kurt, claiming to be relatives. While this was being
investigated, Fritz wrote Kurt letters, signing them "Onkel" Fritz. His wife
became "Mother" Ina. Each month they mailed packages of coffee, presents,
cigarettes, clothing, food and money overseas to Kate and the children. He
began looking for a good lawyer to reopen the case. For the first time since

his capture in Belgium five years before, Kurt's spirits rose.

Finally, Lichtenberg received permission to visit his "nephew." His first words were: "Ach, dear Kurt!" to which Kurt replied solemnly: "Ach, dear Onkel Fritz!"

"He fights stubbornly for a permit to visit me. After a long while we finally meet and utter German words. We are both nearly overcome by the emotion. He shows me pictures of my children and tells me the latest news. I am to be allowed to see him now every four weeks with Maj. Millar."

Lichtenberg's letters to Kate were a joy of deceit and encouragement. "Today I visited our mutual friend. I looked like a pregnant virgin. Everything was hidden in my pockets—letters, chocolate, food. His spirits are good."

The stalwart burghers of Bruges invited Harry to come back to Belgium and celebrate their liberation and honour the dead who had made it possible. In a touching gesture they had named a canal bridge for the Canadians. Two life-sized buffalo sculptures flanked its approaches, emblems of the 12th Manitoba Dragoons, the first troops to enter the city on 12 September 1944 after the German Area Commander had agreed to pull out.

Harry received the red carpet treatment. The Canadian Ambassador, CGS of the Belgian army, old soldiers and members of the Underground all turned out to cheer. Harry delivered a brief but stirring speech at the unveiling of the bridge. When it ended, he was presented with a 20-pound sterling silver buffalo as a memento and an official parchment scroll giving him the Freedom of the City. "After which everybody retired to the Great Hall of the Ancient Order of Archers of the Society of San Sebastian for drinks and dinner."

A few months later, on 8 January 1948, word arrived from Whitehorse in the Yukon that Gilbert Lafayette Foster had died from exposure "while lost in dense bush . . . while prospecting." The only identification the RCMP found on the body was a letter from a Mrs. H.H. Wickwire in Kentville that included a return address. Aunt Sarah telephoned Harry.

"I wanted to weep for him. A brother should weep for a brother. But I couldn't. He had wasted his life. I felt only pity and a little anger over his passing. . . . At least he had the good grace to die sober."

Facts surrounding Gil's death, he uncovered later. His brother had been on a drunk for several weeks. Sick, broke and alone, he had taken a steam bath to clean himself up and immediately afterwards—and apparently sober—had gone out into the –55 degree temperature to borrow money from a friend to buy a meal. A short distance from town he collapsed along the side of the road and had frozen. He was 44.

Harry's heavy smoking, lack of exercise and high blood pressure finally caught up to him. One evening during a dinner party a blood clot suddenly formed in his left leg—phlebitis, the same malady that had killed his father.

The doctors ordered him to diet, sleep with both legs elevated, switch from hard liquor to wine and stop smoking. He returned home wearing an elastic stocking "like some goddam Piccadilly whore." He wore it the rest of his life.

He faced other problems too. Mollie kept after him to leave the army and return to England where "people were more civilized and less pushy." A British block on sterling transfers abroad had prevented her from enjoying the luxuries of life in Canada to the degree she believed still possible in England. "Here I'm nothing but a pauper!" she wailed. Harry nodded sympathetically.

Mollie and his eldest son Tony clashed continuously. They were too much alike, neither prepared to give an inch in any discussion. Finally, one New Year's Eve after a terrible donnybrook resulting from her refusal to allow him to go out on a date with his school friends, he packed his clothes and left. Harry was in tears as his 16-year-old son went out the door. "For God's sake, write if you need anything." He did write, although he never returned and never asked him for anything.

Near the end of his Halifax tour of duty, Premier Macdonald offered Harry the post of lieutenant-governor of the province to replace the retiring J.A.D. McCurdy. It would have been a nice capstone to his career, but he turned it down. There wasn't enough money being provided by the province to support the official residence and its staff and cover the four years of socializing expected from whoever took the job. Nor did he think his health would stand it. Instead, he opted for a two-year appointment in Brussels, heading the Canadian section of the Imperial War Graves Commission.

"We left over 45,000 Canadian dead behind us in Europe from two world wars. Being able to do something that made certain those lives would be remembered for all time seemed a hell of a lot more useful than what I was doing in Halifax. . . . The army no longer held the same attraction. I was bored with it all."

Others remained. Guy Simonds returned home to become commandant of the National Defence College and Canadian Army Staff College in Kingston. When the Korean War started, Brig. J.M. Rockingham was appointed to lead Canada's contingent across the Pacific to assist in the United Nations "police action." Charles Foulkes transferred the outspoken Chris Vokes to GOC Western Command, where he remained until his retirement. Then, in 1951 Foulkes moved up to the newly created post of "chairman of the Joint Chiefs of Staff" to make room for Simonds, who belatedly assumed his rightful position as chief of the General Staff. He held the post until his retirement.

11

There were emotional problems among the Meyer family as well. The years of destitution, living together in confined quarters and trying to survive without proper food, clothing or medical attention, were taking their toll. Ursula became a teenager.

"Mother and Oma have lots of quarrels. We divide up the flat and I belong to Oma. One day Mother takes my brother and sisters and leaves. They go to stay with my mother's cousin in Bodenteich. . . . Another letter from Father. There is a picture on the envelope and a motto 'Joy is everything.' The same motto as our school. The coloured picture is nice—but joy? There is no joy, not even when Mother and sisters suddenly return. She couldn't stay with the aunt. But she doesn't faint because of her heart troubles anymore.

"We get care packages from Father's comrades. An unknown lady from Canada sends us things. Anyone with something extra passes it along." The unknown lady in Canada was a Mrs. Ham from Napanee, Ontario. In a letter sent to Kate at Aurich during the trial she offered to help. Kate accepted. Over the years a steady stream of food packages and presents—children's skates, face powder, lipstick, handbags, dresses and winter clothing—arrived.

"Father writes to me again. . . . He is not here but still with us. We ask each other all the time: 'What would Daddy say?' In each letter he tells us to obey Mother and Oma, they know what is best for us. Consequently no one complains when Irmtraud is given away to relatives. She is only seven. . . .

"Not only grandparents' farm is in the Russian zone but also the farm of mother's brother who was killed in action. Aunt Hedwig writes that one of us can spend the summer holidays there. Inge doesn't want to cross the border so it is me again. I am glad. Mother says: 'You are so thin and pale, a change from the polluted air here will do you good.' No question for Oma: 'I'll get you there.'"

Alma brazened her way past the border guards and Ursula spent a quiet four-week holiday with her Aunt Hedwig in Lüffingen. When time came for school, Alma returned to collect her, once more talking her way back into the Western zone.

"Oma would like to work again. She has asthma and coughs a lot and really can't work although she wants to. She gets only a small pension and Mother, only welfare support. We collect signatures on a petition and send it to the local Health Authorities at Helmstedt."

Late in 1948 life became a bit easier for everyone. "We have enough food vouchers now and are also raising a pig, a sheep, rabbits and chickens. There are regular meals at school. In spring our youngest sister returns. It is difficult to cross the border but an uncle who works in the coal mine hid her in a mine train. These little trains still cross. We are glad to be together again. Irmtraud visits us from Aunty sometimes. Father writes: 'Next year I'll be with you.' We know that Onkel Fritz works hard for him, so we keep waiting. . . .

"Oma gets a message. She is allowed to work again as a midwife, but in Grasleben, another village. She rides her push bike many miles around to the scattered villages delivering babies. . . . Another long year passes. Oma has a bigger flat and I move in with her. Mother says: 'One of us has to go with Oma. We must not leave her alone.' Father writes too: 'I am in good spirits and never without hope.' Why is he still there? Why do I have to leave Mother and sisters again?"

Fritz Lichtenberg sailed for Germany in May 1951. Kate met the boat and brought him home to meet the family. His avuncular manner impressed Ursula.

Lichtenberg had hired H.P. MacKeen,* one of the best—and most expensive—lawyers in the Maritimes. After examining the case and corresponding with Kurt, MacKeen was aghast at the injustice of his family separation and continued incarceration. Even common Canadian criminals were allowed to serve their sentences in prisons close to home and family. He investigated the rules and methods under which the trial had been conducted and found them repugnant and contrary to the basic concepts of jurisprudence. Other war criminals, convicted by the British and Americans, were serving their sentences in Germany, were being given time off for good behaviour and paroled. The war was over. It was time to forgive.

MacKeen started by sounding out Harry before he left Halifax to take up his Brussels posting. MacKeen was blunt: "For you to set yourself up as a judge is about as absurd as me trying to lead an armoured division into battle."

Harry shrugged. "I agree. But then no one ordered you to sit as judge, did they?" But he did agree that Kurt should be released.

"Isn't there something the army can do? After all, he's still a soldier."

"You think we should draft him?"

It was MacKeen's turn to shrug. "You could do worse."

Harry promised to see what he could arrange.

Next, MacKeen tackled the Maritime provinces' attorneys-general for allowing such injustice to exist within their jurisdictions. They replied that it was a federal not a provincial matter, which it was. "By any chance did you gentlemen enjoy tearing the wings off flies when you were children?" MacKeen taunted. To get him off their backs, they promised to write Ottawa suggesting a review of the case. MacKeen was astute enough to know that politicians reacted only to public pressure. He enlisted an assortment of old

---

*MacKeen later became lieutenant-governor of Nova Scotia.

soldiers, newspaper reporters, and broadcasters to the cause while he remained discreetly in the background. The pot started to bubble.

Dalton Dean, one of Macdonald's assistant prosecutors in Aurich, gave a hometown interview stating that Kurt should never have been convicted. CBC Radio ran a special 30-minute feature on the case. Soldiers who had fought against the 12th SS praised its fighting qualities and Kurt's leadership. Legion members began to have second thoughts about what had happened. Feature stories about Kurt appeared in newspapers across the country. The matter came up in the House of Commons. Gradually, pressure began building.

Harry sounded out Foulkes in Ottawa about using Kurt in some military role. This idea was prompted as much from practical considerations as compassion for a former enemy. After years of documented observations, interrogations and interviews in England, Aurich and Dorchester, the army knew exactly what sort of man it had sitting in prison. It knew his capabilities and his limitations.

Kurt had prepared pages of unsolicited tactical recommendations for the Canadian army based on his experience fighting the Russians. From memory he drew detailed maps of various campaigns, citing the errors and omissions on both sides. Everything he produced was turned over to Major Millar and delivered to Harry. After reading the material, Harry passed it on to National Defence HQ in Ottawa. Before long NDHQ staff officers began arriving at Dorchester for private discussions with Kurt. They left marvelling at his talents. For three years this bizarre state of affairs continued.

The army accepted his Nazi outlook; that could never change. Yet he remained apolitical, with no ambitions except freedom. Newspaper suggestions that he could become a new German Führer were nonsense. After a lifetime of hardship his physical powers were already deteriorating. A staff officer like Lieut.-Gen. Hans Speidel was a much more likely candidate to head the new German army than a battlefield commander and convicted war criminal with arthritis, bad kidneys, high blood pressure and an orthopedic shoe. Yet, in Harry's view, "whatever else he may have been, he remained first and always a soldier, with a soldier's sense of honour . . . a first-class front-line commander." Why not use that brilliance while it was still available if it would help get him home to his family?

Foulkes agreed. The question was where to use him? And how to manage it in complete secrecy?

Since the Berlin Blockade of 1948 the Soviet Union had become the bogeyman. Canada held the middle ground in the Cold War between two antagonists. A very real fear existed that Russia would invade the U.S. over the pole. Between the Atlantic and Pacific oceans, 125 miles south of the Arctic Circle, a solitary road—the Alaska Highway—connected Fairbanks, Alaska, to the American heartland. It stretched like a tenuous umbilical cord southeast for nearly 300 miles to the Yukon border, then beyond for another

1,000 miles to Whitehorse, Watson Lake and Fort Nelson until it reached Dawson Creek and the rail link south. The Americans had built it during the war. In the event of hostilities the Canadians were expected to help defend it. Essential to the highway's defence were its bridge crossings. The Canadian army was to fight a delaying action at each until the Americans could airlift men and equipment from the south. Johnsons Crossing at Teslin Lake, the Donjack, the White and several other major rivers were considered key positions and designated as "stop lines" in the event of an overland invasion.

Viewed from the uneasy truce of "Mutually Assured Destruction" by nuclear missiles less than 35 minutes from either continent, tactical considerations such as bridge crossings appear superfluous. But in the late 1940s, before the DEW Line and the thousands of intercontinental ballistic missiles with their multiple warheads, this was state-of-the-art defence.

Brig. John Proctor, Harry's fighting DA* and QMG at 4th Armoured Division, had returned to Calgary after the war to his civilian job in the petroleum business. He remained in the militia, however. Early in 1949 Charles Foulkes and George Kitching, his brigadier of staff planning, visited Proctor in Calgary. They asked him to take command of the 19th Alberta Dragoons, now equipped with new scout cars. One of its duties was defence of the Alaska Highway. Proctor accepted. It sounded like fun.

"Summer militia training exercises consisted of patrolling the Highway and scouting for likely defensive positions along the route. The second year we took over the best hotel in Whitehorse for a few weeks to use as our staff HQ. We divided into four six-man syndicates and were told to come up with ideas for defending the 'stop lines.' . . .

"At the first morning's coffee break I suggested to Kitching that the man we really needed to advise us was Kurt Meyer. I remembered how brilliantly he had thwarted every crossing we tried to make in Normandy. Meyer positioned troops up and down each river in a certain way, covering the approaches with enfilading fire in all directions. Then, after the attack, he would retreat and redeploy on the other bank, where once again he had the attackers by the short hairs. He was a genius at defending a river line from the front end.

"'Who do you think that guy is on your syndicate?' Kitching replied.

"'Meyer?'

"'Meyer,' he confirmed. 'We got him out of the hoosegow but for Christ sakes don't tell anybody! We had one hell of a job getting him! He's given his word of honour not to escape.'"

Kurt, wearing Canadian army battledress and sporting lieutenant's pips on his shoulders, had been introduced as a French Canadian. He remained with the syndicate four weeks before returning to Dorchester. His appraisal

---

*Deputy adjutant.

for defence of the river crossings ultimately became the plan that was adopted by the Canadian army.

The payoff for this cooperation and MacKeen's clever lobbying came on 17 October 1951. The prison's chief-keeper stopped him on the way to his cell, wanting to know his hat size. An hour later he came before Warden Goad and was told that he would be leaving at dawn by air for Germany.

"I spent a sleepless night. . . . The hours crept by slowly. Thank God I had Churchill's memoirs to read. I read the volume where he justified his order to destroy German sea-rescue planes. It shortened the night. At five in the morning I marched up and down my cell. Nobody came. At 0630 hours I got my breakfast and went to work. Disappointed, I looked across the Bay of Fundy where the white sails vanished towards Nova Scotia—like my dreams."

The delay had been due only to fog at Moncton airport. After lunch he was ordered to be ready to leave within the hour. He packed his few belongings, including an inscribed English-German dictionary with his initials embossed on the cover, given to him by the prisoners. Another Canadian army uniform was provided, and after shaking hands with the staff, he left by car for Halifax. That same evening at the Shearwater Naval Air Station he boarded an RCAF transport aircraft for Germany.

"Over Holland the Captain was ordered to divert to Wünstorf instead of Bückeburg because of fog. We overshot the runway and crash-landed, breaking off the landing gear. Nevertheless, I am glad to be home on German soil again."

The air force entertained him at their officers' mess until his escort arrived from Bückeburg. The officers had all seen action in Caen and congratulated him on the accuracy of his infantry's ground fire. After 60 hours without sleep and the better part of two bottles of whisky he felt no pain when the car arrived to take him to military prison at Werl, ten miles east of Dortmund. Its civilian driver, a former Wehrmacht corporal, was personal chauffeur to Colonel Vickers, the British camp commandant. How times had changed! At Werl he joined other imprisoned military leaders—Field Marshal Kesselring and Generals Mackensen, Gallenkamp and Falkenhorst. "I was relieved to be serving under soldiers once more."

12

In some ways Werl turned out to be a much more brutal place than Dorchester. Although under British jurisdiction, the place was staffed mostly by Germans. They were neither pleasant nor accommodating and took themselves far too seriously. A few days later Kurt saw Kate and his mother for the first time in six years. Not a satisfactory reunion. They met facing each other across a wide table with a guard standing over them. No touching was allowed. He went back to his quarters depressed.

Near the end of November, Colonel Vickers accepted Kurt's word of honour not to escape and granted him ten days' compassionate leave. He borrowed a suit and left at once for Offleben. He was astounded by the change in his children. Young Kurt, badly spoiled by his mother and sisters, ruled the roost. Two days before he was due back some Canadian officers returning from behind the "Iron Curtain" stopped off at the flat for a visit and to see if Kate needed anything. Douglas How, a Canadian reporter, accompanied them. His subsequent sensational article about meeting Kurt at home in the bosom of his family while supposedly serving a life sentence in a British prison caused an outcry in Canada. How had carefully omitted the logical explanation.

Despite this furor, MacKeen observed with some satisfaction that the "pro" and "con" Meyer forces in Canada were now about evenly matched. Having managed successfully to get his client out of the country, he pushed next for a reduction of sentence. That had to come from the federal government on recommendation of the Canadian army. Discreetly, MacKeen went to work on the problem. Kurt went back to Werl.

Harry did not like Brussels one bit. "A European counterpart to Ottawa, filled with self-satisfied bureaucrats and political intrigue." To the industrious Belgians the war was now an event to be honoured and revered on appropriate national occasions—like Waterloo—but no longer requiring constant acknowledgment.

When Harry moved into a fashionable flat on Rue Paul Emil Jason, he assumed that past honours bestowed upon him by the Belgians would entitle him at least to some recognition. But fame, he discovered to his chagrin, was at best a fleeting affair. His Freedom of the City of Bruges meant nothing unless he intended using the city's public transport. Tradesmen and shop-keepers were rude, the country's drivers suicidal, and everything cost a small fortune. He found the city's social life consisted of rotating diplomatic dinners and cocktail parties. But the Belgians were definitely not party-goers; they were too busy making money to be bothered. Consequently, he spent as much of his time as possible travelling in Holland and France where the people were friendlier and more appreciative. His younger son, David, he shipped off to Berkhamsted, his old alma mater during World War I.

The War Graves Commission job turned out to be little more than a staffing appointment that could have been handled by any subaltern with a normal IQ. The planning, organizing, cataloguing and reconstruction of Canadian cemeteries from two European wars had been settled efficiently long before his arrival. "I felt useless. A Chairman of a Board of Directors whose members had already decided what they were going to do and expect me to rubber-stamp those decisions without discussion." Which he did. What he did enjoy was travelling through Normandy, Belgium and Holland visiting the grave-yards, reliving the memories of past excitement, old battles, old comrades and the uncertainty of life. Sometimes, when the memories were strong, he wept unashamedly.

Mollie, only mildly interested in these excursions, humoured him. She wanted to go home to England. After decades of cigarettes, Gordon's Gin and overeating, her heart had started to rebel. The first mild attack that felled her resulted in a broken hip, leaving her with a permanent limp. Instead of dieting through her convalescence she consumed more. The doctors gave her five years.

Harry retired from the army in the summer of 1952. Although only 50 and entitled to remain another five years before pension he decided that he'd had enough. "There was no place else to go and nothing else for me to do. I was old and obsolete." They returned to England. Mollie found an elegant three-storey house on an acre of land at the outskirts of Fleet. Nothing like the elegance of The Poplars, but as a retirement home with room for guests and servants it was ideal. She bought the house, Harry bought a dog, and they all moved in.

That same summer Kurt went into hospital with a combination of physical ailments culminating in a tonsillectomy that nearly killed him. Yet there were advantages to being hospitalized. Kate and the children could visit him without the presence of guards. Werl was such a depressing place that for a year he had forbidden them to visit. The sympathetic hospital staff regularly arranged for him to spend a few hours alone with Kate.

Upon his return to Werl the prison chaplain showed the same sort of consideration. Regular family consultations were arranged in the chaplain's office on the pretext of discussing urgent family problems. The padre waited until the guards were out of earshot. "Herr Meyer, there is a box of cigars under my desk. I'll be back in an hour."

It had been suggested to Kate that she and the children move inland so as to avoid a political border "incident" at Offleben. The Russians still wanted Kurt for war crimes, and a cross-border kidnapping of all or part of the Meyer family remained a real possibility. An army friend offered them a summer house in Niederkrüchten until Kurt's release. It was primitive but liveable and considerably shortened the travelling distance to Werl.

Soon after he left hospital, Ursula came to see him. She was 17 and wanted to discuss her future. Their meeting went so badly she never went back.

"I enter the big prison building with much courage but the multitude of doors that had to be opened and closed quite unnerved me. Then, there is Father and a big wide table between us. I want to touch . . . so much. I know I must not cry, otherwise I'll never be allowed to see him again. I say a few words. We have time, lots of time. But he gets up and says: 'Give my greetings to Oma and write your mother. You'll hear from me.' I wanted to say 'Stop, don't go yet,' but he looks so serious, so slim and pale and off he goes."

Later, she learned that he had had a mild heart attack during the visit.

The German chancellor, Dr. Konrad Adenauer, visited him in June 1953, publicly shook his hand and promised to do everything he could to end the imprisonment. For someone of Adenauer's stature to take up the cause provided ammunition needed against the politically fainthearted. Dr. Franz-Joseph Strauss, Adenauer's defence minister, wanted Kurt as his military aide in Bonn. Herr Andreas, a local brewer, offered him a job as sales representative plus an apartment in Hagen.

The months passed. Another commandant replaced the affable Colonel Vickers. The new man, Colonel Meech, "turned out to be a bastard and there were several attempted suicides." Meech placed the war criminals inside a special compound—a prison within a prison. "This of course resulted in everyone playing tricks on him." Kurt included.

Finally, after a formal request from Brig. Sherwood Lett* to Canada's minister of national defence, the government announced on 15 January 1954 that Kurt's sentence would be reduced to 14 years with time off for good behaviour. A release date was set for early September, coinciding almost to the day with his capture ten years earlier. Then, early on the morning of 7 September, a crowd began gathering in front of the prison. Embarrassed by the display, the prison commandant had him spirited out a side door and driven to a local hotel.

The place filled with well-wishers—Kate, war comrades, friends, even 67-year-old Onkel Fritz had flown over to be on hand. Frau Else Weecks, vice-president of the local Red Cross, presented him with a bouquet of flowers. Kurt stood dazed like a man in a dream, nodding, smiling foolishly, stunned by the taste of freedom. Heinz Trapp, a former Leibstandarte Company sergeant-major drove him to the Friedland transition camp where official formalities for his release were completed. His mother was there to meet him with more friends. Everyone was smiling. Then it was on to Nieder-krüchten to see his children.

"Suddenly we stop. The road is blocked by hundreds of people. There is a triumphal arch to greet me. Policemen try to explain. I hear nothing as the drums begin to roll . . . this is my homecoming reception! People holding flares form a laneway, lighting my way home."

Earlier that day townspeople had gone into the woods to cut trees and boughs to decorate his route. The women made patterns with flowers. He

---

*Who survived Dieppe; later, Chief Justice of the Supreme Court of British Columbia.

came home proudly, as a soldier. Most didn't know or didn't care that he had been an ss general.

"After hugging my girls and son I listen to the welcoming speeches and am deeply moved. I am glad to see my old comrades again. The war did bond us together. I tell them now to be law-abiding citizens. 'Believe me, the years behind us have left no hate against former enemies. Don't let's talk about yesterday but work for the future. We must guarantee our children's future and build for them a strong worthwhile Europe.' After 15 years of wanderings I have come home."

RECESSIONAL

The tumult and the shouting dies;
The Captains and the Kings depart.
RUDYARD KIPLING

KURT STARTED his job in Hagen with Andreas Brewery in January 1955, in charge of the 27 sales drivers who covered the district. Typically, he gave the job everything he had. His reputation provided immediate access to owners of every watering hole and family inn throughout the region, and he managed to introduce the delights of Andreas bottled beer to the messes of the Canadian armed forces serving in Europe.

The family moved into a modest three-room flat on the fourth floor of an apartment building with no elevator. It was all he could afford. His starting salary of 700 Deutschmarks provided for basic necessities and little else. He gave up smoking. Young Kurt and the girls slept crowded into one room, but no one complained. For the first time they were together as a family. The teenage girls adored him but found his ideas old fashioned. He treated them like backward adolescents. Secretly, he found them intimidating. Young Kurt, replaced now as cock-of-the-roost, regarded him with the dark suspicion of a ten-year-old.

Yet in spite of his perpetually aching hip, the shortage of money and an inability to give his family all the things he would have liked, his outlook remained one of delight rather than frustration. He felt ecstatically happy just to be free, alive and living with them in a Germany at peace. Union leaders, idealists and politicians from the right and centre parties courted him to join their causes, but the only organization he openly supported was the HIAG, a veterans organization for helping former members of the Waffen-SS. Kurt became a member.

Besides its regular social activities the HIAG provided a financial pool that its members could draw upon for a variety of purposes—an artificial leg for an amputee, rent and food for a destitute member's family, employment opportunities for those who carried the SS stigma in their own communities. By 1956 Kurt had become one of the organization's principal speakers in seeking government recognition for the Waffen-SS as soldiers entitled to pensions on an equal basis with the Wehrmacht. As a convicted war criminal entitled to no pension, he took a personal interest in seeking an equitable settlement for HIAG members.

It was a gigantic task trying to convince the German people and their politicians that the SS were not all criminals like Himmler's Gestapo, the concentration camp guards or the *Einsatzgruppen* extermination battalions.[1] The Waffen-SS had been soldiers, proud soldiers who had given their lives and limbs and reputations out of all proportion to their numbers during a war not of their making. Wherever Kurt spoke—in tents, meeting halls or the open air—the ex-soldiers came to listen. Privately, the politicians agreed the Wehrmacht and Waffen-SS should be treated equally, but felt it to be politically dangerous to voice such opinions in public. With the same tenacity they had shown on the battlefield the members of the HIAG fought on.

While in prison he had decided to write a book of his life in war and prison as a tribute to his young grenadiers. His old commander, Gen. of Panzer Troops, Baron Geyr von Schweppenburg,[2] had begun making a name for himself as a writer, historian and news commentator. Why couldn't he do the same? A Munich publisher gave him an advance for the rights. He wrote it completely from memory during his free time, after work, on weekends and late into the night. *Panzergrenadiere*, published in 1957, sold a respectable 6,000 copies in hardback.*

Life resolved itself around the brewery, the HIAG and his family, with annual summer vacations around the continent seeing the sights and, like Harry, retracing his battle routes. He bored Kate, his son and Gerhild with a five-hour tour and history lesson in Paris; they never got to see the Louvre. He found where Fritz Witt was buried near Caen and wept at the hundreds of tidy and carefully tended graves of his young grenadiers and other comrades that lay scattered across Normandy.

---

*Now in its eighth printing with 24,000 copies sold.

He drove the same road through Belgium where he had been captured. "There's the chicken house where I hid and there . . . *there is the man who betrayed me to the partisans!*" Shocked, he crouched behind the wheel, fearful that the stooped and grey-headed Belgian farmer might recognize him.

By the summer of 1961 his hip had become so painful he had difficulty walking even with the cane he had been using. He believed that his HIAG goals were about to be accomplished. The politicians finally promised to correct the pension injustices to which the Waffen-SS had been subjected for over a decade. After the parliamentary sessions in June many members came forward to congratulate him. But the result was only a wishy-washy statement of support that changed nothing, although the Minister of the Interior agreed to support Waffen-SS members and their families in cases of dire necessity. The gutless decision came as a direct result of the Adolf Eichmann trial in Israel with its horrific publicity and condemnation of the SS in general, plus the building of a concrete wall on 13 August dividing East and West Berlin. Kurt felt betrayed. He had always kept his word and expected others to do the same, politicians included. All his HIAG work had amounted to nothing.

On the evening of 23 December 1961, during dinner with 18-year-old Gerhild, he suddenly put down his fork and touched his heart. "I don't feel well," he muttered and leaned back, pale and trembling. Kate, only two days out of hospital after an abdominal operation, lay resting on the living room sofa. Kurt threw up. Gerhild helped him to lie down.

"Hide the cake, cognac and glasses!" he ordered. After a mild stroke in July he had been told to stay away from coffee, rich foods and alcohol. A second stroke in early November produced the same medical recommendations, as did a third at the brewery two weeks later. Now, too late to make any difference, he didn't want the doctors to discover he had been cheating.

"Phone Schäfer at the HIAG and Owens at the brewery," he whispered, then collapsed. Kate knew he was dying. Gerhild phoned her sister Inge, a trained nurse, for help. Inge's two children answered the telephone singing Christmas carols. Gerhild broke into tears. They gathered at the hospital where he had been rushed to intensive care. He tried to speak, but his head dropped. Inge held his hand as the last sparks of life flickered then died. It was his birthday. He was 51.

He had the largest funeral in Hagen's history. Thousands of condolences poured in. Extra staff were hired by the post office to handle the telegrams, letters and telephone calls. Adenauer and Strauss sent their sympathies. Relatives, family friends and Waffen-SS comrades arrived in droves from all over Europe. Newspaper accounts placed the attendance at 5,000.

Hubert Meyer read the eulogy: "You did not build yourself a monument of stone but erected a shining example in the hearts of your comrades. You worked a lifetime for a Fatherland, happy and free. We will love it as you did. Wherever we are, privately, publicly, at home or abroad we will say with pride: 'I . . . was a comrade of Panzermeyer!' "

2

Mollie died of a heart attack early in 1958. It was not unexpected. She left Harry the use of the house in Fleet for as long as he lived, after which it was to be sold and the proceeds divided equally among her children. He had no reason to stay. Since the war, Fleet had turned into a comatose little town filled with gentry, retired admirals and generals and infected on the outskirts by the "horsey set." Not Harry's cup of tea at all. He thought about it a few days, then signed over his dwelling rights to the heirs, packed his things and booked passage on a CPR cargo/passenger vessel sailing from Antwerp on 9 June.

Ten days later he checked into the Windsor Hotel in Montreal. His eldest son, an executive pilot for TransCanada PipeLines, met him. They had made their peace three years earlier when Tony had visited Fleet for a brief holiday. He had been shocked by Harry's appearance. His father looked old before his time, worn out by Mollie's constant nagging and complaining, and unable to walk more than a few hundred feet because of the constant pain in his leg. Within hours of his arrival Mollie had been at his throat. To keep them apart, Harry took him driving each day around the south of England, returning to Fleet at dark. After a lifetime of mutual suspicion and misunderstanding, father and son got to know each other.

They drank warm English ale and played "shove-ha'penny" at local pubs and ate pork pies in quaint village tearooms. Harry took him on a tour of the old training camps, the stately homes that had once been a divisional or a corps or army headquarters. He told him of the exciting times, the comradeship, the frustrations and the fear. They visited coastal seaports from where the great armada had sailed on D-Day and drove the same miles of peaceful narrow roads once crowded with eager young men and the machinery of their war. They went to London and visited the Imperial War Museum and the Tate Gallery. When his son sailed for Canada, they parted as friends. They met with the same sense of well-being in Montreal.

"What are your plans?"

Harry shrugged. "I haven't the slightest idea."

"You can stay at my place until you decide." Both sons lived in Toronto, the conservative metropolis of Canadian business opportunities. Tony had a penthouse in a new highrise overlooking the centre of the city.

"I accept."

They went in the company's twin-engine aircraft, the one his son flew at tree-top level on twice-monthly checks of the natural gas pipe line running from Burstall, Saskatchewan, to Montreal. Harry, whose flying experience had been mainly in wartime air force bombers, marvelled at the plush interior and comfort. Over Kingston he wanted to circle RMC at low level. His son obliged.

"Foulkes wanted to close it down as an economy measure after the war, did you know that? Can you imagine closing RMC? Bah! He always was a bit of an ass."

"What happened?"

"A group of us got together and fought like hell to keep it open. We won."

They landed at Kingston airport for coffee and a bite before flying on to Toronto. Next morning he borrowed the car and drove to Winona to see Armand Smith, his old brigadier in 1st Brigade. Smith, retired and living in the sumptuous E.D. Smith ancestral home, greeted him like a lost son. He remained in Toronto most of that summer, visiting old friends and comrades-in-arms. Then, one day in August he announced that he was returning to Nova Scotia. "I don't belong here any more than I did in Fleet. I need to get back among my own kind."

He rented a small flat in Halifax's nobby south end and tried to pick up his old friendships. But times had changed. He was no longer the GOC, just another aging warhorse with a pension, a limp and his memories. He felt useless, became depressed and began consuming more wine than was good for him.

Then he met Mona. He had known her as a teenager in Wolfville. She was a year older than Harry. A "fast" girl for her time, she had graduated from Acadia University, gone to a Boston drama school, joined the Ziegfeld Follies and married a Dutch millionaire. During the war their home, outside of Amsterdam, became a hiding place for downed Allied fliers in transit to England. Eventually, they were betrayed to the Gestapo and both were sentenced to death. The sentences were commuted and Mona spent three and a half years in German concentration camps and prisons. Near the end of the war she escaped and, after walking across Germany to Holland, met the advancing Canadian troops. Harry had seen her then—gaunt, pale, her feet in blisters, more dead than alive. Her husband, Billie, survived also but after a series of illnesses died from the accumulative abuses of the concentration camps. Mona, like Harry, had come home to roost.

They were married on 17 June 1959. They got on well together, enjoyed each other's company and friends. They travelled, they read, they entertained, first in Halifax, later in a lovely house on a large property overlooking the ocean at Chester, N.S. During winter, when Atlantic snowstorms thundered along the coast, Harry plowed out the mile of driveway with his new tractor or worked on a boat he was building in the basement. When spring arrived Mona produced a garden, each more beautiful than the previous year's. Harry went sailing. He had finally found his paradise. And, after a lifetime of three packs of cigarettes a day, he stopped smoking. Each year, in midsummer, his sons came for a month's visit.

Mona, who was childless, enjoyed her new stepchildren. "I have the advantage and pleasure of their company with none of the responsibility for their upbringing or present well-being," she informed her friends. "Now what more could any mother ask?"

It was all too perfect to last. Over Easter, 1964, he developed an irritating cough that affected his vocal chords. His eldest son was visiting. "Just a touch of quinsy," he assured him. "It's this damn spring weather. Can't make up its mind whether to rain or snow."

When he finally decided to go to the Halifax army hospital the diagnosis was throat cancer. The doctors gave him four months. He underwent terrible suffering from useless radiation and chemotherapy treatments, all the time losing weight, losing patience, losing hope.

He wrote in July: "I am so weak. I try fighting but it's no use. Some days I actually feel as if I'm going to recover. But then misery comes back from wherever it was waiting. I think it is high time to make up my will."

Finally, he entered hospital. David flew to Halifax.

"Where's your brother, the big-time operator?" Harry demanded.

The big-time operator was in the middle of the agricultural spraying season in southwestern Ontario with his fleet of aircraft. David telephoned him.

"He seems better. In fact he ordered a big meal today."

"I'll be there next week."

Two days later Harry slipped into a coma. The cancer had reached his brain. The new GOC Eastern Command, Maj.-Gen. Bob Moncel, who had served with Harry in the 4th Armoured Division, came to visit at Camp Hill Hospital. He found an emaciated and unconscious body beneath an oxygen tent punctured by plastic tubes. He summoned the doctor.

"What's going on here?"

"He's dying, sir."

"Then for God's sake let him die in peace and dignity."

"I can't do that."

"Doctor, I am going out for one hour. When I return I want to find that bed empty. Do you understand?"

An hour later the room was empty. Harry had gone. He was 62.

The army gave him a proper military funeral as prescribed by the same regulations he had followed so faithfully throughout life. His flag-draped coffin lay atop a gun carriage. Two admirals, three generals, a colour party and a company of soldiers slow-marched behind. An army band played the mournful Chopin Funeral March. Sounds of morning traffic floated in the August sunshine. Flags fluttered in a light breeze. Along the route to the church hundreds of people paused to watch the procession. Men removed their hats. Some straightened their shoulders and saluted, others ignored the whole affair and hurried on about their business. All Saints Anglican Cathedral was filled. The Lieutenant-Governor, the Premier, the Mayor, old soldiers, friends and relatives all turned out. The organist played "Abide with Me" and "O God Our Help in Ages Past."

Mona and her stepsons wept.

Later that afternoon they buried him in the family plot at Kentville next to Janie, Laffy and Margo. Field artillery boomed out a 13-gun salute in the grasslands below the cemetery. Then everybody went home.

His legacy was three photograph albums, two paintings, some pictures, a few pieces of furniture, his cavalry sword, medals and uniform, an unpaid bill for £243 to Jones, Chalk & Dawson, Military Tailors, London, and two sons who were enormously proud of what he had accomplished and very grateful to have had him as their father.

> *When at last the guns fall silent and we've buried all our dead*
> *And the battle flags are folded by those warriors we led,*
> *Then the victor and the vanquished must endure one final pain:*
> *That in the fury of the slaughter their passions were the same.*
>
> FOSTER

Halifax, Nova Scotia
August 1986

APPENDICES

Appendix A
Military Formations

No hard and fast rules exist for structuring the various military formations. Each is designed to fulfil a specific function in the field according to circumstances. The numbers of men, pieces of equipment and parts of units attached or detached for operational purposes may vary widely. Simply put: military formations are nothing more than building blocks with which military commanders assemble armies for battles.

Designation	Avg. No. of Men	Command Rank	
Section	7-10	Corporal	Called a "squad" in the U.S. Army. Can be commanded by a sergeant.
Platoon	30	Sergeant	Or commanded by a 2nd lieutenant. There are 3 sections in each platoon.
Company	90	Captain	Can be in charge of a 1st lieutenant. Normally 3 platoons to a company.
Battalion	540	Major	Usually comprised of 6 companies: 4 rifle companies, 1 machine-gun/mortar company and 1 headquarters company. Can also be commanded by lieut.-col. This is a basic front-line fighting unit.
Regiment	2,000	Colonel	More a ceremonial than fighting unit. Can be commanded by lieut.-col. Consisting of 3 to 5 battalions which, in the case of armoured, Provost, heavy weapons and reconnaissance regiments are attached to other infantry units in company or battalion strength.
Brigade	6,000	Brigadier	Comprising 3 or more regiments with supporting companies and battalions. A brigade is the army's standard battle unit for organizational planning and operational assault against an enemy.
Division	15,000	Major-General	Can have from 12 to 20 thousand troops with three or more brigades.
Corps	50,000 +	Lieut.-General	Three or more divisions. A corps functions for strategic planning purposes only and operates HQ well behind the front line.
Army	100,000 +	General	Two or more corps. Can have as many as a million men. A political more than a military operational unit. Can be commanded by a field marshal.

Appendix B
Waffen-ss Ranks with Their U.S. and British Empire Equivalents

Waffen-SS	*U.S.A.*	*British*
ss Oberst-Gruppenführer und Generaloberst der Waffen-ss	General of Army Five Stars	Field Marshal
	General Four Stars	General
ss Obergruppenführer und General der Waffen-ss		
ss Gruppenführer und Generalleutnant der Waffen-ss	Lieutenant-General Three Stars	Lieutenant-General
ss Brigadeführer und Generalmajor der Waffen-ss	Major-General Two Stars	Major-General
	Brigadier-General One Star	Brigadier-General
ss Oberführer		
ss Standartenführer	Colonel	Colonel
ss Obersturmbannführer	Lieutenant-Colonel	Lieutenant-Colonel
ss Sturmbannführer	Major	Major
ss Hauptsturmführer	Captain	Captain
ss Obersturmführer	First Lieutenant	Lieutenant
ss Untersturmführer	Second Lieutenant	Second Lieutenant
ss Sturmscharführer	Warrant Officer First Class	Regimental Sergeant-Major
ss Stabsscharführer	First Sergeant	Senior Sergeant
ss Hauptscharführer	Warrant Officer Second Class	Company Sergeant-Major
ss Oberscharführer	Master Sergeant	Quartermaster Sergeant
ss Scharführer	Staff Sergeant	Staff Sergeant
ss Unterscharführer	Sergeant	Sergeant
ss Rottenführer	Corporal	Corporal
ss Sturmmann	Private First Class	Lance-Corporal
ss Oberschütze		
ss Mann/Schütze/Grenadier/ Panzerschütze etc.	GI	Private, Rifleman, Tanker, Gunner, etc.

The equivalents are not precise, particularly in the case of generals' ranks where overlapping occurs. Although when literally translated, the rank of Brigadeführer means brigade leader, in actual fact a Brigadeführer normally commanded a division and would be regarded in Allied rank as major-general.

Appendix C
Principal Organizations within the SS

RUSHA—*Rasse-und-Siedlungshauptamt*
The Central Office for Racial Purity. It began innocently enough as a marriage bureau to authenticate the Aryan ancestry of prospective SS brides. Later, with the VOMI, it was to organize the settlement and welfare of SS colonists in the eastern territories that had been conquered. Richard Hildebrandt was its last commander.

VOMI—*Volksdeutsche Mittelstelle*
The Racial German Assistance Office. Formed to look after the welfare of "racial" Germans who had settled abroad. It worked with the RUSHA on the resettlement program under direction of the RKF. Werner Lorenz was its director of operations.

RKF—*Reichskommissar für die Festigung des deutschen Volkstums*
Reich Commissioner for the Consolidation of German Nationhood. Coordinating office responsible for the repatriation of "racial" Germans and settlement of German colonies in eastern occupied territories.

WVHA—*Wirtschafts-und-Verwaltungshauptamt*
Economic and Administrative Office. Controlled all economic enterprises created by the SS and operated the concentration camps. Its chief was Oswald Pohl. Few of the millions of people entrusted to its care survived.

RSHA—*Reichssicherheitshauptamt*
The Reich's Central Security Department. Formed in 1939, it combined the existing police (Gestapo and Kripo) with the Security Service.

KRIPO—*Kriminalpolizei*
The Criminal Police under Arthur Nebe. Nebe was executed for taking part in the assassination plot against Hitler in July 1944.

SIPO—*Sicherheitspolizei*
The Security Police composed of the Kripo and Gestapo and directed by Heydrich.

GESTAPO—*Geheime Staatspolizei*
The Secret State Police under Heinrich Müller.

SD—*Sicherheitsdienst*
The Security Service. Formed in 1932 by Heydrich as the sole intelligence-gathering organization of the Nazi party. The HQ SD and SIPO formed the core of the RSHA.

Totenkopfverbände
Death's Head units originally composed of volunteers from the general SS body. They were organized into four regiments and used as concentration camp guards. In 1939 these units became the nucleus of the SST Division, one of the Waffen-SS's first field divisions.

Waffen-SS
Military combat formations composed initially of *Totenkopfverbände* and the *Verfügungstruppe*. After 1940 it used many non-Germans in its ranks. By the end of the war close to 40 Waffen-SS divisions had been used in the front lines. The

Waffen-ss was by far the largest of all ss groups and at its peak in late 1944 numbered 600,000 men.

Leibstandarte Adolf Hitler

Formed in 1933 from the *Stabswache* (the original Party Headquarters guard), it became Bodyguard Regiment to Adolf Hitler under "Sepp" Dietrich. Oldest of the armed formations, it was transformed into the Waffen-ss. It reached divisional status in 1941 and fought in Poland, Greece, Russia and the West.

Appendix D

Brigadier Harry Foster's Position in the Allied Invasion Forces
Chain of Command on 6 June 1944

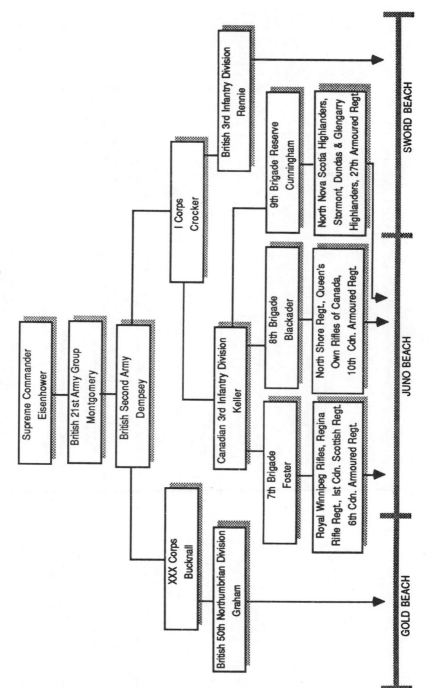

(continued overleaf)

Appendix D (cont'd)

SS Standartenführer Kurt Meyer's Position in the German
Chain of Command on 6 June 1944

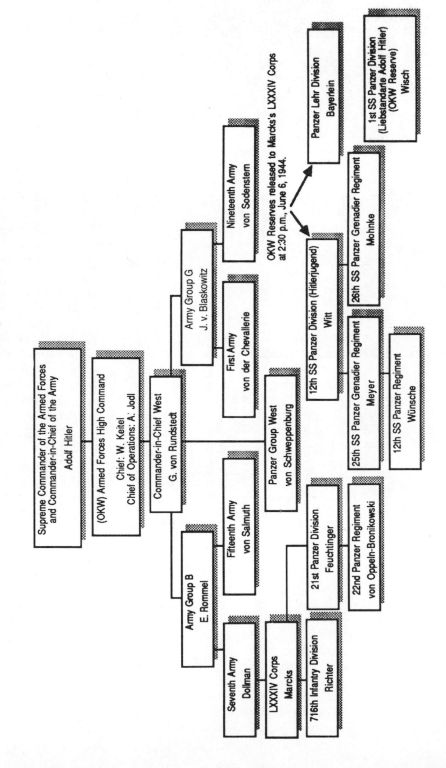

Supreme Commander of the Armed Forces
and Commander-in-Chief of the Army
Adolf Hitler

(OKW) Armed Forces High Command
Chief: W. Keitel
Chief of Operations: A. Jodl

Commander-in-Chief West
G. von Rundstedt

Army Group B
E. Rommel

Army Group G
J. v. Blaskowitz

Seventh Army
Dollman

Fifteenth Army
von Salmuth

First Army
von der Chevallerie

Nineteenth Army
von Sodenstern

LXXXIV Corps
Marcks

Panzer Group West
von Schweppenburg

716th Infantry Division
Richter

21st Panzer Division
Feuchtinger

22nd Panzer Regiment
von Oppeln-Bronikowski

12th SS Panzer Division (Hitlerjugend)
Witt

25th SS Panzer Grenadier Regiment
Meyer

26th SS Panzer Grenadier Regiment
Mohnke

12th SS Panzer Regiment
Wünsche

Panzer Lehr Division
Bayerlein

1st SS Panzer Division
(Liebstandarte Adolf Hitler)
(OKW Reserve)
Wisch

OKW Reserves released to Marcks's LXXXIV Corps
at 2:30 p.m., June 6, 1944.

NOTES

PRELUDE

1. B.J.S. Macdonald, *The Trial of Kurt Meyer* (Toronto: Clarke, Irwin, 1954), pp. 90–91.
2. H. Foster to T. Foster, 1958. Subsequent quotations from Foster are based on his diaries, letters and conversations with T. Foster and others.

PART 1: IN THE SHADOW OF WAR

1. Canada, Department of Militia, *Annual Report* (1898), p. 24.

PART 2: BATTLE'S WAKE

1. Count Alfred von Schlieffen was chief of the General Staff from 1891 to 1906. He wrote a paper on the battle of Cannae to support his favourite theory of encirclement, using Hannibal's crushing defeat of the Romans to prove his hypothesis. His plan for German defence was based on the idea that Germany was surrounded by potential enemies. During a war, one enemy should be selected for decisive defeat and destruction before manoeuvring on interior lines and, aided by a highly developed strategic railway system, allowing the armed forces to turn from the defensive to the offensive against another enemy.

    Schlieffen's Plan was used in part during 1914—heavier forces attacking the West while lighter forces held the front against Russia.
2. Quoted in Adam Smith, *Paper Money* (New York: Dell, 1982).
3. Anti-Semitism was not a recent phenomenon in Vienna or Austria. For over a thousand years discrimination existed against the Jews in Russia and throughout the Holy Roman Empire. Discrimination within Prussia was less pronounced because of its religious tolerance at a time when Catholics were being persecuted and murdered in England.

    However, in the southern states of Germany, all of France and the Austro-Hungarian Empire, anti-Semitism was a way of life for the Jew. Its cruelties were manifested in many different ways over and above the obvious difficulties of employment, worship and social acceptance within the fabric of a host country. For example, during the reign of Austria's Maria Theresa (1740–80), it was discovered that Jews living along the Empire's eastern borders had no surnames. For centuries the Jewish custom had been to use the names of villages and towns for surnames. Registrars were sent out from Vienna to correct the situation and given orders to issue the Jews with proper and distinguishable surnames. Those who could not afford to pay the cost of a fine-sounding name from the list being offered by the registrars were forced to accept whatever they were given. Invariably the supplementary surnames were either demeaning or disgusting. Names like Katzenellenbogen (meaning "cat's elbow") or Arsch (meaning arse) were popular examples of this form of anti-Semitism.

PART 3: THE MAKING OF A WARRIOR: I

1. The Strathconas' dress uniform had

facings of myrtle green with white leather belts, slings and gauntlets; black leather butcher boots and steel spurs; dark blue trousers with a wide yellow stripe down the outside seam; white metal helmet with brass spike and chin chain and red and white horsehair plume; and silvered steel scabbard with sabre.

2. Heinz Guderian, *Panzer Leader* (London: Michael Joseph, 1970), pp. 22–23.

3. The Locarno agreements comprised a treaty of mutual guarantees between Germany, Belgium, France, Italy and Great Britain, and arbitration conventions between Germany and Belgium, Germany and France, Germany and Poland, and Germany and Czechoslovakia. The pact's basic flaw lay in the assumption that Germany would accept a permanent settlement imposed by the Treaty of Versailles for a Polish "Corridor" between East and West Prussia. In the event of a conflict over this question, it was difficult to see how Britain could avoid being drawn into war.

4. E.L.M. Burns, "The Mechanization of Cavalry," *Canadian Defence Quarterly* 1 (3): 6 (April 1924).

PART 4: THE MAKING OF A WARRIOR: II

1. Rosenberg believed that the German peoples were entitled to rule over their racially inferior neighbours because of their having been endowed with special sterling qualities that made them superior. From this basic assumption, Darré went on to argue that German superiority was genetic and that the "Nordic peasantry" held the gene stock "whose blood was as rich and fruitful as the soil they tilled. So great was their virtue that the future strength of Europe depended on the survival of their stock." Darré believed the blood lines of Jews and Slavs were poison to the human race, and he was all for controlled breeding in the SS. Himmler recruited Darré into the SS, appointing him head of the Race and Settlement Office. Originally, this organization was set up to research the genealogy of SS applicants. Later, it became a vehicle for wholesale extermination. Not until Darré's office was satisfied that an SS applicant's ancestry could be traced back to 1750 and be free of Jewish blood would he be accepted.

2. The Enabling Act of 23 March 1933 removed the Reichstag's legislative function and turned it over to the Reich government consisting of Hitler and his ministers.

3. Handwritten notes by Hitler's former senior officer and adjutant, Consul Gen. Fritz Wiedeman; photocopy in the Institut für Zeitgeschichte, Munich.

4. Nuremberg Document PS 3063; IMT, vol. 32, p. 20.

5. *Documents on British Foreign Policy*, 3rd Series, vol. 3 (London, 1950), p. 227.

6. Slovak troops took part in Hitler's war against Poland, and Slovakia received a slice of Polish territory. Under the Prelate Tiso, the Slovakian government remained in power until 1945. Tiso was hanged by the Czechs.

PART 5: THE WHIRLWIND

1. By 1945 Waffen-SS units included regiments and divisions of Yugoslavs, Muslims, Dutch, Hungarians, Italians, Flemish-Belgians, Walloon-Belgians, Russians, French and Danes. Varieties of other nationalities were also inducted into the Waffen-SS—most unwillingly during the latter days of the war. As a result, Waffen-SS troops of Czech, Polish, Russian Ukraine or Hungarian nationality despised their German officers and NCOs even though they were prepared to obey

them. During combat many deserted and surrendered to Allied forces.

2. Two of the men survived the massacre. During that night they crawled away from under the bodies during a rainstorm and were helped by French civilians. A few weeks later they were recaptured by the Germans and after a period in hospital were sent to prison camp. After the war the two had great difficulty convincing British army authorities about the murders. Eventually Knöchlein was brought to justice and hanged in January 1949. During the interim he had risen to the rank of Obersturmbannführer and received both the Iron Cross and Knight's Cross for gallantry.

3. Had Göring concentrated his forces on the British airfields and their installations instead of switching to the indiscriminate bombing of London, he might have crippled the RAF. Just at the time the RAF was reeling from the destruction of its fuel supplies, ammunition dumps and spare parts, the Luftwaffe changed tactics on 7 September, giving the RAF time to replace its losses, rebuild its damaged aircraft and get back in the air.

4. The 58-year-old Graziani had spent the best part of his career as a soldier and administrator of Italy's North African colonies. He had commanded Italian forces in Libya between 1930 and 1934, overseeing the occupation of the Kufra Oasis. He conducted the final pacification of the poorly equipped nomadic Libyan tribesmen with great brutality. After Italy's surrender in 1943, he became defence minister in Mussolini's Republican government. In 1945 he surrendered to the Americans and was imprisoned until 1946 when he was turned over to Italian authorities for trial in 1948. In 1950 he was sentenced to 19 years in prison but was quickly released.

5. In view of such a spectacular success the Wehrmacht could no longer in all integrity ignore the Leibstandarte's fighting ability. General of Cavalry Stumme, commander of XL Corps, issued an Order of the Day expressing his "thanks and fullest recognition for the opening of the Klidi Pass, which resulted from the same unshakeable offensive spirit which the Leibstandarte constantly displays. The present victory signifies for the Leibstandarte a new and imperishable page of honour in its history. Forward for Führer, Volk and Reich!"

PART 6: FORTUNE'S FATE

1. In comparison, D-Day forces on 6 June 1944 consisted of the American 12th Army Group composed of the U.S. First and Third Armies—23 divisions in all. The British 21st Army Group consisted of the Canadian First Army and British Second Army—a total of 17 divisions. By July the Allies had a million men ashore and over 4 million by the end of the war. Although all troops were technically under Supreme Commander General Eisenhower, each army commander ran his own show. None had anywhere near the number of troops commanded by von Bock.

2. The Wehrmacht deployed only 19 panzer and 12 motorized divisions for the Russian campaign. The five Waffen-SS divisions therefore performed a role out of all proportion to their numbers.

3. The four *Einsatzgruppen*—literally, "operation groups"—with 3,000 specialists and over 100,000 assistants were given complete autonomy of action, although officially under the Wehrmacht supervision. The first to be exterminated were Jews, Gypsies and "inferior Asians." To this list Heydrich added "Red Army People's

Commissars, Jews with positions in the Communist Party or State, war-mongers, guerrillas and propagandists."

The "great suppression of Jews" was to begin within hours after a piece of territory had been occupied. Local populations were to be inflamed to the point of assisting in the killing of Jews. Not one Jew was to be left alive. Proudly, each of the SS *Einsatzgruppe* commanders reported his operational results.

Stahlecker of A Unit reported killing 229,052 Jews by the end of August 1941: Nebe of B Unit and Rasch of C Unit weighed in with 45,467 and 95,000 respectively by mid-November. At the beginning of April 1942 Ohlendorf's D Group was up to 92,000. On 29 December 1942 Himmler informed Hitler that 363,211 additional Jews had been liquidated between 1 September and 1 December 1942.

Most victims were exterminated in the death camps by gas chambers or, in the case of the mobile *Einsatzgruppen*, by mass executions. Not only Jews were killed. The invasion of Russia provided a unique opportunity to wipe out several million people to clear the way for German colonization. Historian Christian Streit calculated that of the 5,734,528 Soviet prisoners of war roughly 3,300,000 were either executed or died of cold, disease or starvation. Streit's calculations should include those who died in transit to and from Russian concentration camps after 1945, plus the unknown millions of Poles and Russians who, according to Nobel Prize winner Aleksandr Solzhenitzyn, were murdered later by Stalin as "traitors" or "collaborators." In all, the Soviet Union lost more than 20 million people in World War II and probably half that number again after the war had ended.

4. Former General of Panzer Troops Heinrich Eberbach commanded an armoured brigade during the early part of the Russian campaign. He believed Hitler was correct in ordering his generals to stand and hold during 1941–42. After their earlier successes the generals had panicked at the first signs of defeat. Later in the war, when prudence and common sense dictated no other course of action but to withdraw and fight another day, Hitler, unfortunately, decided to apply the "stand and hold" criterion with disastrous results.

5. COSSAC was the acronym of the title "Chief of Staff to the Supreme Allied Commander" given by British Lieut.-Gen. F.E. Morgan, who headed the invasion planning. The air and naval planners for COSSAC were Air Marshal Sir Trafford Leigh-Mallory and Adm. Sir Bertram Ramsay, who had also planned the Dieppe raid.

6. The *Führungshauptamt*, headed by Obergruppenführer Hans Jüttner, was the operational headquarters for the entire SS and responsible for all training, organization and employment—with the exception of tactical deployment of Waffen-SS field divisions.

PART 7: NORMANDY

1. Soldiers, sailors and airmen of all the warring nations were given a variety of different drugs designed to maintain their alertness under combat conditions. Luftwaffe pilots received pills for duty flying periods of longer than eight hours; Japanese *Kamikaze* pilots took a form of amphetamines before take off. Naval personnel assigned to lookout duties at sea used benzedrine to stay awake.

2. "Pips" Priller had downed 96 aircraft to become one of the Luftwaffe's top scoring aces. He and his wingman, Sgt. Heinz Wodarczyk, attacked the beaches on D-Day. Priller survived the war.

3. Duplex-Drive tanks—American Shermans equipped with dual propellers and canvas flotation collars mounted on support brackets. Forward visibility for the crew came from the tank commander standing on top of the turret; the rest of the DD travelled underwater. Submerged speed was about 4 mph with sluggish control. DDs mounted a 75 mm turret gun.

4. Force 6 on the Beaufort Wind Scale—strong breeze with winds 25 to 31 mph.

5. As a result of the Dieppe experience, British General Hobart's 79th Armoured Division had been assigned the task of dealing with beach obstacles. "Crabs" (flail tanks for detonating land mines), "Crocodiles" (flame-throwing tanks), "AVREs" (Armoured Vehicle Royal Engineers, used for demolishing fortifications and beach obstacles) and DDs were all offered to the Americans. Although Eisenhower was enthusiastic, Gen. Omar Bradley, commander of the U.S. 1st Army Group, would accept only the DDs, citing lack of training time to familiarize his soldiers with the British Churchill tank on which most of the equipment was installed.

This was patent nonsense, since the British Crab device used the American Sherman tank as its carrier, and a conversion course for tank crews from Shermans to Churchills took no more than a week of training. Nor would the Americans accept the need for their assault troops to carry as little equipment as possible when they came ashore at Omaha and Utah beaches. This peculiar streak of pigheaded independence and stupidity cost them dearly on D-Day.

Hundreds of troops jumping from their assault craft into the heavy seas simply rolled over and sank from the sheer weight of their equipment. Then, on the beaches, without specialized armour support, coupled with the earlier failure of the naval and air bombardment and the lack of DD tanks where they were needed most, the infantry was left exposed and vulnerable. Mines, barbed wire and other obstacles had to be cleared by hand. Apart from lightly armoured bulldozers, the Americans had no mechanized equipment for dealing with obstructions and fortifications. Heavy congestion with appalling casualties developed very quickly.

By day's end the British and Canadian armies had landed 81,000 men—of which 14,000 were Canadians. Their combined casualties were 3,168. The Americans, by contrast, landed 10,000 less troops yet had over twice the number of casualties.

6. Cornelius Ryan, *The Longest Day* (New York: Simon & Shuster, 1959), p. 246.

7. From Alexander McKee, *Caen: Anvil of Victory* (London: Pan Books, 1966), pp. 63–64.

8. This glider convoy, carrying most of the 6th Air-Landing Brigade's light tanks, artillery and reconnaissance regiments, was in fact part of the scheduled D-Day planning, and the largest glider force ever launched into battle.

9. SS Obersturmbannführer Hubert

Meyer's narrative of the 12th ss Panzer Division (no relation to Kurt Meyer).

10. Reported to Capt. J.R. Martin. Canadian army historical officer, who landed on D-Day and subsequently interviewed and collected numerous accounts of different actions from a variety of battlefield participants.

11. War Diary, Message Ops. 116/44. 30 June 1944.

12. War Diary, Army Group D (C.-in-C. West) CRS 75144/24.

13. Special interrogation report on Field Marshal von Rundstedt. CMHQ, 1 February 1946.

14. The regiment was trained and commanded by Kurt Meyer until he became divisional commander of the 12th ss. Information from the War Diaries of the North Shore Regiment and Le Régiment de la Chaudière. 4 July 1944. OCMH MS P-164 Waffen-ss Obersturmbannführer Hubert Meyer.

15. War Diary, 7th Infantry Brigade, 4 July 1944.

16. 7,700 tons were dropped. Six bombers were shot down.

17. The Black Watch (Royal Highland Regiment of Canada) was assigned temporarily from the 5th to 6th Brigade by General Simonds.

18. Rommel Papers, 486-87, Rommel document, 15 July 1944, Appx. to OB West Operations 5895/44, 21 July 1944. CRS 751145/5.

19. Lunenburg County residents use a flat *a* followed by a soft *r* in their speech patterns. The word "after," for example, is pronounced "ahrfter."

20. The Katyn Forest Massacre in 1940 of some 4,000 Polish army officers and civilians by the Russians who later blamed the incident on the Germans, for example. Tens of thousands more Polish officers and civilians simply vanished inside Russia.

21. A few weeks later Brigadier Young himself was sacked by Simonds; promoted to major-general, he was appointed quartermaster-general in charge of troop movements between Canada and the U.K.

22. Siebken and Schnabel were tried and convicted of war crimes. They were hanged in 1949.

23. "Spring" was Simonds's first nighttime operation. It was far too complex for the 2nd Division to manage. At no time did he or anyone else down to the brigade level exercise the tight authority and control required as the battle developed. Intelligence was faulty. The Germans survived the opening artillery barrage by hiding in underground mining tunnels and ventilation shafts that spidered across the front. Once Canadian troops passed overhead, the Germans surfaced behind them and began shooting. French civilians had reported the existence of the tunnel network to Corps HQ several days earlier, but no one took the time to investigate or verify the information before going into battle.

24. The U.S. Third Army had arrived in Normandy earlier and remained hidden behind the American lines to keep alive the German illusion that it was still in England and preparing to land at the Pas-de-Calais.

25. In a flash of brilliance, Simonds hit on the idea of converting the "Priest" self-propelled guns that had come ashore on D-Day into armoured personnel carriers. By removing the guns from the tank chassis and welding a steel plate over the resulting gap, he created the first modern APC. The machines were nicknamed

"Unfrocked Priests" or "Holy-rollers." Military bureaucracy formally named them "Kangaroos."

26. Waldmüller and his men had been pulled out of the line three days before. It was customary to remove the remnants of first-class fighting units from battle before they were annihilated in order to provide the necessary cadre for new divisions. A second Youth Division had already been planned around Waldmüller and his men.

27. Relying on approaching Soviet forces to free the city, Polish patriot General Bor-Komorowski led an uprising against the Germans beginning on 7 August whereupon Stalin halted the Russian advance, giving the Germans time to destroy their mutual foe. Bor's underground "Home Army" was starved into surrendering to the Germans on 3 October with a loss of 20,000 soldiers and civilians. The Red Army contended that Bor's uprising was premature and against orders and had nothing to do with ideological conflict between the exiled Polish government in London and the Polish (Communist) "Liberation Committee" formed in Russia.

28. Hubert Meyer's "History of the 12th SS" states that on 1 June 1944 the division consisted of 20,540 officers, NCOs and privates. By 22 August it had lost just over 8,000—roughly 40 percent of its total strength. It must be remembered that most of the remainder were not front-line troops but rear-echelon formations. One may assume that Kurt Meyer's reference in his biography, *Panzergrenadiere*, to only 500 troops remaining in the division after the Falaise Gap refers to front-line soldiers.

PART 8: VICTOR AND VANQUISHED

1. In a typical bureaucratic absurdity, after the war Dudka was denied the pension bonus of a dollar a day for every day in captivity paid to Canadian POWs. To qualify, a man had had to serve 90 days as a POW. Dudka was a few days short. Ironically, any POW who escaped forfeited all benefits, including cost recovery of personal effects taken at the time of capture. After the war he was persuaded not to write the German government in Bonn apologizing for escaping and demanding that he be incarcerated for the extra time needed to qualify for his POW pension.

2. The Canadian army had run out of the large-scale maps it had been using since landing in Normandy. The only available maps were 1:250,000 scale, similar to a tourist highway map covering all of France on a single sheet of paper.

3. This "Court of Honour" was given the distasteful task of deciding which of the conspirators should be handed over to the *Volksgerichtshof* or "People's Court," presided over by former Communist Judge Freisler. Those sitting for the Court of Honour did their utmost to save as many of the accused as possible. It was due to them Lieutenant-General Speidel and others survived.

4. Cooperation between opposing forces in taking care of their wounded was not unusual. During the battle of Normandy, on several occasions German ambulances were allowed through Canadian lines and directed to the nearest field hospital. After their wounded were unloaded, the vehicles were given escort and safe passage back to their own lines.

5. According to Jean de Brackeleer, the

camp closed down on 5 and 6 September. Everyone was transferred to Oranienburg or Sachsenhausen, both north of Berlin. On 16 June 1983 de Brackeleer wrote in the *Calgary Herald*: "They were crammed 80 at a time into totally enclosed freight cars without food, water or sanitation for four days and nights in very hot weather which resulted in the deaths of many men and women during the trip. I know this because I was one of those prisoners. . . . I don't know how many prisoners were transported, but our train was so long I couldn't see the end of it. How come everybody speaks of the millions of Jews who died in the camps but nobody ever speaks of the many hundreds of thousands of non-Jews who died?"

6. The incident quickly became known as the "Malmédy Massacre" and was given great play in the U.S. media. Those members of the Waffen-SS considered responsible were tried in July 1946 at the former Dachau concentration camp. They were convicted and sentenced to death. Five years later the sentences were commuted to life imprisonment by the then American Supreme Commander, Gen. Thomas Hardy, based on his findings that "the offense must be viewed in light of a confused, mobile and desperate fighting action." It created a great uproar at home because one of the soldiers killed had been the son of a U.S. senator.

7. Lieut.-Col. Vladimir Peniakoff, DSO, MC, a Belgian national of Russian parents and educated at Cambridge University, was the manager of the sugar refinery in Cairo when the war started. A sometime spy for the British, he organized a special guerilla force in Egypt attached to the Eighth Army. He commanded the unit throughout the North African campaign and into Italy. It was nicknamed "Popski's Private Army." In December 1944 during a patrol north of Ravenna, he lost his left hand to German gunfire. He recovered rapidly and rejoined his unit in mid-April, where he remained its commander until the war ended.

8. Earlier, in December, Harry had lost another friend when his former ADC, the laconic Capt. Ken Scott, had been shot through the head after rejoining his regiment. Sadly, two of his young drivers were also killed from shellfire after Harry left the 4th Armoured Division.

9. War Diary, Historical Officer, 2nd Infantry Division, 7 May 1945.

PART 9: FLAGS ARE FOLDED

1. Vidkun Abraham Lauritz Jonssøn Quisling became Norwegian defence minister in 1931 and later founded the Nazi party in Norway. His actions during the war made his name a synonym for "traitor." After the German invasion he proclaimed himself prime minister. In 1942 he was appointed "minister-president" of the German-controlled puppet government. He was found guilty of treason and executed after the war.

2. Siebken, as noted earlier, was hanged in 1949 for war crimes. Wilhelm Mohnke, later promoted to Brigade-führer, was commanding SS troops in the Reich Chancellery bunker when Hitler and Eva Braun committed suicide. He lost a leg in the Balkan campaign and wore a prothesis. Fellow officers had nothing good to say about him beyond believing him to be addicted to drugs and a brutal man of violent emotions, quite capable of performing the alleged deeds. Captured by the Russians in Berlin, he was imprisoned in Strausberg camp and later released. He is retired and liv-

ing in West Germany.

3. The Beothuck Indians were New-foundland's original inhabitants. A peaceful tribe, they soon fell victim to the white man's diseases. Early British and Irish settlers hunted the remain-der for sport. By the early 19th Cen-tury they had been wiped out.

RECESSIONAL

1. Ironically, the *Einsatzgruppen*, although given complete autonomy of operation, were under the administra-tive control of the Wehrmacht.

2. In an affidavit dated 12 December 1969 supporting a pension claim by Kate Meyer to the Bonn government, Baron Geyr von Schweppenburg stated: "I was requested as witness for the court-martial trial of Meyer. I was trans-ported from PW Camp Allendorf in Hessen to Aurich. This war trial of the otherwise correct Canadians was a farce from a lawyer's viewpoint. It was conducted under a *special law* of the Canadian Parliament that made every German troop leader personally responsible for the actions of his men. As a former military judge . . . I am well versed in military criminal cases.

"I was singled out as the main witness and questioned by Canadian officers regarding my stand . . . against Kurt Meyer. The Canadians knew that I had lived in the British Army in London for four and a half years [he was actually a military attaché in Lon-don during the 1930s] and not only mastered the language fluently but was knowledgeable about British mil-itary justice. Therefore, I was not even admitted to the trial but sent back with outspoken politeness without appear-ing."

BIBLIOGRAPHY

PRIMARY SOURCES

Directorate of History, National Defence Headquarters. Record of Proceedings (revised) of the Trial by Military Court of S.S. Brigadeführer (Major-General) Kurt Meyer. Vols. 1, 2 and 3. Aurich, Germany, 1945.

_____.Transcriptions of Interrogations by No. 1 Canadian War Crimes Investigating Unit C/F (1944 and 1945).

Foster, Gilbert L. Personal Diaries. [1897–1938]

Foster, Harry W. Personal Diaries. [1939–1958]

Public Archives of Canada. Photographs, Interrogations, Correspondence, and Reports on Kurt Meyer during his Servitude in Dorchester Penitentiary. Dorchester, N.B. [1946–1951]

_____.War Diaries. 4th Canadian Armoured Brigade.

_____.War Diaries. 4th Canadian Armoured Division.

_____.War Diaries. 7th Canadian Infantry Brigade.

_____.War Diaries. 1st Canadian Infantry Division.

Public Archives of Nova Scotia. Photographs, Newspaper Reports, Historical Deeds and Records of Kings County, Nova Scotia.

SECONDARY SOURCES

Appleman, John A. *Military Tribunals and International Crimes*. Indianapolis, Ind.: Bobbs-Merrill, 1954.

Bergander, Götz. *Dresden im Luftkriege; Vorgeschichte-Zerstörung-Folgen*. München: Wilhelm Heyne Verlag, 1979.

Bird, Will R. *The Two Jacks*. Toronto: Ryerson Press, 1954.

Blumentritt, G. *Von Rundstedt*. Odham Press, 1952.

Bond, Brian. *The Victorian Army and Staff College*. London: Eyre Methuen, 1972.

Boussel, Patrice. *D-Day Beaches*. London: MacDonald & Co. Publishers, 1965.

Brett-Smith, Richard. *Hitler's Generals*. London: Osprey Publishing, 1976.

Carell, Paul. *Hitler Moves East*. Translated from *Unternehmen Barbarossa* by Ewald Osers. Boston: Little, Brown, 1964.

_____.*Invasion—They're Coming!* Translated by E. Osers. New York: E.P. Dutton, 1963.

Collier, Basil. *The Defence of the United Kingdom*. London: HM Stationery Office, 1957.

D'Este, Carlo. *Decision in Normandy*. London: Wm. Collins & Sons, 1983.

Dicks, Henry V. *Licensed Mass Murder: A Socio-Psychological Study of Some SS Killers*. London: Chatto-Heinemann Educational for Sussex UP, 1972.

Eaton, Arthur. *The History of Kings County, Nova Scotia.* Salem, Mass.: Salem Press, 1910.

Ehrman, John. *Grand Strategy.* Vol. 5. London: HM Stationery Office, 1956.

Eisenhower, Dwight D. *Crusade in Europe.* New York: Doubleday and Co., 1948. London: Heinemann, 1949.

Ellis, L.F. *Victory in the West.* Vol. 1, *The Battle of Normandy.* London: HM Stationery Office, 1962.

Fetherstonhaugh, R.C. *The Royal Canadian Regiment 1883–1933.* Montreal: Gazette Printing Co., 1936.

Fraser, W.B. *Always a Strathcona.* Calgary: Comprint Publishing Co., 1976.

Greenhous, Brereton. *Dragoon.* Ottawa: Campbell Corporation, 1983.

Guderian, Heinz. *Panzer Leader.* London: Michael Joseph, 1970.

Hamilton, Nigel. *Monty, The Making of a General (1887–1942).* New York: McGraw-Hill, 1981.

Hoffman, Peter. *The History of the German Resistance 1933–1945.* Translated from the German by Richard Barry. Cambridge, Mass.: MIT Press, 1977.

Höhne, Heinz. *The Order of the Death's Head: The Story of Hitler's S.S.* Translated by Richard Barry. Reprint. London: Secker & Warburg, 1970.

Keegan, John. *Waffen-SS, the Asphalt Soldiers.* New York: Ballantine Books, 1970.

Kempka, Erich. *Die letzten Tage mit Adolf Hitler.* Pr-Oldendorf: Verlag K.W. Schütz KG, 1976.

Krausnick, Helmut, and Martin Broszat. *Anatomy of the SS State.* London: Wm. Collins, 1968.

Lachs, Manfred. *War Crimes: An Attempt to Define the Issues.* London: Stevens, 1945.

Lesser, Jonas. *Germany: Symbol and the Deed.* New York: Yoseloff, 1965.

Lucas, James, and James Barker. *The Battle of Normandy, The Falaise Gap.* New York: Holmes & Meier, 1978.

Lucas, James, and Matthew Cooper. *Hitler's Elite Leibstandarte SS.* London: Mac-Donald & Jane's, 1975.

Macdonald, Bruce J. *The Trial of Kurt Meyer.* Toronto: Clarke, Irwin, 1954.

MacPhail, Andrew. *The Official History of the Canadian Forces in the Great War, 1914–19. The Medical Services.* Ottawa: F.A. Acland, King's Printer, 1925.

Maser, Werner. *Adolf Hitler 1889–1945 Manuscripts-Facsimiles.* Translated by Arnold Pomerans. London: Heinemann, 1973.

McKee, Alexander. *Caen, Anvil of Victory.* London: Souvenir Press, 1964.

Meyer, Kurt. *Panzergrenadiere.* Schild-Verlag, 1957.

Moncel, Robert W., et al. *4th Canadian Armoured Brigade—A Brief History, July, 1944–May, 1945.* Mitcham, England: West Brothers, 1945.

Montgomery, Bernard L., *The Memoirs of Field Marshal The Viscount Montgomery of Alamein K.G.* London: Collins, 1958.

———.*Normandy to the Baltic.* London: Hutchinson, 1947.

Myerson, Moses H. *Germany's War Crimes and Punishment: The Problem of Individual and Collective Criminality.* New York: Macmillan, 1945.

Nicholson, G.W.L. *Official History of the Canadian Army in the Second World War.* Vol. 2, *The Canadians in Italy 1943–1945.* Ottawa: Queen's Printer, 1957.

Peniakoff, Vladimir. *Private Army.* London: Jonathan Cape, 1950.

Preston, Adrian, and Peter Dennis. *Swords and Covenants*. Totowa, N.J.: Rowman and Littlefield, 1976.

Preston, Richard Arthur. *Canada's RMC*. Toronto: University of Toronto Press, 1969.

Preston, Richard Arthur, S.F. Wise and H.O. Werner. *Men in Arms*. New York: Frederick A. Praeger, 1956.

Ramm, Agatha. *Germany 1789–1919*. London: Methuen, 1967.

Reitlinger, Gerald. *The SS—Alibi of a Nation 1922–1945*. London: Heinemann, 1956.

Rosinski, Herbert. *The German Army*. London: Hogarth Press, 1939.

Roy, Reginald. *For Most Conspicuous Bravery*. Vancouver: University of British Columbia Press, 1977.

Royce, Hans, Erich Zimmermann and Hans Adolf Jacobsen. *20 July, 1944*. 4th Ed. Bonn, 1961.

Ryan, Cornelius. *The Longest Day*. New York: Simon & Schuster, 1959.

Schneider, Jost W. *Verleihung genehmigt! Eine Bild-und Dokumentargeschichte der Ritterkreuzträger der Waffen-SS und Polizei 1940–1945. Their Honor was Loyalty . . . An Illustrated and Documentary History of the Knights Cross Holders of the Waffen-SS and Police 1940–1945*. Edited and translated by Dr. Winder McConnell, San Jose, Calif.: R. James Bender Publishing, 1977.

Sears, Stephen W., ed. *The Horizon History of the British Empire*. Vol. 2. New York: American Heritage Publishing Co., 1973.

The Simon and Schuster Encyclopedia of World War II. Edited by Thomas Parrish. New York: Simon & Schuster, 1978.

Soviet Government Statements on Nazi Atrocities. London: Hutchinson, 1946.

Speidel, Hans. *We Defended Normandy*. London: Michael Jenkins, 1951.

Stacey, C.P. *Official History of the Canadian Army in the Second World War*. Vol. 1, *Six Years of War*. Ottawa: Queen's Printer, 1957.

————. *Official History of the Canadian Army in the Second World War*. Vol. 3, *The Victory Campaign*. Ottawa: Queen's Printer, 1960.

————. *Canada and the British Army 1846–1871*. Rev. ed. Toronto: University of Toronto Press, 1963.

Stein, George H. *The Waffen SS, Hitler's Elite Guard at War, 1939–1945*. Ithaca, N.Y.: Cornell University Press, 1967.

Summers, Jack L., and René Chartrand. *Military Uniforms in Canada, 1665–1970*. Ottawa: National Museums of Canada, 1981.

Swearingen, Ben. "Readers' Investigations: Hermann Göring—His Suicide," *After the Battle*, 1984, no. 44.

Thomas, Hugh. *The Story of Sandhurst*. London: Hutchinson, 1961.

Tusa, Ann and John. *The Nuremberg Trial*. New York: Atheneum, 1984.

Warlimont, W. *Inside Hitler's Headquarters*. London: Weidenfeld & Nicolson, 1962.

Weingartner, James J. *Hitler's Guard—The Story of the Leibstandarte SS Adolf Hitler 1933–1945*. Carbondale, Ill.: Southern Illinois University Press, 1974.

Wiesenthal, Simon. *The Sunflower*. London: W.H. Allen, 1970.

Wilmot, Chester. *The Struggle for Europe*. London: Collins, 1952.

Zawodny, J.K. *Death in the Forest*. Notre Dame, Indiana: University of Notre Dame Press, 1962.

INDEX

Aa Canal, 181, 187
Aa River, 181
Aachen, 416
Abbaye Ardenne, Kurt Meyer's headquarters at, 312, 316, 320-21, 323, 324-25, 326-27, 336-38, 386-87; discussed at Meyer's courtmartial, 466-78, 480-81, 488
Abbeville, 181, 389, 391
Adak, 262-63, 273-74
Adenauer, Dr. Konrad, 511, 515
Airaines, 390
Aire-St. Omer Canal, 182
Aisne River, 191
Alaperrine, Louis Marie, 317
Alaska, during Klondike gold rush, 4-5, 6, 8; during World War II, 262-63, 272-77
Alaska Highway, 506-7
Albania, 200, 211
Albert Canal, 396, 408
Alençon, 356, 373
Aleutian Islands, 262-63, 272-77
Alexander, Harold, 234, 420, 423
Alexeyevka, 255-56
Algiers, 253
Alkatavka, 255
Allen, "Bogie", 62-63
Allen, Lynn, 186-87
Allen, Terry, 414
Allery, 390
Allier River, 191
Amblie, 329
Amchitka, 263
Amersfoort, 439, 444
Amherst, 169
Amiens, 58, 181, 397
Amsterdam, 444
Ancienne Abbaye Ardenne. *See* Abbaye Ardenne
Andreas, Herr, 511
Andreas Brewery, 511, 513
Andrew, Maurice W., 456, 459-60, 464, 465, 467, 468-69, 470-71, 472-73, 476, 477, 480, 481, 485, 499
Antwerp, 180, 382, 396, 397, 404, 408, 410, 414, 423
Apeldoorn, 433-34, 438-39

Archangel, 226-27
Ardennes, 174-75, 177, 428
Arendsee, 104-5, 125
Argentan, 371-73, 376, 377
Argonne Forest, 35, 397
Arnhem, 409, 434
Arras, 169, 172, 181, 183
Arta, 211
Ashbury College, Ottawa, 55
Ashworth, Edward, 302
Astor, Nancy, 189
Athens, 212
"Atlantic", Operation, 340-44, 349
Attlee, Clement, 451
Attu, 263, 273, 274
Aumüller, Lieutenant, 411-12, 417
Aurich, Kurt Meyer's courtmartial at, 457-85, 486, 487-88, 501, 504, 506
Auschwitz, 486
Austria, 42, 43; annexation by Germany, 135-37
Authie, 311, 312, 314-15, 322, 330, 336-37; atrocities at, 316-17; discussed at Meyer's courtmartial, 464-65, 471-72, 477, 480
Avranches, 354-55, 358, 362, 366-67, 371
Axmann, Reichsjugendführer, 280
Azov, Sea of, 232, 234-35

Baaksonemara, 435
Bad Tölz, ss training centre at, 128
Bad Zwischenahn, 450, 456, 487
Baker, Lorne, 501
Balykov, 232
"Barbarossa", Operation, 217ff.
Barker, R.W., 430
Bayerlein, Fritz, 306-7, 311
Bayeux, 313, 320, 321, 323, 325
Beauvais, 398
Beauvoir Farm, 342
"Beaver Three", Exercise, 244
"Beaver Two", Exercise, 243
Beck, General, 345
Beda Fomm, 201
Belgorod, 266
Belgrade, 203
Belisha, Hoare, 168